ENVIRONMENTAL EDUCATION:
A Sourcebook

ENVIRONMENTAL EDUCATION: A Sourcebook

edited by

Cornelius J. Troost

& Harold Altman

John Wiley & Sons, Inc.

NEW YORK   LONDON   SYDNEY   TORONTO

Dedicated with love to our families:

the TROOSTS—Martha, Roger, Neil, and Shari;

and the ALTMANS—Stel, Steve, Judy, Harvey, Judy, and Ken.

Library of Congress Cataloging in Publication Data

Troost, Cornelius J   comp.
   Environmental education.

  Bibliography: p. 527
  1. Ecology—Study and teaching (Higher) 2. Pollution—Study and teaching (Higher) I. Altman, Harold, joint comp. II.   Title.

QH541.2.T76   301.31'071   72-2321
ISBN 0-471-89100-2
ISBN 0-471-89101-0 (pbk.)

Printed in the United States of America

10 9 8 7 6 5 4 3 2 1

Preface

Few today doubt that our tiny planet is on the brink of ecological disaster. Gradually, but inexorably, man has risen in numbers and technology at a deadly ecological cost. We have, to put it bluntly, misused and defaced our land, water, and air; we are rapidly consuming our nonrenewable natural resources; and we have developed urban environments which, among other things, have bred widespread dehumanization.

Despite the great complexity of many of our problems, some important goals are obvious:

1. Restoration of ecological integrity to ecosystems throughout the world.

2. Rapid reduction of the world's population growth to zero.

3. Development and implementation of urban planning schemes which are ecologically sound.

4. Careful, selective control of our runaway technology.

5. Inculcation of attitudes and values which are enduring—such as the supreme value of each human life, the importance of shared group values, the fundamental importance of respect for our natural environment, and the moral courage to act intelligently to improve the human condition.

To achieve the goals just mentioned, individual and group action must be conscientious, sustained, and as wise as is humanly possible. Scientists, lawyers, engineers, and scholars from the humanities must make a sophisticated response to the ecological crisis. This response is well underway. We are seeing innumerable ecology action groups spring up on campuses, in schools, and among the general population. The growing national commitment to clean up the environment finds strong support in our country's young people. Their awareness of the misuse of our limited natural resources and their dedication to a new way of life to prevent environmental deterioration is one of the most hopeful signs for the future.

Part of the broad response to the ecological crisis is the mobilization of educational forces, completely heterogeneous, which promises to help shape the knowledge, skills, and values of future citizens who must do more than maintain the current level of struggle. The ecologically educated citizen must (1) have some basic knowledge of ecological concepts and facts, (2) have a basic knowledge of the socio-ecological problems of the urban environment, (3) understand his relationship with the natural world, (4) have an understanding of abnormal ecology, or pollution and overpopulation, (5) develop a vigorous interest in local, state, and national politics which bear heavily upon ecological problems, (6) learn to make decisions based upon the best available evidence after detailed analysis of alternatives.

PREFACE

Our schools have a vital role in meeting not just an urgent national need, but an emergency human need. Teachers must gear themselves to understand the problems of pollution and devise effective teaching methods in environmental education. Environmental education should not be the realm of science teachers alone, although they can make a substantial contribution. Elementary and high school teachers of every description ought to play a role in the emerging efforts to restore some semblance of good health to our environment.

This book of readings, activities, and ideas can be used as a general reference source by teachers from kindergarten through grade twelve. It is suitable for the future teacher or the teacher in the field. School administrators, who often have excellent opportunities to assist in developing and interpreting school programs to the community, will find it helpful. It can even be used by community members of environmental quality councils as an orientation to the school's role.

Within these pages is background information on normal as well as abnormal ecology. We provide many of the concepts necessary for a proper understanding of environmental phenomena. Armed with this fundamental information, readers would more readily understand the pathology of environmental deterioration.

We introduce the teacher to the variety of pollution problems, as well as the problems of overpopulation, and depletion of natural resources. Most of the important issues are here, as well as related facts, some concepts, and judgments of various experts. Environmental problems, as you will see, are not simple and subject to quick solutions. For instance, a teacher may enthusiastically encourage use of biodegradable laundry detergents, while in truth, one of the substitutes for phosphates is nitriloacetate, a highly toxic chelating agent. Use of the new substitute with inadequate testing could have far worse effects than the present effects of high phosphate detergents. The message here is clear: dogmatic crusading about particular, narrow issues is untenable. For many of the claims made in this book, there is very great support in the scientific community, but many others are indeed controversial.

This volume addresses itself to two major questions:

1. What is the nature of the environmental crisis?

2. What learning experiences should be provided by this country's schools to meet this crisis?

Parts 1 and 2 provide background information. They are concerned with such topics as the nature of ecosystems and the problems of overpopulation, indiscriminate use of pesticides, increase in air, noise, and water pollution, and depletion of natural resources. They show how the elements of population, atmosphere, water, and land are all interrelated; give a definition of the science of ecology and the role of the ecologist; and present possible solutions to the crisis now facing us.

With a knowledge of the nature of our ecologic crisis, teachers and administrators can begin the process of planning and implementing ecology programs. We have in Part 3 offered everything from a K-12 integrated ecology curriculum proposal to the use of academic games and simulations. A complete blueprint for total school implementation of educational action programs is presented. Specific suggestions for elementary schools, secondary schools, and schools in densely populated urban areas are made. Ideas for in-service teacher training and ecological field trips are included.

PREFACE

We provide a selection of laboratory, classroom, and field investigations which ought to prove very useful. It is hoped that teachers will find them feasible and challenging. They are not integrated conceptually, for that was not our purpose. These are only meant as useful activities to be integrated into the teacher's own program. The editors consider these experiments of major importance since no environmental education curriculum would be complete without firsthand contact with pollution problems.

It is our hope that teachers, both as curriculum directors and instructional agents, will convert these ideas, suggestions, and strategies into reality. A teacher who synthesizes the best of what is in this text will have made a start in the right direction. The bibliography and appendices offer a rich supply of books, materials, and agencies through which he and his students may grow ecologically and make worthwhile contributions to society. The need today for universal environmental education dictates that ecological growth and awareness, if it is to come about, must start now.

Los Angeles, California

Cornelius J. Troost
Harold Altman

Acknowledgments

We gratefully acknowledge the advice and encouragement given us by Professors Paul Mussen of the University of California at Berkeley and Louis S. Levine of San Francisco State College. Dr. Chester A. Lawson from the Science Curriculum Improvement Study was generous in granting certain reprint permissions. Mr. Howard Dvorkin of the Los Angeles County Air Pollution Control District provided a fund of helpful information.

At UCLA, both graduate and undergraduate students offered criticisms and helpful suggestions. In particular, Steve Gottlieb, a very knowledgeable ecology activist, was able to offer many valuable ideas.

The Carthay Center School Ecology Club, sponsored by Mrs. Jean Lamel, Mrs. Hope Arlene Swatt, and Miss Annette H. Willens, offered a varied format of worthwhile procedures and activities. We learned much from that model.

Most of the experiments for the secondary school level were performed and carefully scrutinized by teachers at Thousand Oaks High School and Newbury Park High School in California. Mr. Keith Chartier, Chairman of the Science Department at Thousand Oaks High School, and Mr. Richard McCollough, biology teacher at Newbury Park, deserve considerable credit in this regard.

Mrs. Anne Finch did a substantial amount of the manuscript typing. Mrs. Lee Freis and Mrs. Nadine Hankin performed many necessary and highly valued clerical duties.

Contents

CONTENTS

CONTENTS

xi

CONTENTS

CONTENTS

CONTENTS

CONTENTS

If man is to find his way successfully through the labyrinth of difficulties that confront him in the years ahead, he must, above all, use his intelligence. He can no longer rely upon the unforeseeable fortunate circumstance; future mistakes will have consequences far more dangerous than past ones have been. He must divorce himself from unreasoned slogans and dogma, from the soothsayer, from the person whose selfish interests compel him to draw false conclusions, from the man who prefers indoctrination to education. Man must rapidly accumulate knowledge concerning both his environment and himself, and he must learn how to use that knowledge wisely. He must encourage the emergence of new ideas in all areas. He must learn not to fear change, for of one thing he can be certain—no matter what happens in the world of the next few decades, change will be the major characteristic. But it is within the range of his ability to choose what the changes will be, and how the resources at his disposal will be used—or abused—in the common victory—or ignominious surrender—of mankind.

Harrison Brown
in *The Challenge of
Man's Future*

PART 1

THE ORGANISM AND ITS ENVIRONMENT:

an introduction to ecology

SECTION 1

THE NATURE OF THE ENVIRONMENT

To present ecology effectively in the classroom, every teacher needs a basic grounding in that subject. If you are a biology teacher Part 1 will probably do little for you. If you are not, then Part 1 will provide most of the basic concepts needed for teaching ecology.

In this first section, *The Nature of the Environment,* you will learn something about communities and ecosystems. All of us reside in ecosystems, and young people must learn to appreciate the important relationships such as food chains, food webs, succession, energy transfers, etc., going on within the ecosystem. Biogeochemical cycles, which are discussed in Part 2 by Lamont Cole, are illustrated in this section also.

Physical and biological limiting factors, so crucial in understanding man's relationship to his environment, are briefly discussed. The reader is encouraged to apply the concepts and facts of this section to the situations discussed in Part 2.

Finally, the recently developed concept of homeostasis of ecosystems is treated. The process of succession results in mature, stable ecosystems which represent a high degree of control (homeostasis). The analogy of such a developmental process in nature to human societies is most interesting.

Raymond F. Dasmann

ECOSYSTEMS AND COMMUNITIES

Despite his present position of dominance on earth, man is still dependent upon other living things for his sustenance. Locked up in cities, civilized man may assume that he has risen above nature, but the bread he eats comes from wheat plants formed of soil, air, and sunlight. The soil, with hosts of microorganisms to maintain its health and fertility, was itself formed by the work of generations of green plants and animals, transforming rock and sunlight energy into the organized network of materials needed for the growth of wheat plants. The meat that man demands comes also from soil materials, transformed by a great community of grassland organisms into the plant protein and carbohydrate needed to feed a steer. Beef is soil and sunlight made available to man by plant communities. Like all other animals, therefore, man is dependent upon the ecological interrelationships of living things with their physical environment.

The relationships between organisms and environment are illustrated by the concepts of biotic communities and ecosystems. A *biotic community* is an assemblage of species of plants and animals inhabiting a common area and having, therefore, effects upon one another. A combination of a biotic community with its physical environment is called an *ecosystem. Ecology* is the study of ecosystems to determine their status and the ways in which they function. An understanding of ecology is basic to conservation.

In the broad sense the human environment is the biosphere, which has been defined already as that part of the planet in which life exists and of which it forms a part. It is the surface area of the earth, made up of the atmosphere, the oceans, the upper surfaces of the land areas of the continents and islands and the fresh waters associated with them, and the living things that inhabit this area. In the biosphere, energy from the sun is available to activate living processes; chemicals from air, water, and soil are available as building blocks for living organisms.

The biosphere can be considered as the sum of all the ecosystems of the earth and,

SOURCE. Reprinted by permission from *Environmental Conservation,* 2nd ed., New York: John Wiley & Sons, Inc., 1968, with slight abridgment.

at any one time, people exist as part of a particular ecosystem, although they may travel from one ecosystem to another. What happens to the biosphere and its ecosystems determines what will happen to people. It is impossible to separate an individual human from the biosphere of which he forms a part. The air he breathes, the water he drinks, the sunlight that warms him, and the food he eats, all tie him to his immediate physical and biological environment. Man apart from environment is an abstraction; in reality no such being could exist.

Energy transfer. For a biotic community to exist it must have a supply of energy to activate the life processes of the organisms that compose it. The principal source of energy for any biotic community is sunlight. However, only one group of organisms, the green plants, can make use of sunlight energy directly for the synthesis of foodstuffs. The presence of chlorophyll in the cells of plants makes possible photosynthesis, in which light energy is used in building a plant food (glucose) from simple compounds—carbon dioxide from the air and water from the soil. From glucose, with the addition of other simple chemical compounds obtained from the soil, plants can build more complex carbohydrates, proteins, fats, and vitamins. These materials, required by animals in their diets, must come from the plant world.

The dependence of animals upon plants and of plants upon sunlight brings to consideration a physical law of great importance to the understanding of any ecosystem. This, the *second law of thermodynamics,* states that in any transfer of energy from one form to another, some energy always escapes from the system, usually as heat, no transfer is 100 per cent effective. Always energy goes from a concentrated form useful to a system to a dilute form, in which it is not. Most transfers of energy in natural ecosystems are inefficient. In some instances, of the total

amount of sunlight energy potentially available to green plants, only 1 per cent will be converted finally into chemical energy tied up in foods within the plants. The remaining 99 per cent escapes. Similarly, when herbivores feed on green plants and convert plant starch and protein into animal energy and protein, another high percentage of energy escapes. When carnivores feed on herbivores, there is again inefficiency in energy transfer. The limits of available energy are soon reached. Thus, in some communities, of 10,000 original calories of sunlight energy striking on green plants, only 2 calories may remain tied up in chemical energy within the body of a carnivorous animal.

The operation of the second law of thermodynamics serves to explain many of the characteristics of ecosystems. In any ecosystem the amount of green plants is limited, ultimately, by the amount of sunlight energy and the efficiency of plants in converting it to a useful form. This is a theoretical upper limit, not approached in natural ecosystems, because lesser limits are always set by shortages of required chemical elements or other factors.

In a similar way the final limit on the number of animals in an area is determined by the amount of energy available in green plants and by the efficiency of animals in converting this to a form useful for maintenance, growth, and reproduction. These relationships within an ecosystem are often illustrated in diagrammatic ways, such as the biotic pyramid, food chain, and food web (Figure 1). In the *biotic pyramid* the greatest numbers of organisms, the greatest mass, and the greatest amount of food energy, are to be found in the lowest layer of organisms, the green plants. Partly because of the necessary inefficiency in energy transfer, numbers, mass, and energy decrease as you move up the pyramid. The pyramid is supported by the amount of sunlight energy received and the amounts of essential nutrients, minerals, water, and

THE NATURE OF THE ENVIRONMENT

Food chain   Food chain

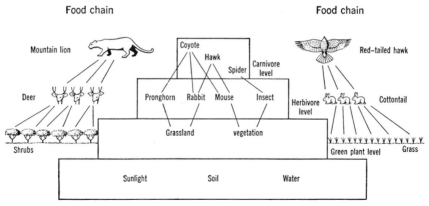

Biotic pyramid showing portion of a grassland food web

FIGURE 1.

essential gases available in the soil or other supporting physical environment. *Food chains* are simply diagrammatic representations of the food relationships within an ecosystem. Although simple food chains may be artificially separated out and studied, most food relationships of the species in an ecosystem are more complicated. In natural systems food chains are interwoven into complex *food webs*. The number of layers in a pyramid or links in a food chain is inevitably limited through the operation of the second law of thermodynamics. Inefficiency in energy transfer keeps pyramids low and food chains short.

Man, as a carnivore, occupies the top layer of a biotic pyramid and the end link of a food chain. However, man can also exist as a herbivore and thus lower the pyramid and shorten the food chain. In those areas of the earth where human numbers are great and productive land is limited, man cannot afford the luxury of being a carnivore nor the waste of energy involved in converting plant protein to beef or mutton. In such areas he must feed on plants directly if his great numbers are to be maintained.

Of perhaps greater importance to man than the limitations imposed by the second

law of thermodynamics is the role played by life in conserving energy. Sunlight energy striking a bare rock or soil surface is soon lost. Much is reflected back into the air; some heats the rock or soil temporarily but is soon radiated back into the atmosphere. The earth as a whole, before life, radiated or reflected back into space an amount of energy equal to that received from the sun. In the absence of life, energy thus became degraded, i.e., dispersed through space until it was no longer capable of doing work. When green plants appeared on earth, this loss of energy was slowed down. Sunlight energy was stored in organisms in concentrated form and transferred in food chains from one to another. With the development of complex biotic communities, a living system was developed that made maximum use of the incoming solar energy and stored a part of it for the future. Man has been dependent upon these stored reserves of energy. When he eats meat, he obtains energy that may have been stored by plants several years before. When he cuts firewood for fuel, he is obtaining energy accumulated and stored by trees for perhaps a century or more. When he burns coal or petroleum, he obtains sunlight energy stored by plant

5

life millions of years before. Man is as yet unable to store significant quantities of energy without making use of the life processes of plants and animals. When living communiteis are destroyed and the land made bare, the energy on which life and man depend is again wasted and no longer is stored for future use.

Chemical requirements. Just as each ecosystem must have a source of energy, so must it have a source of chemical building blocks from which organisms can be constructed. In the oceans this source is seawater; on the land the source is the soil and the atmosphere. Biotic pyramids rest on an energy base of sunlight, and a chemical base of soil or seawater. Both of these sources of minerals, however, are secondary, for minerals come originally from the rocks of the earth's surface or from the atmos-

phere above the earth.

Rocks supply minerals to the soil slowly. Rocks break apart through weathering, the action of cold, heat, wind, and precipitation gradually cracking and shattering them into small particles. They break down more quickly through the action of organisms. Plant roots, for example, penetrate into cracks in rocks, widen them, and eventually split and separate the rock fragments. Acids released or dissolved from plant materials help the process of rock disintegration and free elements for soil formation. Organisms also help to capture elements such as nitrogen from the atmosphere and incorporate them in the soil. Nitrogen, an essential part of protein, must be present for life to exist. The cycle by which it is transferred from atmosphere to organism, to soil, and back to the atmosphere has been well studied (Figure 2).

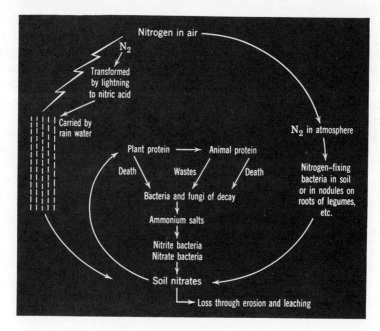

FIGURE 2.

Soil formation. The evolution of soil has accompanied the evolution of life—before life there was no soil—for soil is created through the action of organisms. When life is destroyed in an area, the loss of soil follows.

In an area where rocks have long been exposed to the air we can see the stages through which soil is sometimes formed. Rock surfaces, roughened and weathered, provide a foothold for primitive and hardy land plants, the *lichens* (Figure 3). These

FIGURE 3. **Primary succession on rock. Lichens have occupied the bare rock surface. Where some soil has formed, ferns are established. With more soil, shrubs and trees can take over (photograph by Soil Conservation Service, U. S. Dept. Agric.).**

exert a physical and chemical effect on the rock leading to a more rapid decomposition. Small rock particles may be accumulated and added to the dead remnants of the lichen bodies. When enough mineral and organic material has accumulated, *mosses* next invade the rock surface. These crowd out the lichens, but with their more dense growth habit and more robust plant bodies they hasten the breakdown of rock and add greater amounts of organic debris

to the mixture.

Eventually a layer of materials will be formed deep enough to support the more hardy types of *annual grasses* and *forbs,* and these will invade and overtop the mosses. These in turn break down the rock further and add more organic material. In a forested region they are replaced by larger *perennial grasses* and *forbs* (broad-leaved herbs); these are replaced by *shrubs* and, finally, by *trees.* Each does its part in breaking down rock and adding organic debris to it. Joining in the process are microorganisms of various kinds, bacteria and fungi, which feed on dead plant and animal remains and eventually release from them simple mineral nutrients which may be used again to support new plant growth. Also involved are the larger burrowing animals that churn and mix rock particles together and add to the complex their own waste products and dead bodies. Eventually, with the final stage of vegetation, there has been developed that complex arrangement of minerals and organic materials that is known as mature soil.

The process of soil formation is not always the same. Few of our soils have actually developed in place from underlying parent rock. Most, the *transported soils,* are built from materials carried by wind, water, gravity, or glacial action from other areas and are broken from rock originally by the action of heat, wind, and water. Across the northern United States, the soil materials are mostly of glacial origin, built from fragments ground from underlying rocks by the action of continental glaciers during past ice ages. These have been carried hundreds of miles and deposited where the glaciers finally melted and retreated. Over wide areas in the central United States the soils are derived from *loess,* formed from dust particles carried over long distances by wind currents. But on glacial drifts or loess deposits also the process of plant invation, break-down, and modification of the substrate has gone on. Where the substrate is finely divided, the lichen and moss stage may be skipped and the initial plant invasion be made by herbs, shrubs, or trees. Always, however, there is further development and change until a mature soil and a relatively stable vegetation is attained.

Erosion. Just as the action of living organisms is essential for the development of soil, so it is essential if the soil is to be maintained. Throughout past ages there have been two major groups of forces at work on the earth's surface. One group of forces contributes to land raising: folding up mountain ranges, elevating plateaus, forming volcanic peaks. The other group leads to the degradation of lands, the lowering of the high lands back to sea level. These forces of degradation, or ero-sion, consist of gravity in combination

were stopped in their movement to the sea by the countless small check dams formed from plant life. Instead of washing away, rock particles remained to form soil. But once soil is formed, it becomes highly vulnerable to a much more rapid erosion than that which wears away rocks. Without a covering of green plants and a network of plant roots to hold it in place it can be lost rapidly. When plant cover is destroyed, a few decades can see the dis-appearance of soils that may have been thousands of years in forming. It is this kind of *accelerated soil erosion* that is of concern to the conservationist (Figure 4).

Biotic succession. The role of plants in soil formation illustrates another process fundamental in any ecosystem and basic to much work in conservation. This is the process known as biotic succession. The way in which lichens and mosses are re-placed by herbs and these by shrubs and

FIGURE 4. Accelerated erosion. When overgrazing removed the grass cover, water running off the slope rapidly removed the soil and cut gashes in the hill slope (U.S. Forest Service photograph).

with wind, rain, and temperature, cracking apart the rocks and carrying them to lower elevations. In the long ages before life appeared, *geological erosion* went on as a slow and unchecked process. With the development of life, however, a new force was interposed. The decomposed rocks

trees as soils are being formed is an example of biotic succession. Along with the replace-ment and change in the types of plants, goes replacement and change in the animals dependent upon each type of plant. Biotic succession can be defined as the sequence of biotic communities which tend to succeed and replace one another in a given area over a period of time. The starting point in any biotic succession is always a *pioneer community,* able to colonize and inhabit a bare surface. The end product in any succession is known as a *climax community.* This is a relatively stable community, able to maintain itself over long periods of time and to regenerate and replace itself without marked further change. It is usually the most complex type of community which a particular physical is made possible by the accumulation of soil materials washed into a lake, accumulating around the bodies of plants, and being added to by dead-plant debris. Eventually, unless the process is disturbed, each lake changes to a pond, the pond to a marsh, the marsh into meadow or forest (Figure 6).

There are two general categories of succession. One, which has been emphasized to this point, is *primary succession.* This takes place on areas that have not previously supported life. The other, more

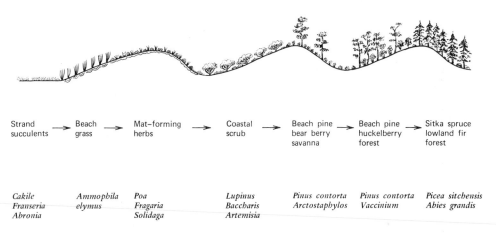

Strand succulents	→	Beach grass	→	Mat–forming herbs	→	Coastal scrub	→	Beach pine bear berry savanna	→	Beach pine huckelberry forest	→	Sitka spruce lowland fir forest

Cakile	Ammophila	Poa		Lupinus	Pinus contorta	Pinus contorta	Picea sitchensis
Franseria	elymus	Fragaria		Baccharis	Arctostaphylos	Vaccinium	Abies grandis
Abronia		Solidaga		Artemisia			

FIGURE 5.

environment will support and makes the most efficient use of sun energy and soil materials. Climax communities represent storehouses of materials and energy accumulated over the long years of plant succession and soil formation.

Throughout the earth, wherever life can be supported, biotic succession goes on. Plants invade and colonize bare areas and are replaced in time by other groups of plants. Succession takes place on bare rock, sand, exposed alluvium in river bottoms, and in the water (Figure 5). Any lake or pond, unless constantly disturbed, tends to be invaded by aquatic plants which are replaced in time by partially submerged reeds and rushes and these in time by sedges and grasses. This aquatic succession immediately important to conservation, is *secondary succession.* This takes place on areas where the original vegetation has been destroyed or disturbed but where the soil has not been lost. This process is generally familiar (Figures 7 and 8). A forest which has been cut down regenerates itself. Ths forest, if not greatly disturbed and if seed sources are available, may regenerate quickly with trees replacing trees. Usually, and particularly after a fire, there are a series of intermediate stages. A weed stage follows forest clearing. Left alone this is replaced by shrubs, then by trees and, eventually, if these have not been destroyed or the environment too greatly changed by disturbance, by the species that composed the original climax forest. The process is

rapid or slow, depending upon the severity of the original disturbance. In a similar way, when a rangeland has been heavily overgrazed, the original climax grassland will go through several stages, characterized by different communities of weeds and grasses, before the climax community replaces itself. Succession tends to be an orderly and predictable process. It is a heartening process for the conservationist, who knows that with care many of our badly abused lands will repair themselves (Figure 9).

FIGURE 6. A climax community. This forest of maple, elm, and ash in Wisconsin is a remnant of the once extensive hardwood forests of the east. An end product of plant succession (U. S. Forest Service photograph).

Succession and land management. The exploitation of biotic resources usually involves the removal and consumption of all or part of the elements that composed the climax communities of the earth. Successful conservation, or land management, often includes the manipulation of biotic succession in such a way that the climax replaces itself as quickly as possible. In this way a continued high yield of resources from an area is obtained.

The lumberman is interested in obtaining the greatest yield of high-quality timber from an area. In some places, such as the

FIGURE 7. Fire has destroyed the chaparral cover on this southern California hillside. Rainfall running off the bare slopes has cut rills as it washed the soil away (U. S. Forest Service photograph).

FIGURE 8. The same area as in Figure 7, reseeded to mustard. These annual plants will help hold the soil in place until normal successional processes lead to replacement of the chaparral cover (U.S. Forest Service photograph).

FIGURE 9. Overgrazing has broken and destroyed the grass cover in this mountain meadow, exposing bare soil or leaving a sparse cover of weeds. With protection, successional processes can restore the original meadow grasses (U. S. Forest Service photograph).

redwood forests of California, the climax forest has the greatest commercial value. Successful redwood-forest management includes a study of the way plant succession proceeds after various systems of logging and the selection of that cutting system which will lead to the most rapid regeneration of the forest. Not all high-value forests are climax, however. In the southeastern United States, the longleaf pine forests represent a subclimax stage in succession. Left alone they will be replaced by climax hardwood trees of lower commercial value. Studies of succession have indicated that the pine forests are best maintained by the use of fire, which kills the seedlings of the climax species but does not injure the fire-tolerant pine seedlings.

On rangelands where climax grasses have the greatest forage value, the range manager attempts to work out grazing systems and levels of stocking which will best perpetuate the climax. Elsewhere, successional grasses may have greater value as forage, and a different system of grazing management will be needed to suppress the climax and maintain the successional forms. In wildlife management it is found that many of the valuable species of game animals are not climax forms, and hence the wildlife manager may be interested in suppression of the climax through the use of fire, cutting, or some other technique which will maintain the necessary level of disturbance. Thus, it can be seen that in many types of wild-land management a knowledge of biotic succession is essential.

Raymond F. Dasmann

LIMITING FACTORS

The human environment, whether in a natural state or in one greatly modified by man's activities, is composed of complex arrangements of matter and energy and is maintained by the interactions that occur among them. Activity within it is ceaseless as energy and materials flow through food chains. Change is also ceaseless, whether it be the relatively rapid change represented by the growth and death of individuals and populations, by the processes of biotic succession, or the slow change represented by the evolution of new races and species of organisms. In places, man accelerates the pace of change, sometimes to his own detriment; but even in the absence of people change goes on.

In the environment, life is distinguished by growth, mobility, and reproduction, among other qualities. Every species that exists tends to increase in numbers, to spread to new and suitable environments, to increase again there, and spread farther. Growth in individual size or in numbers of a population continues usually until some external factor of the environment causes it to cease, although in man and in some other species, self-imposed limitation on growth of populations may occur before external factors bring this limitation. A tree will cease to grow when water or an essential soil chemical ceases to be available in minimum quantity. A population of trees will cease to increase in numbers when the tree seeds encounter conditions that are unsuitable for their germination or for the growth of the new seedling. An animal population will cease to grow when there is no longer adequate food, water, and shelter for the sustenance of individuals, or where weather or other environmental factors result in conditions unsuitable to survival of individuals of that species. Whatever limits the growth in size of an individual or in numbers of a population is known as a *limiting factor* to that individual or population. The ecological principle of limiting factors is stated by E. P. Odum as follows: "The presence and success of an organism or a group of organisms depends upon a complex of conditions. Any condition which approaches or exceeds the limits of tolerance is said to be a limiting condition or a limiting factor." This concept is one of the oldest in ecology and traces its origin to the chemist Justus Liebig in 1840. Liebig, who studied the effect of chemical foodstuffs

SOURCE. Reprinted by permission from *Environmental Conservation,* 2nd ed., New York: John Wiley & Sons, Inc., 1968, with slight abridgment.

on plant growth, first stated this concept as "growth of a plant is dependent on the amount of foodstuff which is presented to it in minimum quantity." This concept, expanded to include organisms other than plants and factors other than chemical nutrients, has been known as The Law of the Minimum.

The concept of limiting factors, combined with a knowledge that the earth is limited in size and in its supplies of energy and materials, leads to the obvious, but sometimes overlooked, conclusion that growth and expansion must have an end. No species, including man, can expand its population indefinitely. Any species, including man, will be better off individually if its growth is limited through its own behavior before the time when environmental limiting factors (shortages in necessities, for example) begin to take effect.

Limiting factors can be divided into two categories: physical and biological. Physical factors that limit population growth would include factors of climate and weather, the absence of water or presence of an excess of water, the availability of essential soil minerals, the suitability of the terrain, and so on. Biological factors involve competition, predation, parasitism, disease, and other interactions between or within a species that are limiting to growth or increases. In the extreme environments of the world, the physical factors are generally limiting. These would include the very cold or very dry environments or, for land organisms, the very wet environments. Droughts, floods, unseasonable cold, or extreme cold are among the factors that limit populations in such environments. In the more optimum environments of the world (the warmer, more humid environments) biological factors more often are limiting. In such environments, complex predator-prey relationships, balances with parasites or disease organisms, and competition for light, soil minerals, or water among species with similar requirements are most frequently limiting to population growth.

Thus fish populations in cold mountain lakes are most frequently limited, both in the growth of individuals and the size of populations, by water temperature and the availability of chemical nutrients. Cold temperatures inhibit biological activity and thus prevent the growth of plankton and of insect populations upon which the fish would feed. The low availability of chemical nutrients inhibits the growth of these organisms during the period when temperatures are suitable to growth. Fish populations are therefore small in numbers. On the other hand, in warm ponds fish populations may grow in size to a point of great abundance where competition among them not only prevents individuals from reaching large size but inhibits further growth of population.

Limiting factors may further be classified into those whose operations are dependent upon the density (the number of individuals per unit of area) of the population and those that have no relation to density. The *density-dependent* factors are those that increase in their intensity, that have greater effects, or that affect more individuals as the population increases in density. Thus the availability of food, grass, and other herbs may be a limiting factor to the increase in numbers of domestic cattle in a pasture. The higher the density of cattle, the less grass there is per cow and the greater number of cows suffer from food shortage. By contrast, a flood sweeping through the pasture would be a *density-independent* limiting factor. It would wipe out all the cows whether there were two or a hundred in the area.

Density-dependent factors usually hold the greatest interest to students of population because of their more general and constant operation. They are usually the factors that set absolute limits to growth, that determine the number of individuals that can be supported—the *carrying capacity* of the area. They are the factors that operate to decrease the individual well-being in a population that approaches the

13

limits or carrying capacity of its environment. In crowded human populations in many parts of the word we see such density-dependent factors in operation.

Cornelius J. Troost

HOMEOSTASIS

In Part 3 of this text you will find an investigation of the phenomenon of ecological succession. As you proceed with that study, keep in mind the fact that succession is a universal process. That is, all communities seem to have stages of development corresponding to an organism—birth, early rapid development, and maturity.

Succession is a natural process whereby communities in the same habitat succeed one another, ultimately ending in a highly stable, *climax* community. This process has both order and direction, and while it occurs the community and the physical environment modify each other. The community controls its succession, while the physical environment acts, by setting limits,

*Eugene P. Odum, "The Strategy of Ecosystem Development," *Science,* Vol. 164, No. 3877, April 18, 1969.

to determine the rate of change, extent of development, and patterns of succession.

According to Eugene P. Odum,* the climax community is characterized by maximum biomass (total mass of living material) and high degree of symbiotic function between organisms as maintained per unit of available energy flow. The "purpose" of succession is to bring the ecosystem to a steady state, that is a state of homeostasis in which the living community and the physical environment are in a state of narrow fluctuation within normal limits— a dynamic equilibrium.

Homeostasis refers to a condition of internal self-regulation involving feedback mechanisms. Living tissues are, of course, homeostatic. The water, salt, and acidity levels fluctuate within normal limits due to homeostatic devices. Such a device may be illustrated as follows:

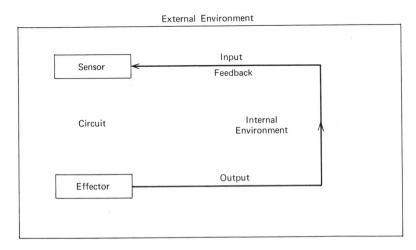

FIGURE 1.   Basic elements of homeostasis.
(Reprinted by permission of the author)

A sensor may be a thermostat, for instance, which controls room temperature by detecting temperature changes (cooling off) and sending messages to the effector (furnace) which responds by producing more heat. The heat acts as feedback which then acts to shut off the thermostat. The room temperature then drops and it starts all over again.*

Homeostasis in ecosystems is the state of balance involving symbiosis, nutrient conservation, stability, decrease in entropy, and increase in biomass. The mature climax community plus its physical surroundings achieves diversity and size as great as is possible within the limits set by available energy and physical factors (water, soil, etc.). The positive feedback mechanisms involve community control of grazing, population density, and nutrient cycling. See Figure 2 for a full list of characteristics of young and mature ecosystems.

*Adapted from *Homeostasis,* by L. L. Langley, New York: Reinhold Publishing Co., 1965.

Ecosystem attributes	Developmental stages	Mature stages
Community energetics		
1. Gross production/community respiration (P/R ratio)	Greater or less than 1	Approaches 1
2. Gross production/standing crop biomass (P/B ratio)	High	Low
3. Biomass supported/unit energy flow (B/E ratio)	Low	High
4. Net community production (yield)	High	Low
5. Food chains	Linear, predominantly grazing	Weblike, predominantly detritus
Community structure		
6. Total organic matter	Small	Large
7. Inorganic nutrients	Extrabiotic	Intrabiotic
8. Species diversity—variety component	Low	High
9. Species diversity—equitability component	Low	High
10. Biochemical diversity	Low	High
11. Stratification and spatial heterogeneity (pattern diversity)	Poorly organized	Well-organized
Life history		
12. Niche specialization	Broad	Narrow
13. Size of organism	Small	Large
14. Life cycles	Short, simple	Long, complex
Nutrient cycling		
15. Mineral cycles	Open	Closed
16. Nutrient exchange rate, between organisms and environment	Rapid	Slow
17. Role of detritus in nutrient regeneration	Unimportant	Important
Selection pressure		
18. Growth form	For rapid growth ("r-selection")	For feedback control ("K-selection")
19. Production	Quantity	Quality

Ecosystem attributes	Developmental stages	Mature stages
Overall homeostasis		
20. Internal symbiosis	Undeveloped	Developed
21. Nutrient conservation	Poor	Good
22. Stability (resistance to external perturbations)	Poor	Good
23. Entropy	High	Low
24. Information	Low	High

FIGURE 2. A tabular model of ecological succession: trends to be expected in the development of ecosystems.

In Figure 2 the P/R, P/B and B/E ratios are unexplained. P/R is the ratio of total photosynthetic food production (P) to rate of community respiration (R). P/R is more than 1 in the early development of an ecosystem. Intense pollution by organic materials lowers the P/R ratio to less than 1. In succession the P/R ratio approaches 1, theoretically speaking that is, the fixed energy tends to be balanced by the energy expended via maintenance (total community respiration) in the mature ecosystem.

When P exceeds R, organic matter and biomass (B) will accumulate within the system. The P/B ratio, then, will decrease as maturity is reached. E is the unit energy flow (P + R), thus the B/E ratio will increase as the system matures. Thus, the amount of standing crop biomass supported by the available energy flow increases, reaching a maximum in the mature stage.

The concept of homeostasis has profound meaning for human ecology. Man must prevent abrupt, often violent interference with stable ecosystems. Monoculture systems of growing crops, building dams, roads, together with the various types of pollution threaten the homeostasis of ecosystems.

The model developed by Odum (Figure 3) illustrates a way to classify ecosystems. Note that Odum prefers for the environment to be compartmentalized, according to biotic function. The model permits a systems analysis approach to be used in order to determine when instabilities are occurring through excesses of certain materials or energy drains caused by pollution, harvest, or radiation.

Odum recommends the use of zoning to establish these specific-use ecosystems. Certainly we will need to preserve as much land (Protective environment) as we possibly can right now, so that we might make carefully considered decisions as to their future use.

The oceans, ironically enough, may be best zoned as Protective environment, since Alfred Redfield* considers the oceans to be

*Ibid, pg. 269.

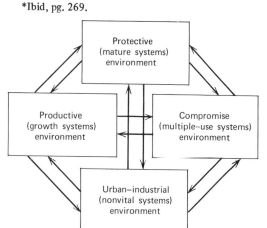

FIGURE 3. Compartment model of the basic kinds of environment required by man, partitioned according to ecosystem development and life-cycle resource criteria.

the major agent in biosphere control, regulating the rate of decomposition and nutrient regeneration, thus creating and maintaining the aerobic terrestrial environment. If we cause entrophication of the oceans in order to feed our exploding billions, we could well greatly reduce the oxygen reservoir of the atmosphere.

Dr. Odum draws an interesting analogy between ecosystem development and human society. "In the early, pioneering stages of a society, high birth rates, rapid growth, high economic profits, and exploitation of accessible and unused resources is advantageous, but as the saturation level is approached, these drives must be shifted to considerations of symbiosis (that is, 'civil rights,' 'law and order,' 'education,' and 'culture'), birth control, and recycling of resources."*

Man today is in the rapid growth stage, heading toward the equilibrium-density stage. Whether man will develop the strong moral, legal, consumer, and technological discipline demanded by this final stage is an ultimate question.

*Ibid, pg. 269.

SECTION 2

THE MAJOR
BIOTIC REGIONS

The "Major Biotic Regions" is a treatment of the naturally occurring climax communities and their physical environments. These are large, relatively stable ecosystems or biotic regions. Some biologists use the word "biome" for these regions.

Using maps, the various world ecosystems are clearly presented, and the teacher has a chance to learn about each of these areas or zones. Certain very interesting features of these areas, such as complexity of flora and fauna, and biomass and productivity, are discussed.

The reader ought to better appreciate the beauty, dynamism, and complexity of this earthly biosphere. He may have gained enough background here to start learning more about man's place in ecosystems, in energy flow, biotic pyramids, biogeochemical cycles, etc. Along the way the reader should gain a deeper insight into the many ways by which man can alter his environment, in particular the ways which are destructive.

Raymond F. Dasmann

PHYSICAL AND BIOLOGICAL FEATURES OF BIOTIC REGIONS

It is generally realized that there are great differences in the productivity and habitability of the various parts of the land surface of the earth. These differences are largely the result of interactions of two climatic factors, temperature and precipitation, with the geology or physiography of the earth. In the water areas of the earth another factor, light, becomes of extreme importance. A cliff face or an active volcano will not support much life no matter how favorable the climate may be. A flat plain with an abundance of available chemical nutrients will not support much life if it is too cold, too hot, or too dry. The depths of the ocean will not produce much in the way of living matter because green plants cannot grow in the absence of light.

Balances between temperature and precipitation are of major significance in determining the suitability of an area for living organisms. Temperature determines the rate at which evaporation takes place and consequently the amount of moisture which can remain in the soil available for plant growth. It also determines whether water can exist in a solid or liquid state. The Antarctic Continent and Greenland are relatively lifeless because they are too cold. The balance between temperature and precipitation in these places is such that both are almost completely covered by hundreds of feet of glacial ice. Although these areas have unusual scientific interest and considerable potential for future use, they have as yet been little used by man. At the other extreme, much of the Sahara desert is inhospitable to life because it is too hot and dry. Evaporation removes much of the rain that falls, and little falls. Only where irrigation can be made available is it possible for such desert regions to support human populations.

In between the areas of extreme climatic or physiographic factors are a great variety of natural areas, a remarkable diversity of climates, geological formations, and biological materials. These constitute man's

SOURCE. Reprinted by permission from *Environmental Conservation*, 2nd ed., New York: John Wiley & Sons, Inc., 1968, with slight abridgment.

original heritage, the diversified earth on which he evolved. Despite our accelerated dissipation of these riches, this diversity of environments remain part of the legacy cession, and the later successional stages are strongly influenced by the climate, soils, and other physical characteristics of a region. As environments vary, so does

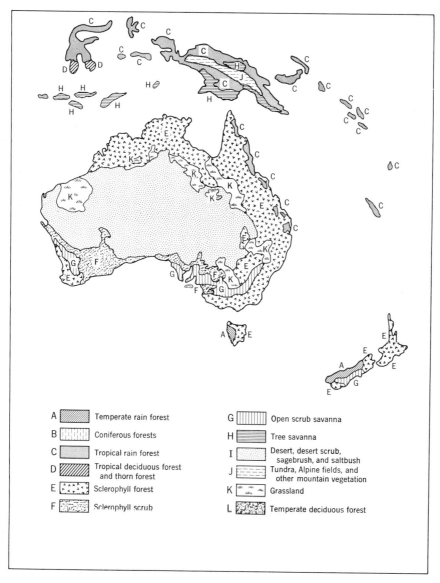

FIGURE 1.

that we enjoy today and can pass on to future generations. This includes the major ecosystems or biotic regions of the earth (Figure 1).

The climax, end product of biotic suc- vegetation and animal life. Hence, if the major natural climax communities of the earth are mapped, the climate and soil regions and thus the major ecosystems are also mapped. A desert in Africa is charac-

FIGURE 1.   (continued)

terized by vegetation, soils, and climate that more closely resemble those of a desert in South America than they do those of an equatorial forest in Africa. Tropical rain forests, too, are relatively similar between Africa, Latin America, and Asia, although the species that compose them may differ. Grasslands in North America present opportunities for human exploitation, difficulties for human occupancy, and penalties for unwise land use similar to those of grasslands in Asia (Table 1).

TUNDRA

In the far north of America is one of the more formidable biotic regions. This area, known as the Arctic barren grounds, or

tundra, is one of long winters and short summers. Winters are extremely cold; summers have moderate to warm temperatures. Precipitation comes mostly as snow and is sufficiently low for the area to be characterized as an Arctic desert. It is preserved from desertlike qualities by the low temperatures and consequent low evaporation rates. Thus, despite the low precipitation, in summer the soils are waterlogged in surface layers. Below the surface of the ground the tundra has a layer of permanently frozen ground, the permafrost. Summers are not long enough for complete thawing to take place.

In such an environment organisms have difficulties. Plants are low growing and thus are protected from extreme cold by

THE MAJOR BIOTIC REGIONS

FIGURE 1. (continued)

the winter mantle of snow. Woody plants are dwarfed or prostrate. Most of the vegetation is grass, sedge, or lichen. All of the plants are adapted to completing their life processes in the short summers: leaves must grow quickly; flowers, fruit, and seed must be produced before the winter cold returns. Summer is a time of great activity.

Animal life is of two kinds: those active or present only in summer and those active through the year. Among the summer forms are vast numbers of migratory birds, including a high percentage of America's waterfowl. Present also are swarms of insects, which pass the winter in egg or larval state and emerge to grow, feed, and reproduce during the period of plant growth. Many mammals also emerge from

hibernation or push northward in migration from the edge of the forest to join the mass of animal life feeding on the burgeoning summer vegetation. The hardy permanent residents, musk ox, caribou, Arctic fox, wolf, polar bear, lay on layers of summer fat to last them through a winter of difficult foraging.

Only a few peoples have been able to adapt themselves to the tundra. In America, the Eskimo tribes developed the cultural skills necessary for survival. Before western culture affected them they were divided into two main ecological groups: the caribou hunters, who depended upon the vast herds of caribou for food and clothing, and the coastal dwellers, who relied upon the ever-present marine life of the Arctic

FIGURE 1. (continued)

seas. Both groups adapted to the climate, concentrating their activities in the summer months and resisting the winter storms in weather-proof dwellings. Compared with most other biotic regions, the tundra is today little exploited or modified by man, although the effects of civilization have been felt on both animal life and vegetation. However, the problems of living in this extreme environment have so far prevented intensive use or settlement.

The tundra ecosystem of North America is repeated in a circumpolar belt across Europe and Asia and reaches southward in modified form along the higher mountain range. It is little developed in the southern hemisphere, where large land masses do not occur within the appropriate latitudes.

BOREAL FOREST

South from the tundra lies timberline, the northern edge of a broad belt of forest extending southward in America into the northeastern United States. This northern forest is characterized by evergreen, coniferous trees, mostly spruce and fir. The region has a climate slightly warmer and with heavier precipitation than the tundra. In summer, the warmest months have enough heat to eliminate the permafrost. Without this ice barrier tree roots can penetrate more deeply, and soils can be more fully developed.

Coniferous forest vegetation helps determine the character of the soil. The leaves and litter that fall from conifers decay slowly in the cold climate and upon

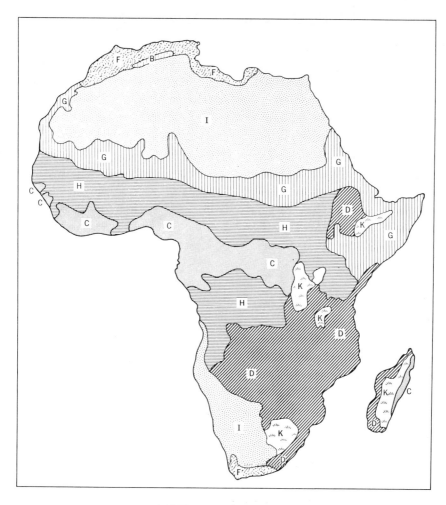

FIGURE 1.   (continued)

TABLE 1.   Relationships of vegetation, soil, and climate

Vegetation	Soil Groups	Climate
Tropical rain forest	Lateritic	Tropical rain forest
Deciduous forest	Red and yellow podsolic	Humid subtropical
	Gray-brown podsolic	Humid continental
Temperate rain forest (Coastal forest)	Gray-brown podsolic	Marine west coast
Transition coniferous forest	Gray-brown podsolic	Mountain
	Red and yellow podsolic	Humid continental
Boreal coniferous forest	Podsol	Subarctic
Tundra	Tundra	Tundra
Desert scrub	Red desert	Low-latitude desert
Sagebrush	Gray desert	Middle-latitude desert
Grassland	Chernozem, Chestnut, Brown, Prairie	Middle-latitude steppe
		Humid continental
		Humid subtropical
		Mediterranean
Broad-sclerophyll forest (Chaparral)	Various	Mediterranean

decaying form acid products which are carried into the soil by rain or melting snow. This mildly acid solution dissolves and leaches out of the top layer of the soil minerals which are important for abundant plant growth. The remaining topsoil tends to be sandy, light gray or whitish in color, and relatively infertile. The deeper layers of soil, in which some of the leached minerals are deposited, become rich in iron and aluminum compounds and darker in color. Such a soil is called a *podzol*. It is of poor quality for agricultural use.

The native animal life of this region, like that of the tundra, is seasonal in abundance. In summer, migratory birds move in to breed, and insects abound. In winter, only the few permanent residents, moose, woodland caribou, lynx, fisher, wolverine, snowshoe hare, and spruce grouse among them, remain to face the period of food scarcity.

Man has settled parts of this region, but much is sparsely inhabited. The fur trapper has led the way in settlement, followed by the lumberman. Only in restricted areas where local conditions have permitted more fertile soils to develop has agriculture been successful. Most of the inhabitants are dependent in whole or in part upon the forests for their livelihood. Forest fires, often man-caused are an important factor.

The boreal-forest ecosystem, like the tundra, forms a broad transcontinental belt in North America and Eurasia, with stringers extending along the high mountain ranges to the south. Like the tundra, and for the same reasons, it does not occur in the continents of the southern hemisphere.

DECIDUOUS FOREST

Farther south, in the eastern part of America, one encounters a third major ecosystem, the broad-leaved deciduous forest. In this area the predominant trees are the traditionally familiar oak, maple, hick-ory, beech, basswood, and other hardwood trees. Unlike the northern conifers, most of these trees shed their leaves in late fall and pass the winter in a bare and dormant state.

In the deciduous forest region precipitation is relatively heavy and well distributed throughout the year. The summer rainfall and warm temperatures provide for abundant plant growth. In general, summers are warm and humid and winters cool to cold with heavy snowfall in the northern part of the region. Southward, as the area of cold winters is left behind, the vegetation gradually changes into the broad-leaved evergreen forest typical of the subtropics.

In primitive times the hardwood forests were widespread between the Atlantic and the Mississippi. However, from early times the influence of man has helped to keep portions of the forest open. Animal life was once abundant and consisted of a greater number of permanently resident species than are found further north. Characteristic of this region are the white-tailed deer, ruffed grouse, cottontail rabbit, red fox, bobwhite quail, fox squirrel, and wild turkey. All played an important role in the pioneer history of the United States.

The forest vegetation determined the soil. Temperate-zone forest litter, whether coniferous or broad leaved, tends to form mild acids on decomposition. These acids, carried into the soil by the abundant rainfall, have a leaching effect. In the deciduous forest, however, because of the greater amounts of litter deposited and the more abundant mineral salts contained in the leaves, the results of leaching are less severe than in the coniferous forest. There is a constant addition of organic material and basic salts to the topsoil which help to maintain its fertility. The *gray-brown podsolic soils* of the northern part of the region, and the *red and yellow podsolic soils* of the southern part are initially fertile and readily worked when they are cleared for agriculture. Without proper care, however, they do not stand up well to continued crop production.

The deciduous forest region, more than most others, has been drastically modified by man. Originally it extended not only through the eastern United States but also through most of western Europe and northern China. However, this type of ecosystem has seen the growth and flowering of western civilization. With this growth the forests have disappeared from most areas, and the lands have been converted for agriculture.

GRASSLANDS

In every continent a grassland region is to be found lying between the forest and the desert and with climates intermediate between the two. It is a region in which relatively low rainfall is normal. Summers are warm and in favorable years moist; winters are cool to cold with snow in the north and rain the south. The rainfall, however, is erratic or cyclic. Wet cycles and dry cycles alternate. Droughts may last for several years, causing major changes in natural vegetation and even more severe changes where the land is used for grazing or agriculture.

The vegetation is dominated by grasses. Tall grasses predominate near the better watered forest border in the *prairie* community. Shorter, sod-forming grasses dominate toward the drier desert side in a region known as *steppe.* The grasses of the climax are perennial, living for several to many years. Annual grasses, which die back to seed each year, are characteristic of disturbed areas.

The climate and grassland vegetation produce grassland soils which differ markedly from forest soils. The topsoil is usually dark in color, and rich in organic matter. Minerals are not leached out of the soil because of the more limited rainfall and the abundant humus. The subsoil is usually rich in lime, whereas forest soils are normally lime deficient. On the scale of *p*H or acidity, grassland soils are neutral or on the alkaline side, whereas the soils of forested regions are typically acid.

Animal life of the grasslands normally includes vast herds of grazing animals, the bison and pronghorn of North America and the numerous antelopes of Africa and Asia being examples. Feeding on these are large carnivores, wolves and their relatives and in Africa the big cats. A variety of mice, ground-dwelling birds, and smaller predators that feed on them are to be found. The abundance of animal life reflects the richness and fertility of the soil.

Grasslands, like the deciduous forest, have long been occupied by man—first by hunters of the great herds of big game, later by nomadic herdsmen with flocks of sheep or cattle, and finally by the farmers with their crops of cereal grains. The fertile soil has favored agriculture since the time when man developed a plow capable of turning the tough, grassland sod.

DESERTS

The dry areas of the world vary considerable in both the amount and the dependability of the rainfall which they receive. Some authorities consider all of those regions that receive an average of 10 inches of rainfall or less per year to be deserts. This includes the extremely dry areas such as the deserts of Chile where no vegetation grows and places such as the northern Great Basin region of the United States where vegetation is relatively abundant.

In the United States there are two main desert regions, the high desert or Great Basin sagebrush region, which extends between the Rocky Mountains and the Sierra Nevada, and the low deserts, Mojave, Coloradan, and Sonoran deserts, which lie to the south of the Great Basin. In the Great Basin the vegetation is characterized by sagebrush and other low-growing shrubs, which form an open cover over the plains, and by the small conifers, junipers, and pinyon pines, which form an open woodland at higher elevations. The low-desert region is an area of desert scrub, where widely spaced creosote bushes are the most common vegetation, giving way in places to various species of cactus.

In both desert regions the vegetation is drought resistant, with various adaptations to prevent or withstand water loss during the long, dry season. It is also adapted to complete its growth and reproduction during the periods when soil moisture is available.

Animal life, like plant life, is adapted to dryness. Animals avoid the heat and drought by being nocturnally active, using sheltered burrows, or remaining in cover in the hot, dry season in the vicinity of the few permanent streams and water holes. Desert rodents often have physiological adaptations that permit them to get along with a minimum of drinking water. Some receive all necessary water from their food and avoid water loss by excreting a highly concentrated urine.

The arid climate and sparse vegetation are reflected in the desert soils. With little leaching there is a minimum loss of soil minerals. With sparse vegetation there is little addition of organic material to the soil, and therefore it may be deficient in nitrogen. Where minerals are in a proper balance and not concentrated in toxic quantities, desert soils are potentially highly fertile when water can be made available.

Deserts have played an important role in human history. The geography of western Asia and North Africa is such that many of the most fertile lands are located on river bottoms surrounded by arid deserts. Western civilization was born on the desert edge, and through history man has had important ecological effects upon the desert. Through turning his flocks of livestock out to graze on the desert vegetation or on the grasslands at the desert edge, man has changed and modified the deserts and has spread desertlike conditions into former grassland areas.

MEDITERRANEAN

On most continents there is a relatively small area with a climate similar to that found around the Mediterranean Sea. Here there are winters with moderate rainfall but little snow and summers which are warm and dry. In North America this is the climate of much of California; elsewhere it is found in Chile, South Australia, South Africa, and in the sections of Europe, Asia, and Africa adjoining the Mediterranean Sea.

The most common type of vegetation in this region, although not always climax, is the dense brushfield dominated by medium-height, evergreen shrubs. This is known in California as *chaparral* and in Europe as *maquis*. It is often interspersed with grassland, tree or shrub savanna or in more sheltered areas with broad-leaved evergreen forest. In California and the Mediterranean region, the evergreen live oaks predominate in this forest and in shrub form in the chaparral. In Australia, *Eucalyptus* forest and scrub dominates the mediterranean biotic region.

In latitude, the mediterranean ecosystem lies between the desert and deciduous forest, or, in the Americas and Australia between desert and temperate rain forest. Its location in Europe has made it the setting for much of the early development of western civilization, which spread from river valleys to mediterranean regions and from there to the deciduous forest.

OTHER TEMPERATE BIOTIC REGIONS

Several other important biotic regions exist in the temperate latitudes, occupying smaller areas than those previously described. One, which can be called *transition coniferous forest,* occupies a zone in the mountains lying between the southward extensions of the boreal forest and the warmer chaparral, grassland, or desert of lower elevations (Figures 2, 5). Pine trees of

FIGURE 2. Transition coniferous forest. Ponderosa pine in Montana (U. S. Forest Service photograph).

various species characterize the climax, or near climax, vegetation of this forest. Transition forest occurs latitudinally in some areas as a belt separating the boreal forest of spruce and fir from the deciduous forest. In the Lakes States and New England it occurs in this role.

On the northwestern coast of North America is an area of high rainfall, well distributed throughout the year, and mild temperatures—a climate of the marine west coast type. This favors the development of an unusually tall, dense, and luxuriant forest, the *temperate rain forest*. In North America this is dominated by redwood, Douglas fir, and other giant conifers (Figure 3). In other continents a similar forest type is dominated by the laurel-leaved hardwood trees. Similar climates and vegetation are found in southern Chile, the South Island of New Zealand, and southeastern Australia.

TROPICAL BIOTIC REGIONS

The most favorable climate on earth for the development of the greatest variety of organic life is to be found in the rain forest region of the tropics, and in the tropics also is to be found one of the least favorable climates for life, exemplified by the virtually rainless deserts of Peru. Tropical rain forest climates have year-round rainfall, without periods when the soil dries out, and temperatures that are always favorable to a high level of plant and animal activity. There are essentially no climatic factors limiting to plant growth. The tropical rain forests are dominated by an unusual variety of broad-leaved evergreen trees—fig and mahogany may be familiar examples—of which dozens of different species often occur in a single acre and many acres may have to be searched to find a second specimen of a particular species of tree.

29

FIGURE 3.   Temperate rain forest. Redwood forest in California (U. S. Forest Service photograph).

The trees in turn support a variety of plants that can survive without contact with the soil, known as epiphytes or perched plants. Orchids, bromeliads, lianas, ferns, mosses, and lichens are in this category. Dense, climax forest has a compact, several-layered canopy that allows little light to penetrate to the ground. The forest floor, therefore, is often relatively free of undergrowth and usually supports little in the way of large animal life. The forest canopy, however, will provide a home for a diversity of birds, insects, arboreal mammals and other animals that may exceed the great diversity of plant species.

Rain forests that have been opened up, either by natural causes or human activi-ties, quickly grow into a dense, second-growth successional forest, the "impene-trable jungle" of tropical travelers. The prevalence of such dense, second-growth jungle in today's tropics indicates the extent of human disturbance. Similar jun-gles occur naturally on the edges of natural clearings, such as stream courses. Since most explorers in the lowland tropics traveled by boat, their accounts of the density of the vegetation were biased by what they saw at the edge of the rivers (Figure 4).

Tropical rain forest soils develop under the canopy of trees, and are enriched by the continual addition of rapidly decaying leaves and litter. The high rainfall and temperatures, however, favor rapid oxida-

FIGURE 4. Tropical forest in Puerto Rico (U. S. Forest Service photograph).

tion of organic matter and leaching of minerals from the soil in areas from which the forest has been cleared. Tropical soils therefore require careful treatment and protection if they are to be maintained in agricultural use. Many of them are poorly suited to agriculture.

Temperate zone writers, in describing the tropics, often overemphasize the importance of the lowland rain forests, since these are the most spectacular and in many ways the most different of the various tropical biotic communities. However, the tropics have a greater variety of biotic communities than all other areas on earth. High on tropical mountains we encounter coniferous forests resembling those of the temperate zone, oak forests similar to those in the eastern United States, as well as purely tropical vegetation such as the puña and paramo of the higher mountains, which are unlike the vegetation of temperate lands (Figure 5).

In those tropical areas where a wet and dry season alternate, a different vegetation replaces the rain forest in the lowlands. This, the raingreen or monsoon forest, is deciduous, the trees shedding their leaves during the dry season. In still drier regions a thorn forest or thorn scrub will replace monsoon forest. With increasing aridity this, in turn, gives way to desert. Leslie Holdridge, working from Costa Rica, has listed 37 different major biotic communities that may occur in any tropical region that displays a wide range in rainfall and altitude. Each of these communities is as distinct and recognizable as the major communities of temperate regions. Compared with the temperate zone, however, the tropics have been rarely studied. They represent a major area for future research.

Until recently, man's influence on the tropics and their biota was slight. With increasing density of human populations, however, and the spread of technology, no large tropical area is any longer secure

31

from disturbance. Without a major effort to preserve representative tropical areas, it is likely that many of the more fascina-

grass in temperate countries, is vegetation consisting of scattered trees and shrubs, or groves and thickets, in an otherwise

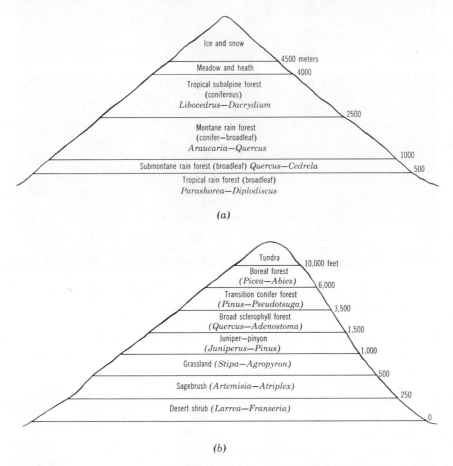

(a)

(b)

FIGURE 5. Zonation of vegetation on mountain ranges. (a) Tropical mountains. (Data from Richards, 1952. Genera are typical of Malayan-New Guinea region.) (b) Temperate-zone mountains with vegetation typical of southwestern United States.

ting living communities on earth will disappear before we know very much about them.

SAVANNA

A glance at a vegetation map of the world will show that large areas in both tropical and temperate regions are covered by vegetation that has not thus far been described in this chapter—savanna. Savanna, sometimes known as parkland or woodland

grass-covered region (Figures 6, 7). It is of natural occurrence along the boundary of forest and grassland where local differences in climate or soil favor an interspersion of vegetation. In such situations also there is normally a greater variety and abundance of animal life than is to be found in either forest or grassland.

Unlike forest or grassland there is no climate or soil that typifies savanna regions, although much savanna occurs within the region characterized by raingreen tropical forest or thorn forest. The great expanse

FIGURE 6. Savanna. Scattered oak trees interspersed with annual grasses in California (U. S. Forest Service photograph).

of savanna over the surface of the earth is now believed to be caused largely by the activities of man and his domestic animals. Man seems to prefer interspersion of vegetation and creates it wherever he goes. Fire and grazing have been techniques used to open the forest and let the grassland enter. Grazing, irrigation, and planting are techniques for spreading woody vegetation into otherwise grassy areas.

The tropical savannas are the home of the great game herds that once roamed widely in Africa and Asia and are still to be found in areas where they have been protected. The enormous variety of wild mammals in the tropics of Africa has long attracted attention. Twenty or more species of large grazing and browsing mammals from elephants to antelope may occur in a single area, each adapted to feeding on or otherwise using different species of plants, or different kinds of vegetation. In addition to these larger creatures a variety of smaller mammals, or predators, and a profusion of species of birds and other kinds of animals will occur.

AQUATIC ECOSYSTEMS

The water surfaces of the earth occupy over 70 per cent of the total world area and support a great variety of living things. However, since they are much more uniform than land areas in conditions favorable or unfavorable to life, they are not as amenable to classification. Classifications of aquatic environments are frequently based on major climatic differences, the amounts of dissolved chemicals, size and relative permanency of the body of water, and the depth of the water relative to the depth of light penetration. The greatest diversity of life is usually found on the edges or interfaces of land and water, the intertidal regions of seacoasts and estuaries, since here the widest range of physical environments will be encountered. By contrast, the open ocean is relatively homogeneous and shows much less diversity in forms of life.

It is worth noting at this point, that the range in productivity of aquatic environments is as great as that to be encountered on lands. The open oceans have sometimes been equated with the world's deserts in supporting and producing relatively little life. Cold fresh-water lakes are also relatively barren. By contrast, warm ponds and estuaries teem with life and are the aquatic counterparts of warm humid forest areas on land.

FIGURE 7. Scrub savanna in Rhodesia, showing effects of heavy browsing by elephants.

COMPLEXITY AND SIMPLICITY

The terrestrial biotic regions of the earth show the effects of gradients that exist in climate. Tropical rainforest climates support the most complex and varied plant and animal life. However, moving out in the tropics along a gradient of decreasing rainfall or increasing evaporation, one would encounter communities that are less complex in which the numbers of species of plants and animals decrease to reach a lowest point in the tropical deserts. Similarly, moving north from the lowland rainforest climate of the tropics along a temperature gradient, we would pass through subtropical rain forests, temperate rain forests, boreal forests, and tundra. Along this line also one passes from the most complex to the least complex biotic community, and the number of species of plants and animals would also decrease along this gradient. Thus, in the boreal forests we find the single species, white spruce, as a lone dominant in great areas of Canada and Alaska.

Within each climatic region, the climax communities will represent, usually, the most complex communities that the climate and geology of the region can support; but the climaxes themselves are more simple and less varied in regions where climatic or geological factors are strongly limiting.

Complexity appears to be accompanied by stability. Tropical forest communities are usually stable communities. They are relatively resistant to change. The numbers and arrangements of species within them vary little from month to month or year to year. By contrast, simple communities, whether of tundra or desert, are subject to regular and often violent changes in the relative abundance of species. The fluctuations of lemmings, a small Arctic rodent, are a legendary example of the instability of tundra populations. The changes in abundance of jackrabbits or mice in arid regions are well known. In the boreal forest, insect pests or diseases sometimes wipe out hundreds of square miles of trees. Locust plagues in dry regions do enormous damage. Similar outbreaks are virtually unknown in humid tropical communities, except where man has intervened.

Man seeks to simplify the complex so that he can manage it. He depends for his livelihood on foods grown in artificially created, simplified ecosystems. Such simplification, however, can be dangerous, since it sets in motion all of the factors that contribute to instability in the normally simple communities of more rigorous natural environments. In the humid tropics, the presence of a great variety of naturally occurring species guarantees competition between species, predation of one species on another, parasitic relations between species, and other complicated interspecies relationships that keep each population under control and prevent any single species population from either increasing or decreasing greatly. When these interspecific controls are removed, as when a plantation of bananas, cacao, or oil palms is established, there is little to keep the pests or parasites that feed on these agricultural crops from becoming abundant. Similarly, in drier or colder regions, simplification

of natural communities also permits the natural enemies of the introduced crop plants to flourish; however, climate offers some periodic control on the abundance of these species.

Plagues and pests have harried man through history, destroying his crops and forcing him to engage in various forms of chemical or biological warfare in his own protection. Unless skillfully employed, however, such activities can make the situation worse, creating a more simple, less stable, more readily threatened system than the one that was endangered in the first place.

BIOMASS AND PRODUCTIVITY

The gradients in complexity and stability that have been described also represent gradients in the mass of living material that a particular region will support (the *biomass*), and in the amount of new living material that can be produced each year (*productivity*). Tropical rain forests support the greatest biomass or *standing crop* of living material per acre or square mile of any naturally occurring community. Extremely dry or cold areas, deserts and tundra, vie for the distinction of supporting the lowest standing crop of living material per acre.

The standing crop of animal life, however, does not follow the same gradient as that of vegetation. Drier tropical savannas support a greater biomass of animal life than do the humid rain forests. Temperate zone grasslands with highly fertile soils supported, before human disturbance, a higher animal biomass than the leached soils of temperate forest areas. These differences appear related to the relative ability of the soils to produce plant proteins essential to animal nutrition. Soils in more humid areas can naturally produce a great bulk of carbohydrates, but lack the chemical balance to supply the quantity of protein per unit of area that can be supplied by the relatively unleached soils of the drier savannas or grasslands. Human populations that live away from the seacoasts in humid tropical areas have difficulty in producing their protein needs. The crop plants of the humid tropics (yams, taro, cassava, and fruits) are poor suppliers of protein.

Natural productivity varies also with the climatic and geological factors that influence complexity. The tropical rain-forest regions, with year-round growing seasons, are capable of producing more living material per acre per year than temperate forest regions where climate is seasonally limiting to plant growth. Temperate forests, however, with adequate rainfall, produce more plant material per acre than grasslands where seasonal drought restricts plant growth.

Man has long had an interest in increasing productivity of both his plant crops and of his domestic animals. To some degree he has been able to improve on natural patterns through supplying nutrients, where these were in short supply, supplying water or providing shelter against climatic factors. However, the highest yield of any land-based crop in biomass gain per acre per year is in sugar cane grown in the humid tropics. In temperate regions, forest plantations are more productive in total biomass gain than are the grainfields that have replaced natural grasslands. In the Arctic, high crop production can only take place where soils and local climate can be modified, and in the desert only the presence of irrigation, which essentially creates a different local climate, makes possible abundant crop yields.

BIOTIC REGIONS AS HABITATS FOR MAN

In this brief description of the major biotic regions, or ecosystems, of the earth, an attempt has been made to describe the physical and biotic setting in which man has operated throughout his history. Since man first appeared on earth, the same general biotic regions have been present, from tundra to tropical rain forest. The boundaries of these regions have shifted as climates have changed, but their general locations upon the earth have not been greatly modified in the time of man. In his development, man has first learned to adapt to the conditions of life within these biotic regions, avoiding those that were too rigorous. With increasing technology, he has learned to modify and change these regions to make them more or less favorable for his existence. Always, however, he has operated within the physical limits set by climate, soil, and vegetation. Even today's technology permits only minor modification of these physical limits. There are prospects of major modifications of climate. We already have means for modifying soils and vegetation. However, such changes are accompanied by risks unless we have an adequate understanding of their ecological consequences. When we replace complex natural processes we must be prepared to exercise human skills if the environment is to be kept healthy and productive.

PART 2

THE DESTRUCTION OF THE ENVIRONMENT:

the effect of man on ecosystems

SECTION 1

OVERVIEW OF
THE PROBLEM

In this, the first section of Part 2, you will be introduced to the general problem, many-faceted as it is, as well as speculation on the causes of pollution.

William Bowen provides a fine general introduction, discussing the fact of universal interdependence among organisms of our biosphere. He also discusses the concepts of limitation and complexity, basic to an understanding of ecology.

The second article, by Donald Whitehead, is an eloquent statement of the problems of pollution, misuse of natural resources, and overpopulation. Whitehead calls for an approach which would create a "steady state" which is a balance between our economic growth, consumer needs, and our finite resource pool and pollution limits of the biosphere.

LaMont Cole, the eminent ecologist, surveys some of the ways in which man tampers recklessly with the balance of nature. After a brief discussion of the destructive acts of men of antiquity, Cole mentions the unplanned perfusion of DDT throughout the biosphere, as well as the fact that if DDT had turned out to have harmful effects upon our bodies we would have suffered a cataclysm. Not only do we use DDT with abandon, we are now mindlessly distributing various other pesticides, plastics, antibiotics, radioisotopes, and detergents.

Professor Cole indicates how the great biogeochemical cycles, involving carbon, oxygen, and nitrogen, can be altered to so great an extent that we may not survive. Fossil fuel burning, he contends, can proceed at a rate which may, in certain areas, exceed the production of oxygen by photosynthesis. If we were to somehow impede the photosynthetic activities of marine plankton, the total quantity of atmospheric oxygen could very well fall to a fatal level.

The article called "The Causes of Pollution" is a detailed study of the impact of a variety of technologies on our environment. It focuses on the "per capita" increase in consumption (production) of products such as plastics which damage the environment far more than the earlier substances they replaced.

OVERVIEW OF THE PROBLEM

The final article, by Louis Levine, Gress LeMaistre, and Jo Ann LeMaistre, outlines the challenge of our times, which is whether or not Homo sapiens can transcend his "functional fictions" to live in harmony with himself and his natural environment. Perhaps this challenge is the ultimate one facing mankind, thus our schools and curricula must turn about and deal honestly and directly with it—before it is too late.

William Bowen

OUR NEW AWARENESS OF THE GREAT WEB

Predictions about anything much less predictable than the rising of the sun are likely to be wrong, or at least seem wrong in hindsight. So we may assume that most predictions put forward in 1937, like those of other years, would now be worth recalling only as examples of fallibility. But at least one prediction published in that year has since come to seem exceedingly perspicacious. It appeared in a book by Kenneth Burke, a literary critic. "Among the sciences," he wrote, "there is one little fellow named Ecology, and in time we shall pay him more attention."

Quite a few years passed before Burke's prophecy was borne out. As recently as 1962 the naturalist Marston Bates wrote: "Ecology may well be the most important of the sciences from the viewpoint of long-term human survival, but it is among those least understood by the general public..." Even a year or two ago, anyone not a biologist or a biology student could easily go for months on end without encountering any mention of ecology.

But now, almost suddenly it seems, ecology is popping out all over—the word, at least, if not the science. We meet ecology at dinner parties, in newspaper editorials, on the covers of magazines, in speeches by public officials, at gatherings of scholars in fields remote from biology, and in the names of recently born or reborn corporations (Ecological Science Corp., Ecologic Resources Corp., Ecology Inc.). At this rate, ecology can be expected to debut before long in *Playboy,* the manifestoes of student rebels, the public utterances of Edward Kennedy, subway-station graffiti, and catch-breeze book titles—*You and Ecology* and perhaps even *Ecology and the Single Girl.* There is an element of fad, of course, in this swift transformation of a mossy scientific term into a conspicuous "In" word. But there appears to be something much more important, too: what Kenneth Burke foresaw, awakened perception by a great many people of an urgent practical need for the kinds of information, insights, and concepts embraced in ecology.

THE COMPRESSED WISDOM

The term ecology was coined a hundred years ago by the German biologist Ernst

SOURCE.   Reprinted, by permission, from *Fortune,* February, 1970.

Haeckel. The eco-, from the Greek *oikos* (house), is the same eco- as in economics, and according to an old definition, what ecologists study is "the economy of animals and plants." In the now-standard definition, ecology is the science of the relations between organisms and their environment.

That will do as a working definition if we bear in mind that neither in nature nor in the thinking of ecologists are there two distinct compartments, organisms and environment. For any organism, other organisms constitute part of the environment. And the physical environment itself is largely created and maintained by organisms. Atmospheric oxygen, necessary to the survival of life on earth, is itself a product of life, accumulated over millennia from the respiration of aquatic organisms and terrestrial plants. A hardwood forest can maintain its stability for many centuries on end because it creates its own peculiar environment, in which seedlings of only certain plant species can grow to maturity. Recognizing that organisms and their physical environment are interacting parts of a system, an ecologist uses the term "ecosystem" to mean the community of living things and the physical environment, both together, in the segment of nature he is studying

Ecologists study all kinds of segments, great and small. One ecologist may investigate how various species of mites coexist in the pine-needle litter on a forest floor by occupying separate "niches," or ways of making a living. (It is a well-established principle of ecology that only one species can occupy a particular niche in any habitat.) Another ecologist may work out the intermeshed food chains of various species in a pond or a forest. Still another, a worker in the sprawling, almost unbounded field called "human ecology," may trace the paths by which radioactive substances and persistent pesticides, created by our interventions in nature, accumulate in the tissues of our bodies.

In all the diverse studies of ecologists, certain basic themes keep recurring. Together, they may be regarded as the compressed wisdom of ecology.

Interdependence. "The first law of ecology," biologist Barry Commoner remarked not long ago, "is that everything is related to everything else." The continued functioning of any organism depends upon the interlinked functionings of many other organisms. Seemingly autonomous man ultimately depends upon photosynthesis for his food. The seemingly autonomous oak in the forest depends upon microscopic organisms to break down fallen leaves, releasing nutrients that can be absorbed by its roots. Interrelations between organisms are often intricate, and some obscure species provide vital linkages not at all apparent to the casual observer. The seeds of the bitterbush, an important food plant for browsing animals in arid sections of Africa, fail to germinate unless several seeds are buried close together below the surface of the soil; that happens in nature only through the intervention of a species of ground squirrel, which buries hoards of seeds and often forgets them. It is unwise for men ever to assume without very close study that any species is entirely dispensable.

Limitation. The saying that trees do not grow to the sky expresses another basic theme of ecology. Nothing grows indefinitely—no organism, no species. Much more commonly than non-ecologists might suppose, animal species limit their own growth: rates of reproduction respond to crowding or other signals so that total numbers remain commensurate with the resources of the ecosystem. In the over-all ecosystem of the earth, total animal energy is limited by the amount of solar energy plants convert into organic compounds. Since combustion consumes oxygen, the amount of combustion the earth can sustain is limited—other limiting factors aside—by the ecosystem's net production of free oxygen.

Complexity. When he looks closely at any ecosystem, the ecologist invariably comes upon complexity, an intricate web of interrelations. A diagram showing the movement of a single chemical element through an ecosystem can get exceedingly complicated. In the ecosystem of man, which includes institutions and artifacts that themselves impinge upon and alter the environment, the interrelations are unimaginably complex. This great web, an ecologist said, "is not only more complex than we think. It is more complex than we *can* think.

CLOSE TO WIPING OUT A SYMBOL

In their complexity, ecosystems exhibit some of the characteristics of complex systems that Professor Jay W. Forrester of M.I.T. recently pointed to in *Fortune* ("Overlooked Reasons for Our Social Troubles," December). In ecosystems as in social systems, causes and effects are often widely separated in both time and space. Accordingly, our interventions often yield unexpected consequences.

After years of spraying persistent pesticides to kill insects, we find that we have come close to wiping out a national symbol, the bald eagle: concentrated through food chains, pesticides accumulate in the tissues of eagles and certain other birds to the point of impairing reproduction. We drain Florida swamplands and learn later on that by reducing the outflow of fresh water into estuaries we have increased their salinity and thereby damaged valuable breeding environments for fish and shrimp. The Aswan Dam impounds silt that would otherwise be carried downstream, so the Nile no longer performs as richly as before its ancient function of renewing fields along its banks. The fertility of the Nile Valley is therefore declining. That is only one variety of ecological backlash from this triumph of engineering. With the flow of the river reduced. salt water is backing into the Nile

delta, harming farmlands there. And in time, some authorities predict, the flow of Nile water to new farmlands through irrigation canals will bring on a calamitous spread of schistosomiasis, a liver disease produced by parasites that spend part of their life cycle in the bodies of snails.

Professor Garrett Hardin of the University of California pithily expressed the principal lesson of all this in pointing out that "we can never do merely one thing." When we intervene in a complex system so as to produce a certain desired effect, we always get in addition some other effect or effects, usually not desired. As Hardin also said: "Systems analysis points out in the clearest way the virtual irrelevance of good intentions in determining the consequences of altering a system."

Ecologists are accustomed to looking at nature as a system, and if we had paid more attention to them we might have been spared a lot of backlash. In trying to reduce insect damage to crops, for example, we might have made more use of specific biological or biochemical means of control and less use of persistent broad-spectrum insecticides. We might now, accordingly, have more birds in our countryside and less DDT in our streams—and in some places, fewer harmful insects in our fields.

THE SUBVERSIVE ASPECT

The recurrent themes of ecology run counter to some old ways of perceiving and thinking that are deeply ingrained in the prevalent world view of Western man. We believe in limitless growth (or did until recently); ecology tells us all growth is limited. We speak (or spoke until recently) of man's "conquest" of nature; ecology tells us we are dependent for our well-being and even survival upon systems in which nature obeys not our rules but its own. Our scientists and engineers, and our social scientists too, proceed by isolating and simplifying; ecology tells us to heed existent complexity and patiently try to trace out its strands. In a sense, then, ecology is subversive. The ecologist Paul B. Sears, a few years ago, called it "a subversive subject," and the editors of a recent compilation of essays on the ecology of man entitled their book *The Subversive Science.* *

To the extent that the recent popularity of the word "ecology" points to the incipient spread of ecological ways of thinking, we may be witnessing the flux of a momentous historical change. Alterations in the ways men perceive and think about reality lead to alterations in the goals and modes of action. It is too early to tell whether an enduring shift to ecological ways of perceiving and thinking is now in progress, but if it is, the effects will surely be beneficial, on balance. Ecology can help us cope with the environmental ills that beset us, if only by enabling us to avoid bringing on

*Edited by Paul Shepard and David McKinley and published by Houghton Mifflin. The book is a rich trove, hard digging in places, but worth it.

new unintended consequences in trying to remedy old unintended consequences.

Less obviously, ecological thinking can help us cope with the social ills that also insistently press upon us. The social sciences are proving to be inadequate as guides to policy, and the inadequacy is inherent in the prevalent methods and mind sets of social scientists. In general, they have aped the successful methodology of the physical sciences, but in the study of complex social systems, simplification too readily slides into oversimplification. The social sciences would benefit greatly—and so would we all—by borrowing from the ecologists their willingness to accept and try to puzzle out complexity and their habit of sustained, open-eyed observation of what actually goes on.

All this may be too much to expect. But it seems possible, to take a cheerful view, that in 1980 or 2000 Americans will be better off in their physical environment *and* their social arrangements because, at the beginning of the 1970's, Kenneth Burke's prediction came true.

Donald R. Whitehead

THIS IS YOUR EARTH . . . LOVE IT OR LEAVE IT

A new era has dawned. Man has entered the age of "environmental awareness" or "the age of ecology." The concerns of a small group of scientists, of naturalists, and of misunderstood and seldom appreciated conservationists have become the focus of society as a whole. Our news media continually report the plight of the environment. The fragile biosphere, that envelope of land, water, and air on which all organisms depend, shows signs of serious deterioration. Lake Erie has become drastically polluted and Lake Michigan is rapidly following the same route. The same applies to innumerable other lakes, and ponds, and also the vast, seemingly limitless reservoir—the sea. The air around many cities and industrial complexes is ladened with dangerous chemicals; vast land areas have been devastated by careless mining operations; unique wilderness areas are threatened by the encroachment of man and his technology; pesticides are beginning to endanger many beneficial species (including man); major cities face insurmountable problems of waste disposal; enormous quantities of litter are accumulating throughout our landscape. All of these and countless more are symptoms of the environmental malaise that is attracting so much attention.

In the past our environmental concerns were less pressing—much appeared to be merely a matter of aesthetics; such as concern for vanishing species or disappearance of natural beauty. We now realize that there is something far more fundamental involved. The symptoms are indications of changes that threaten the survival of the human species. The chemical, physical, and biological changes that we are causing are effectively poisoning our environment, thus endangering man and the vast complex of living organisms on which he is both directly and indirectly dependent for his survival.

Although there is much discussion concerning the deterioration of our environment, the underlying causes and long-range implications of the problems are seldom dealt with directly. Most attention is devoted to ways of dealing with the symptoms rather than the disease itself. Given the frightening pattern of environmental

SOURCE. *Indiana Alumni Magazine,* March, 1970. By permission of the editor and the author.

deterioration and its obvious acceleration, this situation must be rectified immediately. If it is not, we may well have doomed the human race to non-survival.

The threat to human survival comes from several interrelated problems: (1) the explosive increase in human population; (2) an awesome increase in man's ability to alter the environment (largely through the release of vast quantities of gaseous, liquid, and solid effluent), and (3) rapid depletion of resources that are in finite supply. If man is to survive, it is imperative that all three of the problems be dealt with simultaneously. An approach to just one or two will only serve to delay ultimate disaster. Similarly, dealing with the overt symptoms will accomplish little. The purpose of this article is to present the basic facts concerning the causes of environmental deterioration and to indicate what must be dealt with if man is to survive and preserve some of the quality of his environment.

Overpopulation poses the most serious threat to human survival, the quality of life and the quality of the human environment. At present the world's population is increasing so rapidly that it is likely to outrun all resources in the very near future. Although the magnitude of this threat is evident to all who have surveyed the problem, comparatively little has been done to attack it. In fact, society has demonstrated a frustrating reluctance even to talk about its implications.

Certainly the dimensions of the problem are clear. The industrial-technological revolution of the last century has brought about a dramatic decline in death rate (through increased agricultural and medical technology) with no corresponding depression of birth rates. As life expectancy began to creep upwards from a norm of approximately 30 years, a marked acceleration of population growth became evident. The best demographic estimates indicate that the world's population numbered about 250 million at the birth of Christ, about 500 million by the time the Pilgrims landed at Plymouth, one billion at the time of the Civil War, 2 billion by 1940, and had increased to well over 3.5 billion by 1969. The best estimates all suggest that population will exceed 7 billion by the turn of the century and perhaps 15 billion by 2025. The implications of this trend are ominous.

What is even more frightening is that the rate of increase is itself accelerating. It took 1,620 years to double the world's population to 500 million. The subsequent doubling required 240 years and the next, but 80 years. At present the "doubling time" has decreased still further to 37 years—37 years from now there will be twice as many people for the world to cope with. Estimates indicate that by the turn of the century the doubling time will have decreased to 25 years or less.

More and more people at an ever faster rate—that is the basic problem with which man must contend.

Generalized data like those presented here obscure the fact that vast segments of the earth's population face infinitely serious problems. As yet no country has succeeded in checking population growth. Although it is true that many of the more industrialized nations are growing slowly (the doubling time for the United States is 63 years; that for Japan, Sweden, and Hungary about 100 years), the bulk of the world's population lives in less industrialized nations with staggering growth rates. The doubling time for all of Latin America is 25 years—in 25 years the population of that region will have increased from 250 million to 500 million. Individual countries are growing even more rapidly. The doubling time for Costa Rica is approximately 17 years, that for Venezuela about 15. If Latin America faces problems of feeding, housing, educating, employing, and providing medical aid for its present population, how can it possibly cope with twice as many people within the next 25 years? Africa faces similar problems—the doubling times for all of the tropical African nations are close to 25 years. Nigeria, so prominent in the news of late, had a population of 19.9 million in 1931 and 53.7 million in 1963. Clearly the emerging nations of Africa will face even more formidable survival problems within the next few decades. The picture in Asia is equally depressing. India, a nation of some 550 million, adds over one million individuals to its population every month. The population of China grows by almost 1.8 million per month.

The short range consequences of the population explosion are clear. The developing nations will become even more deeply entrenched in the self-destructive poverty cycle—too many people added at too fast a rate to permit any improvement in the standard of living. Unless something dramatic can be done to check the rate of population growth, no amount of agricultural, medical, industrial, technological, and educational aid can alleviate the situation. Without a coordinated international program the less industrialized nations are likely to see increasing deterioration of living conditions—and at an increasingly rapid rate.

The long-range problem is far more serious. The survival of man and all other forms of life will depend on stabilizing world population at some point in the reasonably near future. This necessity follows directly from the nature of the "spaceship earth" on which we live. The earth is clearly finite—it possesses a definite amount of land, finite volume of water, and is surrounded by a finite blanket of air. It follows from this that the earth has a finite—not boundless—capacity for producing food. There is a finite (and measurable) quantity of energy available from the sun and this strikes a finite amount of arable land. Plants grown on this arable land intercept the solar energy and transform a small fraction of it (in the process of photosynthesis) into the stored energy of food substances. The food producing

capacity of the land (and water) is thus limited—and no technological marvels can push productivity beyond this biologically and physically controlled limit.

Consequently, the earth can feed only so many people. If we exceed this maximum number, the survival of all will be threatened by starvation.

Although one could calculate the maximum number of individuals that could be fed, such speculations are academic. In a finite world one should be concerned not with maximizing the number of people, but rather with optimizing benefits. It is clear that every addition to the world's population automatically means a decrease in the per capita holdings of those already present—less food per individual, less living space, less recreational space, fewer material goods and so forth. It is physically impossible to provide "the maximum benefit for the maximum number." Clearly we must reorient our thinking towards "optimizing benefits"—and considerable effort must be directed at defining the optimum level of population—the level which will preserve both the quality of life and the quality of the environment.

Any definition of optimum must take into account the other major facets of the "crisis of the environment": resource depletion and environmental deterioration.

A finite world possesses finite quantities of all resources. At present we are consuming these at an astonishing rate with no apparent concern for the needs of future generations. Some resources pose particularly crucial problems. Such is the case with the "fossil fuels" (coal and petroleum). Once they have been consumed, there is no possibility of replacement. Petroleum provides the most instructive example because it is so crucial for all industrial nations. Although it is difficult to assess the exact status of undiscovered petroleum, most estimates suggest that at present rates of use we will run out of petroleum within the next 100 years, conceivably sooner. The United States, which possesses but 6% of the world's population, uses almost 40% of the world's annual petroleum production. Roughly 90 billion gallons are consumed annually by our 88 million passenger cars! This represents an enormous drain on the world's reserves and this drain is likely to increase. Economists confidently predict over 240 million American autos by the turn of the century. It is clear that we must soon evolve a different philosophy concerning the management of the remaining petroleum supplies, or little will be available for the fundamental needs of the emerging nations.

Analogous problems exist for all other resources. Although it is likely that our burgeoning technology can and will develop substitutes, the fact remains that basic materials such as steel, copper, aluminum and the like are infinitely more practical to meet the most fundamental agricultural and industrial needs of nations struggling to survive. Thus, inevitably, we must consider the status of all such resources and develop management policies consistent with the needs of world civilization. Perhaps equally as important, the concept of "recycling" must be reintroduced into virtually all of the world's industrial systems. In this manner all of the critical items can be retained for use almost indefinitely, rather than being discarded into the world's pollutable reservoir as effluent or used products. If our imaginative technology has the capacity for developing a vast spectrum of substitute materials it certainly has the capacity for evolving efficient ways to reclaim iron and all other nonreplenishable substances.

The development of these priorities will permit a stable human population to live harmoniously with its available resource pool.

Environmental deterioration is the third and most often discussed component of the "crisis of the environment." In large part the deterioration that we can observe results from the release of vast quantities of solid, liquid, and gaseous effluent (much of it highly toxic) into the finite and pollutable mantle of land, water, and air upon which we depend for our existence. Because the biosphere has definable limits, it can only absorb so much effluent without being altered detrimentally. It would appear that we have already exceeded the buffering capacity of our environment.

The dimensions of the world problem are readily apparent when one assesses data on effluent production from the United States alone. Over 200 million tons of solid waste is released into the American environment in a single year. This includes 48 billion tin cans, 26 billion bottles, 4 million tons of plastic materials, 30 million tons of paper, 100 million automobile tires, and 8 million automobiles. This amounts to approximately a ton per person per year—and the volume is increasing by roughly 6% per year. Quite obviously, this can't continue for long, as there is insufficient space to store such waste, burning creates problems of atmospheric pollution, plastics are not degradable, and much of this needs to be reclaimed for further use.

Liquid effluent creates similar problems. In the United States more than 18 billion gallons of municipal and industrial wastes are released into the aquatic environment in a single year. When one considers the character of this liquid waste (much of it consisting of toxic chemicals), the amount released, and adds to the picture thermal pollution from power generating facilities, the input of vast quantities of chemical fertilizers from agricultural lands, radioactive isotopes from reactors and nuclear tests, and an immense volume of pesticides, it is easy to comprehend why all components of the aquatic environment are experiencing serious deterioration.

The earth's atmosphere is no better off. More than 150 million tons of gaseous and particulate matter are released into the air over the United States every year. This pandora's box of pollutants includes roughly 80 million tons of carbon monoxide,

THE DESTRUCTION OF THE ENVIRONMENT

30 million tons of oxides of sulphur (toxic to both plants and animals), and 15 million tons of the equally toxic oxides of nitrogen. The sources of the atmospheric pollutants are reasonably easy to identify. Slightly more than 60% (by weight) of the pollutants derive from automobile exhausts. This includes the 92% of the carbon monoxide and 63% of the hydrocarbons (these are organic compounds resulting from incomplete combustion of petroleum—hydrocarbons are a principal component of the irritating and dangerous Los Angeles-type "photochemical smogs" and many are carcinogenic. Over 80% of the sulphus oxides are released by coal-burning power-generating facilities and industries. The bulk of the particulate pollutants come from these same sources. Almost 50% of the nitrogen oxides come from automobiles and much of the remainder from a combination of industry and power plants.

Our vast arsenal of pesticides poses another tremendous threat to the environment. Over 700 million pounds of 45,000 different kinds of pesticide are released in the United States in a single year. It is estimated that over a billion pounds of DDT is presently circulating in the living mantle of the earth. The beneficial and necessary aspects of the pesticides cannot be denied. Control of disease and agricultural pests clearly requires pesticide use, but the balance sheet is more complicated. We are gradually becoming aware that the debit side of the ledger is more ominous than we realized. This is particularly true of the long-lasting chlorinated hydrocarbon insecticides—a group which includes, among others, DDT. Chlorinated hydrocarbons are now implicated in a vast array of detrimental changes in many formerly balanced aquatic and terrestrial communities. The effects are often long-delayed and frequently at tremendous distances from sites of insecticide application. All evidence indicates that we must rapidly phase out the chlorinated hydrocarbons and be exceptionally careful in assessing the potential

dangers of those that we select to replace them.

The impact of this constellation of contaminants on the total biosphere is enormous. Even the vast and seemingly imperturbable sea has been profoundly affected. Entire communities (ecosystems), both aquatic and terrestrial, have been drastically altered. In most cases these alterations have resulted in the disruption of the intricate fabric of the community through the elimination of many critical species of plants, animals, and microorganisms. The stability (hence survival) of any community depends upon the maintenance of complicated interactions among all components (plant, animal, and microbes). If links in food chains or food webs are lost, or if the microorganisms which are crucial for nutrient cycling within the community are lost, the total community becomes unstable, and, like a sick animal, will have great difficulty in surviving even normal oscillations in the physical and chemical components of the environment.

Our survival depends both directly and indirectly upon the presence of stable ecosystems—stable "natural" ecosystems and stable "cultivated" ecosystems. Environmental pollutants pose two threats to man—a direct threat resulting from the presence of substances toxic to man and an indirect threat from an increasingly unstable world ecosystem.

Man has long considered the sea to be his ultimate reserve—a vast, seemingly limitless reservoir with an enormous buffering capacity—thus capable of absorbing virtually all of our effluents. It is now clear that this concept is false. The sea has a demonstrably finite volume. It is also the ultimate "sink" in which virtually all of the environmental pollutants will accumulate, including the exceedingly toxic lead derived from automobile exhausts, the billions of pounds of persistent pesticides, the sulfur and nitrogen oxides scavenged from the air by precipitation, and so forth. That this boundless array of environmental pollutants will have a detrimental effect on the sea is predictable. In point of fact, serious signs of deterioration are already evident, especially in semi-isolated arms of the sea, such as the Baltic and the Mediterranean.

Fortunately man is becoming aware of the implications of the changes in his environment and accordingly the symptoms of deterioration are beginning to be dealt with. Much legislation has been drafted both here and abroad to cope with specialized aspects of pollution of the aquatic environment and of the atmosphere and attempts are being made to restrict use of persistent pesticides such as DDT and other chlorinated hydrocarbons. As optimistic as these trends appear, it is safe to say that they are doomed to failure unless the underlying causes of the problems are dealt with directly. No attempt to alleviate pollution will succeed unless we simultaneously succeed in checking population growth.

An equally impressive barrier in the path to human survival is our prevailing economic ethic—the ethic which measures the "health" of a nation or the world in terms of economic growth. Our preoccupation is with economic growth—with increase in the Gross National Product or the Gross World Product. Yet, as the economist Kenneth Boulding has pointed out, continued economic growth is incompatible with survival in a finite world. We must reorient our thinking towards establishment of an economic equilibrium—a "steady state" which takes into account the finite nature of the world resource pool and the "pollutability" of the finite biosphere.

One should not take this to mean that we should discourage the economic growth of the agrarian nations. If they are to improve their standards of living, significant industrial development is essential (equally essential is population control). But one must also recognize the fact that as the world's industrial capacity expands, so does the potential for pollution. The more new factories, the greater the volume of contaminating effluent. The way out of this dilemma, as Boulding and others have indicated, is to alter the character of our industrial systems. If the effluents and used products of industry are processed and cycled back into the industrial system, then two problems have been dealt with simultaneously. Recycling facilitates preservation of the resource pool and virtually eliminates the causes of pollution—provided, of course, that we have also checked population and evolved a steady-state economic system.

Such are the basic concerns in this emerging era of environmental awareness. Survival is the long-range issue which must dominate our planning for the future. Survival in an environment of reasonable quality will require (1) stabilization of population at an optimum level, (2) the ultimate stabilization of economic growth, and (3) the recycling of products and by-products of civilization.

Buttons circulated at the Christmas meetings of the American Association for the Advancement of Science carried a picture of the earth as viewed from the moon with the caption "this is your earth, love it or leave it." The message is clear—unless we give the earth's environment careful attention, we may well be eliminated. Man must be considered an "endangered species."

LaMont C. Cole

PLAYING RUSSIAN ROULETTE WITH BIOGEOCHEMICAL CYCLES

In view of the alterations man has made on the world environment, he has been extremely lucky to have stayed around for so long. We humans have presumed to adopt the label *Homo sapiens,* the wise one. We had better start living up to that label quickly if we are going to continue to survive here.

Ever since our Neolithic ancestors started using fire as a tool—probably first to drive game and later to clear forest land for grazing—man has been altering the face of every continent on which he has lived. It was sheer serendipity that these grasslands, created by burning forests, developed soils which eventually made them among the world's most valuable agricultural land. Our own prairies were probably created by fire, and maintained by fire and later by heavy grazing. Many other grasslands in other parts of the world fall into the same category. It is probable that in the continent of Africa, which has perhaps been inhabited by man since his origin, nothing of the landscape is as it would have been without him. The savannas were probably created and maintained by fire, and have become highly productive of a diverse fauna of grazing and browsing mammals. These mammals probably expanded from relative obscurity to tremendous numbers as a result of this alteration of their environment.

From the beginning, however, fire had some other less desirable effects. Smoke polluted the air, and the barren slopes of hills started to erode. The burned materials and erosion polluted streams and, on occasion, blocked them, producing swamps and marshes.

SOURCE.   Reprinted, by permission, from *The Environmental Crisis,* edited by Harold W. Helfrich, Jr., Yale University Press, copyright 1970 by Yale University, with slight abridgment.

OVERVIEW OF THE PROBLEM

Later, man started his serious agricultural efforts on the flood plains of rivers where the land was fertile and well watered and easy to cultivate with simple tools. The valleys of such rivers as the Tigris, the Euphrates, the Nile, and the Indus thus became cradles of civilization. Human populations expanded and felt the need for more land and year-round cultivation. Then they built dams and canals for irrigation, often without providing adequate drainage; under such conditions water will move upward through the soil and evaporate at the surface, depositing a layer of salt there and so destroying fertility. Early men cut the forests from sloping land, causing flooding and erosion and filling of the irrigation works with silt. The grazing of their sheep and cattle accelerated the destruction of the land.

Destruction was so thorough that by the twelfth century Otto of Freising could write in his *Chronicon,* "But what now is Babylon—a shrine of sirens, a home of lizards and ostriches, a den of serpents."

By Otto's time pollution had also apparently come to Europe. He tells us that when Frederick Barbarossa's armies arrived in Rome in the summer of 1167, "The ponds, caverns, and ruinous places around the city were exhaling poisonous vapors and the air in the entire vicinity had become densely laden with pestilence and death." It must have been something like driving into New Haven from the airport.

It is difficult to say how much was known about water pollution in medieval times, but St. Hildegarde had an interesting comment on the Rhine in the thirteenth century. The river's name, incidentally, is supposedly derived from the German word for "clear." She wrote that its waters, if drunk unboiled, "would produce noxious blue fluids in the body."

Certainly, as civilization and urbanization progressed, pollution problems became more acute. By the year 1800, Samuel Taylor Coleridge could write:

"The river Rhine, it is well known,
Doth wash your city of Cologne:
But tell me, Nymphs, what power
divine
Shall henceforth wash the river
Rhine?"

In its early stages urbanization displayed unnoticed detrimental effects which we are barely beginning to appreciate today. Nature's way of dealing with refuse is to recycle it. Dead plant and animal matter breaks down and releases chemical nutrients which are quickly seized by other living organisms and re-used. But a city brings together subsistence materials originating over a wide area and concentrates them in a very small space. When it is time to dispose of the remnants, the materials cannot be recycled locally but must somehow be dispersed. Industry is now encouraging planned obsolescence which further accelerates the accumulation of waste. At the present time the refuse produced in this country is estimated to be increasing about 4 percent per year; this, by no coincidence, is about the same as the yearly increase in the Gross National Product.

The processes I have been discussing, chiefly burning and the acceleration of erosion and siltation, merely accentuate processes that could have gone on without man. A new dimension was added when man began exploitation of fossil fuels: peat, coal, natural gas, petroleum. It is recorded that in 1306 a citizen of London was tried and executed for burning coal in the city; three centuries later this was the way of life, and London had a smog problem. The profession of chimney sweeping was born and with it one of the earliest and the most striking examples of severe industrial pathology: cancer of the scrotum, induced by soot. (I was fascinated to learn recently that Los Angeles has a new law banning the burning of coal in the city. So we appear to have gone full circle.)

THE DESTRUCTION OF THE ENVIRONMENT

Even much earlier, small-scale examples of specific industrial contamination had occurred without appreciation of their significance. The Romans mined lead in Britain and smelted it there. It is said that the sites of those ancient smelting operations can still be recognized from the impoverished vegetation growing on the poisoned soil. However, not until the Industrial Revolution was in full swing could anyone have seen the full portent of such developments.

So man gradually shifted to a way of life based on the exploitation of fossil fuel. Through most of the period coal was the important source of energy, and not until this century was its supremacy challenged by petroleum. Populations multiplied, cities grew, and industry expanded explosively. Now, really just in the period since World War II, we have encountered an entirely new dimension of environmental deterioration. We have become so dependent on fossil fuels that surveys have found farmers expending more calories to run their machinery than they remove from their land in crops. Industrial plants, transportation—especially by automobile—and the heating requirements of an expanding world population have brought the combustion of fossil fuels to the point where we are actually causing measurable changes in the composition of the earth's atmosphere. As we shall see, we are risking much more serious changes in the atmosphere than anything else noted so far.

Never before has man been able to spread a particular pollutant over the entire surface of the earth. DDT is a case in point. It has been recovered from the fat of Antarctic seals and penguins, from fish all over the high seas, and from the ice of Alaskan glaciers. We have been incredibly lucky that DDT has not turned out to be a more noxious pollutant than it is. If it had possessed certain properties that no one had known about until it was too late, it could have brought an end to life on earth. If you are comforted by the thought that DDT is apparently not so bad as it might have been, reflect on this fact: the U.S. Food and Drug Administration estimates that we are now exposing ourselves and our environment to over a half million different chemicals, all of which must eventually be imposed on the earth environment. And this number is estimated to be increasing by 400 to 500 new chemicals per year.

Can our run of luck continue? Consider what new types of things we have asked the environment to assimilate just since World War II: synthetic pesticides, plastics, antibiotics, radioisotopes, detergents.

The detergents make an interesting case. A few years ago on Long Island and elsewhere, people got excited about detergents because suds were coming out of their faucets. They demanded that something be done about it, and the chemical manufacturers came up with so-called biodegradable detergents. People no longer see the detergents, and now they think the problem has been solved. Actually, these biodegradable detergents are more toxic to many forms of aquatic life than the old detergents were, and they are also phosphorus compounds. So, while there is a worldwide shortage of phosphorus, we are throwing it away at such a rate that it has become one of our most significant water pollutants!

Another interesting case involving detergents concerns the tanker *Torrey Canyon* which was wrecked off the south coast of Great Britain and dumped a tremendous amount of petroleum into the ocean. The Royal Navy and Royal Air Force went to work spraying the area with detergent. Fortunately, the Plymouth Laboratory of the Marine Biological Association of the United Kingdom turned over its entire facilities to study the effects of the spraying on marine life. They found some very interesting things. Where petroleum—untouched by the detergent—was washed up on rocky shores, the marine snails went around cleaning up the shore. The snails could eat the oil-soaked vegetation and suffer no harm from it. But where the detergents formed an emulsion with the oil, the snails were killed, and the mess was worse than if they had not used the detergents.

We are at most a few generations away from running out of the fossil fuels on which our economy, including agriculture, now depends. Current thinking holds that our next source of energy will be nuclear fuel.

This raises some very disturbing thoughts. Before scientists learned to control the release of atomic energy, the entire amount of radioactivity under man's mastery consisted of about 10 grams of radium—10 curies of radioactivity scattered among the world's hospitals. Today, a nuclear power plant is being built on the shores of Lake Ontario a few miles from Oswego, New York, that is going to put 130 curies per day into the atmosphere. This is a prodigious quantity of radioactivity, and it will be from a not particularly large reactor. Knowing that exposure to radioactivity shortens life, causes malignancies, and can produce genetic effects that can damage future generations, have we any cause for complacency?

If it turns out that we cannot run our economy on nuclear energy, that we cannot live with the atom and survive, then our remaining hope for a big source of energy is sunlight. This is a very diffuse form of energy, and the problems of concentrating it into usable form will be tremendous.

Past civilizations trusted to luck and disappeared. Modern Iraq could not produce food for anything like the population of the once-great Babylonian Empire; nor could Iran (except for the income from oil) support the Persian civilization of Darius I; nor could modern Guatemala or Yucatan support the Mayan civilization.

Few laymen realize that our atmosphere as we know it today is a biological product, that it has probably remained essentially unchanged in composition for at least 300 million years up to this present century. By volume the atmosphere at sea level, neglecting contaminants, consists of about 78 percent nitrogen, about 21 percent oxygen, 0.03 percent carbon dioxide, and traces of other gases. Nitrogen is actually a scarce element on earth; 99.9 percent of the mass of all known terrestrial matter consists of 18 elements—and nitrogen is not among the 18. So what is so much nitrogen doing in the atmosphere? Oxygen is the most abundant of all the chemical elements, but it is a highly reactive chemical which outside of the atmosphere is almost never found in uncombined form. So what is so much free oxygen doing in the atmosphere?

The answers to both questions are biological. Certain bacteria and algae take nitrogen from the atmosphere and convert it into ammonia, which is a toxic material. If the story stopped at this stage, we should all be poisoned when we breathed.

Two additional types of microorganisms in the soil and water are responsible for converting the ammonia to nitrate. Green plants absorb the nitrate and ammonia and use the nitrogen in building plant proteins. Then microorganisms and animals get the nitrogen for their proteins directly or indirectly from the proteins of plants. When plants and animals die, decomposer organisms—again primarily microorganisms—break down the proteins, mostly to ammonia; and this little cycle, ammonia to nitrate, nitrate to protein, protein to ammonia can repeat.

If the story stopped at this stage, the atmosphere would long ago have run out of nitrogen. Fortunately, there are still additional types of microorganisms that can convert nitrate to molecular nitrogen and so maintain the composition of the atmosphere.

THE DESTRUCTION OF THE ENVIRONMENT

Twice I have heard sophisticated chemists say—and once I read this in a high-school biology textbook—that it would be desirable to block the activities of these so-called denitrifying bacteria. It impressed them as a dirty trick that when some organisms go to all the trouble of giving fixed nitrogen to the soil, others would come along and release it. They did not recognize that what they were proposing, if it could be done successfully, would bring an end to life on earth. So we see that quite a variety of microorganisms involved in the nitrogen cycle are essential for the continuation of life.

But what thought does industrialized man give to the welfare of these forms? With reckless abandon he dumps his half million chemical forms into soil, water, and air, not knowing whether one of these chemicals, or some combination of them, might be a deadly poison for one of the steps in the nitrogen cycle and so cause the extinction of life.

The nitrogen cycle is also very closely tied to the cycles of the elements carbon and oxygen. This subject is perhaps too technical to explore very far here, but the denitrifying bacteria do oxidize organic matter in the soil to get the energy for their activities. So there is a cycling of carbon that goes along with this nitrogen cycle, and there is also a cycle of oxygen involved.

The only reason we have oxygen in our atmosphere is that green plants keep putting it there. The plants take in carbon dioxide and give off oxygen. Animals and microorganisms take in oxygen and give off carbon dioxide; so do our factories, our furnaces, and our automobiles. Seventy percent of the free oxygen produced each year comes from planktonic diatoms in the oceans. But what thought does man give to the diatoms when he disposes of his waste? When he wants a new highway, factory, housing project, or strip mine, he is not even solicitous of the plants growing on land. The fate of Lake Erie and many lesser bodies of water has shown us that man is capable of blocking the oxygen cycle by sheer carelessness.

If this leaves you complacent, let me mention just a few other details. The deciduous forests of the eastern United States appear to produce about 1000 times as much oxygen per unit area as the average cover of the earth's surface. Yet, forests seem to be the first resource that modern man is willing to dispense with. Tropical rain forests, unlike our deciduous forests, carry on photosynthesis throughout the year and so are probably considerably more productive. But several times each year I read of schemes for industrializing or "developing" the tropical regions of Latin America, Africa, and Asia. Recently, a Brazilian official issued a statement that his country must develop the Amazon basin. Tropical soils are typically low in mineral nutrients, and such minerals as are present leach from the soil quickly if the vegetation is unable to trap them and recycle them. Once a tropical forest is destroyed, the change may be irreversible.

I do not think any educated and responsible person would advocate applying defoliants and herbicides to a tropical forest without first making a careful survey of the nutrient status of the soil and vegetation. But ecological understanding is not a prerequisite for policy making.

The U.S. Commerce Department has ordered the suppliers to turn over the entire production of the so-called weed killer 2,4,5-T to the military for use in Vietnam. The military is also taking about a third of our production of weed killer 2,4-D for this purpose. It is taking the entire output of a really horrid new weed killer known as picloram. This is a very persistent chemical. There is one case in Vermont where mules ate vegetation that had been sprayed with picloram. Later, when the manure from the mules was used for fertilizer, it killed the plants it was put on. When picloram has been experimentally sprayed on a forest, typically no woody vegetation has grown for two years. The military is also about to let or may already have let, a major contract for increasing the production of picloram. Presumably, it is going to ship the chemical to Vietnam in tankers. What happens if a few of these tankers sink in the Pacific Ocean? I have seen no experimental data on the effects of picloram on marine diatoms, but I know what it does to terrestrial plants, and I find this a very disturbing project.

Similarly, in the seas, estuaries tend to be much more productive than either the land adjacent to them or most of the open ocean. In Georgia, figures show that the salt marshes and estuaries are two to three times as productive of life as the best agricultural land in the state. These estuaries not only produce oxygen but also serve as nursery grounds for the immature stages of species we harvest for sea food.

Yet, estuaries are where coastal man is likely to dump his refuse. They are the place where commercial developers constantly seek land fill and conduct dredging operations. They are also among the places where it is proposed to locate huge electrical generating plants which would raise the temperature of the water and, in some cases, pollute it with radioisotopes. But who is thinking of the welfare of these green plants or the organisms involved in the nitrogen cycle or of still additional types of organisms which are essential for man's survival?

Perhaps I should mention one more type of organism. Photosynthesis varies tremendously in time and place; it stops at night and, on land areas in high latitudes, it practically stops during the winter, and it is slowed down in other areas by seasonal drought and other factors. Similarly, our oxidative processes vary extremely in time and space. How can these two rates be kept equal? There has to be a governor somewhere in the system, some

feedback mechanism that will release more oxygen as oxygen content starts to fall and vice versa.

We wondered for a long time where this governor was. We suspect now that at least a very important part of it may be in the sulfate-reducing bacteria which occupy oxygen-free environments on the bottoms of lakes, oceans, swamps, and similar places. A number of types of organisms obtain the energy for their activities by oxidizing sulfur to sulfate. When this sulfate is carried down into anaerobic environments, these sulfate-reducing bacteria reduce it to sulfide and conserve oxygen in the process. This is the source of the hydrogen sulfide that comes bubbling off highly polluted bodies of water; it is the source of spherules of metallic pyrites, which are sulfides found by taking the sediment out of a swamp or a lake and examining it microscopically.

As a corollary of our rapid use of oxygen and our threats to the species that produce it, we are adding carbon dioxide to the atmosphere more rapidly than the oceans can assimilate it. This has serious implications for changing the climates of the earth, but the details of what may happen are still uncertain and controversial.

I would like to put one point in the form of a question: Would any rational creature go on changing his environment like this without understanding the possible effects, and at the same time argue that it is necessary to keep the destructive process expanding each year? What is now popularly known as progress begins to look very much like the path toward extinction.

I have attempted some quantitative calculations for the oxygen cycle in order to see where we stand. For the 48 conterminous United States I took the 1966 figures for production and import of fossil fuels. I corrected these for exports and for noncombustible residues and then calculated the amount of oxygen it would take to burn them. Then I made what I believe is the best possible estimate of the amount of oxygen that could be produced within the 48 conterminous states by photosynthesis in that same year. The figure for production of oxygen turned out to be not 60 percent of that for consumption.

The implication is absolutely clear. We are completely dependent on atmospheric circulation to bring to us oxygen produced outside of our borders. This oxygen is most probably produced in the Pacific Ocean. Think again about those tankers carrying picloram to the Far East. If we should seriously attempt to industrialize all of the nations of the earth after our own pattern, I think we would all perish for lack of oxygen long before the transition was near completion.

I've been discussing the atmosphere without unnatural contaminants. There is no secret about the true situation—that over 3000 foreign chemicals have been identified in our atmosphere; that in our cities, particulate matter (soot, fly ash, and, perhaps more importantly, particles of asbestos from brakes and of rubber from tires) pose a health problem; that carbon monoxide, sulfur dioxide, and various nitrogen oxides pose many problems.

Our intense agricultural efforts to produce more food for ourselves raise problems. A few years ago I had a son in college out in Iowa, and at the end of the school year when I went out to pick him up, there was an interesting controversy running in the papers: a lawsuit in which one contingent was arguing that 2,4-D should be considered a normal part of the Iowa atmosphere during summer.

In Florida, and more recently in Montana and some of the other western states, the factories that produce phosphate fertilizer have caused severe problems. Phosphorus is in such short supply that it is going to be the first chemical to run out for man, unless we can learn to mine it from the ocean bottoms. All living things are dependent on phosphorus for their survival. I have already mentioned the way we are throwing it away in detergents, and still it is so necessary to have phosphate fertilizers that we permit severe environmental damage around the industrial buildings that produce them.

In producing the super phosphate fertilizer, tremendous amounts of fluorine are given off into the atmosphere. Fluorine is very toxic to vegetation; it kills the plants growing around or downwind from the phosphate factories. There have been a number of lawsuits involving the death of livestock that have eaten plants polluted with fluorine. In one case in Florida, the plaintiffs were trying to force a manufacturer to put on higher stacks. Of course, this would not reduce the pollution; it would only spread it a little more widely. The company argued that fluorine is so corrosive that it was not practicable to put on higher stacks because the stacks would corrode too rapidly. The company won the suit. So now human lungs are being asked to assimilate something that brick and mortar cannot cope with.

There has been quite a bit published about new prospects for turning petroleum and coal directly into food for man through the activities of various bacteria, yeasts, and fungi. It is a sad fact that the metabolism of bacteria, yeasts, and fungi does not liberate oxygen.

It may be instructive to consider one pollutant in detail in order to appreciate the widespread nature of our problem. I think I could make just as good a story of arsenic, but I have chosen to discuss lead. I have already mentioned the ancient smelting operations in Britain in Roman times. When the lead had been transported to Rome, it went into paint, into water pipes, and to line the vessels used for storing wine. (Apparently, a lead taste is preferable to a bronze taste.) Recent studies of Roman bones have found concentrations of lead which indicate that many members of the upper classes must have suffered from lead poisoning. It has been suggested that this may have contributed to the decline of the empire.

Until recently in this country, lead was a constituent of indoor paint. Lead arsenate was a favorite insecticide, especially for use on tobacco. It got into the soil, and so now we inhale lead with our tobacco smoke. In our city slums, children suffer mental retardation and even die from lead in peeling paint they have eaten. New York City had 509 reported cases in 1964, and the number is steadily rising as more physicians become aware of the problem and capable of diagnosing lead poisoning.

The burning of ethyl gasoline in our cars is putting tremendous quantities of lead into the atmosphere. This is literally polluting much of the world. A recent study of old elm trees has shown rapidly rising concentrations of lead in the wood produced since 1937. A study of snow near the North Pole has shown a 300 percent increase in lead content since 1940. Antarctica is still relatively uncontaminated, but you can detect lead in the snow there. The air over the tropical Pacific contains less lead than that over rural America, although the lead is still present.

Let me seem to digress to consider a very different topic which will, however, bring us back to the problem of lead in the environment. We hear a great deal of talk today about increasing food production from the sea, but any substantial increase will have to come from subtropical and tropical waters. Indeed, many of the sea food populations in higher latitudes are suffering from overexploitation today. In tropical and subtropical waters, especially around islands, there occurs a mysterious type of sea food poisoning known as ciguatera. Fish that have been wholesome food may suddenly become poisonous to man. Or fish on one side of an island may be good to eat, while the same species on the other side of the island is deadly. Apparently, any kind of fish can be in-

volved, including such food staples as anchovies, sardines, and herrings; such sportsmen's favorites as bonefish and sailfish; and such gourmets' delights as pompano and red snapper. Rarely, outbreaks have been attributed to shellfish such as crabs and lobsters. Sometimes, nearly all of the victims recover; in other outbreaks, nearly all die. Nobody knows what causes ciguatera, but I would like to suggest that pollution by man may be involved. It may at least trigger outbreaks.

On the day after Christmas in 1964, the British freighter *Southbank* was wrecked at Washington Island about 1000 miles south of Hawaii. Ciguatera had never been reported there. Salvage crews went to work, and they frequently caught and ate fish. Then, in August, 1965, *Southbank* sank completely, for the first time flooding the main cargo hold. In that same month the fish became poisonous, and those who ate them were taken violently ill. Lead is known to have constituted part of the cargo.

I would not be so rash as to state categorically that lead is the cause of ciguatera. If this should happen to be the case, however, I think it would be ironic that growth of the automotive industry should decrease the potential for food production thousands of miles away. Meanwhile, the lead in exhaust gases is interfering with the attempts of chemists to devise ways of reducing concentrations of other pollutants. There is mounting evidence, which I cannot evaluate, that lead and other heavy metals may play a role in causing cancer.

Obviously, the problem at the base of all the other problems is excessive population growth. Man has been on earth for at least a million years. By the beginning of the Christian era, he numbered perhaps 5,000,000 persons. His population had been doubling about once every 50,000 years. In the summer of 1968 the human population of the world passed the 3.5 billion mark. If the present trend continues, it will continue to double about every 35 years. There is no possibility that the earth can continue to support such growth. In fact, it is very doubtful that the earth is capable of supporting on a sustained basis a population as large as the present one.

I can think of nothing more important for man to do than to bring the world's best minds to bear on these questions: How large a human population can the earth support indefinitely? How much industry of what kinds can be supported indefinitely? What kinds of contamination of the environment can be tolerated? How can waste be recycled? How can we con-serve or reclaim our resources of minerals and energy sources?

We have the technology to regulate the population size. This could be done; but to solve our problems, we will have to call for cooperative efforts of biological scientists, physical scientists, sociologists, psychologists, economists, and political scientists. We must abandon our mania for continued expansion of everything. With so many groups necessarily involved, interaction of scientists with economists and political scientists, and so forth, I cannot feel very optimistic.

Make your own evaluation of our chances.

Barry Commoner
Michael Carr
Paul J. Stamler

THE CAUSES OF POLLUTION

Until now most of us in the environmental movement have been chiefly concerned with providing the public with information that shows that there *is* an environmental crisis. In the last year or so, as the existence of the environmental crisis has become more widely recognized, it has become increasingly important to ask: How can we best solve the environmental crisis? To answer this question it is no longer sufficient to recognize only that the crisis exists; it becomes necessary, as well, to consider its causes, so that rational cures can be designed.

Although environmental deterioration involves changes in natural, rather than man-made, realms—the air, water, and soil—it is clear that these changes are due to human action rather than to some natural cataclysm. The search for causes becomes focused, then, on the question: What actions of human society have given rise to environmental deterioration?

Like every living thing on the earth, human beings are part of an ecosystem— a series of interwoven, cyclical events, in which the life of any single organism becomes linked to the life processes of many others. One well-known property of such cyclical systems is that they readily break down if too heavily stressed. Such a stress may result if, for some reason, the population of any one living organism in the cycle becomes too great to be borne by the system as a whole. For example, suppose that in a wooded region the natural predators which attack deer are killed off. The deer population may then become so large that the animals strip the land of most of the available vegetation, reducing its subsequent growth to the point where it can no longer support the deer population; many deer die. Thus, in such a strictly biological situation, overpopulation is self-defeating. Or, looked at another way, the population is self-controlled, since its ex-

SOURCE. Reprinted, by permission, from *Environment,* Vol 13, No. 3, April 1971, with slight abridgment.

cessive growth automatically reduces the ability of the ecosystem to support it. In effect, environmental deterioration brought about by an excess in a population which the environment supports is the means of regulating the size of that population.

However, in the case of human beings, matters are very different; such automatic control is undesirable, and, in any case, usually impossible. Clearly, *if* reduced environmental quality were due to excess population, it might be advantageous to take steps to reduce the population size humanely rather than to expose human society to grave dangers, such as epidemics, that would surely accompany any "natural" reduction in population brought about by the environmental decline. Thus, if environmental deterioration were in fact the ecosystem's expected response to human overpopulation, then in order to cure the environmental crisis it would be necessary to relieve the causative stress—that is, to *reduce* actively the population from its present level.

On these grounds it might be argued as well that the stress of a rising human population on the environment is especially intense in a country, such as the United States, which has an advanced technology. For it is modern technology which extends man's effects on the environment far beyond his biological requirements for air, food, and water. It is technology which produces smog and smoke; synthetic pesticides, herbicides, detergents, and plastics; rising environmental concentrations of metals such as mercury and lead; radiation; heat; accumulating rubbish and junk. It can be argued that insofar as such technologies are intended to meet human needs—for food, clothing, shelter, transportation, and the amenities of life—the more people there are, and the more active they are, the more pollution.

Against this background it is easy to see why some observers have blamed the environmental crisis on overpopulation. Here are two typical statements:

The pollution problem is a consequence of population. It did not much matter how a lonely American frontiersman disposed of his waste. "Flowing water purifies itself every ten miles," my grandfather used to say, and the myth was near enough to the truth when he was a boy, for there weren't too many people. But as population became denser the natural chemical and biological recycling processes became overloaded, calling for a redefinition of property rights.[1]

The causal chain of the deterioration [of the environment] is easily followed to its source. Too many cars, too many factories, too much detergent, too much pesticide, multiplying contrails, inadequate sewage treatment plants, too little water, too much carbon dioxide—all can be traced easily to *too many people.*[2]

Some observers, for example M. P. Miller, chief of census population studies at the U.S. Bureau of the Census, believe that in the U.S. environmental deterioration is only partly due to increasing population, and blame most of the effect on "affluence."[3]

Finally, some of us place the strongest emphasis on the effects of the modern technology that so often violates the basic principles of ecology and generates intense stresses on the environment.

Dr. Paul Ehrlich provides the following statement regarding these several related factors: "Pollution can be said to be the result of multiplying three factors: population size, per capita consumption, and an 'environmental impact' index that measures, in part, how wisely we apply the technology that goes with consumption."[4] As indicated in the previous passage, Dr. Ehrlich appears to consider population size as the predominant factor in this relationship.

OVERVIEW OF THE PROBLEM

Dr. Ehrlich's statement can be paraphrased as an "equation":

population size x per capita consumption x environmental impact per unit of production = level of pollution.

This equation is self-evidently true, as it includes all the main factors and relationships which could possibly influence the environment. The product of population size and per capita consumption gives the total goods consumed; since imports, exports, and storage are relatively slight effects, total consumption can be taken to be approximately equal to total production. When the latter figure is multiplied by the environmental impact (i.e., amount of pollution per unit of production) the final result should be equal to the total environmental effect—the level of pollution.

Precisely because it is so inclusive, however, this equation does not advance our understanding of the causes of environmental problems. All human activities affect the environment to some degree. The equation states this formally, but we are still left with the problem of evaluating the extent to which different activities cause environmental problems, and the extent to which these environmental effects increase with population growth, with increasing per capita consumption, or with changing technologies. If we are to take effective action, we will need a more detailed guide than the equation offers. To begin with, we must know the relative importance of the three factors on the left side of the equation.

Two general approaches suggest themselves. One is to find appropriate numerical values for each of the four factors of the equation. Another way is to examine specific pollution problems and determine to what degree they are caused, explicitly, by a rising population, by increased prosperity, or by the increased environmental impact of new technologies. What follows is an effort to provide some preliminary data relevant to both of these approaches.

To begin with, it is necessary to define the scope of the problem, both in space and time. As to space, we shall restrict the discussion solely to the United States. This decision is based on several factors: (a) The necessary data are available—at least to us—only for the United States. (b) The pollution problem is most intense in a highly developed country such as the United States. (c) In any study involving the comparison of statistical quantities, the more homogeneous the situation, the less likely we are to be misled by averages that combine vastly different situations. In this sense, it might be better to work with a smaller sample of pollution problem—such as an urban region. Unfortunately, the necessary production statistics are not readily available except on a national scale.

As to time, we have chosen the period 1946-68. There are several reasons for this choice. First, many current environmental problems began with the end of World War II: photochemical smog, radiation from nuclear wastes, pollution from detergents and synthetic pesticides. Another reason for choosing the post-war period is that many changes in production techniques were introduced during this period. The upper limit of the period is a matter of convenience only; statistical data for the two most recent years are often difficult to obtain.

We shall thus be seeking an answer to the following question for the period 1946-68 in the United States: What changes in the levels of specific pollutants, in population size, in environmental impact per unit of production, and in the amounts of goods produced per capita have occurred?

CHANGES IN POLLUTION AND POPULATION LEVELS

Curiously, the first of these questions is the most difficult to answer. Probably the best available data relate to water pollu-

61

tion. These are summarized in a study by Weinberger. For the United States as a whole, in the period of 1946-68 the total nitrogen and phosphate discharged into surface waters by municipal sewage increased by 260 percent and 500 percent respectively.[5]

Here are some additional data which, although sparse, are suggestive of the sizes of recent changes in pollution levels. As indicated by glacial deposits, airborne lead has increased by about 400 percent since 1946.[6] Daily nitrogen oxide emissions in Los Angeles County have increased about 530 percent.[6] The average algal population in Lake Erie—one response to, and indicator of, pollution due to nutrients such as nitrate and phosphate—increased about 220 percent.[7] The bacterial count in different sectors of New York harbor increased as much as 890 percent.[8] Such data correspond with general experience. For example, the extent of photochemical smog in the U.S. has surely increased at least ten-fold in the 1946-68 period, for in 1946 it was known only in Los Angeles; it has now been reported in every major city in the country, as well as in smaller areas such as Phoenix, Arizona and Las Vegas, Nevada.

Rough as it is, we can take as an estimate of the change in pollution levels in the United States during 1946-68 increases that range from two- to ten-fold or so, or from 200 to 1,000 percent.

The increase in U.S. population for the period 1946-68 amounts to about 43 percent.[9] It would appear, then, that the rise in overall U.S. population is insufficient by itself to explain the large increases in overall pollution levels since 1946. This means that in Ehrlich's equation, the increase in population is too small to bring the left side to approximate equality with the right side unless there have been sufficiently large increases in the per capita production and environmental impact factors.

COMBINED FACTORS OF POPULATION AND PRODUCTION

The equation relates total pollution to three component factors: population size, production per capita, and environmental impact per unit of production. As a second step in evaluating the meaning of this approach, it is useful to determine whether the combined factors of population growth and increased per capita production can account for the changes in pollution levels during the period 1946-68.

A rough measure of overall U.S. production is the Gross National Product (GNP). Changes in GNP and in GNP per capita in 1946-68 are shown in Figure 1. GNP has increased about 126 percent in that time and GNP per capita has increased about 59 percent.[10] As a first approximation, then, it would appear that the overall increase in total production, as measured by GNP, is also insufficient to account for the considerably larger increases in pollution levels. However, since the GNP is, of course, an average composed of the many separate activities in the total production economy (including not only agricultural and industrial production and transportation, but also various services), a true picture of the relationship between production and environmental pollution requires a breakdown of the GNP into, at the least, some of its main components.

Under the auspices of the Committee on Environmental Alterations, of the American Association for the Advancement of Science (AAAS), we have begun to collect some of the relevant data for a joint AAAS-Scientists' Institute for Public Information study of the environmental effects of power production. Most of the required data are available from United States Statistical Abstracts and the Census of Manufacturing regarding year-by-year levels of production in different industrial, agricultural, and transportation activities. In order to facilitate comparisons we have

OVERVIEW OF THE PROBLEM

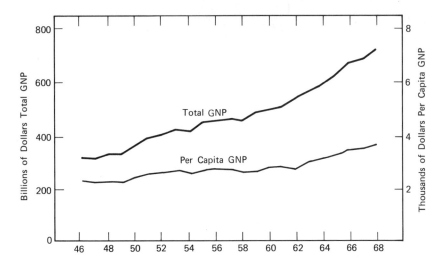

FIGURE 1. Changes in Gross National Product (GNP) 1946-68. The total value of all goods and services produced in the United States (Gross National Product, measured in constant—1958—dollars) is shown in the top curve. The Gross National Product divided by the total U.S. population at the time (GNP per capita) is shown in the bottom curve. The increase in per capita GNP can be taken as a rough measure of affluence.

adopted a standard way of plotting such data: curves are drawn for the period 1946-68 for total production, for production per capita, and production per unit GNP. These curves provide a picture of the trends in overall production, in "affluence" or "prosperity" (i.e., consumption or production per capita), and in the relative contribution made by the particular activity to the overall GNP. Some typical curves of this type are shown in Figure 2.

To obtain a preliminary picture of the results of all of the data of this type that are now available to us, we have prepared a tabular summary in Table 1. This table shows, for each of a series of activities, the percentage change in production or consumption per capita over a ten- to twenty-year period.[11]

It should be kept in mind that Table 1 lists *per capita* changes, so that *total* production figures may be derived by multiplying the listed value by 1.43 (to take into account the 43 percent increase in population in 1946-68). The value of zero

for fish consumption per capita means that total fish consumption increased about 43 per cent.

Several interesting relationships emerge from Table 1. One is that in many cases, the growth in utilization of a particular product is counterbalanced by the reduction in the use of a similar one, the total use of that class of material remaining constant. An example is fiber (or textile) consumption. Total per capita use of fibers of all types increased very slightly (6 percent). However, the major sources of fiber, cotton and wool, declined in per capita consumption by 33 percent and 61 percent respectively. The difference was made up by a very large increase—1,792 percent—in wholly synthetic (noncellulosic) fibers. Thus, we can find in Table 1 a series of pairs in which one item has substituted for another: nonreturnable beer bottles for returnable bottles; plastics for lumber; detergents for soap; truck and air freight for railroad freight; motor vehicles for work animals. Moreover, certain of the

63

THE DESTRUCTION OF THE ENVIRONMENT

STEEL

Total Production

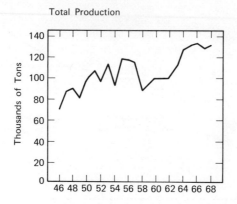

Production per Capita

Production per $1,000
Gross National Product

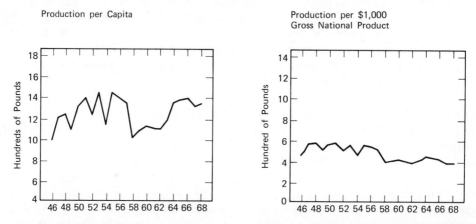

FIGURE 2. Changes in production levels, 1946-68. Examples of production statistics being collected by the Committee on Environmental Alterations, American Association for the Advancement of Science. Such statistics allow one to relate changes in different parts of the national economy to increased stresses on the environment. It can be seen that production of both steel and plastics is increasing rapidly, and that, in fact, both are increasing more rapidly than the population (production per capita is rising). Production of steel per unit of the Gross National Product, however, is declining, which reflects the substitution of other metals and plastics for steel in such applications as packaging; plastic's share of the GNP, while still small, is clearly rising.

other indicated increases in per capita utilization are a result of such substitutions. Thus, mercury use increased partly because chlorine production increased; chlorine production has increased largely because it is heavily used to produce synthetic organic chemicals, which are in turn needed to produce plastics and synthetic fibers. Simi-

larly, one reason for the increase in cement production is the substitution of truck traffic for rail traffic, which necessitates large-scale construction of highways. In the same way, one reason for increased electric power production is the increased production of chemicals, aluminum, and cement, all of which have high demands

64

PLASTICS

Total Production

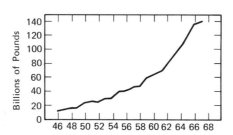

Production per Capita

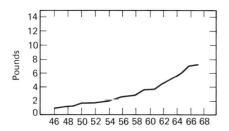

Production per $1,000
Gross National Product

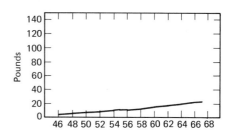

FIGURE 2. (continued)

for power. As we shall see below, most of these changes turn out to be, in environmental terms, unfortunate.

Certain large and basic categories, the necessities of life—food, clothing, and shelter—merit special attention. Data for these categories can be used to determine the degree to which changes in affluence (consumption per capita) or prosperity (production per capita) can account for the large increases in pollution levels for the period 1946-68.

Food production and consumption figures are available from the U.S. Department of Agriculture. Surprisingly, for the period 1910 to 1968, there were very few overall changes in per capita consumption of food materials, especially in the period of interest to us. In 1946-68, total calories consumed dropped from about 3,390 per person per day to about 3,250 per person per day, while protein consumption declined slightly from 104 grams per person per day to about 99 grams per person per day.[12]

It should be remembered that these are *consumption data,* whereas the data of interest in connection with environmental

TABLE I. Changes in production or consumption per capita

Item	Period	% Increase
Nonreturnable beer bottles	1946-69	3,778
Mercury for chlorine and sodium hydroxide products	1946-68	2,150
Noncellulosic synthetic fiber (consumption)	1950-68	1,792
Plastics	1946-68	1,024
Air freight—ton-miles	1950-68	593
Nitrogen fertilizer	1946-68	534
Synthetic organic chemicals	1946-68	495
Chlorine gas	1946-68	410
Aluminum	1946-68	317
Detergents	1952-68	300
Electric power	1946-68	276
Pesticides	1950-68	217
Total horsepower	1950-68	178
Wood pulp	1946-68	152
Motor vehicle registration	1946-68	110
Motor fuel (consumption)	1946-68	100
Cement	1946-68	74
Truck freight—ton-miles	1950-68	74
Total mercury (consumption)	1946-68	70
Cheese (consumption)	1946-68	58
Poultry (consumption)	1946-68	49
Steel	1946-68	39
Total freight—ton-miles	1950-68	28
Total fuel energy (consumption)	1946-68	25
Newspaper advertisements (space)	1950-68	22
Newsprint (consumption)	1950-68	19
Meat (consumption)	1946-68	19
New copper	1946-68	15
Newspaper news (space)	1950-68	10
All fibers (consumption)	1950-68	6
Beer (consumption)	1950-68	4
Fish (consumption)	1946-68	0
Hosiery	1946-68	-1
Returnable pop bottles	1946-69	-4
Calorie (consumption)	1946-68	-4
Protein (consumption)	1946-68	-5
Cellulosic synthetic fiber (consumption)	1950-68	-5
Railroad freight—ton-miles	1950-68	-7
Shoes	1946-68	-15
Egg (consumption)	1946-68	-15
Grain (consumption)	1946-68	-22
Lumber	1946-68	-23
Cotton fiber (consumption)	1950-68	-33
Milk and cream (consumption)	1946-68	-34
Butter (consumption)	1946-68	-47
Railroad horsepower	1950-68	-60
Wool fiber (consumption)	1950-68	-61
Returnable beer bottles	1946-69	-64
Saponifiable fat (for soap products)	1944-64	-71
Work animal horsepower	1950-68	-84

stress are those for *total production* (the difference being represented by storage of farm products and the balance of exports and imports). The difference represents, for instance for the year 1968, no more than about 3 percent of the total value of farm production;[13] the consumption data consequently present a fairly accurate picture of farm production.

The total production figures do in fact reflect the trends evident in per capita consumption. Thus, total grain production, including grain used for meat production, decreased 6 percent in the 1946-68 period. The figures on declining protein intake tell us that increased meat consumption is more than balanced by declines in other types of protein intake, for instance of eggs, milk, and dry beans. Of course, the increased use of beef and other meat (about 19 percent per capita) does represent some increase in affluence. On the other hand, there has been a corresponding decline in another indicator of affluence, the use of fruit. Taking these various changes into account, then, there is no evidence of any significant change in the overall affluence of the average American with respect to food. And, in general, food production in the U.S. has just about kept up with the 43 percent increase in population in that time.

A similar situation exists with respect to another life necessity—clothing. The following items show either no significant change in per capita production, or a slight decline: shoes, hosiery, shirts, total fibers (i.e., natural plus synthetic), and total fabric production. Again, as in the case of food, the "affluence" or "prosperity" factor in the equation is about 1, so that population increase by itself is not sufficient to explain the large increases in environmental pollution due to production of these items.

In the area of shelter, we find that housing units occupied in 1946 were 0.27 per capita, and in 1968, 0.30 per capita, an increase of 11 percent, although there was some improvement in the quality of units.[14] Again, this change, even with the concurrent 43 percent increase in population, is simply not enough to match the large increases in pollution levels.

Another set of statistics also allows us to arrive at an estimate of the "affluence" factor. These relate to average personal expenditures for food, clothing, and housing (including purchased food and meals, alcoholic beverages, tobacco, rents and mortgage payments, house repairs, wearing apparel, but excluding furniture, household utilities, and domestic service). Such expenditures, adjusted for inflation, increased, per capita, about 27 percent between 1950 and 1968.[15] Again, this increase when multiplied by the concurrent increase in population is insufficient to produce the large increases in pollution levels. It is important to note that these expenditures comprise a sector which represents about one-third of the total United States economy.

All this is evidence, then, that the increases in 1946-68 in two of the factors in Ehrlich's equation—population size and production (or consumption) per capita— are inadequate to account for the concurrent increases in pollution level. This leaves us with the third factor: the nature of the technologies used to produce the various goods, and the impact of these technologies on the environment. We must look to this factor to find the sources of the large increases in pollution.

ENVIRONMENTAL IMPACT

Reference to Table 1 enables us to single out the activities which have sharply increased in per capita production in the period 1946-68. They fall into the following general classes of production: synthetic organic chemicals and the products made from them, such as detergents, plastics, synthetic fibers, rubber, pesticides and herbicides; wood pulp and paper products; total production of energy, especially electric power; total horsepower of prime movers, especially petroleum-driven vehicles; cement; aluminum; mercury used for chlorine production; petroleum and petroleum products.

THE DESTRUCTION OF THE ENVIRONMENT

Several remarks about this group of activities are relevant to our problem. First is the fact that the increase in per capita production (and also in total production) in this group of activities is rather high—of the order of 100 to 1,000 percent. This fact, together with the data already presented, is a reminder that the changes in the U.S. production system during the period 1946-68 do not represent an across-the-board increase in affluence or prosperity. That is, the 59 percent increase in per capita GNP in that period obscures the fact that in certain important sectors—for example, those related to basic life necessities—there has been rather little change in production per capita, while in certain other areas of production the increases have been very much larger. The second relevant observation about this group of activities is that their magnitude of increased production per capita begins to approach that of the estimates of concurrent changes in pollution level.

These considerations suggest, as a first approximation, that this particular group of production activities may well be responsible for the observed major changes in pollution levels. This identification is, of course, only suggested by the above considerations as an hypothesis, and is by no means proven by them. However, the isolation of this group provides a valuable starting point for a more detailed examination of the nature of the production activities that comprise it, and of their *specific* relationship to environmental degradation. As we shall see in what follows, this more detailed investigation does, in fact, quite strongly support the hypothesis suggested by the more superficial examination.

Nearly all of the production activities that fall into the class exhibiting striking changes in per capita production turn out to be important causes of pollution. Thus wood pulp production and related paper-making activities are responsible for a very considerable part of the pollution of surface waters with organic wastes, sulphite,

and, until several years ago, mercury. Vehicles driven by the internal combustion engine are responsible for a major part of total air pollution, especially in urban areas, and are almost solely responsible for photochemical smog. Much of the remaining air pollution is due to electric power generation, another member of this group. Cement production is a notorious producer of dust pollution and a high consumer of electrical energy. The hazardous effects of mercury released into the environment are just now, belatedly, being recognized.

The new technological changes in agriculture, while yielding no major increase in overall per capita food production, have in fact worsened environmental conditions. Food production in the United States in 1968 caused much more environmental pollution than it did in 1947. Consider, for example, the increased use of nitrogen fertilizer, which rose 534 percent per capita between 1946 and 1968. This striking increase in fertilizer use did not increase total food production, but improved the crop yield per acre (while acreage was reduced) and made up for the loss of nitrogen to the soil due to the increasing use of feedlots to raise animals (with resultant loss of manure to the soil). For reasons which have been described elsewhere,[16] this intensive use of nitrogen fertilizer on limited acreage drives nitrogen out of the soil and into surface waters, where it causes serious pollution problems. Thus, while Americans, on the average, eat about as much food per capita as they used to, it is now grown in ways that cause increased pollution. The new technologies, such as feedlots and fertilizer, have a much more serious effect on pollution than either increases in population or in affluence.

One segment of the group of increasing industrial activities in the period 1946-68, that comprising synthetic organic chemicals and their products, raises environmental problems of a particularly subtle, but nevertheless important, kind. In the first place, most of them find a place in the economy as substitutes for—some might say, improvements over—older products of a natural, biological origin. Thus synthetic detergents replace soap, which is made from fat—a natural product of animals and plants. Synthetic fibers replace cotton, wool, silk, flax, hemp—all, again, natural products of animals and plants. Synthetic rubber replaces natural rubber. Plastics replace wood and paper products in packaging. In many but not all uses, plastics replace natural products such as wood and paper. Synthetic pesticides and herbicides replace the natural ecological processes which control pests and unwanted weeds. Both the natural products and their modern replacements are organic substances. In effect, we can regard the products of modern synthetic organic chemistry as man-made variations on a basic scheme of molecular structure which in nature is the exclusive province of living things.

Because they are not *identical* with the natural products which they resemble, these synthetic substances do not fit very well into the chemical schemes which comprise natural ecosystems. Some of the new substances, such as plastics, do not fit into natural biochemical systems at all. Thus, while "nature's plastic," cellulose, is readily degraded by soil microorganisms and thus becomes a source of nutrition for soil organisms, synthetic plastics are not degradable, and therefore accumulate as waste. Automatically they become environmental pollutants. Because there is no natural way to convert them into usable materials, they either accumulate as junk or are disposed of by burning—which, of course, pollutes the air. Nondegradable synthetic detergents, with a branched molecular structure that is incompatible with the requirements of microorganisms which break down natural organic materials, remain in the water and become pollutants. Even degradable synthetic detergents, when broken down, may pollute water with phenol, and add another

important water pollutant—phosphate—as well. Thus, these synthetic substitutes for natural products are, inevitably, pollutants.

Because of the considerable similarity of the basic biochemical systems in all living things, an active, but synthetic, organic substance such as a pesticide or herbicide is bound to influence not only the insect or weed which it is supposed to control, but also, to some extent—and often in unanticipated ways—a wide range of other organisms that make up the ecosphere. Such substances are, in effect, drugs. When they are introduced in massive amounts into the environment they become a kind of ecological drug which may affect fish, birds, and man, in unwanted, and often harmful, ways.

The point to be emphasized here is that the modern replacements for natural products have become the basis for the new, expansive production activities derived from synthetic organic chemicals, and are, by their very nature, destined to become serious environmental pollutants if they are broadcast into the environment—as, of course, they are.

There is, however, another way in which synthetic organic materials are particularly important as sources of environmental pollution. This relates not to their use but to their production. Let us compare, for example, the implication for environmental pollution of the *production* of, say, a pound of cotton and a pound of a synthetic fiber such as nylon. Both of these materials consist of long molecular chains, or polymers, made by linking together a succession of small units, or monomers. The formation of a polymer from monomers requires energy, part of which is required to form the bond that links the successive monomers. This energy has to be, so to speak, built into the monomer molecules, so that it is available when the inter-monomer link is formed. Energy is required to collect together, through cracking and distillation, an assemblage of the particular monomer required for the synthetic process from a mixture such as petroleum. (That is, the process of obtaining a pure collection of the required monomer demands energy.) And it must be remembered that the energy requirement of a production process leads to important environmental consequences, for the combustion required to release energy from a fuel is always a considerable source of pollution.

If we examine cotton production according to these criteria, we find that it comes off with high marks, for relatively little energy capable of environmental pollution is involved. In the first place the energy required to link up the glucose monomers which make up the cotton polymer (cellulose) is built into these molecules from energy provided free in the form of the sunlight absorbed photosynthetically by the cotton plant. Energy derived from sunlight is transformed, by photosynthesis, into a biochemical form, which is then incorporated into glucose molecules in such a way as to provide the energy needed to link them together. At the same time photosynthetic energy synthesizes glucose from carbon dioxide and water. Moreover, glucose so heavily predominates as a major product of photosynthesis that the energy required to "collect" it in pure form is minimal—and of course is also obtained free, from sunlight. And in all these cases the energy is transferred at low temperatures (the cotton plant, after all, does not burn) so that extraneous chemical reactions such as those which occur in high temperature combustion—and which are the source of air pollutants such as nitrogen oxides and sulfur dioxide—do not occur. In fact, the overall photosynthetic process takes carbon dioxide—an animal waste product, and a product of all combustion—out of the air.

Now compare this with the method for producing a synthetic fiber. The raw material for such production is usually petroleum or natural gas. Both of these represent stored forms of photosynthetic energy, just as does cellulose. However, unlike cellulose, these are nonrenewable resources in that they were produced during the early history of the earth in a never-to-be repeated period of very heavy plant growth. Moreover, in order to obtain the desired monomers from the mixture present in petroleum a series of high-temperature, energy-requiring processes, such as distillation and evaporation, must be used. All this means that the production of synthetic fiber consumes more nonrenewable energy than the production of a natural fiber such as cotton or wool. It also means that the energy-requiring processes involved in synthetic fiber production take place at high temperatures, which inevitably result in air pollution.

Similar considerations hold for all of the synthetic materials which have replaced natural ones. Thus, the production of synthetic detergents, plastics, and artificial rubber inevitably involves, weight for weight, more environmental pollution than the production of soap, wood, or natural rubber. Of course, the balance sheet is not totally one-sided. For example, at least under present conditions, the production of cotton involves the use of pesticides and herbicides—environmental pollutants that are not needed to produce synthetic fibers. However, we know that the use of pesticides can be considerably reduced in growing a crop such as cotton—and, indeed, must be reduced if the insecticide is not to become useless through the development of insect resistance to the chemicals—by employing modern techniques of biological control. In the same way, it can be argued that wool production involves environmental hazards because sheep can overgraze a pasture and set off erosion. Again, this hazard is not an inevitable accompaniment of sheep-raising, but only evidence of poor ecological management. Similarly, pollution due to combustion could be curtailed and thus reduce the environmental impact of synthetics.

Obviously, much more detailed evaluations of this problem are needed. However, on the basis of these initial considerations it seems evident that the substitution of synthetic organic products for natural ones through the efforts of the modern chemical industry has, until now, considerably intensified environmental pollution.

Two other members of the group of production activities which have shown considerable growth per capita during the period 1946-68, like synthetic organic chemical products, add to pollution problems through their very production. One of these is aluminum, a metal which has increasingly replaced steel (in cans, for example). Aluminum is refined by passing an electric current through the molten ore, and it is therefore no surprise that the total energy required to produce a pound of aluminum (29,860 British thermal units, or BTUs) is about 6.5 times that required to produce a pound of steel (4,615 BTUs).[17] Taking into account that the weight of an aluminum can is less than that of a steel can of equal size, the power requirements are still in the ratio of more than 2 to 1. Of course, a total evaluation of the "pollution price tag" attached to each of these cans requires a full evaluation of the pollutants emitted by steel mills and aluminum refining plants. Nevertheless, with respect to one important part of the environmental cost—air pollution due to power production and fossil fuel consumption, the new product, aluminum, is a far greater environmental polluter than the old one, steel.

This brings us to a distinctive and especially important aspect of the environmentally related changes in production which have taken place in the 1946-68 period—electric power production. Electric power production has been noteworthy for its rapid and accelerating rate of growth. Total power production has increased by 662 percent in the period 1946-68; per capita power production has increased by 436 percent.[18] Electric power production from fossil fuels is a major cause of urban air pollution; produced by nuclear reactors

it is a source of radioactive pollution. Regardless of the fuel employed, power production introduces heat into the environment, some of it in the form of waste heat released at the power plant into either cooling waters or the air. Ultimately all electric power, when used, is converted to heat, causing increasingly serious heat pollution problems in cities in the summer. One of the striking features of the present U.S. production system is its accelerating demand for more and more power—with the resultant exacerbation of pollution problems.

AFFLUENCE AND INCREASED PRODUCTION

What is striking in the data discussed above is that so many of the new and expanding production activities are highly power-consumptive and have replaced less power-consumptive activities. This is true of the synthetic chemical industry, of cement, and of the introduction of domestic electrical appliances.

It is useful to return at this point to the question of affluence. To what extent do these increased uses of electric power, which surely contribute greatly to environmental deterioration, arise from the increased affluence, or well-being, of the American public? Certainly the introduction of an appliance such as a washing machine is, indeed, a valuable contribution to a family's well-being; a family with a washing machine is without question more affluent than a family without one. And, equally clear, this increased affluence adds to the total consumption of electric power and thereby adds to the burden of environmental pollutants. Such new uses of electricity therefore do support the view that affluence leads to pollution.

On the other hand, what is the contribution to public affluence of substituting a power-consumptive aluminum beer can for a less power-demanding steel can? After all, what contributes to human welfare is not the can, but the beer (it is interesting to note in passing that beer consumption per capita has remained essentially unchanged in the 1946-68 period). In this instance the extra power consumption due to the increased use of aluminum cans—and the resulting environmental pollution—cannot be charged to improved affluence. The same is true of the increased use of the nonreturnable bottle, which pollutes the environment during the production process (glass products require considerable fuel combustion) and pollutes it further when it is discarded after use. The extra power involved in producing aluminum beer cans, the extra power and other production costs involved in using nonreturnable bottles instead of reusable ones, contribute both to environmental pollution and the GNP. But they add nothing to the affluence or well-being of the people who use these products.

Thus, in evaluating the meaning of increased productive activity as it relates to the matters at issue here, a sharp distinction needs to be made between those activities which actually contribute to improved well-being and those which do not, or do so minimally (as does the self-opening aluminum beer can). Power production is an important area in which this distinction needs to be made. Thus, the chemical industry and the production of cement and aluminum, taken together, account for 18 percent of the present consumption of power in the United States.[19] For reasons already given, some significant fraction of the power used for these purposes involves the production of a product which replaces a less power-consumptive one. Hence this category of power consumption—and its attendant environmental pollution—ought not to be charged to increased affluence. It seems likely to us that when all the appropriate calculations have been made, a very considerable part of the recent increases in demand for electric power will turn out to involve just such changes in which well-being, or af-

fluence, is not improved, but the environment and the people who live in it suffer.

Transportation is another uniquely interesting area for such considerations. At first glance changes in the transportation scene in the United States in 1950-68 do seem to bear out the notion that pollution is due to increased affluence. In that period of time the total horsepower of automotive vehicles increased by 260 percent, the number of car registrations per capita by 110 percent, the vehicle miles traveled per capita by 100 percent, the motor fuel used per capita for transportation by 90 percent.[20] All this gives the appearance of increased affluence—at the expense of worsened pollution.

However, looked at a little more closely the picture becomes quite different. It turns out that while the use of individual vehicles has increased sharply, the use of railroads has declined—thus replacing a less polluting means of transportation with a more polluting one. One can argue, of course, that it is more affluent to drive one's own car than to ride in a railroad car along with a number of strangers. Accepting the validity of that argument, it is still relevant to point out that it does *not* hold for comparison between freight hauled in a truck or in a railroad train. The fuel expenditure for hauling a ton of freight one mile by truck is 5.6 times as great as for a ton mile hauled by rail. In addition, the energy outlay for cement and steel for a four-lane expressway suitable for carrying heavy truck traffic is 3.5 times as much as that required for a single track line designed to carry express trains.[21] Rights-of-way account for a considerable proportion of the environmental impact of transportation systems. In unobstructed country requiring no cuts or fills, a 400-foot right-of-way is desirable for an expressway, while a 100-foot right-of-way is desirable for an express rail line (in both cases, allowing for future expansion to more lanes or two rail lines respectively).[21] Then, too, motor-vehicle-related accidents might be included in environmental considerations; in 1968 there were 55,000 deaths and 4.4 million injuries due to motor vehicle accidents, while there were only about 1,000 railway deaths, almost none of them passenger deaths. Aside from the loss of life and health, motor vehicle accidents are responsible for the expenditure of $12 billion a year on automobile insurance, which is equivalent to 16 percent of total personal consumption expenditures for transportation.[22] In the case of urban travel it is very clear that efficient mass transit would be not only a more desirable means of travel than private cars, but also far less polluting. The lack of mass transit systems in American cities, and the resulting use of an increasing number of private cars is, again, a cause of increased pollution that does not stem from increased affluence.

It seems to us that the foregoing data provide significant evidence that the rapid intensification of pollution in the United States in the period 1946-68 cannot be accounted for solely by concurrent increases either in population or in affluence. What seems to be far more important than these factors in generating intense pollution is the *nature* of the *production* process; that is, its impact on the environment. The new technologies introduced following World War II have by and large provided Americans with about the same degree of affluence with respect to basic life necessities (food, clothing, and shelter); with certain increased amenities, such as private automobiles, and with certain real improvements such as household appliances. Most of these changes have involved a much greater stress on the environment than the activities which they have replaced. Thus, the most powerful cause of environmental pollution in the United States appears to be the introduction of such changes in technology, without due regard to their untoward effects on the environment.

Of course, the more people that are supported by *ecologically faulty technologies*—whether old ones, such as coal-burning power plants, or new ones, such as those which have replaced natural products with synthetic ones—the more pollution will be produced. But if the new, ecologically faulty technologies had *not* been introduced, the increase in U.S. population in the last 25 years would have had a much smaller effect on the environment. And, on the other hand, had the production system of the U.S. been based *wholly* on sound ecological practice (for example, sewage disposal systems which return organic matter to the soil; vehicle engines which operate at low pressure and temperature and therefore do not produce smog-triggering nitrogen oxides; reliance on natural products rather than energy-consumptive synthetic substitutes; closed production systems that prevent environmental release of toxic substances) pollution levels would not have risen as much as they have, despite the rise in population size and in certain kinds of affluence.

THE CASE OF MERCURY

All of the foregoing discussion is based on overall statistical data rather than on the specific analysis of any particular source of pollution. While such an approach is useful, it is also important to develop data of a more specific kind. This is, of course, a huge task. It calls for a detailed study of the nature of present production technologies and the specific ways in which they affect ecologically important processes. Such studies have hardly been begun; nevertheless it is useful to discuss, at least in a tentative way, a specific example as a means of testing the conclusions derived from the more general statistical evidence.

The use of mercury in the chemical process industries is an informative example. Here its use reflects the increasing value of electrochemical processes, in which electricity is employed to effect chemical reactions, for mercury is unique in combining certain valuable chemical properties (e.g., that it forms an amalgam with metals, such

73

as sodium) with a capacity to conduct electricity. This led, for example, to the introduction in the United States about twenty years ago of a much improved process for producing caustic soda and chlorine. Since both of these substances are very widely used in the manufacture of the numerous synthetic chemical compounds that have been massively produced in the last 30 years, the rapid increase in the use of mercury in an application which permits losses to the environment is one consequence of the increased production of synthetic substances since World War II. Moreover, several major plastics are produced by processes catalyzed by mercury. Plastics production increased about 200 percent in 1958-67;[23] during that time the use of mercury at an industrial catalyst also increased about 200 percent.[24] In that same period the mercury used in chlorine production increased about 210 percent (see Figure 3).[24] These recent changes

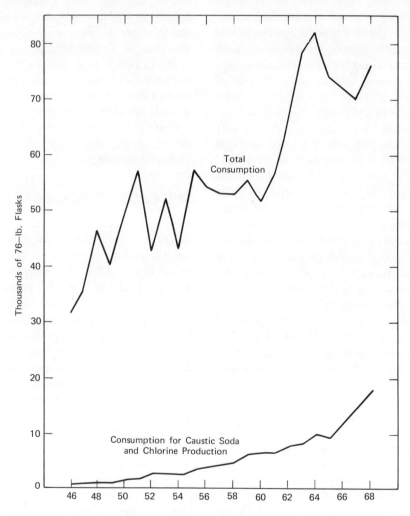

FIGURE 3. Mercury Consumption, 1946-68. Consumption of mercury has increased rapidly, despite occasional erratic fluctuations; the most rapidly growing component of this consumption is in caustic soda and chlorine production, which, although still a small portion of the total, accounts for much of the increase in consumption in recent years.

reflect the trend, beginning with the close of World War II, toward massive technical innovation and intensification of production in the chemical industry (which was discussed in more general terms above). The magnitude of this effect is sharply reflected in the data for the consumption of mercury for electrochemical production of chlorine: an increase of 2,150 percent in the period 1946-68.[24]

These considerations provide an opportunity to test the degree to which population and affluence participate in the generation of environmental pollution by mercury. As already indicated, for the period 1946-68, the U.S. population increased about 43 percent; in the period 1958-68 it increased about 15 percent. In these periods total U.S. consumption of mercury increased 130 percent and 43 percent respectively.[24] A good deal of mercury consumption involves uses in which the mercury is more or less permanently contained (e.g., incorporation of mercury into electrical instruments—although here, too, it becomes important to ask where broken thermometers and burned-out fluorescent and other mercury-containing lamps are disposed of; if they are burned on a dump or in an incinerator, mercury vapor will pollute the air). However, it is perhaps more important to examine uses in those industries, such as chemical processing, which do result in environmental release of mercury. In this connection the following figures are relevant: In 1946-66, use of mercury in the chemical process industries increased about 224 percent; between 1958 and 1968 it increased about 250 percent.[24] These data are sufficient to indicate that the increased industrial activities which are involved in mercury pollution cannot be accounted for by concurrent changes

in the U.S. population. Nor can they be accounted for by the contribution of mercury consumption to increased affluence. As indicated earlier, per capita GNP increased about 51 percent in 1946-66. At the same time, the per capita use of mercury in chemical processing increased 250 percent for all chemical processing and 2,100 percent for chlorine production alone. In effect, goods now produced in the United States which are derived from chemical process industries involve a considerably greater use of mercury than previously. Thus, the increased use—and release to the environment—of mercury reflects changes in industrial chemical technology rather than increased population or affluence.

THE PRIMARY CAUSE

These considerations and the ones discussed earlier in connection with agriculture, synthetics, power, and transportation, allow us, we believe, to draw the conclusion that the predominant factor in our industrial society's increased environmental degradation is neither population nor affluence, but the increasing environmental impact per unit of production due to technological changes.

Thus, in seeking public policies to alleviate environmental degradation it must be recognized that a stable population with stable consumption patterns would still face increasing environmental problems if the environmental impact of production continues to increase. The environmental impact per unit of production is increasing now, partially due to a process of displacement in which new, high-impact technologies are becoming predominant. Hence, social choices with regard to productive technology are inescapable in resolving the environmental crisis.

NOTES

1. Hardin, Garrett, *Population, Evolution and Birth Control,* Freeman, 1969, p. 373.

2. Ehrlich, Paul, *The Population Bomb,* Ballantine, New York, 1966, pp. 66-67.

3. *New York Times,* February 19, 1971.

4. Ehrlich, Paul and John Holdren, "The People Problem," *Saturday Review,* July 4, 1970, p. 42.

5. Weinberger, L.W., et al., "Solving Our Water Problems: Water Renovation and Reuse," reprinted in Hearings before the Subcommittee on Science, Research and Development of the House Committee on Science and Astronautics, *The Adequacy of Technology for Pollution Abatement Vol. II,* U.S. Government Printing Office, Washington, D.C., 1966, p. 756.

6. Patterson, Clair C., with Joseph D. Salvia, "Lead in the Modern Environment," *Environment,* 10 (3) : 72, 1968.

7. Davis, C.C., "Information Bulletin," *Planktol.,* Japan, 12:53, 1965.

8. Molof, A.H., E.R. Gidlund and M. Lang, *Proceedings of a National Symposium on Estuarine Pollution,* sponsored by the American Society of Civil Engineers, Stanford University, Stanford, California, 1957, p. 755.

9. Bureau of the Census, *Statistical Abstract of the United States,* U.S. Government Printing Office, Washington, D.C., 1970, p. 5.

10. Department of Commerce, *The National Income and Product Accounts of the United States, 1929-1965,* U.S. Government Printing Office, Washington, D.C., 1966, pp. 4-5.

11. Bureau of the Census, *Statistical Abstract,* U.S. Government Printing Office, Washington, D.C., 1949: pp. 511, 512, 526, 741, 746, 773, 775, 797, 961, 963, 964, 968, 973; 1953: pp. 92, 93, 821; 1955: p. 830; 1969: p. 509; 1970: pp. 83, 84, 498, 505, 506, 507, 535, 544, 548, 590, 628, 637, 658, 661, 666, 712, 713, 717, 718, 719, 722. Bureau of the Census, "Glass Containers," *Current Industrial Reports,* M32G(69)-13, Washington, D.C., 1970. Department of Agriculture, *Agricultural Statistics 1955,* U.S. Government Printing Office, Washington, D.C., 1956, p. 486. Bureau of Mines, *Minerals Yearbook,* U.S. Government Printing Office, Washington, D.C., 1947: p. 772; 1968, Volume 1: p. 695. *Statistical Abstract, op. cit.,* 1970, pp. 535, 548, 554, 555.

12. *Statistical Abstract, op. cit.,* 1953: pp. 92-93; 1970: pp. 83-84.

13. Department of Agriculture, Agricultural Research Service, Neg. AR5 5593-69 (10), U.S. Government Printing Office, Washington, D.C. Department of Agriculture, *Commodity Fact Sheet - 1970: Wheat,* U.S. Government Printing Office, Washington, D.C. Department of Agriculture, Economic Research Service, *Supplement for 1969 Feed Statistics,* Supplement for Statistical Bulletin No. 410, U.S. Government Printing Office, Washington, D.C.

14. *Statistical Abstract, op. cit.,* 1948: p. 811; 1970: p. 685.

15. *Statistical Abstract, op. cit.,* 1970: pp. 312, 314.

16. Commoner, Barry, "Nature Unbalanced: How Man Interferes with the Nitrogen Cycle," *Environment,* 10(1): 12, 1968.

17. Bureau of the Census, *Census of Manufacturing 1963,* U. S. Government Printing Office, Washington, D.C., pp. 33A-44, 33C-41. *Statistical Abstract, op. cit.,* 1966: pp. 737, 810.

18. *Statistical Abstract, op. cit.,* 1948: p. 493; 1970: p. 507.

19. *Statistical Abstract, op. cit.,* 1970: p. 507. *Census of Manufacturing 1967, op. cit.,* pp. 28A-41, 28B-24, 28D-23, 28E-16, 28F-18, 28G-21, 32B-19, 33C-32.

20. *Statistical Abstract, op. cit.,* 1970: pp. 500, 542, 545, 548.

21. Personal Communications, Missouri State Highway Department, Missouri Pacific Railroad. Forsythe, W., *Smithsonian Physical Tables,* Smithsonian Institution, Washington, D.C., 9th Edition, 1964, pp. 21, 181. Interstate Commerce Commission, Bureau of Accounts, *Transportation Statistics in the United States,* 1968, IC 1.25:968/Part I/Release 2, p. 19. Automobile Manufacturers Association, *Motor Truck Facts: 1969,* p. 52.

22. *Statistical Abstract, op. cit.,* 1969: p. 552; 1970: p. 314.

23. *Statistical Abstract, op. cit.,* 1952: p. 801; 1970: p. 703.

24. *Minerals Yearbook, op. cit.,* 1947: p. 772; 1958, Volume I: p. 756; 1968, Volume I: p. 695.

Louis S. Levine
Gress LeMaistre
JoAnn LeMaistre

SPECIES MAN: EXTINCT OR DISTINCT?

The actions and interventions of species *Homo sapiens* in his natural environment appear to be proceeding at a sufficiently rapid rate to ensure the extinction of the species within the next several generations. An increasing number of individuals hold the position that man will soon become extinct, and they support their position with an impressive array of data, statistics, and theories.

One cannot fail to be impressed with the evidence, the rationale, and the systematic attention which ecologists have given to the problems that threaten the delicate balance among various life forms and their environments. Many ecologists have concluded that we have "drastically overmanaged and mishandled our environment, and the lesson of what our present knowledge is that we must retrench immediately."[1] The implication contained within the "retrenchment" position is that to do

less than improve our environment will lead to global self-destruction.

Having heard the voices of doom and the cries of crisis before, the "clear call of reason" can also be heard above the clamor saying, "You underestimate man and his distinct resources." This call tells us that man's survival potential is great since he is an omnivore and has maximal choices as to what or whom he will devour. Being the most complex of living organisms, he also has the advantages of language, symbols, and he can anticipate the consequences of his own actions. He can pass on via his culture what he has found helpful. He even can pass on his functional fictions. This voice of "reason" tells us that in our lifetime tremendous achievements have occurred through the combination of knowledge, technical skill, and human courage and commitment. True! But for what causes? We are not convinced

SOURCE. Reprinted, by permission, from mimeographed paper, copyright Louis S. Levine, April 1970.

that man will respond to the survival crisis with innovations sufficient to conserve, let alone restore, the diminishing consumable resources of air, water, and soil in ways conducive to the maintenance of life and habitable environments. If such innovations were to become available in order to maintain the delicate balance among organisms and their environments, then such innovations will have to be different than those *relied* upon in the past.

The citizen may not be comforted greatly by those who emphasize the human being's special resources. He may be much more impressed by the irrationality of man's behavior and the absurdity of that to which man chooses to commit his time and talents. Nor will the citizen take much comfort in knowing that our survival crisis has come upon us rapidly and seemingly without our awareness—though we now know that the accelerating rate of the crisis will force us into an immediate action position. Unfortunately, the species survival crisis is, for most of us, an abstraction.

So where are we? Some say that *Homo sapiens* will soon become extinct. Some say that the special talents of our species will result in new discoveries that will save us. If one were to take the most optimistic formulation of both views, one might have the following position: Man, as such, will not survive unless the population growth, pestilence, and the contamination of our air, water, and land resources are controlled. To provide such controls will require new modes of thought to which Einstein directed our attention in 1946 when he said: "The unleashed power of the atom has changed everything except our ways of thinking. Thus we are drifting toward a catastrophe beyond comparison. We shall require substantially new manners of thinking if mankind is to survive."[2] For us, a quarter of a century later, as we examine the evidence, there seems to be considerable doubt whether man can develop new modes of thought and action essential to the continuation of life.

A BASIC QUESTION

The new mode of thought man must develop, if he is to meet the challenges of the species survival crisis of the '70s, will be characterized by the abandonment of the myths that have served us, though not well. As guiding fictions, they have provided the direction for the human efforts which have been expended in bringing us to our present position: the point of no return. Continued use of these guiding fictions will necessitate abandonment of the hope that every man, some day, may be able to live decently—free from hunger, fear, and hate; that man, everywhere, will live in the environments congenial to the development of his intellectual and artistic resources; that the quality of life, as well as its maintenance, everywhere will be given the highest priority. The stupidities that have served us in the past, as our functional fictions, now have to be put aside; the risks are too great for such self-indulgence. For what we risk is the life worth living. Among the stupidities (sometimes referred to here as "guiding fictions" or "petty provincialisms") that can be indulged no longer are:

1. the belief in boundary magic;
2. the belief in the magic of priority permanence;
3. the belief in the magic of environmental permanence.

Belief in boundary magic suggests that nature somehow follows political boundaries. To dispel this magic we must communicate in every manner possible that radiation effects can be as deadly in Oregon as they are in Okinawa. Temperature inversion will result in death in San Fernando as well as in Scranton, and malnutrition will take its toll in Moscow, USA, or Moscow, USSR. Children will die of starvation in Chicago as they will die of starvation in China.

Because boundaries are man-made, man may someday recognize the clear and present danger inherent in maintaining any belief in boundary magic. If there is time and the will to do so, man may turn away from the "territorial imperatives" to which he has no moral or natural prerogative, i.e., the destruction of the air, the water, and the soil.

Belief in the magic of priority permanence will only be dispelled when man finds trecherous the fiction that priorities directed toward destruction have a major claim over those directed toward the reduction of famine, fear, and hate. The obvious equivocal codes go something like this:

If we want to live, we must kill.
If we want to build, we must destroy.
If we want to bring freedom, we must end freedom.
If we want to dignify man, we must degrade him.
If we want to save the air, water, and soil, we must consume them.

In short, if we value the quality of life, we must impair it; if we value life, we must end life.

The irrationality of these beliefs is that the absurd arrangement of the priorities has a set character and is impervious to change; they only can be understood from the perspective of the magician.

Belief in the magic of environmental permanence. Man has a great need to believe that he can control his environment (some people even believe they can control themselves!). This is essential for reasons that we don't quite understand other than that such a need rests on the guiding fiction that the world of people and the world environment are essentially stable and permanent through time. Leaders are leaders. Decisions to use resources for destructive purposes are always defensible. Man has always been around and will continue to be around.

This is indeed powerful magic. The magic of the belief in the permanence of the environment is so great that even the possibility of instability must be dismissed as fantasy. And in the process of converting a disturbing possibility to a harmless notion, the challenger of the myth becomes the enemy, and the spokesman for the "status quo," who acts in a "business-as-usual" fashion, becomes the hero. And isn't this the way it should be? Our heroes soothe our fears; they know more than we do, and they can be trusted to sound the alarm when such an alarm is actually necessary. While the magic works its spell to replenish the power of the powerful, it discourages those who would ask: "Where does the parade of emperors without clothes lead?"

Knowledge increases. Science and technology move toward higher orders of specialization. Information mounts, and there is little interest in changing the political and professional boundaries in search of transprovincial programs directed toward the maintenance and enhancement of life. Such programs could be derived from a human ecology concerned with the molar transactions and interdependencies of man and his environments. Such programs would take seriously the fact that man does have the capacity to sustain and improve the quality of life.

As John Donne so aptly put it in 1623: "No man is an island, entire of itself; every man is a piece of the continent, a part of the main; if a clod be washed away by the sea, Europe is the less, as well as if a promintory were, as well as if a manor of thy friends or thine own were; any man's death diminishes me, because I am involved in mankind; and therefore never send to know for whom the bell tolls, it tolls for thee."[3] Only our responses to the species survival crisis will indicate whether man has sufficient wisdom to act for himself by acting for all men everywhere.

THE DESTRUCTION OF THE ENVIRONMENT

REFERENCES

1. Kennedy, Donald, "Shaking the delicate balance," *Stanford Alumni Association Almanac,* March, 1970, pp. 2-3.

2. Einstein, Albert, *The New York Times,* May 25, 1946.

3. Donne, John, "Meditation XVII," *Major British Writers I* (New York, 1967).

SECTION 2

THE POPULATION EXPLOSION

To many scientists, the quality of life on the planet Earth can be expressed by the following equation:

$$\text{Quality of Life (Q.L.)} = \frac{1}{\text{population size x affluence}}$$

As the denominator increases, the Q.L. decreases. This situation of a constantly increasing population size and a greater affluence appears to be a fact of life in the world today.

The contention that population tends to grow in a geometric progression while food supplies increase in arithmetic progression was first voiced by the Reverend Thomas R. Malthus in 1824. Since that time the "Malthusian" school of thought has been an intellectual and ideological storm center, Malthus believed that if population growth were not checked by such preventative means as continence or delayed marriage, mankind would live in constant poverty and endure unending starvation and disease.

Jean Mayer, Paul Ehrlich, and Durward Allen all agree on the need to check population growth but do not agree on the implications to be drawn from this condition. The burgeoning population is viewed as one of the foremost reasons for such problems as air and water pollution, clogged highways, overcrowded schools, and urban blight. Mayer sees no reason to relate food availability to population growth and assumes a non-Malthusian stance. Ehrlich sees a definite relationship and in that regard is more Malthusian in outlook. Allen is concerned with increased stress which is caused by increased population.

Mayer discusses the implications of population growth in relation to increased affluence. He contends that the nutritional state of the world is not getting worse and that the food supply can keep up with increases in population. He advocates increased use of fertilizers, herbicides, pesticides, and new sources of food. It is his contention that rather than link overpopulation with undernutrition, a more rational approach is

81

to link it with increased affluence. He says rich people disturb the ecology more through increased consumption and therefore create more land, air, water, chemical, thermal, and radioactive pollution than poor people. An approach that worked for a decrease in population as disposable income increased would be more immediately effective than waiting for a hypothetical nutritional disaster.

Ehrlich sees somewhere between one and two billion of the world's three and one-half billion people as presently undernourished or starving. He forsees that prospects for a healthy life which now are far from adequate would become impossible long before the earth's population doubled within the next 35 years. He believes that further attempts at increased food production through the use of fertilizers, herbicides, and pesticides would only poison the environment more. He predicts utter disaster if we do not take immediate steps to limit population growth.

Allen considers the eco-social stress endured by people in urban areas. The city dweller is completely dependent on others for all his services. He is subject to many anxieties in dealing with a wide range of unpredictable situations. Extreme problems are expected to develop when population increase results in an organizational complexity beyond man's abilities to solve.

These three articles with differing outlooks have been purposely selected as a means of stimulating constructive controversy on this all-important issue.

Thomas Malthus

A SUMMARY VIEW OF THE PRINCIPLE OF POPULATION (AN EXCERPT)

But if the natural increase of population, when unchecked by the difficulty of procuring the means of subsistence or other peculiar causes, be such as to continue doubling its numbers in twenty-five years, and if the greatest increase of food which, for a continuance, could possibly take place on a limited territory like our earth in its present state, be at the most only such as would add every twenty-five years an amount equal to its present produce then it is quite clear that a powerful check on the increase of population must be almost constantly in action.

By the laws of nature man cannot live without food. Whatever may be the rate at which population would increase if unchecked, it never can actually increase in any country beyond the food necessary to support it. But by the laws of nature in respect to the powers of a limited territory, the additions which can be made in equal periods to the food which it produces must, after a short time, either be constantly decreasing, which is what would really take place or, at the very most, must remain stationary so as to increase the means of subsistence only in an arithmetical progression. Consequently, it follows necessarily that the average rate of the *actual* increase of population over the greatest part of the globe, obeying the same laws as the increase of food, must be totally of a different character from the rate at which it would increase if *unchecked*.

The great question, then, which remains to be considered, is the manner in which this constant and necessary check upon population practically operates.

SOURCE. Originally written for the 1824 supplement to the *Encyclopedia Brittannica*, then revised and shortened as an independent publication in 1839.

Jean Mayer

TOWARD A NON-MALTHUSIAN POPULATION POLICY

Since the mid-nineteenth century three profound revolutions have been taking place: a demographic explosion, which is accelerating and places the age-old problem of population in an even more dramatic context; a technologic revolution which, despite predictions, promises to accelerate food production even faster; and changes in human attitudes, for which Harlan Cleveland has coined the felicitous expression, "the revolution of rising expectations." It is my contention, in considering these related conditions, that nothing is more dangerous for the cause of a sound population policy than to approach the problem of overpopulation in nineteenth-century terms. If we continue to link the need for population control to the likelihood that food supply will be increasingly limited, the elaboration of birth control programs of sufficient magnitude will be held up for many years, perhaps many generations . . . .

. . . The Malthusian argument (is) that overpopulation can best be appraised with respect to food resources and that the present rate of increase in population is rapidly carrying the world to the brink of or to actual starvation. It is my contention that the legions of conservationists, social scientists and others who have embraced this view have not sufficiently considered the potential of the second great revolution: that of food technology. If anything, this makes me even more of a pessimist about our chances of limiting the world's population at any early date: famine is perhaps the worst method, but it would work. For were we really to starve when the population reaches a certain magic number, this would cause a drastic increase in child and infant mortality, decreased fertility and a shortening of the average life span. It would make the increase in population self-limiting. If the world can continue to feed, however badly, an ever-increasing

SOURCE. Reprinted, by permission, from the *Columbia Forum*, Summer, 1969, Vol. 12, No. 2, Copyright 1969 by the Trustees of Columbia University in the City of New York.

number of people, this safety valve, however unpalatable, is missing.

World War II was not a Malthusian check. In spite of the horrendous numbers of deaths, food production decreased much more than population. By 1945 intake per capita was 16 percent lower than the 1934-1938 average. The difficulties in getting agriculture going while industry and the means of communication were not yet rebuilt led to a general pessimism. Yet very quickly the situation improved. By 1952-1953, the worldwide rate of per capita production of food had overtaken prewar rates. Since then the average rate of increase in food production for the world at large has been three percent per year; the population has increased on the average 1.7 percent. This slight but steady gain of food production over population is part of a secular trend. E. S. and W. S. Woytinski, in their monumental *World Population and Production,* estimate that since 1850 the increase in output has been more rapid than the increase in population. . . . Caloric undernutrition is still found in many parts of the world, and not always as a result of war or civil disorder, earthquakes or floods, invasions of insects and other parasites, or abnormally prolonged droughts. Protein deficiency is encountered in varying degrees of prevalence among the young children of most countries of Asia and Africa and in many of Central and South America. Vitamin A deficiency is perhaps underestimated as a threat to the life, and the sight, of children of most of the same areas where protein deficiency is also seen. Riboflavin deficiency, and a number of other deficiencies are still very much with us. Still, there is no evidence that the situation is getting worse. The food balance sheets on which postwar pessimism was based are imperfect instruments. As an officer of FAO (Food and Agriculture Organization of the United Nations), I spent considerable time attempting to gauge such unknowns as figures for waste at the retail level and within families and that portion of the food supply that does not move within the channels of trade (the estimate of food grown by the farmer for his family is inaccurate, particularly as regards fruits and vegetables, which tend to be underestimated). The nutritional standards against which available supplies are gauged are themselves being refined. As the results of additional experimental and clinical work become available, it is realized that a number of such standards, those of protein and calcium among others, were probably unnecessarily high. Even without such reevaluations, the evolution of food balance sheets, the only instruments we have to judge the race between food and population, make it apparent that most regions do show the same slow increase of per capita supplies exhibited by the world at large. It must be recognized, of course, that many of the worst nutritional scourges of mankind have been historically caused as much by ignorance and callousness as by lack of nutrients. Thousands of children die of protein deficiency in areas where the proteins that would save them do in fact exist and are often consumed in sufficient amounts in the very households where infants and toddlers die for lack of them. A faulty understanding of a child's needs may be the main reason he is denied some of the food consumed by his father and older siblings. As for man's inhumanity to man and its contribution to starvation, it could be illustrated by thousands of examples: cereals being shipped from Ireland under the protection of naval guns during the famine; stocks being withheld during the Congo famine to keep prices up; crop destruction policies in South Vietnam; the food blockade of Biafra. Certainly as far as food is concerned ours is not one world. The United States government rents 20 million acres from our farmers so that they will not grow food on them. Australia, Canada, New Zealand, Argentina, and France have been, or are at present, involved in similar efforts to restrict production.

Nor is this idling of food production restricted to highly developed countries. A recent study estimates that Ghanaian farmers work only an average of two hours a day in the cocoa area, the wealthiest agricultural area of the country.

It is fair to say that in most areas of the world the race between food and population would be more favorable to the development of adequate nutrition if the rate of population growth were decreased. But I believe that there are no grounds for saying in 1969 that the nutritional state of the world is getting worse. It is not. And I believe that improvement in communication, availability of surpluses in certain countries, the existence of solid international organizations and the gradual improvement in international morality make large-scale famines, such as the Irish or the Bengali famine, less likely to occur in this era—except perhaps in Red China because of its alienation from the two richest blocs of countries. (It appears, moreover, that the food situation in China has improved considerably in the past two years, making the recurrence of famine there, as in India, more remote.)

Bad as it is, the present is no worse than the past and probably somewhat better. But what of the future? In absolute numbers, the increase in population is likely to accelerate for some time. Can the food supply be kept up? My contention is that for better or for worse it can and will.

First, let us consider conventional agriculture. FAO's figures indicate that 3.4 billion acres are at present under cultivation. This represents less than 11 percent of the total land area of the world. Some experts—Prasolov, Shantz, Zimmerman—estimate the area that can eventually be made arable at from 13 to 17 billion acres. Colin Clark, director of the Agricultural Economics Research Institute of Oxford, uses the figure of 19 billion acres, but counts double-cropped tropical lands twice. (He considers that, if the land were farmed

as well as the Dutch farmers work their acres today, it would support 28 billion people on a Dutch diet; if Japanese standards of farming and nutrition were used, this area would support 95 billion people.)

The biggest potential increase of food production does not, however, come from extension of the area under cultivation, but from the increase in the use of fertilizers. The phenomenal increase in food production in this country has actually been performed with a reduction in acreage farmed. By pre-World War I standards of cultivation, it took one and one-half acres to support an American. If such standards prevailed today, we would need to add at least 40 million acres, an additional Iowa, to our farm area every ten years. We use fertilizers instead. One ton of nitrogen is the equivalent of 14 acres of good farmland. And our use of fertilizer is less intensive than it is in Japan, where it is well over twice ours, or in Western Europe. (Japan is still increasing its agricultural production at a rate of three percent per year.) India, Africa, and most of Latin America use only an infinitesimal fraction of Japanese or Western amounts of fertilizer, or none at all. Garst has estimated that an expenditure of ten dollars an acre per year for fertilizers would alone add 50 to 100 percent to the low yield in underdeveloped countries. Applying this investment to an area of 1.5 billion acres would be the equivalent to adding at least 750 million acres to the crop areas of these countries, the equivalent of a continent bigger than North America.

Many other advances in agriculture have yet to be applied on a large scale. Identification of necessary trace elements and their incorporation into fertilizers and feeds have opened vast areas to cultivation and husbandry in Australia and elsewhere. Selective breeding of plants and animals has permitted the development of species with superior hardiness and increased yields. In the greater part of the world such work has hardly begun. Advances in animal health and nutrition have permitted mass production of milk and eggs in indoor conditioners on a scale that was unimaginable a few years ago. In some large installations, computers programmed to calculate the cheapest method of providing a diet of known energy and known content in ten essential amino acids, total protein and other nutrients, automatically set the controls that will mix basic staples porviding the cheapest adequate poultry diet as they are informed of the latest commodity prices. Herbicides increase yields; pesticides prevent losses from rodents, insects and fungi. In many underdeveloped countries one quarter of the crop is lost before it reaches the consumer; certain methods of preservation of foods by radiation have just been approved by the Food and Drug Administration. Control of the weather by seeding clouds for rain; speeding cloud formation by heating lakes by atomic energy; desalinization of brackish water by various methods, are entering the realm of practical feasibility.

Powerful though these methods of "classical" agriculture are, I believe they will, within the lifetime of most present inhabitants of this planet, be left far behind as methods of food production. Some of the larger international oil companies have again become actively interested in manufacture of food from petrochemicals (which the Germans started, to feed forced labor groups in World War II). Pilot plants are now in operation. Fatty acids, triglycerides (the constituents of our common fats and oils), and fully metabolizable simpler compounds, such as 1,3-butanediol, may soon be manufactured at very low cost for human food and animal feeds. Though the promise of cheap atomic power, widely heralded for the morrow in the immediate postwar period, has been slow to be realized, it is coming, and it may well be that oil will be increasingly a raw material for food and plastics rather than a fuel.

As a potential source of food production, photosynthesis can be used much more efficiently in algae than in higher plants. With proper mineral fertilization and with the proper rate of removal of the finished products, one square meter may serve to support algae production sufficient to feed one man. And as much as one-half of the calories are derived from protein; vitamins are also produced. The problems entailed in passing from the theoretically possible to the economically feasible are formidable, but their solution is likely to be hastened for an unexpected reason. Interplanetary travel of long duration and the organization of distant stations necessitate the fabrication of food and its integration into the recycling of oxygen, water and excreta. Over the next two decades, an increasing fraction of the several billion dollars that the United States and the Soviet Union will spend every year for space travel is going to be channeled into life-support systems. In many ways, we may have in space exploration what William James called "the moral equivalent of war." We will probably also have in it the technologic equivalent of war, without the corresponding losses in men and resources. The usable "fall-out" of such research is likely to be enormous. Certainly if economic harnessing of photosynthesis, through biologic units or directly, can be realized under hostile interplanetary, lunar or Martian conditions, it should become relatively easy to put it into effect on earth. Obviously, a breakthrough in this field could altogether remove food as a limiting factor to population growth for centuries.

Many writers, generally conservationists and social scientists, concerned, rightly, with the effects of crowding they had observed, have turned to the threat of a worldwide shortage of food as an easily understood, imperative reason for a large-scale limitation of births. Had they consulted nutritionists, agriculturists and chemists, they might have chosen a more appropriate battleground. For if we can feed an ever-increasing number of people—even as badly as many of our contemporaries are fed—their argument fails. Yet there is need for the establishment of a sound population policy for the world at large as soon as possible. And if lack of food is not a component of the definition of overpopulation, rich countries as well as poor ones become candidates for overpopulation—now.

There is a strong case to be made for a stringent population policy on exactly the reverse of the basis Malthus expounded. I am concerned about the areas of the globe where people are rapidly becoming much richer. There, and now, it is possible to see the results of the third revolution, that of "rising expectations." For rich people have the means to occupy more space, consume much more of each natural resource, disturb the ecology more and create more land, air, water, chemical, thermal, and radioactive pollution than do poor people. (The Rhine is in Switzerland, France, Germany and Holland, not China or India; oil pollution is off the coast of California, not Africa.) So it can be argued from many viewpoints that it is even more urgent to control the numbers of the rich than it is to control the numbers of the poor.

Consider some data from our own country. In the United States, our population is increasing faster than ever; our major nutritional problem is overweight, our major agricultural problem is our ever-mounting excess production. Does anyone seriously believe this means we have no population problem? Our housing problems; our traffic problems; the insufficient numbers of our hospitals, of community recreation facilities; our pollution problems—all are facets of our population problem. As just one specific example: four million students were enrolled in U.S. colleges and graduate schools in 1960; six million in 1965. The Bureau of the Census estimates that eight million will seek admission or continued enrollment in 1970; ten million in 1975; 12 million in 1980. No one questions our

ability to feed these youngsters. But are we prepared for a near doubling of the size of our colleges and universities in 11 years?

I may add that in this country we compound the population problem by the migratory habits of our people: from rural farm areas to urban areas and especially to "metropolitan" areas (212 such areas now have 84 percent of our population); from low-income areas to high-income areas; from the East and Midwest to the South and Southwest; from all areas to the Pacific Coast; from the centers of cities to suburbs, which soon form gigantic conurbations, with circumstances everywhere pushing our Negroes into the deteriorating centers of large cities. All this has occurred without any master plan, and with public services continually lagging behind both growth and migration.

This increased crowding of our cities and our conurbations is certainly one of the pictures we have in mind when we think of overpopulation. What of the great outdoors? The earth as an economic system has more to fear from the rich than from the poor, even if we forget for a moment the threat of atomic or chemical warfare.

In 1930, the number of visitor-days at our national parks was of the order of three million (for a population of 122 million); by 1950 it was 33 million (for a population of 151 million); by 1960 it was 79 million (for a population of 179 million); by 1967, 140 million (for a population of 200 million). State parks tell the same story: a rise in visitor-days from 114 million in 1950, to 179 million in 1960, an increase in attendance of over 125 percent for a rise in population of less than 20 percent! Clearly, the increase in disposable income (and hence in means of transportation and in leisure) becomes a much more important factor in crowding and lack of privacy than the rise in population.

THE POPULATION EXPLOSION

Not only does the countryside become more rapidly crowded when its inhabitants are rich, it also becomes rapidly uglier. With increasing income, people stop drinking water as much. As a result we spread 48 billion (rustproof) cans and 26 billion (nondegradable) bottles over our landscape every year. We produce 800 million pounds of trash a day, a great deal of which ends up in our fields, our parks and our forests. Only one-third of the billion pounds of paper we use every year is reclaimed. Nine million cars, trucks and buses are abandoned every year, and although many of them are used as scrap, a large though undetermined number are left to disintegrate slowly in back yards, in fields and woods and on the sides of highways. The eight billion pounds of plastics we use every year are nondegradable materials. And many of our states are threatened with an even more pressing shortage of water, not because of an increased consumption of drinking fluid by the increasing population, but because people are getting richer and using more water for air conditioning, swimming pools and vastly expanded metal and chemical industries.

That the air is getting crowded much more rapidly than the population is increasing is again an illustration that increase in the disposable income is perhaps more closely related to our own view of "over-population" than is the population itself. From 1940 to 1967 the number of miles flown has gone from 264 million to 3,334 billion (and the fuel consumed from 22 to 512 million gallons). The very air waves are crowded: the increase in citizen-licenses from 126 thousand to 848 thousand in the brief 1960-1967 interval is again an excellent demonstration of the very secondary role of the population increase in the new overpopulation. I believe that as disposable income rises throughout the world in general, the population pressure resulting from riches will become as apparent as that resulting from poverty.

It is dangerous to link constantly in the mind of the public the idea of overpopulation with that of undernutrition. It is dangerous to link it necessarily with poverty. It is absurd on the basis of any criterion of history, economics or esthetics. Some countries are poor and densely populated. A few are poor and so sparsely populated that economic development (e.g., road-building, creation of markets) becomes very difficult. It is easy to demonstrate that a couple with many children will be unable to save and invest. It is perhaps also true that, as the comparison to nineteenth-century France, England, and Germany suggests, at a certain stage of development, too low a birth rate decreases the ambition and labor of part of the population so that the savings expected from the decreased birth rate never materialize. The fact is that we are not yet in one world and that even though in general it is true that population increases make improvement in nutrition and in delivery of services more difficult, the relation of changes in wealth to changes in population has to be examined in each area on its own merits.

There is more to the problem of population than the decrease in income consequent to overpopulation. The increase in disposable income creates a population problem that is becoming every day more acute. The ecology of the earth—its streams, woods, animals—can accommodate itself better to a rising *poor* population than to a rising *rich* population. Indeed, to save the ecology the population will have to decrease as the disposable income increases. If we believe, like Plato and Aristotle, in trying for excellence rather than in rejoicing in numbers, we need a population policy now, for the rich as well as the poor. Excellent human beings will not be produced without abundance of cultural as well as material resources and, I believe, without sufficient space. We are likely to run out of certain metals before we run out of food; of paper before we run out of metals. And we are running out of clear streams, pure air, and the familiar sights of Nature while we still have the so-called "essentials" of life.

According to the United Nations report on the problems of the human environment, released June 23, 1969, over two-thirds of the world's forest lands have already been lost. One hundred and fifty species of birds and beasts have become extinct and a thousand more are vanishing. Our fuels have raised levels of carbon dioxide in the atmosphere 10 percent in the last 100 years, and may cause another rise of 25 percent by the year 2000. And, of the pesticides and insecticides we have used to protect our food supply, traces of DDT can reduce by about 75 percent the photosynthetic process in marine algae that is essential to the oxygen in the air and to life in the seas.

Shall we continue to base the need for a population policy on a nutritional disaster to occur at some hypothetic date, when it is clear that the problem is here, now, for us as well as for others? Shall we continue to hide the fact that a rational policy may entail in many countries not only a plateauing of the population to permit an increase in disposable income, but a decrease in the population as the disposable income rises?

Paul R. Ehrlich

THE POPULATION EXPLOSION: FACTS AND FICTION

The facts of today's population crisis are appallingly simple. Mankind at first gradually, but recently with extreme rapidity, has intervened artificially to lower the death rate in the human population. Simultaneously we have not, repeat *have not,* intervened to lower the birth rate. Since people are unable to flee from our rather small planet, the inevitable result of the wide discrepancy between birth and death rates has been a rapid increase in the numbers of people crowded onto the Earth.

The growth of the population is now so rapid that the multitude of humans is doubling every 35 years. Indeed in many undeveloped countries the doubling time is between 20 and 25 years. Think of what it means for the population of a country like Colombia to double in the next 22 years. Throughout its history the people of Colombia have managed to create a set of facilities for the maintenance of human beings: buildings, roads, farms, water systems, sewage systems, hospitals, schools, churches, and so forth. Remember that just to remain even, just to maintain today's level of misery, Colombia would have to duplicate all of those facilities in the next 22 years. It would have to double its human resources as well—train enough doctors, lawyers, teachers, judges, and all the rest so that in 22 years the number of all these professionals would be twice that of today. Such a task would be impossible for a powerful, industrialized country with agricultural surpluses, high literacy rate, fine schools, and communications, etc. The United States couldn't hope to accomplish it. For Colombia, with none of these things, with 30-40% of its population illiterate, with 47% of its population under 15 years of age, it is inconceivable.

Yes, it will be impossible for Colombia to maintain its present level of misery for the next 22 years—and misery it is. Death control did not reach Colombia until after World War II. Before it arrived, a woman could expect to have two or three children survive to reproductive age if she went through ten pregnancies. Now, in spite of

SOURCE. Reprinted, by permission of the author, from the *Sierra Club Bulletin,* October 1968.

malnutrition, medical technology keeps seven or eight alive. Each child adds to the impossible financial burden of the family and to the despair of the mother. According to Dr. Sumner M. Kalman, the average Colombian mother goes through a progression of attempts to limit the size of her family. She starts with ineffective native forms of contraception and moves on to quack abortion, infanticide, frigidity, and all too often to suicide. The average family in Colombia, after its last child is born, has to spend 80% of its income on food. And the per capita income of Colombians is $237 per year, less than one-tenth that of Americans. That's the kind of misery that's concealed behind the dry statistic of a population doubling every 22 years.

But, it seems highly unlikely that 22 years from now, in 1990, Colombia will have doubled its present population of 20 million to 40 million. The reason is quite simple. The Earth is a spaceship of limited carrying capacity. The three and one half billion people who now live on our globe can do so only at the expense of the consumption of non-renewable resources, especially coal and petroleum. Today's technology could not maintain three and one half billion people without "living on capital" as we are now doing. Indeed it is doubtful if any technology could permanently maintain that number. And note that, even living on capital, we are doing none too well. Somewhere between one and two billion people are *today* undernourished (have too few calories) or malnourished (suffer from various deficiencies, especially protein deficiencies). Somewhere between 4 and 10 million of our fellow human beings will starve to death this year. Consider that the average person among some 2 billion Asians has an annual income of $128, a life expectancy at birth of only 50 years, and is illiterate. A third of a billion Africans have an average life expectancy of only 43 years, and an average annual income of $123. Of Africans over 15 years of age, 82% are

illiterate. Look at the situation in India, where Professor Georg Borgstrom estimates that only about one person in fifty has an adequate diet. For the vast majority the calorie supply "is not sufficient for sustaining a normal workday. Physical exhaustion and apathy [is] the rule."

No, we're not doing a very good job of taking care of the people we have in 1968—and we are adding to the population of the Earth 70 million people per year. Think of it—an equivalent of the 1968 population of the United States *added* to the world every three years! We have an inadequate loaf of bread to divide among today's multitudes, and we are quickly adding more billions to the bread line.

As I said at the beginning the facts are indeed simple. We are faced by a most elementary choice. Either we find a way to bring the birth rate down or the death rate will soon go back up. Make no mistake about it—mankind has not freed itself of the tyranny of arithmetic! Anyone, including Pole Paul the 6th, who stands in the way of measures to bring down the birth rate is automatically working for a rise in the death rate.

The death rate could rise in several ways. Perhaps the most likely is through famine. The world has very nearly reached its maximum food production capacity— even with the expenditure of our non-renewable resources. Agricultural experts such as Professor Borgstrom and the Paddock brothers present a dismal picture indeed. The Paddocks' best estimate of the onset of the "Time of Famines," the time when many tens of millions will starve to death annually, is 1975. How accurate their prediction is will depend on many factors, such as the weather, over which we have no control. It will also depend in part on what actions mankind takes to attempt an amelioration of the situation. I must, however, agree with the Paddocks that massive famines are now inevitable.

THE POPULATION EXPLOSION

Plague presents another possibility for a "death rate solution" to the population problem. It is known that viruses may increase their virulence when they infect a large population. With viruses circulating in a weakened population of unprecedented size, and with modern transport capable of spreading infection to the far corners of the globe almost instantly, we could easily face an unparalleled epidemic. Indeed, if a man-made germ should escape from one of our biological warfare labs we might see the extinction of *Homo sapiens*. It is now theoretically possible to develop organisms against which man would have no resistance—indeed one Nobel laureate was so appalled at the possibility of an accidental escape that he quit research in this field.

Finally, of course, thermonuclear war could provide us with an instant death rate solution. Nearly a billion people in China are pushing out of their biologically ruined country towards Siberia, India, and the Mekong Rice bowl. The suffering millions of Latin America are moving towards revolution and Communist governments. An Arab population boom, especially among Palestinian refugees, adds to tensions. The competition to loot the sea of its fishes creates international incidents. As more and more people have less and less, as the rich get richer and the poor poorer, the probability of war increases. The poor of the world know what we have, and they want it. They have what is known as rising expectations. For this reason alone a mere maintenance of current levels of living will be inadequate to maintain peace.

Unfortunately we will not need to kill outright all human beings to drive mankind to extinction. Small groups of genetically and culturally impoverished survivors may well succumb to the inevitably harsh environment of a war-ravaged planet. War not only could end this population explosion, it has the potential for removing the possibility of any future population growth.

Faced with this dismal prospect, why haven't people, especially in an educated country like the United States, taken rational action to bring the birth rate down? Why haven't we led the way toward a world with an optimum population living in balance with its resources? Why indeed have most Americans remained unaware of the gravity of the entire problem? The answers to these questions are many and complex. In the rest of this talk I'd like to discuss one major reason why we have not managed to defuse the population bomb. This reason is the perpetuation of a series of fictions which tend to discount the problem or present fantasy solutions to it. These fictions are eagerly believed by many people who show an all-too-human wish to avoid facing unpleasant realities. Let's look at some of the fictions, and some of the unpleasant realities.

Fiction: The population explosion is over, at least in the United States, because the birth rate is at an all-time low.

Fact: Although the birth rate of the United States has hit record lows (around 16 per thousand per year) for brief periods this year it has not approached the death rate, which is down around 9 per thousand per year. Even at the record low rate (if it were to continue) the population of the United States would double in about 100 years. But the low birth rate will not persist since the large group of women born in the post-World War II baby boom move into their peak reproductive period in the next few years. Birth rates are subject to short-term fluctuations, according to the number of women in their reproductive years, the condition of the economy, the occurrence of wars, etc. Viewing a temporary decline of the birth rate as a sign of the end of the population explosion is like considering a warm December 26th as a sign of spring. The ballyhooing of the temporary decline of birth rate (with, if you recall, no mention of death rate) has done great harm to the cause of humanity.

93

THE DESTRUCTION OF THE ENVIRONMENT

Fiction: The United States has no population problem—it is a problem of the undeveloped countries.

Fact: Considering the problems of air and water pollution, poverty, clogged highways, overcrowded schools, inadequate courts and jails, urban blight, and so on, it is clear that the United States has more people than it can adequately maintain. But even if we were not overpopulated at home we could not stand detached from the rest of the world. We are completely dependent on imports for our affluence. We use roughly one half of all the raw materials consumed on the face of the Earth each year. We need the ferroalloys, tin, bauxite, petroleum, rubber, food, and other materials we import. We, one fifteenth of the population, grab one half as our share. We can afford to raise beef for our own use in protein-starved Asia. We can afford to take fish from protein-starved South America and feed it to our chickens. We can afford to buy protein-rich peanuts from protein-starved Africans. Even if we are not engulfed in world-wide plague or war we will suffer mightily as the "other world" slips into famine. We will suffer when they are no longer willing or able to supply our needs. It has been truly said that calling the population explosion a problem of undeveloped countries is like saying to a fellow passenger "your end of the boat is sinking."

Fiction: Much of the Earth is empty land which can be put under cultivation in order to supply food for the burgeoning population of the planet.

Fact: Virtually all of the land which can be cultivated with known or easily foreseeable methods already is under cultivation. We would have to double our present agricultural production just to adequately feed today's billions—and the population of the Earth is growing, I repeat, by some *70 million people* per year. No conceivable expansion of arable land could take care of these needs.

Fiction: Although land agriculture cannot possibly take care of our food needs, we still have "unmeasurable" resources of the sea which can be tapped so that we can populate the Earth until people are jammed together like rabbits in a warren.

Fact: The resources of the sea have been measured and have been found wanting. Most of the sea is a biological desert. Our techniques for extracting what potential food there is in the sea are still very primitive. With a cessation of pollution, complete international cooperation, and ecologically intelligent management we might manage to double our present yield from the sea or do even better on a sustained basis. But even such a miracle would be inadequate to meet the needs of the population growth. And there is no sign of such a miracle. Indeed there is increasing pollution of the sea with massive amounts of pesticides and other biologically active compounds. In addition, a no-holds-barred race to harvest the fish of the sea has developed among China, Japan, Russia, the United States, and others. This race is resulting in the kind of overexploitation which led to the decline of the whaling industry. All the signs point to a *reduction* of the food yield of the sea in the near future—not to a bonanza from the sea.

Fiction: Science (with a capital S) will find a new way to feed everyone—perhaps by making food synthetically.

Fact: Perhaps in the distant future some foods will be produced synthetically in large quantity, but not in time to help mankind through the crisis it now faces. The most discussed methods would involve the use of micro-organisms and fossil fuels. Since fossil fuels are limited in supply, and much in demand for other uses, their use as a food source would be a temporary measure at best. Direct synthesis, even should it eventually prove possible, would inevitably present problems of energy supply and materials supply—it would be no simple "food for nothing" system. But, I repeat, science holds no hope of finding a synthetic solution to the food problem at this time.

Fiction: We can solve the crowding problem on our planet by migrating to other planets.

Fact: No other planet of the solar system appears to be habitable. But, if all of them were, we would have to export to them 70 million people a year to keep our population constant. With our current technology and that foreseeable in the next few decades such an effort would be economically impossible—indeed the drain on our mineral resources and fossil fuels would be unbelievable. Suppose that we built rockets immeasurably larger than any in existence today—capable of carrying 100 people and their baggage to another planet. Almost 2,000 of such monster ships would have to leave each day. The effects of their exhausts on the atmosphere would be spectacular to say the least. And what if through miracles, we did manage to export all those people and maintain them elsewhere in the solar system? In a mere 250 years the entire system would be populated to the same density as the Earth. Attempting to reach the planets of the stars raises the prospect of space ships taking generations to reach their destinations. Since population explosions could not be permitted on the star ships the passengers would have to be willing to practice strict birth control. In other words, the responsible people will have to be the ones to leave, with the irresponsible staying at home to breed. On the cheery side, getting to the stars might not be so difficult. After all, in a few thousand years at the current growth rate, all the material in the visible Universe will have been converted into people, and the sphere of people will be expanding outward at better than the speed of light!

Fiction: Family planning is the answer to the population explosion. It has worked in places like Japan; it will work in places like India.

Fact: No country, including Japan, has managed to bring its population under rational control. After World War II Japan employed abortion to reduce its birth rate, but it did not stop its growth. Indeed, in 1966, with its birth rate at a temporary low because it was the "Year of the Fiery Horse" (considered inauspicious for births), Japan's population was still growing at a rate which would double it in 63 years. Japan is in desperate straits. Today it must import food equivalent to its entire agricultural production. In addition it depends heavily on its fisheries from which it gets food equivalent to more than one and one-half times its agricultural production. Japan is so overpopulated that *even if her population growth stopped* she would succumb to disaster as her sources of food imports dry up and as her share of the yield from the sea shrinks. But, remember, grossly overpopulated Japan is continuing to grow at a rapid rate.

Family planning in India has had no discernible effect even though it has had government support for some 17 years. During those years the population has increased by more than one half, and the growth rate itself has increased. The IUD (intrauterine device) was promoted by the professional optimists as the panacea for India, but the most recent news from that country indicates a recognition of the failure of the IUD campaign and a return to the promotion of condoms.

Most depressing of all is the point that family planning promotes the notion that people should have only the number of children they *want* and can support. It does not promote family sizes which will bring about population control. As Professor Kingsley Davis has often pointed out, people *want* too many children. Family planning has not controlled any population to date, and by itself it is not going to control *any* population.

These fictions are spread by a wide variety of people and organizations, and for a wide variety of reasons. Some have long-term emotional commitments to outmoded ideas such as population control through family planning. Others wish to disguise the failure of the government agencies they run. Still others have simple economic interests in the sale of food or agricultural chemicals and equipment. Almost all also have genuine humanitarian motives. Most of these people have an incomplete view of the problem at best. The less well informed simply have no grasp of the magnitude of the problem—these are the ones who propose solutions in outer space or under the sea. More sophisticated are those who hold out great hopes for agricultural changes (now often referred to as a "green revolution") which will at least temporarily solve the problem. Such people are especially common in our government.

This sophisticated group tends to be ignorant of elementary biology. Our desperate attempts to increase food yields are promoting soil deterioration and contributing to the poisoning of the ecological systems on which our very survival depends. It is a long and complex story, but the conclusion is simple—the more we strive to obtain increased yields in the short run, the smaller the yields are likely to be in the long run. No attempt to increase food yields can solve the problem. How much, then, should we mortgage our future by such attempts?

I've concentrated, in my discussion, on the nature of the population explosion rather than attempting to detail ways of reaching a birth rate solution. That is because the first step towards any solution involves a realistic facing of the problem. We must, as that first step, get a majority of Americans to recognize the simple choice: *lower the birth rate or face a drastic rise in the death rate.* We must divert attention from the treatment of symptoms of the population explosion and start treating its cause. We have no more time; we must act now. Next year will not do. It is already too late for us to survive unscathed. Now we must make decisions designed to minimize the damage. America today reminds me of the fabled man who jumped off the top of a 50-story building. As he passed the second floor he was heard to say "things have gone pretty well so far."

Durward L. Allen

TOO MANY STRANGERS

The wild creatures of this earth have survived because each performs a useful function in a reasonably stable ecosystem. Any living thing that is too successful destroys the sources of its livelihood and disappears with the community on which it depends. Man's vast power play in using, if not inhabiting, nearly every environment on this planet could be self-defeating if he does not have the insight to impose his own controls and to work for that necessary stability in his ecosystem.

Over the past quarter-century, an increasing body of scientific leadership has been concerned with the accelerating increase of world population. Major advances in the last two decades in the control of infant mortality and epidemic disease and some relief of food shortages have reduced death rates in many tropical countries by about half. Humanity as a whole is on a logarithmic population curve. The 3.5 billion people now inhabiting this globe are on the way to doubling by the end of the century. Unless strenuous counter measures are taken, in the United States our 200 million citizens will increase to more than 300 million in the same period.

It is reasonably certain that worldwide there will be a billion more people to support in another decade. Already more than half the world's people are underfed, and many are starving outright. There is literally nothing to spare for that upcoming billion. Food production technology has made important recent gains, and food scientists are making every effort to rescue mankind from major disaster; yet there are few who expect such efforts to overtake the eruption of human numbers. There is a growing consensus that the chance of avoiding demographic reckoning in the so-called developing countries is small. Within 20 years hundreds of millions will face starvation and death.

Although some sociologists and economists will not agree, I postulate that the problems of human welfare are biological, behavioral, and economic—a spectrum in that order. There are no interfaces where one leaves off and another begins. The whole gamut of conditions and variables is something new in the way of an ecological complex. Understanding and solutions require not only the detailed knowledge of specialists but also the broad appraisal of

SOURCE. Reprinted, by permission, from *National Parks and Conservation Magazine,* Vol. 43, No. 263, August 1969, which assumes no responsibility for its distribution other than through the magazine, with slight abridgment.

the generalist, who has extended his interests enough to communicate with a variety of specialists. The time is not far ahead when generalists will have to be appointed to high government commissions and committees.

It may be that we do not fully grasp what is happening to us and that a re-examination of our primordial heritage will be worthwhile. Long before the human line became human there were millions of years of evolution in which the ancestral stock occupied its functional niche in the ecosystems in which it was found. We pay penalties when the primitive inner man is outraged too far. There could well be clues to human rights and wrongs in the social and habitat adaptations of common animals.

A few of these characteristics are so nearly universal that they are worth reviewing. In temperate latitudes, the young of most species are born in spring and summer, and they develop to a subadult stage in late summer and fall. These adolescents commonly wander widely in a so-called fall shuffle, evidently seeking a place to live where they will not be in competition with their parents. The farther such individuals move in strange country, the higher is their mortality rate. They are at every kind of disadvantage, including the need to invade desirable space already occupied by their own kind.

When the wanderer finds a location where food, cover, the level of competition, and other factors are in useful combination, it settles down into a home range. This is a unit of habitat where the animal becomes familiar with the terrain, develops its routes of travel, knows the location of every necessity, and is best able to escape from enemies. Seasonally, at least, it does not leave the security of its home range. Here it has relationships of tolerance with other individuals of the same species whose ranges overlap. A high-quality home range is a small one, where daily needs can be fulfilled with a minimum of movement. Both economic security and behavioral

ease are found by the animal in its own familiar surroundings. Residents tend to display antagonistic behavior toward strangers.

Let us now consider a human analogy, the resident of a small town in rural America, perhaps in the more simple times of 40 years ago. The person in question has a high degree of self-sufficiency. He has a garden and a cellar stocked with food. He has a well, his own outdoor plumbing, and his supply of fuel for heat and lighting. He disposes of his own trash and garbage.

His home range is small. He commonly gets to his work or wherever else he needs to go by walking. He has recognition relationships with most of the people of his community. Here he has feelings of security and comfort. There is, he says, no place like home. The high degree of independence of this individual becomes particularly evident under "emergency" conditions. He can ride out a winter blizzard with composure, and most of the dislocations that affect him can be met with his own efforts. He needs a minimum of public service.

What of a dweller in one of our large cities? Passing over the social and economic enclaves that produce something akin to small-town conditions, let us select an individual who probably is more representative. Wherever he lives, he is dependent on a wide range of public services. His food, water, fuel, and power are brought to him, and his wastes of every kind are taken away. His work is likely to be many miles removed. To fulfill a specialized function in his community, he must meet a rigid transportation schedule in getting to the place of employment and returning home daily. Likely enough, he passes through territory that is largely unexplored and unfamiliar, and he has continual contacts with individuals with whom he is unacquainted. He has lurking anxieties in dealing with a wide range of unpredictable situations. He may develop the social callouses and aggressive behavior frequently observed in the residents of large cities. In a measure, the city dweller has lost his identity in a social melange that is diffuse and uncertain—a continual fall shuffle.

This individual is dependent for many things. He is vulnerable to every kind of public emergency. A drought or power failure, a strike or riot, a heavy snow that ties up traffic, can immobilize him and jeopardize his security. In this aggregation of largely strange humanity, he finds many of his activities organized and regulated. In turn, he needs protection from his fellow men; in concentrations of people it is evident that aberrant and antisocial behavior must be dealt with, and there are health hazards to be guarded against. It exemplifies the unusual adaptability of the human being that so many can tolerate these essentially unnatural conditions as well as they do.

Inasmuch as all higher animals are socialized in some degree, a measure of association between individuals is beneficial. It follows that with the increase of numbers an optimum density is reached in terms of behavioral needs and available habitat resources. At population concentrations higher than this optimum we see the development of excessive competition for space and other necessities and the consequent breakdown of normal social relationships.

The pressure of dwindling supplies and warped behavior patterns that builds up can be described by the term "stress." Eco-social stress is an elusive phenomenon—difficult to define, analyze, and quantify. For such reasons, scientists have largely avoided this baffling universe of inquiry in their investigations of population mechanics and animal relationships, although the physiology of stress is somewhat better understood.

To help understand the nature of high-density stress in human society, we may look at some of the findings of Alfred Korzybski several decades ago in the field of general semantics. Korzybski explored the incresae in complexity of functional relationships or problems as individuals are added to a managerial system. He noted that the addition of individuals or functions in a relatively simple organization gives rise to an exponential increase in the number of relationships and resultant difficulties. At the root of the problem, said Korzybski, lies the fundamental difference in the rate of growth between arithmetical and geometrical progression. The neglect to differentiate between the growth of arithmetical and of geometrical progressions led him to despair that those who govern could find the wisdom and means to meet their proliferating managerial tasks satisfactorily.

In similar fashion the growth of populations and of nations produces a vast organizational complexity that expands out of proportion to the build-up of population. If, for example, our present world of 3.5 billion doubles by the year 2000, it might be supposed that the problems of government and social affairs would be twice as great. This would indeed be sufficient unto the day, but such a concept probably falls far short of reality. If we assume that the complexity of relations among one billion people is represented by an index of one, then the figure for three billion would potentially be 18 and for six billion 222!

The build-up of stress undoubtedly takes place correspondingly. The phenomenon has not been measured or even dealt with theoretically. It is the resolution of many density-dependent tensions, competitions, stimulations, and interactions. It is a plexus of curves that rise exponentially with every increase in population. The computer is ideally fitted to reveal how these many variables synergize, but programming anything but a simple model using highly "psychic" estimates is beyond present technology in the field.

Americans are accustomed to thinking of mass production as a means of attaining efficiency and lowering the cost per unit. This clearly does not apply to human beings. As people multiply and concentrate, they require more protection and service of every kind, which are correspondingly more costly.

This raises significant questions about our present population level. Is this great and burgeoning complexity related to our always increasing costs of government, our deficits, our inadequacies in dealing with social problems—especially the rising rates of mental and psychosomatic disease and crime? Does it help to explain why municipalities and state governments find it progressively more difficult to collect enough taxes to carry out their commitments to education and other multiplying functions? Adding more land to the tax base does not solve any problems when at the same time it adds enough people to create an exponentially increased demand for public expenditures which more than uses up the new tax income.

Note also that the labor force is growing with the population—at a time of increasing industrial automation. We are committed to a policy of full employment, and surplus labor must be added to private and governmental payrolls. This policy contributes to the tax burden and the cost of goods and degrades the effects of technology as a means of raising living standards.

If population growth beyond an optimum begets problems that increase more rapidly than human numbers, it might be assumed that this only bespeaks the immaturity of our social and economic science—that in due time man and his computers will handle the problem and produce a high living standard despite the difficulties. To an extent, this undoubtedly is true. But whether management skills can overtake a problem that is growing geometrically, and especially whether it can be done in a degree and in time to be a relief to this generation and those immediately ahead, is highly questionable.

It is evident that many of the high-density problems of humanity result from our increasing predilection for urban life. Some 70 percent of the American people now live in cities of more than 50,000, and the proportion is increasing. This fact is relevant also to the usual approach to helping the underdeveloped two-thirds of the world. It is a common economic view that rural populations of these countries must be gathered into cities and their land given over to large-scale mechanized agriculture. It is assumed that industrialization in our image will bring them the blessings of modernity.

Even assuming a drastic Malthusian reduction of population in the next 20 years, as seems inevitable, one wonders whether governments of the countries in question can achieve the sophistication that could make such a change of life possible for their remaining citizens. To an important degree, we ourselves have fallen short in dealing with the challenge of complexity. The President's Council on Recreation and Natural Beauty last year remarked: "No major urban center in the world has yet demonstrated satisfactory ways to accommodate growth. In many areas expanding population is outrunning the readily available supply of food, water, and other basic resources and threatens to aggravate beyond solution the staggering problems of the new urban society."

The concept that industrialization can be the salvation of overpopulated and impoverished countries seems also to neglect the fact that our own system is based on an abundance of native and imported wealth. The inhabitants of North America—only 7 percent of humanity—are using about half the world's yield of basic resources. Sociologist Philip M. Hauser has stated that at our standard of living the total products of the world would support about half a billion people. This seems a dim outlook for the 3.5 billion now alive and those yet to come.

THE POPULATION EXPLOSION

At a cost to themselves and humanity, Americans have shown little understanding or respect for the cultures of other peoples. It might become us—and help us to avoid responsibility for further great errors in dealing with the deveoping nations—to proceed slowly in overhauling their social and economic systems.

There appears to be unmistakable evidence that the world at large has passed the optimum level of population. It has been widely assumed that this does not apply to the United States, but the foregoing considerations seem to indicate that we should be diminishing our problems at the source rather than always trying to outrun them. The population problem has no technological solution. Perhaps the most evident sign of our overabundance is the wholesale degradation of the environment by human works. The technological explosion has been accompanied by a corresponding reworking of the face of the land. The widespread pollution of water and air and the despoliation of natural beauty need no documentation. The solid wastes to be disposed of now aggregate 4.5 pounds per person per day. Thermal modification of natural waters as a result of power production is doubling in 10 years. There is ample evidence that in North America we have exceeded the capacity of the biosphere to degrade and assimilate our wastes.

Not only should we be making strenuous efforts to avoid further population increases, but real and rapid progress toward better standards of life in America probably must await the attaining of a negative birth rate.

Nowhere in the state of nature do we find animals prospering so well, surviving in such large numbers, living so long, and reproducing so abundantly as when a population is expanding to fill a vacant environmental niche. Of course, this is what has happened in North America during the past 300 years. The white man has dis-placed the Indian and has taken over his resources for use at a "higher" cultural level that can support many more people. It is perhaps understandable that modern Americans have been seized by an expansionist euphoria that attributes collective weal to the growth process itself, rather than to the availability of resources on which growth can take place. The "expanding economy" idea has passed from the stage of useful realism to one of economic dogma.

Two of the easy approaches to success in business and industry have become routine. First, we have assumed the right to pollute air, water, and land or to mutilate the scenery as a valid part of the profit-taking process. Second, because we have always had it this way, it is assumed that every enterprise has the right to expand through continuous increases in customers—which takes place through additions to the population. The view that this process goes on indefinitely and that it holds the key to the American dream is behind the huge promotion now under way to attract new industry and build population in practically every community that can support more people through private or public development.

One who reads the transactions of the Western Resources Conferences will learn that as of 1960 there were $22 billion worth of water development projects for 17 states in the files of the Bureau of Reclamation—plans that engineers considered feasible. These projects are planned for construction by the year 2000. It is assumed that every river system must come under complete control, with the total water supply utilized to establish new agriculture, new industry, and more people (estimated at 25 million) in all the undeveloped open space that can be found. There are enthusiastic promoters of this program in Congress and, needless to say, in the local electorates involved. Plans for more economic development for other sections of the country are going forward accordingly.

I do not imply that all such enterprises are not in the public interest, but to make these far-reaching resource decisions, our representatives in Congress must have access to every kind of information and point of view. They are frequently reminded that they represent the construction industry which moves the earth and pours the concrete. But they likewise represent the mass of silent taxpayers who unwittingly support the great works with their baffling cost-benefit ratios. The Congressman must be the reliance of the people at large who need the freedom of open space and the renewal they can draw from scenic beauty and outdoor recreation—people who have little concept of what is happening.

The people know only that we are dedicated to "progress." Where the progress leads or what kind of world is being contrived they are never told. Has someone decided for them that we are to have no hinterland? Are there to be smokestacks in every wilderness, a smog over every countryside, the threat of extinction over every flowing stream? Must inevitably a jostling horde tramp over every wilderness acre?

It needs to be understood clearly that human numbers do not grow in thin air. They are a response to the broadening of the resource base and the opening of vacant or sparsely occupied areas through developments that support new communities. This is one way in which population can be manipulated—increased by creating more centers of build-up or reduced by deliberately preserving open spaces for less intensive uses. It seems evident that we have no public incentive to increase population, yet our planning has been consistently in that direction.

SECTION 3

PESTICIDES AND METALLIC CONTAMINANTS

There is a bitter dispute going on now about the effects of DDT and other pesticides on wildlife and man. In 1962 Rachel Carson's best-selling *Silent Spring* warned us of the potential dangers of massive use of pesticides. Some of the deleterious effects of certain pesticides have been documented, but the debate rages on.

In the first article, Clarence Cottam presents the case against DDT. Parts of his argument are slightly outdated, however the main thrust of the article is supported by recent studies. This intelligent discussion is countered by a letter from Dr. Walter Ebeling, a UCLA entomologist. You, as a teacher, have a clearly defined controversial issue here, with both sides well represented. You would do well to engage your students in this debate.

The last article is an introduction to the potentially deadly metallic contaminant mercury. In this article the sources of mercury are discussed, together with the metal's potential dangers.

Clarence Cottam

PESTICIDE POLLUTION

Like a spaceship the planet Earth has a finite air supply, vast and subject to being refreshed and recycled. Even man's immense use of oxygen over the past highly industrialized century has made only a dent in the available total; the recycling system has been able to produce almost as much elemental oxygen as man has used.

As any good spaceship must be, Earth has also been self-sufficient in many other ways. Working solely with light and heat from the sun, its system has provided a renewable food and shelter supply for a pyramid of living organisms, at the top of which man has elected to place himself. But the ship has been sabotaged.

In 1874 a German chemistry student named Othmar Zeidler unwittingly dropped a rock into the planet's intricate living machinery. The rock rattled around harmlessly for 65 years. Then it jammed and began to chew up the gears, and today our spaceship's life support systems are showing signs of breaking down. Under heavy stress in any case from other human activities, living organisms are disappearing in droves, leaving great gaps in the pyramid.

Some of these gaps serve, as far as we know, "only" to impoverish the human mind and spirit; others threaten the entire biological structure.

Perhaps the least published effect of Zeidler's discovery—now known the world over by the acronym DDT—will be the most damaging in the long run. Scattered scientific reports seem to indicate that the air-freshening system of the Earth, consisting mainly of green plant plankton in the oceans, is breaking down. Although once oxygen production from the oceans was almost able to keep up with oxygen consumption by man, now there are strong signs that production is declining even more under the influence of DDT and a half dozen much more poisonous relatives.

By far the majority of synthetic organic chemicals was synthesized more in an effort to learn the mechanics of organic reactions than to develop a new substance. So it was with Zeidler's synthetic. Zeidler learned how to make DDT, described its basic properties, then put it on a dusty back shelf along with other useless curiosities.

SOURCE. Reprinted, by permission, from *National Parks and Conservation Magazine,* Vol. 43, No. 266, November 6, 1969, which assumes no responsibility for its distribution other than through the magazine, with slight abridgment.

PESTICIDES AND METALLIC CONTAMINANTS

In 1939 the Swiss chemist Paul Mueller was taking part in a concerted effort to find an insecticide that could halt the ravages of the imported Colorado potato beetle. Zeidler's creation was one of thousands of chemicals tested for insect-killing properties. Mueller found it potent. Either on contact or after ingestion, minute quantities scrambled an insect's nerve endings and caused death. The small amounts that could be expected to reach a human through a treated crop proved unable to strike the human dead on the spot; and as far as the researchers were concerned, these two considerations meant that their hunt for an ideal pesticide was successful.

Shortly after Mueller's discovery the U.S. armed forces began to use the chemical to control insect disease vectors, and the popularity of DDT was assured. By 1948, when Mueller was awarded the Nobel Prize for his work, one of mankind's greatest assaults on his environment was well under way.

At first satisfaction with DDT knew no bounds. During World War II it generated wild enthusiasm. It controlled malaria-carrying mosquitoes, typhus-carrying lice, and the arthropod vectors of some two dozen other diseases. It has been extravagantly estimated that the use of DDT in this war averted about 10 million deaths and 200 million cases of pest-borne illness. To many people after the war, DDT seemed the final answer to control of agricultural pests. It was cheap, effective in microscopic amounts, and, most important of all, it was persistent.

No one knows precisely how long DDT takes to break down in nature, but it has been estimated that it has a half-life of at least 15 years. This means that half a given application will have broken down in 15 years, half the remainder in another 15 years, and so on. One application indeed goes a long way—just what a tragically long way should have been realized, but no one wanted to be a Jeremiah. With the mix of childish enthusiasm and arrogance typical

of the technological revolution in America, DDT by the thousand tons was spewed over the surface of our planet.

Few bothered to ask what effect a chemical with such demonstrated biological potency could have on living organisms other than insects or considered that not all insects harm man—that some, in fact, are beneficial. If such simple questions were so poorly considered, it could hardly be expected that DDT's effect on the "balance of nature" would be seriously weighed. The fledgling science of ecology was then only beginning to publish the idea that no member of a community of life, or ecosystem, is independent of the others; that no matter how useless or annoying the smallest creature might seem, it has a function in the planet's system; that before eliminating any organism, therefore, it might be wise to consider what that function is. Meanwhile, DDT in dust, spray, and fog continued to blanket the land. If in a year or so an application washed into the soil out of range of target insects or ran off into drainage ditches, more DDT was applied. If mosquitoes bothered suburban taxpayers, out came a fogging truck to spread DDT. By the time the first small sign of trouble appeared in 1949, DDT had been applied to every crop from tomatoes to timber and was treated around people's homes almost as carelessly as oatmeal. Then someone noticed DDT in milk.

Now, inasmuch as milk involves children, it constitutes a sensitive part of the American political anatomy. So people paid some attention to this small fact. How did DDT, an insecticide, get into cows? In a demonstration of several of its more obvious faults, traces of DDT dust and spray intended for fields under crops had drifted to neighboring pastures. Dust from croplands blown into pastures carried more DDT. There its persistence allowed it to accumulate on alfalfa, and cows ate the alfalfa. DDT is practically insoluble in water, but it is soluble in various hydrocarbons and in animal fat. Traces of DDT, not detectable on the alfalfa, are concentrated by the cow in fatty tissues and, of course, in the butterfat of its milk.

After a few such early instances, it was decided that perhaps DDT should be used more carefully—"in moderation on crops, only in amounts sufficient to get the job done" as one agricultural bulletin advised in 1950. No one suggested not using it at all.

hysterical denunciations of the author, her scientific credentials, conclusions, and even writing style. Her basic message was: Man's assault on the living environment with chemicals, principally DDT but including a large supporting cast, had succeeded in poisoning the environment for higher creatures such as birds, fish, and mammals (presumably including man). This assault had succeeded in tearing askew the delicate ecosystems of the earth that ultimately

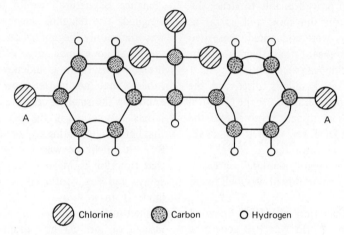

Chlorine   Carbon   Hydrogen

DDT molecule. Related pesticides are made simply by substituting such atoms as fluorine and bromine at point A.

In the two decades since, while bits of evidence have shown DDT to be a global pollutant, production of DDT in the United States has grown to an industry with a sales peak in 1962 of nearly $30 million, declining to about $20 million in 1969. Chemists, following the lead of DDT's molecular structure, went even farther by developing a whole class of DDT-like compounds called chlorinated hydrocarbons, many of which are much more poisonous than DDT. All these poisons pose substantially the same problems as DDT even if they are not yet used on the same scale.

The evidence was assembled for the public by the late Rachel Carson in her bestseller *Silent Spring,* published in 1962. This book, which in the light of more recent evidence and discussion seems a model of reason and restraint, sparked

keep man alive. But—a cruel irony—it was on the verge of failing utterly to control insect pests.

Complex higher animals have generation times ranging up to man's 20-odd years and generally produce few offspring per female. So the trial and error of evolution can proceed only slowly. Insects, on the other hand, may have generation times of only a few days or weeks, each female producing huge numbers of offspring. Consequently, if 99 percent of a population of flies is killed by DDT, the 1 percent surviving because of a slight inborn resistance can produce a new crop of flies very quickly. The new crop, all stemming from resistant flies, may have up to 2 percent able to survive a DDT application. And so it goes—each generation a bit more resistant. By now scientists have been able to produce houseflies in the laboratory that can stand wetting down with a concentrated DDT solution!

Since the attacks on Miss Carson 7 years ago, action on a wide front has vindicated her. Michigan has banned the use of DDT except in a few minor circumstances. Wisconsin has placed stringent limitations on its use. Many states have restricted it and probably will ban it. Abroad, Australia has banned its use on pastures because Australian meat was not meeting residue requirements of the U.S. Food and Drug Administration. Sweden, which had given Mueller the Nobel Prize, has banned it.

It is too late to avoid serious consequences, however, and no one really knows what the final biological outcome will be. Enough DDT already has been released to play all sorts of havoc, yet there is even more lying in the soil to eventually seep into water supplies; therefore, even if the use of DDT were to halt tomorrow, concentrations of the poison in the water of the world would continue to rise before falling.

The various properties of DDT (and the chlorinated hydrocarbons in general tend to follow the pattern) may be summarized as follows:

- DDT is among the most pharmacologically active substances known. In many cases it behaves like hormones, those trigger chemicals secreted by organisms in tiny amounts to control their bodily functions.
- It is soluble in animal fat but not in water. Most of an organism's fluids are aqueous; only its fatty tissue can dissolve and retain DDT, so DDT tends to be deposited in these tissues.
- It is chemically stable. Chemical and biological forces that may encounter DDT in the environment break it down only with difficulty, and it breaks down spontaneously only very slowly.
- It is not easily metabolized in the systems of animals (an extension effect

of its stability and its insolubility in most body fluids). Thus, once deposited in fat, it tends to stay there (half-life 15 years!). With continued ingestion of polluted food by an animal, DDT accumulates to ever higher levels. This leads to the phenomenon of biological magnification, discussed later.

- It is nonspecific. This potent substance hits friend as well as foe, often wiping out a predatory insect that has been able to control a pest better than DDT ever could. Consequently the target pest's population rises instead of drops. Even DDT's side effects share the shotgun appraoch, striking not at species or genera but whole orders of creatures.

The biological potency of the chlorinated hydrocarbons means that, whereas a particular dose may not poison an organism outright, it is capable of altering living systems in several harmful ways. Early signs indicate that chlorinated hydrocarbons, including DDT, can cause cancer and mutations. Autopsies of people dead of blood and liver diseases have shown higher than normal DDT residues. However, as the pesticide industry never fails to point out, no human deaths have been proven to be due to the direct effects of DDT under prescribed controls. But "prove it!" seems the most childish of all possible arguments in the face of a possible link.

The chemical's potency, its affinity for fat, its ability to accumulate, and its persistence all combine to suggest that there is no safety in tolerance levels set by the U.S. Food and Drug Administration unless these levels are zero. There is no such thing as a sensible degree of poisoning.

One fallacy in FDA tolerance levels is due to the fact that the effects of the chlorinated hydrocarbons may be additive. Tolerances for each are set, but a farmer often uses more than one chemical on a particular crop. Thus a vegetable may carry half the legal limit of four different chlorinated hydrocarbons—say, DDT, dieldrin, chlordane, and lindane for a hypothetical example. Animal tests have demonstrated that the effect is roughly like having twice the legal limit of any one chemical on the product. When a diet containing theoretically harmless levels of 2 parts per million each of DDT, lindane, toxaphene, chlordane, and methoxychlor—a total of 10 parts per million of chlorinated hydrocarbons—was fed to laboratory rats, liver damage resulted.

The phenomenon of biological magnification underlies another fallacy of "acceptable" tolerance levels. Americans who eat normal amounts of the normal American high-fat diet produced from farms using normal practices of insect control ingest "normal" levels of DDT in their food. These levels are not permitted to exceed the FDA's tolerances, so the food is "safe." Yet DDT accumulates in fatty tissues, and mother's milk, for example, is made from fatty tissue. A nursing baby receives a concentrate of the DDT its mother ate and thus ingests even higher levels. The FDA would consider mother's milk unsafe for human consumption were it a marketable item, so high is its content of DDT.

A clear illustration of biological magnification comes from the Green Bay area of DDT-laced Lake Michigan. There, the bottom muds were found to contain 0.014 parts per million of DDT. But tiny crustacea living in and on the mud absorbed and concentrated DDT in their bodies to a level of 0.41 ppm. Fish eating the polluted crustacea in large volumes accumulated 3 to 6 ppm of DDT in their bodies. Herring gulls eating large amounts of these fish accumulated the DDT from their diet until it reached *99 parts per million.* This amount is enough to kill them during times of food scarcity when they are forced to draw on their own poisonous fat reserves.

Biological magnification has economic effects, too, although other effects are much more serious. In the 1930's the people around the upper Great Lakes ate fish—beautiful big lake trout, whitefish, and

other species; and commercial fishing was their livelihood in some places. Then sea lampreys and alewives appeared, let around formerly impassable Niagara Falls by the Welland Canal, an ecological blunder in its own right. The parasitic lampreys wiped out the whitefish and trout industry. The alewive's population exploded to fill the void, nothing checking their increase but the physical size of the lake. Killed finally in millions by overcrowding, stinking windrows of alewives rimmed the lake as a memorial to man's meddling.

Years went by, a way to deal with the lamprey was found, and the lakes were safe again for commercially valuable fish and sport fish. Lake trout, coho salmon, and chinook salmon were stocked. As expected, the stocked fish found the environment empty of predators and competitors and full of prey in the form of alewives. All three species did well, but the coho waxed incredibly fat. The Lake Michigan fishery was reborn. It was estimated that the influx of sport fishermen alone would net the state $100 million a year. Released as fingerlings in the spring of 1966, the coho had grown to 15 or 20 pounds by the fall of 1967. Anglers went on something like a piscatorial gold rush. State officials dreamed rosy dreams. The 1968 fall season was anticipated with the eagerness usually reserved for Christmas by lakeshore dwellers, who were eating well again.

But DDT got there first. The FDA, finding DDT levels as high as 20 parts per million in coho harvested from the lake by commercial fishermen, seized the fish and forbade the sale of Lake Michigan coho. Few anglers wanted to go after fish the FDA said were poisonous. If the FDA's interim tolerance level of 5 ppm becomes permanent, it will eliminate the sale of about 80 percent of the commercial coho catch and severely limit sport fishing. Moreover, fingerlings apparently are killed by 20 ppm of DDT in their bodies, so natural spawning of all three stocked fish probably will be prevented until DDT levels in the lake fall considerably. With DDT's 15-year half-life, it could take 35 to 40 years before the residues in the fish get down to 5 ppm. The coho, chinook, and lake trout are at the top of a food chain that passes through the alewives from the microorganisms in the mud of the lake. DDT in the mud is magnified as it passes up the chain.

The principal arguments against DDT and its relatives must rest on their drastic alteration of the living environment. These alterations are subtle but profound and in the long run may threaten man's survival.

One of the most dangerous areas of concern is the effect of DDT on oxygen production. Marine biologists subjected five common species of oceanic plant plankton to roughly the DDT levels found in the surface waters of the open ocean. Addition of the DDT was followed by a severe reduction in the rates of photosynthesis and cell division in all species. In one case the reduction in photosynthesis was more than 50 percent. Photosynthesis is the process by which green plants convert carbon dioxide, water, and the energy of sunlight into food for their own growth. Oxygen is a by-product of this process. Between 50 and 70 percent of the Earth's oxygen is produced at sea by phytoplankton (plant plankton). Even without considering DDT, oxygen production is lagging behind oxygen consumption because of man's vast demands. If the effect found in the laboratory is widespread—and it is reasonable to believe it is—the results could be more disastrous than a nuclear war. Decreased conversion of carbon dioxide to oxygen, accompanied by the buildup of carbon dioxide from air pollutants, could result in planetary overheating due to the greenhouse, or heat-trapping, effect of this gas in the atmosphere. As a result, polar caps would melt, and sea levels would rise perhaps 200 feet. It can be hoped only that there is enough flexibility in the oxygen cycle to prevent such drastic con-

sequences until the DDT in the oceans decomposes.

Even supposing that this long-term effect does not occur, a relatively short-term consequence probably cannot be avoided. Zooplankton (animal plankton) also is highly susceptible to DDT. Reduced amounts of zooplankton along with reduced photosynthesis and cell division in photoplankton means a decrease in the amount of plankton available for organisms that eat it and a consequent drop in their population, a drop in the population of organisms that feed on *them,* and so on. Plankton lies at the bottom of almost every marine food chain. It is unfortunate that this basis of marine productivity is being eroded just when optimists are proposing to feed ocean products to the increased billions of human population predicted in the next few decades.

A second area of concern, DDT's effect on hormones, has been receiving some publicity lately, due mainly to the fact that the bald eagle is the Union's symbol. Raptorial birds, of which the eagle is one, have been the first victims of the hormonal effects of DDT pollution because of their position at the top of food chains. In concentrations of a very few parts per million—in mammals and birds at least and perhaps in other animals—DDT stimulates the liver to produce enzymes that destroy many other enzymes and hormones. Among the destroyed substances is estradiol, which in birds regulates the withdrawal of calcium from bone for the manufacture of eggshell in the oviducts. Consequently these birds lay thin-shelled eggs—in some cases eggs with no shell at all. Such thin-shelled eggs cannot be incubated properly, so a potential eagle, hawk, or fish-eating bird is lost. Because of their position in their food chains, raptorial birds in the United States have been reduced to desperate straits by chlorinated hydrocarbon pollution. The once-numerous peregrine falcon is now extinct as a breeding bird in the East and is surviving only precariously elsewhere, partly because of breeding success depressed by DDT and its relatives and partly because of direct effects on these birds. The Everglades kite, pushed to the brink by man anyway, may be doomed to rapid extinction by pesticides. The Southern bald eagle is endangered, with perhaps only 600 birds surviving. The American osprey or fishhawk, once numerous, because of its feeding habits is especially liable to ingest DDT, and its population is in sharp decline and already at the danger point. The osprey feeds on fish; and fish, of course, are prime biological magnifiers.

Too many farmers dislike hawks and as a group are not inclined to mourn their demise. What once again goes unrealized, however, is the importance of the falconiforms in maintaining ecological balances. Birds of this order that do not eat mostly carrion, one valuable service, likely include rodents as a major item of their diet as another valuable service. One team of writers has estimated that, were the rodent control performed by these birds removed, mice would cover the United States from coast to coast 2-1/2 inches deep. This example is a statistical trick, but it indicates the important service that, if not done by hawks and other predators, would have to be done by some agency of man's devising.

Hawks and eagles are merely the first birds to be affected by DDT's action on the liver. Brown pelicans are now in a dangerous decline, and other birds with less DDT in their diet must follow suit to some degree as they accumulate the chemical. Then there are the mammals to worry about. (Man, of course, is a mammal. What effect might DDT accumulation have on human biochemistry?)

The third area that greatly worries scientists is the possible mutagenicity of DDT. Whether DDT can cause mutations is not definitely known. It is known that many chemicals, including some that are widespread as pollutants, can cause changes in the gene structures of certain organisms, so biologists keep a sharp eye out for this phenomenon. (What effect might chlorinated hydrocarbons have on human genes?)

Obviously there are many unanswered questions about persistent pesticides, as well as demonstrable harmful effects.

What can concerned Americans do to protect themselves against DDT and other chlorinated hydrocarbons? It is impossible to escape the chemicals now. DDT has been found everywhere, even in the fat of Antarctic penguins. The best that can be done at this point is to totally halt the use everywhere of DDT and its relatives; dieldrin, aldrin, heptachlor, lindane, chlordane, and endrin are the principal offenders among the chlorinated hydrocarbons. The latter chemicals can be hundreds of times as poisonous as DDT, depending on the animal being poisoned. They have avoided being a worse problem only because they are more expensive so have not yet been used as widely. President Nixon's Environmental Quality Council has been considering the effect of the use of persistent chlorinated hydrocarbons on the environment in this country. If the Council decides that these chemicals are harmful, it has the duty to recommend to the President that he use the power of his office to halt their production and use. (It may be noted that 125 million pounds of DDT were produced in the United States in 1968. True, the bulk of it went abroad, but it will work its way back to us through the winds and waves, or through shock-waves in the planetary ecosystem.)

Meanwhile there are many control methods for insects other than chlorinated hydrocarbons, and the homeowner would be wise to seek them out. Japanese beetles, for instance, usually can be more effectively controlled with milky spore disease, a natural check on their population, than with chemicals. Often one application of MSD does a permanent job.

If a homeowner wisely decides to dispose of his stock of chlorinated hydrocarbons, he should use foresight or he will do worse damage than he could by using them on his garden. They should not be flushed down the toilet; this is the fastest route to the aquatic environment where they can begin their trip up the food chain. They should not be burned, because aerosol cans would explode, and besides higher temperatures than a simple bonfire are needed to break down the substances; they would either remain in the ash or go up in lethal smoke. Neither should they be thrown into the garbage can unless one knows for certain that they will go into an incinerator with temperatures of 1300°F. or above. The best recommendation, other than incineration over 1300°F. is to bury pesticide containers in the backyard encased in the heaviest polyethylene bag obtainable and well knotted—or better yet, encased in concrete or asphalt—under *at least* 2 feet of soil.

Having urged his state and federal governments to protect him from a poisoned environment and having buried any chlorinated hydrocarbons he may own, there is something more the citizen can do. He can stay alert to technological propaganda. Those who would develop and apply technology without sufficient foresight and at any cost are fond of casting their pet project as an irresistible force that we must all go along with, else we will be considered reactionary fossils or butterfly chasers.

Technology has but one justificiation: to serve man's needs for food, shelter, and clothing so that he can be free to develop his unique assets—mind and spirit. Technology whose end result is an impoverished setting for the human mind—let alone technology that kills people—is worthless, a total failure. Man may survive the DDT blunder; he may survive the automobile; he may even survive the invention of the hydrogen bomb. But there must be a limit to narrow escapes, and that limit will be reached soon, barring a change in the present attitude of awe and enthusiasm for every new product of technology.

Walter Ebeling

DDT IS ONE OF MANKIND'S MAJOR TRIUMPHS

Like the majority of my colleagues engaged in entomological research, I have devoted much time to attempts to develop safer insecticides or pest control measures not requiring the use of toxic chemicals. I am as concerned as anyone with the quality of our environment. However, I believe it is also important to bring to the attention of your readers a side of the DDT controversy to which most of them have probably never been exposed.

DDT is one of mankind's major triumphs. Probably no other compound, not even penicillin, has saved as many lives. It has been the principal insecticide in the control of insect vectors of yellow fever, typhus, elephantiasis, bubonic plague, cholera, dengue, sleeping sickness, and dysentery. In mosquito control it has been applied principally to the inside surfaces of homes and other buildings, with little or no opportunity for environmental contamination.

In Ceylon where the age-old scourge of malaria was virtually eradicated by DDT, the spray program was abandoned for political, emotional, and unsound reasons.

Within a few years the incidence of malaria increased to about 1 million in a population of 11 million. Orders were then placed in the United States for rush deliveries of DDT which totaled nearly 10 million pounds within one year. DDT was banned in Sweden, Norway, Finland, Ontario, Canada, and Maine, but all had to rescind their ban as soon as the disastrous consequences in field and forest became evident.

Among the hundreds of thousands of persons applying DDT throughout the world and among the hundreds of millions whose homes have been treated, no harm has been observed from its use except for a few isolated cases of accidental consumption of a large quantity or attempts at suicide. The amount of DDT required to produce adverse effects can be judged by the fact that single doses of 5-gram quantities (over two teaspoonsful) and higher have been administered to man in the successful treatment of barbiturate poisoning. This is about four times the quantity taken in by the average person in a 70-year lifetime. All patients rapidly recovered

SOURCE.   The *Los Angeles Times,* April 10, 1971.

from the barbiturate poisoning and without noticeable side effects.

Propaganda implying a causal relationship of DDT to cancer was based on an investigation in which doses of DDT 3,000 to 160,000 times the dose (per unit of body weight) found in the average person were found to produce nonmalignant tumors in the livers of rodents (and no other order of animals). The tumors disappeared when the dosage was reduced to only 1,000 times the average human intake. The words "cancer" and "cancerous" were never used by the investors.

When DDT usage was at its height in the United States, the average concentration of DDT in mothers' milk was 0.13 ppm, but, along with the continuous decline in DDT usage in this country, the concentration in mothers' milk has likewise declined to between 0.03 and 0.04 ppm. A mother's milk contains nicotine, 500 times more poisonous than DDT, if she has been smoking. Milk and other foods contain cholesterol, carcinogenic to experimental animals, when administered in sufficiently high quantities. Arsenic is present in cow's milk at levels of about 0.3 to 0.5 ppm on a dry-weight basis and occurs naturally in many foods.

Pesticides are not tolerated by state and federal agencies at concentrations greater than 1% of the maximum levels found to be safe in extensive experiments with rats and other laboratory animals. If the same criterion were used for naturally occurring substances, some common vegetables grown "organically" as well as vitamins A and D in egg yolk and butter, D in milk, and zinc in seafood would be ruled out as foods.

The decline of the brown pelican on Anacapa Island, blamed on DDT, happened not when DDT usage was at its peak, but after the greatest oil spill in Southern California history. Mercury, lead, arsenic, and polychlorodiphenyls in ocean water, and the incursions of ecologists in helicopters into breeding areas, are not mentioned as factors deleterious to pelicans in the current emotional campaign against DDT.

In California the precipitous and ill-advised substitution of the much more poisonous organophosphorus insecticides for DDT, for the protection of certain agricultural crops, has resulted in the death of personnel applying them, more treatments per year at much greater expense to the farmer, and less effectiveness against pests.

I would be the first to admit that mankind is faced with some difficult problems, all deriving in some way from unbridled population explosion. To feed and clothe a rapidly increasing population, an increasingly more efficient agricultural production is required—greater production on continuously shrinking acreage of arable land. Pesticides used under adequate controls and supervision will continue to play an important role. Pollution problems from this gigantic enterprise have been relatively trivial compared with the problems related to pollution of air and water, sewage disposal, solid waste disposal, noise, etc., that result from urbanization and industrialization.

MEDDLESOME MERCURY

Last spring, Federal agencies, after discovering mercury in fish in Lake St. Clair and Lake Erie, thought they had a fair idea of where it came from: chlorine-alkali plants on the St. Clair and Detroit Rivers. The Federal Water Quality Administration moved to clean up the industrial effluents, and the Department of the Interior reported in September that mercury discharges had been cut by 86 percent. Use of mercury as a slimicide in paper and pulp plants—a use that made it practically impossible to clean up effluents—dropped from 296 flasks (a flask is 76 pounds) in the first quarter of 1970 to 6 flasks in the third quarter.

There is no doubt that large quantities of environmental mercury came from these direct industrial sources. But in recent weeks, there have been increasing numbers of reports of high mercury levels in marine organisms, and it is almost impossible to learn where the mercury comes from. Scientists are now beginning to wonder if mercury in the environment is not an inescapable concomitant of increasing industrialization.

For example, says John West of the U. S. Bureau of Mines, there seems to be an association between trace amounts of mercury and bituminous coal. When the coal is burned, the mercury, which is volatile in its elemental form, enters the air. Likewise, says Dr. Edgar H. Bailey of the U. S. Geological Survey, mercury is sometimes associated with crude petroleum, and in one oil field—the Cymric Field in California's San Joaquin Valley—there is so much mercury in the oil that metallic mercury collects in pipelines. The source of the mercury there is probably nearby mercury deposits. But there seems to be a more general kind of association—not yet explained—between trace amounts of mercury and hydrocarbons. With energy consumption increasing at a prodigious rate, mercury discharges into the air from burning of fuels are bound to keep increasing.

Speculation that major amounts of environmental mercury may have a natural source probably has little basis in fact, says West, and Dr. Bailey agrees that such a source is unlikely. Most naturally occurring mercury is in the form of cinnabar, a sulfide of low solubility and volatility. "Any volatilization that takes place is extremely small," says Dr. Bailey. West adds that in the few instances where metallic mercury occurs naturally, it is in dry areas where conversion to soluble forms is unlikely.

SOURCE. Reprinted, by permission, from *Science News,* Vol. 99, No. 1, January 2, 1971.

PESTICIDES AND METALLIC CONTAMINANTS

The largest industrial use of mercury is in the chlorine-alkali plants, and losses to the environment from this use have largely been halted. But there is a wide range of other possible direct industrial sources. Industrial mercury consumption rose from an annual average of 48,147 flasks in 1949-53 to 79,104 flasks in 1969. Mercury is used in electrical appliances, for mildew-proofing compounds in paint, in dental amalgams, in industrial instruments, as a catalyst in plastics manufacture, in agricultural fungicides, in pharmaceuticals and for a number of laboratory purposes. Probably, says West, most of these uses involve loss of mercury to the environment. Control will sometimes be difficult.

Whatever the source, the Food and Drug Administration now believes that human intake can be minimized through careful selection of fish, so far the only major foodstuff in which large amounts of mercury have been found. Mercury, like DDT and other persistent pesticides, concentrates in organisms up the food chain. Thus large predators generally have larger concentrations than smaller ones.

"All the data aren't in yet," says Richard Ronk of FDA's compliance branch, "but indications are strong that if fishermen will select smaller fish, then the mercury concentrations will be low." For example, the highest concentrations so far—up to 2.4 parts per million—have been found in large swordfish. But 6-to-12 pound skipjacks have virtually no mercury. Because canned tunafish actually comes from several different species of fish, it will be possible, says Ronk, to select the smaller species, especially where seining methods are replaced by hook-and-line fishing—the practice on Japanese fishing boats, the prime source of tuna. In the meantime, FDA is removing all contaminated fish from markets and is setting up machinery for future monitoring.

Although there have been a number of deaths in Japan in the past from mercury-contaminated fish caught near mercury-using industries, Ronk says FDA is fairly certain there has been no poisoning in the United States from contaminated fish. The FDA limit of 0.5 parts per million of mercury in foodstuffs has, he says, a 10-fold safety factor. Mercury is cumulative in human tissues from continual exposure, but its half-life in humans is about 70 days. Because Americans generally eat little fish, the mercury is excreted far faster than it can accumulate; this would be the case even if fish consumption were markedly increased.

And fish apparently is the only dietary source of mercury in the United States. FDA checks on chickens, bread, eggs, flour, dry milk and other foodstuffs tentatively show essentially no mercury contamination. Sampling of marine animals low on the food chain show negligible amounts. A few shrimp samples, for example, had mercury concentrations of 0.1 parts per million.

But there has been little research into the effects of low-level chronic doses of methyl mercury, and it is possible that even the lowest doses may have at least some toxic effect not now measurable. At least one synergism has been discovered through which methyl mercury's toxicity is greatly increased: combination with nitrolotriacetate (NTA) a substitute builder for phosphates in detergents.

Far more research is needed, not only into the low-level toxicity of mercury compounds but also into the way the compounds are formed. The exact mechanisms through which elemental or inorganic mercury are converted into the much more toxic methyl mercury are still not clear. As with so many environmental by-products of industry, scientists have just begun to learn about the complex ramifications of mercury contamination.

SECTION 4

WATER POLLUTION

Howard G. Earl's introductory article on water pollution provides a framework within which the problem may be examined. He discusses the amount of water available to our nation, how much of it is currently being used, and the purposes for its use. The term water pollution is defined and evidences of pollution throughout our country are cited. He explains the danger to human health, touches upon methods of eliminating sewage from our waters, and speculates upon future water purification and reclamation methods.

Pollution is a simplification of the ecosystem with a resulting instability in the aquatic community. The kinds of water pollution which are causing this simplification and instability are detailed in the next article by the Izaak Walton League. Pollution caused by heat, oil, irrigation, agricultural run-off, acid mine drainage, and sediment is discussed. In addition, the special problems caused by storm water overflows, destruction of estuaries, and eutrophication of lakes are presented.

The next group of articles focuses more intensively on typical pollution problems as found in estuaries, lakes, and oceans. Their importance can be realized when considering the following estimate: By the year 2000 more than 50% of the population of the United States will probably be living within 100 miles of the shore of the sea or of the Great Lakes.

Niering examines the dilemma of the coastal wetlands, a tidal-marsh estuarine ecosystem which must rank with rivers, lakes, and oceans as a vital natural resource. Barry Commoner gives the reasons for the eutrophication of Lake Erie, a process which could affect many other of our nation's lakes. The threat to ocean life because of oil pollution is examined in the next article. This problem is global in nature and constitutes one of the most serious threats to the oceanic ecosystem.

On the bright side of the picture is the possibility that more modern methods of water treatment and governmental planning on a regional basis would help solve the contamination problem. The last article deals with this possibility. Bylinsky questions the manner in which the federal government has waged the "war" against water pollution but concedes some limited gains. He advocates a regional approach and cites as a promising example the river-valley program evolving along the Great Miami River in Ohio. His exposition of waste water treatment methods is made within the context of the entire water pollution problem.

116

Howard G. Earl

THAT DIRTY MESS: WATER POLLUTION

Water, water, everywhere, but not a drop to drink!

The continental United States has not reached the situation experienced by Samuel T. Coleridge's *Ancient Mariner,* who found himself surrounded by water but not a sip fit to drink.

It is quite unlikely that conditions will reach such a state in this country if remedial action is taken not only to stop the unnecessary pollution of our water resources but also to put an end to the shameful waste of our potable water. The culprits in this thievery of one of the most vital elements to the existence of all living things range from raw sewage of municipalities to the waste products of industries, detergents, and the residue of agricultural fertilizers, insecticides, pesticides, and fungicides all being dumped into our streams, rivers, and lakes.

Across the vast expanse of America, the great river basin areas are getting their waters dirtied at such constantly accelerating rates there is fear we shall run out of potable water or, at least, in the next decade or two experience the dire risk of serious inadequacies of useable water.

Starting at the Atlantic seaboard, the once-beautiful Hudson River has become a slimy, brackish cesspool in many areas. Continuing on across the country, the Schuylkill, Potomac, Susquehanna, Allegheny, Illinois, Des Moines, Mississippi, Missouri, Platte, Red, Colorado Rio Grande, Snake, and Columbia Rivers, and many others, together with their tributaries, are polluted to such an extent in some places that it is impossible to reclaim the water even for industrial uses.

Pollution is a costly waste of our water resources, endangers our health, is a threat to outdoor recreation, destroys fish, and in most cases is unnecessary. Taking a cool survey of the water situation in our country, we find some interesting facts to ponder.

First, we are not in danger of a water crisis, although there are areas in the nation—the New York City area is one example—where a water shortage has existed during the past few summers because of a substantially decreased rainfall. This caused the region's reservoirs to be drained to dangerously low levels where pressure levels dropped to the extent that tap water was

SOURCE. Reprinted, by permission, from *Today's Health,* March 1966, published by the American Medical Association, with slight abridgment.

hard to draw. But let's take a little deeper look into the available water supply for the United States.

In 1900, this country used 40 billion gallons of water daily. Consumption today runs between 75 to 100 billion gallons every day. It is estimated that by 1980 daily water consumption will reach 150 to 200 billion gallons. At the same time, the current estimate of economically available fresh water in lakes, streams, and reservoirs is between 300 to 400 billion gallons. It is anticipated that this available gallonage will increase by 1980 to 600 billion gallons, or thereabouts. So, although the demands on the water supply will double within the next 20 years, we still will have a sufficient margin between deliverable supply and water actually used, some 600 billion gallons—or three times the projected consumption.

A water crisis, then, is not one of overall shortage but one of serious shortages of transmission and processing and storage facilities. This means pipelines, pumps, filtering, storage, and other equipment to transmit the water from where it is to where there is an inadequacy in supply.

How do we use water? It's estimated that a home with running water consumes at least 60 gallons a day per person. Broken down into more understandable figures, we use five gallons daily to wash, shave, and brush our teeth. Every minute you stand in the shower with the water turned on, you use at least five gallons, and each time you flush a toilet five to seven gallons of water are used. The homemaker requires 27 gallons of water for all three cycles in a load of laundry. Air conditioners, garbage disposers, and automatic dishwashers place a heavy demand on the water supply.

Turning to the farm, the combined consumption of a cow, hog, sheep, and chicken will average about 40 gallons of water a day. It requires 375 gallons of water to grow a one-pound sack of flour. A one-acre orange grove in California will use 800,000 gallons of water. And more than

77 billion gallons of water a day are pumped from rivers, reservoirs, and ponds in the widespread irrigation network that feeds Western agriculture:

But the greatest user of water today is American industry. The figure used becomes so astronomical that it becomes meaningless stated in total amount of gallons. Another way to explain industry's use of water would be to use comparisons with agriculture per capita. Industry's water use today is placed at about 900 gallons per person in this country per day, as compared to agriculture's 700 gallons per person daily.

Reducing this water usage to specifics, it takes 236 gallons of water to make one gallon of alcohol; 1000 gallons to make a pound of high grade paper; 600,000 gallons for a ton of synthetic rubber; 29 million gallons for the 30,000 pounds of aluminum required for a bomber.

But the real problem concerning our water supply is the polluting of our available water and otherwise wasting it through leaks in municipal water systems and failure to use the valuable supply to its fullest potential.

The pollution problem is exceedingly shameful and an inexcusable one. Foremost, water pollution stands as a constant threat to the nation's health. The United States Public Health Service (USPHS) defines polluted water to mean the presence of any foreign substance (organic, inorganic, radiological, or biological) in water, with such pollution tending to degrade the water's quality to the extent that it constitutes a hazard or impairs the usefulness of water. The USPHS further holds that the water supply shall be obtained from the most desirable sources which are feasible and that an effort should be made to prevent or control pollution at the source. Further, if the source is not adequately protected by natural means, the supply shall be adequately protected by treatment.

The USPHS Drinking Water Standards for 1962 state:

WATER POLLUTION

"Drinking water shall not contain impurities in concentrations which may be hazardous to the health of consumers. It should not be excessively corrosive to the water supply system. Substances used in its treatment shall not remain in the water in concentrations greater than required by good practice. Substances which may have deleterious physiological effect, or for which physiological effects are not known, shall not be introduced into the system in a manner which would permit them to reach the consumer."

Despite these water drinking standards, water pollution problems are prevalent throughout the country. For instance, at Newburgh, New York, the breathtakingly beautiful Hudson River is polluted. Cast iron pipes, some six feet in diameter, spew raw sewage into the river. In fact, statistics show that between Troy, New York, and where the river empties into the ocean, the wastes of some 10 million people are dumped into the stream each day. In fact, three types of pollution get into the river; raw sewage dumped from the city; primary-treated sewage from New Jersey, which contains 70 percent of the germ content of raw sewage, and industrial wastes from New Jersey and Staten Island factories.

This example of pollution is duplicated across the country, in such places as Portland, Oregon, on the Columbia River; the Iowa cities of Council Bluffs and Sioux City on the Missouri; St. Louis on the Mississippi, and Savannah on the Savannah River.

What are the dangers to health from such pollution?

The *Bacillus coli,* now known as *Escherichia coli* is present in fecal matter from humans and other mammals. It is included in what is called today the coliform (resembling *Escherichia coli*) group of bacteria. The latter is a pollution indicator. It is an indirect approach because the identification of disease-producing bacteria or viruses is time-consuming and costly.

If coliform organisms are found in a water supply or a stream, it may indicate fecal pollution because these microorganisms suppose the presence of fecal matter and there always is the possibility that this fecal matter may be associated with disease-producing bacteria found in the lower intestines of ill persons.

Two families of viruses are excreted from the feces: the *enteroviruses* (which include polio, Coxsackie, and Echo viruses) and the *adenoviruses.* The enteroviruses multiply in the human intestine, are discharged in the feces and may cause summer fever illnesses in infants and children. Several members of this virus family may cause paralysis.

Adenoviruses apparently multiply in the human intestine and are found in significant amounts in fecal matter. This family of viruses is associated with upper respiratory diseases, causing inflammation of the mucous membrane of the respiratory and ocular (eye) systems. The Coxsackie viruses are highly infectious among the young, especially. Loss of appetite, a general feeling of illness, nausea, and abdominal discomfort are the early symptoms. These viruses also may cause paralysis and inflammation of the heart.

Echo viruses, excreted by healthy and ill children, cause acute summer diarrheal diseases in infants and young children. Sometimes there is only nausea and vomiting and generalized abdominal pain. Sick infants and children may manifest clinical poliomyelitis, usually the non-paralytic form.

There have not been any actual cases of waterborne disease from drinking water contaminated by Coxsackie, Echo, and adenoviruses. But hepatitis, Coxsackie, polio, Echo, and adenoviruses are excreted in feces and can be found in urban sewage. Bathing in water heavily contaminated with human feces or sewage is flirting with the threat of infection. Since it is established that effluents from sewage treatment plants do contain bacteria and viruses, it is not difficult to understand why streams receiving raw sewage pose threats to health.

THE DESTRUCTION OF THE ENVIRONMENT

The effects upon fish in our polluted streams is best exemplified by 1963 statistics which showed that more than 50 million fish were killed in U. S. coastal waters and rivers. How? Radioactive wastes were blamed for kills in the Colorado River. Many streams in Pennsylvania and West Virginia were fouled by acid draining into them from mines. Elsewhere the wastes of unsewered septic tanks seeping into underground waters, and chemical pesticides and oil spills have been involved in fish kills.

It was disclosed last October that research by the U. S. Department of the Interior scientists found that amazingly small amounts of pesticides can kill shrimp, crabs, and other aquatic life. One part of DDT in one billion parts of water was found to kill blue crabs in eight days. One part per billion, a spokesman for the department said, is the same relationship as one ounce of chocolate syrup would bear to 10 million gallons of milk.

The researchers also found that commercial brown and pink shrimp exposed to less than half of one part of heptachlorendin or lindane in one billion parts of water were killed or immobilized in 48-hour laboratory tests.

These chemicals, like DDT, are chlorinated hydrocarbon insecticides. In the laboratory, paralyzed fish or shellfish, it was found, may live for days and even weeks. However, death may result almost immediately in the sea where only the fittest survive.

A large petrochemical plant on a tributary of the Ohio River produces a very complex waste which, it has been estimated, contains at least 300 chemical substances in solution. An attempt was made to identify the major individual chemical compounds contained in samples of the receiving stream below the plant outfall. But it was decided that the complex mixture in a simple sample would require many years of man-power effort by highly competent organic chemists to ferret out all the toxic mixtures involved.

The problem of identifying the myriad pollutants that may appear in water supplies is formidable. Studies made at the Public Health Service's Sanitary Engineering Center, Cincinnati, Ohio, have revealed that new and unusual contaminants are appearing in the drinking water of the nation. Among these compounds are such items as DDT, o-nitrochlorobenzene, pyridine, detergents, diphenyl ether, kerosene, nitrites, and a variety of substituted benzenes. Unfortunately, waste treatment processes do not remove many of these contaminants, and purification processes fail to cleanse the water of the impurities. The concentrations of such materials in drinking water are usually low, but they cannot be considered insignificant.

Even users of wells sometimes experience trouble in finding water that doesn't contain "ABS"—alkyl benzene sulfonate—the chemical residue left by detergents. There are no proved effects on health by detergents in the water. Water begins to foam if there is as much as one part of ABS in a million parts of water. In a test cited by the Public Health Service, six people took oral doses of ABS in a concentration equal to 50 parts of ABS per million parts of water, every day for four months, with "no significant evidence of intolerance." Detergent producers point out that it is extremely unlikely that anyone would drink water with such an amount of ABS, since it would be about the same as drinking from a washing-machine drain.

PHS adopted a standard for drinking water that allows up to one-half of one part of ABS in a million parts of water. Soap and detergent manufacturers say most large streams have less than one-half of one part of "ABS" per million parts of water, even before the water is purified for human consumption. In fact, records show that many of our rivers receiving detergents from sewages and other sources contain even less than two-hundredths of one part of ABS per million parts of water—far less than half as much as the drinking water standard permits.

But, aside from this, there is a new development in the detergent problem. Detergent producers say that about 80 percent of the detergent residue is "biodegradable." This means that about 80 percent of the detergent residue can be broken down or decomposed. This is made possible by the chemical companies supplying the detergent manufacturers with raw materials which are more degradable than the detergents used in the past.

It would now appear that the detergent situation is being brought under control. But what of the other pollution problems? Are they receiving the proper attention? Considerable work is now directed toward remedying the pollution situation both from the dumping of raw sewage into rivers, streams, and lakes, and also spilling chemical wastes into our water resources. One example may be found at Newburgh, New York, where the sewage spillage into the Hudson River has been a disgrace.

Late in 1965, Newburgh received the state of New York's formal order to build a primary sewage plant at a cost of about $3 million. When completed, Newburgh's sewage plant will put a stop to pouring raw sewage into the Hudson.

Newburgh offers an example of what can be done to end the dumping of raw sewage into our rivers, streams, and lakes. Other cities throughout the country which do not have any sewage plants are not beginning to construct them.

Industry, too, is attacking the problem. Many industrial wastes are harmless and easily eliminated. Some have no value, but others can be put to good use. A few are deadly and must be controlled. Industry is attacking the control problem by employing special equipment to utilize or dispose of leftover production materials and waste.

The distilling industry is an example. It now recovers about 90 percent of its fermentation residue and converts it into dry livestock feed, which also reduces the pollution potential.

The brewing industry is following a similar program. The young antibiotic industry is moving from conventional waste treatment to in-plant recovery. Other industries are working on similar programs which not only are cutting down on pollution but also saving on the nation's water resources by re-using it.

There is no attempt here to give industry a clean bill of health. Like many of our cities and communities, there also are industries which are not taking any steps toward cleaning up the dirty mess of water pollution.

Conservation of water, of course, can be greatly increased through re-use and through reduction of evaporation. San Diego, California, often is cited as a city which fails to re-use water. The city gets most of its water from the Colorado River, some 300 miles away. The water is used only once and then spewed into the ocean. It is claimed that if modern purification methods were employed, the water could be used again in industry, agriculture, or even for replenishing ground water resources, as is done elsewhere. Some cities through reclaiming and purification methods are re-using water as many as five times.

As for means of reducing evaporation, research in this field has progressed to where it is possible to stop up to 63 percent of evaporation in reservoirs and other places where water is stored for use. The evaporation is reduced by spreading a chemical film over the water's surface. The achievement is the more impressive when you consider that in many reservoirs evaporation exceeds the amount of water withdrawn for use.

It is now estimated that the water utilities of the United States supply our homes, stores, offices, and factories with almost 20 billion gallons of water a day— or 150 gallons daily for every man, woman, and child served by these systems. There is little doubt that the demand for water will increase with the rise in our population and the increase in the number of industrial uses to which water will be put.

Although there is no danger of a water shortage, precautions are being taken and methods developed by which more water may be made available. One of the most talked-about methods is the use of water from the oceans. This may be accomplished through a desalting process by which the salt and other impurities are removed from the ocean water.

Conversion of sea water into fresh water on a scale large enough to yield an important supply is a technical reality. Modern desalting plants now are producing fresh water for about $1 per 1000 gallons. Many water engineers see in the not-too-distant future reducing this cost to about 30 cents per 1000 gallons. And from a West Coast plant there are indications that production of 150 million gallons of fresh water daily, using nuclear energy, can be achieved at a cost of about 22 cents per 1000 gallons.

So the reduction of pollution and increase in conservation of our water supplies move ahead on many fronts. A major recent step may prove to be President Lyndon B. Johnson's signing of a bill which substantially strengthens the federal government's hand in cleaning up the nation's waterways. Pledging that water pollution "is doomed in this century," the President called for more and stronger laws to go on with the job.

The new law adds $50 million to the previously committed $100 million set aside for federal grants to aid state and local bodies to build sewage treatment plants. It requires states to establish water quality standards by July 1, 1967, or have the federal government do it for them. Cities and industries reserve the right under the law to appeal the cleanliness standards to a public water conference and to the courts.

President Johnson has promised that Washington's Potomac, which he called "a river of decaying sewage and rotten algae" would be one of the first bodies of water to be cleaned up.

"I pledge to you," said the President, "that we are going to reopen the Potomac for swimming by 1975. And within the next 25 years, we are going to repeat this effort in lakes and streams and other rivers across the country."

It's a promise that will cost the country billions of dollars, but it will be worth every cent spent.

POLLUTION PROBLEMS AHEAD

Some of the following top priority pollution sources and locations require development of improved control techniques.

Thermal pollution. Power plants and some industries use large volumes of water for cooling. Use of cooling water will increase dramatically over the next several decades as more power stations are built.

Cooling water returned to source streams without pre-cooling may raise stream temperatures 10 to 30 degree F. above normal temperatures. Many discharge temperatures now range up to 115 degrees F., often resulting in river temperatures above 95 degrees F. as far as five miles downstream from a power plant.

Water temperatures exert a profound influence on aquatic life. Heat, for example, reduces water's capacity to hold oxygen. With less oxygen present, water becomes less efficient in assimilating wastes and may harm fish and other aquatic life. While limited temperature increases may benefit some aspects of fish growth and reproduction, uncontrolled temperature increments could have disastrous ecological effects, particularly in fine trout streams and sensitive estuaries.

Given the growing use of nuclear power plants, which require greater volumes of cooling water than fossil fuel stations, and the present lack of regulation to control heated discharges to streams, thermal pollution is one of the major problems to be overcome in the next few years. Two types of water cooling facilities, cooling towers and closed circuit cooling systems, now exist. The job ahead is to get these essential facilities included in the design for power plants. States should not grant exceptions to water quality standards to allow hot water discharges to their waterways.

Storm water overflows. There are two kinds of sewer systems, combined and separate. Combined sewers carry away both water polluted by human use and water polluted as it drains off homes, streets, or land during a storm. In a separate system, sanitary sewers carry only sewage and storm sewers handle the large volumes of water from rain or melting snow. Most old-

SOURCE. Reprinted, by permission, from *Clean Water,* published by the Izaak Walton League of America, April 1968, with slight abridgment.

er and larger cities have combined systems. During storms, because of increased water volumes, much of the combined storm and sanitary water by-passes the local treatment plant. Thus, completely untreated sewage enters local waters during storm periods. Separation of combined sewer systems would relieve as much as 50 percent of the pollution problem in some areas, although even where sewers are separated surface water run-off problems may still exist.

Oil pollution. Pollution of ocean surface, coastlines and beaches, estuaries, harbors, rivers, lakes, and land from oil spills, whatever the source, is a serious problem. Oil damages and destroys important land and water areas and essential forms of life as well.

Tankers, handling terminals and commercial and naval shipyards where oil can be loaded or unloaded, tank cleaning companies, on-land and offshore drilling rigs, refineries, petrochemical plants, other industrial operations, storage facilities, sunken tankers and other ships, and natural oil seeps off certain coastlines are all sources of oil pollution. Another source is service stations and garages which may dump used crankcase oil into community storm and sanitary sewers. The effect on local water quality is considerable since the used oil also contains detergents and other chemicals.

Vessel pollution. Studies have shown that vessel pollution poses a growing threat to harbors, bays, lakes, estuaries, and other heavily used waterways. It is senseless to expect cities and industries along these waters to clean up their waste discharges only to have the water remain polluted by sewage; oils; litter; bilge, ballast, and wash waters; sludge; and other substances discharged from vessels. Federal regulations governing such discharges have been proposed for vessels of all descriptions.

Irrigation pollution. Irrigation of crop lands can damage water quality. Water

leaching through the soil collects salts and minerals which increase in concentration as the water is repeatedly reused. Further concentration occurs as water is lost through transpiration by plants and from evaporation. The brackish water resulting may not be fit for municipal purposes or for further agricultural uses downstream. Better methods must be found to reduce concentrated salts and minerals from irrigation return flows.

Agricultural run-off. Rains washing agricultural lands carry wastes from animal feedlots as well as non-degradable pesticides and herbicides (chemicals which do not break down on reaching the water but remain to produce harmful effects on plants and animals). Land drainage pollution is hard to control because all the waters in a given watershed cannot be collected and treated as wastes from cities and industries can. Because of its detrimental effect on water quality, land run-off must be controlled.

Acid mine drainage. Acid mine drainage from active or abandoned underground and surface mines harms fish, wildlife, plants, and aquatic insects. While low acid concentration may not kill fish and wildlife, it can change their physical condition or growth rate. High acid concentration may suppress or prevent reproduction of desirable fish species or may prove lethal. Preventive control measures being tried include recontouring disturbed land and grouting, flooding, or airsealing old mines to stop the flow of polluted water. Water treatment methods are also being studied.

Sediments. Large volumes of soils, sands, and minerals washed from the land and paved areas of communities into our waters cause another pollution problem. Sediment fills stream channels and harbors, requiring expensive dredging, and fills reservoirs, reducing their capacity for a useful life. It erodes power turbines and pumping equipment and reduces fish and shellfish populations by blanketing fish nests and food supplies. More importantly, sediments reduce the amount of sunlight penetrating water. Sunlight is required by green aquatic plants which produce oxygen necessary to normal stream balance. Sediment greatly increases treatment costs for municipal and industrial water supply and for sewage treatment where combined sewers are used.

Estuaries. Destruction of estuarine areas by pollution, by dredging to improve navigation channels or harbors, or by bulkheading or filling (for land development) threatens U. S. commercial and sport fisheries, and wildlife populations. Estuaries—including sounds, marshes, bays, lagoons, and coastal waters—are critically important in maintaining the food chain of water and water-dependent creatures. Complex areas encompassing both land and water, they are fertile in the production of plant life, shellfish, sport and commercial fish, waterfowl, and shore birds.

Experts claim that over 50 percent of our annual commercial fish harvest (in volume and in value) consists of species spending some part of their life cycle in estuarine environments. The estuarine fishery harvest annually yields over 3 billion pounds valued at nearly $400 million. It includes shrimp (our most valuable fishery resource), salmon, oysters, clams, and about 70 other commercial and sport species.

Estuaries are also valuable recreation areas. Half of the people in the U. S. live within an hour's drive of an estuary. But given the smallness of our estuarine areas and the large public demands being made on them, we could totally destroy them in 20 to 25 years. Water quality management and land and shoreline management (including enlightened zoning practices) must be included in preservation attempts. Presently, no national regulations protect our estuaries.

Eutrophication. Lakes, like men, are born, grow old, and die. The natural aging process of a lake (due to enrichment of the waters with nutrients) occurs in terms of geologic time—hundreds, thousands, even millions of years. Most lakes were born in the glacial ages and probably supported no aquatic life at birth. Gradually nature added nutrients and these, accompanied by gradual warming, encouraged growth of plants able to feed fish and other aquatic life. Throughout the youth of a lake the aquatic plants increase and die. As the lake ages, organic deposits pile up on the bottom, making the lake shallower, smaller, and warmer. Organic decay depletes the water's oxygen supply until it once again sustains no life. Over thousands of years the lake becomes a marsh and "dies" by merging into land.

Man's activities add excessive nutrients (fertilizers) which greatly accelerate the natural process, sometimes aging a lake as much in 20 years as nature would in 1000 years. The nutrients, principally phosphates (commonly found in municipal sewage, human wastes, agricultural fertilizers, detergents, and industrial discharges) and nitrates cause algae and other water weeds to flourish—first along the shoreline and then farther and farther into the lake. This causes several problems: slime and odor on beaches, disappearance of game fish (deprived of oxygen by the dying algae), fouling of fishermen's nets, taste in drinking water supplies. The sooner these signs of eutrophication are detected and remedied, the greater the chance of saving the lake.

Scientists think phosphates may be the chief cause of the problem because even extremely minute amounts of these encourage the excessive plant growth which eventually chokes and kills a lake. If phosphates are controlled, other nutrients will be less harmful. To slow down this aging process we must prevent phosphate from reaching the water. Lakes have little or no flushing action to remove the excessive nutrient loads and present biological waste treatment does not remove enough of the nutrient material either.

If we are to save our lakes from extinction, we must utilize on a much larger scale the existing waste treatment methods which are capable of removing as much as 80 percent of the phosphates from waste water. We must also develop even better phosphate-removal techniques.

William A. Niering

THE DILEMMA OF THE COASTAL WETLANDS: CONFLICT OF LOCAL, NATIONAL, AND WORLD PRIORITIES

The creeks overflow: a thousand
rivulets run
'Twixt the roots of the sod, the blades
of the marshgrass stir;
Passeth a hurrying sound of wings
that westward whirr;
Passeth, and all is still; and the
currents cease to run;
And the sea and the marsh are one.

In his descriptive poem, "The Marshes of Glynn" (which are located along the shoreline of Georgia), Sidney Lanier has beautifully defined the coastal wetlands where, truly, "the sea and the marsh are one." The tidal-marsh estuarine ecosystem should be of vital concern to everyone. An aquatic complex stretching along the Atlantic and Gulf coasts from Maine to Mexico and along the Pacific from California to the Arctic, it seems almost limitless in extent. Actually it is quite limited; it represents something like .00003 percent of the acreage of our entire country!

The Department of the Interior recognizes 20 different kinds of wetlands in the United States. Originally, they comprised some 127 million acres, but now only 70 million acres—about 60 percent—remain.

The coastal wetlands are strategically located, and consequently they are subject to constant conflicts in multiple use. Sixty percent of this nation's population lives in a band 250 miles wide along the Atlantic, Pacific, and Gulf shorelines. Two thirds of the factories producing pesticides, two thirds of those turning out organic chemical products, about 60 percent of those making inorganic chemicals, 50 percent of the pe-

SOURCE. Reprinted from *The Environmental Crisis*, Harold Helfrich (Ed.), New Haven: Yale University Press, 1970. By permission of the publisher.

troleum refining plants, and two thirds of the pulp mills are located in the coastal states. Thus, the evidence is impressive that these lowlands along the shore, these estuaries, are becoming places where the pollutants merge and concentrate, often with deleterious effects on terrestrial and aquatic wildlife.

The estuarine zone serves many purposes, among them transportation, harbors, national security, commercial and industrial sites, waste disposal, abiotic and biotic resources, recreation, and natural beauty. So the many competing possibilities for the use of a single limited region are bound to precipitate conflict and an inevitable dilemma. Our only hope of finding a solution is to evaluate this complex potential ecologically and to establish priorities, rather than to continue the past destructive *laissez-faire* operation.

Of the 27 million acres which are important as fish and wildlife habitat in the 27 states sharing the estuarine zone, about 7 percent—close to 570,000 acres—has been eradicated. The greatest deprivation has occurred in California and northeastern Florida. California leads with a loss of 67 percent, or 256,000 acres out of 382,000 acres of estuarine habitat. Between 10 and 15 percent of the true estuarine environment has been wiped out in New York, New Hampshire, Connecticut, and New Jersey. (In the case of Connecticut, 50 percent of the tidal marshes have been obliterated. The destruction continues daily, eating into the remaining 14,000 acres at the rate of about 200 acres every year.)

A biogeological analysis of this tidal-marsh estuarine system as a natural landscape may more easily resolve some conflicting uses and establish some priorities. Those, in turn, may spotlight more sharply the public's concern at the local, state, federal, and international levels.

Tidal marshes such as those on the Connecticut-Rhode Island border, in southern France at the mouth of the Rhone, exemplify estuarine ecosystems characteristic to the temperate zone. In the latter case, much has been filled in, but surviving marshes contain bands of rushes, glasswort, and sea lavender, which are some of the typical salt marsh plants common in temperate regions. The coastal zone of the tropics such as in southern Florida is dominated by mangroves, rather than the temperate zone's salt marsh grasses, and is very productive in wildlife and aquatic resources.

The tidal-marsh estuarine ecosystem is an interface where the water and land meet, and where nutrients tend to concentrate. In our temperate zone it is a place dominated by grasses, primarily the cordgrasses, which can play an extremely important role in the total marsh ecosystem. Basically, the grasses supply one of the major forms of nutrients that make the estuary a rich and productive area. Each year about half of the grasses that fall onto the marsh flat are partly decomposed by bacteria. About three-quarters of a ton of the dead marsh grass in the form of detritus is swept annually from each acre. As a result of this bacterial action, the total protein content of the grass vegetation is actually increased or even doubled. Therefore, the grasses represent one of the most productive units in the estuarine system.

The mud algae represent another facet contributing to the productivity of the estuarine tidal-marsh complex. Diatoms coating the surface sediments of the mud flats serve as the base of the food chain. They are beautifully adapted to their changing environment, carrying on maximum photosynthesis at high tide in the summer and when the tide is out in the winer and the flats are warmed. Diatoms form a tremendously important contribution to the primary producer biomass.

A third aspect of the estuary's productivity is the phytoplankton, the microscopic plants suspended in the water which serve as another major source of food for zooplankton and other aquatic organisms.

These three major components—the grasses, diatoms, and phytoplankton—make the estuarine tidal marsh one of the world's most productive ecosystems, with an output of up to six times more protein than the cornfields of Iowa. To these one must add the macroscopic algae (seaweeds) which decay; their detritus also makes a sizable contribution to the total productivity.

We have to think of this particular ecosystem as a place where nutrients accumulate and are trapped. Studies by Lawrence Pomeroy, a biologist at the University of Georgia, have indicated that there are about 0.1 parts per billion phosphorus above the marsh and about 10 times more below it, which means that most of the phosphorus is not coming from the land but from the marsh complex. In addition to their production, the nutrients are trapped and held within the estuary. During the tidal cycles the lighter fresh water flows over the salt water, and in the vertical mixing which follows the nutrients are retained within the estuarine system.

The nutrients are trapped not only by this physical aspect of the estuary's hydrology, but also by ribbed mussels embedded within the marsh. These abundant bivalves help stabilize the banks of tidal ditches which have been dredged for mosquito control. As the water sweeps over them, each of these organisms can siphon up to four quarts of water per hour. In that process, they accumulate detritus and phyto plankton in such quantities that they often eject some as pseudofeces, providing further enrichment in the estuary. Thus, the ribbed mussel, commonly regarded as an inedible and unimportant species, actually serves as an important mechanism for keeping the fertility of the estuary high.

The estuary serves as a nursery and a spawning ground for many species, particularly the flounder. Here certain fish spend the early stages of their lives. Providing a nutrient-rich medium, the estuary serves as the base of the food chain for the larval stages of many marine forms during this critical part of their life cycle.

The base of the food chain for shellfish and finfish originates in the estuary. It is the energy derived from this system that accounts for the high shellfish and finfish productivity of our coastal waters. However, it is worth noting that the whole shellfish industry in Connecticut has gone downhill, primarily due to marsh destruction and pollution. Through the 1920's the taking of clams annually netted up to $20 million—equivalent to $48 million in today's economy. At the moment, net clamming profits are down to about $1.5 million.

Significantly, 90 percent of our total seafood harvest is dependent in one way or another upon estuarine environment. In 1960 in New England the fleet landed 800 million pounds of fish valued at over $60 million. About 500,000 pounds of that fish were directly dependent upon the marsh. I have already mentioned the shellfish value which has gone downhill because of a complex of factors; but it can be brought up again, especially if the pollution is abated.

The Sport Fisheries Institute has valued a managed estuarine acre off the Maine coast at $33,563. This figure is based on the potential harvest of shellfish and bait worms. Where such acreage is not managed, about one half that value is estimated. By comparison, the market value of a good acre in upland Maine is about $2000.

In various parts of the world, production of shellfish and finfish has greatly increased when estuarine acres are managed. That may be necessary in this country if we hope to help in feeding our world population. With the population doubling every few decades, and with more than half of humanity suffering from malnutrition, it seems to me that on a long-range basis we cannot afford to lose this tidal marsh habitat.

Commercial oystermen are attempting to increase oyster productivity by submerging strings of scallop shells in unpolluted bays where the young oyster spat settle on the shells and grow. Without any special fertilization, it is possible to achieve tremendous quantities of these young spat, which can be eventually seeded in the estuary to mature to marketable size.

The production of wildlife is another important characteristic of the estuaries. The spectacular water birds associated with the marsh attract millions of people annually. The marshes along the east coast are in the path of the Atlantic flyway. Tremendous numbers of birds stop on the marshes to rest and feed during the migration periods. Many also nest. In fact, it is estimated that during an average year 300,000 ducks—and in the best years 700,000—are produced along the eastern coastal wetlands. This particular environment is quite literally a duck factory!

Among the most distinctive birds of the marsh are the rails. The clapper rail, one of the most common, is a secretive bird seldom seen by the casual marsh visitor. In addition, the spectacular waders, the herons and egrets, are most frequently seen as they search for food along the mud flats at low tide.

Because of its declining numbers, the osprey has excited most attention at this particular moment. Studies by Peter Ames, University of California ornithologist, have documented a correlation between the amount of DDT found in the eggs of the osprey and their hatchability. In the Connecticut eggs he found that it took two nests to produce one offspring, while there was one bird per nest in Maryland. Checking the DDT content, he discovered about five parts per million in the Connecticut eggs and only three parts per million in those from Maryland. In simple terms: less DDT in the Maryland eggs and a little bit better hatchability, more DDT in the Connecticut eggs and poorer hatchability. Normally, one can expect two or more young ospreys to hatch per nest.

Although only a correlation, Ames' findings stimulated the examination of some other factors. Lucille Stickel, at the

U. S. Department of the Interior's Patuxent Research Center, correlated differential eggshell thickness in pesticide-fed birds. Mallard ducks particularly, which were fed DDT in their diets, produced eggs with shells measuring 13 percent thinner than those produced by birds that had not been fed the pesticide. Joseph Hickey, wildlife biologist at the University of Wisconsin, analyzed the eggshell thickness of hawk eggs from various museums, collected before 1945, and compared them with more recent eggs of the same species. Here his correlation indicated a 19 percent decrease in the thickness of the eggshell, which means increased breakage in the nest and fewer birds hatched. Hickey also found that the change in the thickness of the eggs occurred about 1947. This correlation is significant because we began to use persistent pesticides at about that time. This adds further evidence regarding the role of pesticides in the declining population of our birds of prey.

Now that we have examined the various roles of the tidal marshes, let us consider some of the conflicts concerning them. An obvious conflict occurs over the encroachment of filling, which reminds me of Shakespeare's statement that "when you take my life, you take the place in which I dwell." A classic example in Connecticut was the creation of a parking lot by marsh filling at Sherwood Island State Park. Dredging for the installation of a marina is another case in point. Although more marinas may be needed they need not be located in a tidal marsh.

A second conflict: are we going to have marshes for ducks, or are we going to have them for the production of finfish and shellfish? These marshes can be impounded and converted to fresh water areas. They are unquestionably able to produce more ducks, but certain of their other productivity qualities are lost. Other disturbances include the blasting of holes into the marsh in duck management programs.

WATER POLLUTION

Agricultural pollution can also be a problem. A survey has found that the duck farms at Moriches Bay on Long Island contributed tremendously to the transformation of the bay's whole phytoplankton population. Instead of the normal diatom population of many different species, the result was two species of chlorophyllaceous algae which were not beneficial to oysters. The bay's ecology had actually been changed by a particular enrichment with organic matter. Laboratory tests indicated that these two species of algae were favored by the organic nitrogen available in such tremendous quantities.

How do we resolve the conflicts that imperil our estuarine marshes? We will continue to need navigation, transportation, and harbors along the nation's coastline. Obviously, oil discharges, whether from ships or underwater wells, show the necessity for more stringent regulation. Also essential is sewage control from ships, industry, and agriculture, and even domestic sources.

The cleanup process will be long and costly. It could start with strict rules and enforcement for vessels, and then similar provisions for pulp mills where effluents deplete the estuarine waters of oxygen. Oysters there have been found to be 500 times more sensitive to the effluent than fish. Or the cleanup campaign could aim at another critical problem, chemical wastes where Pacific salmon move through the estuary. Many aquatic and terrestrial organisms are extremely sensitive to metals such as cobalt, copper, and mercury which are being flushed into the water flowing into the sea. Again, it is obvious that new and stricter regulations on effluents are required.

Agricultural chemicals create a more difficult problem. How can we prevent leaching of pesticides off the landscape into surrounding estuaries? The lower Mississippi fish kill in 1963 was a dramatic example where extensive numbers of catfish were killed by the pesticide endrin. A chemical company was largely responsible, but some of the insecticide presumably came from surrounding agricultural lands.

Control of materials that get into the estuary is complex and difficult but must be governed from the source where possible. Oysters not only are sensitive to insecticides but can accumulate great quantities of them—in one experiment up to 70,000 times the average amount in the surrounding water. This is the problem of biological magnification. Even if the pesticide content entering a stream is relatively low, animals such as the bivalves become accumulators of the deadly material.

Obviously, we need more than new regulations and enforcement. The treatment of our addiction to pesticides requires an entirely new approach, integrated biological control systems with pesticides serving as only part of the total design. Various cultural techniques can be employed. In the case of cotton in California, scientists learned that by planting alternate rows of alfalfa they have been able to divert some insects from the cotton to the alfalfa. We must expand our search for such integrated control techniques so that only minimal amounts of pesticides are necessary. It will cost a lot of money and require government subsidy. Marketing inspectors and consumers must modify their demands for insect-free produce. High-powered advertising has accustomed us to the idea that every commodity must be virtually perfect; this is not necessary.

Thermal heating is another industrial conflict in the estuarine environment. Senator Edmund Muskie of Maine criticized the Atomic Energy Commission in 1968 when it failed to consider thermal heating, in addition to radioactive contamination, as its problem. Muskie's reflections have also alerted some utilities to be more careful. Daniel Merriman of Yale University has been carrying on studies at the Connecticut Yankee nuclear energy plant on the effects of thermal heating, and Nelson Marshall at the Rhode Island Oceanographic Institute has started long-range research at the plant under construction at Millstone Point. These experts and others are attempting, as the AEC has done for many years in the case of radioactivity, to determine the ecological changes likely to evolve from nuclear power plant operations.

A utility executive recently said that the demand for electricity will double in the next ten years. Actually, the estimates range from 32 to 512-fold by the year 2000. That will put a tremendous demand on the utility systems. It also will pose a rather interesting ethical point: do we really need all the electricity utility companies plan to try to sell us? The question may encroach a little on the free enterprise system concept, but remember that we are all on this planet together. Conceivably, sooner or later we will face the choice of sacrificing some electricity or certain estuarine ecosystems.

Domestic pollution is a serious threat to our environmental welfare. Our rivers are so polluted that we cannot swim in them. The Thames River flows by my house here in Connecticut. It looks beautiful from the distance, but I cannot swim in it and certainly do not want to fish in it. Millions of gallons of sewage come daily into the Thames from the cities of Norwich and Taftville. Of course, this problem will be solved soon if the federal and state governments can match enough funds. But funds are in short supply and the pollution is increasing.

There is no doubt that we recognize the crisis. Appropriate legislation has been passed in an attempt to clean up the nation's water, but it will take some time. In fact, it is going to take quite a bit of time, because so much of our tax money is being diverted to other uses. In the first year after the Clean Water Restoration Act was passed in 1966 the demand from cities for matching federal funds far outstripped the money available. It all boils down to getting enough financial aid to help cities clean up first, so that the estuarine environment can be salvaged too.

Another conflict centers on our abiotic resources. This, basically, involves the taking of sand and gravel from beneath estuaries for such purposes as construction of the Connecticut Thruway or parking facilities on the marsh at the Sherwood Island State Park. That resource below the estuary is immensely valuable, and some shrewd businessmen with their eyes on it have approached the Connecticut Resources Commission several times to suggest a rather interesting kind of dredging ditch—one which would serve only a single purpose, to get at the sand and gravel deposits. Such a venture was undertaken in Florida with the predictable result that after ten years of dredging an estuary, very little bottom fauna remains. The removal of such a resource is wanton, unforgivable destruction.

Mining oil on the coastal shelf can create problems. The incidents of the leaking oil wells off Santa Barbara, California, speak for themselves as a potential future threat to the biota of the coastal zone.

Another threat to our existing marshes is filling in conjunction with recreational development. In the recently acquired Bluff Point State Park in Groton, Connecticut, the initial plans proposed the filling of about one third of the wetlands, leaving what somebody has designated as the "valuable wetlands." However, no one has demonstrated that the ill-fated one-third of the wetlands is not valuable; until such proof is offered I would suggest that we leave it inviolate. In my opinion, it does not have to be filled, because there are alternate ways which we have not yet even considered for getting people to shoreline parks. For instance, if they have driven a long distance, they might enjoy a boat ride as the last lap of their jaunt to the park. Or how about busing the swimmers from a nearby inland parking area, rather than filling in the wetlands so they can put their cars on the former marsh? Nobody has really explored all of the alternatives available in trying to preserve this invaluable resource, but the need is critical.

At the global level, the International Union for the Protection of Nature held a conference in the early 60s in an attempt to stimulate the preservation of wetlands on an international scale. Many constructive resolutions were passed. At the federal level we have a Water Pollution Control Administration, and a Clean Water Act. A national survey is also underway to inventory and evaluate estuaries, and to make recommendations on what should be preserved.

Two bills are pending in the Connecticut General Assembly. [Since the presentation of this paper a Connecticut Wetlands Bill was passed in the 1969 legislature.] They would provide good wetlands legislation similar to that already in effect in Massachusetts, Rhode Island, and Maine.

The land trusts, of which 12 are already established in Connecticut, make up another—and one of the finest—methods of generating local interest and getting action started from the ground level.

I strongly recommend that we declare a moratorium on any further destruction of wetland resources until all have been inventoried and ecologically evaluated. Then we should develop a national wetlands policy in cooperation with other countries.

This responsibility cannot be delegated to state and local governments; it must begin at the federal level, because the marshes and estuaries cross political boundaries. Our system has proved to be archaic at resolving some of these situations. All kinds of conflicts, not only at the state and local levels, but even at the federal level, have developed because we lack a wetlands policy. The Army Corps of Engineers has fought with the Department of the Interior over problems concerning the Everglades. We have seen one federal agency try to preserve wetlands for ducks, while another wants to fill them for agriculture. We have even seen the Department of Commerce making grants to communities to study the feasibility of using coastal wetlands as loca-

tions for developments to stimulate the local economy. It is clearly evident that there is no national wetlands policy.

We need broadly trained advisers who can examine the total ecological system, rather than people just looking at the problems of ducks or food production. This opinion has been supported by a recent Harvard study under IBM sponsorship on "The Impact of Technology on Society."[1] The researchers found that the impact has provided the individual with a greater sense of worth (a questionable conclusion). It was also evident from their discussion that our affluence has resulted in many effluents.

One of the difficulties with modern technology has been that the profit-making corporation is not yet entirely geared to deal with social problems or pollution. Another is that it has not been anyone's business to look at this problem. The consequence has been unrestrained technological individualism, much like the unbridled economic individualism of the pre-New Deal days. This is why I recommend that a broader group start looking at the big, the total, ecological picture.

In summary, a statement by Senator Henry M. Jackson in *Bioscience* (December 1967), pointedly touches at the heart of the issue. Senator Jackson said:

> *In the future we must strive to improve the methods of economic analysis by which environmental management decisions are made. We must recognize that the marketplace often deals in illusions, that much of the profit of yesterday turns out today to be shortsighted because the price tag did not include all the social and economic costs.*

[1]Emmanuel G. Mesthene, "The Impact of Technology on Society," Fourth annual report of the Harvard University Program on Technology and Society.

Barry Commoner

THE WORST LOSS: LAKE ERIE

About 10 million people live in the Lake Erie drainage basin, and the treated effluents of the sewage systems which serve their communities are discharged into the lake or into rivers tributary to it. The total mass of organic waste which is dumped into Lake Erie each year requires, for its conversion to inorganic salts, the consumption of about 180 million pounds of oxygen. However, in 1964 it was found that the oxygen deficit in the bottom waters of the central basin alone was 270 million pounds of oxygen. Since this deficit developed over a period of only several weeks in only a part of the total mass of lake water, and must have been partially mitigated by oxygen entering the lake water, it is clear that Lake Erie, as a whole, must receive annually sufficient oxygen-demanding material to require the consumption of very considerably more than 270 million pounds of oxygen. If the organic wastes reaching the lake in a year can account for the consumption of only 180 million pounds of oxygen, somewhere in the lake there must be a very much larger oxygen demand, which is the real culprit in causing the dangerously low levels of oxygen in lake water in recent summers.

The explanation for this discrepancy is now at hand. Most of the inorganic products released into the lake as a result of waste treatment do not flow out of Lake Erie into the sea, but are reconverted into organic matter, much of which remains in the lake, where it forms the huge demand for oxygen that has been so disastrous for the lake's biology.

Algae are crucial in this process. Nitrate (as well as other inorganic salts) are necessary for the growth of all green plants. In the lake, nitrate fertilizes the growth of algae which readily convert it into their own organic cell-substance. One of the symptoms of the sickness of Lake Erie has been the appearance in each recent summer of huge algal "blooms"—vast areas of the lake where, under the impact of excessive nutrients, algal growths give the lake the literal appearance and consistency of pea soup. In recent years such massive algal growths have discolored vast reaches of the

SOURCE. Reprinted, by permission, from *Providing Quality Environment in Our Communities,* published by Graduate School Press, United States Department of Agriculture, with slight abridgment.

134

lake waters, and great mounds of algae have washed up on beaches. Algal blooms grow quickly; they die off equally fast and sinking into the lake foul it with algal organic matter. This process, eutrophication, or over-fertilization, is largely responsible for Lake Erie's growing oxygen deficit: the inorganic nitrogen salts added to the lake are converted to algal oragnic matter which accumulates in the lake bottom . . . the lake's nitrogen balance has been upset by a stress about equally derived from the city and the farm. Much of this material has accumulated, largely as organic matter, in the lake bottom. Instead of Lake Erie forming a waterway for sending wastes to the sea, it has become a trap which is gradually accumulating in its bottom waste material dumped into it over the years—a kind of huge underwater cesspool!

Until recently, the oxygen-demanding materials which have been accumulating in the lake bottom were largely isolated from the biology of the lake. The special capability of the ferric, or oxidized, form of iron to join in insoluble complexes with other substances has formed a kind of protective skin on the surface of the lake mud. This insoluble film keeps the oxygen-demanding material of the mud from chemical contact with the waters of the lake. But this barrier can remain intact only so long as the overlying water contains sufficient oxygen to keep the iron in its oxidized form. For in the absence of oxygen, the iron is converted to its reduced (ferrous) form, which is highly soluble and no longer forms an insoluble, protective layer on the mud. It now appears that during the serious oxygen depletion which has occurred in Lake Erie in recent summers, the protective barrier of oxidized iron on the mud surface has begun to break down—exposing the biology of the lake to the heavy impact of the accumulated waste materials for so long stored in its bottom . . .

Glynn Mapes

POLLUTION OF THE SEAS AND BEACHES BY OIL POSES MAJOR GLOBAL PROBLEM

Not long ago oceanographers aboard the research vessel Chain were collecting surface samples from a lonely expanse of the Atlantic south of Bermuda known as the Sargasso Sea. They had planned to study marine life inhabiting the great quantities of drifting seaweed found in the area.

Instead, the scientists made a disturbing discovery. Their nets quickly became fouled with oil and tar—thick sticky globs up to three inches in diameter. Day after day along a 630 mile stretch they cleaned the nets with solvent only to see them gum up again a few hours later. Finally, they abandoned the project in disgust because they were picking up three times as much oil as seaweed.

It wasn't an isolated incident. "Just in the past few years we're finding we can't sail anywhere in the Atlantic—even a thousand miles from land—without finding oil," says Howard Sanders, senior scientist at the Woods Hole Oceanographic Institution, which operates the Chain.

As the vessel's unhappy voyage suggests, world wide oil pollution—even diluted by the ocean's vastness—is nearing crisis proportions. Beach-goers in such widely scattered spots as the New Jersey shore, Bermuda, the Riviera and the Red Sea complain of gooey black lumps of jellied oil that frequently wash up on shore. Floating oil spills—almost always of unknown origin—each year kill many thousands of seabirds in North Atlantic and Mediterranean waters, according to surveys by conservationists. Indeed, scientists believe the growing quantity of oil dumped into the sea is

SOURCE. Reprinted, by permission, from *The Wall Street Journal,* November 26, 1969, with slight abridgment.

threatening marine life of all sorts—and perhaps man as well. The oil industry itself is exhibiting mountain concern.

Where's all the oil coming from?

Ships that routinely discharge oil wastes at sea are the biggest offenders, pollution control experts agree. Tankers, for example, wash out their cargo tanks with salt water after each load. Not infrequently, the washings—along with a heavy residue of oil—are dumped into the ocean. Moreover, passenger lines and freighters often fill their empty fuel tanks with water for ballasting purposes. This highly concentrated mixture is always pumped over-board before the ships enter port to refuel. And vessels of all types normally discharge oily bilge sludges over the side.

Often major sources of unwanted oil includes spills from manufacturing plants, refineries and oil terminals. In Boston Harbor alone, a spill of several tons of oil can be expected every three weeks, according to officials of the Massachusetts Division of Natural Resources. Seepage from off-shore drilling rigs and spills from wrecks of oil barges and tankers also add to pollution levels.

In recent years, a few widely publicized disasters—like the grounding of the supertanker Torrey Canyon off Britain and the blowout of a well in the Santa Barbara Channel—have focused public attention on oil spills. Yet, damaging as these occasional catastrophes can be, they're only one part of a far larger problem, the experts say.

"It's the day-to-day stuff that's killing us—the chronic oil pollution that nobody reads about in the headlines," says Lieutenant Commander Paul Sova, a Coast Guard law enforcement officer in New York. Adds a biologist for the U. S. Fish and Wildlife Service: "A great deal of oil is washing ashore all along our coasts. What's its cumulative effect on our environment? That's what we ought to start worrying about."

Statistics on oil pollution are scarce. The Coast Guard lists 714 major oil spills in U. S. coastal waters last year, up from 371 in 1966. No one counts the spills on a world-wide basis.

Things are expected to get worse. On one hand, world-wide off-shore petroleum production is expanding at a rate of 10% a year—and presumably the inevitable minor spills and seepages will grow correspondingly. So far, major blowouts have been rare. But a Presidential panel set up after the Santa Barbara disaster recently warned that by 1980 the U. S. can expect a major pollution incident from off-shore wells every year.

Ocean shipments of oil are also climbing rapidly. Capacity of the world's tanker fleet has doubled since 1960 and is continuing to grow. Many of the new vessels are supertankers. These behemoths, with capacities of 100,000 tons or more, will be hauling half of all marine shipments of oil by 1975, it's estimated. (The biggest supertanker afloat today carries 312,000 tons; by comparison, the Torrey Canyon's capacity was 117,000 tons.)

What's more the imminent tapping of the vast North Slope oil fields in Alaska is adding greatly to pollution fears, especially among conservationists. Tankers will likely be hauling oil through treacherous icebound waters. Even small spills during transport or drilling operations would be especially damaging to the fragile Arctic environment, since oil tends to persist far longer in cold waters than in warm.

Talk of growing oil pollution is most unsettling to Kenenth Battles, co-owner of the Sea Crest Hotel, a resort in Falmouth, Mass., on Cape Cod. He has already had his fill of the stuff.

Sticky black globs of oil washed up on the Sea Crest's beaches three times in August alone, Mr. Battles says. Disgruntled guests had to clean their feet with kerosene—and some cut their visits short. "We're sure the oil came from ships heading into Boston, but there's no way to prove it," he says.

Topping off Falmouth's summer, a barge ran aground on a nearby shoal in mid-

THE DESTRUCTION OF THE ENVIRONMENT

September, spewing diesel oil over the town's shoreline. The spill took a month to clean up (the Sea Crest used bulldozers to remove oil from its beach), and for several days Falmouth smelled like a refinery, Mr. Battles says. "The cape should be a refuge for the pollution problems of the city," he adds angrily. "Why drive all the way from New York to find the same damn thing here?"

The Falmouth spill also caused extensive mortality in some 24 species of fish and killed large numbers of crabs, lobsters, and scallops, according to scientists who surveyed the scene.

But more disturbing were the subtle effects on the creatures that survived the spill. Weeks later divers from the Woods Hole laboratory found fish and crabs whose natural instincts were strangely altered. Flounder that appeared outwardly healthy allowed themselves to be handled by the swimmers; ordinarily they would have scooted away. Normally skittish fiddler crabs also seemed to have lost their escape reaction; most boldly held their ground as the divers approached.

Max Blumer, a noted organic chemist at Woods Hole, observes that many marine animals produce minute quantities of chemicals that perform functions essential to maintaining the cycle of life. These chemicals act as attractants during the mating process. They also aid predators in locating their prey and, conversely, give warning to potential victims that they're being stalked by predators. Oil—whether from a single big spill or a buildup of repeated small doses—may well upset these vital, chemically triggered responses, Mr. Blumer theorizes, and thus could have a disastrous effect on the survival of many species, including those that are commercially important.

Dumping of oil in the sea may also be creating a new risk of cancer in man. Some crude oils contain compounds that tend to produce cancer in animals. (Researchers, for example, have already found a high incidence of cancerous tissue in certain types of fish taken from the oily waters of the Los Angeles harbor.) Fish and shellfish that are eaten by man can ingest these oils. Hence, Mr. Blumer and other scientists speculate that chronic oil pollution may be leading to accumulation of cancer-causing agents in human food.

Gene Bylinsky

THE LIMITED WAR ON WATER POLLUTION

COLIFORM ORGANISMS

VIRUSES

INORGANIC CHEMICALS

Ammonia	Iron
Arsenic	Lead
Barium	Manganese
Boron	Nitrates and nitrites
Cadmium	Phosphorus
Chloride	Selenium
Chromium	Silver
Copper	Sulfate
Fluoride	Zinc

ORGANIC CHEMICALS

Cyanide

Phenols

Pesticides

    DDT

    Dieldrin

    Endrin

    Heptachlor

    Heptachlor epoxide

    Toxaphene

RADIOACTIVE SUBSTANCES

Radium 226

Strontium 90

To judge by the pronouncements from Washington, we can now start looking forward to cleaner rather than even dirtier rivers. The Administration has declared a "war" on pollution, and Secretary of the Interior Walter J. Hickel says "we do not intend to lose." Adds Murray Stein, enforcement chief of the Federal Water Pollution Control Administration: "I think we are on the verge of a tremendous cleanup."

The nationwide campaign to clean up ravaged rivers and lakes does seem to be moving a bit. For the first time since the federal government got into financing construction of municipal sewage plants in 1956, Congress has come close to providing the kind of funding it had promised. Assuming the Budget Bureau allows Interior to spend all of the $800 million appropriated for the current fiscal year, that will come to almost two-thirds as much as all the federal funds invested in the program so far. There are other signs that the war is intensifying. Under the provisions of the Water Quality Act of 1965 and the Clean Water Restoration Act of 1966, federal and state officials are establishing water-quality standards and plans for their implementation, to be carried out eventually

SOURCE. Reprinted, by permission, from *Fortune*, February 1970, with slight abridgment.

through coordinated federal-state action. Timetables for new municipal and industrial treatment facilities are being set, surveillance programs are being planned, and tougher federal enforcement authority is being formulated. Without waiting for these plans to materialize, Interior is talking tough to some municipal and industrial polluters, with the possibility of court action in the background.

Even with all this, however, the water-pollution outlook is far from reassuring. Although the nation has invested about $15 billion since 1952 in the construction of 7,500 municipal sewage-treatment plants, industrial treatment plants, sewers, and related facilities, a surprising 1,400 communities in the U. S., including good-sized cities like Memphis, and hundreds of industrial plants still dump untreated wastes into the waterways. Other cities process their sewage only superficially, and no fewer than 300,000 industrial plants discharge their used water into municipal sewage plants that are not equipped to process many of the complex new pollutants.

Since the volume of pollutants keeps expanding while water supply stays basically the same, more and more intervention will be required just to keep things from getting worse. Within the next fifty years, according to some forecasts, the country's population will double, and the demand for water by cities, industries, and agriculture has tended to grow even faster than the population. These water uses now add up to something like 350 billion gallons a day (BGD), but by 1980, by some estimates, they will amount to 600 BGD. By the year 2000, demand for water is expected to reach 1,000 BGD, considerably exceeding the essentially unchanging supply of dependable fresh water, which is estimated at 650 BGD. More and more, water will have to be reused, and it will cost more and more to retrieve clean water from progressively dirtier waterways.

Just how bad water pollution can get was dramatically illustrated last summer when the oily, chocolate-brown Cuyahoga

River in Cleveland burst into flames, nearly destroying two railroad bridges. The Cuyahoga is so laden with industrial and municipal wastes that not even the leeches and sludge worms that thrive in many badly polluted rivers are to be found in its lower reaches. Many other U. S. rivers are becoming more and more like that flammable sewer.

Even without human activity to pollute it, a stream is never absolutely pure, because natural pollution is at work in the form of soil erosion, deposition of leaves and animal wastes, solution of minerals, and so forth. Over a long stretch of time, a lake can die a natural death because of such pollution. The natural process of eutrophication, or enrichment with nutrients, encourages the growth of algae and other plants, slowly turning a lake into a bog. Man's activities enormously speed up the process.

DESIGNED FOR A SIMPLER WORLD

How clean do we want our waterways to be? In answering that question we have to recognize that many of our rivers and lakes serve two conflicting purposes—they are used both as sewers and as sources of drinking water for about 100 million Americans. That's why the new water-quality standards for interstate streams now being set in various states generally rely on criteria established by the Public Health Service for sources of public water supplies. In all, the PHS lists no fewer than fifty-one contaminants or characteristics of water supplies that should be controlled. Many other substances in the drinking water are not on the list, because they haven't yet been measured or even identified. "The poor water-treatment plant operator really doesn't know what's in the stream—what he is treating," says James H. McDermott, director of the Bureau of Water Hygiene in the PHS. With more than 500 new or modified chemicals coming on the market every year, it isn't easy for the understaffed PHS bureaus to keep track of new pollutants. Identification and detailed analysis of pollutants is just beginning as a systematic task. Only a few months ago the PHS established its first official committee to evaluate the effects of insecticides on health.

Many water-treatment plants are hopelessly outmoded. They were designed for a simpler, less crowded world. About three-fourths of them do not go beyond disinfecting water with chlorine. That kills bacteria but does practically nothing to remove pesticides, herbicides, or other organic and inorganic chemicals from the water we drink.

A survey by the PHS, still in progress, shows that most waterworks operators lack formal training in treatment processes, disinfection, microbiology, and chemistry. The men are often badly paid. Some of them, in smaller communities, have other full-time jobs and moonlight as water-supply operators. The survey, encompassing eight metropolitan areas from New York City to Riverside, California, plus the State of Vermont, so far has revealed that in seven areas about 9 percent of the water samples indicated bacterial contamination. Pesticides were found in small concentrations in many samples. In some, trace metals exceeded PHS limits. The level of nitrates, which can be fatal to babies, was too high in some samples. Earlier last year the PHS found that nearly sixty communities around the country, including some large cities, could be given only "provisional approval" for the quality of their water-supply systems. Charles C. Johnson Jr., administrator of the Consumer Protection and Environmental Health Service in the PHS, concluded that the U. S. is "rapidly approaching a crisis stage with regard to drinking water" and is courting "serious health hazards."

Clearly, there will have to be enormous improvement in either the treatment of water we drink or the treatment of water we discard (if not both). The second approach would have the great advantage of making our waterways better for swimming and fishing and more aesthetically enjoyable. And it is more rational anyway not to put poisons in the water in the first place. The most sensible way to keep our drinking water safe is to have industry, agriculture, and municipalities stop polluting the water with known and potentially hazardous substances. Some of this could be accomplished by changing manufacturing processes and recycling waste water inside plants. The wastes can sometimes be retrieved at a profit.

SEWAGE ON THE ROCKS

A great deal of industrial and municipal waste water now undergoes some form of treatment. So-called primary treatment is merely mechanical. Large floating objects such as sticks are removed by a screen. The sewage then passes through settling chambers where filth settles to become raw sludge. Primary treatment removes about one-third of gross pollutants. About 30 percent of Americans served by sewers live in communities that provide only this much treatment.

Another 62 percent live in communities that carry treatment a step beyond, subjecting the effluent from primary processing to secondary processing. In this age of exact science, secondary treatment looks very old-fashioned. The effluent flows, or is pumped, onto a "trickling filter," a bed of rocks three to ten feet deep. Bacteria normally occurring in sewage cover the rocks, multiply, and consume most of the organic matter in the waste water. A somewhat more modern version is the activated sludge process, in which sewage from primary settling tanks is pumped to an aeration tank. Here, in a speeded-up imitation of what a stream does naturally, the sewage is mixed with air and sludge saturated with bacteria. It is allowed to remain for a few hours while decomposition takes place. Properly executed secondary treatment will reduce degradable organic waste by 90 percent. Afterward, chlorine is sometimes added to the water to kill up to 99 percent of disease germs.

Secondary treatment in 90 percent of U. S. municipalities within the next five years and its equivalent in most industrial plants is a principal objective of the current war on pollution. The cost will be high; an estimated $10 billion in public funds for municipal treatment plants and sewers and about $3.3 billion of industry's own funds for facilities to treat wastes at industrial plants.

But today that kind of treatment isn't good enough. Widespread use of secondary treatment will cut the amount of gross sewage in the waterways, but will do little to reduce the subtler, more complex pollutants. The effluents will still contain dissolved organic and inorganic contaminants. Among the substances that pass largely unaffected through bacterial treatment are salts, certain dyes, acids, persistent insecticides and herbicides, and many other harmful pollutants.

Technical "tunnel vision," or lack of thinking about all the possible consequences of a process, has often been the curse of twentieth-century science and technology. Today's sewage plants generally do not remove phosphorus and nitrogen from waste water, but turn the organic forms of these nutrients into mineral forms that are *more* usable by algae and other plants. As one scientist has noted, overgrowths of algae and other aquatic plants then rot to "recreate the same problem of oxygen-consuming organic matter that the sewage plant was designed to control in the first place." The multibillion-dollar program to treat waste water in the same old way, he says, is "sheer insanity."

Yet the U. S. has little choice. Most of the advanced treatment techniques are either still experimental or too costly to be introduced widely. To wait for those promising new methods while doing nothing in the meantime could result in a major pollution calamity.

MATS OF ALGAE AND MOUNTAINS OF FOAM

The pollutants that secondary treatment fails to cope with will increase in volume as industry and population grow. Phosphates, for instance, come in large amounts from detergents and fertilizers, and from human wastes. Phosphorus has emerged as a major pollutant only in recent years. Nitrogen, the other key nutrient for algal growth, is very difficult to control because certain blue-green algae can fix nitrogen directly from the air. Since phosphorus is more controllable, its removal from effluents is critically important to limiting the growth of algae.

A few years ago, when it looked as if America's streams and lakes were to become highways of white detergent foam, the manufacturers converted the detergent base from alkyl benzene sulphonate to a much more biologically degradable substance, linear alkylate sulphonate. That effectively reduced the amount of foam but did almost nothing to reduce the amount of phosphates in detergents. The mountains of foam have shrunk, but green mats of algae keep on growing. The developers of detergents failed to consider the possible side effects: such lack of systematic thinking and foresight is precisely what has led to today's environmental abuses.

It might be possible to substitute non-phosphorus bases in detergent manufacture—and work is in progress along those lines. There is a bill before Congress that would ban phosphorus from detergents by the middle of 1971. But this certainly wouldn't do much to restore algae-clogged lakes such as Lake Erie, where farms, cities, and factories all contribute phosphates.

There is little prospect of substituting something else for the phosphate in fertilizer. It's hard to visualize a fertilizer that is a nutrient when applied to land and not a nutrient when it enters the water. One way to reduce water pollution from farmlands would be to reduce the amounts of chemical fertilizers farmers apply to their fields—it is the excess fertilizer, not absorbed by plants, that washes into streams or percolates into groundwater. Through some complex of social and economic arrangements, farmers might be persuaded to use less fertilizer and more humus. By improving the texture of soils, as well as providing slowly released nutrients, humus can reduce the need for commercial fertilizer to keep up crop yields. The U. S. produces enormous quantities of organic wastes that could be converted to humus. Such a remedy for fertilizer pollution, of course, might seem highly undesirable to the fertilizer industry, already burdened with excess capacity.

DISPENSING WITH BACTERIA

Even if phosphorus pollution from fertilizers and detergents were entirely eliminated —an unlikely prospect—phosphates from domestic and industrial wastes would still impose a heavy load upon rivers and lakes. As population and industry grow, higher and higher percentages of the phosphorus will have to be removed from effluents to keep the algae problem from getting worse. The conventional technology being pushed by the federal water-pollution war cannot cope with phosphorus, or with many other pollutants. But there are advanced technologies that can. Advanced water treatment, sometimes called "tertiary," is generally aimed at removal of all, or almost all, of the contaminants.

One promising idea under investigation is to dispense with the not always reliable bacteria that consume sewage in secondary treatment. Toxic industrial wastes have on occasion thrown municipal treatment plants out of kilter for weeks by killing the bacteria. "We've found that we can accomplish the same kind of treatment with a purely physical-chemical process," says a scientist at the Robert A. Taft Water Research Center in Cincinnati.

In this new approach, the raw sewage is clarified with chemicals to remove most sus-

pended organic material, including much of the phosphate. Then comes carbon absorption. The effluent passes through filter beds of granular activated carbon, similar to that used in charcoal filters for cigarettes. Between clarification and absorption, 90 percent or more of the phosphate is removed. The carbon can be regenerated in furnaces and reused. Captured organic matter is burned. Carbon absorption has the great additional advantage of removing from the water organic industrial chemicals that pass unhindered through biological secondary treatment. The chemicals adhere to the carbon as they swirl through its complex structure with millions of pathways and byways.

A PRODUCT RATHER THAN AN EFFLUENT

Other treatment techniques are under study that make water even cleaner, and might possibly be used to turn sewage into potable water. One of these is reverse osmosis, originally developed for demineralization of brackish water. When liquids with different concentrations of, say, mineral salts are separated by a semipermeable membrane, water molecules pass by osmosis, a natural equalizing tendency, from the less concentrated to the more concentrated side to create an equilibrium. In reverse osmosis, strong pressure is exerted on the side with the greater concentration. The pressure reverses the natural flow, forcing molecules of pure water through the membrane, out of the high-salt or high-particle concentration. Reverse osmosis removes ammonia nitrogen, as well as phosphates, most nitrate, and other substances dissolved in water. Unfortunately, the process is not yet applicable to sewage treatment on a large scale because the membranes become fouled with sewage solids. Engineers are hard at work trying to design better membranes.

New techniques are gradually transforming sewage treatment, technically backward and sometimes poorly controlled, into something akin to a modern chemical process. "We are talking about a wedding of sanitary and chemical engineering," says David G. Stephan, who directs research and development at the Federal Water Pollution Control Administration, "using the techniques of the chemical process industry to turn out a product—reusable water—rather than an effluent to throw away." Adds James McDermott of the Public Health Service: "We're going to get to the point where, on the one hand, it's going to cost us an awful lot of money to treat wastes and dump them into the stream. And an awful lot of money to take those wastes when they are going down the stream and make drinking water out of them. We are eventually going to create treatment plants where we take sewage and, instead of dumping it back into the stream, treat it with a view of recycling it immediately—direct reuse. That is the only way we're going to satisfy our water needs, and second, it's going to be cheaper."

Windhoek, the capital of arid South West Africa, last year gained the distinction of becoming the first city in the world to recycle its waste water directly into drinking water. Waste water is taken out of sewers, processed conventionally, oxidized in ponds for about a month, then run through filters and activated-carbon columns, chlorinated, and put back into the water mains. Windhoek's distinction may prove to be dubious, because the full effects of recycled water on health are unknown. There is a potential hazard of viruses (hepatitis, polio, etc.) being concentrated in recycling. For this reason, many health experts feel that renovated sewage should not be accepted as drinking water in the U. S. until its safety can be more reliably demonstrated.

Costs naturally go up as treatment gets more complex. While primary-secondary treatment costs about 12 cents a thousand gallons of waste water, the advanced techniques in use at Lake Tahoe, for instance, bring the cost up to 30 cents. About 7-1/2

cents of the increase is for phosphorus removal. Reverse osmosis at this stage would raise the cost to at least 35 cents a thousand gallons, higher than the average cost of drinking water to metered households in the U. S. Whatever new techniques are accepted, rising costs of pollution control will be a fact of life.

SLICING UP RIVERS

The General Accounting Office recently surveyed federal activities in water-pollution control and found some glaring deficiencies. The G.A.O. prepared its report for Congress and therefore failed to point out that in some of the deficiencies the real culprit was Congress itself. Still largely rural oriented, Congress originally limited federal grants for construction of waste-treatment facilities to $250,000 per municipality. The dollar ceiling was eventually raised, but was not removed until fiscal 1968. In the preceding twelve years about half of the waste-treatment facilities were built in hamlets with populations of less than 2,500, and 92 percent in towns with populations under 50,000.

In drafting the legislation that provides for new water-quality standards, Congress again showed limited vision, leaving it up to the states to decide many important questions. Each state is free to make its own decisions on pollution-control goals in terms of determining the uses to which a particular stream or lake will be put. Each state is to decide on the stream characteristics that would allow such uses—dissolved oxygen, temperature, etc. Finally, each state is to set up a schedule for corrective measures that would ensure the stream quality decided upon, and prepare plans for legal enforcement of the standards.

It would have been logical to set standards for entire river basins since rivers don't always stay within state boundaries. What's more, there were already several regional river-basin compacts in existence that could have taken on the job. But with the single exception of the Delaware River Basin Commission, of which the federal government is a member, the government bypassed the regional bodies and insisted that each state set its own standards. Predictably, the result has been confusion. The states submitted standards by June 30, 1967, but Interior has given full approval to only twenty-five states and territories. It has now become the prickly task of the Secretary of the Interior to reconcile the conflicting sets of standards that states have established for portions of the same rivers.

Some states facing each other across a river have set different standards for water characteristics, as if dividing the river flow in the middle with a bureaucratic fence. Kentucky and Indiana, across the Ohio from each other, submitted two different temperature standards for that river: Kentucky came up with a maximum of 93° Fahrenheit, while Indiana wants 90°. Similarly, Ohio set its limit at 93°, while West Virginia, across the same river, chose 86°. Up the river, Pennsylvania, too, decided on 86°. One reason for such differences about river temperature is that biologists don't always agree among themselves about safe temperatures for aquatic life. At one recent meeting in Cincinnati, where federal and state officials were attempting to reconcile the different figures for the Ohio, the disagreement among biologists was so great that one exasperated engineer suggested, "Maybe we should start putting ice cubes at different points in the river."

A FAILURE OF IMAGINATION

The biggest deficiency in the federal approach is its lack of imagination. Congress chose the subsidy route as being the easiest, but the task could have been undertaken much more thoughtfully. A regional or river-valley approach would have required more careful working out than a program of state-by-state standards and subsidies, but it would have made more sense eco-

nomically, and would have assured continuing management of water quality.

A promising river-valley program is evolving along the Great Miami River in Ohio. The Miami Conservancy District, a regional flood-control agency, began two years ago to explore the concept of river management. The Great Miami runs through a heavily industrialized valley. There are, for instance, eighteen paper mills in the valley. Dayton, the principal city on the river, houses four divisions of General Motors and is the home of National Cash Register. To finance a three-year exploratory program, the Miami Conservancy District has imposed temporary charges, based on volume of effluent, on sixty plants, businesses, and municipalities along the river. These charges amount to a total of $350,000 a year, ranging from $500 that might be paid by a motel to $23,000 being paid by a single power-generating station.

With this money, plus a $500,000 grant from the Federal Water Pollution Control Administration, the district has been looking into river-wide measures that will be needed to control pollution even *after* every municipality along the river has a secondary treatment plant. (Dayton already has one.) The district's staff of sanitary engineers, ecologists, and systems analysts has come up with suggested measures to augment the low flow of the river as an additional method of pollution control. The Great Miami's mean annual flow at Dayton is 2,500 cubic feet a second, but every ten years or so it falls to a mere 170 cubic feet a second. To assure a more even flow, the Miami District will build either reservoirs or facilities to pump ground water, at a cost of several million dollars. The cost will be shared by river users. District engineers are also exploring in-stream aeration, or artificial injection of air into the river to provide additional dissolved oxygen. The state has set an ambitious goal for the Great Miami—to make the river usable "for all purposes, at all places, all the time."

To meet this goal, the district will introduce waste-discharge fees, which will probably be based on the amount of oxygen-demanding wastes or hot water discharged. Will these amount to a charge for polluting the river? "No," says Max L. Mitchell, the district's chief engineer. "Charges will be high enough to make industry reduce water use."

Federal money would do a lot more good if it were divided up along the river-basin lines instead of municipality by municipality or state by state, with little regard for differences in pollution at different points in a basin. To distribute federal funds more effectively, Congress would have to overcome its parochial orientation. Also, Congress should be channeling more funds into new waste-treatment technologies and ways of putting them to use. Unless pollution abatement is undertaken in an imaginative and systematic manner, the "war" against dirty rivers may be a long, losing campaign.

SECTION 5

AIR POLLUTION

Nearly every major city in the world has an air pollution problem. The generation of life-damaging substances is occurring on so vast a scale that geochemists, along with other scientists, are profoundly concerned. To introduce you to the nature of the problem, the article by O. C. Taylor is simple, direct, and defining.

The second article has, as its purpose, the description of the atmosphere, with particular reference to the types of pollutants present in it.

In the third reading, Tom Alexander provides a hard-hitting discussion of the demands for more energy by our ever-increasing population, together with the effects of this pursuit upon our atmosphere. He not only discusses the usual pollutants, he directs attention to the increased production of carbon dioxide and its possible long-range effects upon global climates. Finally, Mr. Alexander conducts a journey through the variety of ways, in use or pending, by which sufficient electric power generation can be sustained. This complex, awesome problem is an ultimate one. That is, unless we are willing to make compromises in performance, along with self-denial and greatly increased costs, we are faced with inevitable threats to our health and even our survival.

Finally, the fourth article clearly describes the possible effects of air pollution on human health. Although some known effects may be depressing, it is necessary for everyone to know the truth about the dangers of air pollution.

O. C. Taylor

WHAT IS AIR POLLUTION?

Webster defines pollution as "a state of being polluted: defilement or impurity." Air is defined as a colorless, odorless mixture of gases—78% nitrogen, 21% oxygen, 0.3% carbon dioxide, and about 0.7% rare gases—which envelops the earth. In the strictest sense then, one might consider the fragrance of a rose, the odor of a pine forest, a lady's perfume or a fluffy rain cloud as air pollution. The impurity is, however, usually not considered to be a pollutant unless it has an objectionable odor, irritates one's senses, obscures visibility, soils property, or is toxic to man, animals, or plants. Natural phenomena — volcanoes, windstorms, and fires ignited by lightning for example—release large amounts of gases and particulates into the atmosphere, but the terms "air pollution" and "smog" are generally reserved for the contaminating materials generated by man.

Energy conversion has certain material by-products. When they become airborne, in sufficient concentrations to be irritating or injurious to man and his surroundings we call them "air pollutants." By-products from processes other than energy conversion also occur, but they are seldom as widespread or as highly concentrated.

The enormous increase in world population now taking place, an increase apparently destined to continue, and the congregation of masses of people in relatively small regions continue to multiply the tonage of by-products released in a limited air supply. Geographic barriers and unique meteorological conditions which provide a comfortable climate much of the time also limit the dispersion and dilution of pollutants leading to an intolerable condition of stagnation and air pollution.

The greatest single product of energy conversion processes—water—is usually of least concern as an air pollution problem. Only occasionally in localized areas does water vapor become objectionable. Next in quantity of waste products is carbon dioxide. It is naturally abundant in the atmosphere and man and other organisms are well adapted to live in comfort in

SOURCE. Reprinted, by permission, from a University of California (Riverside) air pollution symposium publication; published by the Air Pollution Research Center at U. C. Riverside, 1969, with slight abridgment.

widely ranging levels of it. Incomplete combustion yields carbon monoxide, a gas which is toxic to man and animals but apparently not injurious to plant life.

Toxicants in polluted atmospheres which have caused greatest concern include: (1) sulfur dioxide; (2) oxides of nitrogen; (3) hydrogen fluoride; (4) chloride; (5) ethylene; and (6) the photochemically produced oxidants—ozone and peroxyacetyl nitrate.

Mercaptans, hydrogen sulfide, aldehydes, and other organic gases have objectionable odors and minute quantities can be highly objectionable. Offensive odors from these and other compounds of polluted atmospheres are often sufficient cause for a concerted effort in air pollution control even if they are not toxic to living organisms.

The earliest manifestation of air pollution which comes to the attention of citizens in a community is usually the deterioration of visibility because of the smoke, haze, or aerosols suspended in the atmosphere. The occurrence of specific types of plant injury may be expected to appear soon after this and irritation of the eyes and respiratory system follows as the pollution condition becomes acute.

Waste products from energy conversion and processing of raw materials is inevitable, but satisfactory methods of limiting the discharge of toxic, irritating, and corrosive wastes of the atmosphere must be developed and used if man and the living organisms upon which he depends for food, fiber, and enjoyment are to survive.

THE ATMOSPHERE

Man's atmospheric environment is both narrow and finite; comprehension of its limitations and normal conditions is necessary to understand how it became polluted. The density of the atmosphere decreases with altitude, and approximately half of the atmosphere by weight lies below 18,000 feet. It contains about 21 percent oxygen which animals, including man, require for life and, because the average person requires available oxygen at pressures approximating 3 pounds per square inch, man cannot survive for long if oxygen is not available in close to that proportion and at that pressure. Other constituents of air include variable amounts of water vapor, nitrogen (78 percent), and carbon dioxide, carbon monoxide, and certain other gases, all of which total less than 1 percent by weight. The proportions of the gases are about the same in all parts of the world. The water vapor (water in a gaseous form) amounts to 1 to 3 percent by volume throughout the world's atmosphere. For our considerations, the water vapor can be regarded as an independent gas mixed with air.

There are several atmospheric layers. The *troposphere* is the layer adjacent to the earth and varies in height from about 28,000 feet over the poles to 55,000 feet over the equator, the depths being subject to seasonal change. Normally, tropospheric temperature decreases with increasing altitude and we term this phenomenon the lapse rate. Where an abrupt change in the rate of temperature fall with altitude increase occurs, we reach a region called the *tropopause.* This atmospheric region separates the troposphere from the *stratosphere* (26 to 29 miles thick). Our discussion will principally be concerned with the effects of man's activity on the troposphere and, to some degree, the stratosphere.

The atmosphere is influenced by many forces, both natural and man-made. Chief among them is heat energy from the sun. Heat is a form of energy as well as an expression of molecular activity. Since air is composed of atoms and molecules, air temperature is also a measurement of heat or molecular activity. Because different materials have different molecular structures, they will develop different temperatures (molecular activities) when the same amount of heat is applied. Accordingly, substances are said to have different spe-

SOURCE. Reprinted, by permission, from the workbook *Air Pollution,* published by the Scientists' Institute for Public Information, 1970, with slight abridgment.

cific heats or heat capacities. Land, for example, becomes hotter than water when identical amounts of heat are applied and cools faster than water, as at night. Heat to the earth is largely supplied by the sun and this incoming radiation is offset roughly by outgoing or reflected radiation (terrestrial radiation). At night, cooling occurs by terrestrial radiation. Temperatures of land masses rise and fall more rapidly than water masses, and, therefore, the land is warmer by day and cooler by night than the sea. This results in breezes toward land in coastal regions during the day which often reverse at night.

Atmospheric pressure is the force exerted by the weight of the atmosphere on a unit measurement of area (example, per square inch). We measure this force with an instrument called a barometer, one form of which is an evacuated tube with its open end placed vertically in an open container of mercury. At sea level, the weight of the atmosphere acts as a force on the mercury causing some of it to rise as a column in the tube, on the average about 29.9 inches. Mercury is used rather than lighter substances such as water because the displacement of a heavier substance in terms of column rise is considerably less, thus requiring a shorter tube. Differences in atmospheric pressure between points on the globe account, among other forces, for movement of air from regions of high to low pressure. When this movement is parallel to the earth's surface, we refer to it as *wind*. Other factors responsible for air movement include the earth's rotation about its axis, its yearly revolution about the sun, the uneven heating of the earth's surface by the sun, and the tilt of the earth's axis, to mention a few. However, solar energy is the predominant force responsible for weather phenomena.

In discussing the tropopause earlier, we defined it as the altitude zone where an abrupt change in the lapse rate occurs. Actually, lesser changes occur quite frequently and even closer to the earth. For example,

there may be a narrow layer within the troposphere in which temperature *increases* with altitude for several hundred feet; we call this an *inversion* (or temperature inversion) of the usual decrease of temperature with altitude. Inversions can, thus, impede the rise of the air below and if the latter air contains impurities (pollutants) the inversion acts as a lid to seal them below. If no significant lateral movement of air (wind) occurs, then the stage is set for an acute air pollution episode in the volume of air below.

If the earth did not rotate on its axis one might conceptualize air movement occurring by another means. We could conceive of warm air rising over the equator where it is more heated and less dense. It would rise high and flow laterally resulting in atmospheric pressure below lower than that in the surrounding adjacent area where the air is more dense because of its cooler temperature. Thus, cool air from the poles would move toward the low equatorial pressure where it in turn would be warmed, rise, and spread laterally toward the poles in a continuing cycle. For example, under these conditions, a lighter than air balloon turned loose over the equators would rise and drift toward either pole. It would then descend over the poles and simply skim the earth's surface toward the equator thence to rise again. However, the earth *does* rotate and this rotation results in a force which deflects the southern winds toward the east in the northern hemisphere and toward the west in the southern hemisphere; we call this the Coriolis force. Other influences on local weather include differential cooling and heating between mountains and flat land, desert and cultivated land, green and pavement, etc. All contribute to weather phenomena.

MIXING POLLUTANTS WITH THE ATMOSPHERE

We should regard the atmosphere as a gigantic reaction-vessel in which countless largely unidentified chemical reactions take place, a reaction-vessel whose properties change as temperatures and pressures change, a truly dynamic state.

However, we have some knowledge of the basic constituents of the atmosphere and of atmospheric chemistry. In addition to the oxygen, nitrogen, water vapor, and oxides of carbon mentioned earlier, "pure" air includes minute amounts of nitrogen and sulfur.

The oxygen-carbon dioxide cycle is of fundamental importance to animal-plant relationships. Atmospheric oxygen is produced by photosynthesis, a process by which plants exploit solar energy and trap carbon dioxide to synthesize organic (carbon-containing material) matter; a by-product of this process is oxygen. Photosynthesis has been taking place for millions of years, and must continue in order to maintain the oxygen content of the atmosphere. While plants thus get their energy for growth and reproduction from the sun, animals extract energy from chemical packets (plants or other animals). In essence, animals burn material in the presence of oxygen and with the assistance of numerous chemical catalysts called enzymes and coenzymes. The result of this combustion in the presence of oxygen are oxides of fuel materials, for example, carbon dioxide. When man burns other materials in manipulation of his environment, other oxidized forms are generated, such as oxides of sulfur and nitrogen, etc.

CARBON MONOXIDE

The complete combustion (oxidation) of carbon in the presence of oxygen results in the development of carbon dioxide (CO_2). Carbon monoxide (CO) results from incomplete combustion and is an almost exclusively man-made pollutant. Its chemical fate in the atmosphere is not certain, although it may include conversion to CO_2, reaction with certain reactive chemicals (hydroxyl radicals) or assimilation by

plant life on land or ocean absorption and biological oxidation. It is toxic to humans at concentrations of 100 parts per million with exposure for several hours. Carbon monoxide is produced almost entirely from incomplete combustion of fuel and predominantly by automobile engines, but tiny amounts are normally produced by man and other animals.

CARBON DIOXIDE

Carbon dioxide (CO_2), on the other hand, occurs naturally as a by-product of animal respiration. However, a major contribution results from the combustion of fossil fuels such as coal, oil, and gas. Since the advent of the industrial revolution, man has increased CO_2 emissions, principally by electric power plant and internal combustion engines. It has been estimated (by Rohrman, *et al.,* in *Science* 156:931, 1967), that man-made emissions of CO_2 will show an eighteen-fold increase from 1890 to 2000. Because of pollution from these major sources, carbon dioxide enters the air faster than the natural cycle of carbon dioxide can adjust to the accelerated input. Besides assimilation of carbon dioxide by both aquatic and terrestrial plants, the oceans provide a huge sink for CO_2 with exchanges taking place at air-water interfaces and shallow and deep water mixing. Limestone (calcium carbonate) is formed by hydration of CO_2 and reaction with calcium ion. However, the movement of CO_2 from shallow to deeper parts of the ocean occurs slowly and thus is one of the rate-limiting parts of the cycle of release into air, diffusion into water, etc. This is one reason for the slow but measurable buildup of carbon dioxide in the atmosphere.

Carbon dioxide has an effect on global temperature because of its ability to absorb heat energy (infrared radiation) and reflect energy back to earth much as the glass on a greenhouse does, allowing less heat to escape to outer space. Since short wavelength energy (ultraviolet) passes through carbon dioxide, an increase in CO_2 concentration with a more or less constant supply of solar energy should result in increasing global temperatures. Many scientists attributed the rise in mean global temperature in the 60 year period after 1880 to the seven percent increase in atmospheric carbon dioxide concentration. A *decrease* in mean global temperature has been noted since 1940, and may be due to increases in water vapor and atmospheric turbidity from air pollution, resulting in less incoming energy reaching the earth, since they exert their own greenhouse effect in a reverse direction. Changes in solar activity could be another source of this decrease in temperature.

OTHER WEATHER CHANGES

Indeed, various climatological changes are increasingly being attributed to air pollution. Dust particles (800 million tons produced worldwide per year) are effective cloud forming agents since their attraction for water vapor permits condensation and ice crystal formation on the dust nuclei. With sufficient moisture present, the droplets grow and fall, resulting in the increased precipitation potential, rainfall, and weather change already believed to have occurred in many locales. For example, one investigator noted an apparent increase in cloudiness along the heavily traveled jet aircraft corridors between New York and Chicago; a pound and one-quarter of water is released per gallon of jet fuel burned. At altitudes of 20,000 to 40,000 feet the rarified atmosphere and cold temperatures permit large volumes of air to be saturated by relatively small quantities of water. In addition, particulate exhaust from the jets contributes to the "seeding potential," setting up good conditions for cloud formation. Thus, even a seemingly innocuous substance such as water vapor can, under certain conditions, invoke profound environmental change.

NITROGEN OXIDES

Oxidation of nitrogen and release of nitrogen oxides into the atmosphere comes largely from automobile and electric power plant sources. Man-made sources do not account for all or even the largest part of global nitrogen emission; other sources include biological processes and lightning. Another source suggested by Dr. Barry Commoner is the possible contribution of the application of nitrate-containing fertilizer.

Some of the oxides of nitrogen are oxidized further to nitrogen dioxide which strongly absorbs ultraviolet light from the sun, creating nitric oxide and atomic oxygen (O); the latter can form ozone (O_3) in the presence of molecular oxygen (O_2). This highly reactive form of oxygen has been responsible for ozone "alerts" in Los Angeles. During an ozone alert, out-of-doors exercise by school children is restricted in order to avoid lung damage. These ingredients in the presence of hydrocarbons (compounds containing carbon and hydrogen) react to form an eye-irritating mucous-membrane damaging substance called peroxyacyl nitrate, or PAN, a principal component of photochemical smog. Other sources of hydrocarbons are natural bacterial decomposition of organic matter and release from forests, so that photochemical smog, while common in most of our major cities, has the potential of forming even in rural areas given the presence of nitrogen oxides and sunlight.

PARTICULATES

Particulate matter is enormously widespread. In New York City, dust fall levels as high as 30 tons per square mile per month were recorded in 1969. Dust fall tends to consist of relatively heavy particles which settle close to their source. Finer particles settle at greater distances. Particles larger than 10 microns emanate from grinding, spraying, and erosion. Particles less than 5 microns in size may reach the lower respiratory passages and lodge in the tiny air sacs which terminate them. Here there are none of the defenses which tend to expel the larger particles from the upper respiratory passages. Sulfur dioxide may be absorbed on those particles, and slowly released into the air sacs. Other harmful components such as radioactive isotopes of polluted air can also be carried into the lungs on these tiny particles. Other aerosols, such as DDT, are blown from the forest, field or garden where they were originally sprayed and passed through food chains from plant to animal to man or even directly to man. In this way, DDT has contaminated animal (including human) fat tissue in virtually all areas on the globe including the polar zones. Indeed, DDT has made its way into mothers' milk, resulting in the mother contributing to the contamination of her infant.

As indicated earlier, particles can scatter sunlight, reducing the amount of energy reaching earth and provoking global temperature decreases. Global dust levels are rising in the atmosphere and include products from all phases of human activity, including fossil fuel burning, and natural products such as volcanic eruptions and forest fires. Dustfall can also come from thermonuclear explosions which have radioactive isotopes as additional by-products.

SULFUR OXIDES

Oxides of sulfur are emitted largely from man-made sources and are primarily released as sulfur dioxide, which may be oxidized to sulfur trioxide. The latter can combine with water vapor to form sulfuric acid mists which are highly corrosive to building materials, including stone and marble. Indeed, the oxides of sulfur can, in several decades, deteriorate statuary that has survived the ravages of several thousand years of normal weathering. When precipitated into water via rainfall sulfate salts increase acidity and can destroy aquatic

life, most of which cannot survive at pH's (an index of acidity) lower than 4.0. Salmon kills occur at pH 5.5. While pH of lakes and rivers vary with seasonal changes in temperature and biological activity, the threat from sulfur oxides is formidable. Natural sulfur oxide sources include volcanoes, geysers, and decomposition of sulfur-containing organic material.

Other emissions deserving mention include lead emanating largely from gasoline burning but also from smelting and certain glazing operations. About 65 percent of the lead in combusted gasoline is released into the atmosphere and results in both local and distant fallout. It is estimated that the northern hemisphere contains a thousand-fold surplus of lead above and beyond natural base levels because of man's contributions.

Radioactive pollutants vary from short-lived isotopes, such as radioiodine with an 8-day half life to radiocarbon with a 5,000-year half life and many intermediates. Those entering the environment as a result of nuclear explosions are discussed in "Environmental Effects of Weapons Technology" and "Nuclear Explosions in Peacetime"; those that come from nuclear reactors in "Environmental Cost of Electric Power"—all workbooks in this series.*

Obviously, a variety of compounds are released into the atmosphere from all of man's activity with little regard for the how, when, or why of release. This anarchy of pollution results in the formation of many poorly understood or unidentified compounds, the short and long range biological effects of which are even less well understood. For example, the combustion of many plastic containers can result in the formation of totally new products reacting chemically in the atmosphere in ways completely foreign to us and producing effects which are as yet undetected or at least

*These workbooks are published by the Scientists' Institute for Public Information (SIPI) 30 East Sixty-Eighth St., New York, N. Y. 10021.

unknown. Polychlorinated biphenyls, used as plasticizers in the manufacture of many products, are chemically similar to DDT, and are also appearing in the environment.

Tom Alexander

SOME BURNING QUESTIONS ABOUT COMBUSTION

Civilization has been formed in the crucible of fire. Combustion, or the rapid chemical reaction of oxygen with carbon, has propelled human advancement. But Prometheus' presumptuous gift of fire to man is calling down a punishment not anticipated by the ancients. For where there's fire, there's smoke.

Fossil fuels that accumulated over hundreds of millions of years are being converted to gas and ash in a combustive gluttony that began a century ago. In the U. S., the tonnage of these fuels consumed now doubles every twenty years. All this combustion—the internal combustion of transportation and the external combustion of industries, power plants, home heating, and incineration—is by far the principal contributor to the dirtiness of cities and the foulness of air. Still, if pollution is the brother of affluence, concern about pollution is affluence's child. Air pollution is not a recent invention: some nineteenth-century cities with their hundreds of thousands of smoldering soft-coal grates coughed

amid a richer and deadlier smog than any modern city can concoct. But while in some ways air pollution is not as bad as it used to be, it threatens to get a lot worse than it is unless society revises the traditional orientation of engineering toward efficiency and economy.

The best antipollution intentions come up against certain gritty realities. The hunger for energy seems insatiable. Combustion of fossil fuels—particularly coal and petroleum products, which are the worst polluters—is likely to increase for quite some years to come, probably reaching several times present levels by the end of the century. The only courses left open, then, appear to be cleaning up combustion and substituting noncombustive modes of energy production. Whichever course society chooses—or even if it chooses to do nothing—men will pay a higher price for their energy.

Byproducts of combustion make up roughly 85 percent of the total tonnage burden of air pollutants in the U. S. Most

SOURCE. Reprinted, by permission, from *Fortune,* February 1970, with slight abridgment.

of the emissions commonly classified as pollutants are not inherent in combustion, but are rather the results of inefficient burning or impure fuels. The pollutants fall into two main types, particles and gases. The particles include fly ash, which is an unburnable mineral fraction of ordinary coal; soot, which is burnable but unburned carbon; and lead, the unburnable additive in gasoline. Less visible but more damaging are the gases. These include sulphus dioxide (SO_2), a product of the combustion of coal or oil that contains sulphus; carbon monoxide (CO), emitted when insufficient oxygen is present during combustion; and various oxides of nitrogen, products of very high combustion temperatures. A great many complex hydrocarbon compounds, both particulates and gases, also result from incomplete combustion.

SOMETIMES IT RAINS ACID

Few would quarrel with the view that air pollution is aesthetically objectionable. Numerous studies confirm it to be an economic drain upon society as well. Government economists at the National Air Pollution Control Administration in North Carolina have taken several routes to arrive at admittedly broad-brush estimates that air pollution costs U. S. citizens somewhere between $14 billion and $18 billion a year in direct economic loss.

The potpourri of airborne particulates is the main cause of soiling—whether of shirt collars or of office buildings. But sulfur dioxide accounts for most of the damage to materials and much of that to agriculture. SO_2 combines with oxygen and then with moisture to form sulphuric acid. Sometimes this takes place in the lungs of animals, sometimes on the leaves of plants, sometimes in droplets of rainwater, and sometimes simply in the atmosphere where the acid persists as a fine, floating mist. The atmosphere of many industrialized areas is more corrosive to metals and other materials than sea air.

Under the influence of sunlight, several of the hydrocarbons react with the oxides of nitrogen to form ozone and a variety of complex organic compounds. Many of these "photochemical" substances are particularly damaging to plants. Because of the prevalent photochemical smog, leafy crops such as lettuce and spinach can no longer be grown in parts of southern California.

Sulfur dioxide has been implicated as the cause of many deaths in several air-pollution disasters, including those in the Meuse Valley in Belgium in 1930, in Donora, Pennsylvania in 1948, and in London in 1952. These occurred when atmospheric temperature inversions combined with low wind ventilation to trap coal smoke over populated areas. Few doubt that any of the pollutants, not just SO_2, are harmful in concentration. The real question concerns the hazards of the long-term, low-level exposures encountered in everyday life. A great many studies strongly suggest that SO_2 is a cause or intensifying agent in various respiratory ailments even without inversion situations. The gas seems to do its worst in conjunction with particle pollutants, which can carry the SO_2 deep into the lungs and hold it there against sensitive tissue.

Similar evidence is also building up against nitrogen dioxide as a contributing cause of respiratory ailments. Carbon monoxide, a well-known poison, has been measured at toxic levels in the streets of certain cities. Hydrocarbons and ozone are implicated in the eye-irritating smogs typical of Los Angeles and other sunny cities. Some animal experiments suggest that the hydrocarbons also cause lung cancer.

But the medical evidence against most air pollutants is far from conclusive. Even in the most polluted areas, citizens still breathe air whose contaminants are many times less concentrated than the pollutants in a lungful of tobacco smoke—and it took years to establish a tight case against cigarettes. After one surprising series of experiments, an independent laboratory under contract to the electric power industry has found that guinea pigs that have spent their life breathing an atmosphere with a fairly high concentration of SO_2 seem to live longer on the average than guinea pigs breathing pure air.

THE MISSING GREENHOUSE

One combustion product that worries some scientists a great deal is not usually classified as a pollutant. This is carbon dioxide (CO_2), which unlike CO, SO_2, and the rest, is an inevitable result of carbon combustion. Hundreds of millions of tons of CO_2 are discharged into the atmosphere each year. Though CO_2 constitutes less than a tenth of 1 percent of the earth's atmosphere, the amount has increased roughly 25 percent during the past hundred years or so, and is expected to increase another 25 percent by the year 2000. CO_2 probably poses no direct threat to health, but quite a few scientists maintain that in the long run it may prove to be the most important pollutant of them all.

In theory, at least, an increase in atmospheric CO_2 should tend to raise the average worldwide temperature. The CO_2 acts like the glass in a greenhouse in trapping heat near the earth's surface. Accordingly, it is sometimes argued, the continued buildup of CO_2 will inescapably lead to calamitous overheating of the earth. Despite the theory, however, the average worldwide temperature has actually registered a slight drop since 1940. To account for this puzzling phenomenon several meterologists are pointing suspiciously at another combustion product, suspended particulate matter, or smoke. Careful measurements indicate that the global atmospheric "turbidity"—or murkiness—has indeed increased over the past century, and thus could have offset the CO_2's "greenhouse effect." The particles not only shade the earth, but also act as "condensation nuclei" to promote cloud formation and so further

reduce the amount of solar energy reaching the earth. Some meteorologists have even begun to worry in advance about the widespread operation of supersonic transport planes, because their release of condensation nuclei at high altitudes might greatly increase the cirrus cloud cover over much of the earth.

Whether the climate gets warmer or cooler, the implications are serious. Man and his institutions everywhere are critically adjusted to just the climatological conditions that prevail. Remarkably little is known about the interactions between earth and atmosphere, but it may well be that the nature of our environment is such that relatively small perturbations could trigger latent instabilities. Taken individually, the various inflictions that man imposes upon his environment may be tolerable; but in combination, they could work to disastrous effect. For instance, the expected exponential increase in worldwide combustion could combine with man's widespread destruction of the vegetation that removes CO_2 from the atmosphere. This, in turn, could lead to a world warming trend. Since water's capacity to absorb CO_2 decreases as the water gets warmer, the result might be still more CO_2 in the atmosphere and further warming from greenhouse effect, and so on.

WHERE TIME AND SPACE ARE LACKING

In terms of sheer tonnage, the automobile is the prime U. S. air polluter, contributing about 40 percent of the 200 million tons of emissions that human activities put into the air in a year. The wide range of demands upon automotive engines—both cold and hot starting, high and low speeds, rapid acceleration, idling—entails compromising both combustion efficiency and fuel purities. Share of nationwide tonnage to be sure, does not tell all the story. Given enough time and space to do her job, nature can cleanse the air of almost anything. Pollution is still very much the special bane of places where the time and space are lacking—where there is high traffic density, for example, or where people live too close to smokestacks. Much of the automobile pollution is discharged in open country where nature has a chance to work. Moreover, the auto emits little SO_2.

While efforts to find a substitute for the internal-combustion engine have captured much recent attention, probably the most productive approach to the problem of auto pollution for a couple of decades at least will prove to be what the auto companies have been maintaining—cleaning up the present internal combustion engine or its fuel, or both. Despite intensive and expensive efforts, no one yet appears to have come close to devising a marketable alternative propulsion system that can do more than nibble at the edges of the national problem. No prospects are in evidence for inexpensive, lightweight batteries or fuel cells that could supply the combined range, speed, and hill-climbing ability that Americans will probably continue to demand. Several planners have pointed out another objection to battery propulsion: if most Americans were to drive electric autos, the power for charging the batteries would doubtlessly have to be drawn from the electric-utility system. This would mean something like a doubling of electric-power capacity and immense additional air pollution from power plants.

Neither the steam engine nor the gas turbine looks like a panacea at present either. It is probably no fluke that the internal combustion engine won out during the evolution of the automobile. Despite centuries of engineering attention, steam systems are still heavy and complicated in comparison with internal-combustion engines. Because they operate under more uniform conditions, gas turbines emit less carbon monoxide and hydrocarbons than piston engines per pound of fuel. But gas turbines burn more fuel per mile, especially in city traffic.

Even if alternative modes of propulsion do emerge, the sheer economic, political, and social inertia represented by all the institutions that have grown up to feed and care for conventional automobiles would seem to preclude a sudden shift. Happily, the near-term problems posed by the internal-combustion engine appear to be somewhat less pressing now than they did a year or so ago. Federal auto-emission standards, which were first applied to 1968 models and will become increasingly more stringent through at least 1975, have already begun to have discernible effects. The inevitable CO_2 aside, federal authorities estimate that auto pollutant tonnages, which totaled about 80 million tons per year in 1968, will be reduced to around 75 million tons this year and will continue to decline. If new exhaust standards that the government is pushing are adopted, the emissions should drop to around 55 million tons per year in 1985. After that, however, with continued increases in the number of cars and car-miles, the levels may begin to climb again. Adoption of some of the contemplated standards will hinge upon the development of a workable device—such as an afterburner—that would complete the combustion of unburned components of exhaust.

For the near term, at least, this process of modification will be less costly in either money or performance than alternatives to conventional internal-combustion engines. Conceivably, however, with sufficient attention to development, a respectable alternative could emerge. One possible approach is a "hybrid" vehicle with electric propulsion and a small combustion engine used to charge the batteries, but only in open country. Because this engine would turn at constant speeds and be equipped with exhaust afterburners, it would emit only a tiny fraction of the pollutants now put forth by the conventional engine.

THE POWER PREDICAMENT

The most nagging prolems of pollution and pollution-control policy for the future appear destined to spring from the electric-power industry. Though electric-power generation now produces only 13 percent of the total pollutant tonnage, it accounts for more than 50 percent of the sulphur dioxide, about 27 percent of the oxides of nitrogen, and nearly 30 percent of the particulates. Present trends indicate that soft-coal consumption by electric utilities will increase by a factor of roughly three and a half between now and the year 2000. This projection reflects anticipated demand for electric power as well as the great economic inertia provided by long-life coal-burning plants that are already built or committed. Nuclear energy's role will rapidly increase, but its rate of growth will be restrained by limitations in manufacturing capacity and by practical policies—in the electric-power industry and in government—of maintaining both a competitive alternative to nuclear power and a viable coal-mining industry—a large, labor-intensive activity that cannot be turned on and off with ease. While implying no inevitability, the projection for coal points to the magnitude of the air-cleaning tasks ahead. If sulphur dioxide and dioxides of nitrogen are of concern now when electric utilities emit some 25 million tons of these pollutants a year, how much worse will the problem be when they burn three and a half times as much coal?

Since coal disappeared years ago from the cellars of most houses, Americans have come to think of it as old-fashioned. But coal still provides most of the energy propelling the U. S. economy. While estimated reserves of oil, gas, and uranium are reckoned in terms of a few decades, coal reserves are apparently ample for centuries.

The roughly $1 billion the electric-utility industry has spent so far for controlling air pollution has gone mostly into filters and electrostatic precipitators for removing particulate matter, and partly into premium prices paid for fuels with low sulphur content, including desulphurized oil and natural gas. For the future control of gaseous emissions most people in the industry would prefer to rely upon these measures, plus tall smokestacks. Tall stacks, industry spokesmen say, would permit the emissions from even very large plants to be adequately diluted before reaching the ground. One appealing quality of tall stacks is that compared to alternatives they are cheap, costing considerably less than other control devices to put in and nothing to operate. But outside the industry there is sharp disagreement about the effectiveness of tall stacks, especially as more and more generating plants dot the landscape. Great Britain has been equipping power plants with tall stacks, and one apparent consequence is that Scandinavian countries across the North Sea are occasionally pelted by rains and snows with a high content of sulphuric acid.

For control of sulphur dioxide, federal authorities would prefer removal of sulphur before the fuel is burned, or removal of sulphus dioxide from the flue gas. Both oil and certain kinds of coal can be desulphurized at an additional cost of about 10 percent. Already a great deal of desulphurized oil is being sold in cities, New York for example, that have imposed stringent standards on SO_2 emissions. Potentially, at least, SO_2 could be removed from stack gases through any of a variety of approaches. Each of these approaches is likely to be expensive, adding somewhere between 10 and 20 percent to the cost of generating power, compared to about 1 percent for the tall-stack approach. The actual penalty for sulphur removal depends upon a number of variables difficult to quantify. In terms of capital outlay, the cheapest method involves injection of limestone into the combustion flame, where it combines with oxides of sulphur to form a solid, calcium sulphate. Calcium sulphate in copious quantities—1,100 tons per day from, say, a 1,000-megawatt power plant—would present an expensive waste-disposal problem, and, if not carefully managed, a potential water-pollution problem as well.

Other methods of SO_2 removal involve higher capital and operating costs but yield as a byproduct either sulphur or sulphuric acid that might be sold to offset some of their cost. By the 1990's, however, power generation might produce these chemicals so abundantly as to wreck the market for either. In that case, they too would become costly liabilities. Even now, while U. S. sulphur producers are busy extracting some 12 million tons a year, fossil-fuel burners are putting more than 16 million tons into the atmosphere.

STAMPING OUT FIRE

Imposition of stringent and expensive controls on pollutants from combustion of coal or oil would no doubt lead to broader use of alternative fuels, and would also hasten the emergence of alternatives to the combustion process itself. One alternate fuel is natural gas, which has little sulphus content and in burning emits smaller quantities of oxides of nitrogen and hydrocarbons than coal, oil, or gasoline. Some urban generating plants now operate part time on gas. A number of enthusiasts envision a large future for compressed natural gas as a motor fuel. But natural gas is the least abundant of the fossil fuels, and this fact alone will limit its role largely to the requirements for residential heating.

Proper economic inducements—including stricter emission standards—would also make the gasification of coal attractive. Relatively pollution-free, coal gas would necessarily cost a lot more than its thermal equivalent in solid coal, but its use as a fuel might prove cheaper than the other technological approaches to cleaning up coal combustion.

Noncombustive means of generating electricity have a long history; at one time, indeed, the term "generator" called up in the public mind an image of dams and water turbines. But hydroelectric power, which amounts to about 12 percent of total installed capacity in the U. S., is already approaching full exploitation here, as in most other industrialized nations. A number of clean and noncombustive technolo-

gies, including geothermal power, tidal power, and solar power, are under development, but their potential uses appear to be limited to certain regions or special applications.

Fuel cells can produce electricity directly from a variety of substances. The use of hydrocarbon fuels such as natural gas, entails—as always—emission of carbon dioxide. But other fuel cell reactions do not even produce CO_2. With pure hydrogen and oxygen, the byproduct is nothing more objectionable than water. Other possible fuels are hydrazine and reformed ammonia, both compounds of nitrogen and hydrogen, which react with oxygen to produce electricity plus nitrogen and water. Though the potential cost of some of these fuels could approach that of coal, fuel cells will be far too expensive for widespread use until the cost—especially of their catalysts —can be brought down. Costs of catalysts now range around $2,400 per kilowatt of generating capacity. This compares with *total* costs of around $100 per kilowatt of capacity for steam-power plants.

THE FEAR OF A NUCLEAR NEIGHBOR

Ultimately, it seems inevitable that nuclear reactions will largely supplant combustion reactions in the production of electric power, especially in the very large central generating stations that are increasingly the fashion. Right now, though, nuclear energy is being slowed by some fundamental problems, aside from high costs and slow deliveries. One particular difficulty is the fear that leads citizens to prefer a fossil-fuel plant as a neighbor to a nuclear plant. A lot of concern has been voiced about radiation, including the possibility of such substances as iodine 131 finding their way into food chains and thence into the bodies of human beings. But actual measurements seem to show that the radioactive substances normally emitted by nuclear plants are virtually undetectable in the surrounding environment. Some nuclear plants actually emit less radioactivity than many fossil plants. Assuming that a continuing increase in electric-power demand is inevitable and a choice must be made, the evidence available suggests that nuclear plants pose less threat to the environment and to human well-being than fossil plants.

A valid objection to nuclear power is the thermal pollution that present-day plants pour into rivers and streams. To prevent their fuel elements from melting, nuclear plants produce steam at a lower temperature than fossil-fuel plants. This means that for an equivalent amount of electricity nuclear plants produce more steam. After passing through the turbines, the steam must be rapidly condensed; otherwise the power plant could not operate efficiently. To accomplish this condensation, the power plant draws large volumes of cooling water from a stream, pumps it through a condenser, and then returns it to the stream. The warmed-up water discharged by a nuclear plant is at about the same temperature as that from a fossil-fuel power plant, but there is about 40 percent more of it. By 1980, nuclear plants alone will require about one-eighth of the total volume of stream flow in the U. S. for cooling. Possible remedies include paying a penalty in generating efficiency by operating with less coolant volume; discharging the heat far out at sea; channeling the warmed water to cooling towers that discharge heat into the atmosphere; or, finally, putting the heat to use for space heating or industrial purposes. A bonus of the last approach is that it would reduce the burden of pollutants from combustive activity. By the mid-1980's the thermal problem should be moderated by the introduction of other kinds of reactors, notably breeder reactors. Breeders can operate with high-temperature fuel elements. The result is higher thermal efficiency and less discharge of waste heat.

As things stand now, there is reason for concern about the adequacy of the re-serves of cheap nuclear fuel. Reasonably assured reserves of uranium in the U. S. would be insufficient to last beyond the 1980's if nuclear technology were limited to present types of reactors. More uranium will no doubt be discovered, but there is no way of knowing how much or what it will cost to find and mine. Worries about fuel, however, should vanish for practical purposes with the development of the breeder reactor, which will create more fissionable fuel than it consumes. Even so, the fast breeder under development now is a difficult and skittish device, the safe operation of which may require expensive safeguards and so keep the price of electricity high.

THE ULTIMATE ENERGY SOURCE

In the past few months, scientists have gained renewed encouragement over the prospects for controlled nuclear fusion. The new optimism comes from experimental evidence—mostly obtained by Russian scientists—apparently indicating that the long-standing technical barriers to fusion are soluble, at least in principle. If and when they are overcome—five, fifteen, or thirty years from now—man will then have available an inexhaustible, cheap, clean, and safe source of energy. That could spell the end of man's grand-scale need for his ancient friend and enemy, combustion.

But the widespread deployment of fusion reactors is a long way off—perhaps half a century or more. Meanwhile, unless all the people of the world adopt new and unlikely attitudes that radically deflate the value of energy as an index of human advancement, we are likely to see fossil-fuel consumption continuing in its recent trend, at least doubling every twenty years. Even at present, some 15,000 cubic miles of air are fed into the flames of combustion each year, emerging greatly depleted in oxygen and poisoned as well. The time has come when the earth's atmosphere can no longer be regarded as limitless, but must be regarded rather as an exhaustible resource.

The traditional goals in engineering have been maximum performance and minimum cost in the objects being engineered. Now the objects being engineered must often include the very biosphere itself, the earth's thin, life-supporting peel of rock, soil, water, and air. All costs must be refigured, and many will increase. The costs may be paid in the form of nonproductive capital or operations, in compromised performance, and sometimes perhaps in simple self-denial. But if the payments are not made early, mankind will end up paying far greater penalties later—to property, to peace of mind, to health, or to life itself.

BIOLOGICAL EFFECTS OF AIR POLLUTION

In any metropolitan area, acute air pollution episodes can occur whenever atmospheric conditions prevent rapid dispersal or dilution of the pollutants. Acute air pollution episodes resulting collectively in the deaths of thousands in Belgium's Meuse Valley (1930), Donora, Pa. (1948), London (1952, 1959, 1962), New York City (1953, 1962, 1966) have been well documented. All of these episodes shared certain characteristics:

A high population density with a correspondingly high concentration of combustion processes.

Seasonal influence—occurrence was in the winter when fuel consumption was increased and upper respiratory diseases were prevalent.

A stagnant air situation and temperature inversion for several days to a week with accumulation of pollutants in the air.

In general, the fatalities and severe illnesses resulted from acute, chemically irritative changes to the lining of the air tubes (bronchi) leading to the lungs. In London, the leading causes of hospital admissions during those episodes were respiratory disease, often with heart failure complicating the processes in the lung. The heart in a person with preexisting heart-lung disease could not take the added burden of moving blood through the chemically irritated lungs.

No single smog component in either London or Donora was present in concentrations very much higher than usual. Thus, an increased duration of exposure is implicated, with the possibility of additive or synergistic factors. (The latter is a biologic effect produced by two or more agents together which is greater than the sum of the effects of the individual agents.) Other membranous body surfaces reflected the same irritative mechanisms, consequently, sore throat and burning of the eyes were frequent complaints, as were headache and nausea. While no specific offending agents have been indicted in the London and Donora disasters, oxides of sulfur, common to both, were probably acting in concert with particulates and possibly other pollutants. Infecting agents may also have

SOURCE. Reprinted, by permission, from the workbook *Air Pollution*, published by the Scientists' Institute for Public Information, 1970, with slight abridgment.

been operative. In Donora, 5,910 people were affected and 17 died. In London, 4,000 to 6,000 more deaths occurred between December 5-9, 1952 during a dense smog; in December, 1962, 340 more deaths occurred than was normal, during a similar period of smog.

For a long time the medical profession has been preoccupied with infectious causes of disease to the neglect of the physical and chemical aspects. While this was justifiable in the early part of the twentieth century when people were dying from diseases such as pneumonia, influenza, meningitis, and tuberculosis, it no longer seems valid at this time in the United States when most people are dying from non-infectious diseases. Indeed, the diseases which appear to be killing Americans today seem not only to be non-infectious in origin but to have other common characteristics, namely multiple rather than single causes, insidious onset and development over a 20 to 30 year period and extremely difficult to treat when full-blown. Included in this group are cardiovascular disease, stroke, cancer, particularly bronchogenic cancer, and chronic pulmonary disease (bronchitis and emphysema).

Although complicated by many variables, the evidence linking chronic lung disease with air pollution is impressive. Bronchitis, an inflamation of the bronchi, is characterized by excessive mucous secretion accompanied by chronic or recurrent cough productive of sputum. Bronchitis is not considered chronic unless these manifestations are present on most days for at least three months of the year and for two successive years. Using these criteria, a 20 percent incidence is estimated in urban men in Great Britain between the ages of 40 and 60 years.[1] In Great Britain, illness from chronic bronchitis is related to the population size of cities,[2] suggesting that air pollution, which also increases with the size of cities, may be implicated. Another study showed a correlation between the bronchitis mortality rate and the amount of fuel burned for domestic and industrial purposes.[3] In England and Wales, places with higher mean annual sulfur dioxide measurements had associated higher mortality rates due to chronic bronchitis.[4] Using decreased visibility as an index to pollution, British investigators showed an association between pollution and illness-absenteeism among postmen.[5] The postmen's counterparts working indoors suffered less work loss due to bronchitis, an association not attributed to weather alone. A number of observers have related aggravation of symptoms of bronchitis to air pollution increases.

Bronchial asthma, a disease in which the muscles of the bronchi constrict and impede outward movement of air, seems unquestionably to be influenced by air pollution. Thus, in Donora, 87 percent of asthmatics became ill, while illness struck 43 percent of the rest of the town's population.[6] Bronchial asthma generally responds well to certain medications which dilate the air tubes or combat allergy and infection. In contradistinction, another type of lung disease, indistinguishable from asma by physical examination but distinguishable by negative response to these medications has been described among American military personnel in Yokohama. Evacuation seemed to be the only form of therapy for "Yokohama respiratory disease," pointing to some offending local environmental contaminant.[7] New Orleans has experienced epidemic outbreaks of asthma, typically in October.[8] Dr. Murray Dworetsky, in the presidential address to the American Academy of Allergy in 1969,[9] pointed out that "the literature strongly suggests that the frequency of death from asthma has recently been increasing," and said that although "inappropriate management" is probably one cause, "There is much reason to believe that in and of itself air pollution may be increasing the number of deaths from asthma."

Emphysema, another chronic respiratory disease, appears to be adversely affected by air pollution. In this disease, the small air sacs into which the air passages empty become distended, rupture and/or coalesce. The lining of these sacs is the site of gaseous exchange between air and blood. Thus, the larger sacs for the same volume present less surface area for exchange. Lung emptying is impeded, coughing is less effective, and victims become predisposed to infection. Heart failure is a common complication. Emphysema prevalence in the United States is increasing; this disease has doubled in incidence and mortality every five years for the past two decades[10] Not only is emphysema aggravated by air pollution, especially in conjunction with smoking, but one California study showed that lung function could be improved simply by placing the patients in an air pollution-free room.[11]

While most authorities agree that cigarette smoking plays the dominant role in the development of lung cancer, there would appear to be some further agreement that an urban factor plays a much smaller although detectable role as well. Data suggest a higher incidence of lung cancer in urban than in rural areas among smokers. Thus the incidence of lung cancer among smokers who emigrated from Great Britain to South Africa was higher than among white native South Africans who were even heavier smokers.[12] Immigrants to Australia and New Zealand from Great Britain had higher lung cancer mortality than native New Zealanders and Australians in spite of similar smoking backgrounds.[13, 14].

Air pollutants frequently have been concentrated and applied to the skin of mice. This has resulted in the

> . . . induction of a kind of cancer called squamous cell carcinoma. Tumors under the skin have been induced in mice exposed to air pollutant tars collected from a number of American cities. The induction of lung cancer (adenocarcinoma) in mice has been achieved by exposure of

mice in dust chambers to asphalt road sweepings and also by the same type of exposure to soot . . . . On the other hand rats and mice are quite resistant to induction of lung cancer. Even when exposed to aerosols of pure carcinogens, the animals do not develop lung tumors but do get skin tumors from this type of exposure although rats are normally resistant to skin tumor induction. Both species, however, develop lung cancers when the exposure is sufficiently intense. Thus, when the carcinogens are implanted in the lung in high dosages the animals develop lung cancer . . . .[15]

It must be cautioned that such evidence is not definitive, although certainly suggestive. A one-pack-per-day smoker of cigarettes exposes himself to several hundred times more inhaled organic matter than an individual in a congested traffic area of New York. The major difference is that the smoker can stop smoking, while the pedestrian can hardly be expected to stop breathing.

New York City's 1953 episode was not really recognized until approximately nine years later when a comparative analysis of hospital records,[16] and air pollution data revealed an excessive number of deaths during a period of severe air pollution. It is, therefore, hardly unreasonable to assume that many deaths from pollution may take place without ever coming to the attention of Public Health officials because of the unavailability of the necessary measurements or the necessary data analysis, or because the numbers are so small as to fail to give significant results.

Only three parts per million of sulfur dioxide exposure to a healthy person can produce a slight increase in airway resistance, that is, the ease with which expired air passes through the airways. Yet, people with chronic bronchitis or similar conditions may be aggravated by levels as low as 0.25. Twice as many acute respiratory illnesses were found at exposures to 0.25 ppm for twenty-four hours as at 0.4 ppm among those aged 55 or over with chronic bronchitis.[17] Increased airway resistance can frequently occur even at extremely low levels of sulfur dioxide when it is combined with inhalation of particulate matter or sulfur trioxide, which combines with water to form sulfuric acid. Twelve-hour averages of sulfur dioxide (parts per million) in New York City have been known to exceed 0.8. The major source of sulfur dioxide in that city was the combustion of high sulfur content fuel oil and bituminous coal. The implication of these figures to New York's over one million estimated sufferers[18] of asthma and hay fever could well be profound. Fortunately, some steps have been undertaken to reduce the sulfur content of New York fuels.

Obviously, the respiratory system is most directly affected by breathing polluted air, and we have concentrated so far on cardio-respiratory diseases in terms of possible cause and/or aggravation. Not infrequently, however, certain pollutants can attack an organ system far removed from the portal of entry to the body. Lead, for example, can have diffuse and confusing effects, as experience with occupational exposure, and with exposure of children to lead paints has shown. Lead can enter the body via lungs, intestinal tract, or skin and by poisoning certain enzymes which are present in most organs can affect blood-forming, nervous, gastrointestinal and excretory (kidney) systems among others. Lead toxicity can occur after chronic as well as after acute exposure.

The biological effects of carbon monoxide are different than many other air pollutants. First, it cannot be tasted, smelled or otherwise sensed by the body and second, it does not directly affect the eyes, nasal passages or lungs. Instead, it passes unchanged through the walls of the lung into the blood, where much of it actively combines with hemoglobin, the substance in the red blood cells normally responsible for carrying oxygen to all the tissues of the body. (A very small amount of CO is produced by normal body metabolism; we are concerned here only with *additional* exposure to CO from the environment.) This combination forms a substance called carbomonoxyhemoglobin, and has the effect of decreasing the oxygen-carrying capacity of the blood. Since CO is about 100 times more strongly bound than oxygen to hemoglobin, a small amount of CO in the ambient air has a greatly magnified effect on the oxygen transport function of the blood. All tissues of the body may suffer from oxygen deprivation, but the two tissues most sensitive to lack of oxygen are the heart and the brain. Thus, at low levels, effects on these two tissues are well documented. (At higher levels, about 1,000 ppm and more, CO can be lethal.) As Table 1 indicates, such effects can range from

TABLE 1. Health effects of carbon monoxide (CO)*

Concentration of CO in air	% Carbomonoxyhemoglobin in blood	Symptoms
Up to 300-500 ppm	30-40% and above	Severe headache, dim vision, nausea, collapse.[1]
100 ppm	Up to 20% depending on exposure and activity of subject	Headache at 20%. Impaired performance on simple psychological tests and arithmetic above 10% CO in blood.[1]
	20% in dogs exposed for only 5.75 hours per day, for 11 weeks	Brain and heart damage found at autopsy.[2]

THE DESTRUCTION OF THE ENVIRONMENT

TABLE 1. (continued)

Concentration of CO in air	% Carbomonoxyhemoglobin in blood	Symptoms
50 ppm and	2-4% and above Maximum of about 8% (calculated from [5])	Ability to detect a flashing light against dim background worsens with increasing amounts of CO. 4% was lowest point shown, but authors state that even the CO from a single cigarette could be shown to cause rise in visual threshold.[3] It is, therefore, obvious that smoking and exposure to CO from auto exhaust interact. Subjects presented with two tones and asked to judge which is longer. Judgment impaired at this level of CO in the air; lower levels of CO not studied.[4] Results interpreted as impairment of ability to judge time.[5] Not known whether this may influence people's ability to drive safely. Another author[1] concluded that 1-2% CO in the blood should cause a detectable number of errors on psychological tests if a sufficiently large-scale experiment were done.
15 ppm	Up to 2.4% (calculated from [5])	New York's air quality goal. Even this amount of CO could cause some of the effects on vision and loss of judgment of time that are mentioned above.

*Prepared by D.M. Snodderly, Jr., New York Scientists' Committee for Public Information

1. J.H. Schulte, "Effects of Mild Carbon Monoxide Intoxication," *Archives of Environmental Health*, 7, 1963, pages 524-30.
2. F.H. Lewey and D.L. Drabkin, "Experimental Chronic Carbon Monoxide Poisoning of Dogs," *American Journal of Medical Science*, 208, 1944, pages 502-11.
3. R.A. McFarland, F.J.W. Roughton, M.H. Halperin and J.I. Niven, "Effects of Carbon Monoxide and Altitude on Visual Threshold," *Journal of Aviation Medicine*, 15, 1944, pages 381-94.
4. R.R. Beard and G. Wertheim, "Behavioral Impairment Associated with Small Doses of Carbon Monoxide," *American Journal of Public Health*, 57, 1967, pages 2012-22.
5. J.R. Goldsmith and S.A. Landau, "Carbon Monoxide and Human Health," *Science*, 162, 1969, pages 1352-59.

changes in various psychological capabilities in humans, such as time discrimination, to permanent heart and brain damage in experimental animals. (Concerning this last point, many scientists feel the now well-documented correlation between smoking and heart disease may well be due in part to the CO in cigarette smoke.)

The effects determined in the laboratory and described in Table 1 should be compared with the actual measured levels of CO, culled from several sources, listed in Table 2. The overlap is clear; the only uncertainty concerns how long people in urban areas are exposed to these various levels.

TABLE 2. Carbon monoxide levels at various locations

Location	CO Levels (in average ppm's)
Los Angeles Freeways	37
Los Angeles Freeways, slow, heavy traffic	54
Los Angeles, severe inversion	30 for over 8 hours
Parking garage	59
Cincinnati intersection	20
Detroit, short peak	100
Detroit, residential area	2
Detroit, shopping area	10
Manhattan intersection	15 all day long
Allowed industrial exposure for 8 hours (for comparison)	50 recently lowered from 100

AIR POLLUTION

One of the air pollutants resulting from the aniline dye and benzene industries has, by careful epidemiologic analysis, been shown to result in the increased occurrence of bladder cancers among workers in these industries.[19, 20] In this instance, the target organ, the baldder, was certainly distant from the portal of entry, the lungs. Since bladder cancers are responsible for only a few percent of all deaths from malignancy, these pockets of disease could be expected to attract attention, and did. The disease was found to be heavily concentrated in workers within these industries and in residents in the *immediately surrounding vicinity*. Laboratory confirmation by the provocation of experimentally induced aniline dye tumors in dogs using beta-naphthylamine has been reported.[19] An increased frequency of tumors of the bladder paralleling the increased occurrence of lung cancers in smokers has been reported.[21] and as one might expect, cigarette smoke contains these same contaminants. In the case of this pollutant, short term exposure revealed no ill effects; it was exposure for a long time to a relatively low level that resulted in disease.

Similarly, the results of airborne radioactive isotopes are slow in developing. In 1954, 53 Marshall Islanders were subjected to radiation fallout including iodine 131 from a nuclear bomb test. Iodine 131, although a short-lived isotope, concentrates in the thyroid and can damage the thyroid tissue as it emits its energy and decays. Eleven and twelve years later, 18 of these individuals were reported to have thyroid abnormalities. In 11 cases, surgery was performed, and one cancer of the thyroid was found.[22] Fallout was not blamed for the malignancy found in another patient, who was reported to have received less exposure from iodine 131. However, in a population of this size, one would not expect even a single case of thyroid cancer to be present in 15 years. It should be remembered that this represents also a rather brief period between exposure and disease. The mutagenic properties of radiation are well known, and would lead us to expect effects on later generations. Experience has taught us that it may be as many as five generations after exposure before the effects of a recessive mutation appear. These concerns are probably quite applicable to the long-term effects of release of radioactive materials into the environment from whatever source.

There is much that we don't know about what pollutants are in the air. The term "particulate matter" is a general one that includes numerous pollutants, many as yet unidentified. There are also gaseous pollutants emitted by various industries or released in the burning of wastes that are not monitored. If we knew more about *what* is in the air, this would be only the first step toward studying the biological effects of single pollutants and pollutants in various combinations.

Early concern with the effects of air pollution was largely confined to effects on man which, while quite proper, was also somewhat misleading. By the time we started noticing damage in man, a devastating toll had been taken in plants and possibly in lower animals. Long before the health effects of air pollution became a matter of serious concern, enormous areas of formerly fertile ground surrounding ore processing mills in this country and others became bare as a result of fumes emanating from the mills. This occurred during the days prior to the development of high stacks which promoted more rapid dilution. Sulfur dioxide from stack gases tends to burn vegetation, particularly alfalfa and soft-leafed vegetables. Hydrofluoric acid has been described as being damaging to plants and fluorosis has been described in cattle. By the end of the late 1940's more and more complaints from farmers were heard concerning smog injury to crops. Virtually every crop in New Jersey has been adversely affected by air pollution.

The effect of smog on plants can be quite variable and consequences can include the reduction of crop yield, growth retardation or outright destruction of the plant. Visible damage is probably best known since it is the most easily observable, as when pine trees lose their needles,

oxygen. Statistics on how fast land is being consumed are not available for many sections of the country. However, according to the U. S. Department of Agriculture, roughly 420,000 acres a year are being converted to urban use (which includes buildings and roads), and approximately the same amount is going underwater as new dams and reservoirs are built. In addi-

POLLUTION AND ITS SOURCES

Five major pollutants and their sources are shown below. The total for industry is obviously incomplete, since it includes only the six major industrial polluters. Putting all pollutants into the same units—millions of tons—is somewhat misleading. Some pollutants are harmful even in very small amounts. Some are more harmful than others, and some are more harmful together than separately. (From "The Sources of Air Pollution and Their Control," Public Health Service Publication No. 1548, Washington, D.C., 1966.)

TABLE 3.   Annual Emissions of Five Major Pollutants in Millions of Tons, as of 1966. Total: 142 Million Tons

Carbon monoxide	66	Sulfur oxides	9	
Hydrocarbons	12	Particulates	6	
Nitrogen oxides	6	Hydrocarbons	4	
Sulfur oxides	1	Nitrogen oxides	2	
Particulates	1	Carbon monoxide	2	
Total Automobile	**86**	**Total of 6 Major Industries**	**23**	

Sulfur oxides	12	Sulfur oxides	3	Carbon monoxide	1
Nitrogen oxides	3	Carbon monoxide	2	Hydrocarbons	1
Particulates	3	Nitrogen oxides	1	Particulates	1
Carbon monoxide	1	Hydrocarbons	1	Sulfur oxides	1
Hydrocarbons	1	Particulates	1	Nitrogen oxides	1
Total Electric Power	**20**	**Total Space Heating**	**8**	**Total Refuse Disposal**	**5**

or when lawns become brown after an intense smog assault. Of continuing concern should be the fact that the more extensive the damage to plants, the greater the reduction in oxygen production by green things. For example, phytoplankton, microscopic marine plants which produce oxygen, can be destroyed by air or water pollution or DDT.

City growth, increased miles of highways, and the spreading out of more and more people over the countryside reduce the area given to plants producing life-giving

tion, approximately 160,000 acres are being converted each year in rural areas for highways and airports. It is estimated by the USDA that cropland furnishes roughly one half of this million acres. Thus man, with his exponentially increasing population and his soaring per capita energy use, at least in this country, may ultimately threaten one of his own basic life-sustaining systems, the oxygen cycle.

The measures taken so far to reduce air pollution are being offset by increases in the sources of pollution—more and larger

AIR POLLUTION

power plants, more and larger industrial plants, more automobiles and trucks. So far, controls are being imposed on industry slowly, and principally to reduce sulfur dioxide and particulate matter. Knowledge of what comes out of industry's stacks is often limited, and authority to control it is even more limited. For example, the Committee for Environmental Information found that while industries reported to the city's Air Pollution Control officer what was coming out of their stacks, this was sometimes privileged information, not available to the public. The Air Pollution Commissioner could order reductions in industrial emissions only for sulfur dioxide, hydrogen sulfide, oxidants and particulates—the pollutants for which standards have been adopted by the city. He has authority to reduce emissions of other pollutants only if he can show that they present a danger to the health of the people in the vicinity or constitute a nuisance. Direct cause and effect on human health is extremely difficult to prove in connection with any environmental contaminant, and for new and untested chemicals would be impossible to prove until after the tragic fact. (The dye industry example described previously is a good case in point.)

At a recent conference on air pollution and the automobile at the University of Missouri, William H. Megonnell, Assistant Commissioner for Standards and Compliance, National Air Pollution Control Administration, said:

> In my judgment, the best we can expect from the Federal standards now in effect is that hydrocarbon and carbon monoxide emissions will in 1980 dip to approximately 60 percent of current emissions, or roughly what they were in 1953. And after 1980, when these standards have passed the saturation point of their effectiveness, as vehicle use continues to increase, the levels of pollution will resume their upward climb.

At the same conference, Dr. Robert Karsh, president of the St. Louis Committee for Environmental Information, said:

> The 1968 automotive emission standards reduced carbon monoxide emissions by 50 percent and hydrocarbons by 70 percent of uncontrolled levels in new cars only. The devices are not maintained because they do not have to be maintained in most areas. Because of increased numbers of cars and increased driving, under existing controls automotive pollution will double in the next 30 years.

Since that conference, new federal standards have been proposed which would reduce carbon monoxide emissions to half of present emissions, hydrocarbons to a fourth, particulates to a third and nitrogen oxides to a sixth. These stringent standards would not go into effect until the 1975 model year, and therefore would not reduce the total automotive pollution by those amounts, and then only if the control devices are maintained, and the number of cars does not increase.

According to the U.S. Bureau of Public Roads, the number of registered motor vehicles is increasing every year—in 1969 the increase was three million over 1968. But this tells only a small part of the story. The amount of air pollution from cars is more closely related to miles travelled, and particularly to *urban* miles travelled. In 1946, urban miles travelled were 170 billion. Twenty years later this had more than doubled, to 470 billion, and it is still rising. What this indicates is that our control efforts continue to lag behind our capacity to pollute the air.

REFERENCES

1. H. Heimann, "Effects on Human Health," *Air Pollution,* World Health Organization Monograph No. 46, pages 159-220.

2. Register-General, *Statistical Review of England and Wales,* 1953, H.M.S.O., London, 1954.

3. A.E. Martin, "Mortality and Morbidity Statistics and Air Pollution," Symposium No. 6, from "Medical and Epidemiological Aspects of Air Pollution," *Proceedings of the Royal Society of Medicine,* 57, October, 1964, page 966.

4. J. Pemberton and C. Goldberg, "Air Pollution and Bronchitis," *British Medical Journal,* 2, 1954, page 567.

5. A.S. Fairbairn and D.D. Reid, "Air Pollution and Other Local Factors in Respiratory Disease," *British Journal Preventive and Social Medicine,* 12, 1958, page 94.

6. H.H. Schrenk, H. Heimann, G.D. Clayton *et al.,* "Air Pollution in Donora, Pa., Epidemiology of the Unusual Smog Episode of October, 1948," *Public Health Bulletin,* No. 306, Washington, D.C., 1949.

7. T.E. Huber, S.W. Joseph, E. Krablock, P.L. Redfairn and J. Karakawa, "New Environmental Respiratory Disease (Yokohama Asthma)," *Archives Industrial Hygiene and Occupational Medicine,* 10, 1954, pages 399-408.

8. R.E. Carroll, "Environmental Epidemiology. V. Epidemiology of New Orleans Epidemic Asthma," *American Journal of Public Health,* 58, 1968, page 1677.

9. Murray Dworetsky, "Presidential Address," *Journal of Allergy,* 43, June, 1969, page 315.

10. "Mortality," Part A, from *Vital Statistics of the United States,* 1965, Volume 2, U.S. Department of Health, Education and Welfare, Public Health Service, National Vital Statistics Division, Washington, D.C.

11. H.L. Motley, R.H. Smart and C.I. Leftwich, "Effect of Polluted Los Angeles Air (Smog) on Lung Volume Measurements," *Journal of the American Medical Association,* 71, 1959, page 1469.

12. G. Dean, "Lung Cancer among White South Africans," *British Medical Journal,* 2, 1959, page 852; G. Dean, "Lung Cancer among White South Africans, Report on a Further Study," *British Medical Journal,* 16, 1961, page 1599.

13. G. Dean, "Lung Cancer in Australia," *Medical Journal of Australia,* Volume 49, 1962.

14. D.F. Eastcott, "The Epidemiology of Lung Cancer in New Zealand," *Lancet,* 1, 1956, page 37.

15. Benjamin L. Van Duuren, "Is Cancer Airborne?" *Environment,* January, 1966, page 5. Original sources for these statements are: *Motor Vehicles, Air Pollution and Health,* A Report of the Surgeon General to the U.S. Congress, U.S. Department of Health, Education and Welfare, Public Health Service, U.S. Government Printing Office, Washington, D.C., 1962; *and,* M. Kushner, S. Laskin, E. Cristofano and N. Nelson, "Experimental Carcinoma of the Lung," *Proceedings of the Third National Cancer Conference,* 1957, pages 485-495.

16. L. Greenberg *et al.,* "Report of an Air Pollution Incident in New York City, November, 1953," *Public Health Reports,* 77, 7, 1962.

17. Bertram W. Carnow, Mark H. Lepper, Richard B. Shekelle and Jeremiah Stamler, "Chicago Air Pollution Study," *Archives of Environmental Health,* 18, May, 1969.

18. Assuming 15 percent of the population is affected, a conservative figure according to several studies of the incidence of these ailments in the general population.

19. W.C. Hueper, "Aniline Dye Tumors of the Bladder," *Archives of Pathology,* 25, June, 1938, pages 856-866.

20. M.W. Goldblatt, "Occupational Cancer of the Bladder," *British Medical Bulletin,* 4, 1947, page 405.

21. J. Clemnessen *et al.,* "Smoking and Papilloma of the Bladder," *Danish Medical Bulletin,* 5, 1958, page 121.

22. Robert A. Conard, Leo M. Meyer, Waturu W. Sutow *et al.,* "Medical Survey of the People of Rongelap and Utirik Is-

lands Eleven and Twelve Years after Exposure to Fallout Radiation (March, 1965 and March, 1966)," Brookhaven National Lab., Upton, N.Y., April, 1967.

SECTION 6

NOISE

Although there are many unsettled questions in the area of noise pollution, there is no question that changes of a permanent or temporary nature can take place when an individual's threshold of noise tolerance is exceeded. There is no problem in measuring the permanent hearing loss of a jackhammer operator. It is more difficult to accurately assess the frustration and irritation caused by sonic booms, motorcycle engines, automobile horns, or construction activities. The effect of disruptions such as these on a person's mental health ranges from simple annoyance to unbearable anguish.

This section contains a summary of recent efforts at home and abroad to combat the problems of noise pollution. Although it details the situation in New York City, the problems encountered would be typical of any major city. Information is provided on what noise is, the mental and physical health problems it causes, and the possibilities for remedial action in the future.

GENERAL ASPECTS OF THE NOISE PROBLEM

The sounds of New York City were once regarded with familiar affection as agreeable signs of the busyness and hubbub of a thriving center of human activity. Throughout our history, natives and visitors have often expressed enchantment with the hum of our multilingual chatter, the gentle clicking and whirring of sewing machines and printing presses, the babble of our children at play, the vocal enterprise of our street vendors and the voluble sales resistance of their customers.

Some of the colorful sounds are gone; the hurdy-gurdy and the pitch of the hawker on the street are memories. The other human sounds have nearly all been drowned out by a mechanical screeching and pounding and roaring that is altogether out of human scale. This is noise. And there is so much of it that it seems inescapable. The New Yorker's day is filled with the nerve-wracking shriek and clank of the subway, the deafening cacophony of pneumatic hammers, construction equipment, traffic, jet planes, and electronically amplified sound that becomes noise when he has to listen to it against his will.

The fact that the City has grown noisy is often regarded as an unpleasant but immutable part of the deterioration of the urban environment. This is not true acceptance of the burden of excessive noise, but is rather an attitude of futility. It is based partly on lack of awareness that a quieter city is indeed possible, and partly on despair that a campaign for quiet could succeed. The attitude of many New Yorkers on the noise question, and on other important environmental factors is often mis-called "apathy." It is not apathy at all but rather silent desperation.

Fortunately, a substantial number of citizens do not share this attitude. The Task Force has noted with great appreciation the past and continuing anti-noise efforts of such groups as the Upper Sixth Avenue Noise Abatement Association, the Emergency Committee Opposing the Pan Am Heliport, the Queens Borough President's Committee on Aviation Problems, the Central Brooklyn Citizens Union, the Thruway Noise Abatement Committee of Westchester, and many civic associations, particularly those in neighborhoods under airport ap-

SOURCE. Reprinted, by permission, from a report of the Mayor's Task Force on Noise Control, "Toward a Quieter City," New York Board of Trade, Inc., 1970, with slight abridgment.

175

proach and take-off paths. It has been gratifying to the Task Force to see the establishment of Citizens for a Quieter City, Inc., which, with the good efforts of other interested individuals and groups, may importantly serve the New York community by volunteer efforts in support of present and coming municipal action on noise abatement. In a relatively short space of time, this organization has significantly sparked the interest of machinery suppliers, the hopes of citizens, and the concern of legislators for a quieter New York.

While there has been this salutary development of articulate and intelligent anti-noise sentiment, there continues to be a simultaneous increase in noise. This is, in part, the result of population increase and concentration around our City. By 1975, over 75 percent of America's population will crowd into tightly-knit megalopolises, cities that have overflowed their boundaries. Concentrations of large populations invariably result in higher noise levels, for the building and rebuilding of metropolitan areas never ceases and the press of traffic never lets up.

The suburbs no longer offer havens of quiet. Overhead jet aircraft, increased road traffic, banging garbage cans, and whirr of power lawn-mowers, and the seemingly inexorable urbanization of the suburbs have already brought high noise levels to the entire region.

What one associates, then, with a city like New York, is tension, a nervous energy which, despite its attraction for those who revel in it, is nevertheless a debilitating thing. Though the City will never be fully rid of all irritating noises, there is presently too much noise in terms of human health and efficiency.

Largely because the problem of noise has grown in proportion to the urbanization of this country, and urbanization is growing explosively, physicians and psychologists have begun to study the effects of noise on the individual. Many research-

ers now believe that the harmful effects have been seriously underestimated.

MENTAL AND PHYSICAL HEALTH

Exposure to excessive and sustained noise can cause not only physical damage but also harmful psychological effects. It can cause loss of hearing, sometimes permanently. Researchers estimate that a minimum of six to sixteen million industrial workers sustain degrees of hearing loss from exposure to noise on the job. Nationally, claims for compensation because of hearing loss amount annually to two million dollars.

More subtle effects have been described by recent experiments conducted by Dr. Samuel Rosen, consulting ear surgeon at New York's Mount Sinai Hospital. He showed that noise causes tension which may contribute to high blood pressure and heart disease.

Dr. Rosen also carried out a significant experiment on noise with an isolated tribe in the Sudan. In the people there he found an almost total absence of presbycusis—hearing loss due to aging—which is commonly found in modern industrial nations like the U.S. and has been attributed to old age. Dr. Rosen's studies suggest that one of the causes may be a noisy environment and not age alone.

Although physiological research has only begun, one subject has received much scientific attention: effects of noise on sleep. Everyone knows that intense noise prevents sleep. But what if a sleeping person is subjected to noise not so great as to awaken him?

Recent reserach has shown that sleep, accompanied by dreaming, is essential to mental health. Dr. Jerome Lukas, psychologist at Stanford Research Institute, looked into this noise problem and found that his volunteer dreamers, subjected to noise while sleeping, woke up extremely fatigued. Dr. Lukas concluded that this fatigue was caused by the effort to maintain sleep in spite of the noise. The close relationship between that fatigue and that noise suggested that a sleeping person suffers from noise even when it is not so intense as to awaken him.

IS NOISE RELATIVE?

As we have become increasingly aware of the effects of noise, some myths and misconceptions about noise have been exposed. One myth is that some people "can take it" and others cannot, and that those who cannot are overly sensitive, even neurotic. Curiously, the truth may be exactly the opposite. Some studies suggest that a sensitivity to noise may be the sign of an integrated and healthy personality. This point was underscored by the Medical Subcommittee of the Task Force.

Noise, therefore, is open to differing definition. Below the level of painful sound, what is perceived as "noise" depends very much on how sensitive the ear is and on the duration and intensity of the sound it receives. Sound becomes noise when it is too loud, lasts too long, or is too unpleasant, and these are subjective judgments.

Scientifically, it is nearly impossible to arrive at an adequate definition of noise. The Task Force's Technical Subcommittee says:

> A definition of noise as those sounds which arouse these negative responses—unpleasant, discordant, disturbing or painful—is about as objective as possible, provided the group consulted was large enough and diverse enough.

Nevertheless, there are ways to measure noise. Certain standards and scientific equipment can be used. The following three measurable quantities are used in nearly all testing of noise: (a) the "level" in decibels, which is the volume of the sound; (b) the "frequency" in cycles per second, which is pitch—high frequencies, for example, correspond to a soprano's voice, low ones to a basso profundo's; (c) "duration" in seconds, hours, or some other measurement of time.

Human sensitivity to sound, as the Task Force's study makes clear, is a function of all three factors working simultaneously and interdependently. No single factor is adequate to determine the quantity of noise.

WHAT CAN BE DONE ABOUT IT?

There are ways for the citizen to make his voice heard above the din of other problems competing for attention.

One avenue open to him is to protest to his federal and state representatives in an effort to get corrective legislation. The more he objects to the rising level of noise, the more likely he will get some action.

Another avenue opens to the marketplace. As a consumer, he can be highly selective about products he buys, insisting upon products which make a minimum of noise. Businesses, often priding themselves on being attuned to customer's needs, will not ignore such demands at the risk of losing sales. Even now one can see some evidence, especially in the manufacture of refrigerators, of noise reduction features in home products.

Of course, if all his efforts fail, he can move to a less noisy environment by changing his job or moving his family to a quieter place. In periods of general national affluence, he will find opportunities for work or residence elsewhere. This fact has not been lost to his employers. More than ever before, businesses are finding it economically justifiable, in view of the trend to large turnovers, to improve the working environment and making it acoustically satisfactory for the employee.

The victim of noise has a fourth resort— to join forces with others who want to get action. Unless he can identify himself with a consumer movement for quieter equipment, or with his community group acting to prevent a noisy threat such as a heliport or stolport, he is ineffective in combatting the big noise problems of the City. Only the City Administration, in concert with federal and state bodies, can effectively control these sources and make the difference between success or failure of noise abatement in the City.

WHAT IS BEING DONE: AT HOME AND ABROAD

Many U.S. Cities have been interested in the need to control noise. Some states, for example, Wisconsin, Illinois, New York, California and Oregon, have inaugurated limited noise abatement programs.

The City of Memphis, with the backing of its press, has successfully reduced horn noise and relegated noisy trucks to a few specific routes. Paris effectively silenced the Parisian habit of auto horn blowing.

Paris, London and other European cities have regulated landing of aircraft during the hours of sleep. New Orleans, Los Angeles, Chicago, and Boston are studying plans for off-shore airports. The FAA has given its backing to the feasibility of the idea. The Port Authority, it may be hoped, will give serious consideration to the proposed relocation of its noisy operations to offshore runways connected to the existing terminals and maintenance complexes by causeways. There are many benefits to such a proposal beyond the noise relief provided hundreds of thousands in New York City and other municipalities. First, with a relatively unlimited amount of space available for runways, a triple parallel runway system will increase the capacity for air traffic at Kennedy and LaGuardia. Second, if the runways are built on fill, the solid waste disposal problem can also be solved. Third,

the release of large land areas now tied up at Kennedy and LaGuardia airports for runway use can be freed for expanded passenger, cargo, and aircraft maintenance terminals as well as industrial parks, creating many job opportunities.

In the Congress, Hon. Theodore R. Kupferman presented the most comprehensive bills on noise control that the House of Representatives has seen. His bill, which would have established an office of noise control within the Office of the Surgeon General among other far-reaching provisions, was not passed. Nevertheless, HR 3400, the F.A.A. Aircraft Noise Certification Bill, did pass to become Public Law 90-411. Although the intended effect of this Act is highly controversial, it may attest to the growing interest of Congress in such legislation.

The most recent evidence of national concern was in the form of President Johnson's announcement in November 1968, of a concerted, stepped-up federal program of noise abatement. In "Noise—Sound without Value," prepared by the Federal Council for Science and Technology, which recommends a program of research, education and compliance at the federal level, the President gave an important stimulus to noise control programs in New York and other cities.

While this represents a gain, several European countries have done more to give their citizens a less noisy environment. Noise abatement laws are in effect in countries such as Switzerland, France, Germany, the Soviet Union and the Scandinavian countries. England, for example, published an exhaustive report on noise in 1963 and subsequently passed a national noise abatement act. Several European countries have also established noise control regulations in their building codes. The United States is only beginning to realize the need for such laws and to take steps to reduce unnecessary noise.

SECTION 7

WASTE DISPOSAL

We only recently gained awareness of the threat posed by our own wastes. As consumers we throw away millions of tons of garbage, lawn trimmings, leaves, ashes, newspapers, magazines, toys, rags, furniture, autos, etc., per year. In addition industries spew out poisonous and non-poisonous materials used in fiber-processing, chemical refining, metal processing, and glass making. The sheer quantity of waste materials threatens to engulf us.

Waste materials not only cause a litter problem; they also contribute to soil, water, and air pollution. This condition once again illustrates the interactions between one phase of the environmental problem, waste disposal, with other phases, such as population, water pollution, and air pollution.

In the first article, Arsen Darney argues that our waste disposal systems are archaic. He asserts that the whole consumer industry is geared toward the throwaway package, while the increase in population raises the demand for such products. He discusses techniques by which waste processing can be vastly improved. Processing techniques in which the wastes are discarded must give way to techniques in which the wastes are reused. Darney recommends reorienting industries away from the use of virgin materials toward the use of secondary materials.

In a somewhat similar vein, the second article by Richard H. Gilluly shows how waste products from water sewage can be recycled and used to advantage. He tells about experiments now being conducted at Pennsylvania State University in which sewage effluent is used to stimulate plant growth. The Penn State project may serve as the major model for water treatment. This article provides another dimension to Bylinsky's article on water treatment plants in the Water Pollution section of this unit.

The third article points out the many problems associated with disposal of radioactive wastes. The Atomic Energy Commission proposes to bury these radioactive materials in an abandoned salt mine in Kansas. Geologists from the state of Kansas question this procedure and outline its hazards.

179

Arsen J. Darnay, Jr.

THROWAWAY PACKAGES – A MIXED BLESSING

The rising national concern about pollution emphasizes an aspect of life that most of us would just as soon forget—the problem of solid waste disposal. The discussions about solid waste in our newspapers and magazines are not so much a sign of progress as an indication that one activity which we had taken for granted is failing. And this fact intrudes on our consciousness. However irritating that may be, only one sane course is left: the ailment must be diagnosed and some sort of remedy prescribed.

In 1967 and 1968, Midwest Research Institute (MRI) took part in such a diagnostic endeavor. MRI economists spent nine months attempting to discover the role that packaging materials play in solid waste disposal in a study undertaken for the Solid Wastes Program, U.S. Department of Health, Education, and Welfare.

Packaging materials are only one part— and a relatively small one—of the total solid waste problem. Food wastes (garbage), lawn trimmings and leaves, ashes, newspapers and magazines, discarded toys and tools, rags, and furniture, and a variety of other items such as Christmas trees, old tires, aged swingsets, and an occasional washer or drier, account for about 80% of all residential wastes. Packaging accounts for about 20%. Materials other than packaging wastes represent 92% of total industrial and commercial discards; packaging represents the remainder.

A discussion of packaging in relation to solid waste handling necessitates a review of the entire solid waste disposal problem. What emerges is the fact that no one specific group—solid waste handling agencies, packaging companies merchants, and the like—can be blamed for the problems we face. Rather, the problems result from the many individual activities pursued in ignorance or innocence of the ultimate consequences.

What are the solid waste problems? To say that solid wastes cause environmental pollution is too simple a characterization of the situation. In my view, solid waste handling presents six clearly distinct aspects, each of which constellates a different set of difficulties. Packaging relates to

SOURCE. Reprinted, by permission, from *Environmental Science and Technology*, Vol. 3, No. 4, April 1969, with slight abridgment.

each difficulty in a greater and lesser degree. Furthermore, each set of problems suggests a set of solutions.

Several general observations are worth noting:

- Solid waste disposal, viewed as an art or technique, is very much behind the times. Our waste collection practice is analogous in many ways to water distribution practice on the American frontier in the mid-19th century. With few exceptions, disposal techniques in use today are indistinguishable from the techniques used by the Romans. We do not fight, communicate, build, or educate as they did, but our smoldering dumps are very much like theirs.

- The materials flowing into this antique waste processing system are the products of sophisticated industries—fiber-processing, chemicals refining, metal shaping, and glass-making. In short, the kinds of waste are changing.

- The availability of goods at throwaway prices, the rapidly rising economic well-being of a large segment of the population, and the growth in population are increasing the quantity of wastes. At the same time, very little money seems to be available for so mundane an activity. Ghettos, inadequate housing, a burgeoning crime rate, archaic water treatment and sewage disposal systems, crowded airways, decaying downtowns—all vie for municipal dollars. Little remains to expand and modernize waste disposal facilities.

COLLECTION

Ninety cents of each dollar spent on solid waste disposal is spent picking up and transporting wastes to disposal sites. Of the $2.8 billion spent on collection in 1966, about 80% was for labor. In that year, 46.5 million tons of packaging materials were discarded and subsequently collected at a cost of at least $373 million.

The role of packaging materials in this connection is significant because consumption of these materials is rising steadily—absolutely and in terms of per capita use. In 1966, each person threw away 121 pounds more of such materials than in 1958; by 1976, we shall be discarding 136 pounds more per person than we did in 1966. This per capita increase, coming on top of the normal population increase, will mean that in 1976—when packaging consumption has risen to 73.5 million tons per year, or nearly 23 million tons higher than in 1966—nearly 15 million tons of the additional tonnage will be accounted for by increased per capita consumption, and only 7 million tons by normal population growth. However, these figures are for total packaging consumption; only about 90% of the total enters the solid waste stream, the remainder is recycled.

Collection labor costs are rising, too, as well as the prices of collection vehicles. Moreover, as disposal sites near population centers are filled and engulfed by expanding subdivisions and industrial parks, collection vehicles must travel farther. This, in turn, adds to collection costs. But even if unit costs are the same in 1976 as they were in 1966, to collect and haul the *increase* in packaging materials alone will cost $157 million, or nearly half of the amount spent on collecting *all* packaging wastes ten years earlier. The increase in waste will necessitate nearly 4.75 million more collection trips than were required in 1966, and some 9,500 more collection vehicles (costing about $265 million currently) would have to be added to the present fleet of about 150,000 trucks.

Clearly, packaging materials will cause serious strains on waste disposal systems. For one thing, total residential waste tonnage will increase by 34% in the 1966-1976 period, according to Public Health Service estimates. At the same time, packaging materials thrown away by residential sources will increase by 42%.

Forecasts also indicate that packaging materials will be less dense in 1976, and will require more space in collection vehicles. The reason for this is that packaging materials in 1976 will contain more paper, more plastics, and less metal than in 1966.

The solution to collection problems in solid waste handling is not to be sought in the reduction of tonnages to be collected, but through automation of the collection process. Processes worth examination are on-site reduction by grinding, and pipelining of wastes to collection or separation sites. Piping of solid wastes could be piggy-packed on sewer systems, especially in areas where new storm or sewer lines are being built or where underground tunneling is being used for subway construction. Some development work along these lines is underway.

WASTE PROCESSING

Once collected, wastes usually are transported to one of four basic types of disposal operations—open dumps, landfills, municipal incinerators, or composting plants. In addition, there are a number of other disposal routes which need to be mentioned. Among these are the various on-site burning installations, such as backyard burners, tepee burners, and apartment house burners. Ocean dumping is another technique; wastes are dumped at sea either unburned or as ashes. The feeding of swill to swine is still practiced, but it is generally an activity on the way out.

The one characteristic marking all these disposal processes is the lack of sophisticated equipment and techniques. Roughly 75% of all wastes end up in open dumps. Sanitary landfills, which sound good on paper, frequently are quite unsanitary. The average incinerator, in the words of one federal official, is "nothing more than a dump roofed over." And composting plants, usually started up amidst optimism, tend to fail with regularity, either because their products cannot be sold or because the plant attracts undue public interest by its odor.

Against this backdrop, an attempt at serious analysis of the disposability of packaging materials is handicapped at the start. Packaging materials may cause difficulties in a few well-operated incinerators, landfills, or composting plants, but, for the most part, their final destination is a facility which does no processing and accepts a paper carton as readily as a polyethylene bottle, a kraft bag as readily as an aluminum can, a pop bottle as readily as a pressurized CO_2 container.

There is a vast gulf in waste disposal technology between the leading practitioners and the rank-and-file that forces one to a schizophrenic approach, in which it is impossible to generalize. The literature on solid waste handling is produced by the avant-garde—people who worry about plastics in incinerators because grate-fouling can result, or about liquefied glass deposits on refractory walls. These are people who are concerned about plastic and aluminum containers which persist in landfills and, when the fills are put to some other use, may rise to the surface. There are also the people who dislike film plastics because these materials are difficult to remove mechanically in composting. Over against these leaders are many others who have fewer or no problems with packaging because they do not operate at the leading edge of technology.

The result of this general situation is that you can assert, in the same sentence, that some packaging materials are troublesome and that they aren't—it depends on your point of vantage. More curious, however, is the fact that even advanced practitioners do not have at their command the best technology available, either in their own field or in related fields. There is, for instance, the materials handling expertise of such companies as American Machine and Foundry, which has developed a fully automatic short-order kitchen; Link-Belt; and Union Tank Car. Computer-controlled chemicals processing is a multimillion dollar reality. A score or so companies making

WASTE DISPOSAL

How Packaging Relates to Aspects of Solid Waste Problems

Aspect	Basic problem	Packaging contribution	Possible solution
Waste collection	Collection is labor-intensive, thus costly	Proportion of packaging materials in municipal waste growing	Automation of collection On-site volume reduction and disposal
Waste processing	Disposal technology is relatively backward Insufficient support of research and development Land available for waste disposition is dwindling	Packaging materials are usually nondegradable by natural processes	Retooling of financial support for waste processing Development of new disposal technology Modify packaging materials to make them more degradable
Aesthetic blight from littering	Public carelessness and/or indifference	Packaging is major component of litter	Intensive anti-litter publicity Rigorous anti-litter law enforcement Economic incentives for returning containers
Soil and groundwater pollution from decomposition of organics	Inadequate waste processing Poor selection of disposal sites	Packaging plays indirect role; some materials may contain organic residues	Relocation of adequate sites Replacement of dumps by incinerators
Air pollution from waste combustion	Existence of burning dumps Poorly operated or designed incinerators	Role of packaging same as for solid waste in general	Elimination of burning dumps and inadequate incinerators R&D on improved combustion equipment High quality pollution abatement equipment for incinerators
Loss of potentially valuable raw materials	Solid waste has low value because of contamination by intermixing Low cost of virgin material reduces demand for secondary materials	Many high value raw materials combined in single package Exploitation of concept of throwaway containers	New technology for low cost automated separation of heterogeneous solid waste Incentives for wider industrial use of secondary materials Modifications in package design which would utilize more homogeneous materials

farm equipment have made giant strides toward the elimination of hand-picking in fruit, berry, and vegetable harvesting. Numerical controls have been used for some years now in guiding machine tools. And, finally, sensing technology has been advanced as aerospace and medical electronics have developed under government sponsorship.

All these techniques could be harnessed to breach the barrier to sophisticated solid waste processing—that of material mixing and contamination. Proper control of incinerator operations, for instance, could be achieved by segregating waste into its components, batch-loading wastes of the same combustion characteristics, and bypassing noncombustibles around the incinerator. Waste reduction techniques—shredding and grinding—could reduce all landfill materials to a uniform consistency. Small bits of aluminum or plastics would be far less objectionable than full-sized containers.

Such techniques, however, suggest more processing and processing adds value. In this case, the value is added to a material which has no value; it is waste by definition. It might appear that any increment of solid waste processing is an increment of money thrown away. Indeed, such seems to be the prevailing attitude, and it translates into an absence of funding for solid waste disposal activities.

This attitude—insofar as it is general, and I have little doubt that it is—stems from an era of abundance: abundant land, abundant water, abundant clean air. The American Indian moved his campsite periodically when the wastes of his daily activity began to get underfoot. We inherited his light-hearted ways. Today, however, the unwillingness to add value to our wastes perpetuates open burning dumps, creates black plumes atop office buildings of large cities at 5 p.m., permits municipal incinerators to violate laws which private citizens break at their peril, and adds to the pollution of groundwaters.

Given this general state of affairs, the contribution to the problem presented by packaging materials is slight. Waste processing must be upgraded, and the only way to do so seems to be a retooling of the financial infrastructure on which solid waste disposal rests. In one area of the nation with which I am particularly familiar, the average householder's expenditures on water services are $10 a month, compared with $1.75 for waste disposal. Both are vital utilities, and their costs should be much closer than they are.

Litter is one of the signs of affluence, a phenomenon corresponding to belching smokestacks in the 19th century that were viewed as so many badges of prosperity. However, litter is a nuisance. Unlike the dump, which is probably on the other side of the tracks, litter is everywhere, and is a reminder that we have a solid waste problem.

This is one aspect of solid waste handling in which packages play a dominant role. On a tonnage basis, packages may not be the greatest contributors to litter. A few discarded tires, bumpers and bedsprings—all actually found along a mile-long stretch of a Kansas highway surveyed for litter—easily outweigh a large number of cigarette packets and aluminum cans. On the other hand, discarded packages account for the majority of items in litter.

In spite of efforts by civic organizations, there is good reason to believe that littering will intensify in the future, fed by a powerful expansion in the production of one-way beverage containers. Looking only at beer and soft drink containers—bottles and cans—10 billion nonreturnable units were produced in 1958, 25.6 billion units in 1966, and 58 billion units will be produced in 1976 unless legislative dampers are placed on this growth.

A good part of the reason for expansion in nonreturnable containers rests on their appeal to both consumer and merchant. The consumer need not return the empties, and the merchant need not receive, store, and handle them. Another part of the reason derives from the fact that beverage packaging is a last growth frontier for package makers, especially glass makers. Each deposit-type bottle displaced from the market means the sale of 20 one-way containers, since deposit bottles make an average of 20 trips to the home before they are broken. In 1966, for instance, 65 billion containers were filled, but only 28 billion containers were produced. If all containers were of returnable type, a market for 37 billion units would have been up for the taking, and that's a lot of bottles or cans.

All this, of course, would not mean more litter if the population would be more thoughtful or conscientious. Littering cannot be blamed on industries which produce the ammunition, even though in future wars against the litterbug, the first casualties may turn out to be can and glass makers. Laws limiting the use of such containers have been introduced by the score in state legislatures, and some may pass in coming years. In 1967, 32 proposed bills were presented in 19 states, but none survived as law.

Such laws may well act, indirectly, to make the population aware of the extent of littering and create strong incentives to buy returnable containers by touching off discussions in the press and on radio and TV. A look at bills already put forward suggests that future legislation probably will take the form of outright bans, taxes on one-way containers to make them less attractive to purchase, or deposits on cans and bottles. The difficulties inherent in a regulation requiring a deposit on cans can be imagined. Such a law, for instance, suggests that merchants would have to store empty beer cans. This, in turn, would mean special collection bins that would contain the odor of fermentation. Also, would the thousands of cans thrown away before passage of such a law be redeemable?

Just how effective such laws would be in curbing litter is an open question. The state of Vermont, which banned one-way bottles for a brief period in the mid-1950's, found that the ban had little effect on collection costs.

SOIL AND GROUNDWATER POLLUTION

Soil and groundwater pollution can be caused by solid wastes. Pollution of this type occurs predominantly because the disposal site is at an elevation below that of the surrounding terrain and, thus, becomes a natural collection basin for runoffs, or because the site is placed in an area where the groundwater table is relatively high and pollution is likely to take place. Another situation that tends to bring about

such pollution is establishment of a dump or landfill in a region where heavy rainfall is usual or soil conditions are not favorable to landfilling. By and large, such pollution is preventable. Packaging materials play an indirect role in this aspect of solid waste handling. In themselves, packaging materials are not very degradable, and are unsuitable for composting but harmless to underground storage.

AIR POLLUTION

In addition to gaseous effluents generated as wastes are burned, solid waste handling also results in unpleasant odors and dust at all points where wastes are transferred or processed.

How do packaging materials relate to air pollution from solid waste handling operations? First, the various materials involved—paper, metal, glass, wood, plastics, and textiles—do not contain sufficiently high percentages of hazardous compounds to rate as dangerous fuels. One packaging material, polyvinylchloride (PVC) decomposes into undesirable chlorine compounds; about 36,000 tons of this material were used in packaging in 1966. However, more than one million tons of PVC were sold in the same year in the form of garden hoses, rainwear, shoe soles, floor coverings, construction materials, and the like, indicating that PVC occurs in solid waste at a much higher rate than a look at the packaging component alone would suggest.

The sulfur content of packaging materials is lower than that of most hydrocarbon fuels. Test results developed by Elmer R. Kaiser, and MRI estimates of packaging materials markets, show that a typical ton of packaging materials in 1966 contained 1.80 pounds of sulfur, or 0.9%. Our estimates also indicate that sulfur content will increase only slightly by 1976, to 2.02 pounds.

Solid wastes leave considerable residue when burned—ash, noncombustible components, and unburned leftovers. These must, of course, be disposed of in a land-fill or dump. In some operations, incinerator residues are sufficiently free of unburned organics to be sold as clean fill. Handling of these residues may cause air pollution, and some particulates escape through incinerator chimneys.

In the usual case, incinerator residues account for 20-40% of the original weight. Calculations conducted on a typical ton of packaging materials in 1966 indicated that about 35% by weight of these materials is left over, a percentage close to the maximum. However, more than 90% of these leavings consists of cans and glass containers, not fine ash, leading to the conclusion that particulate air pollution from packaging sources is relatively low.

LOSS OF VALUABLE RAW MATERIALS

In 1966, materials valued at $16.2 billion entered the packaging market, and, of this total, probably 90% was thrown away. This illustrates the nature of the final aspect of solid waste handling to be discussed here. We may ask ourselves why it is that we find uses for the bark of trees, process trash fish to make nutritious fish meal, are able to utilize every component of an animal carcass to produce valuable goods, and squeeze high-priced commodities from every fraction of crude oil, but are unwilling to prevent the squandering of valuable natural resources after they have been converted into finished goods. The answer seems to be that whereas we have perfected the technologies necessary to harvest, separate, refine, and convert virgin materials— no matter how complicated their chemical structure or how heterogeneous the mixtures in which we find them—we have not made any strides toward using secondary materials resources because we have had no need to do so.

If one takes a sober and unemotional look at the situation, there is indeed, no immediate need to be concerned about our wasteful behavior. We have sufficient timber in the U.S. and Canada to supply domestic needs for many decades without any strain. (We are, however, a larger exporter of paper, and shortages may occur within 30 years if we put export demand on top of domestic demand.) Our resources of hydrocarbon stocks will last for a long time, and we have yet to tap tar sands and shale oils. There is no foreseeable shortage of iron ore. Our aluminum is derived largely from imports (about 80% is imported), and aluminum conservation would make good sense, if for no other reason than to limit the outflow of gold.

Only if we look well beyond the year 2000 does it seem as if shortages may begin to be felt, especially if an across-the-board industrialization of backward nations is assumed and current population growth rates persist. Although the 21st century is still a long way off, we should be working on reuse and recovery of secondary materials in anticipation of faroff eventualities. We should now be creating the technologies, distribution networks, and financial structures that will give us flexibility in the next century. Nevertheless, the opposite trend is perceptible, especially with reference to packaging materials.

PAPER

Let's look at paper supplies. Right after World War II, 35% of all U.S. paper fiber requirements was met by waste paper (or paperstock, as it is called in the trade). In 1956, paperstock accounted for slightly more than 26%; in 1966, for 21%; and by 1980—extending the trend—paperstock should supply only 17.5% of total paper required. The decline in percentage figures does not mean that tonnage of paperstock used has been declining. On the contrary, it rose from 7.3 million tons in 1946 to 10.2 million in 1966. But, proportionately, secondary paper fiber consumption is trending down when—to anticipate shortages in the long term—it should be trending up.

WASTE DISPOSAL

The declining popularity of waste paper as a raw material may ultimately be traced to cost. On one hand, pulp-tree harvesting and processing have been improved by new technology, driving down virgin pulp prices. On the other hand, costs of handling secondary paper have been rising, partly because labor costs are increasing, but, more significantly, because the waste papers are more and more contaminated. Papers are coated with plastics, printed with inks that resist de-inking, and are laminated to metals. To separate the useful and useless components of waste paper takes hand labor, and the more sorting that is required, the higher the price. Not surprisingly, paper-stock dealers prefer to buy from sources such as printing shops and binderies, where the waste is already fairly clean, rather than from office buildings or residential sources where paper wastes are frequently mixed with organic materials.

Much the same situation characterizes salvage of other materials used in packaging. To give one last example, to make a ton of cullet (broken glass of uniform color), a dealer has to handle between 1900-4600 bottles; and for a ton he can obtain $15, at best. In some cities, sorting costs exceed $30 a ton, and consequently cullet is not handled at all.

The composite picture which emerges from even a cursory look at waste salvage is one where this activity slowly is being squeezed out of existence because of adverse economics. In other words, we are once more faced with the need to add value to something that seems to have no value. Thus, increased use of secondary materials can be brought about only by an indirect tax on virgin materials—for instance, by subsidizing secondary materials handlers, giving tax incentives to potential users, or investing in research and development on automated processing of wastes for reuse. To ban the use of one-way beverage containers would also be an indirect tax on bottle and can makers. Yet, to turn about at this time and reorient various industries from a virgin-materials focus to a secondary materials focus may well be the thing to do—in the long run. In the short run, it may not be justifiable.

There is no doubt that the contribution of packaging to solid waste problems cannot be assessed without also passing some judgment on current practices for handling solid wastes. Large inputs of packaging materials into the solid waste system cannot be blamed for all the distress signals which are perceptible. Rather, the problems illustrate that the entire field of solid waste handling is a neglected area and should now be overhauled.

Richard H. Gilluly

NEW DIRECTIONS IN WATER POLLUTION ABATEMENT

Last year was clean air year in Congress, as major amendments were passed strengthening air pollution abatement programs. This year promises to be clean water year, as Sen. Edmund Muskie's (D-Me.) air and water pollution subcommittee holds hearings on a rash of water bills, including Muskie and administration bills that would greatly increase funding for Federal sewer grant programs.

Hard-pressed cities and towns desperately need the money if they are to build new sewage treatment facilities. But scientists are concerned that the Environmental Protection Agency's Water Quality Office has in the past placed far too much emphasis on 50-year-old water treatment technologies that get the job done only imperfectly and forego major benefits that can come from new innovations. In addition, critics such as Ralph Nader say that WQO, the Administration and Congress have ignored special problems that come from the addition of industrial wastes to municipal sewage systems (SN: 4/17/71, p. 262). These

critics hope the forthcoming new legislation will emphasize the innovative approaches. Fortunately, there is evidence Congress and the Administration are becoming aware of these approaches.

One of the reasons clean air received first legislative priority was the general belief that air pollution abatement problems are far more complex and difficult to solve than water pollution problems, a view recently expressed by EPA's Administrator William D. Ruckelshaus.

This view has prevailed because water treatment is an old, established technology and officials often assumed that the treatment was being done right. But scientists increasingly point out that the old ways may not always be the right ways and that there is as much room for innovation in water pollution abatement as in air pollution abatement.

"I don't disagree entirely with Ruckelshaus," says Dr. Robert C. Ball, head of Michigan State University's Institute of Water Research. "Water pollution abate-

SOURCE. Reprinted, by permission, from *Science News,* Vol. 99, No. 19, April 24, 1971, with slight abridgment.

ment is better known." But, he adds, a higher level of research and development than now provided for in WQO's budget is needed—especially into techniques for in-house treatment of industrial wastes so that pollutants can be removed before they enter municipal systems.

(Ruckelshaus was quoted April 14 to the effect that he viewed the Nader report on water pollution as a valid criticism of WQO. This suggests his views on the need for new innovative technologies may have changed.)

Most of the new innovations rely on considering sewage as "resources out of place" rather than wastes. Dr. Howard A. Tanner, also of Michigan State University, says a policy of requiring industries to pay fees to municipalities for treating their sewage may be exactly the wrong approach in this context. If the ecological goal of recycling wastes is to be met, then dumping industrial effluents into municipal systems simply makes it more difficult to recover valuable materials. "Never dilute 40 percent ore to 4 percent," is an old resource recovery principle that should be applied to sewage treatment, Dr. Tanner says.

But there are more immediate problems than losing resources, says Mary Fulmer, a sanitary engineer and chairman of the Columbus, Ohio, Sewer and Water Advisory Board. She points out that where industrial wastes are dumped into municipal systems, scheduling is often haphazard and communication nil. Thus a municipal sewage plant can get hit with a dollop of toxic industrial wastes without time for preparation and sometimes even without knowing what the substance is. Bacteria for biological treatment are sometimes killed. Or, Dr. Ball points out, some pollutants, such as mercury, go right on through the system and enter waterways.

Mrs. Fulmer says one of the problems is that sewage treatment traditionally has been aimed at public health goals, rather than ecological ones. Removal of phos-

phates, for instance, is primarily an ecological goal of a kind only recently adopted. Cost, she says, can be immense, with a sodium aluminate process for precipitation of phosphates possibly doubling the cost of treatment. And Dr. John R. Sheaffer of the University of Chicago says even the public health goals probably are not being met. Coliform bacteria—traditionally gauged by a count of *E. coli*—may be killed in conventional treatment, but there is evidence, says Dr. Sheaffer, that pathogenic viruses are getting through.

Dr. Sheaffer, now on leave from Chicago to work with the Army Corps of Engineers, is a major architect of a scheme now getting under way in Muskegon County, Mich., that is being watched with great attention by water scientists everywhere because it promises to solve almost all of these problems and, in addition, provide major by-product benefits. (WQO, incidentally, is financing more than half the $30 million cost of the Muskegon plan, partly with R&D funds, partly with construction grant funds.) And there are similar projects getting under way elsewhere in the country.

The Muskegon project, on which construction will begin this year, relies on some surprisingly simple principles. One is that dirty water filtering through soil is quickly cleansed by the soil. Another is that such enrichment of soil makes it far more fertile. Putting these two facts together, scientists at Pennsylvania State University conceived the notion of spraying sewage effluents on marginal soils instead of dumping them into waterways. They tried it, and it worked. Not only was soil fertility greatly increased, but also a decline in the water table was slowed as excess irrigation water filtered through the soil into the water table.

Dr. Sheaffer and others decided there was no reason not to try the idea on a far larger scale, and Muskegon County (population 170,000) officials were willing. The sewage outlets of cities and towns in the county will be turned away from the lakes they now pollute, including Lake Michigan, and will go into a larger collector system that will take the sewage to marginal land in the eastern part of the county. First, the effluent will go into aeration lagoons for biological treatment by bacteria. Then it will go into storage lagoons capable of holding the effluent during the non-irrigation season. From there it will go to spray-irrigation devices. Corn will be grown on the irrigated fields.

The aeration lagoons will be large enough to accommodate a large dose of industrial wastes toxic to the bacteria in them without killing all the bacteria in any given lagoon. Thus the bacteria killed could be replaced by regrowth.

Another advantage is that the viruses not removed by conventional sewage treatment will be filtered entirely out of the effluent as it goes through the 6,000 acres of soil to be irrigated. One estimate of the annual return from the corn growing on the now marginal soil is $740,000. There are many other side benefits, the major one perhaps being that recreational development of Lake Muskegon and two other small lakes in the county will be possible because they will no longer be polluted.

The plan is an expensive one, but most scientists are optimistic about its eventual success. Mrs. Fulmer and others, however, believe there simply have not been extensive enough pilot projects for many of the innovative new approaches. Sometimes, she says, a so-called pilot project for a new sewage treatment technique is conducted with glassware and quarter-inch tubing. And she is still leary of industrial wastes in connection with techniques that use sewage —either effluent or sludge—as fertilizer.

There is little doubt that far more extensive R&D is needed. In its fiscal 1972 budget, the Nixon Administration is emphasizing increased sewer construction grants and assistance to local and state enforcement agencies. The fiscal 1972 R&D budget of WQO is actually down from 1971—from about $60.5 million to $56.5 million. Thus projects such as the Muskegon one will get shorter shrift, while enforcement, which may compel construction of more of the conventional treatment plants, will be stressed.

But the Muskegon project will be completed in 1973. Dr. Sheaffer points out that most major cities have the right combination of nearby marginal soils and inadequate sewage treatment plants to make similar projects feasible. If the Muskegon project works as planned, it may serve as the major model for sewage treatment.

THE KANSAS GEOLOGISTS AND THE AEC

With the growth in the number of nuclear power plants comes the problem of how to dispose of the radioactive wastes they create. For some time the Atomic Energy Commission has been seeking repository sites for the wastes, and on the recommendation of two studies by the National Academy of Sciences it decided last year on an abandoned salt mine near Lyons, Kan. In its budget for fiscal 1972, the AEC accordingly requested $3.5 million to begin work on the planned repository.

But the plan has met with opposition from Kansans fearful of the possibilities of contamination of their land, water and air from the stored wastes. The Kansas State Geological Survey asked the AEC to delay its plans until adequate studies could be made of their safety (SN: 8/8/70, p. 115).

Last August, the Survey, headed by Dr. William W. Hambleton of the University of Kansas, began studies of the surface geology, ground water hydrology and subsurface geology of a nine-square-mile area surrounding Lyons. The researchers recovered two deep cores from opposite corners of the proposed 1,000 acre site, one of which penetrated through the salt to a depth of about 1,300 feet. They also drilled some 40 shallower holes.

The Survey's preliminary report is highly critical of the AEC, accusing it of giving insufficient consideration to several serious problems.

The report tentatively concludes that the geologic conditions of the site are satisfactory. But problems relating to heat flow and surface subsidence remain largely unsolved, it says, and AEC models for solution of the problem have been based on simplified theoretical conditions, rather than on the actual geology of the mine area.

The interaction of subsidence, thermal expansion and heat flow, the Kansas scientists found, could break the seal of overlying rocks permitting entry of ground waters that form the primary water source for the area.

SOURCE. Reprinted, by permission from *Science News,* Vol. 99, No. 10, March 6, 1971, with slight abridgment.

THE DESTRUCTION OF THE ENVIRONMENT

The waste containers would eventually deteriorate, but according to the AEC plan the salt itself would act as the primary container for the wastes. The AEC says the earth pressures and thermal effects of the waste would cause the salt to close about the containers and seal them in place.

The Kansas geologists, however, see dangers in this plan. Studies of radiation effects on salt show high heat storage, they say. Rapid thermal excursion from sudden release of this stored energy could cause temperatures in the affected region to rise to 620 degrees C. "These high temperatures," according to the report, "could result in greater flow of salt around the containers, and could cause an explosive effect due to this sudden thermal expansion." These effects could cause the containers to migrate to lower depths, possibly to shale layers, and could create faults in overlying rocks, the report claims.

Furthermore, the geologists point out, the metal containers are expected to deteriorate within six months, and the ceramic material containing the wastes will last only several years. Radioactive particles could therefore migrate through the salt. The ceramic material itself, the researchers say, can store energy, and gamma radiation can cause chemical breakdown of salt. Radiolysis could result in formation of new chlorine compounds capable of leaching plutonium.

The AEC, the report concludes, has "exhibited remarkably little interest" in the heat-flow problem and in studies of radiation damage.

One of the more vocal critics of the AEC plans has been Rep. Joe Skubitz (R-Kan.). An exchange of letters between Skubitz and AEC Chairman Glenn T. Seaborg, in which Dr. Seaborg apparently failed to satisfy Skubitz' objections, culminated last month in a letter from Skubitz to Kansas Governor Robert B. Docking. Citing the "paucity and unsureness of facts by those who are scientifically best informed," Skubitz urged state officials to oppose "making Kansas an atomic garbage dump."

Dr. Seaborg responded to these charges on Feb. 23 with a point-by-point rebuttal. "The Commission," he said, "has no intention of burying wastes in this facility until all the pertinent data are available to support the safety of this operation."

On the question of retrieval of wastes, Dr. Seaborg said that once radioactive wastes are placed in the repository, retrieval would be considered only in case of safety problems which at present the AEC does not foresee. However, he added, the facility would be designed to allow retrieval.

Studies will continue, Dr. Seaborg said and "as we proceed, if exploratory studies were to develop objective data which raise serious questions as to the suitability of the site for radioactive waste storage, the Commission would cease work on the project. To date, we have no reason to believe that this important project should not proceed if authorized."

Final agreement on the location of the nuclear repository site will have to await settlement of these differences between Kansas geologists and the AEC. The situation seems increasingly typical of many problems in today's technological age: Both sides cite scientific evidence to reach opposite conclusions.

SECTION 8

DEPLETION OF NATURAL RESOURCES

The treatment of natural resources as an inexhaustible supply appears to be a habit deeply ingrained in our country's heritage. When the pioneers pushed west, the forests and buffalo felt the impact of their invasion. In the process of conquering the wilderness, timberlands were demolished and buffalo were killed off.

Present day habits in relation to natural resources appear not to have changed. Typical examples of current callous indifference are the mismanagement of timber lands, the disregard for certain species of animals which are in danger of complete extinction, and the rape of land and streams through stripmining.

Today, eighty-three species of animals in the United States face extinction. These species are endangered because of man's activities, such as changing the form and use of land, or polluting the natural environment. One of these endangered species is our national symbol, the bald eagle. In the article, "Symbol of a Nation," J. Richard Hilton discusses this indignity to our national pride.

In the second article, Malcolm Margolin cites alternatives to the wasteful practices employed by the forest products industry. Because of gross mismanagement he foresees a timber crisis by the 1980's.

The final article, by Wayne Davis, tells about stripmining. In this highly lucrative surface operation, three times as much coal can be mined as underground. The more rapid depletion of coal foreshadows its extinction as well as the already predicted end of oil and natural gas. Other outcomes of stripmining with its removal of surface soil are permanently scarred land resources and the destruction of streams. Loss of timber resources, fisheries, and recreation areas all accompany this desecration.

J. Richard Hilton

SYMBOL OF A NATION

As the so-called superior form of life, man has long challenged the existence of lower creatures. Dozens of wild birds and animals have been driven into extinction as a result of man's attitude. Even the national bird of American man reflects his greedy nature. Today the bald eagle's endangered status symbolizes an advancing civilization confused and unsympathetic to other forms of life. More clearly, it reflects what man is doing to his very own environment and his apathetic attitude towards improving its quality. For the almost 200 years since the date of its inauguration as our national bird, the eagle has met resistance and depravation much like many other species of wildlife less publicized. It has been shot, poisoned, trapped, stuffed, and caged—all the while representing freedom, nobility, and courage to the American people.

The bald eagle belongs to an avian order called Falconiformes, which includes other such winged predators as hawks and falcons—nearly all of which have faced great population crashes within the last century. Even as our symbol, the eagle has not evaded prejudice, and it is now virtually extinct within much of its former range. Only Florida and Alaska can count bald eagles in appreciable numbers. Not only are all Fal-

coniformes vital to a wildlife community—their diets balancing rodent and insect populations, but they have served as a barometer to environmental pressures applied by man. Although they represent the wildlife community in a royal and dignified manner, their limited and declining populations are a disgrace to all forms of life; they reflect man's pressures many wildlife species face as a result of environmental conditions. The bald eagle's cousins, the golden eagle and gyrfalcon, receive equal rank as symbols of countries, although little more in protection and respect. Few are treated as anything but symbols; their territorial declines representing in some way or another man's enthusiasm to control their abundance in any way possible. From eagle bounties in the United States, exploitation of nests in Iceland, to a lack of protection in Mexico, bird of prey populations have suffered greatly. It is sometimes argued that the Hawks represent only one order of birds; their decline only being characteristic of their inability to adapt to a changing world. However, of the 28 orders of birds, more than half contain species also unable to withstand current ecological pressures.

SOURCE. Reprinted, by permission, from a brochure published by The Society for the Preservation of Birds of Prey, with slight abridgment.

DEPLETION OF NATURAL RESOURCES

The multitude of mammal species threatened with extinction has been so widespread it has caused some preservationists to literally give up all hope for the future existence of some species. The path to oblivion for wildlife, and the destruction of undisturbed habitat will reach even greater proportions in the future if man continues his environmental slaughter. As a result of this outlook, optimistic conservation groups have evolved. Some specialize in protecting a species; there are groups to save the alligator, sea otter, tule elk, whale, and whooping crane. Others strive to educate man; some alarm him into acting on his own behalf. All agree that *we are at a time now when the most radical action isn't enough.* Something must be done now to combat environmental abuses. Legislation and wildlife protection measures will serve only as a foundation to the solution. Robert M. Hatch, Bishop of Western Massachusetts, once spoke of bird of prey declines: "Of course our predatory birds cannot be saved solely by legislation . . . the struggle is less a legal one than it is a war on ignorance, prejudice, stupidity, and cruelty in human minds and hearts . . . it is an effort to replace these traits with reason and humaneness, and it is basically the same struggle that man faces in his attempts to achieve a just and peaceful world."

Just as Hawks in a wildlife community serve as a stabilizer in the balance of nature, so too must man act in his community. The imbalances of our natural environment are with us primarily because we are not utilizing existing alternatives. It is essentially a question of priorities. Are we going to erect oil platforms within a wildlife sanctuary and threaten the very existence of 50 remaining condors? Should we continue to allow industrial plants to pollute the air simply because it may be financially infeasible for them to seek alternatives? American man, especially, has the knowledge and intellectual capabilities to come up with a few answers. If we can design computers or land men on the moon, then surely we

have the potentials. Then why aren't we using them? We aren't using them simply because to place a man on the moon is more important to many of us than is the quality of life here on earth.

One of the major factors in the American public's apathetic attitude towards improving the environment is our inability to recognize an ecological crisis when it occurs. The use of strong pesticides such as DDT illustrates this point clearly. Biologists have warned against the use of chlorinated hydrocarbons (non biodegradable insecticides) for use on crops and fruit trees for the last 20 years. Yet only within the last three years has a groundswell of scientific evidence emerged against such chemicals. It began with startling affects on bird of prey reproduction; the causal factor in the decline of bald eagles. It was not until a correlation between cancer and DDT concentrations in man that public protest began. As a result, concern over the continued use of chlorinated hydrocarbons has come to light in 1970, only now it is not simply a matter of the survival of an eagle, peregrine falcon or osprey, as much as it is to all forms of life—including man.

For some reason, man has for centuries found great joy in persecuting something which is the very dream of his ambitions: strength, superiority, ability, and courage. These are the qualities of the hawks; it is no wonder that man chose them as his symbol over a multitude of other wildlife species. Man has long been associated as a predator—it is only his ignorance as a predator that has caused him problems. Now he is an endangered species, his very existence balancing on his own self-destruction. He pollutes the air, fouls the water, and rapes the land of its wealth. His hypocritical attitude is to talk about the problem he has created; he may even enact legislation—it takes him years to do this, and by the time he does it is too late. This is an American attitude clearly reflected by the lack of concern for the very symbol which represents him. Only now, the American eagle is no longer just a symbol, its present status being a reflection of the environ- mental hardship and depravation that man has ignorantly bestowed upon himself.

Malcolm Margolin

THE HABIT OF WASTE

"We had better worry about wood," warns *Pulp & Paper,* a trade journal, and statistics from the U.S. Forest Service are certainly ominous. They predict: two and a half times the current demand for pulpwood by 1985; well over twice the demand for all wood products by 2000; and millions fewer forested acres to grow it on.

We could, of course, simply use less wood. We could take advantage of substitute materials for home building—materials not being used because of a reactionary building industry and a jungle of obsolete building codes that only the most preposterous overuse of wood can satisfy. "We're still building houses the same way we did in the 1890's," notes Gov. Daniel Evans of Washington.

Or we could recycle paper, thus eliminating simultaneously a good part of the garbage, air pollution and conservation problems. If *The New York Times* were de-inked and recycled instead of being burned, that would save nearly 36 square miles of mature Canadian forest each year. Add just a few more cities on the East Coast to this recycling plan, and we would save something close to a national park's worth of standing timber a year. Yet a recent conference on recycling attracted what one journal called "widespread disinterest."

It is insane to suppose that if the public sits on its hands long enough, industry will lead the way to conservation of wood. The forest products industry is the fourth largest in America; and, typically American, it thinks only one brute thought: bigger! The very companies that yell "timber shortage" the loudest spend millions of dollars to develop "disposables"—throwaway evening gowns, tuxedos, tablecloths, and the like. For every scientist seeking to save wood, there are a hundred searching for new ways to waste it. Would you believe wooden pipes for conducting liquids underground?

When the Defense Department stops ordering pinewood ammunition cases, the loggers do not rejoice at the salvation of the Southern pine forests; they demand (and get) a House Small Business Committee conference to find out why. And last year when the price of lumber suddenly jumped 30 percent and plywood nearly 80 percent, Congress held three separate hearings to discuss, not how to decrease the demand but how to squeeze more timber out of the forests.

SOURCE. Reprinted, by permission, from *The Nation,* Vol. 210, No. 8, March 2, 1970, with slight abridgment.

Congress might have examined that 1968-69 timber famine more closely. Why, for instance, wasn't the 20 percent restrictive tariff on plywood imports dropped? Or why, during the crisis, did the industry's profit ratio double, climbing "beyond what should reasonably be expected," according to George Romney.

There were other oddities. The industry unanimously demanded that the National Forest increase the allowable cut on public lands by 10 percent. At the same time, industry had purchased 26.6 billion board feet of national forest timber which they were not cutting—a backlog equal to twice the annual cut. "It's beginning to look like someone here is pulling our leg," commented Bert Cole, State Land Commissioner of Washington.

Finally there was the puzzling business of exports to Japan—2.23 *billion* board feet of prime Pacific Northwest logs in 1968, 35 percent more than was exported in 1967, ten times what was exported in 1960. Fat, healthy logs were jamming the West Coast harbors within view of sawmills that had closed down for lack of supply. Yet Japan was so glutted with wood at this time that companies like Germain Lumber of Pittsburgh were actually forced to *import* plywood from Japan.

This adds up to something worse than collusion or a deliberate manipulation of the market. (Collusion, if it existed, could have been stopped by already existing laws.) The timber crisis indicated how extensive is the mismanagement and nonmanagement of the timber supply.

Where will the wood come from? Ask a logger or a forester, and you will get a very tempting answer: from intensified forestry. Weyerhaeuser is squeezing 33 percent more lumber out of its forests by intensive cultivation methods. International Paper, Potlatch Forests, St. Regis and others use fertilizers and genetically improved "supertrees" to get 50 percent to 60 percent more wood per acre. And from legislation now being pushed through Congress (The Na-

tional Forest Conservation and Management Act), the national forests will soon be enjoying *intensive cultivation* to increase yield by a whopping 66 percent. It sounds marvelous—until you get out of your car, walk through the gates of Weyerhaeuser, International Paper, or any of the others, and take a look at the "Forests of the Future." The trees are arranged in straight rows precisely the same distance apart. They are all the same species, the same age, the same height and the same shape. They were selected from genetically improved stock to remove any imperfections that might give the trees individuality. These tree farms are sometimes fertilized, sprayed for insects and fungi, and are regularly thinned. They are wildlife deserts and have no more recreational value than do cornfields. In fact, that is the first association of every one who sees them: "wheat fields," "corn fields." Yet today nearly every logged-over acre of industrial timberland in the South and Northwest is artificially reforested in this manner—more than 1 million acres last year alone, about 1,600 square miles.

If tree farms were as visible as smog there would be an enormous protest; but they are mostly on private land, as far removed from the public eye as logging itself, and they are well padded by public relations lullabies. Except for industry, only the Sierra Club, the Wilderness Society, and a few others are aware of tree farms; and they have been waging an unsuccessful battle to preserve at least the publicly owned land from such a fate.

If this is what threatens America's remaining forests, the first question to ask is: are there alternatives? I have already touched upon a few: use of substitute materials, recycling of paper, stopping exports (which now account for 10 percent of America's timber production). There are many more. American logging, milling, and home-building practices were developed during an age when forests were plentiful, even a nuisance. The attitudes and technologies from this era still cling. In its progress from forest to its ultimate destination—the dump—we find wood outrageously wasted at every step.

To begin at the beginning, logging, especially on the steep slopes of the Northwest, is still exciting; but once the chain saws have stopped whining, the engines have stopped roaring and the donkey whistle is silent, what remains are hillsides littered with slash. Ten to 20 percent of the volume is left behind, to be burned or buried. It could all be used. Portable chippers, sky-lining, and ballooning (lifting whole trees with balloons as they do in Russia) make it possible, and according to a Wilderness Society estimate would increase the national timber supply by 10 percent.

Next comes the sawmill, where fat logs go in one end and skinny planks emerge from the other. Bark, which is about 10 percent of the log, is burned or sold as mulch: it could be converted into bark board. Sawdust, which accounts for about 7 percent of the log, could be halved with thinner blades. New methods and patterns of cutting Southern pine could increase output by another 8 percent. Few mills have special equipment to process undersized or defective logs. And finally there are the thousands of marginal, small-town sawmills that stink up the air by burning ends, edgings, and slabs instead of converting them into fiberboard, particle board, or pulp.

What I am describing are ways of applying *existing* technology. Why haven't they been applied? They are, unfortunately, economically marginal, or worse. Good forestry and good milling are simply not profitable—not when the price of lumber is artificially depressed by overcutting private land and by raiding the national forests. Deliberate action will be needed to bring them into harmony: perhaps a steep price rise, perhaps legislation to promote better practices, or maybe something sweeter like tax relief or subsidies to insure proper treatment of wood.

The next stage on the journey through the sawmill is past the grader. Although devices for grading accurately exist, it is still done haphazardly. A man glances at one side of a passing board and puts on the grade. The standards are set by industry, and they are entirely voluntary. Strong wood is occasionally misgraded (and misused) as weak. But a recent check by *The Washington Post* found that half the lumber bought from randomly selected dealers was "much weaker" than it was supposed to be. Architects and builders know this, and they automatically compensate, using 2-by-10s instead of 2-by-8s, etc. More accurate grading, the Western Forests Industries Association thinks, could reduce the amount of lumber used in the average house by 15 to 30 percent. Rep. John Dingell (D., Mich.) thinks that the waste from misgrading "could amount to as much as *25 percent of the total resource.*"

Then there is the matter of proper seasoning, to make wood last longer and reduce the rate of replacement. The antiquarian Eric Sloane has compared the suburban house which sags, rots, and sports termites after a single generation, with the New England barn that lasts centuries—without paint or preservatives. The difference is in the seasoning.

It is impossible to estimate how many Yellowstones could be saved by recycling, using slash and sawmill leftovers, increasing mill efficiency, halting exports, grading properly, seasoning adequately, and using alternate materials. Yet there is more to the subject. I have not even touched upon the attacks by hundreds of critics against numberless stupidities: the Jones Act, for example, which in effect forces Alaska to ship nearly all of its lumber to Japan; the telephone poles which devastate forests and scenery at the same time; power transmission lines that destroy more than 30,000 acres of forest a year; flood-control dams in areas where reforestation would not only control floods but would produce commercial timber; failure to use bagasse (sugar refinery refuse) instead of pulp for certain grades of paper; failure to encourage use of groundwood paper (which uses 90 percent of a log) over finer grades (which convert only 50 percent.

We steadily reduce our wild varied forests to mono-cultural tree farms; yet we allow 2 million logged-over acres in Southern Florida and millions more in nearly every state to be taken over by brush. If an Oregon landowner wants to strip his land of mature firs, cedars, hemlocks and larches, and replant with colonnades of genetically improved Douglas firs, he will benefit from millions of dollars worth of research, state nurseries, and the visitations of public foresters. But if he wants to rehabilitate his brushland, there is nothing he can do but buy the one book available on the subject. "And if this represents the state of the art," comments one of them, Bruce Starker, "I could have spent my money more effectively on an ax."

At the present rate of waste, we shall certainly have a timber crisis by the 1980s. We shall also see a large part of our forests brutalized by "intensive cultivation." Every one will blame the sad state of affairs on overpopulation, but they will be wrong. The real cause of that double disaster, timber famine and tree farms, will be the current gross mismangement.

Various solutions have been put forth. They include price rises, price controls, federal or state regulation, tax reforms to promote efficiency, subsidies, and others more radical. Every one who views the situation would like to take the villain by

the throat, but he is not to be found. The four largest timber producers combined control less than 10 percent of the market. There is not one hole in the barrel but a thousand.

Whenever the industry itself speaks of the approaching timber famine, it casts the entire blame on three evils: the refusal of small landowners to let their land be logged; the withdrawal of timberland for national parks and wilderness areas; and the failure of the government to cultivate the national forests more intensively. In effect they have only one solution: we must cut more and that is ridiculous.

Many individuals and groups have looked into aspects of the timber situation—they range from the Sierra Club to Ervin Peterson, former Assistant Secretary of Agriculture and now president of Sonic Jet Processes Corp.—and they usually come to the same conclusion. We need, at this moment, a high-level commission, a sort of Hoover Commission, to study the whole seedling-to-dump timber problem, to sort out fact from public relations propaganda, to collect for the first time adequate statistics, and finally to make recommendations.

The call for "more study" always tends to sound pale and timid, yet in this case it is the first and necessary step. Without such an authoritative, comprehensive study, critics of timber mismanagement are left with nothing but the current scatter-gun attack on a gigantic, fragmented industry that doesn't care, that never responds honestly, and that wastes, wastes, wastes, the very last of the wild forests.

Wayne Davis

THE STRIPMINING OF AMERICA

Kentucky is being destroyed by stripmining. Not slowly and surely, but rapidly and at an ever accelerating rate. And the disease that affects Kentucky soon may spread to more than half our other states.

Most Sierrans are aware of the problem of acid mine drainage. Sulfur impurities in coal, when excavated and exposed to the air, invite invasion by bacteria which manufacture sulfuric acid. The result is streams with a pH so low that nothing survives but bacteria. The damage is permanent; some sickly red streams run dead a hundred years after mining operations have ceased, with little prospect of improvement in sight.

The extent of the problem is enormous. Keith O. Schwab, of the Federal Water Quality Administration in Cincinnati, has data showing 12,000 miles of degraded streams from mine acid drainage in the Appalachian states. "We can ill afford to lose more streams to mining pollution," he said, "but this is exactly what is happening."

Acid mine drainage has been with us as long as we have been mining coal. It comes from deep mines and surface mines. It has long been accepted by most local people as a price they must pay for an economy which removes the coal and burns it up as quickly as possible. Progress means removing the wealth, destroying it, and leaving the land and streams permanently impoverished.

Acid mine drainage, considered one of the most vicious of industry by-products, is trivial however compared to the massive onrush of destruction caused by the incredibly rapid move to surface mining.

In surface mining heavy machinery removes the soil, including trees, grass, and everything else on the surface, to expose the coal seam beneath. In the steep hill country of Eastern Kentucky, this means pushing massive amounts of soil down the mountainside. Even the largest trees are broken and pushed over. The magnitude of the devastation is difficult to imagine for anyone who has not seen it. Man's ever accelerating technology, now rushing forward faster than the speed of thought, has designed machinery which will move 100 cubic yards of dirt with a single bite. Such

SOURCE. Reprinted, by permission of the author, from the *Sierra Club Bulletin*, Vol. 56, No. 2, February 1971, with slight abridgment.

shovels, standing as high as a 12 story building, are used around the clock, as is the smaller equipment at many of the mountain stripping sites. With profits running as high as 50 percent annual return on the dollar invested and the minimum price of Eastern Kentucky coal having doubled over a 6 month period last year, the rush is on while the getting is good. Western Sierrans who watched the timber barons' frenzied efforts to cut as many big trees as they could before Congress established a national park will understand the rape of Kentucky. As stripping grows and as people become more informed, the opposition forces encompass an ever larger segment of the public.

When rain falls upon a strip mine site massive quantities of mud wash into the streams. A study by the U.S. Forest Service in Kentucky showed streams carried as much as 46,000 ppm of suspended sediment, compared to a maximum of 150 ppm in adjacent forested watersheds. Stream bed burdens of as much as 66,500 cubic feet of sediment per square mile of watershed were observed in the stripped areas. In addition to the stream beds, the woodland flood plains were also made a muddy mess from silt. Subsequent rains not only brought down more silt but moved part of the previous loads on downstream, affecting more of our watercourses.

Bethlehem Steel Corporation has mined the high quality low sulfur coal needed for processing steel from deep mines in Eastern Kentucky for many years without arousing the displeasure of conservationists. However, their decision in 1969 to strip 40,000 acres in several counties changed them from an acceptable responsible corporation into the number one target and rallying point for the anti-stripping forces. Stripmining not only puts permanent scars on the mountainsides, but it also kills the streams, which are public property.

Silt kills streams by destroying the nature of the bed. Many aquatic invertebrates upon which fish feed live beneath stones in the gravel-covered bottom of a stream. A fine load of silt from the clay banks above glues down the stones, making them inaccessible and preventing the free movement of oxygen-carrying water among the gravel and beneath the stones.

The effect upon spawning of fish is similar. Most species of game fish lay eggs in the gravel of the stream bottom. If a fine layer of silt washes off the strip mine, spoils, and covers the eggs, they are deprived of sufficient oxygen for development and fail to hatch. Thus the stripminers rob the public of a valued resource.

Although land destruction, acid mine drainage, and silt are the best known effects of stripmining, a less known but equally dangerous factor may be the raising of the mineral ion concentration of the water affecting its usability by man and his industries. The U.S. Public Health Service sets standards for drinking water quality and the various industries have their own tolerance levels depending upon the purpose of the water they use.

The U.S. Forest Service has done studies on the effects of stripmining on water quality in Eastern Kentucky. In a report they point out that although the U.S. Public Health Service's Maximum Permissable Level for sulfates in water is 250 ppm, on severely disturbed watersheds in Eastern Kentucky they found concentrations ranging up to 2100 ppm. Whereas the tolerance level for manganese is 0.05 ppm, concentrations of up to 74 ppm were found, and for iron, whose recommended maximum level is 0.3 ppm, concentrations ranged up to 88 ppm.

Why the tremendous increase in stripmining activity? Many reasons have coalesced to result in today's frenzy.

The use of electrical power, pushed along by Madison Avenue's request that we live better electrically, has been growing at 7 percent per year, a rate which doubles consumption every 10 years. Coal is a major energy source for power generators.

DEPLETION OF NATURAL RESOURCES

Even with nuclear reactor power generators increasing at a rate that doubles their numbers every 2.4 years, with this rate expected to continue at least through 1980, the demand for power is increasing so fast that coal powered generators also are being built.

The scarcity of natural gas, which caused gas companies in the East to deny service to many new industrial customers in 1970, and the ever increasing dependency of this country on foreign oil sources, has increased the interest in coal, one resource which is still in abundant supply.

The new mine safety law has helped push operators out of deep mining into the stripmining business. Stripmining produces three times as much coal per man as an underground operation and requires less machinery and investment. It is safer for the workers and more profitable to the operators. The result has been that the strip mine has risen from 29 percent of the production 10 years ago to 36 percent today. In the steep Appalachian hills of 9 states strip mine benches now extend for 20,000 miles. Since only 4.6 billion of the estimated 108 billion tons of strippable coal have been harvested, one can see what the future holds.

As the acceleration of stripmining proceeds, attempts to regulate it are frustrated. Although Kentucky has a fairly good mining reclamation law and some honest, conscientious people in the Division of Reclamation, law enforcement has broken down. An employee of the Division told me that during the summer of 1970 permits were issued to over 100 new operators. Since anyone who can borrow enough to get a bulldozer into operation can go into business and get rich now, there is a flood of new people into stripmining. The enforcement officer said that some of these inexperienced operators could not operate within the law even if trying to do so and spills of soil onto public highways and into the streams are the result.

The business is so lucrative that an operator has been quoted as saying that if we will leave him alone for just two years he doesn't care if we outlaw stripmining, for by that time he would be rich enough to retire.

Operators are getting rich and selling out to the big corporations. The giants of oil and steel, smelling the killing at hand, have been rushing into the fray like a pack of sharks to a bleeding swimmer. The major stripmining operations are subsidiaries of such corporations as Gulf Oil, Humble Oil, U.S. Steel, and Bethlehem Steel. TVA is also heavily involved.

If you think coal mining is only a problem for Kentucky and such well known coal states as West Virginia, Pennsylvania, and Illinois, you are in for a surprise. A total of 26 states have strippable reserves of coal. We easterners will not even be in the running when the big time arrives, because the states with the largest reserves of strippable coal are North Dakota, Montana, and Wyoming. If we draw a line from Pennsylvania to the coal-laden northwestern tip of Georgia, every state west of the line except Wisconsin, Minnesota, and Hawaii has some coal deposits. With the industry's trend toward building power plants where the coal is, the destruction of parts of your state may be even now on the shallow horizon.

Stripmining as a big business has moved into Ohio. Ben A. Franklin of the *New York Times* reports that 5 billion tons of low grade fuel, long considered too marginal for mass mining, lie near the surface in Ohio, and the boom is on from Cincinnati to the east central border to recover it. In 346,000 acre Belmont County alone, 200,000 acres have been sold, leased, or optioned to the strippers. Two giant electric shovels, each 12 stories high, scoop up farms, barns, silos, churches, and roads to uncover the coal, piling the rubble into strip mine soil banks. Franklin quotes Ohio Congressman Wayne Hays, whose home is in

Belmont County, as saying "They're turning this beautiful place into a desert," but Ford Sampson, head of the Ohio Coal Association is credited with the line, "Are we going to cut off the electric power because some guy has a sentimental feeling about an acre of coal?"

Perhaps a better example of what we are up against is illustrated by the opinion of James D. Riley, a vice president of Consolidation Coal Company, who spoke to the American Mining Congress in Pittsburgh in 1969. To the thunderous applause of the assembled strip miners, Mr. Riley declared that the conservationists who demand a better job of land reclamation are "stupid idiots, socialists, and commies who don't know what they are talking about. I think it is our bounden duty to knock them down and subject them to the ridicule they deserve."

What can be done? First we must insist that Americans take their heads out of the sand and recognize the act that power demand cannot continue to rise as it has been. Nothing—whether the power demand, the production of coal, the number of people, the number of cars, or the gross national product—can continue indefinitely to rise at an exponential rate in a finite world. The sooner we face reality on this the sooner we can begin to attack the problems.

So the next time the power tycoons tell you they must double power capacity by 1980 you should reply, "Nonsense—long before 1980 we must plan and put into practice a program to level off power consumption at something like present levels or less."

Second we must have federal regulations of mining practices. Any local efforts to regulate this or any other industry encounter the standard and somewhat justified reply that regulation would put them at a disadvantage with their competitors in other states.

Dr. Robert Kuehne says that in Kentucky we could not have designed a better system to ruin the maximum number of streams in a shorter period. Instead of mining watersheds that are already destroyed until all the coal is gone, the economic system assures that we skip around in such a way as to kill all our streams in the coal country.

The Committee on Resources and Man of the National Academy of Sciences-National Research Council has pointed out that the culmination of oil production in this country is now at hand and the culmination of natural gas will arrive at the end of this decade. We are now dependent upon foreign sources for 20 percent of our oil supplies, and by the end of this decade this is expected to rise to 40-45 percent. Although coal reserves are much greater, we should not continue to treat them as the common enemy to be destroyed with all speed by the system found to be so effective in getting rid of our oil and gas.

We simply cannot afford to continue the present pattern of exploitation of the fossil fuels.

SECTION 9

TOWARD A SOLUTION

In this final section of the second part of the book there is presented a group of articles on a local, national, and international level which deal with possible solutions to the problems of environmental deterioration. In every type of arena, battle lines are drawn between forces favoring immediate economic and material gain against those forces concerned with present and future ecological effects. At the heart of the solution to the problem is the very way man thinks about himself in relation to the environment, the imponderables associated with determining what future effect within the ecosystem could stem from a present cause, the manner in which mankind has organized his socio-political systems to handle these problems, and the intensity of his determination to solve the environmental problems. These issues of human attitude, ecological cause-effect, and governmental institutions of management are the major points of emphasis in this section.

Irving Bengelsdorf makes the point that the solution is mainly a matter of attitude, not merely more technology. He says that to survive man must follow in the footsteps of nature and learn to recycle his goods and resources.

Although cause and effect within a complex ecosystem are often difficult to determine, Luna Leopold's report on the Everglades Jetport is a masterpiece because of the attempt it makes to chart specific environmental deterioration which could take place in event certain specific jetport development programs were initiated. The building of a jetport would upset natural balances existing within the Big Cypress Swamp of southern Florida's Everglades National Park and probably cause changes within the entire state of Florida as well. Although Leopold's projection pertains to a marsh-estuarine system somewhat limited in area, the same situation could be applied to a wider geographic region, sub-continent, or continent. The problem boils down to whether there is a greater public benefit through immediate financial gains that would accrue from development or from future human gains that would accrue from maintenance of the ecosystem.

205

THE DESTRUCTION OF THE ENVIRONMENT

The next article by Frank Potter, raises questions on the effectiveness of governmental institutions as presently constituted in dealing with the pollution problem. Potter makes the point that it is the government itself which will have to clean up pollution. He defines the problems involved in governmental efforts. Some of these problems concern the manner in which citizens can initially demand governmental action. Other problems concern the inertia of government itself. The absence of clear environmental policies, certain legislative practices, governmental bureaucracy, and the ineffectiveness of the courts are all factors contributing to the difficulty in arriving at a solution. He urges the adoption of stronger tools to bring about the necessary executive, legislative, and judicial reform to halt environmental pollution.

While national plans could have a great impact, pollution knows no local jurisdictional boundary lines. The earth's atmosphere and waters touch all nations. The United Nations could have a part to play in a solution to the problem. The next article tells about the reasons for a planned United Nations world conference on the environment. The final article makes an eloquent plea for the continued existence of the human animal on the planet Earth.

Irving S. Bengelsdorf

DEAR STUDENTS: OUR SPACESHIP EARTH'S IN TROUBLE; SO ARE WE

This is an open letter to all high school, college, and university students who will participate in the First National Environmental Teach-In to be held in schools from coast-to-coast during the week of April 20-25.

As you listen to speeches delivered by professors, politicians and businessmen, particularly on Earth Day, April 22, remember that they are talking about the environment in which you will spend *your* adult life.

Earth is a tiny cosmic spaceship with finite dimensions and finite resources. There are speculations that life may exist elsewhere. But, at present, our planetary home is unique; it is the only known haven of life in the universe. Our spaceship is the *only* environment we have. The maintenance of its quality is a trust for you and your children. We must stop behaving as if the word "posterity" no longer exists.

Man produces nothing; he only consumes. We are clever at making things, but the only producers on the surface of our planet are green plants. In the presence of sunlight, green plants combine carbon dioxide with water to produce food and release oxygen. And animals breathe the oxygen and eat the green plants. And men eat both the animals and the plants. So, the sun provides us with the food to eat and oxygen to breathe. No sun, no life.

Unlike industrialized man, nature abhors waste. Miserly nature runs a taut, thrifty spaceship. Everything is reclaimed and recycled. Plants and animals die and are decomposed into reusable molecules that become parts of new plants and animals. And nature recycles its water—from oceans to clouds, to rain, to rivers, and back to oceans.

Thus, to survive on our spaceship we must learn to do as nature does—to reclaim and recycle our manufactured goods and resources. We cannot continue to turn out products that are used only once and then discarded.

SOURCE. Reprinted, by permission, from the *Los Angeles Times,* April 16, 1970, with slight abridgment.

THE DESTRUCTION OF THE ENVIRONMENT

So, beware of the man who talks about "cleaning up" the environment. He does not really understand what is involved in the management of our spaceship. He talks as if all we need are a few billion dollars and a few years time and we then can sit back on our fatty acids and relax. But the environmental crisis will be with us from here on out. We must learn to become stingy, efficient stewards of our tight little planet.

And do not be upset by the intimation that your concern for the environment is "anticapitalistic." Pollution is a global problem; it respects no political boundaries or ideologies. The bulldozer knocking down trees in California or the Soviet Union is not cognizant of the political convictions of the man in the driver's seat.

And do not be misled by economic arguments. Pollution problems cannot be solved on economic terms alone. How much are two bald eagles worth, particularly if they are the last pair on earth? The American Great Lakes contain more than one-fourth of all the fresh water on the surface of our planet. All show rising levels of pollution. How much are these five lakes worth, and Lake Erie in particular?

Our spaceship naturally came equipped with the laws of biology and geology. The laws of economics are man-made. There is no natural law that says we have to burn 8 million gallons of gasoline each day in Los Angeles, or double our demand for electricity every nine years.

Listen to Dr. Georg Borgstrom, renowned population-and-food authority at Michigan State University, East Lansing: "We have almost exclusively gauged our advances by adding up only the credits. For the first time, we have to present a complete accounting with all the debits posted. Our wasteful civilization cannot be copies on a global scale. The rest of the world deserves better and more viable advice than we have given them so far. A new technology has to take shape, recognizing the laws of biology. Nature can only be governed by obeying it."

Finally, be wary of the man who claims that technology alone will solve our environmental problems. The beauty of technology is that it provides alternatives—we *can* do things differently. But, *shall* we? Solving environmental problems is mainly a matter of attitudes, not technology.

EVERGLADES JETPORT

National Parks Association has been much concerned in 1969—as have conservationists across the nation—about developments in the controversy over Dade County Port Authority's determination to build a giant jetport just north of Everglades National Park in south Florida. There was editorial comment about the threat in *National Parks Magazine* in January and July, and a special section of the July issue was devoted to graphic evidence of the enormous damage already caused in the Everglades by the construction of merely one training runway—a hint of the physical and ecological destruction that would be wrought on all south Florida by the proposed 39-square-mile commercial jetport.

The course of events surrounding this problem has moved swiftly since National Parks Association, National Audubon Society, and others assembled a coalition of some 20 national conservation, environmental, and economic organizations last spring to oppose the plan. On April 17 this Everglades Coalition signed a joint letter of protest to Secretary of Transportation John A. Volpe; on April 23 it gathered in NPA's board room for a press conference; and it met on May 14 with Assistant Secretary

of Transportation James D'Orma Braman. Subsequently, Secretary of the Interior Walter J. Hickel and Secretary of Transportation Volpe announced creation of a joint interdepartmental committee to investigate the possible environmental effects of the proposed jetport, and alternatives, before any further federal financial commitment would be made. On June 11, NPA's President Smith testified by invitation at hearings of the Senate Interior Committee on the jetport plan and on the Army Engineers' so-called Central Florida Flood Control Project.

An announcement by Secretary of Transportation Volpe of a decision agreed to in a September 10 meeting he held with Interior Secretary Hickel and Governor Claude R. Kirk Jr., of Florida, represented at least a partial victory for conservationists and a stunning setback for promoters of the jetport—a spokesman for whom had publicly waxed intemperate in remarks about the interference of butterfly-chasers and bird-watchers. "We have agreed that the Everglades National Park should not and will not be damaged," Secretary Volpe said. "We believe that a training facility which is the only thing that has been constructed can

SOURCE. Reprinted, by permission, from *National Parks and Conservation Magazine,* Vol. 43, No. 266, November, 1969, which assumes no responsibility for its distribution other than through the magazine, with slight abridgment.

—with proper safeguards—be utilized without having an adverse environmental impact on the ecology of the Everglades . . . an acceptable solution [for the full-scale jetport problem] must be found including the seeking of alternative sites."

Conservationists heartily agreed with the alternative-site idea, but many disagreed that the completed training runway (shown on the centerspread of our July issue) should be allowed to remain. NPA's President Smith and other conservation leaders called for dismantling even the training runway. A telegram sent to President Nixon, the Secretaries of Transportation and Interior, and Governor Kirk by the United Automobile Workers of America—a member of the Everglades coalition—states the case clearly and forcefully:

"The struggle to save America's beauty seemingly has few victories. This undoubtedly is one. But it would be more complete, more assured, if the jetstrip now being constructed supposedly for airline pilot training were also abandoned. That runway and the facilities that surround it would, in time, serve to encourage revival of the original huge jetport plans which would seriously damage the Everglades National Park. All scientific data on air pollution, water pollution, and noise, and the obvious hacking at our woodlands and forests cry for more attention in protecting our environment."

On September 18 an environmental research report prepared for the Joint Committee of the Departments of the Interior and Transportation was released by the Department of the Interior. The study was made by a team of environmental experts from the Interior Department and the state of Florida, headed by Dr. Luna B. Leopold, noted scientist and ecologist of the Interior Department's Geological Survey. The report documents the ecological and to some extent the social reasons why even the training strip should not be tolerated.

A few days later the Everglades Coalition met again at NPA headquarters and issued a statement calling upon federal and Florida governments to make no more funds available for the project; to eliminate the present runway and restore the environment there; and to prevent the construction of highways to the site. Further, the statement noted that assistance given to the Dade County Port Authority has been considered by competent legal authority to have been given in violation of law, and it questioned whether further assistance in the completion of the existing runway or its operation might constitute a continuing violation of law.

The Leopold report is important, projecting the controversy into some larger environmental questions; therefore we present here a summary of its findings.

For a nonecologist the following definitions may be helpful in reading the report:

ecosystem: Ecological system; a community of living organisms and its physical environment. All living organisms interact interdependently with each other and with their environment. Alteration of one element—the amount of water, say, or the decrease of a certain kind of fish or plankton on which other life forms depend for food—affects the entire system.

hydroperiod: The length of time during which a soil area is waterlogged. This period varies considerably with seasonal rainfall and other factors, and life cycles in the ecosystem are tied to this fluctuation. Drainage of any area in the Everglades would hasten the runoff of slow water flow and shorten the period of wetness.

eutrophication: Condition of rich nutrition and decreased oxygen. Increased nutrients in water stimulate growth of algae faster than it can be eaten by higher organisms. As the algae die and rot, the amount of free oxygen in the water is decreased and life forms requiring oxygen die (including certain kinds of fish), eventually the water is covered with algae as a malodorous slime, and it will support little other than anaerobic life.

TOWARD A SOLUTION

biological magnification: The concentration of substances by a food chain. Some very stable chemicals accumulate in bodies of higher organisms instead of being metabolized or excreted. In this way crustaceans may accumulate a level of DDT higher than in surrounding waters; fish eating the crustaceans and birds eating the fish in turn concentrate even higher levels.

The DDT level thus may be magnified to a dangerous point.

evapotranspiration: The portion of water returned to the air by direct evaporation and transpiration of plants. Transpiration produces the water vapor "exhaled" by plants in the process of photosynthesis. Much water is lost in this manner from standing water and its accompanying water plants.

Luna B. Leopold

LEOPOLD REPORT SUMMARY: EVERGLADES JETPORT

FINDINGS AND RECOMMENDATIONS

Development of the proposed jetport and its attendant facilities will lead to land drainage and development for agriculture, industry, housing, transportation, and services in the Big Cypress Swamp that will destroy inexorably the south Florida ecosystem and thus the Everglades National Park. There are three alternatives for future action:

1. *Proceed with staged development of training, cargo, and commercial facilities.* Regardless of efforts for land-use regulation, the result will be the destruction of the south Florida ecosystem. Estimates of lesser damage are not believed to be realistic.

2. *Proceed with final development and use of a training facility of one runway, with no expansion for additional use. Obtain an alternative site for expansion, pro-* *bably through an exchange of excess lands at the current site for public lands at a new site. Permit no new or improved surface access to the current site.* This alternative would not preclude eventual development of lands in the vicinity of the current site. It could, however, reduce pressures for development and secure time for the formation of sufficient public interest in environmental conservation to achieve effective planning and land-use regulation.

3. *An alternative site be obtained capable of handling the training operation as well as the fully developed commercial facility; and when appropriate, the training activities at the present site be abandoned and transferred to the new site.* This alternative would inhibit greatly the forces tending toward development in Big Cypress Swamp and would give an impetus to developing effective land-use controls that could lead to permanent protection of the south Florida ecosystem.

SOURCE. Reprinted, by permission, from *National Parks and Conservation Magazine,* Vol. 43, No. 266, November 1969, which assumes no responsibility for its distribution other than through the magazine, with slight abridgment.

TOWARD A SOLUTION

SUMMARY OF ENVIRONMENTAL IMPACTS

In simplified form, the following represents the views of the study group on environmental impacts of the jetport and its associated developments:

Phase 1/The Training Facility

1. The construction of each training strip will destroy about 400 acres of natural habitat of the Big Cypress Swamp.

2. No significant problems are expected from sewage, industrial wastes, or pesticides in the training phase, because they will be very limited. Air pollutants from engine exhausts will be substantial in an environment that has not been degraded previously by local activity. The effect of such pollutants on a natural aquatic system is almost entirely unknown. There may be adverse effects on the Indians. The introduction of air pollutants may increase the incidence of local fog under some weather conditions.

3. The Miccosukees will suddenly and involuntarily be subjected to round-the-clock noise levels commonly experienced by urbanites who live very near airports in many cities. There will be frequent high-level noise intrusion on the wilderness character of the northern part of Everglades National Park and even more on the Big Cypress Swamp and Conservation Area No. 3.

4. A severe bird strike problem [airplanes hitting birds] may develop within the airport boundaries, over Conservation Area No. 3, and in the quadrant southwest from the training strip. This problem would involve large water birds, including several rare and endangered species at altitudes ranging from ground to 2,000 feet. Small animals that seek refuge on the runways in flood periods will add to this problem when they are crushed and attract carrion-eating birds.

5. With sufficient culverts provided through runways, ramps, roads, and other facilities, interference with overland water flow will be negligible.

6. The combination of bird strikes, pest insect problems, and incidence of small animals on runways will probably lead to drainage of at least part of the jetport property. This is the Federal Aviation Administration recommendation in wetland areas for control of bird strikes. The Dade County Port Authority has announced no such plans but has the capability and authority to construct canals for drainage within and without the port boundary and to use eminent domain authority on exterior lands. To be effective, any drainage effort would have to cover a large area using a grid of drainage canals. Drainage canals, however, almost surely would be prohibited in Conservation Area No. 3, on which much of south Florida depends for water; birds would continue feeding there, probably in increased numbers. Drainage would materially increase the occurrence of fires.

7. Construction and imminent operation of the first training strip have elevated surrounding land prices and sales. Economic and social pressures for further development within and without the port property will mount rapidly, the one encouraging the other. Such development for housing, trade, or industry will lead inexorably to land drainage outside the jetport property. Land development and drainage will be accompanied by increased nutrients in the water, will alter the hydroperiod, and will promote eutrophication. To the extent and at the rate these changes take place, the south Florida ecosystem will be altered.

Phase 2/Cargo Handling

1. The volumes of aircraft exhaust emissions, and subsequent pollution of the surface waters, will increase according to the air traffic, the extent of which is not known to us.

The advent of heavy auto traffic will add to the air pollution load and probably will be a more important source of pollutants than aircraft.

Sewage and industrial wastes will no longer be insignificant. A large number of airport employees will be required, as well as flight maintenance operations and, possibly, some aviation-oriented industries. This situation will require the provision of full waste treatment facilities, including removal of dissolved nutrients if the ecosystem is to be protected. A system capable of treating a wide range of materials will be essential at this time, both on-port and for the surrounding area. An analysis of the possible alternative waste treatment systems will have to be made, with initial construction of some essential portion of the total treatment plan (for full development) becoming operational in the cargo phase.

If adequate treatment is not provided, then deterioration of water quality will ensue, including eutrophication and introduction of toxic materials.

With large-scale human occupation of the area, heavy use of pesticides and fertilizers, both within and without the jetport, will occur. Further increase in pesticides in the aquatic system would add to the biological magnification problems and possibly would lead to the destruction of several birds that are at the higher levels of the food chain. Extensive use of fertilizers will lead to eutrophication.

2. The numbers of flights will increase, and traffic will be in all quadrants. Noise will be a common characteristic of much of the Big Cypress Swamp, Conservation Area No. 3, the park, and all Indian lands.

3. Bird strikes will increase because of the added numbers of flights and the flight patterns being extended into all quadrants.

4. An improved highway corridor will be necessary for transport of cargo and personnel. If sufficient culverts and bridges are provided, interference with southward flow of water can be minimized. The corridor will destroy the habitat it occupies, will increase developmental pressures, and will intrude on the social and economic life of the Miccosukees.

5. In this stage, development outside the port will be vigorous. Pressures for land drainage will be administratively insurmountable. The canal systems will be decisive for the ecosystems of the Big Cypress Swamp and the western portion of the park. We know of no conventional drainage method that could simulate natural flows and prevent this. Should storage reservoirs be built, the waters they contain would be subject to such intense competition—economically and administratively—and to such high evapotranspiration losses that there would be little likelihood of maintaining the hydroperiod of the Big Cypress and of the western park.

In this phase, the adverse effects on the ecosystem of massive technological intrusion and general inability to implement plans for protection of environment will become evident. Inasmuch as the Big Cypress Swamp is actually a portion of the Everglades ecosystem, the effects of its deterioration will be reflected over a much larger area.

A given ecosystem cannot indefinitely be reduced in size and complexity and still survive. As parts are successively removed or altered, biologic balances are continually changed and the stability of the system is undermined. The degree and rate of land drainage, eutrophication, and alteration of the hydroperiod will be greater than similar changes brought about by the training facility. Thus the degree and rate of destruction of the ecosystem will be increased.

Phase 3/Full Development

1. All environmental problems will be maximum with full development. Noise levels will be excessive throughout the ecosystem. Auto traffic will be very dense along the corridor, and parking facilities for thousands of automobiles will be in use.

2. The high-speed ground transport system will be in full operation, with individual units traversing the Everglades at very frequent intervals. Thus, the roar of jet

engines will be added to the noise background at ground level, and their exhaust materials will be trailed across the landscape.

3. Sewage waste volume from the jetport would be in the order of 4 million gallons per day; industrial wastes would be about 1.5 mgd. Surrounding urban areas would increase vastly the volumes of daily wastes. Despite the availability of adequate technology, there is no precedent to indicate that legal, administrative, or social practice would in fact result in the maintenance of water control and water quality necessary for continued operation of the natural ecosystem.

4. Any resemblance of the new hydroperiod of the entire Big Cypress drainage to the present one would be accidental and incidental. Thus, the single most significant element of the natural, complex, and highly diverse environment—the hydroperiod—would be lost. The interaction of water, plants, and animals would bear little resemblance to its present condition, and the south Florida ecosystem as it presently functions would be destroyed.

5. The Miccosukee tribe will be totally absorbed in the intensive development, with virtual elimination of its social customs and way of life.

CONCLUSIONS

The construction of the airstrip for training in south Florida presents an issue in the public interest. Public interest consists of two general aspects—a monetary consideration and a nonmonetary one. The monetary or financial gains that result from development in the modern sense—urban, agricultural, and industrial—are monetary gains that redound primarily to the locality and, to some lesser extent, to the adjoining region and the nation. The public interest in the preservation of an environment is primarily nonmonetary; it is one that affects a large part of the whole society, and in a diffused way.

The south Florida problem is merely one example of an issue that sooner or later must be faced by the nation as a whole. How are the diffused but general costs to society to be balanced against the local, more direct, and usually monetary benefits to a small portion of the society? Concurrently, the society must ask itself whether the primary measure of progress will indefinitely be the degree of expansion of development, such as housing, trade, and urbanization, even at the expense of a varied and, at least in part, natural landscape.

- Some benefits to society flow from failure to develop, but this entails a cost. To reap the benefits of nondevelopment—benefits that accrue generally to a broad part of society—may often burden a small segment of society. Under such circumstances, public policy must be so stated or redefined that the inequities are redistributed. At the present time, the operation of public policy in dealing with redistribution of such equities is inconsistent and ill defined.

- The second main conclusion of this report is that the benefit to society accruing from the maintenance of an ecosystem is of a different order than that due to the preservation of a few species. The effects of the jetport and the surrounding development should not be thought of in terms of the possible elimination of some rare and endangered species such as alligator, wood stork, and others. These effects, however, can be thought of as indicators or touchstones as to what is happening to the total ecosystem. Unfortunate as it would be to lose some of these rare species, the problem is larger. Society has an interest in the functioning of an ecosystem as a whole. The substitution of a controlled state of a biologic community for a naturally functioning ecosystem leads to one or more of the following consequences: (a) More controls and increased management are necessary to keep the new unnatural system in reasonable balance; (b) unforeseen consequences are usually costly and often long continued; (c) these costs are usually borne by the public through the expenditure of tax revenue from a large part of society to compensate for unforeseen consequences of actions taken to benefit a small segment of a society.

- The third main conclusion is that ecosystem destruction in south Florida will take place through the medium of water control, through land drainage and changed rates of discharge. It will come about through decrease in quality of water both by eutrophication and by the introduction of pollutants, such as pesticides.

- The fourth main conclusion is that the training airport is intolerable, not because of its flight operations, but because the collateral effects of its use will lead inexorably to urbanization and drainage that would destroy the ecosystem. The development in the surrounding land is already beginning, as a result merely of the probability that the airport will grow in size and importance. Assuming the present types and operation of land-use controls, this development tendency will proceed uncurbed. Planning procedures and their application are presently not sufficiently uniform, sophisticated, effective, or enforceable to provide any optimism that use of the jetport for training would proceed without concomitant land development and thence by stages to destruction of the ecosystem. So long as the training airport is in use, pressures and plans for its expansion will continue and will inexorably and surely lead to ecosystem destruction completely. Elimination of the training airport will inhibit land speculation and allow time for formation of public awareness of environmental degradation—the awareness prerequisite for effective and practical action in the field of planning and land-use control.

Frank M. Potter, Jr.

EVERYONE WANTS TO SAVE THE ENVIRONMENT BUT NO ONE KNOWS QUITE WHAT TO DO

It is difficult to find a newspaper today that doesn't have at least one story on environmental problems. People who read these stories react to them and, with increasing frequency, their reaction is sympathetic. Environmental concerns are no longer the private preserve of the birdwatchers: the same bell tolls for us all.

In 1969, the National Wildlife Federation commissioned two polling organizations to investigate American attitudes on environment. The polls reached the conclusion that most people are actively concerned about environmental problems and would prefer that a greater proportion of their taxes be devoted to the costs of solving them. The level of concern here rose with income and varied inversely with age. Over fifty percent of those interviewed felt that the government was devoting insuffi-

cient attention to environmental problems and was providing insufficient funds to resolve them. Over eighty percent felt a personal concern, and most of these registered "deep concern." What, then keeps them from the barricades?

Apathy, one might think, but the surveys rule that out. The most significant inhibitor of action may be that we are too easily convinced of our own political impotence. The larger the grouping, the more difficult it is for any person to make a significant impact upon social decisions.

On the other hand, when they are really aroused, people can take and have taken effective action. For example, a coalition of citizens joined forces in 1969 to require a reluctant U.S. government to quadruple the amount of funds to be used for wastewater facilities. They did so by informing

SOURCE.   Reprinted, by permission, from *The Center Magazine,* Vol. 3, No. 2, March 1970, a publication of the Center for the Study of Democratic Institutions in Santa Barbara, California, with slight abridgment.

their elected representatives that this was a matter of specific, personal, and urgent priority; their representatives listened and responded. Again, a few years ago, a small group of citizens banded together against the largest utility in the United States, opposing plans to construct a major hydroelectric plant within fifty miles of New York City. They stopped the utility company in its tracks. That company was Consolidated Edison, the plant was the Storm King project. The Federal Power Commission, which must decide whether or not the plant should be built, has still not made its decision. The strong case made by the citizens depended in large measure on the fact that they were able to propose alternatives to the project and to support their case by a wealth of technical and engineering detail that showed New York's serious power problems could be met by less damaging methods. Although Con Edison has not yet given up the project, it has adopted the alternatives, and many sophisticated agency-watchers now consider it unlikely that the Storm King plant will ever be built.

Collective action, then, can make a difference. Individually or collectively, we are confronted with a clear option: Are we to live well only for a short period, or must we cut back economic growth in favor of long-term survival for the species? For the most part we appear to have adopted the former course of action, and it is by no means clear that we would act much differently if the choice were clearer. "*Après moi, le déluge*" is an attitude confined neither to France nor to the eighteenth century. As individuals, we tend to be somewhat ambivalent about the importance of what might be called an environmental conscience.

With very little effort, we could educate our children about the importance of environmental responsibility: yet it is the children who seem to be taking the lead in educating us. In schools and colleges across the country, there are signs that problems of pollution are occupying a rapidly in-

creasing portion of the attention of young people.

It is important to distinguish between the actions and attitudes of individuals and those of the citizen groups organized to consider environmental problems. The biggest problem faced by such groups is seldom a lack of motivation; it is financial. It is still rare for anyone whose economic interests are involved to oppose a polluter; this means that concerned citizens must themselves assume these costs, although the financial burdens of speaking out and working against a powerful and well-financed industry or government agency may be great. The costs of carrying on a major controversy may exceed five hundred thousand dollars. We cannot reasonably expect any private group to bear such a burden, nor should we as long as the group is acting to protect assets that are common and valuable to all of us.

It is important to note, though, that even concerned citizens do not always organize themselves to protect the environmental system as a whole—one group may be interested only in visual pollution while another is interested in noise. It is an unfortunate fact of life that a normal resolution of a pollution problem often means pushing it into another area which may not be so vigorously defended. For example, the public concern with power-generation facilities producing air pollution in the form of coal dust, oil droplets, and increased sulphur dioxide emissions encouraged the building of nuclear plants, which involve none of these pollutants but may well present other problems in terms of radioactive and thermal pollution of cooling water.

To look to private business for solutions to pollution may be futile. Its horizons are deliberately limited to those factors which are considered to be of immediate importance, principally economic, and the hidden costs to the society at large tend to be ignored. These costs still exist, however, and they must be borne by everyone if not by the industry which creates them. A classic example would be a pulp processing plant which emits fumes of hydrogen sulphide, causing foul air and peeling paint for miles downwind. The resulting inconvenience, possible health hazards, and certain increases in maintenance costs have not traditionally been imposed upon the agency which created them. Instead, they have been borne by our whole society, regardless of the capability or willingness of individual members to bear them.

To be sure, some private companies have taken steps to limit the anti-social consequences of their operations and have done so at considerable cost, quite beyond what they have been required to assume by law. But a voluntary approach to reducing environmental problems, it is clear, is just not good enough. For one thing, the forces of competition tend to minimize such voluntary efforts. Few men or companies, however public-spirited they may be, are prepared to expend large sums on the internalization of indirect costs. Nor can they do so without incurring the wrath of profit-seeking stockholders, who are even further removed from the environmental mischief they have indirectly created.

Polluting industries have most often resisted pressure to clean up their operations by claiming that the measures proposed are unduly prohibitive or confiscatory. Their chief means of resistance has usually involved threats to pull up stakes and move elsewhere. This last resort has been adopted infrequently, if at all, and is only likely to occur where a producer has found himself impossibly squeezed between falling profits and rising costs. It has also been alleged that these are the marginal producers whom the next strong wind will blow away in any case, so that little lasting economic damage to the area ever occurs.

The mechanics for balancing social costs against economic values, then, must be found outside the private institutions themselves, and they are—this is a major function of the government. The laissez-faire philosophy which at one time characterized the attitude of American government toward American industry won't work today. It is also apparent that the government is likely to expand its program in this area. Public attention has already been focused on air and water pollution. But there are other areas in which governmental action must be anticipated—among them, noise, solid-waste disposal, and the by-products of energy transfer are mentioned with increasing frequenty.

Governmental over-view, if impartially and reasonably imposed, need not be hostile to the private sector; it may even be in its interest, both short-termed and long-termed. The National Association of Manufacturers has never been known as a hotbed of social activists, yet members of N.A.M. operating committees have endorsed proposals for a strong federal body to oversee environmental issues. Businessmen have to breathe, too, and most of them are prepared to accommodate themselves to the ecological imperative—as long as their competitors are subject to the same rules. We cannot assume, however, that increased governmental concern will take place without some economic disruption. Marginal producers will feel the pinch most strongly, and some may not survive. Nevertheless, the important consideration is that the rules must be enforced fairly and impartially upon all parties.

It is important to bear in mind that the mass of government workers—the *Lumpenbürokratie*—marches to a drumbeat that only it can hear. Higher levels of government, presumably more responsive to broad social needs, generally find their choices so circumscribed by business-as-usual decisions farther down the line that their options are dissipated by the inertia of the machinery. This is by no means peculiar to the solution of environmental problems, though these tend to be somewhat more acute because of the high stakes involved and because the new issues do not fit easily into the existing bureaucratic patterns.

THE DESTRUCTION OF THE ENVIRONMENT

In practically every agency of government, at almost every level, strong pressures to maintain the status quo are built up. As one progresses from local to national bureaucracy the inertia increases. A random example: early in the nineteen-fifties, the Eisenhower Administration stated a strong preference for private power development as against public power, but it was not until the Kennedy Administration took office eight years later that the direction of bureaucratic thinking had changed enough to give effective support to the idea of private power. Nor could the Democrats reverse the trend.

There are also powerful personal influences that, in current bureaucratese, are "counter-productive." As one observer put it, "the paramount objective of the permanent bureaucracy is permanence." This contributes directly to the institutional resistance to change. Agency employees tend to react self-protectively. This was probably the principal roadblock encountered by Ralph Nader's "Raiders" in their government agency investigations during the past two summers. They often ran up against a bureaucratic wall which blocked the publication of several unfavorable agency reports on the controversial supersonic transport until the reports were wrenched from unwilling bureaucratic hands by actively concerned congressmen. To combat this reaction Congress passed the Freedom of Information Act, requiring disclosure of all but certain specified documents—a public law which has been honored far more in the breach than in the observance.

This problem is compounded by a frequent lack of clear policy guidance from the upper levels of government to the lower. New policies may be found in new regulations and pronunciamentos which either go unheeded or trickle down by word of mouth. This communications system serves as an efficient filter for any content that may fortuitously have crept into the public statements of the man or men at the top.

Such difficulties should not be ascribed solely to bureaucracy. The problem for bureaucrats is essentially the same as that of the private citizen: they are unable to relate everyday decisions to any specific action of the government machinery. Moreover, the results of yesterday's decisions are rarely communicated to the decision-makers as a corrective for tomorrow's programs. To be sure, there is enough feedback for everyone to know when a dam doesn't hold water (which happens), but when a dam destroys a delicate ecological balance and wreaks havoc in the local community, the mischief is rarely perceived as a genuine problem.

Still another troublesome aspect is that government agencies compete with one another. For decades, to cite an example, the Departments of the Interior and Agriculture have carried on a polite war; its prime casualties have frequently turned out to be considerations of the environment. Countless examples of this competition have been observed: timber-cutting practices on public lands and in national forests, pesticide regulation (if that is the correct term for it), dam building, and soil conservation are just a few. The same kind of competition may occasionally be found between the public and private sectors of the economy; once again, concern for the environment usually loses out.

In some respects, such competition is healthy. Occasionally, the public may even benefit from it. Several years ago, for instance, the Army Corps of Engineers conceived a plan to build a high dam on Alaska's Yukon River which would flood hundreds of thousands of acres of land in the process. The dam was successfully opposed by the Fish and Wildlife Service of the Interior Department on the ground that it would do untold damage to the wildlife in the region. The operative word here is "untold"; no one knew just how much damage would have been done and the Corps was not really interested in finding out.

There are other consequences of government competition. Although they operate with public funds, governmental agencies are under pressure to make the most of the funds they expend. The budgetary restrictions placed upon the head of a large operating government agency are no less severe than those upon the directors of a large corporation, and the body to which they report is no more aware of the importance of environmental factors than the average stockholder of American Telephone & Telegraph. This comparison ought not to be pressed, however, since while it will be difficult to improve the ecological understanding of the average citizen, it is not beyond our grasp to educate Congress.

The essential function of the Legislative Branch of government is to formulate and to review policy. In so doing, it operates under constitutional or other social restraints, and it must of necessity paint with a broad brush. Translating basic policy decisions into specific go and no-go decisions, never an easy task, is often complicated by pressures within the Executive Branch to change the policy decisions themselves. More important, policy is only as good as the information upon which it is based, and this information tends to be biased, conflicting, fragmentary, and/or out-of-date.

Consider the effect of the following factors upon the theoretical non-bias with which a congressional policy decision is supposed to be approached:

The nature of the proposal—Most legislation enacted by the Congress is originally proposed by agencies in the Executive Branch. (This, incidentally, may not be quite so common today; the legislative proposals of the present Administration have been criticized as somewhat sporadic. Many of the bills now before the Congress, however, are holdovers from earlier years, and the basic pattern seems to have changed

very little.) Support for these measures tends to be channeled well in advance of their consideration—facts are marshaled, charts are drawn up, witnesses are prepared. A frequent result of this process is that the Congress may focus on the wrong issues.

The congressional committee structure—Committees of the Congress, and especially their ranking members, are among the principal focal points of power in Washington. This apparatus determines which bills are considered, whether testimony in opposition will be considered, and if so, how it will be rebutted. Unless the issue is getting the attention of the press and the public, or unless a maverick congressman digs in his heels, those controlling the committee have a relatively free hand in developing the arguments for and against the bill; hence they control its future.

The bias of congressional leaders—The environmental crisis is a relatively new phenomenon, and the young are more concerned with the problems than their elders. This is as true in the Congress as elsewhere. The result is that many of the older members, who exercise greater control over legislative action than their younger colleagues, are less inclined to meet the new challenge. Exceptions can easily be found, but the general truth of this observation is not seriously questioned. There is, then, a bias favoring inaction. It ought not to be discounted.

The adequacy of the testimony itself—Assuming that the measure is reasonable and that the controlling committee is interested in developing the real issues, the witnesses called to testify may nonetheless not be the best available. Witnesses on environmental issues have tended to be the elder statesmen—established scientists and professionals whose views on new problems and on the need for new approaches have been colored by their own studies and viewpoints, which are frequently considerably out-of-date. A review of non-governmental scientific testimony over the past few years shows that several names pop up again and again; these individuals (who may be spectacularly well qualified in their own areas of competence) occasionally edge into areas in which they are not well qualified to speak, and they often seem to be responding to the unspoken needs of some committee members to be reassured that things are not all that bad, and somehow technology will find a way. Although not every expert witness falls into this category, it happens often enough to constitute a real problem. There is, consequently, a need to develop a base of scientific testimony available to the Congress on environmental issues and to see that younger scientists, whose factual knowledge is more current, are heard.

The context of the legislative decision— Another conflict, not at all restricted to environmental issues, faces the legislator who must decide whether to favor the good of his own constituency over national interests. Thus congressmen and senators from the West are generally inclined to favor legislative proposals to open public lands for development (mining, grazing, lumbering, oil exploration, etc.), whereas the interests of the entire country might seem to favor retaining these lands in a less exploited condition. How to measure the interests of local areas against those of society is a serious question. Resolving the conflict may be one of the most significant functions of government.

The broad nature of the authority and responsibility of the legislature may prevent it from exercising effective control over the actions of the organizations theoretically under its direction. The policies the legislators are called upon to define are so broad they cannot possibly be spelled out in detail, and yet it is in such details that the actions of government become manifest.

The legislative mechanism may also be criticized for its slow reaction time. The Congress is a highly conservative body— deliberate in adopting new courses of action, and slower to change them once they are adopted. This is, of course, a source of strength, preventing today's fad from becoming tomorrow's straitjacket. But it is also a real source of danger to the system. Science and technology have transformed the world of the mid-twentieth century into something that was quite unimaginable fifty years ago. The rate of change is accelerating, and it is a brave man who will claim that he can predict the state of the world in the year 2000. Shrill voices may decry technology and demand that there be a halt to new technological development; they are no more likely to be heeded than were the machinery-wrecking Luddites of nineteenth-century England. Whether they are right or wrong is quite beside the point; barring massive catastrophe, technology will not be significantly curbed and the rate of technological change will almost certainly continue to speed up.

New technology creates new social conventions, which in turn affect legislative policy. Yet the mechanisms for determining that policy are keyed to technological considerations that may have already been out-of-date in 1800, and to decision-making processes that have remained essentially unchanged since the days of Roger Bacon.

Consider massive changes in climate. Scientists tell us that urban development and energy transfer now have a significant effect upon global weather patterns. We hear on the one hand of the "greenhouse effect," which tends to raise atmospheric temperature as a function of increased carbon dioxide production, and on the other of increased amounts of pollution in the air, which tend to lower atmospheric temperature by decreasing the amount of solar radiation reaching the earth's surface. Some scientists, extrapolating present activities, speculate that it would take ten years to decide which is the more powerful effect, and that by then large-scale climatic changes may be irreversible. This view is by no means commonly held, but it is under serious consideration by men whose voices ought to be heard. They are not given a hearing before Congress; if they were, they might well be outnumbered ten to one by men saying, "We are not certain, we do not know, and we should take no action until we do."

Our ecological problems, then, are not the exclusive province of the Congress; they are those of the scientific community and of all of us who have an interest in human survival. There seems as yet no way to force these problems to the forefront, conjoined as they are with an historically validated precedent for doing nothing—at least not yet.

Legislators tend to focus upon institutions rather than individuals—to see the needs of the larger groups whose existence depends upon traditional thought patterns and legal fictions. A water pollution problem is perceived as that of a municipality or an oil company, an air pollution problem as that of a manufacturer. Yet it is individual citizens whose favor the legislator must seek if he is to survive. This suggests in turn that if individuals can organize themselves to be heard as an institution concerned with environmental survival the legislators will respond. This has not yet happened generally. No significant environmental lobby has yet made its voice heard on the national level.

The courts exist to see that the written and unwritten rules of society are followed; that the policies formed by the people and their elected representatives are observed. Within narrow limits, the courts have been successful in this function. As a means of achieving rational decisions on environmental issues, however, the courts are usually ineffective. Their influence could increase, but this would require a significant departure from the usual legalistic approach. It would involve the recognition of a basic and inalienable human right to a livable environment. Such a decision appears to be a remote possibility. Without this new constitutional approach, the courts will almost certainly be hamstrung by inadequate policies adopted by the legislature and by common-law rights which were defined centuries before the current environmental problems appeared.

Only in rare instances can the courts make decisions with more than local force and effect. The U.S. Court in southern New York may properly hold that the federal Department of Transportation must observe certain procedures specified by statute that may have escaped the Department's notice, and for this reason a highway shall not be built over the Hudson River. At the same time, the same Department favors the construction of longer runways into the Columbia River. Technically, the decision of the New York court is not binding in Oregon; the Oregon courts are free to disagree with their East Coast brethren and such disagreements are in no way uncommon. A means does exist for resolving interjudicial disputes—the Supreme Court of the United States. The Court, however, is already operating under a fearful load and can devote only a limited amount of its energies to environmental questions, however important they may appear to be.

The courts also lack the information upon which to base their decisions. The common-law system is grounded upon the adversary system, the theory being that each side will present the most favorable case it can and that the court will then resolve the dispute on the basis of the evidence before it. The environmental problems arising today are very complex—very different from the land disputes and tort actions of centuries ago. In theory, expert testimony ought to be available to both sides to support their cases; in practice, this simply does not work. Even if environmentalists can afford to hire experts (and often they cannot), experts cannot always be found. It is a rare electrical engineer who will agree to take the witness stand on behalf of opponents to a power plant or transmission line; he knows that other utilities may thereafter hesitate to contract with him for services even in circumstances that may be wholly unrelated to the present controversy. Conscientious men do exist and some may be found to testify, but it is not easy to find them. Cases have been lost and will continue to be lost for this reason alone. Without that interplay of expert testimony, the court is at a major disadvantage.

Even if experts can be found by all parties, the court's information problems are not thereby solved. Technical questions are already difficult, and they are growing more complex every day. Judges spring from different backgrounds, but the law operates according to the theory that their experience is essentially irrelevant to the issues that they must decide. Historically, ignorance has been a prime virtue, the court acting as the *tabula rasa* upon which the cases of the opposing parties may be written. This is a manifest absurdity, but it is the way the law grew, and it is a fact that lawyers with weak technical cases prefer judges with little technical competence.

Another weakness built into the judicial system is its tendency to delay decision. Combined judicial and administrative delays have postponed the Storm King decision by five years already. If the parties fight down to the wire, a longer delay is likely. In many respects this delay has worked in favor of the conservation group, but this happy state of affairs is not the rule. Citizens opposed to a particular proposal or project are usually forced to seek injunctive relief from the courts; they may and often do find that this relief cannot be obtained without their posting a substantial bond which is quite beyond their means. The result is that while they work their way through the courts, the opposition is busily building or digging or chopping down. By the time that the court is ready to decide, the essential question has become moot. Injunctive relief is typically the only possible hope for environmentalists, since the alternative is a damage suit, and it is a basic tenet of such organizations that money cannot replace what is threatened.

Constitutional revision has been proposed as a means of providing a clearer and more enforceable definition of our rights to a satisfactory environment. New York State has adopted such a program, and similar efforts have been mounted on a national level. An Environmental Bill of Rights would indeed be a valuable tool, but no such proposal has a chance of even being seriously considered without vastly increased pressure upon the Congress and upon the legislatures of the several states.

Pollution will be inevitable until we can develop adequate tools for dealing with it. The government will never do the job by itself. The solution seems to lie, rather, in putting stronger weapons into the hands of the people—helping it to bring about the necessary reforms through legislative and judicial channels.

A WORLD CONFERENCE ON THE ENVIRONMENT

That life on earth, all of it, and certainly human life, may be entering upon a sickness unto death, unless resolute curative action be taken soon, is the burden of the recent report of the Secretary General of the United Nations on the projected environmental conference authorized by the General Assembly for 1972.

The decision of the Assembly last year to convoke the gathering came none too soon. The invitation by Sweden to hold the sessions in that country has coincided with a commendable decision by the Swedish Government to outlaw DDT. The report of the Secretary General, his advisory group, and his staff is a masterly statement of the peril in which we find ourselves and the first steps which must be taken.

Few of the facts which have been marshaled in the document are new, but seldom have they been compressed so briefly into a single statement.

Biocides are being poured into the earth's waters, mainly, but by no means without parallel, in the United States, and they may have the effect of reducing photo-synthesis in marine algae by as much as 75%. This means a possibly catastrophic reduction in the production of oxygen for the replenishment of the atmosphere.

There has been a 10% increase in the proportion of carbon dioxide in the earth's atmosphere in the last 100 years, with a possible rise to 25% by the year 2000. Because this gas traps the heat of the sun by what is known as the greenhouse effect, temperatures can be expected to rise ineluctably, with possible disastrous effects on weather, and thus on crops.

Offsetting such events in some measure, but precariously, and bringing other dangers, is the increase of particulate matter in the atmosphere from urban-industrial processes, which may entail cooling sequences.

Contributing to the danger of reduced oxygen supply has been the destruction of the world's forests. Two-thirds of the world's forest lands are said to have been lost for the production of timber. Can this trend be reversed and the forests of the earth restored?

SOURCE. Reprinted, by permission, from *National Parks and Conservation Magazine,* Vol. 43, No. 262, p. 2, August 1969, which assumes no responsibility for its distribution other than through the magazine.

THE DESTRUCTION OF THE ENVIRONMENT

The soil situation is perilous. Well over a billion acres of arable land have already been lost through erosion and salination at a time when worldwide famine impends; such a statement speaks for itself in terms of human misery.

While the dangers of the biocides are stressed in the report, and the fundamental problem of overpopulation is touched upon, the mortal nature of the complex of issues which centers here may not have been sufficiently stressed. Many human societies are caught in an expansion of population at a rate faster than the capital growth which might otherwise provide the means of survival.

A short-circuit, bypassing industrialization in the developing countries in favor of accelerated agricultural production, might conceivably save the day temporarily until populations can be stabilized. But accelerated agricultural production depends on more mechanization, new crops, more pesticides, and more fertilizers. The use of both pesticides and fertilizers (phosphorus as a pollutant, nitrogen as a food poison) may have to be very severely curtailed if they are not to become the ultimate agents of death. This is a grim dilemma.

The ecological structure of life on earth, including man, has already been seriously impoverished by the extinction of more than 150 species of birds and other animals, and the impending loss of perhaps 1000 more. The resilience of the biosphere, its ability to adapt to new climatological and ecological shocks, is reduced every time any creature is lost; the organic underpinnings of life are weakened; for man, the esthetic and scientific losses in terms of beauty and knowledge are irreparable.

For perhaps the first time in a major public document the report notes that the developing and the developed countries are caught together in a trap called urbanization. This process does not create cities in a cultural, nor even in an efficient economic sense; it gathers conglomerates which are largely uninhabitable.

The environmental crisis is as broad as human society; the industrial countries cannot hope to escape it. Smothering by air pollution, poisoning by water pollution, psychic trauma by urban congestion, these enemies respect no boundaries.

Irresponsible acts like the disposal of radioactive wastes and the proposed dumping of nerve gases into oceans must cease. The agencies of the United Nations which wrestle with environmental problems in the future will necessarily have to engage in serious dialogue with the military operators in all countries; whether environmental pollution or nuclear war becomes the greater menace may be in question; in any event, the problems are closely related.

The financing of the proposed conference will be difficult. We trust that both private and public money will be forthcoming. The conference itself must face the issue of the long-range fiscal measures required for effective United Nations action. There will be strong arguments for shifting money from military to environmental activity. The challenge of environmental survival may offer a moral equivalent of war.

The problems, the conference, the possibility of worldwide action, present an alluring potential for the development of international law. Each time a new convention is proposed and accepted, or a new agency of the United Nations is created to deal with environmental issues, an addition will have been made to the network of worldwide institutions which moves in the direction of representative world government under law.

NEEDED: A REBIRTH OF COMMUNITY

Man has had his Age of Exploration, and proved himself a master at discovering the riches of his planet. He has moved on to an Age of Exploitation, and demonstrated great skill in putting those riches to use. Now the time is long overdue for an Age of Conservation to begin, and so far man has shown little talent for replenishment.

The habits that must be re-formed, the attitudes that must be reshaped are so deeply ingrained that the entire task might be given up as hopeless if it were not so urgent. Perhaps, as some fear, it will take a major disaster to shock mankind into mending its ways. The human animal is the most adaptable of creatures, and the challenge of preserving his environment may well be his greatest test.

Somehow industry and consumers alike must be persuaded that their present binge of expansion and accumulation is a ruinous mistake. It is difficult to see this being accomplished without accepting some fairly important modifications of the American traditions of free enterprise and free choice. In a nation that has just managed, after 43 years, to reduce from 27-1/2 percent to 22 percent its oil depletion allowance, a government subsidy that actually encourages exhaustion of nature's petroleum supplies, these changes are not going to proceed easily.

Nor will it be easy to restrain the impulse for industrial growth when, in the world as a whole, there is a host of less-developed countries clamoring for what they see as the blessings of industrialization, and when—in the United States—there are millions of poverty-stricken citizens whose main hope for relief under the present system lies in business expansion. The dilemma is neatly illustrated by a controversy currently raging in the Atlantic resort town of Hilton Head, S.C. Local citizens, fishing interests and resort developers are up in arms against a German company that plans to construct a $123 million dye and chemical complex on the coast. But the new plants would offer desperately needed jobs to hundreds of the county's unskilled blacks.

The battle against pollution must also overcome the jurisdictional boundary lines that carve the planet into separate sover-

SOURCE. Reprinted, by permission, from *Newsweek,* January 26, 1970, copyright Newsweek, Inc., 1970, with slight abridgment.

eignties. It does a city little good to pass strict water-pollution laws if another city upstream runs its sewers into the river. No state can legislate against the dirty air that drifts from its neighbor. A nation's laws for the conservation of ocean fisheries are useless if other nations practice no such restraint. Any rational approach to a worldwide affliction such as pollution requires that national and local rivalries be put aside.

That, of course, is really the fundamental lesson that ecologists would have us learn: that people cannot seal themselves up as individuals or nations or species—like it or not, they depend on each other and on other creatures and things. What is needed, the ecologists suggest, is a rebirth of community spirit, not only among men but among all of nature. "We can change our ways," says Rockefeller University's noted microbiologist René Dubos, "only if we adopt a new social ethic—almost a new social religion. Whatever form this religion takes, it will have to be based on harmony with nature as well as man, instead of the drive for mastery." There was a glimpse of this new ethic, perhaps, and of man's predicament at last summer's Woodstock music festival. The overcrowding was horrendous. Food and sanitary facilities were scarce. The weather was terrible. "If we're going to make it," someone told the crowd, "you'd better remember that the guy next to you is your brother."

And not only the guy next to you, but the guy in the next century, too. Many of man's depredations upon the environment amount to what conservationist David Brower calls "grand larceny against the future." As veteran ecologist Eugene P. Odum points out, "the American creed is get rich today and to hell with tomorrow." In order to rescue the environment, man must learn to consider time in longer stretches. He will have to perceive disasters that do not occur with dramatic suddenness—the tiny increments of waste that gradually overwhelm a river's powers of self-cleansing, for example—and he must grow accustomed to undertaking cures that will show no results until after his lifetime.

These obstacles to reform—man's traditional notions of growth, sovereignty, individualism and time—are formidable in themselves, but all of them might be overcome if it could be persuasively demonstrated that man's survival is at stake. The trouble is that despite all the cries of the ecological doom-sayers, it cannot. Perhaps the greatest obstacle to rescue of the environment is man's own uncanny adaptability. "Modern man," as Dubos notes ruefully, "can adjust to environmental pollution, intense crowding, deficient or excessive diet, as well as to monotonous and ugly surroundings." And these adjustments are reinforced by the process of natural selection; so that the human beings who take most readily to regimentation, overcrowding, and esthetic privation rise to positions of leadership and also outbreed their less adaptable fellows. The real specter that pollution casts over man's future is not, perhaps, the extinction of *Homo sapiens* but his mutation into some human equivalent of the carp now lurking in Lake Erie's fetid depths, living off poison.

PART 3

EDUCATIONAL IMPLICATIONS:

an action program for school, classroom, and field

SECTION 1

THE NATURE OF
ENVIRONMENTAL
EDUCATION

We as teachers already have preconceptions of the nature of environmental education. Many are those who are making some effort in this direction. What we are battling is, however, a truculent, intransigent enemy—ourselves. The processes of rampant technology, land development, irrational consumerism, and indifference toward destruction of nature have been long cultivated, so that the educational process must indeed depend upon more than good intentions.

A major source of hope is our youth. One can hope that they will respond in coming generations to transform technological impact and assorted other ills, achieving ultimately a reasonable balance between man and nature. The inheritance of teeming cities, polluted air and water, refuse-filled streets, clogged highways, littered national parks, and so on, must be improved, and education will make a necessary contribution.

The young, or anyone else, cannot act wisely without knowledge, thus they need the facts and concepts related to topics like ecology, environmental law, economics, specific polluting industries, environmental medicine, meteorology, geochemistry, urban planning, architecture, and so on. Obviously the process of environmental education will be far more specialized (with exceptions) at the college and university levels. The effect of pre-college environmental education will be at least as important, because the minds and habits of the multitudes are molded in these early years.

We as teachers have a deeper obligation than transmission of knowledge, important as that is, and that is the development of values, habits, and problem-solving skills which will really make a long range difference. The articles in this section begin the job of spelling out the nature of the kind of education we need in order to survive. It is as clear and inevitable as that—education for survival is what we must be about.

THE NATURE OF ENVIRONMENTAL EDUCATION

William Stapp, in the first article, precisely outlines a definition of environmental education, together with a strategy for development and implementation of a K-12 curriculum. Le Von Balzer, in the second article. "Environmental Education in the K-12 Span," provides a model for the kinds of cognitive, affective, and process components needed in the complete curriculum. The author presents many topical areas within which specific performance objectives could be developed.

The third article by Irwin Slesnick involves some ideas for teaching about population. The need for this type of education is obvious. The reader is also referred to the discussion of the Population Curriculum Study in Section 5.

In an article on in-service teacher training, William Stapp presents a set of excellent suggestions as to what such a program ought to contain. There are specific criteria for use in the design of future teacher training programs.

Carl Berger stresses the importance of discovery learning in ecological education. It is most interesting that Berger believes that children can learn how to "think" and make decisions about specific issues like DDT (and probably the SST, ABM, etc.), while Balzer seems to prefer training in facts and values in the elementary grades. All authorities agree that there are skills related to critical thinking that elementary level students can develop. Therefore, there is definite value in following through on Berger's suggestions.

Finally, since the passage of the Environmental Education Act of 1970, the U.S. Office of Education became vigorously involved. The last article is an excerpt from a USOE bulletin entitled, "Environmental Education: Education That Cannot Wait." Note the emphasis on community involvement.

William B. Stapp

ENVIRONMENTAL ENCOUNTERS

Today's youth in elementary and secondary schools will soon be assuming important roles as adult citizens in society. As citizens and voters, no matter what their occupations may be, they will be asked to make decisions that will affect not only the immediate environment in which they live, but also that of their country. To an increasing extent the votes they will cast and the choices they will make will be concerned with their environment. They will be asked to make social and economic decisions about recreation, transportation, beautification, water needs, and air and water pollution control. Since these issues affect the total environment in which we live, we must assist our young people (and adults) to acquire the experiences, knowledge, and concern necessary for making informed environmental decisions.

In our political system we depend upon the wisdom of individuals of the populace for making decisions. A major responsibility for assisting future citizens to obtain the knowledge and incentive necessary to make informed decisions has been delegated to school systems. Since environmental education is essential to our type of political system, it is important for the public to ask if school systems are effectively fulfilling their responsibility to society.

One of the most important challenges of education today is to develop an effective method of implementing environmental education into elementary and secondary school systems.

A STRATEGY OF CURRICULUM DEVELOPMENT

If individuals are to be prepared to make the kind of environmental decisions that our nation will face in the future, schools must embark on a comprehensive environmental education program that will span the curriculum—kindergarten through the twelfth grade—and link subject areas that relate most closely to the environment.

The information that follows reflects the author's 8 years of experience in serving as conservation consultant with the Ann Arbor Public School System; a graduate seminar[1] in environmental education,

1. The members of the seminar were: Donald Austin, Marion Baker, William Bryan, Ellen Jackson, Katherine Lien, Jean MacGregor, Paul Nowak, Cynthia Russell, Sara Segal, James Swan, and Professor William Stapp.

SOURCE. Reprinted, by permission, from the *Journal of Environmental Education,* Vol. 2, No. 1, Fall 1970, with slight abridgment.

THE NATURE OF ENVIRONMENTAL EDUCATION

School of Natural Resources, The University of Michigan; and a comprehensive review of the literature.

A school system (K-12) that is interested in developing an *environmental education program* might consider the following strategy:

Phase I: Identify the *need* for developing the program

Phase II: Establish an environmental education *committee* to develop and implement the program and to facilitate communication

Phase III: Establish the *goal* and *subgoals* of the program

Phase IV: Establish the *objectives* (in terms of behavioral predispositions) of the program

Phase V: Review of the literature regarding *theories of learning and instruction* that apply to the formulation and implementation of the program.

Phase VI: Establish the *curriculum organization* of the program

Phase VII: Establish the *curriculum* of the program

Phase VIII: Establish a comprehensive in-service *teacher education program*

Phase IX: Develop instruments to *evaluate* the effectiveness of the program

Phase I: The Need for Developing an Environmental Education Program

Within the past 50 years, the United States has become a predominantly urban nation, both in thought and in physical character. Large and middle-sized communities, many within complex urban regions, have evolved to where over 70 percent of this country's population resides on 1-1/2 percent of the nation's land surface. By 1980, eight out of ten Americans will probably live in an urban environment. Consequently, the independent rural-oriented living that once characterized this country's social and political heritage is no longer a dominating influence in the lives of most Americans.

In rural surroundings, direct daily contact with the basic natural resources was prevalent, especially within man's immediate environment. As man became progressively urbanized, his intimate association and interaction with natural resources diminished, and with it his awareness of his dependency on them. Yet, it is imperative that man, wherever he lives, comprehend that his welfare is dependent upon the "proper" management and use of these resources.

Man should also have an awareness and understanding of his community and its associated problems. Our communities are being plagued with problems such as lack of comprehensive environmental planning, indiscriminate use of pesticides; community blight; air and water pollution, traffic congestion; and the lack of institutional arrangements needed to cope effectively with environmental problems. While these problems are legitimate concerns of community governmental officials and planners, the responsibility for their solution rests, to a large extent, with citizens.

To an increasing extent citizens are being asked to make decisions that affect (directly and indirectly) their environment. Specifically, citizens make these decisions as they *cast* votes on community issues; as they *elect* representatives to policy-making bodies; as they directly act upon the environment itself. Citizens can be effective in influencing sound policy in other ways. They can ask informed questions, at the proper time, of the right people. They can serve on advisory and policy-making committees. They can support sound legislation directed at resolving environmental problems. To perform these tasks effectively, it is vital that the citizenry be knowledgeable concerning their biophysical environment and associated problems, aware of how they can help solve these problems, and motivated to work toward effective solutions.

The Supreme Court decision regarding the one-man, one-vote concept, that has enabled the increasing urban majority to ac-

233

quire greater powers in decision-making, makes it imperative that programs developed for urbanites be *designed with them in mind*. It is important to assist each individual, whether urbanite or ruralite, to obtain a fuller understanding of the environment, problems that confront it, the interrelationship between the community and surrounding land, and opportunities for the individual to be effective in working toward the solution of environmental problems.

Most current programs in conservation education are oriented primarily to basic resources; they do not focus on the community environment and its associated problems. Furthermore, few programs emphasize the role of the citizen in working, both individually and collectively, toward the solution of problems that affect our well being. There is a vital need for an educational approach that effectively educates man regarding his relationship to the total environment.

Phase II: Establish an Environmental Education Committee to Develop and Implement the Program and to Facilitate Communication

An essential component of most successful school programs is effective communication between the community and school system. The introduction of any new school program requires the involvement and preparation of the community, administration, teaching staff, and student. One reason many well-conceived programs have failed is because teachers and students were not involved in program development.

In developing an environmental education program, it is important that an environmental education committee[2] be formed to develop and implement the program and to facilitate communication

between the community and the school system. The committee should consist of elementary teachers (representing each grade level), secondary teachers (representing each discipline), school administrators, community citizens, and students. The environmental education committee should report to the superintendent of schools (or to an individual or committee designated by the superintendent).

In developing an environmental education program for a school system, it is strongly recommended that an environmental education consultant *position* be created. The environmental education consultant[3] could provide the leadership and guidance essential to the success of any program. One of the major responsibilities of the environmental education consultant would be to assist in the development and implementation of the in-service teacher education program.

Some important duties of the environment education committee (or committees) would be to:

. . . Assist in the development of the philosophy and structure of the program.

. . . Become familiar with the existing instructional material relevant to environmental education.

. . . Identify community resources, both physical and human, to serve the program.

. . . Assist in the development and distribution of instructional material (such as environmental encounters).

. . . Provide a comprehensive in-service teacher education program.

. . . Train community citizens to serve the program.

. . . Assist in the development of school sites to serve the program.

. . . Administer the program.

. . . Make presentations to parent-teacher and other community organizations regarding the program.

---

2. It should be recognized that part of the responsibility for developing and implementing an environmental education program might be assigned to an existing instructional committee.

3. The environmental education consultant could serve as chairman of the environmental education committee.

. . . Evaluate the effectiveness of the program in achieving stated objectives

Phase III: Establish the Goals[4] and Sub-Goals of the Environmental Education Program

Without a clear statement of goals, an environmental education program would become a series of unrelated experiences, focusing perhaps on limited program objectives. The goal of environmental education is to produce a citizenry that is knowledgeable concerning the biophysical environment and its associated problems, aware of *how* to help solve these problems, and motivated to work toward their solution.

The major sub-goals of environmental education are to help individuals acquire:

1. A clear understanding that man is an inseparable part of a system, consisting of man, culture, and the biophysical environment, and that man has the ability to alter the interrelationships of this system.

2. A broad understanding of the biophysical environment, both natural and man-made, and its role in contemporary society.

3. A fundamental understanding of the biophysical environmental problems confronting man, how to help solve these problems, and the responsibility of citizens and government to work toward their solution.

4. Attitudes of concern for the quality of the biophysical environment which will motivate citizens to participate in biophysical environmental problem-solving.

Phase IV: Establish the Objectives[4] (in terms of behavioral predispositions) for an Environmental Education Program

There are various ways to state the expected and desired outcomes of an en-

vironmental education program. Perhaps the most significant and dynamic approach is to state them in terms of behavioral predispositions. In other words, the product of an environmental education program (K-12) should be a citizen who is:

1. Interested in his environment and its relationship to society.

2. Sensitive (total awareness) to his environment, both natural and man-made aspects of it.

3. Sensitive to the dimension of quality of his environment and able to recognize environmental problems.

4. Inclined to participate in coping with environmental problems.

Phase V: Review of the Literature Regarding Theories of Learning[5] and Instruction that Apply to the Formulation and Implementation of an Environmental Education Program.

A recent review of the literature reveals the following points that should be considered in the formulation of an environmental education program:

. . . Behaviors which are reinforced are most likely to recur. It is important that desired behaviors be reinforced by the home, school, church, youth organizations, etc.

. . . The most effective effort is put forth by youth when they try tasks which fall in the "range of challenge"—not too easy and not too hard—where success seems likely but not certain.

. . . Youth are more likely to throw themselves wholeheartedly into any project if they themselves have a meaningful role in the selection and planning of the enterprise.

. . . Reaction to excessive direction of the teacher is likely to be: apathetic con-

---

4. The local environmental education committee might consider the goals and sub-goals expressed in the following phase.

5. The local environmental education committee might consider the theories of learning and instruction expressed in the following section (these are not unique to environmental education).

formity; defiance; escape from the whole affair.

. . . What is learned is most likely to be available for use if it is learned in a situation much like that in which it is to be used and immediately preceding the time when it is needed. Learning in youth, then forgetting, and then relearning when need arises is not an efficient procedure.

. . . The learning process in school ought to involve dynamic methods of inquiry.

. . . Research shows little correlation between cognitive achievement and concern and values. Able students who achieve well in traditional "content-centered courses" do not necessarily demonstrate commitment to positive social goals.

. . . Learning takes place through the active behavior of the student. It is what he does that he learns, not what the teacher does. The essential means of an education are the experiences provided, not the things to which the student is merely exposed.

. . . One of the keys to motivation is a sense of excitement about discovering for one's self, rather than having a generalization presented by a teacher and requiring a student to prove it.

. . . Attitudes may not be formed through a rational process by which facts are gathered and a reasonable conclusion drawn, but rather through the repeated exposure to ideas.

. . . Helping citizens to acquire technical knowledge alone regarding an environmental problem, may not increase their concern for the problem.

. . . Citizens are more likely to become involved in environmental issues if they are aware of how they can have some effect upon decision-making.

Phase VI: Establish the Curriculum Organization[6] of the Environmental Education Program

6. The local environmental education committee might consider thoughts on curriculum organization expressed in this section.

An important criticism of our public school system is the lack of adequate articulation between the various divisions of the school organization. Instead of a well-developed series of instructional units and activities commencing at the kindergarten level and terminating at the twelfth grade, many school systems present a series of units that have little relationship between what has previously been taught and what will be taught in future years. The K-12 approach seems to be the most sound way to plan a curriculum for environmental education.

It is also important to plan curriculum projects horizontally as well as vertically. Disciplines, such as science and social studies, should not be studied in isolation. A curriculum should be planned so that students can see the contributions of interdisciplinary studies in assisting the learner to better understand the environment and to be more effective in solving environmental problems.

Furthermore, a curriculum program should recognize individual differences. There is no sequence that will meet the needs of all groups of youth. Therefore, a curriculum program should be flexible in design so that material can be presented in different ways depending on the background, needs, and aspirations of the students.

A set of guiding principles that should be considered when structuring an environmental education program are:

. . . Span the curriculum, kindergarten through the twelfth grade, so that environmental experiences can be presented at every grade level, thereby capitalizing on the cumulative effects of the program.

. . . Link subject areas that relate most closely to the environment, especially science and social studies, so that both the social and scientific knowledge important in understanding and solving environmental problems are properly developed.

. . . Integrate and correlate the program with the existing curriculum in a manner that will enhance the instructional goals of the school system.

. . . Focus on the local environment, but do not neglect regional, national, and international environmental issues.

. . . Stress attitudes and problem solving skills. The most important environmental impact that most of our urban citizens will have upon our environment is through their action as community citizens.

. . . The learner should play an active role in the learning process. The learner develops attitudes through personal experiences and thinking and not through the presentation of predigested conclusions.

. . . Provide a comprehensive in-service teacher education program which would operate throughout the school year and which is directed at assisting teachers to increase their understanding, interest, awareness, and teaching skills in environmental affairs and to involve them in curriculum development.

Phase VII: Establish the Curriculum[7] of the Environmental Education Program

In establishing an environmental education program for a school system (K-12), consideration should be given to the development of a series of *environmental encounters*. The encounters should focus the attention of elementary and secondary youth on their environment and in a manner that would link relevant ecological, economic, social, technological, and political information.

The environmental encounters could be designed to provide the learner with meaningful environmental experiences at each grade level, both elementary and secondary. The encounters could be used to enhance and extend an existing instructional program or to serve as the core of a comprehensive environmental education program.

7. The local environmental education committee might consider *environmental encounters* as an integral part of their program.

Environmental encounters would provide the flexibility that a program needs to meet varying local environmental conditions and situations, as well as individual class needs.

Some examples of topics that the environmental encounters might focus upon, are: land resources, water resources, air resources, plant resources, animal resources, environmental design, environmental planning, transportation, solid waste disposal, and recreation. The class could select with the teacher environmental encounters to extend an existing class unit or to serve as the central thrust of a major teaching unit.

In developing environmental encounters, the following guidelines are recommended:

. . . At each grade level the learner should be exposed to *meaningful* environmental encounters that relate relevant ecological, economic, political, technological, and social information. However, greater emphasis in the earlier grades should be toward developing in youth an interest, awareness, understanding and respect for the environment, and in the latter years emphasis should be on "honing" problem solving skills.

. . . Environmental encounters should provide the opportunity at each grade level for the learner to become personally involved in positive action toward the solution of environmental problems in which he has been exposed.

. . . The learner should play a major role in both selecting and designing environmental encounters.

. . . Environmental encounters should fall in the range of challenge—not too easy and not too hard.

. . . Environmental encounters should involve dynamic methods of inquiry.

. . . Environmental encounters that relate to environmental problems should expose the learner to the following problem solving procedure: (1) Define the environmental problem or issue. (2) Become informed about the problem. (3) State the alternative solutions. (4) Develop a plan of action. (5) Implement the plan of action.

Every environmental encounter should contain a list of the outcomes that are desired. The outcomes desired should be expressed as *behavioral objectives*. They (behavioral objectives) provide: direction for the learning process; guidance in selecting content and experiences; greater focus on the learner—what the learner does; and the opportunity to appraise (evaluate) the effectiveness of a particular learning experience and of the total program. Behavioral objectives can be stated at different levels of complexity and in the cognitive (knowledge), affective (concern), and action domains.

An *example* of an environmental encounter recommended for a sixth grade class, is as follows:

INVESTIGATING A POND COMMUNITY

"An Environmental Encounter
for a Sixth Grade Class"

Behavioral Objectives:

In the completion of a successful encounter, the student should be able to:

1. Draw an accurate map of the drainage area of the pond community.
2. Describe in writing four ways that the land in the drainage areas affects the pond community.
3. Draw two (2) food chains illustrating organisms observed in the pond community.
4. List (*number*) major problems affecting the pond community.
5. Describe in writing the major steps in solving one (1) of the problems noted in question 4.

Activity:

1. What is the bottom of the pond community like? How does the type of bottom affect the kinds of plants and animals found in the pond community?
2. As you look from the center of the pond community toward the shore, are there plants growing under water, on the surface, and out of the water? Why are plants important to the pond community?
3. Dip a small jar into the pond and note if there are small organisms (these are probably plankton organisms). Why is plankton important to the pond community? What would cause plankton to increase or decrease?
4. Make or obtain a dip net and sample around the edge of the pond community. How are the animals you have caught important to the pond community? Draw a food chain linking some of the plants and animals you have noted in and around the pond community.
5. On a map of your community color in the land area that drains toward the pond. How has the use of this land changed over the past 15 years? What changes are occurring at the present time? How does the use of this land affect the pond community?
6. Do both children and adults visit the pond community? What do people do when they visit the pond community?
7. Do you see any problems that are affecting the pond community? Who is responsible for creating the problems? What could your class do to help solve one of the problems noted above (define the problem, become informed about the problem, state alternative solutions, develop a plan of action, implement the plan)? Is your class motivated and concerned about *one* of the problems to the degree that they desire to work toward its solution?

An example of an environmental encounter recommended for a high school *American Government* class, is as follows:

FLOOD PLAIN ZONING

"An Environmental Encounter for an
American Government Class"

Behavioral Objectives:

In the completion of a successful encounter, the student should be able to:

1. Draw *on* a map of his community the flood plains (50 year flood line) of the   (name)   River from   (location)   to   (location)   and record accurately how each flood plain is developed.

2. Describe in writing the number of floods and flood damage that has occurred on the flood plains of the   (name)   River from   (location)   to   (location)   over the past 60 years (or over the time that records have been filed).

3. Describe in writing the major provisions in the laws of his state and community regarding flood plain zoning.

4. Identify the power structure (pressure groups, governmental committees, governmental policy makers) of his community regarding who influences and makes policy on flood plain development and zoning.

Activities:

1. Take a tour (or illustrate by slides) along the   (name)   River from   (location)   to   (location)   and note the following:

   a. Are there a series of flood plains?

   b. How are the flood plains developed?

   c. Are there homes or buildings on the flood plain? Are they flood proofed?

   d. Are there provisions for protecting the flood plains from flooding?

   e. What trends regarding land development are occurring on the flood plains of your community?

2. Seek information from reliable sources regarding the flood plains of the   (name)   River from   (location)   to   (location) :

   a. Has flooding of the flood plains occurred during the past 60 years?

   b. List the years in which flooding has occurred.

   c. Approximately how much damage (dollars, lives, inconveniences) has occurred on the flood plains as a result of flooding over the past 60 years?

   d. What does your *state* flood plain ordinance say? If none exists, is it considering an ordinance?

   e. What does your *community* flood plain ordinance say? If none exists, is it considering such an ordinance?

   f. How is the undeveloped land on the flood plain zoned?

   g. Are there any current proposals to utilize the undeveloped flood plains of your river for recreational, residential, commercial, or industrial development?

   h. What proposals seem wise or unwise in light of the hazards you have identified?

3. Draw *on* a map of your community the flood plains (50 year flood line) of the   (name)   River from   (location)   to   (location)   and record how each flood plain is developed.

4. Determine by interviews the points of view of land developers, community citizens, realtors, chamber of commerce officials, planning commission members, city council members, and students of your class regarding the future development of the flood plains of the   (name)   River from   (location)   to   (location) .

5. Based on the information collected, have the class formulate alternative solutions to the development (or preservation) of the flood plains on the   (name)   River from   (location)   to   (location) .

6. Draw a chart of the power structure (pressure groups, governmental committees, governmental policy makers) of your community regarding who influences (underline the influencers) and makes policy (circle the policy makers) on flood plain development and zoning.

7. If the solution advocated by the class members is different from the point of view held by the planning commission and policy makers of your community, then develop and implement a plan of action (presentation to the ap-

propriate authority, develop a fact sheet, publicize your position, etc.).

Each environmental encounter should also provide data regarding sources of additional information relevant to the topic.

If the environmental education for a school system revolved around environmental encounters, a twelfth grader may *not* be exposed to all aspects of the environment. However, through the inductive (inquiry) approach advocated by this system, a twelfth grader that had been exposed to this program *should* be more sensitive (total awareness) to his environment, better able to recognize environmental problems, more sophisticated in the utilization of problem solving skills essential to the solution of emerging environmental problems, and more inclined to participate in coping with environmental problems *than* the product of other forms of instruction known to the author. The learner would also have an understanding and should see the importance of relating ecological, economic, social, technological, and political information when working toward the solution of environmental problems.

The environmental encounters should be produced by the local environmental education committee and by youth and teachers from throughout the school system. The environmental encounters produced at the local level could be mimeographed and distributed to all schools in the system. Many school systems might need and desire consultant help (which is available) to orient the local environmental education committee to the task of developing environmental encounters. However, *samples* of environmental encounters could be developed and produced by a national publishing house according to elementary grade levels (lower elementary, middle elementary, upper elementary) and secondary subject matters (general science, American Government, biology, economics, social problems, etc.). Environmental encounters produced at the national level could be adapted

to meet local needs and situations by the local environmental education committee.

Phase VIII: Establish a Comprehensive In-Service Teacher Education Program.

If our youth are to acquire the interest, awareness, understandings, and skills essential in understanding and contributing to the solution of environmental problems, then it is imperative that our schools provide environmental learning experiences. However, few teachers are prepared in our colleges and universities to use the environment to enrich instructional goals. For this reason a comprehensive in-service teacher education program is essential to a successful environmental education program (K-12).

An effective in-service teacher education program should be developed by the local environmental education committee. An early task would be to formulate a comprehensive in-service teacher education plan, which might include the following:

a. Clear statement of objectives.

b. Time sequence regarding when offerings will occur throughout the school year.

c. Involvement of teachers at all grade levels and subject areas.

d. Development of written material and instructional aids to assist the teacher in understanding and presenting environmental information.

e. Blending of community environmental experiences with indoor presentations.

f. Provisions for experiences to occur on school sites.

g. Promotion and publicity of local collegiate offerings and scholarship programs.

The first stage of an in-service teacher training program would be to orient all teachers and administrators to the philosophy of environmental education, structure of the environmental education program, and ways to effectively utilize environmental encounters.

The second stage of an in-service teacher training program would be to plan a bus tour of the community to provide teachers with first hand experiences regarding their local environment and associated problems. Information should be provided to all teachers regarding community citizens and governmental officials knowledgeable on the environment and available to serve the school system as resource persons on environmental matters.

The third stage of the in-service teacher training program would be to assist the teachers in ways to effectively integrate environmental encounters into the school program.

Phase IX: Develop Instruments to Evaluate the Effectiveness of the Environmental Education Program

It is imperative that instruments be developed to evaluate the extent to which behavioral objectives are attained and the effectiveness of the total environmental education program. An evaluation should be a continuous process involving pupil and teacher feedback.

It is imperative that the evaluative instruments be objective, reliable, and valid. It should be noted that behavioral objec-

tives provide an excellent opportunity to appraise the effectiveness of particular learning experiences and of the total program. The evaluative instrument could be developed by the local environmental education committee.

SUMMARY

If we are to bring urbanized man to a fuller understanding of his environment, our schools must embark on a comprehensive environmental education program. The program should be aimed at helping our youth to be more knowledgeable concerning the environment and associated problems, aware of how to help solve these problems, and motivated to work toward their solution.

One of the most important challenges of education today is to develop an effective method of implementing environmental education into our elementary and secondary school systems.

This paper provides one strategy as to how a school system might develop a comprehensive environmental education program (K-12). The environmental encounters could be used to enhance and extend existing class units or to serve as the core of a comprehensive environmental education program.

LeVon Balzer

ENVIRONMENTAL EDUCATION IN THE K-12 SPAN

A widely accepted definition of environmental education is not available at the present time, in spite of the extensive emphasis upon the environment and environmental education. In addition, various terms are being used with a wide range of meanings. To clarify discussion in this paper, a brief discussion of some of these terms follows.

Nature study. This complex and diverse movement was initiated at the turn of the century by Liberty Hyde Bailey and associates at Cornell University. A major purpose was to get children to know and love their environment by observing their surroundings. The beautiful, the curious, and the unusual were often emphasized more than the understanding of scientific principles. Actual content included such aspects as field work, soils, aesthetics, farm and city locations and landscapes, building construction, economics, and politics. In addition, form, making and modeling, work with numbers, colors, drawings, and music

were activity areas emphasized. There was emphasis on the out-of-doors, field trips, and plant and animal identification, measurement, comparisons, and representation of results. There was much concentration on aesthetic, emotional, and moral values.

Conservation education. The efforts and achievements of conservation education will not be detailed here, but mention of some major areas of attention seems appropriate. Content aspects have traditionally included soil, water, air, plant and animal identification, wildlife, and forestry. Other areas that have often been included are human resources, agriculture, rocks and minerals, space, energy, and basic ecology, including succession. Techniques of field-trip organization, sampling, collecting, and recording have commonly been taught.

Many organizations have been actively involved in conservation education over the years. State departments of natural resources, county soil and water conservation

SOURCE. Reprinted, by permission, from *The American Biology Teacher*, April, 1971, with slight abridgment.

districts, and various park boards and commissions are often involved at the state and local levels. Other organizations are National Wildlife Federation, Nature Conservancy, National Aeronautics and Space Administration, National Audubon Society, National Park Service, Sierra Club, Soil Conservation Service, Tennessee Valley Authority, U.S. Atomic Energy Commission, U.S. Department of Agriculture, U.S. Forest Service, state departments of education, state game and wildlife commissions, state departments of conservation, and the Ozark Society. Often, private industries make free or inexpensive educational materials available, but the educator should be aware that these materials are likely to represent and promote the particular view of conservation that is suitable to the industry involved. The same can also be said, of course, about the various interest groups and governmental agencies listed above.

Outdoor laboratories and outdoor education. A clear-cut distinction cannot be made between current usage of the terms conservation education and outdoor education. It is possible, however, to suggest a distinction on the basis of overall goals. Conservation education has often focused extensively on the many content topics listed above, while outdoor education has been seen as education executed under the ideal conditions of the out-of-doors. Thus, the goal of outdoor education is to provide a learning climate (out-of-doors) which facilitates the achievement of various educational objectives. Accordingly, the literature of outdoor education often deals with such aspects as management of an outdoor laboratory, programming, and the planning of grounds and facilities.

The content to be achieved may be similar to that described above for conservation education, but it often includes also objectives in the areas of language arts, industrial arts, music and art, social studies, mathematics, health, and physical education. Various individual programs also suggest affective (value, appreciations, etc.)

and inquiry objectives in addition to the content areas already suggested.

Outdoor recreation. Camping, hiking and Scouting are other outdoor educational endeavors often emphasized. Achievements include working together, preparation of temporary shelters, food preparation, helping one another, sharing and taking responsibility, and physical conditioning. Various other content and affective objectives may be incorporated as well.

Environmental education. Obviously, much of what is being attempted in environmental education is not new. At the same time, it is apparent that past efforts to generate favorable attitudes and behaviors toward the environment have not been particularly successful. Americans pollute and destroy their environment with little or no evidence of reluctance.

THE NEED FOR OBJECTIVES

The major objectives of nature study, conservation education, outdoor education, and outdoor recreation are not readily disputed. They continue to be appropriate areas of concern. However, if environmental education is to become effective in changing behavior, objectives with behavioral foci will have to be developed. Curriculum development must then proceed in a manner compatible with these objectives, incorporating instructional strategies which develop behavioral changes. It appears, then, that environmental education must be an attempt to alter the behaviors of modern man by persuasion. There may be differences of opinion regarding the form this persuasion should take. Perhaps one individual will be persuaded on the basis of individual inquiry; perhaps another is persuaded on the basis of appreciations developed in contrasting environments. In any case, the individual is to be persuaded to behave in a manner less detrimental to, and more in harmony with, the environment than the past behaviors of modern man have been. We might expect these behaviors to be expressed in at least two forms: (i) behaviors implying concern about the effects of personal environmental destruction; and (ii) behaviors implying concern about the environmental destruction caused by others. Thus environmental education must be that which facilitates the achievement of such behaviors. As a science educator, I would say that such education should also be scientifically legitimate.

As those who have been involved in curriculum development can recognize, the specific behavioral objectives of environmental education will be very numerous. Behavior that is in harmony with the environment has many facets. Some of the areas of concern and behaviors are discussed in the next section.

AREAS OF OBJECTIVES

In Figure 1 are shown some of the major areas of interest to the biology educator, in which behavioral objectives might be specified in environmental education. The activities and experiences of environmental education would constitute the volume of the grid and a given experience (visualized as being *within* the box) would normally have components in each of the three dimensions. In some cases, attitudes might be more heavily emphasized and in other cases one of the other dimensions might receive more attention. Such an encompassing view of objectives is appropriate if people learn individually and are persuaded individually through a variety of means.

A complete discussion of the grid is not possible here, but several features should be noted. Several of the unifying themes of BSCS (see E. Klinckman, ed., 1970: *Biology Teachers' Handbook,* 2nd ed., John Wiley & Sons, New York) appear to be particularly appropriate in environmental education and have been incorporated in the cognitive dimension. Second, various applications of our scientific knowledge must be incorporated if values concerning the environment are to be addressed, so technology is included in the cognitive dimension. Third, if we have the kind of faith in scientific inquiry that we usually claim to have, inquiry should be a major method used. Thus, various processes of science have been incorporated, including those of the process approach (see A. Livermore, 1964: "The process approach of the AAAS Commission on Science Education," *Journal of Research in Science Teaching* 11: 271-282).

Certainly the grid of Figure 1 should not be seen as complete or final. The major emphasis here is on science, with various other curriculum areas only mentioned. As our understanding of environmental education develops, additions, deletions, or other modifications will be necessary. The point is that if the major behavioral outcomes described in the previous section are to be realized, decisions will need to be made regarding emphasis upon at least these three dimensions in the educational experience. Furthermore, activities considered should be analyzed to ascertain their strengths in these dimensions and to avoid a curriculum heavily imbalanced with respect to the dimensions.

Figure 2 is an attempt to illustrate some of the major relationships of environmental education. At the center of the scheme are the individual and the environment, which interact as indicated. Associated with the individual are numerous areas of objectives within which behavioral examples can be specified. Also associated with the individual are the various types of activities in which he will be participating, thus gaining experience in the performance of the types of behaviors being specified. Associated with the environment are various areas of information with which the student will have experiences and in which cognitive behavioral objectives may be specified. Also associated with the environment are examples of educational techniques in terms of environmental setting. Specific behavioral objectives may also require behaviors

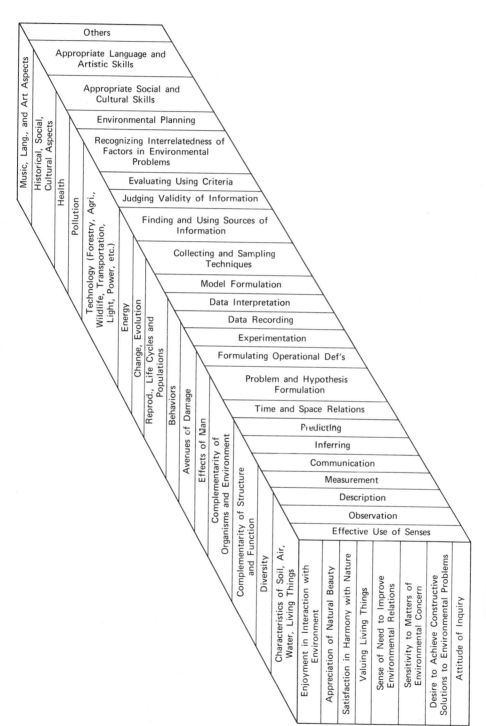

FIGURE 1. Grid suggesting some major areas of objectives in environmental education.

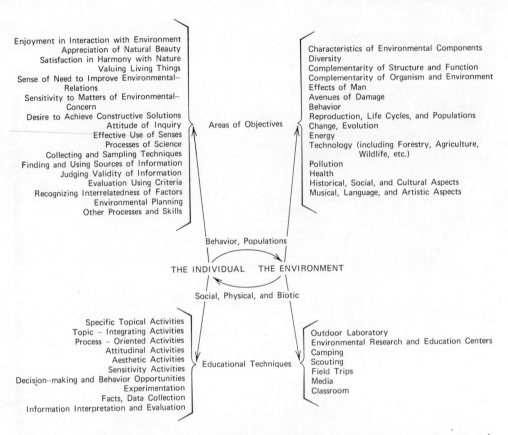

Enjoyment in Interaction with Environment
Appreciation of Natural Beauty
Satisfaction in Harmony with Nature
Valuing Living Things
Sense of Need to Improve Environmental--
Relations
Sensitivity to Matters of Environmental--
Concern
Desire to Achieve Constructive Solutions
Attitude of Inquiry
Effective Use of Senses
Processes of Science
Collecting and Sampling Techniques
Finding and Using Sources of Information
Judging Validity of Information
Evaluation Using Criteria
Recognizing Interrelatedness of Factors
Environmental Planning
Other Processes and Skills

Areas of Objectives

Characteristics of Environmental Components
Diversity
Complementarity of Structure and Function
Complementarity of Organism and Environment
Effects of Man
Avenues of Damage
Behavior
Reproduction, Life Cycles, and Populations
Change, Evolution
Energy
Technology (including Forestry, Agriculture,
Wildlife, etc.)
Pollution
Health
Historical, Social, and Cultural Aspects
Musical, Language, and Artistic Aspects

Behavior, Populations

THE INDIVIDUAL   THE ENVIRONMENT

Social, Physical, and Biotic

Specific Topical Activities
Topic -- Integrating Activities
Process -- Oriented Activities
Attitudinal Activities
Aesthetic Activities
Sensitivity Activities
Decision--making and Behavior Opportunities
Experimentation
Facts, Data Collection
Information Interpretation and Evaluation

Educational Techniques

Outdoor Laboratory
Environmental Research and Education Centers
Camping
Scouting
Field Trips
Media
Classroom

FIGURE 2. Preliminary scheme of major relationships involved in environmental education.

integrating these two groups of objectives. The experiences themselves occur in an integrated manner.

ILLUSTRATIVE BEHAVIORAL OBJECTIVES

To illustrate, let us consider some specific examples.

1. For the primary grades, let us consider the following behavioral objective: "The child will respond enthusiastically and provide reasonable answers when asked what he enjoyed about the walk he and his classmates took through the woods."

2. For the intermediate grades, let us consider the following behavioral objective: "The child will spontaneously or voluntarily suggest the need to improve a situation, based upon his interpretation of data provided."

Behavioral objective #1 may deal with enjoyment in interaction with the environment, appreciation of natural beauty, or valuing living things (Figure 1). In any case, the affective dimension (attitudes) (#1) is represented. Though other concepts or knowledge might also be represented, the child will usually provide or imply characteristics of such features as soil, air, water, or living things, thus representing the cognitive dimension (knowledge, concepts). Typically, at least the processes of observation and description are represented in the achievement of this objective. To repeat for emphasis: the above does not suggest that all specific behavioral objectives will have equal components in all three dimensions of the grid (Figure 1); indeed, this would be unnecessarily difficult to accomplish. However, broad goals and specific objectives should be developed and implemented with an awareness and deliberate evaluative decision regarding all three dimensions in the curriculum.

The attitudes and processes described above are examples from the areas of objectives that describe the individual (Figure 2), and the information about the environment stated or implied by the individual partially describes the environment. (The behavior itself also partially describes the individual, of course, but the information conveyed pertains more directly to the environment than the individual in this case. The attitudes and processes conveyed, on the other hand, pertain more directly to the individual than the environment.) Quite likely the teacher would consider the activity to have an attitudinal, aesthetic, and sensitivity orientation, though it could be a combination of others as well. Facility-wise and environment-wise, it is a field trip, although it may also be taking place in an outdoor laboratory or other specifically designated facility.

It should be apparent in the example provided that there is an environmental influence upon the child through the social, physical, or biotic context that is provided. It is also clear that achievement of this specific objective is consistent with our over-all goal of persuading the student to behave in a manner less detrimental to the environment, though the two are certainly not synonymous. This transfer of behaviors will continue to be very difficult and much will continue to depend upon teacher strategies and behaviors. A bit more will be said about this later.

In the second behavioral objective provided above, the child provides evidence that he senses the need to improve environmental relations (Figure 1) and perhaps implies achievement of other areas of affective objectives. The knowledge or concepts reflected depend upon the nature of the data, of course, but population, pollution, effects of man, and "major applications" would all be fertile areas. Some of the processes likely involved would be inferring, predicting, problem-formulating, and especially, interpretation of data. Attitudes, processes, and information can be related to the child and the environment (Figure 2) in much the same manner as in example #1. The activity would probably be topical and focus on information interpretation and evaluation (Figure 2). As described here, the activity could take place in the classroom.

ORGANIZATION OF CONTENT AND LEARNING EXPERIENCES

A major goal of environmental education has been presented, and various subsumed areas of objectives within three dimensions have been suggested. The bases of these selections include such considerations as goals, student interest and appropriateness, validity, and significance of content. Similarly, the organization of content and learning experiences must incorporate considerations such as child development, interest, logical structure of disciplines, the nature of learning, attitude development, facilities, social context, and teacher preparation. In actual curriculum development, such considerations are highly numerous and detailed. Furthermore, since curriculum development is a continuous process, content and organization will undergo more or less continuous change. Let us not be distracted here by the current hypothesis, however, that children should determine their own learning experiences. The potentiality for these experiences must still be provided at least in part through the curriculum; hence, a certain degree of structure and organization is needed for planning.

In the primary grades, consideration such as the following appear to be defensible:

Basic skills and processes of science (use of senses, measurement, etc.)
Characteristics of soil, air, water, organisms (observation, description)
Diversity (from obs., classif.)
Life Cycles (change, time relations)
Population (numbers, time)
Change (obs., inference, time relations.)
Homes and habitats, needs
Gardening, foods
Weather, seasons
Behavior
Effects of man (obs., inf., likes, dislikes)
Avenues of damage (obs., inferences)
Pollution
Health
Enjoyment in interactions with environs
Valuing living things
Appreciation of natural beauty

Obviously, the above list is neither complete nor adequate. However, it should provide an overview of the kinds of areas in which specific behavioral objectives should be developed for the primary grades.

In the intermediate grades, the areas listed for the primary grades should be reinforced and deepened. Beyond these, the following areas of objectives should be emphasized:

Integrated processes of science (experimentation, model formulation, etc.)
Collecting and sampling techniques
Finding and using sources of information
Energy (light, heat, temperature, etc.)
Local changes, historical considerations
Complementarity of structure and function.
Food webs (organism and environment)
Environmental factors and living things
Communities
Agriculture, food production, and simplicity

Forestry
Wildlife conservation
Satisfaction in harmony with nature
Attitude of inquiry
Sense of need to improve environmental relations

In the middle schools and junior high schools, many of the previously mentioned areas should again receive additional attention. The following additional areas or more specific examples within areas of objectives should be incorporated at the middle school level:

More complex instances using integrated processes of science
Greater independence in finding and using sources of information
Environmental changes, succession
Interaction
Ecosystems
Decision-making (local issues, committees, interest groups, etc.)
Health and medical considerations
Local cultural and social studies (special speakers, etc.)
Sensitivity to matters of environmental concern

In the high schools, much of the attention of environmental education must be given to experiences that will provide increased sophistication in the areas already listed for the previous levels. In addition, considerable emphasis should be given to such areas as the following:

Evaluation using criteria
Judging validity of information
Recognizing interrelatedness of factors in environmental problems
Environmental planning
Desire to achieve constructive solutions to environmental problems

The areas of objectives as organized for the various school levels obviously should not be taken as mutually exclusive or strictly sequential. Evaluation as a skill will be taught before the high school, but it should be emphasized at the secondary level. Hence, the content of environmental education should not be seen as strictly sequenced, but an overall pattern does emerge. Needless to say, future experience may indicate a need for extensive modifications.

A few words should be said about the complexity and messy appearance of the environmental-education curriculum. First, we should attempt synthesis and simplications of this proposal. Second, we should be prepared to accept that environmental-education-curriculum development that is specific enough to facilitate implementation may be highly complex. The problems of the environment and environmental education are highly complex and pervasive. The writer is impressed that the task before us in environmental education may well be the most important and the most difficult one we have ever faced.

COMMENTS CONCERNING IMPLEMENTATION

Environmental education should not be "tacked on" or added to the existing K-12 curriculum. My suggestions for environmental education in this paper are strongly science- (especially biology-) oriented, but simply increasing the science content is not the solution either. The entire curriculum must be infused by the activities that facilitate improving man's relation to the environment.

Irwin Slesnick, in a paper presented at the 1970 convention of NABT, illustrated a mechanism for accomplishing such infusion in the area of population education by bringing together various areas of the curriculum (such as art, social studies, health, science, etc.) on a grid. Space does not permit detailed treatment of this mechanism here, but this process must be carried out in environmental education. When the potential contributions of all these areas toward the ultimate behavioral goals of environmental education are worked out, we will be moving toward the total curriculum of environmental education in the K-12 span. In the process, we may even evolve some major themes around which our objectives can be more simply structured.

Irwin L. Slesnick

POPULATION EDUCATION – A RESPONSE TO A SOCIAL PROBLEM

The phenomenon is excessive human population growth. It originates at the interface of modern technology, traditional culture, and biotic potential. It contributes to war, poverty, hunger, disease, pollution, the erosion of freedom, and the loss of individual identity. The phenomenon is a current social problem, and the action is toward stabilizing world population, with the ultimate aim to achieve and maintain levels of optimum population size.

In recognition of the consequences of overpopulation, each institution of society has begun to move in the direction of population control. Governments are establishing new population policies: liberalizing abortion laws; removing pronatalist tax incentives; funding research in family planning. Similarly, the churches are re-examining their pronatalist policies, and families of two or fewer children are becoming symbols of social responsibility. The school and its external arm, the mass media, have assumed the tasks of disseminating knowledge about the population phenomenon and establishing attitudes that, when translated into behaviors, will prevent the recurrence of population imbalance.

Population education, therefore, is one effort to change the reproductive behaviors of modern man through a deliberate program of persuasion. Failure to recognize this as the real goal of population education may lead curriculum pacesetters to statements of vague goals and the staking out of topical territories that only appear to be related to the educational need. A snowfall of instructional materials that results from a perfunctory response to the population problem would do little to support the cause of population control. A random and administratively convenient placement of informational packages about population will not change reproductive behaviors.

SOURCE. Reprinted, by permission, from *The Science Teacher,* Vol. 38, No. 2, February 1971, with slight abridgment.

THE NATURE OF ENVIRONMENTAL EDUCATION

The failure of conservation education is a case in point. For the last 50 years or so schoolchildren have been expected to develop wholesome attitudes and acquire knowledge about their physical and biological environments. In classrooms they read and talked about environmental dynamics, saw films and demonstrations, and some even planted trees and lived in the woods. Today the American adult, a product of conservation education, is a world champion polluter. Our environment is being consumed and defouled to such an extent that the citizen must now be controlled by threat of imprisonment and fine, lest he further desecrate his environment. The population education parallel is obvious: Unless individuals learn to control their fertility voluntarily, their reproductivity will be directed by legislated sanctions, not unlike the laws that now attempt to control littering.

Two categories of causes have contributed to the failure of population control efforts thus far. One category is motivation toward family size limitation. Most of the people of the world are driven by a long-established cultural tradition to achieve high fertility. Such forces as religious doctrines, moral codes, public laws, community customs, marriage habits, family organization, and children's literature explicitly and inexplicitly demand high child productivity. Parenthood is fulfillment; and children, especially sons, are wealth, security, and demonstrations of virility. Although motivational problems are more pronounced in developing countries, studies of family size expectations in the United States reveal only slight effects on reducing the present growth rate. The second category is the availability of the means to control conception and birth. No matter how motivated couples may be not to conceive, they must still know how to prevent a conception, where to obtain contraceptives, and how to use them. And all this learning should occur before the first act of sexual intercourse. Population education focuses on the task of motivating individuals to avail themselves of the means to limit their reproduction.

Approximately 50 percent of world population is under the age of 16. It is not realistic to expect to reach these people at the instant of marriage and then change their behavior with information about population and family planning. The mass media messages of the crisis of overpopulation and the benefits of family size limitation occur too late, since the behavior of adults is directed in large measure by the attitudes which develop in childhood. The society that wishes to control the size of its population must influence its youth by creating an awareness of the consequences of overpopulation, the virtues of a small family norm, and an understanding of what they must do individually as adults to achieve the goal of a population of optimum size.

The first task of curriculum development is to state objectives in ultimate behavioral terms. The primary objective for population education is that each couple voluntarily contracepts, or takes equally effective measures, to limit the size of its family and to space its children. The unfortunate reflex against this objective challenges the propriety of teaching contraception to children, and it becomes necessary to point out that attitudes which produce high fertility behavior are established during childhood in the absence of any instruction of the techniques of producing babies. Societies that are notoriously prudish or Victorian are efficient in perpetuating the attitude that large families have economic and social advantages, and they do this without doing violence to the highly classified information about sexual reproduction. Patterns of adult sexual behavior are established in childhood, and we must realize that any position the school takes within the spectrum of sexual morality has an impact upon ultimate behaviors. Abjection of responsibility is a strong negative position that ensures the persistence of the *status quo.* Even so, there are those who would proceed in the development of a population education while denying or ignoring the ultimate objective. The condition is symptomatic of a kind of cultural schizophrenia, and does not contribute to the development of a curriculum for which the goal is clearly achievable.

Population education, in my view, is distinct from sex education (family life education) and environmental education (conservation education), even though a considerable amount of the content of the programs will overlap. Where population education seeks to change the reproductivity of modern man, sex education seeks to influence the establishment of interpersonal ethics. Where population education seeks to control the number of human consumers of natural resources, environmental education seeks to optimize the relationships between each human and his environment.

A reasonable approach to population education, considering the present subject-centered structure of the educational system, is an infusion of instructional activities appropriately placed in the subject areas of the K-12 span. The alternative is to peg core topics at appropriate grade levels in schools where curriculum is organized to enable an interdisciplinary problems approach to learning. In either case the thrust of population education will occur in areas of the social studies and science. But since the consequences of abnormal population growth permeate all aspects of life, it is logical to expect that every school subject area involve itself in the population curriculum, whether the curriculum is an integrated core or traditionally subject centered.

The resources on population as they relate to the objectives of population education are widely scattered. In the past several years a dozen or so organizations have addressed themselves to various tasks of instructional materials development. These projects include the preparation of bibliographies, the establishment of clear-inghouses, and the production of instructional materials. Most of the action is being carried by international organizations for non-American audiences.

Possibly the greatest need in population education is the development of a comprehensive sourcebook. The sourcebook would identify and explicate a solid core of content and be not only a book of knowledge but also an anthology of ideas for the effective presentation of the content. The sourcebook would be useful to teachers who wish to incorporate population education into their programs. Coverage would include all grade levels and all subjects. The sourcebook would also be a fountainhead for the development of such instructional materials as monographs, films, and games.

The sourcebook may resemble in format the initial productions of the recent curriculum developments in biology and earth science, where content and curriculum specialists collaborated in brainstorming on the ingredient topics of the subject. In population education, for example, an anthropologist and a curriculum specialist in the social sciences could prepare jointly a section on the evolution of the human family, and suggest ways to communicate to children through educational media the modern trend toward the small family norm.

An overall curricular design for population education would have to be reflected in the sourcebook, even though the ultimate working structure of a program would emerge only after extensive classroom trials. As a beginning, we might envisage a curriculum grid that includes school subjects and grade levels.

For illustrative purposes let's trace, through a curricular grid, the development of two possible themes, one horizontally at the third-grade level and the other vertically through several years of science. In the first illustration assume that it was determined appropriate to concentrate during the third grade on the evolution of the small family norm. The study focuses in the social studies with other subjects providing support. In the second illustration, assume that the sequence of science studies, spanning the intermediate elementary school

Despite intensive inputs into population control programs, world population continues to grow at the alarming rate of about

Horizontal Development of a Population Education Theme in Grade 3.

GRADE LEVEL	SOCIAL STUDIES	SCIENCE	LANGUAGE ARTS	HEALTH
3	Modern family no longer depends on many children as a labor force and old age security	An inquiry into family structure, size, and role in animal population	Supportive literature portraying happy small families, childless married couples, and even secure and contented unmarried adults	Assurance that immunization and other modern health practices provide child survival and longevity

HOME ECONOMICS	FINE ARTS	MATHEMATICS
An examination of the modern home providing comfort, privacy, and care for the small family	Studies of family art, possibly noting the current art of India depicting the small happy family	Story problem support to theme of greater individual wealth to members of the small family

Vertical Development of a Population Development Theme. This Sequence of Science Studies Would be Supported in Other Subject Areas.

GRADE LEVEL	SCIENCE
4	The formal introduction of reproduction and sexuality using the flowering plants as vehicles in establishing a noncontroversial entree to the sexual reproductive cycles of organisms.
5	Plant population studies emphasizing biotic potentials and limiting environmental factors.
6	Reproduction in animals including studies of reproduction as a life process, sexuality as an adaptation, anatomy, physiology, behavior, mating, fertilization, development, biotic potentials, and parental care.
7	Human reproductive anatomy, physiology, and behavior—an upward extension of previous studies, coinciding as closely as possible with the onset of puberty.
8	Human population dynamics and the mechanisms of population control.

and junior high school, would be supported in other subject areas.

More important than the content of population education or its sequence will be the method by which it is learned. The phenomenon of excessive human population growth lends itself well to teaching and learning by inquiry. A teacher's mastery of this method will determine the ultimate effectiveness of his program in influencing his students in realizing objectives.

2 percent. The failure of these programs has been attributed to powerful cultural demands for high fertility. Efforts to influence acceptance of family planning means will fail until the attitudes of couples toward the small family norm overcome the traditional pressures for large numbers of children. New attitudes which will change reproductive behaviors can occur through the formal schooling of children in a program of population education.

William B. Stapp

INSERVICE TEACHER TRAINING IN ENVIRONMENTAL EDUCATION

Someday our youth will be adult members of a community, perhaps your community. As citizens and voters, no matter what their occupations may be, they will make decisions affecting not only the community in which they live, but also their country. To an increasing extent the votes they will cast and the choices they will make will be concerned with our natural resources and their wise use. They will be asked to make decisions about recreation, parkways, beautification, water needs, and air and water pollution control. Since decisions on problems like these will affect the total environment in which we live, we must help our young people (and ourselves) obtain the experiences and the knowledge necessary to assure wise decisions.

If we are to assist youth to be more effective in helping to solve environmental resource problems, we must provide them with the proper "tools." It is imperative that these tools be identified and that instructional programs be provided to help our youth acquire them as they proceed through our school systems. These tools must also be taken into consideration as *inservice teacher training* programs are developed. Some of the tools that I consider to be minimum prerequisites for informed citizen action are:

1. *Strong general education*—educational training that will enable students to think clearly and critically; to be able to articulate their thoughts through speech and writing; to widen their interest range in daily experience; and to develop a "questioning mind."

2. *Understanding of our natural resources*—their characteristics, status, distribution, and importance to man.

3. *Ecological awareness*—a blending of field and classroom experiences that will help youth develop a greater inter-

SOURCE. Reprinted, by permission, from *The Science Teacher,* Vol. 34, No. 4, April 1967, with slight abridgment.

est, awareness, understanding, and respect toward man's environment.

4. *Economic awareness*—an understanding of economic theory so to better understand the role of economics in resource decisions.

5. *Political awareness*—an understanding of the American political process at the national, state, and local level, and ways that the individual can be effective in helping to promote sound environmental resource decisions.

6. *Problem solving*—inherent in this is the ability to define the problem, consider all related viewpoints, and, on the basis of substantial facts, determine the best solution.

7. *Understanding that man is a part of the human ecosystem*—recognition that man is a part of his environment and is expected to make contributions to society according to his ability.

If an understanding of man's environment is indeed essential to the educational development of our youth, then our schools must give appropriate priority to environmental education and designate an individual or committee to appraise the total instructional program of the school system and to make recommendations.

Some school systems have employed conservation consultants to help develop instructional programs aimed at transmitting and inculcating into the minds of the youth they serve a fuller understanding of man's environment and the role of the citizen in helping to solve environmental resource problems. Other school systems have improved their instructional programs in environmental education through the work of a committee composed of administrators and teachers representing various disciplines and levels of education. Regardless of who leads the effort, attention must be directed to the total school curriculum, to class activities, and to the *inservice teacher training program.* These should not be thought of as separate entities but as vital components of a total

environmental education program which involves the entire staff.

Some points to consider in relation to the curriculum are:

1. Identify "understandings" which are minimal prerequisites for informed citizen action regarding natural resources and the natural environment of urban regions.

2. Survey the total existing curriculum and determine the most effective way of integrating the understandings into the total school curriculum (K-12) in a manner that will provide the logical continuity and progression.

3. Give the learner an opportunity to study community natural resources under natural conditions. This will provide certain learning experiences that can not be duplicated within the school building.

4. Stress attitudes and not vocational skills. The most important conservation impact that our urban youth will have upon natural resources will be through their action as community citizens.

5. Emphasize local resource problems but do not neglect state, national, or international resource problems.

6. Give the learner the opportunity to play an active role in the learning process. The learner develops attitudes through personal experiences and thinking and not through the presentation of predigested conclusions.

7. Provide a comprehensive inservice training program which operates throughout the school year and is directed at helping teachers increase their understandings, interest, awareness, and teaching skills in conservation.

If our youth are to develop proper attitudes concerning their environment, we should provide environmental learning experiences. However, few teachers are trained in our colleges and universities to use the community environment to enrich instructional goals. For this reason a comprehensive *inservice teacher training* program should be developed so that teachers are more effective in helping youth to acquire the skills and the knowledge essential in contributing to the solution of environmental resource problems.

An effective *inservice teacher training* program can be developed by a conservation consultant employed by the school system or by a school committee that is assigned this responsibility. In either instance, the first task is to formulate a comprehensive inservice teacher training plan, including the following:

1. Clear statement of objectives.
2. Time sequence regarding when offerings will occur throughout the school year.
3. Blending of community environmental experiences with indoor presentations.
4. Provision for experiences to occur on school sites.
5. Development of written material that will offer information as well as methodology.
6. Involvement of teachers at all grade levels and subject areas.
7. Promotion and publicity of local collegiate offerings and scholarship programs that relate to conservation.

Inservice teacher training programs—or self-help programs—could revolve around a broad theme that would serve as a major thrust for the year. For example, let us take "Water and Its Importance to Man."

The *first* stage of the inservice teacher training program should be to plan a meeting to orient teachers to the characteristics, distribution, status, and uses of water resources. The emphasis of the presentation should be on the local water situation and ways of integrating information and activities into the curriculum. It would be helpful to circulate written material on water resources at this initial meeting.

The *second* stage of the inservice teacher training program should be to plan a bus excursion in the environs of the community to provide teachers with firsthand experience regarding local water resources. Discussions should focus on topics such as landuse patterns and their effect on water uses, access to water areas for public recreation, variations in water quality, and examples of beautification or absence thereof along waterways. Adequate time should be provided for questions and answers and a discussion concerning activities that students might pursue in the field and classroom regarding water resources. In the development of the field excursion, community public officials could be involved.

The *third* stage of the inservice teacher training program should be to provide teachers with subject matter and activities that focus on water resources. A few meaningful activities in the area of water resources that could be suggested to elementary and secondary school *teachers* as examples of activities that would help students better understand water resources in their own community, are:

1. Locate an aquatic habitat in close proximity to the school and collect the following information (involves several subject-matter areas):
   a. What is the drainage area of the aquatic community? How have land uses changed in the drainage area over the past 50 years? What is the quality of the water?
   b. Is the aquatic community relatively productive? What factors might affect its productivity? How will its productivity affect the role of succession?
   c. What is the dissolved oxygen and carbon dioxide level of the water area? Do these levels fluctuate? If yes, why?
   d. How would you determine the volume of water in the aquatic community? What effect does water volume have on aquatic biota?
2. Visit the community water treatment plant to determine the following information:

a. What is the source of the community drinking supply?

b. What chemicals are used to treat the water?

c. Is fluoride added to city water to reduce tooth decay? If yes, for how long? If not, has it been proposed?

d. Has the treatment plant been enlarged in recent years? If yes, how were the funds appropriated? Have there been bans on water usage in recent years?

3. Visit a local community that is bordering a water area and obtain the following information:

   a. Is there good access to the park? If not, is it possible to improve it?

   b. Is there swimming available at the park? If no, why not?

   c. Is the water dirty? If yes, where does the dirt come from?

   d. Does your community have enough parks located around water areas? If not, is there land bordering water in your community that could be used for a park?

   e. What are the recreational uses of water in your community?

4. Visit a local industrial plant in your community and find out the following information:

   a. What is its source of water? Is the source adequate?

   b. If the industrial plant had to move, would water supply be important in the selection of its new location?

   c. Does the industry have a waste disposal plant? Has the industry solved its waste disposal problem?

5. Visit the community sewage treatment plant to determine:

   a. Does your community separate sanitary wastes from storm runoff?

   b. What type of sewage treatment is employed by the plant? Is the type of treatment considered adequate for the present time and for the next 20 years?

   c. How is the sewage treatment plant financed? Is it self-supported?

   d. Does the sewage treatment plant receive waste from local industrial plants? If yes, are any of these wastes unusually difficult to treat?

   e. Is the plant effluent (treated sewage) discharged into a stream or a lake? Is the effluent chlorinated to protect downstream recreational users? What downstream communities use the water for municipal purposes?

6. Other assignments might include essays or class discussions on questions such as the following:

   a. What might be considered a pollutant of a river?

   b. What effect do different kinds of pollutants (inorganic, organic, toxic, radioactive, or hot wastes) have on river life?

   c. Can a river purify itself?

   d. How could your community enhance the beauty of its waterways?

If we are to bring urbanized man to a fuller understanding of his environment, our schools must embark on a comprehensive conservation education program. This program should be directed at helping students increase their interest, awareness, and understanding of their environment, as well as *their* responsibility to help solve environmental resource problems. Therefore, our schools must provide a strong *inservice teacher training* program that will assist teachers in acquiring the skills and the knowledge necessary in guiding the youth they serve.

Carl F. Berger

SCIENCE OR FAIRY TALES?

There was a time in the not-too-distant past when the objectives of science education could be dealt with purely theoretically. A layman's influence on scientific decisions seemed slight, and most of us were bent on producing young scientists rather than clear-minded citizens. Today this is no longer true. We have discovered that we are facing situations in our environment which will have serious repercussions for future generations. It's hard to pick up a newspaper or magazine that does not have some article relating to the problems of mercury poisoning in game birds, offshore oil spillage, cancer-producing agents placed in our environment, and the even greater problem of pollution on a broad scale in our water and the very air we breathe. Most distressing is the realization that few researchers seem to agree on what can be done, and indeed, many do not even agree that a given problem exists. Experts cannot agree. What are we to do when we, who are not scientists, are asked to make decisions on the basis of scientific evidence?

An example of the controversies that face us involves the eggs of the brown pelican. One researcher reports that the eggshells of the brown pelican have become so thin that these birds actually crush their own eggs when they sit on them. He notes the rise in DDT measured in these eggs and concludes that the brown pelican may become extinct because of DDT. An English researcher raises birds exposed to DDT and finds that the shells of their eggs are somewhat thicker than before DDT was introduced. Still another claims the shell-thinning may be due to tetraethyl lead from gasoline exhaust in the environment. What are we to do when faced with such conflicting information: ban DDT? tetraethyl lead? While we remain confused about causes, an important seashore population is dying out. We could influence the decision-makers if we just knew what to tell them.

What can be done to increase the decision-making ability of the next generation of adults? One method has been to give young children the latest facts so they can

SOURCE. Reprinted, by permission, from the *SCIS Newsletter,* No. 18, Summer 1970, published by the Science Curriculum Improvement Study, University of California at Berkeley, with slight abridgment.

make decisions based on these facts. Indeed, that is what science education has been doing for many years.

This method of giving children facts, while being an effective means of raising test scores, is failure-prone in relation to decision-making for two very basic reasons. First, it places undue emphasis on the scientist as *the* authority, with the result that we believe authority and exclude actual evidence. How many of us have not heard or used the phrase "scientists say," or "science knows," as if science, or the word of a scientist, were based on a special kind of knowledge using special techniques and special tools unknown to "normal" man. Although experiments may be carried out in the traditional fact-oriented classroom, they take the form of verifying facts; the experiment "fails" if the results are not consistent with the facts already known.

Second, and more important, the giving of facts is based on the assumption that young children think like miniature adults and can understand and absorb abstract evidence. We have learned from the work of Jean Piaget, and from our own experience at the Science Curriculum Improvement Study, that this is incorrect. We have seen that young children go through stages of thinking, beginning in the early school years with what Piaget terms the preoperational stage. At this level children are generally incapable of handling abstractions, even when concrete material is present. Many of the elementary school years are spent in the concrete operational stage—from the age of about six to twelve—during which abstractions and generalizations may be juggled and considered, but only when they concern experiments or concrete materials at hand.

Not until the stage of formal operations can children state hypotheses and make predictions based on theories of a general, rather than a specific, nature. From this we can conclude that facts, as abstractions,

will not have any reality to most elementary school children.

Yet traditional methods have not recognized that young children think differently than adults. In one textbook series, for example, the concept of the molecule is introduced to second-grade children. After seeing the confusion with which young children approach a simple Piagetian demonstration, we must conclude that if they believe in molecules it is on the same level as their belief in fairy tales. Tell a young child that he can smell something across the room because a tiny invisible particle floats through the air and into his nose, and it will be as real to him as a knight on a white horse being able to climb the glass mountain to save the princess. Indeed, giving children even our best facts at an early age is on the level of giving them fairy tales. They'll believe you, they'll go along with you, but the facts they learn will have as much relationship to their understanding of reality as a fairy tale has to a true story. Whether the authority is the teacher, the television announcer, or the Grimm Brothers, the result—unquestioning acceptance—is the same.

Is the introduction of facts to young children an incorrect objective in science teaching? Yes, if it is unrelated to reality—but no, if it is related to the child's real world and is presented at the proper moment in a teaching sequence. We should introduce the fact after the children have had enough experience to relate the fact to reality. Children in the first and second grade in SCIS classrooms use terms such as material, property, detritus, habitat, interaction, and life cycle. The difference is that the children have learned—through their own experience—what these concepts mean before they learn the terms to apply to them.

What difference does it make if children are given direct experiences? What significance does this have for the problems society is facing today? Contrasting two groups of older children—those whose background has not included an experiential approach with those who have participated in the SCIS program—gives us an interesting parallel to adult society.

During the developmental stages of *Ecosystems,* a unit dealing with the interplay of the community and the environment, we looked for a discrepant event to stimulate the children's investigations. Sixthgraders "know," they literally *know,* that plants give off oxygen and take in carbon dioxide. They "know" this because they've seen it on television and they've read it in books. Actually, this is not always the case. We asked the students to apply their "knowledge" in an experiment.

The children placed small sprigs of an aquatic plant in vials containing water and an indicator for carbon dioxide. The solution was green—showing that a quantity of carbon dioxide was dissolved in it. They reasoned that if plants do breathe in carbon dioxide, there would be less carbon dioxide in the water the next day, turning the solution from green to its original blue. Placing their vials throughout the classroom, the children sat back, secure in their prediction.

When the vials were collected the next day, the room was in chaos. Some of the children were delighted, for their predictions had borne out, but other children . . . . The color of their liquids had not turned back to blue; if anything, the liquid had become a pale yellow, indicating that carbon dioxide had been released into the water. What caused it? These fact-oriented students were quick with their answers. "It's a dirty vial," "It's dirty water." "You gave us the wrong liquid." "Maybe the plant's dying." For them, the experiment had not worked.

Finally one student ventured the idea that maybe plants don't all *always* take in carbon dioxide. Maybe, just maybe, plants give off carbon dioxide sometimes. His classmates would have torn him apart, had he not quickly placed a disclaimed: "Well, it's only a hypothesis." No further tests

were suggested which would have led the children to discover that plants *do* give off carbon dioxide in the dark. At twelve years old, they had closed their minds.

In the other sixth-grade class, where SCIS experience had shown the importance of relying on evidence, the children were also amazed by the results of their experiments. They, too, had predicted that the solutions in the vials would return to blue. Their initial reaction brought out similar complaints: "Something went wrong." But when one child suggested that he thought plants might give off carbon dioxide sometimes, his classmates were willing to try out his idea. Experimental vials were set up again to find out what conditions would cause plants to give off carbon dioxide. Some vials were placed on tabletops and desks, others went into cupboards, boxes and closets. The children were delighted with the results the next day: solutions in the light turned blue, but those in the dark had paled to yellow.

Let's examine closely and see the relationship of what happened with these children and what has literally happened to us in our society. The first group of children *knew* the answers. They had heard the answers from a source of authority. However, when they did their own experiments, they came up with contradictory evidence. Did they believe the evidence? No. The first thing they did was to try to explain away the contradictions with every tool at hand. The second group of children, who were willing to test out an idea even though it countered their preconceptions, had the valuable experience of finding out for themselves.

The similarities for decisions in adult society are great. First, we learn the answers to environmental problems from many sources: newspapers, television reports, and radio broadcasts. Since reports on controversial issues are frequently given in an authoritarian manner, we accept them. Then, knowing the answer, we find it very difficult to accept contrary evidence. We are either unequivocally *for* DDT, or violently against it. How many of us consider the conditions under which experiments are conducted: Were the birds studied by the English researcher similar in hormonal makeup to the brown pelican? Have other animals been found to respond to traces of tetraethyl lead? What other unnatural substances may be found in the pelican's environment or food supply? Is, in fact, the brown pelican's plight due to environmental conditions, or to disease, or some other natural cause?

If we continue to use the techniques in the classroom as we have done in the past, we will continue to decide answers on the basis of the person whose voice is the loudest, who is in the most eminent position of authority, or who can sell the very best idea, whether or not this idea is consistent with available evidence. The broad aim of science education is to help develop a group of adults who can weigh and sift evidence for themselves, who will remain open-minded, who will listen to hypotheses, and who will then make decisions on the merits of the evidence. In order to meet this aim we must change the procedures of science education. The change must be away from the introduction of general facts at an early level—away from fairy tales—and toward an emphasis on experience in processes and content so that the child will be continually challenged to examine discrepant events. So that he will say, "Hey wait a minute, look what's happening here."

PROGRAMS OF ENVIRONMENTAL EDUCATION

Programs of environmental education will involve the entire American educational system, both formal and nonformal. A formal educational system in this context is one which is targeted on specific student-teacher relationships, through specific curricula. A nonformal system is less definitive and structured and is directed toward the public at large, or particular segments of the general public.

The formal education system, from pre-school through continuing education, will directly affect about 50 percent of the American population in this decade. Initially, the principal effort in environmental education should be that of developing supplementary materials that are designed for the traditional curricula such as English, biology, mathematics, and history. In addition, the development of new curricula applicable to nearly all teaching and learning situations should be initiated. The approach is to infuse environmental and ecological concepts into all studies which lend themselves to changing man's life style to one of harmony with his world.

Another approach for school systems might be that of developing a special environmental curriculum through which the traditional subjects would be learned. A third approach, but less desirable at the primary and secondary level, would be the creation of a new course called environmental studies.

The challenge for formal education is the establishment of curricula with relevant ecological content, presented in a way to meet the present high motivation of students. This means that we must take advantage of all opportunities to relate learning experiences to actual environmental improvement and problem solving in the community (frequently referred to as "issue orientation").

The school must divorce itself from the traditional classroom concept and expand its frame of reference to make full use of all community resources in the curriculum.

SOURCE. Excerpts from *Environmental Education: Education that Cannot Wait,* published by the U.S. Office of Education, 1971, by permission of the U.S. Office of Education.

THE NATURE OF ENVIRONMENTAL EDUCATION

Environmental study areas, museums, libraries, local businesses and industries, and local government agencies all have a role to play in formal education.

The school administrators and teachers should orchestrate these resources into a workable curriculum, rather than concentrating on classroom materials. To accomplish this, it is imperative that a close working relationship (and frequent dialogue) be established among students, educators, businessmen, union leaders, and representatives of government at the local, state, and regional levels.

This will assist in formulating educational programs and activities that are relevant to real life issues . . . and give students the values, attitudes, and methods they will need to solve present and future problems deriving from pollution, increasing population, growing technology, resource depletion, and other environmental issues.

Nonformal education will reach important segments of the general public (and in some cases the entire population of a locality) with environmental education programs. This will be a major responsibility of local and national media, volunteer agencies, business and industry, and other private organizations.

It is essential that both local and network television, radio, film studios, newspapers, magazines, and book publishers contribute increasingly to informing the public about critical environmental problems and their possible solutions. In addition, the vast advertising and promotional resources of business and industry may be directed toward environmental and ecological issues.

Many private and volunteer organizations look to school facilities and personnel—as well as to the children, their parents, youth, and others directly related to the educational activities of the schools—for full utilization of the programs and activities these organizations offer. Such programs presently include square dances, spring and winter festivals, musical and dramatic productions, nature hikes and bird walks, and similar activities. In addition, museums and libraries frequently arrange for special exhibits, films, or discussions of interest to general or special groups.

Increasingly, as part of a comprehensive effort in environmental education, these voluntary and private agencies may wish to orient their programs toward EE objectives and to plan them in cooperation with local schools and colleges capable of providing assistance and publicity.

It would be desirable for a national nonprofit organization to accept as its primary task the creative role of encouraging, advising, and assisting private organizations and business to orient their considerable resources in nonformal education, information, promotion, and advertising toward EE objectives.

The emerging role of the local school system as participants in nonformal education should be emphasized. Everyone can recall situations in their hometowns and communities where administrative staff and teachers of local schools have contributed their talents and services, as well as the school facilities, to worthwhile community projects such as curtailing drug abuse. A vastly broadened activity of this nature is called for if all the varied educational resources of any community are to be coordinated in a nonformal EE effort.

Nonformal environmental education, sparked by local schools, may include sponsorship of seminars, briefings for businessmen and community leaders, public forums and exhibits, informational programs and contributions to media, operation of centers for volunteer activities, and development of clearinghouses for environmental information.

Correlation is the key to full utilization of community resources, and the local school system may be the best or only public agency available to carry out the responsibility.

SECTION 2

PSYCHOLOGICAL CONSIDERATIONS

This section of the book, containing Adah Maurer's article, is intended to appraise teachers of the likelihood of certain fears being raised in children as a result of environmental studies. Information of this type would prove useful to the teacher in more accurately assessing possible outcomes of particular lessons. It would also provide useful background in answering questions from concerned parents.

Environmental hazards such as polluted air or water fit into Maurer's natural hazard category. Apprently, most children fear animals, people, and machinery more than natural hazards. At ages 5 and 6, children have no fear at all of such natural hazards as storms, fire, water, waves, floods, volcano, etc. Between the ages of 7 to 14, from 26% to 35% of the subjects questioned in Maurer's study expressed such a fear.

Paul Mussen reported on a replication of Maurer's study.[*] Two-hundred children from kindergarten through sixth grade (approximately thirty per grade) were interviewed. Previous to grade six, children expressed no fear of pollution. At the sixth grade, 13% of the children did express this fear.

One of Maurer's conclusions has tremendous implications in environmental education. It is that the things children are taught to fear (traffic, germs, and kidnappers) are not the things they actually fear. Apparently children are likely to remain as blasé about stories of poisoned air and putrid water as they currently are about constant parent and teacher admonitions on America's number 1 threat to life—traffic hazards.

Maurer does find relationships between what a child fears and his maturity. As the child matures, the emotion of fear fastens upon more and more realistic objects. Experience learning becomes more significant than formal instruction.

[*]Based on personal correspondence between Dr. Paul Mussen, Professor of Psychology, University of California at Berkeley, and the writer.

Adah Maurer

WHAT CHILDREN FEAR

Children do not fear the atomic bomb.[1,11] They do not even fear the things they have been taught to be careful about: street traffic and germs. The strange truth is that they fear an unrealistic source of danger in our urban civilization: wild animals. Almost all 5- and 6-year-olds and more than one-half of 7- to 12-year-olds claim that the things to be afraid of are mammals and reptiles (most frequently): snakes, lions, and tigers. Not until age 12 or more do most children recognize actual sources of danger and, when they do, these dangers are almost always highly personal rather than politically or socially determined.[2]

One 12-year-old boy said that the things to be afraid of are "Wild animals, fierce dogs and cats, and snakes." Another of the same age answered "Not being able to get a job." Both boys had earned intelligence scores within the normal range (low 90s) on the Wechsler Intelligence Scale for Children. Both had mild learning problems, but there the similarity ended. After an assessment that included achievement tests, the school history, parent interviews, and a study of the family dynamics, a marked difference became apparent. The first boy had been overprotected and lacked opportunity to care for himself and to make

decisions. He was the youngest of a large family and had been babied and restricted in experiences. The second boy had been overwhelmed with excessive demands from his parents. His irresponsible father had drifted from one menial job to another and was unemployed at the time of the study. The boy, the eldest of his siblings, had borne the brunt of his father's disgust at the latter's incompetence and had been belittled and criticized to an excessive degree. Compared to that of the first boy, the conversation of the second boy seemed mature.

Did the answers these boys gave to the question about fears reflect in some measure the underlying problem? In the second case, it would seem that it did, yet without knowing the kinds of answers one might expect from normal children, it would be easy to jump to unwarranted conclusions. Was the first boy's fear of animals due to some traumatic experience? Had he lived in a primitive area where wild animals actually were a threat to his safety? Or had his father been a pioneer and entertained the boy with tales of the dangers of the woods? And if any of these suppositions had been true (which they were not) did they relate in any way to his learning prob-

SOURCE. Reprinted, by permission, from *The Journal of Genetic Psychology*, Vol. 106, 1965, with slight abridgment.

lems? To answer questions such as these and to determine the etiology of fear in children became the purpose of a year-long study of normal children.

A 5-year-old boy, referred because of excessive aggressiveness, answered the question thus: "Dogs!" He was encouraged to go on. "And what else?" He grimaced and said, "Dog, dog, two dogs!" In the silence that followed he screamed, "DOGS!" Again he was asked, "Anything else?" More quietly, but still firmly he said, "Ten dogs." He proved to be a very fearful child, uncertain of the stability of his home and of his place in it. His belligerence in school seemed to stem from a psychological need to defend himself.

Children's fears have been explained by several diverse theories. The first, a folklore, denies that children fear by calling the emotion "stubbornness." The parents of the boy who feared dogs, dogs, ten dogs said, "We've told him that dogs won't hurt him but he won't listen!" The attempted cure had been repeated spankings for this and much else, and spankings again for passing the punishment on to his contemporaries.

The Freudian considers fear as a displacement of the son's fear of the father who, so the child believes, will retaliate for the son's incestuous desire for his mother by castrating the son. The Freudian postulates that, during the oral stage characterized by sucking, the child fears being eaten because he feels guilt about his desire to eat (or bite) his mother's breast.[3] Psychoanalytic therapy has consisted of an effort to resolve an oedipal triangle, thus permitting the child to enter the genital phase of his development. The American Academy of Child Psychiatry has re-evaluated this formulation, as have many of the neo-Freudians; but the emphasis remains firmly rooted in the dynamics of the child's emotional involvement with his parents.[5,9]

The behaviorist finds that fears are conditioned responses based upon associational ties with one or another of the fears present at birth. John B. Watson, the earliest behaviorist to apply the theory to child rearing, was certain that the fear of dogs proceeded from a traumatic experience in which the loud barking of a dog had triggered the original fear of loud sounds. His recommended cure consisted of unconditioning the fear by the introduction of a dog or a toy dog at some pleasant time, such as during a meal, and gradually bringing it closer until it could be tolerated on the tray.[12] This theory, too, has undergone considerable modification; but the emphasis remains upon the learning, unlearning, and modification of fear through environmental experiences.

A follower of Jung's early theories[6] would explain a fear of animals as an expression of the collective unconscious. In more primitive times, the boy's ancestors feared the rampaging wolf, the stealthy poisonous snake, and other natural enemies. Although the boy lives in the midst of the trappings of civilization, and the descendants of the wolf have been tamed to family pets; yet deeply submerged is the tribal fear, built in perhaps to the neutral network present but dormant at birth. Thus the child goes through a stage that he outgrows as he matures into succeeding phases of the ontogenetic recapitulation of the history of his race. This theory has been muddied by mysticism and has been neglected in the ongoing debate between the psychoanalysts and the experimentalists. Animal ecologists,[7] however, have demonstrated the specificity of fears in animals, notably in the giraffe which animal, though born in captivity and raised on a bottle, nevertheless startles and shies away from the mock-up of a lion, the traditional enemy of his species; but approaches and sniffs at the mock-up of a giraffe. Humans, however, generally are considered to have lost their instincts and to have become dependent upon learning.

Gesell[4] and the maturation theorists have demonstrated the primacy of growth in physical and mental functions, yet for the most part they have omitted similar studies of the maturation of the emotions, especially of fear. It may be that they have thought of fear as an abnormal manifestation or a malfunctioning rather than as an aspect of normal growth.

The eclectic finds it difficult to choose among the theories for they have little in common. Psychoanalysts have been concerned chiefly with the abnormal, and their preemption of the subject of fear has colored general thinking along these lines. The behaviorists have dealt with fear largely as a means to eliminate unwanted responses. Their use of punishment is empirical, with no discussion of fear it arouses since fear is a subjective phenomenon. Yet it should be obvious that a judicious, rational fearfulness is life preservative and therefore an inescapable aspect of the normal child.[8] Excessive, irrational fears are widely known to be intimately connected with learning difficulties, delinquency, and withdrawal. Preventive methodology requires more knowledge of the normal fears of normal children thus defining, highlighting, and permitting evaluation of the unique and the aberrant.

Based upon the results of this study, each of the major theories appears to contain some part of the truth. It also becomes clear that the amount, depth, and kind of fear as well as its objects is ascertainable and definitely of diagnostic value.

METHOD

Over a period of a year, each child who was given the Wechsler Intelligence Scale for Children was asked an additional question. At the conclusion of the comprehension subtest, in the same neutral tone used for other questions, the examiner said, "What are the things to be afraid of?" Each answer was recorded as nearly verbatim as possible, as were all answers for all subtests. Silent approval and recognition that the fears were legitimate was given by a sympathetic nod. When the child stopped speaking he was encouraged to go on. "And what else?" and then, "Anything else?" Four children replied "Nothing." One answered "You shouldn't be afraid of anything." In these cases, to provide the ease of replying by projection, the question was rephrased, "Some children are afraid of some things some of the time, aren't they?" All nodded or said "Yes." The examiner continued: "What are these children sometimes afraid of?" In all cases this brought a satisfactory reply.

The direct question "What are you afraid of?" was not used because children might interpret this as critical and tend to reply defensively. Since the question necessarily came after four failures (except for the brightest who scored very high in comprehension) most of the children seemed relieved by an "easy" one and, with some exceptions, the answers flowed smoothly and without shock. For severely disturbed children, the question was omitted.

SUBJECTS

The subjects of the study consisted of 130 children of whom 91 were boys and 39 were girls. In age they ranged from 5 years and 5 months to 14 years and 6 months. All of them were in regular attendance at elementary schools in middle- or lower-middle-class suburbs. Eighteen of them proved to be mentally retarded (nine boys, nine girls), two of them severely (one boy, one girl). Since the study was for the purpose of tabulating the fears of normal children, these 18 were eliminated from all calculations except one. In this one calculation, the attempt was made to determine whether replies conformed to a chronological or mental-age pattern and the retarded were included in the group of their mental-age mates. In all other tabulations and discussions, the subjects are the 112 students whose IQs fell between 80 and 144 (see Tables 1 and 2.)

EDUCATIONAL IMPLICATIONS

TABLE 1. Subjects in the Study by Age and Sex

Age	Boys	Girls	Total
5 and 6	13	7	20
7 and 8	20	9	29
9 and 10	21	10	31
11 and 12	18	1	19
13 and 14	10	3	13
Total	82	30	112

TABLE 2. Subjects in the Study by IQ Scores*

| | Intelligence quotient | | |
| | Slow | Average | Bright |
Age	80-89	90-110	111-144
5 and 6	2	14	4
7 and 8	8	12	9
9 and 10	7	18	6
11 and 12	4	12	3
13 and 14	8	5	0
Total	29	61	22

*The distribution approaches the normal probability of 22, 68, 22 percent in the three divisions, respectively, closely enough to consider this a fair sample of school children.

RESULTS

Of the 467 responses, 233 or 50 percent, consisted of a single category: animals. Seventy-two of the 112 children, or 64 percent, replied solely or partly by naming animals in general or one or more specific animals including: alligator, ape, bat, bear, bee, bird, black widow, bobcat, buffalo, bull, cat, centipede, cow, crocodile, deer, dinosaur, dog, eel, elephant, fox, gorilla, hawk, hippopotamus, horse, insect, leopard, lion, lizard, mosquito, mountain lion, parakeet, pinchbug, rat, reptile, rhinoceros, scorpion, shark, snake, spider, spit-monkey, tarantula, tiger, turtle, wildcat, whale and wolf.

The most unpopular animal is the snake. Thirty-three of the subjects, 23 boys and 10 girls (28 percent and 33 percent respectively) mentioned them. Next in order came lions, mentioned 28 times; tigers, 14 times; and bears, 9 times.

The most striking fact that emerged from the study, besides the near universality of fear of animals, is that fear of animals decreases sharply with age (from 80 percent of the 5- and 6-year-olds to 23 percent of those 13 and 14 years old). The older children also tended to qualify their responses. Rather than simply "Lion, tiger," they said "Wild animals if you are in a jungle without arms," "Dogs with rabies," "A cow that might kick you," or "A parakeet that's infected."

Fear of the dark seems to disappear after age 7, with only two stragglers who admitted to it after that age, both of them qualifying their responses: "Little kids are afraid of the dark," and "Highways at night." Similarly, fears of nonexistent entities, such as monsters, the boogie man, ghosts, witches, and animated skeletons, are left behind after age 10. Thus the questions about the effect of television dramas highlighting horror becomes a matter of age. Fright films would seem to be traumatic before the child thoroughly understands that they are only imaginary; after that age, the possibility of their being therapeutic may enter. Age 9 to 10 appears to be the dividing line.

PSYCHOLOGICAL CONSIDERATIONS

Unique and individual responses rise from zero at 5 and 6 years to 46 percent as children reach early adolescence. The subject matter becomes more realistic and more closely tied to learned or experienced objects and situations (see Table 3).

TABLE 3. **Subject Matter of Fears**

Age	Animals	People	Dark	Spooks	Natural hazards	Machinery	Misc.
5 and 6	80	20	20	33	0	20	0
7 and 8	73	17	3	17	34	34	14
9 and 10	61	42	3	10	35	35	16
11 and 12	68	42	0	0	26	42	26
13 and 14	23	39	0	0	31	46	46

*In each age group, the percent of subjects who replied that things to be afraid of were such as to be classifiable under the categories. "People" includes "bad men," "kidnappers," "people who . . . ," "if somebody . . . ," as well as members of the family and playmates mentioned by name. "Spooks" includes "monsters," "ghosts," "witches," "man made of iron," "Frankenstein," etc. "Natural hazards" includes storms, fire, water, waves, flood, volcano, etc. Machinery includes all man-made gadgets and inventions, such as weapons, cars, electricity, trains, etc.

The question arises: Is this maturational trend a function of chronological age or does intelligence play a part? Two severely retarded children, whose replies were not tabulated with the above, gave immature replies. The boy (age 14:7, IQ 44, MA 6:8) said, "Cow, horse, goat, snake." The girl (age 15:6, IQ 46, MA 7:5) said, "Bears, lions, train if you go in front of it, and alligators." On the other hand, an exceptionally bright boy (age 9:6, IQ 134, MA 14:2) answered the same question, "Things you can't overcome." Asked to explain, he added, "Well, if you are afraid of water, for example, you probably will never overcome it." His home life showed an excessive responsibility for his mother who lived under the constant tension of having her husband away from home for long stretches on cruise as a Lieutenant Commander in the Navy.

Fear of fire is the traditional example used to prove that children learn by experience. "A burnt child fears the fire" seems to imply that the unburnt child does not or that only by experience does the child learn to fear or learn what to fear. The folk saying is older than central heating and seems to have little specific pertinence in today's world. Among our 20 children of 5 and 6 years (who gave a total of 91 replies), 54 replies were of animals, only one was fire. Four percent of the 7- and 8-year-olds, five percent of the 9- and 10-year-olds, 16 percent of the 11- and 12-year-olds and nine percent of the oldest group included fire (forest fire, burning house, etc.) among the things to be feared. In no case, however, could it be ascertained that this response sprang from a personal experience. The one child known to have suffered extensive burns, a girl (age 11:6, IQ 60, MA 6:9) replied with a standard "Lion, tiger, dog, cat, snakes, rattlers, spiders." Her scars, which extended from neck to buttocks on her back, had been covered with grafts from her thighs. They had come to be her one claim upon her contemporaries for awed attention and upon adults for sympathy. Accordingly, she valued them and was quick to lift her skirts for strangers, a habit that tended to be misinterpreted. Asked directly if she feared fire, she looked puzzled and then smiled happily, "I guess so."

Other natural hazards mentioned by this group of children included storms, deep water, waves, earthquake, volcano, hurricane, tornado, quicksand, sharp rocks, cliffs, a tunnel cave-in, avalanche ("snow falling down from the hill"), poison oak, and the desert. No one of them was mentioned often enough to have any general significance. Individually, some seemed merely to represent the most recent subject of adventure stories read or viewed; others proved to have deep personal significance in the light of subsequent parent interviews. As a group, natural hazards (including fires) supplied one of the responses of the 5- and 6-year-olds, but from one-fourth to one-third of the responses of the 7- to 12-year-olds. The age of adventure thus begins at 7.

Machinery is perhaps an inadequate title for a category that includes cars, trucks, trains, construction, buildings, airplanes, guns, knives, electricity, a trapdoor, explosions, a submarine, helicopter, firecrackers, rusty nails, bicycles, a tractor, a crane, a hatchet, electric chair, gas, falling bricks, trolley car and a stairwell. What was intended was a grouping of those hazards that are man made and that are elements of an industrial civilization. Here it is obvious that learning has taken place. There is no possibility that a collective unconscious could have suggested to a boy that tractors are dangerous because "you might move the wrong lever and it would start up." The amazing discovery lies in the fact that teaching has had so little effect.

Surely every kindergartener and first grader listens to lengthy lessons about the dangers inherent in highways, traffic, cars, and trucks. Yet when asked what are the things to be afraid of, not one gave evidence of having learned his lesson. Among older children—7 to 14—only 15 percent of the replies referred in any way to the Number 1 threat to life in America today. Automobile accidents account for more deaths and disabilities among school-age children than any disease and far more than all the dangers that children fear put together. Perhaps this is just as well. We would not want our children to be terrified of crossing a street in the same unreasoning sense that some of them are terrified of dogs. Es-

tablishing the habit of stop, look, and listen before you cross is apparently enough; to add warnings of peril is ineffective because, for whatever reason it is not learned.

Trains, usually qualified, were mentioned 11 times; weapons only seven times. All the others were unique replies. Many of them were qualified or explained. Some children went on to tell of personal experiences that gave important clues to their life style. The boy who replied "Walking down the highway at night you might be hit by a car" had indeed been doing just that. His wanderings in search (it would seem) of a 1st father helped to explain his listlessness in school. Another who listed "Big cranes, big trucks, when you're tearing down a house" was describing his father's occupation and admitting inadvertently both his fear of his father and his fear that his father would leave.

The category "people" was also revealing of underlying difficulties. Forty-five replies involved "people who . . . (come with guns, hit you, try to give you trouble," etc.) or specific persons. Alas for learning only five mentioned "Somebody who tells you to get in his car." All children should have been warned against child enticers; perhaps most had been, but spooks, monsters, and ghosts remained frightening to more children than kidnappers. One boy blurted out "My brother! He comes up behind me in the dark and says, 'Boo!' " Another, a girl, replied "People who might try to make you nervous or give you a heart attack." She was describing, not her own, but her mother's palpitations. Five children said, "If your parents get a divorce." This should perhaps be a separate category since it indicated not a fear of people but a resurgence of the separation anxiety of infancy. In these cases there was little need to hunt further for the cause of poor school work. A family break up, almost without exception, causes at least a temporary emotional upheaval in the children that is often reflected in an inability to concentrate.

Miscellaneous responses included: war, 5; the atom bomb, 2; punishment, 4; disease, 4; separation ("if you're all alone," "if you get lost," etc.), 4; breaking the moral code, 2; death, 6; unemployment, 1; and Hell, 1. Some of these seemed to be thoughtful assessments of dangers in the abstract. Others were obviously specific to the particular life situation of the child. A few were so strange as to be baffling. One boy replied "My little brother sleeps with me" possibly implying that otherwise he would be afraid of the dark or that there was danger in this arrangement either for the brother or himself. It could not be determined, and was not necessary. The parents, with very little persuasion, agreed to provide bunk beds. Another changed the subject: "We planted some flowers in our garden," and would say no more. There is a farfetched possibility that the "flowers" might have been marijuana and that the girl sensed her parents' concern about being caught or that a body was buried in the garden and camouflaged, but such speculations were considered out of bounds and the matter was not pursued.

CONCLUSIONS

The question, "What are the things to be afraid of?" asked routinely in the course of the Wechsler test proved to be an important clue to the emotional dynamics of the child being tested.

Eighty percent of children of 5 and 6 reply to the question by naming one or more wild animals, with snake, lion, tiger, and bear predominating. Sixty percent or more of children between the ages of 7 and 12 answer similarly but, after mental age 12, it is rare.

One-third of children under 7 admit to fear of imaginary beings (monsters mainly), and a fifth of them fear the dark. Both of these replies drop off sharply after age 7.

The things that children are taught to fear (traffic, germs, and kidnappers) are rarely mentioned. Punishment, war, and the atom bomb are also scarce replies at any age although it is likely that children would answer "yes" if they were asked directly "Do you fear . . . any of these?"

As children mature, the kinds of things they regard as frightening become diverse, unique, and are often tied directly or indirectly to their central concern.

Refusals to answer, replies of "Nothing," long pauses, changes of volume or pitch of the voice, and facial expressions (while not common) provide clues to the intensity of the fear.

An "immature" reply may characterize the well-protected child and in some cases the mentally retarded. The child who has been burdened with excessive responsibility or hardship is more likely than others to give a unique, "mature" reply, as is also the bright child with a mental age of 12 or more.

Much caution is needed in interpretation, for recent events and the child's mood during the examination may be the fleeting cause of any particular answer.

All four of the major theories of childhood (psychoanalysis, behaviorism, the collective unconscious, and maturation) contribute, albeit incompletely, to an understanding of childhood fears.

A strong maturational factor, partly influenced by intelligence and partly influenced by the amount of responsibility thrust upon the child, seems to be at work upon an archaic instinctual base. The child is born with the capacity to fear, apparently more than is necessary to preserve his life. Although he feels fear, the child does not know with the same certainty as the smaller-brained mammals just what objects or situations are to be feared. Much infant questioning,[10] especially that relating to life and death, is prompted by a curiosity about the missing information and by a desire to locate accurately the causative objects of the amorphous sense of possible danger. If archaic instincts to avoid specific hazards are lacking, it may be that the fear of being eaten by wild animals or poisoned by snakes retains a certain ease of arousal. Among the uneducated, the folk habit of enforcing obedience by supplying incorrect information to children for the purpose of controlling them ("The wizard man will eat you if you stray!") is enormously effective, but also, by rousing archaic fears,

it may be a limiting factor to the full use of mental powers.

As the child matures, the emotion of fear fastens upon more and more realistic objects depending upon experience learning rather than upon instruction.

The intensity of the child's fear depends for the most part upon the family relationships.

REFERENCES

1. Escalona, S. "Children's responses to nuclear threat." *Children,* 1963, **10**, 137-142.

2. Freud, A., & Burlingame, D. *War and Children.* New York: Willard, 1943.

3. Freud, S. Analysis of a phobia in a five year old boy. In *Collected Papers. Vol. III.* London: Hogarth Press and the Institute of Psycho-Analysis, 1925. Pp. 149-288.

4. Gesell, A., & Amatruda, C. *Developmental Diagnosis.* New York: Harper, 1941.

5. Josselyn, I. Concepts related to child development: The oral stage. *J. Child Psychiat.,* 1962, **1**, 209-224

6. Jung, C.G. The Archtypes and the Collective Unconscious. *Collected Works— Bollinger Series.* New York: Pantheon Books, 1962.

7. Masserman, J. Ethology, comparative biodynamics and psychoanalytic research. In Scher, M.D. (Ed.), *Theories of the Mind.* New York: Free Press, 1962. Pp. 15-64.

8. Maurer, A. The child's knowledge of non-existence. *J. Exist. Psychiat.,* 1961, **2**, 193-212.

9. _____. Did little Hans really want to marry his mother? *J. Hum. Psychol.,* 1964, **4**, 139-148.

10. Piaget, J. *Language and Thought of the Child.* New York: Meridian, 1955. Pp. 171-240.

11. Schwebel, M. Nuclear cold war: Student opinions. Unpublished manuscript read at the convention of the American Orthopsychiatric Association, March, 1963.

12. Watson, J.B. *Behaviorism.* Chicago: Univ. Chicago Press, 1959.

SECTION 3

PLANNING A SCHOOL PROGRAM

The six articles presented in this section provide the keys to a successful school-wide ecology action. Although each article stands on its own and may be read independently of the others, the reader will find it more productive to read them in sequential order.

The first article provides the theoretical rationale upon which the other articles are grounded. It cites research from the behavioral sciences which suggests the manner in which organizational members should proceed in order to achieve institutional goals. Organizational structure, leadership roles, communication channels, and relationships between participants are all considered within the context of environmental education. The precepts suggested are applicable to curricular change in all subject areas. Inasmuch as environmental education is our concern, examples are given from this field.

The second article uses the framework established by the first article to show how an environmental program is evolved within an elementary or secondary school setting. The staff environmental committee constitutes the nucleus for environmental planning. It is a guiding agency for all ecological activities within the school. There is an elucidation of the roles of staff and student ecological groups and discussion of relationships between intra-school planning and community agencies and resources.

The third, fourth, and fifth articles focus upon student action groups in greater detail. They deal very practically with the problems of organizing and conducting elementary and secondary school ecology clubs. Goals, membership, activities, etc., are discussed in considerable detail.

"Organization and Activities of an Elementary School Ecology Club" is general in nature and provides a broad framework upon which to establish an elementary school action group. The fourth article by Hope Swatt and Annette Willens is more specific and gives details on exactly how one particular club in one particular group conducted its program. Examples of dramatizations, newspapers, and club announcements are given.

The fifth article, by Cornelius Troost, stresses the organization and activities of a high school ecology action group. High school students, being more mature than their elementary counterparts, can become involved in fairly ambitious projects, some of which are listed in the article.

273

Harold Altman

ENVIRONMENTAL EDUCATION: A VEHICLE FOR INNOVATIVE PRACTICES AND INSTRUCTIONAL CHANGE

The enthusiasm demonstrated by people who have rallied under the environmental banner is in many ways equaled by their impatience with traditional premises and procedures. They reject previously unquestioned basic assumptions and adopt a wholly different outlook on such sacred cows as technological advance, industrial growth, and population expansion. They are committed to the preservation and improvement of the environment. They recognize that implicit with this commitment is a call to action which may include anything from minor reforms to drastic changes in the way of life as we know it today.

INNOVATIVE TECHNIQUES

To achieve these changes it is often necessary to use newer techniques for improved processes of communication and decision-making. Successful citizen's action committees in such places as the Florida Everglades and San Francisco Bay employed such innovative techniques as *action research, temporary systems, change agents, and collaborative efforts.* They relied on an *overall strategy* in directing their goal oriented efforts.

Teachers involved in a program of environmental education who wish to retain the same spirit of dedication among students and teachers would be well advised to consider some of these same strategies. The development and retention of student and teacher zeal is basic to the program's success. These strategies employ the natural built-in motivation for growth and change which exists in every individual and is la-

SOURCE. By permission of the author.

274

tent in every organization (Rogers, 1967; McGregor, 1960).

They can be used by the principal and/or the school-wide teacher chairman, the teacher advisor to the student ecology club, or the classroom teacher. They would prove equally useful for the development of any newer curricular program within a school or classroom setting.

ACTION RESEARCH

A method of on-the-spot research which enables a participant to determine answers to his own problems as he attempts to perform organizational tasks is often referred to as *action research* (Corey, 1953). This type of research is aimed at the solution of an immediate problem arising as part of the operation of the school.

Action research usually starts with the collaborative diagnosis of a problem situation. In this first step, data is collected as a means of "arousing dissatisfaction" (Miel, 1946). A study of data produced by survey instruments or opinion polls arouses interest and attention. In environmental studies, the field trip, classroom investigation, and common concern over an existing ecological nuisance also serve as interest producing devices.

The second step usually involves interpreting the data and forming a diagnosis. It must be emphasized that the group members are the ones who review the data, form the diagnosis, and if necessary, request help from a *change agent* to better serve their needs (Havelock, 1967).

The third step involves testing of various prescriptions as treatment is applied. Research is used in interpreting, diagnosing, setting up programs, getting material assistance, and designing evaluations. The participant is the one to initiate the request for research data and "reaches out" to obtain information needed to effect desired changes in his group (Wiles, 1966). In a classroom setting, students use all resources at their command to test their original

hypotheses and find answers to their questions. Rich assortments of books, periodicals, or audio-visual aids to accommodate student inquiry are needed. Volunteer personnel from local environmental agencies are often a helpful source of information.

If change is seen as something that is very much wanted, if it comes as a result of certain dissatisfactions on the part of the person who will be most affected by the change, rather than the top echelon handing it down, there is a far greater possibility for a new program to take place.

BUREAUCRATIC STRUCTURE

The *structure of the system* itself is an important consideration in the adoption of innovative programs and practices. School systems are bureaucracies. The bureaucratic model is characterized by fixed and official jurisdictional areas, hierarchical authority structures, and administration by full-time trained officials. Authorities administer on the basis of written documents, established regulations, and comprehensive general policies (Presthus, 1962).

In a bureaucracy, innovation is restricted for several reasons: (1) Authority and initiation cascade down from the top in hierarchical fashion. (2) Bureaucratic organizations are conservative, and novel solutions appear threatening. (3) Innovative behavior is sometimes interpreted as unreliability. (4) Strong subunit identifications arise so that people are more concerned with internal distribution of power than organizational goal accomplishment (Thompson, 1965).

ROLE OF THE SCHOOL ADMINISTRATOR

The administrator plays a key role in the ultimate success of change efforts. In most cases, he is charged with responsibility for the ongoing success of the school's educational programs and is given authority commensurate with this responsibility. His prestige and authority can play a great part in determining a final outcome. "The administrator is powerful because he has authority. Authority is a critical element in innovation because proposed changes generate mixed reactions which can prevent consensus among peers and result in stagnation" (Brickell, 1964:503). The authority of the classroom teacher is generally limited to those factors immediately and directly related to his own classroom. It is the administrator who can allocate school-wide resources in terms of people, money, or time.

ROLE OF THE CHANGE AGENT

While the school administrator holds a responsibility for the total and ongoing educational program, he can best exercise this responsibility through *change agents* who act in a consultant capacity. A change agent can achieve his fullest potential when the administrator allows the school staff sufficient freedom for experimentation and innovation. When staff members seek to develop their own programs to achieve desirable environmental objectives, they voluntarily and willingly call on change agents for assistance.

A change agent intervenes at different structured points at different times. He uses the strategy of making an appropriate selection of the proper variable at the proper time. One of the best descriptions of the change agent's role is made by Howes, when he states that a modern teacher moves away from being a transmitter of knowledge toward behaving as a responder controlled by the pupil; moves away from being the initiator-developer toward being a contributor-reactor; and moves away from being a programmer-director toward being a co-designer-assister (Howes, 1967).

The change agent could hold a variety of roles such as researcher, trainer, counselor, teacher, or line manager. He could be an insider who works in the local school, or an outsider from central headquarters. He may come from another organization entirely. He could be a paid person or work in a purely volunteer capacity. An outsider may have greater detachment and perspective in promoting change, but an insider generates less suspicion. It is possible that there may be a great value in the use of teams of insiders-outsiders (Lippitt, 1965). An environmental inside-outside team could be the school chairman working collaboratively with a local expert from the National Wildlife Federation.

NEWER STRUCTURES

In order to increase innovation, it is possible that the future will see structures of diverse problem-solving specialists linked together with coordinating specialists. These new structures will either replace the bureaucratic structure of school systems or function alongside it. Task forces linked by expertise much more than vertical status role may work on a particular issue rather than a whole series of diverse issues. This problem-oriented group may well produce the looser, more untidy structures necessary for improved self-actualization. From this technique may come the authentic relationships necessary to engender the freedom and creativity needed for innovation in bureaucracy. Improved collaboration between superiors and subordinates would lead to increased worker self-control, improved decision-making, and a better climate for innovation (Bennis, 1966).

Temporary systems are one example of these newer structures. They may be the keystone to a future organizational structure which will mitigate some of the harsher effects of formal organizations and enable people from varying ranks and echelons to work in a collaborative manner in a solution of common tasks (Miles, 1964). A *temporary system* consists of a group of people, selected according to aptitude and attitude, working within a narrowed time perspective, and focusing on a sharply defined goal.

Participants are chosen according to skill and competence rather than rank. They experience greater creativity and improved freedom because they focus on a particular problem of mutual interest, find it easier to develop new norms since they are unhampered by the status roles assigned to them in the permanent system, and work in an atmosphere of reduced anxiety in a "mini world" of physical and social isolation.

The temporary system has some of the features of action research through its organization around issues to be solved and the enlistment of aid from those people most competent to solve them.

In Part 2, the article "Everglades Jetport" describes a temporary system composed of a coalition of 20 national conservation, environmental, and economics organizations. It was designed to keep a commercial jetport out of the Everglades and used a research report by a recognized expert, Luna B. Leopold. This report so adequately documented possible ecological damage to the Everglades that plans for the jetport were abandoned.

GROUP EFFORTS

Collaborative efforts by administrators, teachers, and an outside resource team are better than reliance on any one role alone (Fox and Lippitt, 1964). Group target setting offers advantages that cannot be achieved by individual target setting. Many significant objectives and measures of performance can be developed for the group. Participation of all members of a subsystem towards organizational goals results in better achievement and improved decision-making as all members work toward a common purpose. The use of the inside-outside team is a good collaborative technique on either the classroom, school building, school system, or community system change levels.

Collaboration between teachers is often called *team teaching*. In this type of or-ganizational pattern, two or more teachers take responsibility for all or part of the instruction of the same group of students (Shaplin and Olds, 1964). Team teaching has the advantage of providing better opportunities for teachers to be assigned jobs most suitable to their interests and abilities. It could be of particular value in the study of environmental problems since the subject is interdisciplinary and requires familiarity with a diversity of science and social studies fields. Rarely does one teacher possess all of the ecological, economical, and political understandings needed to deal with this subject. Team teaching also provides opportunity for differentiated staffing in which teacher assistants, paraprofessionals, and specialists may supplement the regular teaching staffs.

In environmental education, as in all other activities, school staffs must get together and develop methods to improve the vertical (hierarchical) and horizontal (peer group) information flow. One way to do this is through the use of survey instruments as a source of data for freer communication. These instruments improve morale and enable school staffs to work toward goal classification and action research type of activities. Groups can more easily focus upon their needs as they feel them.

OVERALL STRATEGY

Change within a social system involves an appropriate blending of a variety of techniques according to a preconceived master plan. It could include telling, showing, involving, training, restructuring, or value orientation change (Guba, 1968). It would involve inside and/or outside change agents, much use of action research, and the traditional type of inservice and college training to develop technical skills.

Environmental education is more than acquisition of facts. It requires a change in values, attitudes, and interpersonal relations. It is socio-cultural change. Strategic models for socio-cultural change utilize a variety of programs and recognize that a length of time such as 2-5 years may be needed before change takes place.

The change program shows a "concern for people" and a "concern for production," therefore, it has emotional and intellectual content. The organization is approached as a system, rather than a series of tasks to be performed. The need for cooperation of top management is taken for granted, and the program is phased so it evolves from individuals, to group, to intergroup, to overall organization (Bennis, 1966).

A truly successful program of environmental education would more nearly resemble a crusade than still another curricular program superimposed on the work load of already overworked teachers. It would be heralded as "teacher-proved," rather than "teacher-proof." It would make use of modern, imaginative, innovative practices. These practices would be applied to the organizational framework of the school and take into account the structure, the status roles, and the needs of the various people within the local school in effecting overall change strategies.

REFERENCES

Bennis, Warren G. *Changing Organizations.* New York: McGraw-Hill Co., 1966.

Brickell, Henry M. "State Organization for Educational Change: A Case Study and a Proposal." *Innovation in Education* (Mathew B. Miles, ed.) New York: Teachers College, 1964.

Corey, Stephen M. *Action Research to Improve School Practices.* New York: Teachers College, 1953.

Fox, Robert S., and Lippitt, Ronald. "The Innovation of Classroom Mental Health Practices." *Innovation in Education.* (Mathew B. Miles, ed.) New York: Teachers College, 1964.

Guba, Egon G. "Diffusion of Innovations." *Educational Leadership,* 25, 292-295. January 1968.

Havelock, Ronald G. "Linking Research to Practice: What Role for the Linking Agent?" Research paper prepared for the AERA Symposium on Training Linking Agents, February 16, 1967. (Mimeo)

Howes, Virgil, et al. *Individualization of Instruction, A Search.* Los Angeles: Educational Inquiry, Inc., 1967.

Lippitt, Ronald. "Roles and Processes in Curriculum Development and Change." *Strategy for Curriculum Change.* Washington, D.C.: ASCD, 1965.

Miel, Alice. *Changing the Curriculum.* Appleton-Century-Crofts, Inc., 1946.

Miles, Mathew B. "On Temporary Systems." *Innovation in Education.* (Mathew B. Miles, ed.) New York: Teachers College, 1964.

McGregor, Douglas. *The Human Side of Enterprise.* New York: McGraw-Hill Co., 1960.

Presthus, Robert. *The Organizational Society.* New York: Alfred A. Knopf, Inc., 1962.

Rogers, Carl. "A Plan for Self-Directed Change in an Educational System." *Educational Leadership* 24, 717-731. May 1967.

Shaplin, Judson T., and Olds, Henry F., Jr., (eds.). *Team Teaching.* Harper, 1964.

Thompson, Victor A. "Bureaucracy and Innovation." *Administrative Science Quarterly,* 10, 1-20. June 1965.

Wiles, Kimball. "Curriculum Change: Where and When." Address to the Florida ASCD Annual Conference. St. Petersburg, Florida, January 1966.

Harold Altman

Cornelius J. Troost

PLANNING A SCHOOL PROGRAM FOR ENVIRONMENTAL EDUCATION

Few, if any, educators today doubt the need for the universal adoption of environmental educational programs. The need is obvious and urgent. Our environment is being degraded at a rapid rate. Educational programs can make a substantial contribution to the production of informed, willing citizens who can involve themselves in the complex business of trying to stem the tide of ecological disaster.

BACKGROUND

The stage is set for substantial advances in environmental education. At no time before have we had such an outpouring of magazine articles, TV programs, and public discussions on this topic. But we cannot rest on mere consciousness of our socioecological problems. The knowledge, practices, and intellectual skills essential to mature,

systematic action can be obtained best in organized school programs. Young people must grow up in an environmental education curriculum which is continuous and which prepares them to confront the polluted, overpopulated world which is their inheritance.

Environmental education will take on many forms. Certainly many school districts are hard at work developing curriculum guides in this broad area. State curriculum committees have already adopted and will be adopting broad guidelines for curriculum development in environmental education. National environmental curriculum projects in the separate fields of science and social studies have already gone through the trial stages and are now being published commercially. School districts all over the country are in the process of developing innovative environmental education pro-

SOURCE. By permission of the authors.

grams. The precise form of environmental education programs depends upon many variables. These include such factors as the following: nature of the guidelines, structure of the curricula developed on paper, administrative talent and interest, teaching personnel and their commitment, student values, interest and abilities, facilities and equipment, and type of community surrounding the school.

MAKING A START

Through the broad guidelines provided in this text (especially William Stapp's *Environmental Encounters*—Part 3) interested school personnel and students can indeed begin the process of developing environmental education programs which fit local circumstances. Careful study and utilization of the activities and ideas in Part 3 should prove very helpful to groups and individuals trying to develop and implement ecological topics and programs.

Whatever type of program you become involved in, it must at a minimum contain ecology and related topics introduced into the regular fare, as well as extracurricular activities. At the elementary level environmental instruction can be readily integrated within the self-contained classroom, but the organization of the secondary school curriculum requires in most cases integration of ecology topics into regular courses like English, social studies, or biology; or the development of new interdisciplinary courses which are normally team-taught, or both. Finally, both elementary and secondary curriculum decision makers can adopt a total prefabricated science curriculum which has been built by major groups such as SCIS, ISCS, or ECCP. You will learn about these and other projects in this Part 3. The discussion which follows may seem unnecessary to those who simply decide to use a total program like SCIS, ISCS, or BSCS. However, an overall strategy within a school involving all phases of curriculum, the concerted "extracurricular" efforts

of students and faculty, and the participation of community agencies will achieve a higher degree of success than the reliance upon only one approach.

ROLE OF THE ADMINISTRATOR

A school-wide environmental education program could be given necessary leadership by the principal and/or a teacher chairman. In either event, the principal's support is vital. As the school's educational leader, he possesses the ability to allocate resources of time, money, and personnel to make the program a success. With his backing, there is the greatest assurance of success. Once this is obtained, a teacher or group of teachers interested in developing a worthwhile school-wide environmental education program could feel ready to begin.

ROLE OF STAFF MEMBERS

A small group of teachers and other staff personnel interested in developing an environmental education program emphasizing the crisis ought to get organized. The size of the group is not important. What is important is the dedication and willingness of its members. The greatest pitfall to avoid is that of attempting to superimpose a program on a group not yet ready to accept the need for one. The road to failure is paved with the best intentions of enthusiastic "leaders" plunging ahead with a plan not yet approved by the local staff. Successful change efforts involve a system-wide approach in which local school staffs working in a cooperative manner with outside personnel and community groups act upon issues perceived by themselves as educationally relevant.

Later in the semester a request could be made for additional participation by all school personnel interested in this type of project. The recruitment of willing volunteers rather than appointment of "noncommitted" committee members is critical to the ongoing success of the program.

Designation of personnel particularly dedicated to the objectives of the environmental movement insures that measure of enthusiasm and zeal needed to set it apart from routine types of "extracurricular" assignments.

FORMATION OF STAFF ENVIRONMENT COMMITTEE

The collaborative local committee could consist of the principal, interested teachers, the school nurse, the librarian, and several local citizens. They should familiarize themselves with content similar to Parts 1 and 2 of this book. From time to time, the committee could call upon the advice of specialists from organizations such as the Audubon Society, community health agency, or local community environmental council.[1]

OPERATING TECHNIQUES OF STAFF COMMITTEE

Further needed information could come from engineers, physicians, research scientists, and other experts called in to help on a particular problem. These resource persons often perform as *change agents* because they impart more than information to committee members. Such experts may also induce a change in attitude of the committee or a change in the ways of perceiving a problem.

The maintenance of an open-ended committee structure enhances a feeling of flexibility and diversity in viewpoint. It helps reinforce the attitude of spontaneity and enthusiasm which originally sparked the formation of the committee.

It is recommended that the environmental committee make use of many temporary groups. This organizational technique consists of a group working on a specific project with limited objectives. It seeks advice from resource persons who assist the group in its problem-solving efforts. Once the objectives have been attained, the group may disband or it may ascertain new goals and reorganize itself to include others. Examples of temporary systems are Earth Days, special environmental assemblies, and campaigns directed against a specific environmental nuisance. The temporary system may be as readily used by the student environmental committee.

Committee members keep the total school staff informed on developments and solicit added suggestions from them. Faculty meetings, school bulletins, and informal exchange of information between staff personnel constitute a large measure of the communication network needed to keep the total school informed.

ACTIVITIES OF STAFF COMMITTEE

The staff environmental education committee is the nucleus of all faculty efforts directed toward environmental education in a local school. Plans for special student assemblies, teacher ideas for classroom presentations, or suggestions for purchase of special audio-visual materials are all filtered through this group. It can carefully analyze new science, health, or social studies curricula with an eye toward ecological content. Committee members coordinate environmental education within the normal classroom program, or sponsor a student ecology committee.

STUDENT ECOLOGY COMMITTEE

The student ecology committee (or club) may be considered an organizing nucleus for environmental education among students A more detailed exposition of its procedures on an elementary and secon-

---

1. See Appendix E for a list of available organizations. Also, see AAAS plans for Environmental Councils in article "Curriculum Projects with Ecology Content," in section on *The Secondary School Curriculum*, Part 3.

dary school level are presented in this section.

COLLABORATION OF STAFF WITH STUDENTS

The staff committee works in a collaborative manner with the student committee to analyze school and community environmental problems. It is possible that certain pollution conditions exist within the school itself and a combined teacher-student approach is needed to find an apt solution. For instance, there could be a problem in noise pollution in the cafeteria or hallways. Perhaps the school's appearance is spoiled by litter all over the front lawn. Maybe the drinking fountains or lavatories could be maintained in a more sanitary manner. Any number of school environmental problems could be a fit subject for educational activities.

PROBLEM SOLVING APPROACH

Certain problems come from the outside community but must be faced by the school which is part of that community. Examples include: smog conditions so severe that vigorous physical exercise must be curtailed, noise so annoying that proper study conditions are impossible, or overcrowded classrooms and/or schoolyards that endanger student safety. The presence of these problems provide relevant opportunities for a school to develop educational programs which give students an understanding of the cause and correction of environ-mental pollution. They may act as a springboard to action research, a scientific method of obtaining answers to one's own problems.

EVALUATION

The most successful environmental education programs are the ones which motivate students toward further learning and ethical action. For example, an assembly devoted to a once a year event such as Earth Day may have significance. However, its true value may be measured in terms of the amount of in-depth constructive activity that it engenders. In the last analysis, it is the ongoing educational program of the classroom itself that balanced and sequential environmental understandings are formed. Intelligent action cannot be separated from such understandings.

SUMMARY

The solid foundation upon which successful classroom activities are built is the school-wide, collaborative approach to environmental education. In this method, educators and students work cooperatively on real problems. They consult with specialists whenever necessary. They coordinate school programs with wider community programs. The staff and student environmental committees provide the solid undergirding necessary for the development of responsible environmental citizenship through relevant school and classroom educational programs.

Harold Altman

ORGANIZATION AND ACTIVITIES OF AN ELEMENTARY SCHOOL ECOLOGY CLUB

This article is designed to give general information to teachers who wish to sponsor an elementary school ecology club. It will tell about club structure and function, recruitment of club members, the teacher's role, student leadership, and club activities. In the succeeding article, the specific experiences, activities, and programs of the Carthay Center School Ecology Club (Los Angeles) will be recounted.

STRUCTURE AND FUNCTION

The ecology club should be viewed more as a loosely formed nucleus of interested volunteers from which student environmental activities are generated and to which school environmental problems are presented. It is not a "governing body" and need not be considered a representative section of the school. Therefore, membership does not have to be on the traditional basis of equal representation from every classroom or grade level. The criteria for membership could be the student's interest

in the subject and his ability to make a contribution to the entire school. It would be permissible for certain students to drop out and other students to come in as work progressed. One of the primary functions of the ecology club is to infuse an attitude of awareness and concern toward environmental problems. It sets up common understandings and paves the way for students and teachers to conduct successful environmental studies.

RECRUITMENT OF CLUB MEMBERS

The teacher advisor to the ecology club will find very little problem in recruiting elementary students interested in this subject. The media of television, newspapers, and periodicals has already set the stage. Reports of environmental teach-ins, Earth Day observances, and Nader's-Raiders investigations have effectively appealed to students' imaginations. It is quite possible that more students would volunteer than would be

SOURCE. By permission of the author.

283

desirable for one teacher to handle. If this happens, it may be wise to have two or more teachers work as a team in planning the initial club program.

ROLE OF TEACHER ADVISOR

Once the club program "jells" into specific activities, subcommittees may be formed (ecology newspaper, school assembly, dramatizations, etc.). The activities of the teacher representative or representatives may be coordinated with the student subcommittees. Teachers may elect to work as a team with the entire club, work individually with subcommittees, or combine both procedures.

The teacher advisor works in the capacity of a change agent who facilitates students' learning activities. He uses techniques which enable students to share responsibility for ongoing club activities. The teacher's shift in role from director to facilitator emphasizes the process of learning as much as teaching in the "teaching-learning" cycle.

CLUB NAME AND INSIGNIA

Students should be given the opportunity to decide if they wanted a specific name for their club or if they wished to be known by the national name of Protect Your Environment (PYE) Club. One group in a local school calls itself the Help Our Polluted Earth (HOPE) Club. Another group chose the name, Save Our Spaceship (SOS). Students enjoy making up catch-word phrases. They may decide on such slogans as, "Keep the Earth Clean and Green," "Help Nature Keep *You* Alive," or "Ecologize!" A club insignia could be designed as part of an art lesson. Students may wish to incorporate the nationwide ecology symbol into their insignia.

STUDENT LEADERSHIP

Election of student officers is a purely optional activity. There could be no need of club officers if most of the club activities

are performed by subcommittees. In this instance, subcommittee chairmen could help assume the major club leadership responsibilities. Chairmen could be chosen on the basis of demonstrated leadership and expertise from within the subcommittee membership. If the total club does elect officers, it is well to understand that few elementary school children possess the skills necessary to preside over large group discussions. These skills are sometimes difficult for trained professionals. The teacher advisor may find it desirable to work in a collaborative capacity with the club president.

COMMUNICATIONS

Vital to understanding and continued support of student activities is an adequate communications network. The use of a club ecology newsletter is highly recommended. Supplemental announcements for the community newspaper, articles in the PTA or Advisory Council bulletins, and occasional inserts in the faculty newsletter serve to keep all participants informed and knowledgeable of student activities.

CLUB ACTIVITIES

The student membership should determine the activities. It may decide to develop a scrapbook of environmental newspaper articles or cartoons. It may wish to write articles for an ecology newspaper or deliver speeches in the regular classrooms. It could make school-wide plans for Earth Day. It could act as a clearinghouse of environmental information with data on pertinent television programs, newly published books, or recently acquired audio-visual materials. It could invite outside speakers, or mount a campaign to help correct a school or community environmental imbalance. The range of possible activities is limited only by available imagination, time, and resources.

The following informational bulletin from a local school is indicative of the kinds of activities and projects that could be conducted.

PLANNING A SCHOOL PROGRAM

ECO 71

CHILDREN
AND THEIR
ENVIRONMENT

BUCHANAN ST. SCHOOL &
OCCIDENTAL COLLEGE

Ecology
Program

Principal—Mary McKnight
Manager—Jane Forker
Chairman—Rebecca Nasori

JANURY—WATER POLLUTION
FEBRUARY—WILD LIFE & NATURE APPRECIATION
MARCH—VISUAL POLLUTION AND ENVIRONMENTAL PROBLEMS
APRIL—AIR POLLUTION
MAY—SOLID WASTE & NOISE POLLUTION

SCHOOL MOTTO:

QUALITY
ENVIRONMENT
THROUGH
EDUCATION

PROJECTS

PROJECTED
PROJECTS

School Newspaper
Live Animal Exhibition
Lunch Area Table Painting
Can Drive
Field Trips:
    to City Hall, Occidental
    College, Los Angeles Times
Basketball League
Pom Pom Girls
Language Tutoring
Hallway & Library Painting
Operation Olympiad

Vegetable Garden
Plant Exchange
Street Tree Planting
Film Making (Completed)
Paint Up & Clean Up of Neighborhood
School Yard Redevelopment with
    Assistance of Cal. Poly, Pomona
    Environmental Design Students.

The succeeding article is an account by Mrs. Hope Arlene Swatt and Miss Annette H. Willens of their experiences as teacher advisors of the Carthay Center Ecology Club. The model they present may provide ideas, suggestions, and inspiration for other leaders.

Hope Arlene Swatt

Annette H. Willens

CARTHAY CENTER'S ECOLOGY CLUB IN ACTION

ORGANIZATION

Carthay Center's Ecology Club was conceived as a small, highly motivated nucleus group of youngsters ranging from intermediate to upper grades with primary children joining according to special interest and aptitude. The group was fluid and allowed its members freedom to leave upon completion of a particular project in which they had been involved. Conversely, new children could enter as activities evolved which stimulated their interest, however, the club maintained a group of about twenty throughout the year. Meetings occurred weekly from 2:15-2:50, but could be more or less often depending upon the projects involved.

GOALS

The goals of our club have been to educate and develop an environmental awareness for its members with a fanning out through them to the total school population by projects which capture interest and create involvement. Close teacher communication was necessary as is evidenced by the message which follows this article. Community action thus far has been exerted, hopefully, through education and pressure on parents and other adults who have been exposed to our information and projects. An article from a community newspaper is included at the end of this article. It has been decided that the club will move toward more direct action techniques next year.

BACKGROUND INFORMATION

Many areas of background information were drawn upon. Participants were encouraged to bring in or read the pertinent articles abounding in newspapers and magazines and to watch for TV discussions and special programs on these subjects. These were shared, discussed, and evaluated by our group.

SOURCE. By permission of the authors.

286

We have also used films, guest speakers from ecological organizations, and representatives from ecology health products to educate and stimulate, encouraging student evaluation as to value and completeness of content.

For the future we are considering trips to the local Museums of Natural History or Science and Industry as well as a visit to the water purification plant for our area. In brief, opportunities abound all around us. It just takes motivation and an educated eye to seek them out.

ACTIVITIES

The first year's project centered around a play presented to the total student body on Earth Day. This was done in a simple, unsophisticated manner. Our costumes were made mainly from paper bags to represent the flora and fauna involved. Some of the ecological phenomena such as rivers, smoke, and leaves were made from pompoms of appropriate colors. An equally primitive sound tape was devised with nature sounds supplied by classical music, child-made imitations, and city sounds taken from modern music, taped on the spot, or duplicated by our sound technicians. Guest speakers spoke briefly on pertinent aspects of ecology, stimulating discussion for possible action and solutions. A copy of the play follows this article.

In the future another technique for dramatization might be initiated. Several small bands of "traveling performers" could go from room to room presenting puppet shows, TV scrolls, songs, or parodies on popular songs. At the conclusion the children might present a brief discussion with a plea for some major action program that would be forthcoming.

NEWSPAPERS

Our culminating activity for the first year was our *Carthay Ecology News* written by club members and many other students. It was printed by Trade Tech., a local college. In this our second year of publication, we are experimenting with mimeographing our newspaper. This process helps to save money and allows more students to contribute. An example of the mimeographed newspaper is included at the conclusion of this article.

ART FAIR

This year the club members voted to have an Art Fair rather than a play. This project involved the total school. Entrants prepared work from one or more of these categories: posters, mobiles, collages, diaramas, assemblages, or junk art. Club members created examples and presented them to the classrooms to stimulate interest. Entries were received over a period of six weeks. The exhibit was presented throughout the entire first floor of our building and judged by club members who made their choice for each category. Prizes presented at the school assembly included one plant free from DDT, one bottle of unpolluted water, one bottle of smog-free air, one fish free from mercury poisoning, and one corner free from noise pollution. Two conspicuously green and elaborately decorated certificates were bestowed upon a couple of prolific but unartistic participants for "outstanding interest in the field of ecology."

One of the most delightful though poignant posters was submitted by a little kindergarten girl. It was a scribble of felt-pen lines discernible in the center with a small rectangle crossed with something resembling a ribbon. On the bottom was her dictated caption, "Presents for all the people who have died from pollution."

DIRECT ACTION

Finally, children can be involved in action programs on a direct level involving recycling of cans, bottles, or newspapers. Petitions or letter-writing to officials in industry or government can be initiated with booths set up and manned by club members.

This year, graphs were made to show the electricity used per day in the student's home, the water used throughout the day, and the litter picked up. The graphs could be expanded throughout the school and displayed in the hallways.

There are many possibilities for educational activities and action. We found it important to keep our program fluid, fun, dynamic, and innovative. We not only encouraged awareness of ecological problems through attuning all of our senses to the environment around us, but we also found it psychologically important to encourage children to recognize that which is still positive and beautiful in our world and to help them to strive to preserve and, if possible, extend it.

The following are specific examples of activities of club bulletins, news articles, newsletters, and dramatizations.

WRITTEN COMMUNICATION FROM TEACHER REPRESENTATIVE TO OTHER CLASSROOM TEACHERS

Our first Ecology Club meeting got off with a bang. The members plan to start a newspaper, so if your class has some pertinent stories, cartoons, poems, etc., about environment, please send them to room 17.

We also plan to observe *Earth Day* April 22 with plays and an assembly. Let us know if your class would like to present a skit about ecology, pollution, litter, or the balance of nature.

We'll have our second meeting this Thursday at 2:30 in room 17.

P.S.—

Of interest: *This Land is Mine* Tonight at 7:30, channel 7 *Pollution is a Matter of Choice* Tuesday at 7:30, channel 4.

ARTICLE FROM COMMUNITY NEWSPAPER

Carthay Center School Slates "Earth Week" Program Tomorrow

Youngsters at Carthay Center Elementary School, 6351 Olympic Blvd., are making "Earth Week" this week to learn more about man's environment.

The week was the idea of the school's Ecology Club, a group of youngsters who have been studying environment problems as they relate to air, water, and land pollution.

Members of the club wanted to let other pupils at the school know the things they have learned in their club activities, so they have planned two assemblies tomorrow, and they're at work on a school newspaper issue on environment problems.

At the assemblies, third and fourth graders will hear a report on "Spaceship Earth" from Sierra Club member Anita Girard.

Fifth and sixth graders will listen to Richard Gaines, director of air conservation and environmental health program for the Tuberculosis and Respiratory Disease Association of Los Angeles County. Gaines also is a member of the National Air Conservation Commission.

Club members also will present dramatizations of environment problems during the assemblies.

The club also is producing a newspaper, "Carthay Ecology News—Help Our Polluted Earth (HOPE)," to be published at the time of the assemblies.

The club is coordinating its ideas with its teacher representatives, Jean Lamel and Hope Swatt.

Talking of the school activities, Principal Harold Altman said, "It is expected that the subject of environmental education will be a continuing and ongoing study at Carthay Center School."

The intent of the week was expressed by Ecology Club member Allison Cane in a poem, "What the World is Coming to." Part of the poem goes:

"Once the world was clean and bright,
Bur something happened overnight.
I've looked up and seen the air,
I can tell you that we don't care."

DRAMATIZATION WRITTEN AND GIVEN BY STUDENTS DURING EARTH DAY ASSEMBLIES

HELP OUR POLLUTED EARTH

Narrator #1:

What is ecology all about? When we study ecology, we discover how plants and animals live together. Plants help animals by giving them oxygen; and in turn, animals give plants carbon dioxide and fertilizer. Did you know that 25 square feet of grass gives a man enough oxygen for one day?

Without plants, then, fish and land animals would die. On the other hand, plants need animals, too. Plants and animals depend on each other to live. This is ecology. Even insects belong in this chain of life, for birds need insects to eat. So, everything has its place in nature. Ecology is the biggest life cycle of them all.

Narrator #2:

Do we protect nature and our earth's ecology? What happens when we build homes and highways over many plants, dirty our water with oil and garbage, use up natural resources, and pollute the air we breathe?

Now there are 200 million people in the United States. In 35 years there will be 400 million. All of these people need homes, clothes, and food. Everyone helps cause pollution. Carthay's Earth Day brings us all together to try to solve these problems, and to save our earth.

The Ecology Club would like to tell you a story about our ecology.

Curtain Opens
(On stage are students dressed as trees, birds, flowers, fish, and animals)

Narrator #3:

Once there was a planet that was very clean and full of life. The air was so clean, you could see straight through it. Trees were green with leaves and fruit, and many birds were in them. Flowers grew all around. There were clean rivers full of fish and water life. Animals like deer, tigers, and leopards ran in the forests. Then came something called the human race, and our planet changed.

At first, man was very clever. He learned how to build a wheel, light fires, and even build machines to do his work. Here comes a modern man. Let's see what he's doing . . . Oh, he's building a factory. *(Large cardboard to rear of stage resembles facade of a factory)* Let's watch how the things men do spoil our environment.

Narrator #3 continues and explains each pantomime:

(Man and Factory pantomime)

Man has built a factory. The *factory* throws out black smoke *(black strips of paper are used for smoke)* which pollutes the air—Let's watch and see what happens to the *flowers*—and the *trees*. After a while the *river* becomes polluted—and the *frogs* and *fishes* die off. *(frogs and fish fall down)*

(Automobile exhaust pantomime)

Oh, oh—Here comes a *car*—its exhaust smoke pollutes the air—and more *flowers* and *trees* die. *(flowers and tree fall down)*

EDUCATIONAL IMPLICATIONS

Listen to the *noise pollution (sounds from drum)* from the cars and factories—Now the birds are forced to fly away! *(some birds leave stage)*

(Hunter pantomime)

Here comes a hunter. He is *coughing* from the polluted air—Let's see what will happen next—Yes, the cruel hunter has killed 3 of Earth's rare, big cats. *(leopards and tiger).*

(Extinction of species pantomime)

The hunter has sold the leopard's skins. Here comes a thoughtless girl who has bought a coat made from the skins! Now she is littering our environment with trash.

(Tree pantomime)

Next a woodsman comes into the forest *(chops trees)*—and our world is poorer by 2 trees. *(another 2 trees fall down)*

(Pesticide pantomime)

And last comes a man with a flit gun)— *(sprays trees—leaves fall off—bird dies)* You're right! The spray was DDT. It poisons our animals, defoliates the trees, and spoils some of the food that you and I

would eat. *(paper leaves fall off, remaining tree and bird fall down)*

As you can see, if man continues to be cruel, careless, and thoughtless, he will *ruin our world.*

Stage is silent.
Cast sings "Where Have All the Flowers Gone."

Curtain Closes

Narrator #3 continues:

If we go on, what will we have in fifty years? Is this how we keep America beautiful?

But we can, and must, end on a note of Hope, the slogan of our <u>Carthay Ecology Newspaper</u>. *(four students walk on stage in front of curtain, each carrying a sign with one of the letters, H-O-P-E)*

"H" stands for Help.

"O" stands for Our.

"P" stands for Polluted.

"E" stands for Earth. Remember, if we all work together, there is HOPE for a cleaner world.

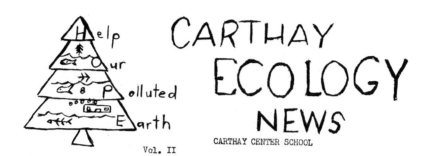

CARTHAY ECOLOGY NEWS

CARTHAY CENTER SCHOOL

Vol. II

OUR ECOLOGY ART FAIR
by
Paul Cohen
12 years old

On March 10 at assembly, awards were presented for ecology posters and diaramas. The posters were based on pollution and our environment.

For the best diarama, Paul Cohen got one bottle of unpolluted smog-free air. For her poster Penny Diener won one fish free from mercury. Jackie Parker won one plant free from DDT for her poster. Jayne Alweil won a bottle of unpolluted water for the best collage. Robin Sedor won one corner free from noise pollution for the best assemblage. Mark Cohen and David Safran received honorable mention for their efforts.

POLLUTION
by
Lisa Work
12 years old

Awhile ago, the air was clean
Life seemed to be a beautiful dream.
But like everything else
It was too good to last
And dirtiness took its place
    filthy and fast.

How do we live in such a messed-up
    place?
Pollution is all a filthy waste.
And the people of the world have
    caused this crime
But to clean it up is going to take
    some time.

SPECIAL ECOLOGY ISSUES FOR CARTH AY
CENTER'S POSTAL SERVICE

by
Irving Adlen

by
Pom Witt

SING ALONG WITH OUR ENVIRONMENT

Sung to "Spinning Wheel"
by Cindy Fried
12 years old

Stopping pollution is my bag
Why don't you see our world is a drag?
'Cause nobody cares about ourselves,
People let me tell you we're not a
  bunch of elves!

Speeding cars, going top speed
Trying to find out who's in the lead.
Making exhaust to come out stronger
If this keeps up, we won't live much
  longer.

Trash falling out all over the place
Why can't we form a human race?
Cleaning the streets and cleaning
  the air
And keeping it this way, I'll know
  that you care.

California Smog
(To the tune of Tia Juana)
Smalls
by Phillip Weingarten

California Smog
Smog it isn't fine, fine, baby
  for you will die maybe
You know it is war,
Y ou know it is war.

Cars leave it there
Y ou breathe the air, air, baby
  for you will die maybe
You know it is war,
You know it is war.

Industry too
It will kill you, you baby
  and you will die maybe
You know it is war,
You know it is war.

How to Play "Dirty Water"
by Adam Weiss
8 years old

There are four players. Each

one starts with one hundred dollars.

Y ou roll the dice and go around

the board gathering fish and bacteria

to fill up your lake. Whoever fills

up his lake first wins.

This game teaches you all about

different kinds of pollution and the

effect on you and how to prevent it.

I like this game because you play

with money and you learn about ecology.

POLLUTION
by
Elaine Rosenes
11 years old

The problem is pollution
No one can find the solution.
Wear a gas mask
Because of another attack.

The pollution is killing me
Not only me, but every pea, bee,
  and tree.
Soon everything will die
And over the earth will lie.

Then the earth will be a disgrace
  to thee,
And to everyone including me.

CARTHAY ECOLOGY NEWS 1971
CARTHAY CENTER SCHOOL
6351 W. Olympic Blvd.
Los Angeles, California
Masthead design-
  Demetra Spanos
  Eli Glickman
Ecology Club Advisors: Mrs. H. Swatt
                      Miss A. Willens

2

HELPFUL HINTS

If You Want to Save Our Country

Helpful Hints from the
Sierra Club Bulletin
by
Barrie Friedman
9 years old

1. Don't use colored facial tissues, paper towels or toilet paper. The paper dissolves properly in the water, but the dye lingers on.

2. Have your cats sprayed. Ten thousand unwanted puppies and kittens are born an hour in the U.S. As strays they kill more wildlife than hunters do.

3. Refuse to purchase any objects of clothing or decor made from the bits and pieces of dead wild animals.

4. Use lunchpails instead of paperbags.

5. Refuse to use DDT or any of the other persistent environment oxides like RAID.

6. When buying a new car, make sure that it has an anti-smog device.

7. Use detergents low in phosphates. We recommend Ivory Soap Flakes with Washing Soda.

8. Save vegetable peels for fertilizers. Bury them 5-6 inches deep around plants.

9. Take your own paper bags to the market. Re-use paper bags and packages.

10. Avoid styrofoam and reduce your use of plastics. They never decompose.

11. Use more bicycles and less cars to stop pollution.

Poisons
by
Victoria Shepard
11 years old

Have you ever stopped to think what our world is coming to? Our world is turning into a big piece of waste land because nobody cares. You can help by stopping things which you have done but didn't notice. If your parents use spray for plants, tell them not to because sometimes the spray not only gets on the plants but also gets in the air.

Not only do sprays cause air pollution, but so do factories. Most factories have smoke stacks. When the factory wants to get rid of certain wastes, it is sent out from the smoke-stacks in the form of smog.

What about water? Our water is being polluted too. Most water pollution is caused by factories. When the factory gets rid of wastes, some of it is thrown into the water.

Mercury is also a poison. It gets in the ocean from chemicals that come

3

from operating factories. There are
thousands of dead fish that have been
struck by pollution.

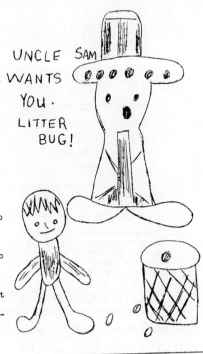

Copy of a letter sent to Mr. Nixon
by
   Jackie Parker
   10 years old

May 13, 1971

Dear Mr. Nixon,

I am concerned about the smog
problem. I don't have to study it or
know when it's there. All I have to do
is go outside and let my eyes get all
bloodshot. Also people are rushing too
much. They think that airplanes are
better, but actually there are not. It
may help the person get where he is going to faster than the train, but it
does not help the world environment.
A train pollutes too, but not half as
much as the airplane.

There are ways to stop smog, water
and other pollution too. For instance,
use your lunch bag over and over or
bring a lunch pail. Don't use colored
toilet paper. Use the money that you
save for the space race for a clean
city. Don't spend money on spraying
plants. There are some solutions to
pollution. Please try to help.

4

Thank you.

Book Reviews

Today we are trying to recycle our garbage and many people have found many uses for their "Junk". An old beer barrel can be a chair; tin cans can be turned into lamps, and things like large telephone cable spools become patio tables. The saying today is "One man's trash is another's treasure."

Beautiful Junk by Jon Madian with photographs by Barbara and Lou Jacobs, Jr. is an outstanding example of recycling. Once there was a man who went to trash cans to collect junk. He made beautiful stuff out of the junk. The man used broken glass and broken tile and built what is known as Watts Towers. Simon Rodia is the person who built the Towers out of the junk he found that other people threw away. He built the Towers during his spare time. He was a very poor person who wanted to be remembered by building something beautiful. He collected the

junk in his wheelbarrow. There was a pull test on the Towers to see if it could be pulled down as some people thought it was not very strong. But, they found out that it was very, very strong. Also the people in the Watts section of L.A. did not want it pulled down. Today you can go and see the Towers.

By

Steven Horowitz
10 years old

The Sea Around Us

Rachel Carson said, "No organism in biological history has survived for long if its environment became in some way unfit for it. But no organism before man has deliberately polluted its environment."

I have just finished the book called The Sea Around Us by Rachel Carson. In this book it tells about water pollution and how it's killing all the things in nature like reptiles and amphibians. Pollution is caused by people dumping things in the water

5

like cans, paper, or gas. The part
I like best is the way to find oil.

I think this book is very interesting for 9-10 year olds especially
because of our interest in ecology.

By

Mark Ritz
8 years old

Interviews

Today I had an interview with
Mrs. Gold. Mrs. Gold and Mr. Gold are
very concerned with the world we live
in. The reason why she got started in
ecology is because everybody is interested in his child's future and what will
affect his life. You start working on
different goals and find out that
ecology is most important for their
future.

Cars are one of the most contributors to smog in the world, and G.M. is
the biggest manufacturer of cars in the
world. They were found guilty of an
anti-trust suit last year. If G.M.
would make a smog proof car, all the
rest would have to follow.

The best soap to use is an old
fashioned soap. It is really the
best or a little baking soda gives
you a clean wash.

Some of our electricity is not
made from water turbines. The electricity made by S.C.E. which they use
with gas causes SMOG. It is highly
recommended that we use white tissue
because the dye comes out in water.

Children can do lots for ecology
like saving newspaper. A stack 36 in.
high of newspaper is equal to a tree.
Watch for unnecessary lights, water
also. Please take cans and glass to
reclamation centers. DO NOT BUY
PLASTIC. It cannot be reused. The
key is to recycle.

By

Irving Adlen
11 years old

POLLUTION
by
Melody Weiss
10 years old
We need a solution
to air pollution.
Pollution is bad,
It's almost a fad.
It's driving me mad,
It's killing every lad.

6

Shaklee Products

Shaklee products are made from organic vegetables and fruits. They make vitamins and household cleaners. Now the 99 year old Dr. Shaklee makes household products from the leftovers of the vitamins. Dr. Shaklee believes in good neighborhood policy. Now this product helps stop pollution.

I would like to thank Miss Zilberstein for coming to talk with me. If you want some Shaklee products, you may contact her or other representatives through Miss Willens in the library.

by

Karen Weinstein
9 years old

CAN WE STOP POLLUTION?
by
Benjamin Tysch
11 years old

Can't we stop pollution?
    Is there no solution?
We've made a bomb and a rocket,
    a radio, an electric socket.
Can't we stop pollution
    before it is too late?
Can't we stop pollution on
    this very date?

POLLUTION
by
Sonny Finck
11 years old

Pollution is everywhere
On the streets and in the air.

There is so much smog in the sky
It almost wants to make you cry.

If we don't get it out of the sky
Pretty soon we will all just die.

MANY YEARS AGO
by
Nancy Kleinrock
11 years old

The air was fair
    many years ago.
You could breathe with ease
    many years ago.

But the air's not fair
    anymore today.
You can't breathe with ease
    anymore today.

We could try to buy
    some new fresh air.
But they don't sell this
    anywhere.

LOOK AROUND YOU
by
Mandy Wasserman
11 years old

Look around you
What do you see?
A dirty brook, a dying tree.

Look around you
What is here?
Filth and dirt is always near.

Look around you
How do you feel?
As hopeless as a dying seal.

7

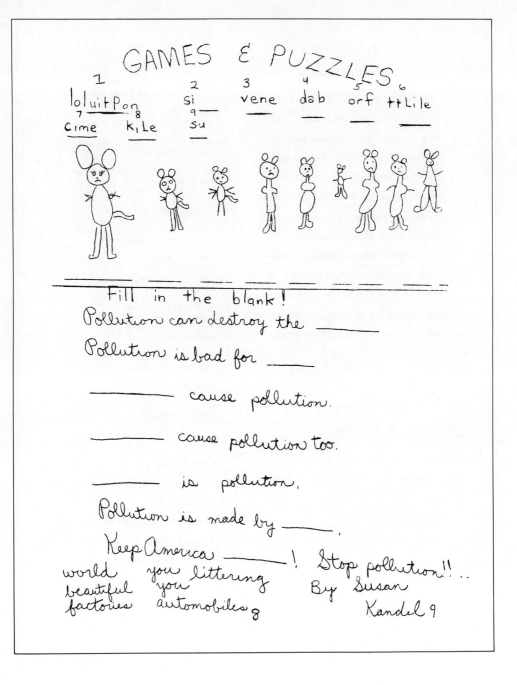

GAMES & PUZZLES

1 loluitPon 2 si 3 vene 4 dab 5 orf 6 ttLile

7 Cime 8 kiLe 9 su

Fill in the blank!

Pollution can destroy the _____

Pollution is bad for _____

_____ cause pollution.

_____ cause pollution too.

_____ is pollution.

Pollution is made by _____.

Keep America _____! Stop pollution!! ..

world   you littering   By Susan
beautiful you   Kandel 9
factories automobiles 8

298

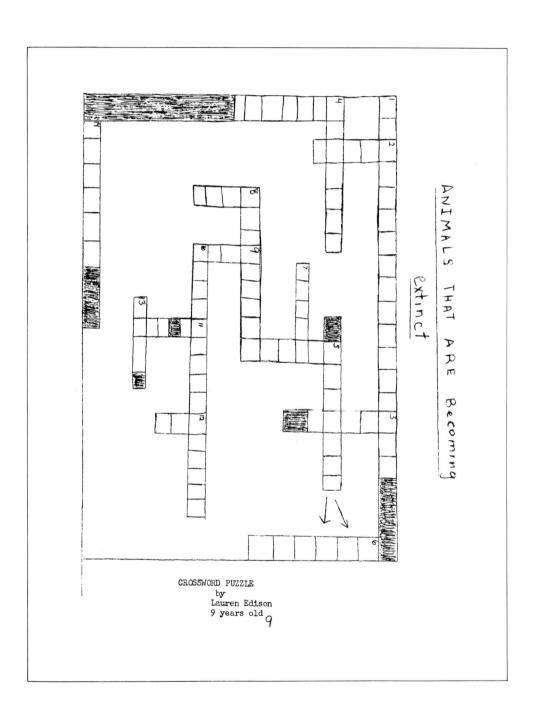

ANIMALS THAT ARE Becoming extinct

CROSSWORD PUZZLE
by
Lauren Edison
9 years old

299

CROSSWORD PUZZLE CLUES
by
Lauren Edison

ACROSS

1. Found living in swamp (2 words)
4. Bird that doesn't chew what he eats.
5. Fastest cat in the world.
7. American buffalo
8. Small creature found only in Australia (2 words)
10. Big mammal with big ears (2 words)
13. Can't live without salt water
14. Mammal with two big teeth coming out of his mouth that looks like horns.

DOWN

2. Symbol of America
3. Striped cat
5. Biggest bird — wings spread up to 20 feet
6. Breed of horse similar to donkey or wild ass
9. Big giraffe-like animal
11. Very large bird
12. Moose

UNSCRAMBLE THE WORDS AND FIND THE STORY
by
Lauren Lipsky
9 years old

1. llpotuoin
2. si
3. abd
4. ofr
5. het
6. howel
7. rowld
8. ew
9. ttrebe
10. od
11. thsoemning
12. uobta
13. ti
14. forbe
15. we
16. vahe
17. no
18. rowdl
19. nad
20. no
21. omer
22. goxyen

SAVE
OUR
WILDLIFE

10

Pow

by
Jack Williamson
8 years old

300

ANSWERS TO SCRAMBLED STORY

Across

1. American alligator
4. Pelican
5. Cheetah
7. B ison
8. Koala Bear
10. African elephant
13. Seal
14. Walrus

Down
2. Eagle
3. Tiger
5. Condor
6. Onager
9. Lama
11. Crane
12. Elk

Pollution is bad for the whole world.

We better do something about it before

we have no world and no more oxygen.

FIND THE SOLUTIONS TO POLLUTION: UNSCRAMBLE THE WORDS
by
Jackie Parker
10 years old

1. tissues colored use don't

2. buy don't cans aluminum

3. not do kid school drive to you need unless to

4. your bag over use over and lunch

T

Answers should look like this:

1. Don't use colored tissues.

2. Don't buy aluminum cans.

3. Do not drive kids to school unless you need to.

4. Use your lunch bag over and over.

11

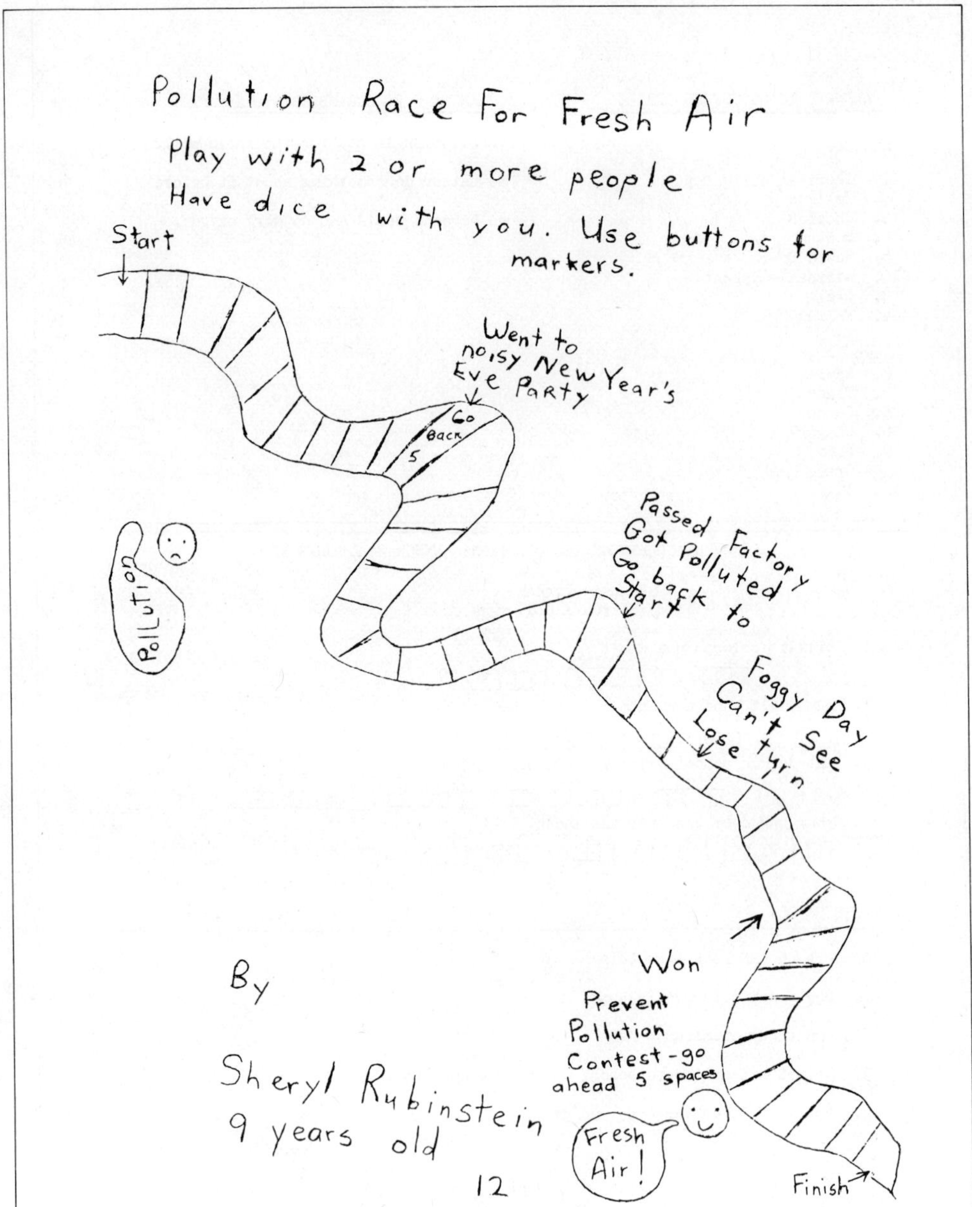

Pollution Race For Fresh Air

Play with 2 or more people
Have dice with you. Use buttons for
markers.

Start

Went to
noisy New Year's
Eve Party

Go
Back
5

Pollution

Passed Factory
Got Polluted
Go back to
Start

Foggy Day
Can't See
Lose turn

By

Sheryl Rubinstein
9 years old

Won
Prevent
Pollution
Contest - go
ahead 5 spaces

Fresh
Air!

Finish

303

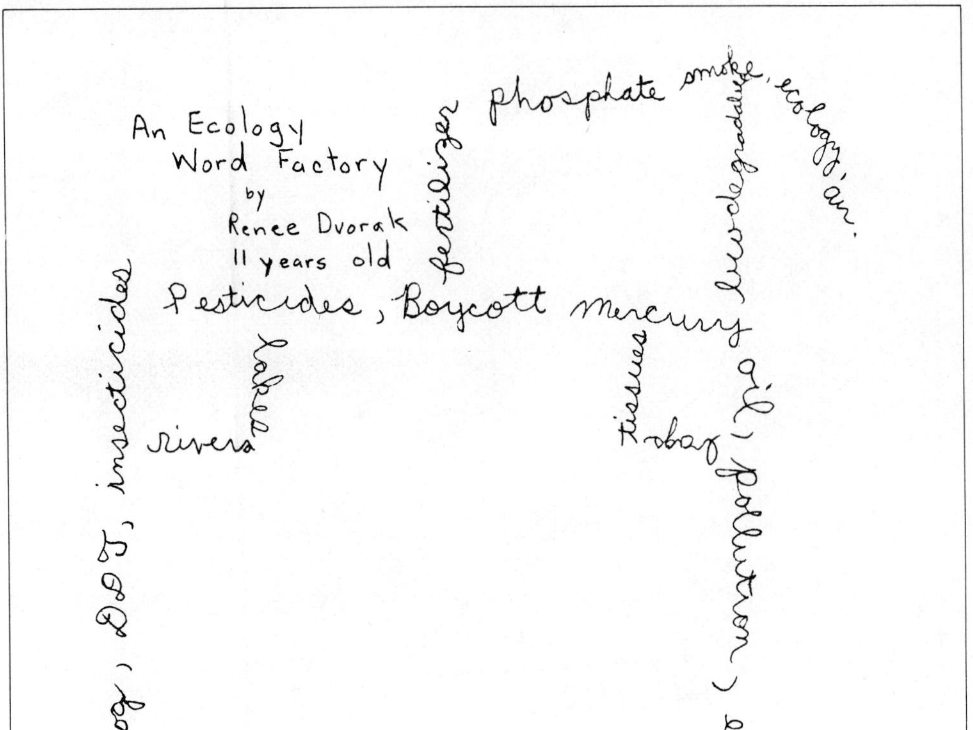

An Ecology
Word Factory
by
Renee Dvorak
11 years old
Pesticides, Boycott mercury

fertilizer phosphate smoke, ecology, air.

biodegradable

detergents, smog, DDT, insecticides

rivers

labels

tissues

oil) pollution

bar

Progress

water

automobile manufacturers

I hate
flying because
the pollution
is in my way.

by
Pamela Shepard
8 years old

14

EVEN MICKY MOUSE

HAS A HARD

TIME BREATHING

Gas Mask.

By
Phillip Weingarten
11 years old

WORLD VIEWS

First there's big industry,
    Polluting our air
        and filling our fish
With mercury.

Then there's the poor, poverty,
Receiving their welfare checks.
Their homes are wrecks.
They need help,
But they've no place to go.

Then there's the problem of cars,
And half of the drivers in bars.
They make so much smog and noise,
And they aren't exactly as harmless as toys.

                    By
        15   Dori Kramer
                    10 years old

Cornelius J. Troost

ECOLOGY ACTION BEYOND THE HIGH SCHOOL CLASSROOM

The community is an excellent "lab" for teachers and responsible students. That is, a high school ought to organize an ecology action program—both educational and practical—which bridges the gap between school and community.

As proposed in the article, "Planning a School Program for Environmental Education," an environmental committee or council should be set up. Teachers may take the lead in organizing such a group, but administrators, students, PTA, and other community groups ought to be represented. In addition, a student ecology group (club) should be formed, with direct assistance from faculty sponsors. Both faculty sponsors and several student representatives should report periodically to the environmental committee.

An organizational framework and objectives can be worked out so that various projects can be undertaken—some in conjunction with regular courses and others independent of the school curriculum.

Some community agencies and organizations potentially helpful to the ecology action group are:

1. Local air pollution control agency
2. News media
3. Museums
4. Local university urban ecology institutes or centers, i.e., Washington University's Center for the Biology of Natural Systems
5. Local parks and recreation division
6. Water reclamation plant
7. Local and state conservation organizations
8. Service clubs and Jaycees
9. Ecology action councils
10. State and local environmental councils
11. Boy and girl scout organizations
12. Churches and other religious organizations
13. Family planning agencies

Students should be encouraged to contact these groups and others in planning various projects. Many community agencies have education programs and liaison person-

SOURCE. By permission of the author.

nel who are ready to assist young people. The projects themselves should be well organized, with stated objectives and a well-conceived plan of operation. Problems such as released time, official permissions, legal questions, parent approval, transportation, etc., must be solved beforehand.

1. Take field trips to polluting industries.

2. Develop ecology exhibits for the school and for local shopping centers.

3. Invite guest scientists, engineers, sociologists, and others to discuss various aspects of environmental problems.

4. Plan an Earth Week.

5. Develop a "Camera Squad" which photographs pollution sites. Contact local news media to help publicize need to correct these situations.

6. Run recycling campaigns for local school families, involving glass, aluminum, and paper.

7. Develop a special educational group responsible for ecology workshops for the *community*.

8. The education group ought to establish good connections with politicians, environmental councils, ecology action councils, conservation clubs (like the Sierra Club) to keep well informed of current events and to formulate ways in which the group can help.

9. Plant and maintain tree-belts around industrial areas.

10. Purchase ecology action bumper-stickers for members and parents.

11. Conduct anti-littering campaigns.

12. Develop an organic food garden and maintain it. Perhaps the cafeteria manager can be convinced to offer such products.

It is obvious from this list of activities that they are interesting, relevant, and hold potential for legal difficulties when school and community meet. Teacher sponsors must be extremely careful in this regard. Prior to every trip or project, the school principal should be fully informed, so that he can act as liaison between the environmental committee and the school board.

There are other problems, such as the incompatibility of politically motivated ecology extremists and those who wish only to commit themselves to constructive action. The very serious, high-achieving students could be repulsed by the obstructionist, illegal tactics of the few extremists.

Another potential problem is "fraternal" behavior of industries. That is, if pollution detecting equipment is borrowed for purposes of "pollution eavesdropping," most industries will refuse to cooperate.

Of course, many practical obstacles lie in your way. The adult environmental committee should be sanctioned by the local school board. Also, the school principal ought to act as liaison between his environmental committee, the school board, and when necessary, the city council. Every project must have the principal's approval.

In the article, "Curriculum Projects with Ecology Content" in Section 5, the author discusses the AAAS system of environmental councils. Such councils will operate independent of the schools, yet should offer a community source of great potential value to the student group. Thus, it would be judicious for any newly emerging group to contact the local or state environmental council.

Ecology action is relevance with a capital R. The risks are many, but they are worth the effort.

SECTION 4

THE ELEMENTARY SCHOOL CURRICULUM

In this section, activities and experiences suitable for elementary school students are detailed. The first article provides for the elementary teacher specific information on the objectives, concepts, procedures, and available learning materials in the field of environmental education. It describes the role of the teacher as a resource consultant and the student as a problem-solver. The value of group discussion in solving problems is pointed out. Relevant curricular programs, teacher guides, and classroom organizational patterns are explained. One manner in which skill subjects such as language arts and mathematics may be integrated into the natural and social science environmental field is presented.

The second article, from the *Grade Teacher,* provides a sample activity unit for a study of land pollution. Many of the suggested activities may be readily adapted for units on other types of pollution.

The next two articles give a more detailed description of two major natural science environmental curricular programs: The Science Curriculum Improvement Study (SCIS), and the Elementary Science Study (ESS). A perusal of these two articles brings into focus the contrasting philosophy of the two programs. SCIS is oriented to a development of the biological concept of ecosystems. Students are led through the processes of exploration, invention, and discovery to attain scientific literacy. ESS has a variety of units which provide for open-ended student investigations. Teachers may use these units in whatever sequential order that meets their requirements. It is likely that both programs provide ingredients vitally needed for a successful environmental education program.

Other important classroom activities for both elementary and secondary students are described in the special sections devoted to field trips, urban activities, academic simulation games, and experiments.

Harold Altman

ENVIRONMENTAL EDUCATION FOR THE ELEMENTARY CLASSROOM

INTERDISCIPLINARY LEARNING

Environmental education is interdisciplinary in nature. It involves subject matter from the natural sciences and the social sciences. It focuses on topics such as water or air pollution which cut across the various subject matter disciplines.

It is a fusion of subject matter (content) and inquiry skills (process). Subject matter is the product of the process of investigation. It is fruitless to speak of content or process as being more important. They are equally important and should be regarded as an entity.

With the subject matter of environmental education as a central theme, students in an elementary classroom can use inquiry skills to explore almost every facet of man's interaction with his biophysical and social environment. They are able to gain a clearer, more unified, and better related understanding of the world in which they live since in the real world, all subject matter is interrelated and not arbitrarily categorized according to special fields.

The elementary self-contained classroom is often more conducive to interdisciplinary studies than the secondary school departmental classroom. In a departmentalized school, team teaching is often necessary in order to better relate subject fields. Team teaching can combine the skills of a group of teachers with differing subject matter specialties to offer programs revolving around an interdisciplinary theme. While team teaching, or at the very least, team planning, is a most desirable activity on an elementary level, it is not necessary for development of interdisciplinary learning.

The elementary teacher is charged with teaching all subject matter fields. It is therefore easier for him to combine subjects. Doing so enables him to save time and also help children gain clearer concepts of the world around them.

SOURCE. By permission of the author.

EDUCATIONAL IMPLICATIONS

INTERACTIONS WITH THE ENVIRONMENT

Concepts represent abstractions based on observations over a long period of time. Young children between the ages of five and ten are considered by Jean Piaget (1964) to be at the concrete level in the development of their thinking. He believes that a child who has the opportunity for interaction with his environment will move more readily from the concrete to the abstract level of thinking. A school environment so structured as to enhance active exploration of reality aids the elementary child's intellectual development. The need for inquiry activities in which a student assimilates external experiences and integrates them into his internal mental structure is crucial to cognitive growth. In the words of an old Chinese proverb:

> I hear, and I forget;
> I see, and I remember;
> I do, and I understand.

Many of the primary schools in England have adopted a method of education which involves intensive interaction between the child and his environment. The school day is so structured that it no longer has the traditional rigid timetable which mandates a succession of short periods. In its place there are longer periods during which students may be engaged individually or in small groups exploring their environment in the immediate classroom or in the area immediately adjacent to the school.

SITE EXPERIENCES

The use of areas either immediately adjacent or within walking distance of the school site provides many opportunities for ecological investigations (Yasso and Brovey, 1970). This site model for environmental investigations differs from the traditional field trip. The site model has the following advantages over the traditional field trip model.

1. It is more easily accessible for frequent visits.

2. There are no strong time limits to in-depth student investigations.

3. Changes over a period of time may be observed, measured, classified, and then recorded in a variety of ways including reports, graphs, charts, or sketches.

The reader is urged to check the materials in the section, *Urban Activities* (Part 3) of this sourcebook. Schneider outlines certain ways that ecological studies may be made of areas near the school. "A Place to Live" published by the National Audubon Society, provides a complete outline of learnings associated with nearby environmental walks. The section, *Experiments for Elementary School Students* (Part 3) also gives many ideas for out-of-the-classroom experiences. Of course, the traditional field trip still possesses certain advantages. It may provide specific learning resources which are not readily available near a school. While not downgrading the value of the field trip, it is urged that careful consideration be given to the many learning opportunities that are readily available near most school sites.

GOAL OF ENVIRONMENTAL EDUCATION

The goal of environmental education is to produce an *active environmentally-oriented* citizen. *Active* describes an individual who is personally involved in decisions and practices regarding man's interaction with his environment. *Environmentally-oriented* describes an individual whose values and attitudes are sympathetic to responsible use and management of the earth's resources. Citizens must be able to make decisions on environmental problems by using the most current and accurate information from the natural and social sciences. Educators must provide students with a set of experiences that give them the skills and concepts necessary to make effective decisions.

THE ELEMENTARY SCHOOL CURRICULUM

PROBLEM-SOLVING APPROACH

Environmental education should employ a problem-solving approach. That is, ecological issues are presented and pertinent questions are raised. A tentative hypothesis is made. Research is done in order to support or negate the hypothesis. The conclusions reached form the basis for intelligent decisions and actions on environmental problems.

Problems may be school or community related. They could be raised as a result of a field trip, experiment, or television program. They could even result from the teacher reading to the class a short story similar to the following:

> It was mid-twenty-second century when a visitor from another planet stepped from his spaceship onto Earth. No vegetation, no water, no human or animal life were visible. As the visitor surveyed the desolate scene, he was intrigued by the fragments of white, crumbling rocks that wound in and out over the barren landscape. Scattered here and there on the frayed slabs were high piles of rusted, four-wheeled contraptions. The visitor eagerly took photographs of the blighted area and cautiously collected samples of rocks and pieces of metal in small plastic bags. Upon returning to his home planet, he and his fellow scientists would spend hours attempting to fathom why the civilization on Planet Earth had disappeared. They would search for clues which they hoped might save their civilization from a similar fate. (Burgdorf and Harney, 1970:103)

Following the reading of the story, students engage in discussion and are encouraged to make tentative hypotheses of what happened on the planet Earth. The use of a discussion circle in which class members face one another promotes the exchange of ideas and enhances their clarification.

The teacher assumes the role of a resource consultant rather than the dispenser of knowledge. He enters into the discussion when there is an obvious lag, when an arbitrator is vitally needed, or to reinforce a point made by a student. He withdraws from the discussion when students are able to get along on their own. He uses the strategy of the change agent by intervening at different structured points at different times. The challenging part of his job is to know when intervention is necessary.

Class discussion is useful when problems are raised and tentative hypotheses posed. It is also useful in clarifying the research findings of class members. It is most helpful as a means of testing hypotheses, generating conclusions, and determining the next course of action. Oral reports made to the class by individual members on results of research findings help to precipitate class discussions. An oral report is a monologue in which information is presented. The class discussion is a give-and-take in which information is presented, analyzed, evaluated, and then denied, supported, or modified.

TOPICS THAT CAN BE STUDIED

The broad range of topics that could be studied are similar to those outlined in a bibliography developed by the Conservation Education Association. The subject categories are listed as follows:

1. Interrelationship of resources (Ecology)
2. Natural resources
   a. Air
   b. Water
   c. Plants
   d. Animals
   e. Soil
   f. Land as space (farm, range, forest, towns, cities, transportation, recreation)
   g. Earth materials
   h. Energy resources (the sun, fossil fuels, water power, atomic energy, etc.

311

3. Role of man
   a. Man and his resources
   b. History of conservation
   c. Quality of environment (air and water pollution, pesticides, solid wastes, atomic wastes)
   d. Social implications of conservation (economics, politics, esthetics, ethics)
   e. Population
   f. Planning

(Conservation Education Association, 1968)

INTRODUCTION TO CURRICULAR PROJECTS

The National Science Foundation has funded several major curricular programs in science, each of which have their own objectives, learning experiences, materials, and teacher-training aids. None of these projects employs an interdisciplinary approach with emphasis on both science and social studies. One of them, the Science Curriculum Improvement Study (SCIS) emphasizes ecology in its life science program. It has developed a conceptual framework with an increasingly more sophisticated hierarchical structure. It is published commercially by Rand McNally and Company. Another one, the Elementary Science Study (ESS) has many units with environmental content. The teacher is given flexibility in determination of the sequence in which they are taught. As of 1969, ESS had devised at least 50 of these independent science units. They are published by McGraw-Hill Book Company. The third major project, Science—A Process Approach (AAAS), emphasizes the process skills of a scientist. Various subject matter including topics about the environment are the vehicles through which process skills (observing, measuring, etc.) are developed. The publisher is Xerox Corporation. Man: A Course of Study (MACOS) emphasizes the social sciences rather than the life sciences in its consideration of environmental problems.

SCIENCE CURRICULUM IMPROVEMENT STUDY

The Science Curriculum Improvement Study has developed sequentially-organized, materials-centered, conceptually-oriented units of instruction in ecology for grades 1-6. The six levels of the SCIS life science program are: Organisms, Life Cycles, Populations, Environments, Communities, and Ecosystems. A capsule description of Ecosystems, the culminating-level, is given immediately after this article. With this science program as a basic framework, it would be possible to blend in the social studies needed for a truly interdisciplinary understanding of environmental problems.

The National Academy of Sciences and National Academy of Engineering in their publication *Institutions for the Effective Management of the Environment* (1970) have this to say about environmental education programs at the elementary (K-6) level:

There are at least three federally assisted programs of national importance, the major ones being Elementary Science Study (ESS), Science—A Process Approach (AAAS), and Science Curriculum Improvement Study (SCIS). Of these, SCIS is the most promising for environmental education, because it centers attention on ecological and biological questions. Also, it is unique in that it provides a variety of living organisms for classroom demonstrations and experiments as part of a complete elementary science course. The educational materials consist of textbooks, teachers' manuals, films, demonstrations, and experimental kits. At present the course is being taught to 200,000 children, and that figure is expected to rise to between 2 and 5 million within a few years....It impresses us as an excellent beginning program in environmental science for

young children.
(p. 30-31)

An account of SCIS at the first grade level is given by Al Cline in the *Sierra Club Bulletin* (1970). He tells about Mrs. Louise Brown who is a science teacher at the Jefferson Elementary School in Berkeley. She teaches only first graders. They spend an average of two and one-half hours per week with her and study about ecosystems, pollution, smog, DDT, organisms, and habitats. No subject concerned with planet Earth is taboo.

The major goals to Mrs. Brown, a vivacious woman with 20 years experience in the classroom, 18 in Berkeley, are scientific literacy and environmental education. Trained in the University of California Berkeley-developed Science Curriculum Improvement Study (SCIS) technique, a system stressing exploration, invention, and discovery, Mrs. Brown emphasizes the diversity of organisms, both plants and animals. Her students observe the life cycle birth, growth and death. They learn what makes water turn green, what the black stuff is at the bottom of the fish bowl, what sustains life, and what causes death.

When the students bring something from home, and they do this consistently, it is discussed with enthusiasm. The science room is covered with articles of interest: a news story and pictures of a Minnesota fish kill; an article on a new and complex system of converting salt water to fresh; that not so scenic Sierra Club poster depicting the rape of a redwoods stand.

"I try to make the children aware of what's going on around them," Mrs. Brown says. One lad spelled out his theory for eliminating smog, a simplistic idea perhaps, but to the point. "Make difrent ingin for cars,

trucks and motor cicles." Others in a free-wheeling discussion on air pollution called for development of an electric auto, a steam driven car, and a return to the use of feet. In a discussion of pesticides, a girl gave a lucid explanation of the role of DDT in the demise of the pelican. Using the Redwood poster as a take-off, another girl left no doubt that she understood the cause and meaning of erosion.

This is Mrs. Brown's second year of working with first graders and she acknowledges that no one really thought her program would succeed to the extent that it has. The argument was that the kids just weren't ready for such advanced material, that their attention span could not be held for such a long (one hour) period. But it is working.

"There is a terrific increase in vocabulary, in the ability to describe things," the teacher reports. "I get tremendous feedback from both parents and teachers. And the second graders continue to be as enthusiastic as they were last year."
(p. 12-13)

ELEMENTARY SCIENCE STUDY

The Elementary Science Study (ESS) takes a less structured approach to environmental education than SCIS. It is not as concerned about the development of a scope and sequence for the elementary grades. School systems can use it to develop their own scope and sequence in relation to their own objectives. ESS is concerned with using concrete materials to promote the student's active involvement with learning. The importance of allowing children to follow their own inclinations as they interact with materials is emphasized. Following this article is one written by Edith H.E. Churchill which originally appeared in *Nature Study* and was reprinted in the *ESS Newsletter*. It expresses the ESS philosophy toward environmental studies.

MAN: A COURSE OF STUDY

A curricular project for upper elementary grades with emphasis on social science is Man: A Course of Study (MACOS). This program is produced by the Education Development Center in Cambridge, Massachusetts, under grants from the National Science Foundation. MACOS has produced ethnographic film studies, games, booklets, and teacher guides. It is based on three questions: What is human about human beings? How did they get that way? How can they be made more so? The course explores, in human terms, some basic ecological considerations about man and animals in the web of their relationships to their environment. The EPIC Clearinghouse for Education and Science reports, "The [MACOS] materials are elegant and exciting, but the approach is overly prescribed" (Henderson, 1970).

PEOPLE AND THEIR ENVIRONMENT

School systems may wish to develop their own instructional plans for environmental education. South Carolina is an excellent example of a state system which developed its own K-12 curriculum guides. Four agencies, the State Department of Education, the State Advisory Council for Conservation Education, the University of South Carolina School of Education, and the Belle W. Baruch Foundation collaborated in their formulation. Paul F. Brandwein who contributed his conceptual scheme and Mathew J. Brennan who provided editorial supervision served as guidance consultants. There are three major concepts around which these guides are designed:

> 1. Living organisms are interdependent with one another and with their environment.

> 2. Organisms (or populations of organisms) are the product of their heredity and environment.

> 3. Organisms and environments are in constant change.

All of the eight guides entitled, *People and Their Environment,* are now available from the J.G. Ferguson Publishing Company.

STUDENT ACTIVITIES

Students should participate in a variety of activities to help solve environmental problems. They could engage in committee projects, write stories, do individual research, write to environmental agencies, conduct scientific investigations, make opinion surveys, invite environmental experts to school, go on field trips, prepare ecology scrapbooks, or construct monitoring stations. Suggestions for various investigations are located in section 9, Part 3 of this book. Located in the appendices is a bibliography of curriculum materials for environmental studies. It lists a variety of programs, curriculum guides, books, periodicals, audiovisual aids, and experimental activities.

At the present time there are no curricular programs available which provide for the elementary teacher an interdisciplinary course in environment. Although this situation may at face value appear to be a liability, it is actually an asset. In the absence of a ready made source of reading and audio-visual materials, the student must himself seek out answers.

THE ROLE OF THE TEACHER

Instead of the teacher presenting information which the student digests and then regurgitates, he gets involved and finds his own information. Environmental studies are exciting and dynamic. Real answers are found to real problems. Often there are questions with no clearcut answers. Controversial issues are frequently subjects of classroom discussions. The teacher must learn to handle traditionally taboo areas in an honest personal way. He is challenged by the need to use new teaching strategies and by opportunities to explore new roles.

A promising aid to the classroom teacher are the public broadcasting programs on environmental improvement planned by the Public Broadcasting Environmental Center (Los Angeles Times, May 29, 1970). The U.S. Office of Education granted funds to the Corporation for Public Broadcasting to start this center. With money also coming from private sources, an eight million dollar a year array of programs is expected. The new center plans to work with public and private organizations to transmit programs over 191 television and 425 radio stations. Educational and entertainment techniques used by the children's show, *Sesame Street,* will be employed. These shows will inform the average citizen how to change his style of living to preserve the environment.

READING MATERIALS

It is recommended that every classroom assemble a set of reading materials on the environment. Available are books written primarily as children's literature but having environmental implications, ex., *Just Right* (Parents' Magazine Press); books written as texts on environmental abuse; ex., *Let's Go to Stop Air Pollution* (G.P. Putnam's Sons); or single copies of books from various natural science or social science textbook series, ex., *Concepts in Science* or *The Social Sciences: Concepts and Values* (Harcourt, Brace and World). The environmental reading collection should include a diversity of books with reading levels geared to the reading abilities of the students in the class.

An excellent source of material may now be found in such nationally distributed children's periodicals as *My Weekly Reader* (American Education Publications) and the *Junior Scholastic* (Scholastic Publications). The National Wildlife Federation publishes *Ranger Rick's Nature Magazine.* The National Audubon Society has recently pro-

duced a study work-text and accompanying teacher's manual called, *A Place to Live.* It is designed for grades 4-6, covers basic ecological concepts, and is a useful resource for walking trips near the school site. See Section 7 of this part.

CHILD AUTHORED BOOKS

Even kindergarten children are capable of engaging in meaningful environmental activities. The following are examples of stories that were dictated by kindergarten children to their teacher. A picture was drawn by each child to accompany the text.

Smog by Kevin
> The house is in the smog, and the window is open.
> The people inside will get sick.

My Smog Story by Linda
> I hate the smog because it makes me cough.
> Cough, cough, cough,
> Cough, cough, cough.

The Pollution Story by Allen
> The people are coughing inside because the air is getting through the screen.

My Pollution Book by Diane
> This is my house. I am coughing because of the smoke coming out of the chimney.
> This is the President. He is asking the people to make clean air.

It is recommended that every elementary child should have the opportunity to author a book of his own. If allowed to author more than one book, he not only improves the product but gains skill in discriminatory selection of reading material. These child-authored books enhance the class's environmental reading collection and increase the amount of reading material available on the subject.

The teacher will find the following procedures helpful in having students write child authored books:

EDUCATIONAL IMPLICATIONS

GETTING READY

Children who have enjoyed books of many kinds will need little time to study physical features of books.

Children with limited experience with books will need more time to enjoy a variety of books with the teacher and other adults.

Children need to talk, talk, talk about the books they enjoy.

I. Explore many books.
   A. Concepts.
      1. Books are written about a theme or subject.
      2. Books provide pleasure and enjoyment.
      3. Books provide needed information.
   B. Physical features.
      1. Sizes and shapes vary.
      2. Covers give clues to content.
      3. Each book has an author who is unique.
      4. Some books have illustrators.
      5. Some books tell a story only through pictures.
      6. Most books have title pages.
      7. Most books have sequence and page numbering.
      9. Additional features: style of writing, index pages, work lists, etc.

II. Become familiar with a subject.

Young children develop concepts through touching, smelling, tasting, seeing, hearing, and talking about their experiences.

Older children enjoy this type of motivation but frequently receive stimulation from pictures related to experiences they have had.

Some children are full of ideas without teacher provided motivations. They may only need support, encouragement, and sources of information.

Children have keen interest in:

A. Animals
   1. The teacher needs to bring animals into the environment and to help children find animals in their outdoor environment-rabbits, hamsters, etc.
   2. The children need time to observe and *talk* about animals.
      • how they look—fur, shell, skin, features, etc.
      • how they move—walk, crawl, slither, etc.
      • how they eat—nibble, peck, gobble, chew, etc.
      • what they eat—meat, grain, vegetables, fruit, etc.
      • how they drink—suck, lap, sip, absorb, swallow, etc.
      • how they talk—squeak, bark, whistle, chatter, etc.
      • how they sleep—standing up, lying down, etc.

B. Machines and energy
   1. The teacher needs to provide machines of many kinds and help the children observe machines at work in the school environment—trucks, wagons, cars, etc.
   2. The children need time to observe the machines and energy at work and to cause the machines to work in many ways. They need to *talk* about these experiences.
   3. Machines and energy may be classified to help organize a sequence for a book.
      • machines: *kinds of work* —grinders, movers, etc.
      sounds of work—buzz, clang, whirr, etc.
      where used—city, home, water, air, etc.
      • energy: manual electricity, heat, light, etc.

THE ELEMENTARY SCHOOL CURRICULUM

C. People
1. The teacher needs to provide opportunities for children to *talk* to adults and peers.
2. The teacher needs to help children ask interesting questions and react verbally to information received.
D. Water and other land forms
1. The teacher needs to provide many experiences with
a. Water—siphoning, floating, polluting, etc.
b. Sand, both dry and damp —molding, pouring, etc.
c. Soil, both dry and damp —digging, eroding, etc.
d. Rocks of many shapes, sizes and composition— weighing, chipping etc.
2. The children need time to repeat activities, make comparisons and classifications, and *discuss* discoveries with peers and adults.
3. Older children will apply discoveries to geography and history as related to problem solving in social studies.
E. Shapes and sizes
1. The teacher needs to help children see the many shapes in their environment, use materials of many shapes and sizes, and begin to classify these materials in many ways — big, little, square round, etc.
2. Older children will apply geometry and statistical data to social studies problems and other content areas.
F. Additional themes
Add ideas of high interest to you or children in your classroom.

WRITING A BOOK

I. Talk about your ideas.
II. Stories or parts of stories may be dictated for the teacher or teacher aide to write or type.
III. Children may write or type their own stories.
IV. Illustrations may be made before or after recording.
V. If each page has one or two ideas, pages may be put in order and assembled later. This may help to develop sequence.
VI. Blank book may be preassembled for children to use as needed.

(Los Angeles Unified School District, 1969)

MATHEMATICS

Problems in mathematical reasoning may be based upon the subject of environmental abuse. The following are some examples of these:

One American is responsible for one ton of garbage per year. How many pounds is that per person each day? What happens to all the garbage?

The air that makes city dwellers sneeze and wheeze costs every American $65 per year—a total of $11 billion in medical bills, corrosion, crop damage, cleaning, and so on. Can you cite examples of these expenses?

It costs $35 in taxes to pick up a pop bottle, candy wrapper, or other similar item discarded along our highways and in our parks. Take a walk with the class around the school grounds or a nearby park, picking up bottles and papers, and putting them in trash cans. Keep a record of the items picked up. How much did the class save the taxpayers?

Scientists say that if air pollution is not halted by 1985 the amount of sunlight reaching the earth will be reduced by one half. Today air pollution shuts out 45 percent of the sunlight over Los Angeles and 25 percent of it over New York City. An estimated 5 percent is shut out over rural areas. Discuss why this is so. Estimate how much sunlight your area receives.

Other problems may be developed on the amount of existing forest land in relation to newsprint production; comparisons between urban and rural population during the preceding fifty year period; or the amount of pollution-caused fish kill in proportion to the source of pollution. These statistics can be easily found in a standard almanac.

Graphs can be constructed on noise levels at various times of the day at a particular school location. The volume needle of a battery operated tape recorder could be used as an indicator. Other data that can be graphed over a period of days include the smog report as announced by the air pollution control agency, and the reduction in visibility on smoggy days as recorded by a photographic light meter.

AUDIO-VISUAL MATERIALS

Among some of the most valued aids to students are the growing amounts of films, filmstrips, film loops, and recordings on the subject of environmental education. In most instances, these can be adapted to students with a wide range of intellectual abilities. They can be used with the entire class to raise questions on environmental problems, or as a resource for research designed to find solutions to those problems.

They are also useful for review purposes as part of an environmental learning center. This center functions as a study carrel for small groups of students. It provides a convenient physical location for students to pursue independent investigations. Located there is audio-visual equipment such as filmstrip projectors, record players, and headphones. These devices are useful for viewing and listening activities. Laboratory materials for science experiments are readily available. This ready accessibility to work materials enhances the opportunity for various types of individual research activities.

EVALUATION

Self-evaluation on the part of the students and teacher is an integral and ongoing feature of all class activities. The teacher should check himself, and encourage students to examine themselves, for evidence of understanding of certain major concepts. Concepts cannot be taught. They must be developed within the student. An adequate development involves a growing sense of environmental values and a commitment to the action programs necessary for responsible citizenship to implement these values.

The following concepts are central to the environmental curriculum:

1. An interdependence exists between all living things and their environment.

2. All components of the environment are in constant change.

3. Our biophysical environment is characterized by complexity and diversity.

4. All resources within the environment are in limited supply.

The process of education through which these concepts are assimilated will have some of the following features:

1. Situations are structured for improvement of skills in problem solving.

2. Opportunities are provided for manipulation, investigation exploration, experimentation, and discovery.

3. Provision is made for development of concepts.

4. Stress is given to values as well as knowledge.

5. Relationships are established between the natural and social sciences.

6. Application is made of environmental understandings to language arts and mathematical skills.

A successful program in environmental education cannot be detailed in recipe fashion. Every teacher has his own style and method of approach. All students differ in intellectual, emotional, and social characteristics. Each class is an ecosystem with its own personality and unique interrelationships. A creative and stimulating curricular program which grows from students' needs and interests will be the one with the greatest possibility for making responsible environmental citizenship a way of life.

REFERENCES

Burgdorf, Lucille P. and Harney, Irene F. "Challenge of the City." *Instructor* 79:103; April 1970.

Cline, Al. "Conservation Education." *Sierra Club Bulletin* 55:12-13; April 1970. (Reprinted by permission).

Conservation Education Association. "Conservation Education—A Selected Bibliography." Compiled by Joan Carvajal and Martha E. Munzer, 1968.

Henderson, Martha T. "Environmental Education: Social Studies Sources and Approaches." Boulder, Colorado: ERIC Clearinghouse for Social Science Education, October, 1970.

Landsmann, Leanna. "Earth Day—How You Can Observe It." *Instructor* 79:108; April 1970. (Reprinted by permission).

Los Angeles Times. "Environment Series Set by CPB Branch." May 19, 1970.

Los Angeles Unified School District. Supplementary Aid, *Child Authored Books*. Submitted by Mary Niceley, Academic Supervisor, Prepared by Communications Skills Coordinator. November 1969. (Reprinted by permission).

National Academy of Sciences—National Academy of Engineering. *Institutions for the Effective Management of the Environment*. Report of the Environmental Study Group to the Environmental Studies Board, Part I. Washington, D.C. January 1970.

Piaget, Jean. "Cognitive Development in Children: Development and Learning." *Journal of Research in Science Teaching* 2:176-186; 1964.

Yasso, Warren E. and Brovey, Daniel J. "Earth Science Experiences: Expanding the Child's Awareness of His Natural Physical Environment." *Science and Children* 8:30-33; October 1970.

Dorothy Needham

THE EARTH – AN ACTIVITY UNIT

TEACHER BACKGROUND

In addition to helping children discover the causes and effects of land pollution, the activities in this unit provide a further insight into the manner in which one type of environmental pollution invariably leads to another.

With their emerging awareness of how man's misuse of technology has taxed the natural purification processes of air and water beyond the limit, children will almost intuitively perceive the role of land in the environmental pollution cycle. In America, it was with land that man committed the first of his many ecological sins, through his erosion-producing farming practices and his forest-clearing operations.

Today man uses highly-advanced technology and accomplishes the same result on a larger scale and manages to pile up more than 100 million tons of refuse on the land every year in the process. Man's creative skill in production emphasizes his meager knowledge of disposal.

The major causes of land pollution are erosion, the indiscriminate clearing, removal, filling in, mining, drilling and paving of land, the widespread use of chemical pesticides and herbicides and the accumulation of industrial, municipal and domestic waste. Population growth is also a factor which can no longer be ignored.

The effects of land pollution are unsightliness, loss of valuable topsoil for food production, the pollution of waterways by silt deposits, the destruction of wildlife habitats in field, forest and marsh, the extinction or near-extinction of several hundred species, rat-infestations, and the appearance in food of chemicals with which man has had no previous biological experience.

Under certain conditions, land can renew itself, but, as with other natural purification and renewal processes, time is of major importance. (For example, it takes nature several centuries to build up a six-inch depth of rich topsoil.)

The children's activities in the air and water pollution units should provide a good base for problem-solving experiences in the land pollution study. The culminating activities involve all three units and stress the role of the individual and the

SOURCE. Reprinted, by permission, from *The Grade Teacher,* October 1970, with slight abridgment.

individual family and school in attacking the problem of environmental pollution.

THE APPROACH

I. Prepare some table and bulletin-board displays designed to stimulate interest in land pollution and to stress its relationship to other forms of environmental pollution.

A. Bulletin board (large)

1. Cover with black background paper. Staple on it 12" squares of white construction paper to achieve a large checkerboard effect. In dead center place a large solid circle cut from bright yellow oaktag. In the center of the circle, print "Pollution." Completely around the edge of the circle, print "Round And Round It Goes."

B. Bulletin board (small)

1. Cover with bright yellow paper. In dead center place a large box form (with the lid partially opened) cut from black construction paper. With white chalk, label it "Pandora's Box." During the course of the unit, children will add three large demons (labeled "Air Pollution," "Water Pollution" and "Land Pollution"). The demons are rising from the opened box, and assorted smaller cutout demons (labeled "erosion," "refuse," "cars," "algae," etc.) tumble in appropriate positions around the central demons. (Charcoal is an excellent "demon" medium.)

C. Table (placed under small bulletin board)

1. Books and magazines. Story books, factual books, and poetry books about land, magazine and newspaper articles, pamphlets and brochures about land pollution.

2. Materials. A "Twenty Questions" box (a covered shoe box with a slit in the top); some index cards for those children who wish to make a land pollution file; a second box, labeled "Trash or Treasure?" filled with such scraps of litter as twigs, labels, bottle caps, plastic pieces, rusty bobby pins, glass, dry leaves, etc.; an oaktag

envelope (about 12" long and 6" wide) labeled "Quiz Your Neighbor" and containing a set of teacher-made flashcards on which are printed questions about pollution with answers on the back; baby-food jars filled with different types of soil (topsoil, gravel, sand and clay, for example); a stack of pre-cut solid white oaktag circles, 10" in diameter, and the "Earth Bingo Game" (see "Developmental Activitis," Section I-K).

3. Pictures mounted on cardboard, labeled and placed in a folder so they may be borrowed from the display for study. Include pictures of dumps, slums, arid lands, farms, factories, people spraying pesticides, abandoned mines, bare hillsides, potholes in streets, a forest fire, oil-drilling operations, an eagle, a cheetah, rats, a junked car, a junk yard, piles of debris, etc., etc.

4. Maps: Local outline maps, community land use map (usually obtainable from zoning boards), local road maps.

5. Charts: Some Audubon "Food Chain" charts, mounted on cardboard and covered with clear contact paper to prevent damage. (These are inexpensive and may be purchased from The National Audubon Society, 1130 Fifth Ave., New York City 10028.)

II. Tell the children the Greek myth about Pandora's Box, stressing the idea that the box had been given to Pandora by Zeus for *safekeeping*. Have a general discussion about the legend. Questions: What has been freely given to us and to all people not only for safekeeping, but for use (natural resources)? What are those natural resources? Has man safeguarded his natural resources? Will he ever receive any more resources than what he has right now? Can we throw away this planet and get another one tomorrow?

Ask the class to imagine a different ending to the Pandora myth, to imagine that air, water and land pollution were the demons that escaped from the box, to imagine that Pandora was very clever and an excellent problem solver. Write an ending to the story and tell how Pandora rounded up all the demons, put them back in the box and slammed it shut forever. (This exercise should identify those children who have thought about the problems in terms of possible solutions. Make sure at least one of these is in each group. Ask them to submit names of children with whom they have not worked in a group situation in the other two units. Use the lists in group-forming for the unit.)

III. Show the children the question box. Hand each child 10 small strips of paper. Have them construct 10 good questions about pollution (to which they know the answers) . . . one on each strip, with their names on the back. Check all questions for errors and for too many duplications. Have the children rewrite or recopy if necessary. Fold the strips in thirds and place them in the question box. Questions will be used in an activity described in "Ongoing Projects." (See "Developmental Activities," Section I-A, below.)

IV. Make a master of as many circles as you can place on a duplicating sheet. These should vary in size from two to four inches in diameter. Give each child two copies. Instruct the children to draw, in each circle on one sheet, different things in nature that are more or less round. Have them use the circles as rough outlines, labeling each drawing. Flowers, eyes, the earth, sun, moon, berries and faces are standard. More imaginative children tend to draw such things as turtle shells, a ram's horn, paw pads, leopard spots, fern sori, etc. When the page is complete, have a child list his drawings on the chalkboard. Continue this until all the different things from the children's sheets have been added to the list.

Discuss the concept of the circle as an abstraction. (Relate it, if necessary, to the known concept of a "number" as an abstraction.) On the second sheet, have chil-

dren draw anything in nature that *reminds* them of a circle or a cycle. Tell them that they may use arrows, words or other symbols to express this. Day-to-night-to-day, the seasons, the tides and the earth's orbit are typical responses. Other children envision birth-life-death, the hydrologic cycle, the metamorphosis of a frog or butterfly, simple food chains. Collect the second sheets. These will be checked and returned to the children with certain ideas designated for further research and development for the checkerboard bulletin board (see Section I-B).

DEVELOPMENTAL ACTIVITIES

I. Ongoing projects
A. The children use the "Twenty Questions" box by taking one question from it each day for 20 days. Each child constructs a personal "Twenty Questions" booklet consisting of 20 sheets of lined paper and an oaktag cover, appropriately designed and titled, into which he copies his daily question and answers it with as much detail as possible. (Examples of titles are "Twenty Answers," "The Expert Answers" and "Ask Away.") Sketches further delineating the answers should also be included on each page. (Second choices are allowed only when a child has already answered the question in his booklet.) Remind the students to return their questions when they're through. Students may use any research source to discover the answers.
B. The children are responsible for making finished copies of their "nature cycles" on the 10" white oaktag circles. (Further "roughs" may be submitted before the final drawings are made.) Ballpoint pens, India ink or crayon are excellent media for this project. As the circles are completed, pin them on the white sections of the bulletin board checkerboard. Ask the children to write a few paragraphs explaining their cycles and center them on the adjoining black section of the checkerboard. Cutouts of "circular things in na-

ture" can also be placed in the black sections. At the end of the unit, a large "Environmental Pollution Circle" chart can replace the yellow center circle. This may be patterned after the one issued, free, by the New York Department of Health, Albany, N.Y. As the focal point of the bulletin board, it will suggest how environmental pollution intrudes upon other ecological cycles.

C. Specific groups begin to design the three big demons for the "Pandora's Box" bulletin board. Others will fashion the small demons as the unit progresses.

D. Children add appropriate pictures to the file.

E. Each group produces a wide variety of pictures (crayon, water color or tempera) relating to land pollution for the "Tape-Slide Show." A description of this show is located near the end of this article.

F. Children write lab sheets on each experiment and demonstration performed during the unit, including materials, procedures, observations and conclusions. These should be kept in a lab folder.

G. Allow short "buzz" sessions after each experiment and field trip so groups may share their ideas and observations.

H. Each class member saves any local newspaper clippings relating to new construction in the community and any changes in zoning laws.

I. One group is responsible for discovering the names and addresses of all members of the local zoning board, the editor of the local newspaper, the mayor or town manager and other local officials.

J. The children play "Quiz Your Neighbor": Two or more classmates sit together and flash each other the question cards for reinforcement.

K. Make a master of a chart resembling the one used in a bingo game. Print the letters E-A-R-T-H in the top five spaces, and number from 1 to 5 down the left side. Paste copies on oaktag and cover with clear contact paper for protection. Print "pollution" words on small oaktag squares (words starting with the letters in "earth"). On another set of small squares, print each letter in "earth" plus a number from 1 to 5 (E-1, E-2, etc.). Play as regular bingo is played. A good small group game.

II. Discovering the existence of land pollution

A. Hold up the "Trash or Treasure?" box. Statement: "Yesterday when I left our room, I decided to pick up every bit of litter that was in my path between the room and my car. This is what I found." Hold up each item for comment and place it on the table. Comment, "I have called the box 'Trash or Treasure?' why do you suppose I have done so?" Lead children to understand that organic matter (leaves, twigs, nuts, shells and paper made from wood pulp, for example) will eventually decay and become part of the soil if left outdoors, and that iron will be broken down by rust. Questions: What about this aluminum twist-off top? What about this piece of glass? The plastic? (Accept all answers.) On the chalkboard, write "biodegradable." Have the children find the prefix *bio* in their dictionaries. Write "a living organism" next to the prefix. Following the same procedure for "degrade" (to wear down) and "degradable" (capable of being worn down). Questions: Who will now put all the parts of the definition together and tell me what a *biodegradable material* is? What is a *non-biodegradable* material? Invite the children to the table to assist in separating the biodegradable and non-biodegradable materials. Questions: Which ones seem to be treasures? Which ones seem to be trash? How can we find out about our "undecided"? (Accept all suggestions for now.)

B. Take a "litter walk" around the school playground. Give each group a large bag and designate areas to be covered. Give one child a separate bag and a large magnet to "sweep" the area and to probe into sidewalk or asphalt cracks for metals. (This activity should take about 10 minutes.) Still outdoors, have the children empty the bags and sort the contents. Estimate the number of pieces of paper, bottles, string, etc., and record the estimates. Recollect the litter and dispose of it.

C. Write the estimates on the chalkboard and have children make bar graphs to show the incidence of certain types of litter on the playground. How much of it was biodegradable? Can they imagine the amount of litter on all the playgrounds in the community? In the state? In the country? In the world? Can some types of litter be called pollutants? What kinds? As homework, ask the children to collect the litter in their yards, to estimate the incidence of certain types and to prepare a bar graph to compare with the one made in school.

D. Make some "litter gardens" to further establish the concept of biodegradability. Line six or seven shoe boxes with plastic wrap and half fill with soil. Plant two identical rows (the long way) with four items each. (For example, a hair clip, a piece of plastic, a piece of aluminum foil and a piece of newspaper in each row.) Use different items in each of the boxes. Identify each piece with a tag on a toothpick. Keep the soil slightly damp at all times.

At the end of a week, the children can carefully dig up one row in each box, allowing time between each "dig" for observations to be recorded. At the end of the second week, have them dig up the second row in each box and record observations. Questions: Which materials showed signs of wearing down? Which materials remained the same? Which materials are biodegradable? Which ones could pollute the landscape indefinitely? Can materials be "degraded" in any other way?

E. Take all the materials that did not show signs of deterioration in the soil and hold each, in turn, with tongs over a candle flame. Ask the children to observe which materials burn, do not burn, give

off smoke, give off odor. Which of these make the most undesirable litter? Which could contribute to air pollution? (Hold up a small piece of copper.) "Copper is getting pretty scarce, but millions of pieces are thrown away or left in the engines of junked cars. Can you think of any ways that copper—and iron, aluminum and steel—might be reused?" Discuss.

F. Visit the community dump or invite a qualified guest to discuss how garbage is disposed of in your community and in other places. Discuss advantages and disadvantages of each method (open burning, incineration, sanitary landfill) with special reference to air pollution (burning and odors), to water pollution (dumping or burying) and land pollution (accumulation of non-degradables).

G. Place two large pieces of newsprint on the front table. On them place two (tissue) boxes. Fill one with bare, dry soil, and the other with grassy sod. Ask one of your boys to stand on the table and drop water on the bare soil with a medicine dropper. Show the children the splash pattern of the bits of soil on the newsprint. Repeat the action, dropping water on the grassy area. Point out that grass helps to hold the water in the soil. Introduce the word *erosion*.

Cut a "V" on the front edge of each box. Give a child an empty glass and ask him to hold it under the "V" of the bare soil box. Tilt the back end of the box to simulate a hillside. Pour a half glass of water on the soil, and catch the runoff in the glass under the "V". Repeat with the grassed soil. Have the children compare the runoff in the two glasses. Discuss and record on lab sheets.

H. Take an "erosion walk" around the school neighborhood. Note (or take pictures of) such signs of land erosion as bare soil, exposed tree roots, gullies, holes, etc. Invite speculation on whether different instances of erosion were caused by wind, water, or the freezing and melting of ice. Question: If water caused the erosion,

where did the soil eventually go? (Call the children's attention to soil heaped in road gutters. Reinforce water pollution studies.) Have children note streets and paved playground areas in need of repair.
I. Take a "land use walk" around the neighborhood. Do any of the buildings look "out of place"? What zone is the neighborhood in? Is property being taken care of? Is there any "open land" left? What suitable use might be made of it in the future?

III. Discovering causes and effects of land pollution.
A. Show, explain and discuss (according to the achievement level of your class) the community land use map. Circle your school neighborhood (specifically, the area covered in the land use walk). Place the map on an opaque projector so that enlarged details will facilitate discussion. Discuss the purpose of zoning. Questions: On our field trip, did you see any violations of zoning? Did any structures contribute to land pollution? Air pollution? Water pollution? Keeping our zoning laws in mind, how could we improve our school neighborhood? Can zoning laws be changed? How?
B. Invite a member of your local zoning board to speak to your class. Ask him (in advance) to discuss how and why certain zones are set up, how a zoning board meeting is conducted, and how citizens can make their ideas or feelings known to the board. Have the children construct a brief outline of the speaker's remarks. Afterwards, write thank-you notes to the guest.
C. Hold a "Current Events Day." Have children share their newspaper clippings concerning new construction or zoning changes being proposed in the community, if any. Discuss the advantages and disadvantages of the proposals, with special reference to environmental pollution. (If the children seem to feel very strongly about one particular thing, an impromptu mock zoning board could be set up, with

the petitioners and the complainants heard.) The entire class can vote on the decision.
D. Make a master copy of a chart, plotted in half-inch squares. Down the left-hand side, on the lines, type: glass, bits of paper, plastic bags, waxed paper, food, cans, bottles, metal fragments, gum, lollipop sticks, strings, boxes, fabrics, other materials. At lunch-time, distribute copies to three children and ask them to monitor the playground, with one child acting as a recorder and two as "spotters." The recorder places a checkmark denoting each piece of material dropped or thrown away by children.

Discuss the listing. Hand out copies of the chart to all children and have them construct simple bar graphs as the data are read by the recorder. Discuss ways of reducing playground litter.

Questions: Are there laws against littering? Should playground litterbugs be punished? Allow children to buzz in their groups and make a group list of suggestions for playground improvement.
E. Give children a fresh copy of the chart to use for homework. Ask them (with their parents' permission) to stand for about 20 minutes that afternoon near a store, restaurant or garage and to tally the litter dropped or thrown by adults (either walking by or passing in cars). Make a second graph. Compare graphs the following day and draw conclusions.

Problem: "Our community has a ($50) fine for littering. How much money would have been collected yesterday in just our neighborhood if that law were enforced? Have the children figure their individual totals; then help them compile a final class total. Lead children to an appreciation of the economic effects of littering. Have them consider the cost to taxpayers for streetcleaning, the cost to businessmen, etc.
F. Make some miniature friezes to illustrate cause-and-effect relationships in various types of land pollution. Distribute white construction paper and have the children fold it once one way and twice the other

EDUCATIONAL IMPLICATIONS

way to make eight sections. This will help the children formulate a sequence of events and will serve as a model for larger friezes. Here's an example: "Once there was a beautiful forest on a high hill." (Sketch the forest in Section 1.) "Many animals lived in the forest" (Section 2). "Men cut the trees for lumber" (Section 3). "Animals lost their homes" (Section 4). "Much of the land was bare" (Section 5). "Heavy rains formed deep gullies in the hillside" (Section 6). "Windstorms picked up soil and blew it everywhere" (Section 7). "Silt filled the streams in the valley below" (Section 8).

As the unit develops, groups can illustrate other sequences for large friezes. Assign different parts of a planned frieze to group members (or have leading group members assign them). Preliminary sketches are made on newsprint. Each section of a pollution story is done on a large piece of white oaktag, on which a water color background has been painted. The children glue on the details, using any available materials. (Some "stories" may require six sections; others, four; others, 10.)

Display the finished friezes in their proper sequences on an outside bulletin board. The caption could read: "What happens when . . ." If the children need help in getting started, suggest: "Hard pesticides are sprayed on trees"; "the garbagemen go on strike"; "a factory is built near our school"; a dam is built in a river."

G. Discuss why silver is no longer used in our national currency. (It is becoming very scarce.)

H. Discuss or show a film on pesticides, herbicides and biocides. Plant weeds in the tissue box used in Section II-G. Ask the children to imagine that it represents a beautiful apple orchard. Spray the "orchard" with whatever spray paint you have available. Ask the children to imagine that you are spraying a chemical guaranteed to get rid of all insect pests. Pour water over the plants. Ask the children to imagine that a rainstorm has occurred. The children

will observe the "chemical" being washed from the leaves and into the ground.

Statement: "Last week in my newspaper I read that a biologist found an osprey's nest in a tree near a polluted lake. The eggs in the nest were all broken because the shells were so thin. The little ospreys never hatched. When the biologist examined the eggs, he found traces of pesticide in them . . . just like the pesticide I used on my apple orchard. Ask the children to explain, in writing, how the pesticide got into the eggs.

I. Instruct different groups to research these topics: Animals That Are Extinct, Animals That Are Almost Extinct. Natural Causes Leading to Animal Extinction, Man-Made Causes Leading to Animal Extinction, Importance of Wild Animals, How Our Wildlife Can Be Saved from Extinction. Reports will be shared with the class.

J. Take a field trip to the nearest wildlife sanctuary. (Guides are always available on request.) Point out differences in natural forest "litter" and city "litter." Questions: Is forest litter biodegradable? How do the trees improve the quality of the soil? Are pesticides used in the sanctuary? Are there signs of erosion in the sanctuary? Can people hunt in the sanctuary? Do the trees show any signs of air pollution damage? Does the sanctuary pond show any signs of water pollution? (Teacher's note: It probably will, since even the relatively protected sanctuary has no control over the content of ground water. More often than not the ponds show signs of heavy algae growth from detergents used in area homes.) Is that decaying log an ecosystem? How does the sanctuary soil differ from the playground soil? What helps rain to percolate gently through the sanctuary soil? (An abundance of leafy trees and the ground cover of the forest floor "stop" the rain from pounding relentlessly on soil.) Write letters to the sanctuary director describing enjoyment of the trip and telling the most memorable experiences. Mail the letters in one envelope, unedited and unexpurgated.

326

K. To promote recall of the sanctuary field trip, write some adjectives on the chalkboard and have the children list as many things as they can remember from the field trip that each adjective describes. Adjectives might include soft, hard, moist, rough, smooth, red, cool, beautiful, round, noisy, quiet, funny, unusual, tiny, unexpected, etc. Share the lists orally.

L. For fun, and to reinforce understanding of air, water and land pollutants, play "What Am I?" (Close the room door—it may get beautifully noisy.) Attach a piece of paper, with the name of a pollutant on it, to the back of each class member. Allow the children to roam about, asking whoever will listen, such questions as, "Am I something in the air? What color am I? How did I get where I am?" Only one question may be asked of any single individual. When a child accurately says to another child, "I'm hydrocarbon" (for example), he may place his card in front of him, but continue to participate in the game until all children have identified themselves.

M. Take the baby-food jars containing different kinds of soil to the front table. Place small amounts from each jar on different pieces of newsprint. Have the children examine the soils. Questions: Which soil contains the largest particles? The smallest? Which soil reminds you of the sanctuary soil? Playground soil? Beach soil? What is in between all the particles of soil? (Air) How does air help the plants that grow in the soil? How was each of these soils made by nature?

Pour an identical amount of water into the jars containing the rest of the soil. Have the children note and record the percolation rates. Problem questions: Which soil could contribute to land pollution by holding rain in puddles on its surface? How? Which soil does not mix well with the water? What effect would this have on land? Could we say that soil which can absorb and hold water may be best for some things? What? Why?

Variation of (M): Place dry samples of soil in juice cans that have holes punched in the bottoms of them. Pour exactly one-half cup of water in each can and catch the runoff underneath. Measure the runoff of each soil type. The greater the runoff, the less water-holding power of the soil. Discuss the usefulness of this knowledge to farmers . . . to community planners . . . to house builders.

N. Show, explain, and discuss food chain charts. To visibly demonstrate the "pyramid of numbers" in food chains, ask 10 children to stand next to each other at the front of the room. Tell them that they represent *billions* of tiny plants and animals on and near the bottom of a body of water. In back of them place five children. Tell them that they represent *millions* of snails, shrimp, and other little animals who feed on Row 1. In back of them place three children, who represent the *thousands* of small fish who feed on shrimp and snails. In back of them place two children, who represent the *hundreds* of larger fish who feed on smaller fish. In back place *one* child, who represents the comparatively few eagles, ospreys, hawks, and falcons who feed on the larger fish.

To further emphasize the idea of a chain, give each child a piece of string about a yard long. The other end of the string is held by the "predator." Have children plan and show, in the same manner, a forest food chain.

Lead children to understand that the animal at the top of the pyramid gets everything in concentrated form from all the animals in the food chain. Stress the concept of plants as producers, animals as consumers, and bacteria (and fungi) as decomposers.

Questions: Does nature recycle her materials? Does land play an important role in the recycling? Can land contaminants affect food chains? Can land contaminants affect recycling?

(Note: A simple explanation of natural recycling that fascinates children is the story of a carbon atom. The atom is in the air. It enters the plant. An animal eats the plant. The atom enters the animal. The animal dies. The atom enters the soil. The atom returns to the air to be used by a plant, etc.)

Questions: Could man take a lesson from nature and recycle some of the materials that he uses in production of things? Would this eliminate some land pollutants? Would it save valuable metals?

O. Devote a lesson to a discussion of no-deposit bottles (which some communities are hoping to outlaw). They are virtually nondegradable litter and cannot at present be recycled. Have groups of children discuss the topic and suggest solutions. (Some soft-drink manufacturers are currently test-marketing plastic disposable bottles.)

IV. Seeking solutions and applying pressure
A. Write a letter to the editor protesting a specific problem that has come to light in the study of land pollution (methods of garbage pickup or disposal, the proposed building of a factory, the condition of school neighborhood roads, unsightly debris piled in fields, unnecessary tree-cutting, dirty gutters, etc.). Make each problem the subject of a separate letter, signed by all the students. Send copies of the letters to the town officials, the sanitation department head, and the zoning board (if applicable). Make your principal aware of what you are doing—he likes to be "in" on such things, and his prior knowledge will assure you of his backing.
B. Present your principal with a *complete plan* (drawn up by the class) for school-ground improvement. Such a plan might include a suggestion that segments of the student body be assigned to monitor and clean up specific sections of the school-grounds, at specific times each week; that school littering be considered a "school crime"; that the town maintenance department be advised of cracks and holes (state which ones, specifically) in paved and grassed areas; that litter cans on the playground be painted by the school art

department (preferably with interesting designs); that the school conduct a "button" sale so that trees may be purchased and planted (in definite places) on the school grounds (the buttons can proclaim a simple statement, such as "I love trees" or "Trees are good people," and may be ordered in quantity from a button manufacturer); that permission be given to erect some bird houses or feeding stations (made by children) on the school grounds, and that the practice of observing Arbor Day be revived (if your school has no such program).

Discuss all suggestions made by the children before the list is drawn up. The plan could be printed on a scroll, stating, "We, the people of Grade ———, Room ———, ———————— School, respectfully request that you, as principal . . ." etc.
C. Interest your PTA in the schoolground improvement program and enlist their help.
D. Make a list of environmental pollution books that are not in your school library. (Also include nature magazines like *Ranger Rick* and *The Conservationist*.) Submit the list to your librarian and ask if the books could be considered for purchase in the next order.
E. Submit to your principal a list of the materials or equipment used in these pollution units which you had to borrow or purchase. Ask if the materials could be included in next year's middle-grade budget.
F. Have each child make an oaktag poster, reading:

SAVE US . . .
    a breathe of fresh air
    a drink of clean water
    a patch of green grass
PLEASE!

(signed)
The Clean Environment Class,
Grade ———, Room ———,
———————— School

Each child must persuade a local merchant to display his poster.
G. Write a class letter to your superintend-

ent of schools, requesting that Earth Day be considered a culminating activity rather than a beginning one . . . a day when results rather than attempts are applauded. Perhaps Earth Day could develop into a "school tour" day for boards of education, garden clubs, conservationists and other interested citizen groups.

H. Make car and boat litter bags. Use a double thickness of newspaper. Fold in half where it folds naturally. Spread bright tempera on it with a sponge. When it is dry, print "I Hate Ugly" on it in a contrasting color. Designs may be added if desired. Spray with clear acrylic. Fold in half and staple the sides and bottoms. Attach yarn handles. Each child should make several.

V. Culminating activities

A. Divide the class into three groups to prepare materials for the major activities that wrap up the pollution units. Groups will work on the large environmental pollution circle, the "Tape-Slide Show," and a "What-Can-I-Do?" open letter to parents.

1. The "Environmental Circle" group. All members make an idea chart to organize their thoughts. Divide paper into three columns: Air Pollution, Water Pollution and Land Pollution. Start with any one and list the pollutants. (Land, for example, might be "open dumps," "erosion," "pesticides," "junk cars," "fertilizers." Have the children consider the effects of these in other areas. (Example: erosion leads to silt in the soil or dust particles in the air.)

Have the group members compare lists and decide on six pollution cycles. To dramatize the six cycles, have a child draw six evenly spaced, concentric circles. Using light lines, divide the circle into thirds and label the sections "Air Pollution," "Water Pollution" and "Land Pollution." Label the bull's-eye "Environmental Pollution." (A ball-point pen and a compass, or different-sized round objects can be used to make the circles.)

Then have the child demonstrate a cycle by writing the name of an air pollutant

on one curved line, the name of the water pollutant it becomes on the continuation of the line, and the land pollutant that in turn becomes on the remaining section of the curve. Four more cycles can be done similarly. (Make sure that pollutants lead into each other correctly.)

Suggest that the children practice a while on newsprint. When a perfect model is produced, have it copied on a yellow oaktag circle and place it in the center of the large bulletin board.

2. The "Tape-Slide Show" group. (Note: If necessary, ask your multi-media department for help with this project well in advance. Most such departments will lend you a small camera with a viewfinder—or send someone to assist—and will supply you with film. If you cannot get a camera this way and do not own one yourself, send out a plea for parents to help. Invariably, you will get not only a camera but the services of a photo buff, as well.)

Have the group sort all the crayon, tempera and watercolor pictures submitted during the course of the units, according to the content (air, water, land). From the various efforts, have them select as many pictures as possible that best illustrate pollution.

Place the camera on a stand and focus it on the blackboard. Tape one picture at a time on the blackboard to line up with the viewfinder on the camera. Snap each picture. (You can't miss with this one.)

When the slides are developed, the group re-sorts and numbers them. (Have them include any other slides taken on field trips.) If you offer your slides for use by other schools you might be able to get the money for developing them from the PTA or the multi-media department.

Project the slides for the whole class to see. Discuss each one and ask for comments that describe the action and tell a story of pollution. If a "story line" is not forthcoming suggest "Pandora's Box, Circa 1970," and let the children take it from there. The simpler the story line, the more effective the show.

A starter: "Once upon a time in (*your community*) there lived a girl named Pandora. One morning when she went out to bring in the milk, she saw a strange black box on her doorstep. She was very curious . . ." etc.

When all the "lines" are decided upon, give them to different children to practice before taping. Remember to leave a few seconds of blank tape between each line so the slide may be projected. The name of your show, the producers, and "The End" may be typed on slide-sized pieces of acetate and inserted in slide mounts, or written on the chalkboard, and photographed.

A tape-slide show can always be simulated by using the children's art work on the opaque projector instead of making real slides.

Present the "Tape-Slide Show" as an assembly program for your school and for parents and other interested adults after school. Send invitations in advance.

Name a panel of 10 or 12 children to answer questions from the audience after the show. If possible, tape the question-and-answer session.

3. The "Open Letter" group. Members of this group make lists of everything they can think of that their families can do to help reduce pollution. When a final list is decided upon, type a master entitled "An Open Letter to Parents." These will be distributed (with principal's permission) to all classes, to the "Tape-Slide Show" audience, to the local newspaper, town officials, etc. The letter might include a greeting, a paragraph about the seriousness of the pollution problems, and a comment about the children's course of study.

Suggestions about how individuals can help might include (1) Do not use any pesticides or herbicides which would pollute the air, the water, and the soil. (2) Plant some trees and increase the available oxygen supply while beautifying property. (3) Reduce the use of detergents which pollute water. (4) Plant grass seed in bare spots. (5) Protest, whenever and wherever possible, about the continued use of no-deposit bottles. (6) Compost leaves instead of burning them. This prevents air pollution from smoke and gives you some good material for your soil. (7) Repair all leaky faucets in your home so water will not be wasted. (8) Use white instead of colored toilet paper and facial tissues. White paper is degraded more quickly. (9) Keep your yard spruced up and free of litter. Clean the gutter in front of your house, too. (10) Talk to your neighbors and friends about pollutants and conservation. (11) Write to your elected representatives and tell them how you feel about environmental pollution. Be sure to inquire how they voted on pollution bills. (12) Voice an opinion at zoning board meetings. (13) Have the exhaust on your car checked. If you can see waste materials coming from it, you are polluting the air more than you have to. (14) Protest, in all possible ways, any industries in your neighborhood contributing to pollution. (15) Try to cut down on noise. This, too, is a form of pollution. (16) Join and work for a conservation group. (17) Reuse as many materials as possible (paper bags, aluminum foil, etc.). (18) Save metal scraps and newspapers, both of which can be recycled. (19) Plant a vegetable garden. (20) Keep water cold in your refrigerator instead of letting the water run every time you want a drink. (21) Clean leaves and twigs out of roof gutters. (22) Reuse gift wrappings.

4. Add the "Twenty Questions" booklets, lab sheets, litter tally sheets, bar graphs, and the original art work from which the "Tape-Slide Show" was made, to the display table.

5. Hold a short "Open House" in your classroom, preferably the tape-slide show, and assign different children to explain the environmental pollution and Pandora's Box bulletin boards, friezes, experiments, booklets, "Earth Bingo" game, "Quiz Your Neighbor" game, etc. Give each visitor a

copy of the "Open Letter," a button (if you had them made) and a litter bag. Have one child act as a "roving reporter" with a cassette tape recorder to obtain guests' impressions of the exhibit.

GLOSSARY

Biocides—long-lasting, hard pesticides, such as DDT; literally, life-killers, not simply pest-killers.

Biodegradability—the ability of a living organism, or anything that was ever part of a living organism, to deteriorate.

Ecosystem—any size community of living things and their special environments; a decaying log is an ecosystem—so is a pond.

Frieze—a series of pictures which tell a story or express an idea.

Herbicide—chemical used to kill or inhibit plant growth.

Incineration—the process of causing materials to burn to ashes.

Landfill—a method of waste disposal. Refuse is placed in trenches, compacted by a bulldozer, and covered with soil.

Non-biodegradable—Not capable of deteriorating through decomposition (examples: glass, plastic, aluminum).

Osprey—a large brown-and-white hawk that feeds on fish; presently near extinction in many areas.

Percolate—to trickle; specifically, the action of water filtering through soil.

Sori—spore spots on the undersides of fern fronds.

ECOSYSTEMS

Public interest has recently turned to the ways in which changing conditions in the environment can disturb the organisms interacting with it. Federal and private funds are now being allocated to control the wastes that are contaminating our air, water and soil, but money alone will not solve the problem of man's indifference to his ecosystem. When the SCIS Life Science Program began in 1965, Chester A. Lawson, director of the program, chose the ecosystems concept to serve as a framework for the program because of its basic biological importance. In addition, he felt that an understanding of the organism-environment relationship would lead children to a greater concern about the ecosystem of which they are a part. This spring, coinciding with the new public awareness, the culminating unit of the life science program,*Ecosystems,* has been published in trial edition.

The children's initial activity of building composite aquarium-terrarium systems leads them to review the ideas introduced in the five earlier units. The organisms living in the containers with a land area and a "pond" include peas, grass, Anacharis, Daphnia, crickets, snails and guppies. These repre-sent plants, plant eaters and animal eaters that flourish under varying environmental conditions. Based on the children's obser-vations of the natural changes occurring in their containers, the ecosystem is intro-duced as the system made up of a com-munity of organisms interacting with its environment.

The observation of water droplets on the inside of the aquarium-terrarium sys-tems leads the children to a series of experi-ments in which they seek to clarify the role of water in an ecosystem. The children discover that all organisms, soil, and water itself, release moisture to the environment. From experience with Freon (a substance which boils and evaporates at a low tem-perature) and with vials of ice water, the children develop the water cycle model to explain their observations; water evaporates where it is warmest and condenses where it is coolest. From further discovery activities, the children can infer how the water cycle operates outdoors.

The children investigate another facet of the environment on which organisms are dependent: the oxygen-carbon dioxide cycle. Children of this age generally have established a theory of the relationship of

SOURCE. Reprinted, by permission, from the *SCIS Newsletter,* Spring 1970, published by the Science Curriculum Improvement Study, University of California at Berkeley, with slight abridgment.

organisms and these gases: plants take in carbon dioxide and give off oxygen, animals take in oxygen and give off carbon dioxide. The principle tool for their investigations is the indicator Bromothymol Blue (BTB), which the children have used in earlier SCIS units. A BTB solution turns yellow when it interacts with carbon dioxide and other acids. From their experiments, children find that their theory applies to plants and animals in the light. In the dark, however, BTB solutions, in which the children placed plants, turn yellow. The children conclude that their theory was not complete: plants in the dark release carbon dioxide to the environment. The results of this experiment not only have biological significance, but also reinforce an important process concept: the children must accept a conclusion based on evidence, even though that conclusion might contradict what they formerly considered to be "fact."

The last series of investigations revolves around pollution, which refers to any harmful deviation in an environmental factor from its natural condition in the ecosystem. In some cases the children will observe that an organism is directly affected by a pollutant—as when fish behave erratically when the children subject them to large quantities of carbon dioxide. When the children investigate the effects of excess thermal energy on Daphnia and algae, they are asked to consider the entire food chain in a river into which hot water wastes are pumped. Thus, thermal energy may be considered a pollutant to fish and fish-eating animals living nearby, as well as to the Daphnia and algae. An experiment with the movement of fertilizer through soil demonstrates the potential pollution of an area far removed from the original source of a pollutant.

In the final activity of the unit, the children subject containers of land plants and aquatic organisms to the smoke produced by smoldering string. The devastation of the environment and the resulting death of animals and plants is a realistic example of what can happen when the delicate interrelationships in an ecosystem are disturbed.

By considering the exchange of matter and energy between organisms and their environments, the *Ecosystems* unit draws on the entire SCIS program, both physical and life science. Teaching of *Ecosystems* has begun in trial center schools in Berkeley, Los Angeles, and Oklahoma. A revised final edition of the unit, based on feedback from this trial, will be published next year. Individual copies of the teacher's guide and student manual may be purchased from the SCIS offices.

Edith H. E. Churchill

ENVIRONMENTAL STUDIES IN CITY SCHOOLS

Telling people about environmental problems does not seem to change people's behavior. Yet it is people's behavior and, even, their priorities, which must change before anything can be accomplished. We are faced with a question which challenges the entire structure of education and applies equally to suburban and urban situations. How can we educate a generation of children to work for goals more socially responsible than those presently held by most people?

The components of effective change which we see as necessary are briefly as follows:

1. Teachers need to change their classroom behavior and need to have different attitudes about the way classrooms are run, and about how they as teachers relate to children. When this happens, we are convinced that children will grow up with different attitudes.
2. The attitudes we hope teachers will foster in children are

(a) that they have an understanding and respect for the environment
(b) that they value human life
(c) that they believe in their own power to change things and to control what happens

With experience, we have changed our thinking about the best approach to science teaching. The earlier units were developed to illustrate a concept. For example, *Small Things* was conceived to illustrate the universality of the cell as a biological building block . . . . This study fits easily into existing classrooms and differs from the classical biology instruction only in that each child has his own microscope and the teacher tries to get the child to describe what he has seen, instead of telling him what he is supposed to see and having him struggle to convince himself that he has actually seen it.

In contrast to *Small Things*, a more recent unit, *Pond Water*, is a good example of how our thinking has changed. Instead

SOURCE.   Reprinted, by permission, from *Nature Study,* Winter 1969-1970, published by the American Nature Study Society, with slight abridgment.

of starting with a concept we hoped to make clear to the students, we have started with actual material: a trip to a pond, bringing water back to the classroom, and in-depth study of the material—drawing the animals, writing about them, watching changing populations develop, and then relating these ideas to what happens outdoors. This gives children the opportunity to begin to generate their own concepts based on their experience.

The role of the teacher has changed also in the more recent units. The guides now give much less in the way of formal directions and detail, and each teacher is free to develop the exact direction of the study with his own class. Thus the teacher can develop each unit as he goes along, following the children's interest and adapting the material to his situation. We have found that a teacher who is deeply engaged in the work himself generates a much livelier learning situation.

Approaching the natural world through examples seems to be more child-appropriate and produces better results in terms of involvement and active learning. *Crayfish, Earthworms, Budding Twigs, Starting from Seeds* ... in each case the study starts by isolating a small piece of the environment, looking closely at it, and then fitting it back into the total scene. The indoor work then helps to solve outdoor problems, and the relation to the larger scene makes the study exciting . . . .

So much for choice of materials. But how does this relate to teacher preparation? . . . We are convinced that teacher preparation which hopes to change teachers' behavior and beliefs must begin by involving the teachers completely in the materials. Once they have responded to the materials and have had a *highly personal experience* with them, most teachers have no real problem in transferring their own experience to what the same material will do for children.

Beyond an opportunity to become involved with the actual curriculum materials, teachers need a chance to discuss and question the philosophy which suggests substituting this active approach, via material, for the work-book-memorize-and-regurgitate cycle they have experienced themselves in school or have learned from their teacher-training institutions. They need to begin to think about the hard questions. Is there a body of knowledge which every child must acquire and is this the same for all children? Do children really learn to read adequately by the graded reader-workbook system, or do they perhaps learn to read in spite of it? How and why do we grade students? Do our practices promote the kind of learning we want? Do marks help children learn or only teach them the "game of school"?

Last, but by no means least in teacher preparation, is the response of children to these materials . . . .

Teaching environmental studies in a way that will change people's attitudes and behavior requires *much* more than telling. It requires real involvement with living organisms. It requires respect for life, in-depth experience with a life process, and the growth of a sense of personal responsibility and personal effectiveness. We feel that we begin to reach these results when we offer teachers and children the opportunity to start with the specific example be it a twig, a seed, a paramecium, or a frog's egg and learn enough about it to be able to relate it to the whole complex world of out-of-doors . . . .

SECTION 5

THE SECONDARY SCHOOL CURRICULUM

In this section you will be introduced to suggested topics to be included in your school program, ways of modifying traditional courses to enhance their ecological value, and examples of major curricula with ecological content. In addition you will be introduced to some ways of encouraging critical thinking through ecological studies.

The first article provides a list of topics which would be important for any environmental education curriculum. Each topic is followed by several related subtopics, but these are not comprehensive. Although several areas are expanded, each teacher will have to organize and develop the topics into a logical arrangement within a syllabus before they make complete sense.

In the second article there is a group of suggestions for modifying traditional courses to include more ecology content. There is no intention here to monopolize traditional content in these subject areas, only to extend our efforts to create a strong environmental conscience in each student. In fact the addition of ecological content to most courses may even enhance the achievement of the usual goals of the teacher.

The third article describes most of the major curriculum projects which have a reasonable degree of ecology in them. Those interested may contact these projects directly for more details.

In the fourth article an effort is made to suggest how environmental topics can be used to cultivate habits of critical thinking. In an era when intellectual skills are being stressed as never before, this article may be welcomed by those determined to emphasize such process skills.

Cornelius J. Troost

Steve Gottlieb

ENVIRONMENTAL EDUCATION TOPICS FOR THE SECONDARY SCHOOL

The following sketch of topics to be covered in various courses, traditional and interdisciplinary, should prove helpful. We have only developed one broad topic, namely population (#8), one subtopic, food and nutrition, and have briefly developed an aspect of air pollution. The expanded development is both an elaboration of subtopics, a series of questions, and a Concept, Questions, Suggestions format. This is a suggestive treatment, not meant to be a prescription for a curriculum framework. The suggestions for topics, concepts, and activities, are, we think, very useful starting points.

1. Ecology. Here the concepts of ecosystems, communities, populations, energy flow, biogeochemical cycles, and homeostasis, etc., need to be emphasized.

2. Geography. Some discussion of the nature and distribution of soils, water, and minerals. Human geography—

the relationship of culture to physical features of the earth. Biogeography.

3. Man and Energy. The concept of energy and its relationship to human needs. The history of man can be surveyed in terms of energy usage. The hunting, agricultural, and industrial stages of man can be stressed. What energy sources exist today? Which are threatening to our ecosystems and our health? Which industries demand the greatest amounts of the energy from fossil fuels?

4. Pollution. Effects of pollution on air, water, land, and health. The nature of various gaseous, liquid, and solid wastes. Introduction to the toxicology of wastes and pesticides. How are pollutants formed and circulated? Exploitation of wildlife, fisheries, and forests. The effect of technological growth on remaining fossil-fuel reserves.

5. Technology and Pollution. Man's use of machines. The computer and

SOURCE.   By permission of the authors.

automation. The rise of mass transportation and communication. The internal combustion engine—its consequences and alternatives. Potential energy sources for tomorrow.

6. Political Problems. Effects of political policies on population growth rates. Relationship of huge industries to political power structures. Factors in the ABM, SST, and nuclear testing decisions. What effect does the U.S. Congress have on the total pollution situation?

7. Ethical Values. The contributions of our Judaeo-Christian heritage. Values of technologists. The nature of ethics and the need for a new set of ethical standards. The relationship of class or race membership to the problem of ethics. Abortion. Family planning. Individual responsibility.

8. Population.
   A. Growth of World Population
   History and explanation of human population growth; world situation today, by continents and selected countries; population projections and forecasts for the U.S., world, and selected countries.
   B. Population Analysis
   Basic demographic concepts, data, and measurements; composition and structure of human populations (urban/rural and geographic distribution; sex and age pyramids; race, nationality, language, religion, and educational, economic and marital status); fertility; mortality; migration; demographic transition; DC (developed country) and UDC demographic behavior.
   C. Control of Populations
   Carrying capacity; limiting factors; control of plant populations (competition for water, light, nutrients, space; role of herbivores); population control in animals (predator-prey interactions; dominance-hierarchy; territoriality; etc.); population

density and social pathology; man's role redistribution and size of plant and animal populations.
   D. Birth Control
   Human reproductive anatomy and physiology; regulation of numbers in preindustrial human societies (restrictive practices: infanticide, abortion, sexual taboos, treatment of aged and ill, migration, contraception, marriage restrictions; expansive practices: larger resources, defense, etc.; war, disease, famine; eugenic practices); methods of birth control (contraceptive techniques, abortion, sterilization); cultural, religious, and governmental attitudes on birth control and population control; family planning and population control.
   E. Food and Nutrition
   Human food requirements (essential food elements and their sources); malnutritional diseases; hunger (in the U.S.; in the world); geography of food production and consumption; food from the sea; possibilities for increasing world food production.
   F. Population Problems
   Natural and social theories on population growth; determining optima and carrying capacities; problems in UDC's (food; economic development; social stresses); population-related problems in DC's (environmental deterioration; resource adequacy; distribution; socio-economic considerations); policies of the U.S. and other countries; solutions?

QUESTIONS

1. GROWTH OF WORLD POPULATION
What is a "population"? Can you picture 3.5 billion of anything? 200 million? 200 million Americans, no less? How

many persons have ever lived on earth? When did they live? How do you answer such a question? Why bother to ask it? How is world population distributed? How was it distributed in the past? How will continental distribution patterns change in the future? How many aborigines were living in Australia before the White Peril descended? How many Eskimos over how large an area? Likewise, how many American Indians? How many people can the earth support with a hunting-and-gathering economy? primitive agriculture? How healthy, wealthy, well-fed, clothed, housed, educated, etc., are most of the peoples of the world? What percent are as well fed as the average American? How many people are reasonably adequately fed? What is a doubling time? What has happened to doubling times for the world population, or to the time required to add increments of one billion? Is there a difference between absolute and relative growth? How quickly has the U.S. added increments of 100 million? If Adam and Eve lived 6000 years ago, and had doubled their numbers every seventy years, how many descendants of the primal duo would be living today? How long would it take one bacterium, doubling every one half hour, to fill the earth, and what happens in the last hour? How fast is the world population increasing?

2. POPULATION ANALYSIS

What's a ratio? Rate? Proportion? How do we know how many people there are in the U.S.? OK, then, how does the U.S. Census Bureau know? What are "vital statistics?" To whom are they vital? How is the census conducted? Why? Why does it ask how many toilets you have in your home? Is this an invasion of privacy (lock the door)? Who uses census data and for what purposes?

How can we characterize a population or describe its composition? What is meant by the age structure of a popula-

tion? Why is it important? Can you tell an ODC from an UDC by its age structure? Can you read a sex and age pyramid? What is a "baby boom?" Are you a baby boom? What are various measures of fertility (CBR, GRR, NRR, fertility rates, child/woman ratio); What accounts for variations in the birth rate in the U.S.? Re birth rates, what transpired during the depression? after World War II? thru the fifties? 1970? What variables affect fertility? What is a crude death rate? How crude is it? Are people living longer than they used to? Has the maximum life span been increased? Does fertility or mortality have a greater effect on the age structure of a population? How does population tend to distribute geographically, past, present, and future? Urban/rurally? Do you want to bother with life tables or survivorship curves? How many people have died in auto accidents since the conception of the first iron horse? How about other causes of mortality? Are wars effective population control measures? Does man have any predators? Why are death rates more amenable than birth rates to induced lowering? Why can we just ignore the boys as far as population growth is concerned? What is migration? What are the immigration policies of the U.S.? Australia? Others? Can you think of any large relatively recent migrations? Have you and/or your family migrated? Why? How important is in-migration to our lovely state? What is the state of our state demographically speaking? Would you sign a letter "Demophobially yours?" What sort of transition is the demographic transition? Under what conditions of natality and mortality (and migration) will population continue to grow? What would you say to somebody who says the U.S. birth rate is the lowest ever so let's not fret?

What happened after World War II, re the death rate in UDC's? Who did it?

EDUCATIONAL IMPLICATIONS

3. CONTROL OF POPULATIONS

What is a carrying capacity? How is it determined and with what accuracy? How does the concept apply to natural populations? How do you identify limiting factors? What are some factors limiting or affecting the size and distribution of natural plant populations? What do we mean by "natural?" What roles do herbivores play (especially insects and browsing or grazing mammals)? If all species have the ability to produce a lot more offspring than they customarily do, what happens to the excess? Why don't you see sick or dead or dying animals in nature? What controls the size of animal populations? What is the significance of a population being density independent? Can any population be density independent? What is extinction? How are insect populations kept under control in natural communities? Are insect pests inherently pesty or are they born (created) that way? What is the role of complexity, diversity in ecosystems as related to stability? What is meant by stability, diversity? How is it measured? What happens when prairie dog towns are poisoned? To deer populations when all their predators are destroyed? In social animals, what are various means of population control (baboons, certain birds, lions, etc.)? What do Calhoun's experiments on population density and social pathology show? What is the role of *Homo sapiens,* Superpredator, the Wise Guy, concerning the size and distribution of plant and animal populations?

4. BIRTH CONTROL

What regulates the numbers of hunting-and-gathering tribes? How long have humans been using which birth control methods? What is the most common form of birth control today? Is birth control necessary? Why? Are there any really effective methods of birth control? Is sterilization of the male or female easier? Why do women have abortions? Does family planning constitute population control? Is the U.S. a perfect contraceptive population? How successful has India's family planning program been? What are the advantages and disadvantages of each contraceptive technique available to women in this country? What are your attitudes towards birth control? What are the attitudes of your parents? Friends? Society? Government? How do you know? What is the origin of religious opposition to contraception? What are the politics of other countries? Do Catholic countries in Europe have higher birth rates than non-Catholic nations?

Mankind is entering the *Age of Food.* The quantity and quality of food available to a rapidly growing human population will be of paramount concern in the coming decades.

Concepts, Questions, and Teaching Suggestions

Several dozen elements and compounds found in foods are necessary for life and health in human beings. The essential nutrients fall into five general categories: carbohydrates, fats, proteins, vitamins, and minerals.

- Discuss human nutritional requirements, with special emphasis on calories and on the quantity and quality of protein (eight essential amino acids).

- Distribute to students *A Guide to Good Eating* (1968, 3rd Edition, National Dairy Council, Chicago 60606), which illustrates how nutritional needs can be met by choosing some foods from each of four food groups daily.

- To illustrate the differences in traditional diets of various peoples around the world, ask for volunteers to investigate and report to the class on the diets of other cultures. Include people from all continents, hunting-and-gathering societies like the Eskimos and Australian aborigines, and a comparison of

European and American diets of today and of the past. Nutritional requirements can be satisfied by many combinations of foods.

- Introduce the concept of cultural food preferences. What are the implications of food preferences concerning attempts to alleviate hunger and malnutrition through new crops, food aid, or new products (fish protein concentrate, Incaparina, etc.)? Ask individual students which foods they don't consider food. People must be taught how to prepare unfamiliar foods. Give some examples of people resisting changes in their diets.

Air pollution is a critical environmental problem of global importance, affecting the health and economic well-being of millions of persons.

Concepts, Questions, and Teaching Suggestions

Meteorological conditions govern the flow, dispersion, and dilution of atmospheric pollutants.

- Discuss the normal composition of the ambient air. What is the basis for determining if the air is "polluted" (define pollution)?
- Examine several meteorological factors which help to determine the severity of air pollution, including temperature inversions, wind, sunlight, fog and air temperature. What causes inversions, where do they occur and how often, and how do they restrict the vertical dilution of pollutants? Wind speed and direction affect horizontal movement and dilution of substances in the air.
- Show slides and films depicting inversions and air flow in the Los Angeles and San Francisco regions.
- Cite evidence of the global travel of air pollutants, including DDT, lead, and radionuclides. What goes up must come down?

The air-contaminating activities of civilization fall into three general categories: (1) attrition, (2) vaporization, and (3) combustion.

- Combustion is most basic to the air pollution problem, especially combustion of fossil fuels. At what sites do burning processes occur, and how do these sites differ in their combustion products? In how many places does combustion occur in the home?
- Use the automobile to illustrate all three processes (gas tank and carburetor evaporation; tires and brake linings—attrition).

Five major sources are responsible for the five major air pollutants.

- Discuss the relative quantitative contributions of the four stationary sources (industry, power plants, refuse disposal, and space heating) and moving sources (transportation) of carbon monoxide, sulfur oxides, nitrogen oxides, hydrocarbons, and particulate matter.
- Discuss the chemical properties of the various airborne contaminants, indicating which are colorless and odorless. Demonstrate the reaction of nitric oxide (NO) to give reddish-brown, acrid-smelling nitrogen dioxide (NO being colorless and odorless) by releasing a *small* quantity of NO from a bottle in a well-ventilated room. Relate the amount of NO in the bottle to the quantity which issues from the exhaust pipe of an auto per mile driven, with and without controls.
- Discuss other pollutants, most of them locally important, including odors, beryllium, arsenic, aerosols, and heavy metals. Lead and asbestos deserve a more extensive treatment. Ask the students what substances they breathe in their homes besides good old-fashioned air, e.g., hair sprays, deodorant sprays, insecticides, cooking odors, etc.
- What natural sources of air contaminants exist, and what is their significance (volcanoes, forest fires, products of bacterial decomposition, salt spray, etc.)? Why are the Great Smoky Mountains smoky? Are there desired forms of air contamination (incense, cigarettes, cigars, pipes, logs burning in the fireplace)? Desired by whom?

The nature of the air pollution problem in different areas varies with the sources, meteorology, and topography of each locality or region.

- The original smog refers to London smoke plus fog. Rural or small-town, local air pollution (give examples) caused by a specific industry affects many people not living in large urban areas. Distinguish between reducing and oxidizing atmospheres, the former being more prevalent in cities with many sources of sulfur oxides.

New, undesirable substances are produced in the ambient air by the interaction of the radiant energy of the sun with chemicals in the air. This process, which produces Los Angeles-type *photochemical smog,* becomes of serious concern when four conditions are satisfied: (1) inversion and stagnant air prevent dilution, (2) resplendent sunshine abounds, (3) photoreceptors are lurking to receive resplendent sunshine, and (4) many sources pour many pollutants, notably hydrocarbons and other organic compounds, into the air to react with the nascent oxygen released by the photoreceptor (usually NO_2 produced from NO, most of the latter courtesy of the internal combustion engine, gratis).

- Discuss the properties of the new substances, especially ozone, other oxidants, PAN, and aldehydes.
- Demonstrate the photochemical process (or the concept of the atmosphere as a huge but finite and very complex reaction chamber in which many reactants are present in extremely low concentrations) by irradiating for 30 minutes a flask containing ordinary air with a bactericidal lamp* to produce ozone, adding hydrocarbons in the form of lemon oil by squeezing a lemon peel, and then watch a bluish haze form. This is the haze which reduces visibility in

*This is an ultraviolet lamp. One brand is called Pen-Ray and is available from Ultraviolet Products, 5114 Walnut Grove Ave., San Gabriel, Calif. 91778.

certain forest regions. Students should not breathe the aerosols in the flash directly. Ozone is harmful to lung tissues.

Air pollution adversely affects the health of human beings. The health effects are determined from four kinds of evidence: (1) acute air pollution episodes, (2) epidemiological studies, (3) animal research, and (4) industrial hygiene standards.

- Discuss the difficulties involved in unequivocally assessing the health effects of air pollution, and in particular the shortcomings of each of the above four methods (generalizing from animals to man; too many variables, especially smoking; industrial hygiene standards meant for healthy persons; etc.).
- Nevertheless, what is known about the health effects? What substances were identified as the culprits in the several air pollution disasters? (Now is an appropriate time to introduce the important concept of synergisms, in which the whole is greater than the sum of the parts.)
- Another important consideration is the basic fact of human biology that people are different, e.g., in their sensitivity to various pollutants. Explain the meaning and significance of a *dose-response curve.* Who suffers most from air pollution (elderly, young, hypersensitive, and persons suffering from chronic respiratory and cardiac disease)? Point out that cigarettes at least involve a voluntary abuse of the body. To what extent can man adapt to the air pollution challenge to his health (in the context of W.H.O.'s definition of health as a complete state of physical, mental, and social well-being, and not merely the absence of infirmity or disease)?
- Treat separately the effects at various concentrations of CO, SO_2, NO_x and O_3, presenting the basic anatomy and physiology of the respiratory system as background material. The meaning of ppm can be illustrated as 1 cc in 1 cubic meter. Compare health effects findings with official air quality standards and

with actual levels in our air in Los Angeles. How serious is the air pollution problem in the Los Angeles region? Serious enough to impair athletic performance, to prevent children from exercising in school, for several thousand persons per year to be advised to leave Los Angeles by their doctors, to prevent the growing of certain crops in the area?

Air pollution also affects materials, plants, animals, visibility, and probably the weather.

- Which pollutants affect which plants, and what is the general mechanism? What is the significance for agriculture and horticulture?

- When, where, and to whom is the reduction of visibility due to air pollution a problem?

- Which pollutants do the most damage to materials, including paint, clothing, rubber products, corrosion of metals, etc.?

- Explain the *greenhouse effect.* CO_2, ozone, and water vapor have the ability to absorb and reradiate infrared radiation, and the CO_2 content of the atmosphere is increasing. On the other hand, atmospheric dust is also increasing, which could have a heating or cooling effect. Do scientists understand the long-range meteorological consequences of man's air-contaminating activities?

- What are the economic costs of air pollution? What effects does this figure not take into account? Compare who pays the costs to who creates the most pollution.

Steve Gottlieb

Cornelius J. Troost

ECOLOGY WITHIN THE HIGH SCHOOL CURRICULUM

Within the curriculum of most high schools, there are many opportunities for teachers of different subjects to provide environmental education for their students. The suggestions that follow are by no means exhaustive, but may stimulate or help secondary school teachers to create instructional units or courses of study that embrace environmental topics.

ART—Opportunities in art are tremendous. Displays can be created which depict any of a variety of pollution problems. Paintings may represent world-wide famine, population density, and other problems. Collages on pollution may be impressive.

BIOLOGY—The biology teacher has the opportunity to provide a program of ecology. Students receiving ecology instruction ought to be exposed to pollution problems. Field trips to pollution sites are in order. Possible projects for students might be noise pollution and its effects on human hearing, effects of various pesticides on local animals, effects of ozone on plant life, and other topics treated in this book.

The biology of populations can be followed by discussion of birth control methods. Use fruit flies to demonstrate rapid population growth.

CHEMISTRY—Encourage critical thinking about environmental issues by discussing the long range effects of fuel combustion on the oxygen level of the atmosphere. Calculate the amount (in pounds) of oxygen required to burn one gallon of gasoline and compare this result to the oxygen consumed by one person in 24 hours. Test the biodegradability of various waste materials, such as paper, wood, aluminum, glass, plastics, steel, leather, etc. When discussing nuclear reactions, include problems associated with peaceful uses of nuclear energy. Emphasis might be placed upon the problems associated with disposal of radioactive wastes into the oceans.

ENGLISH—If letter writing is treated, have the students write to various politicians, their state and federal congressmen, and senators about pollution problems. When teaching Henrik Ibsen's "Enemy of

SOURCE. By permission of the authors.

the People," relate it to water pollution in the U.S., indicating how business and government have behaved in these crises. Encourage critical analyses of TV and magazine advertising of large scale polluters such as the oil and auto industries. Develop a love of nature through the poetry of Frost, Tennyson, Whitman, Thomas, and others. Read and discuss Paul Ehrlich's *The Population Bomb,* Robert Theobald's *Dialogue on Technology,* and Wesley Marx's *The Frail Ocean.*

GOVERNMENT—Students ought to know which federal agency or department has jurisdiction over each aspect of pollution:

All types—Environmental Protection Agency

Water pollution—Department of Interior

Solid wastes—HEW (Bureau of Solid Waste Management)

Land management—Department of Interior, FAA, Army Corps of Engineers, TVA

DDT—HEW, Interior, Department of Agriculture

Radiation Atomic Energy Commission, Federal Radiation Council

Air pollution—HEW, National Air Pollution Control Administration, Council on Environmental Quality

HEALTH—Every type of pollution has some effect upon health. Among the topics to be discussed are pollution of recreational areas, litter, sewage, radiation, etc. The great problem of population density and its effect on human beings (psychological and social) ought to be discussed. A study of the effects of mercury and lead on human health would be worthwhile.

SOCIAL STUDIES—The study of the industrialization of America can be analyzed in relation to population growth. The dangers of population explosion can be discussed, particularly by projecting the current trends into the next few decades. Recalling the warning of Thomas Malthus, can food production in the U.S. keep pace with the population growth? If famines occur in other countries, what implications do these have for Americans?

When discussing a particular country's population size, also provide related data on population growth rate, standard of living, family size norms, demographic history, and population composition.

Cornelius J. Troost

CURRICULUM PROJECTS WITH ECOLOGY CONTENT

In this article we will survey some of the science and social science curricula which have some degree of concern with ecology and the problem of pollution and over-population. The description of the work of the AAAS Commission on Science Education, while not in the curriculum category, is included here because it offers assistance to those planning various kinds of environmental studies program.

INTERMEDIATE SCIENCE CURRICULUM STUDY

The Intermediate Science Curriculum Study (ISCS) of Florida State University is a junior high school science curriculum project. They have produced a series of instructional materials which allow each pupil to proceed at his own rate. The units are commercially produced by Silver Burdett Publishing Co.

One unit is called *Environmental Crisis*. In this unit pupils are given a chance to investigate such phenomena as biochemical oxygen demand in yeast solutions and raw sewage, as well as the effects of deter-gents on elodea and radish seedlings. They also investigate pesticides, thermal pollution, temperature inversions, and smog, auto emissions, and other topics.

One of the features of the ISCS units is that they encourage students to make their own decisions as they solve problems. Problems are posed, such as the locating of a new chemical industry in a small town. This plant would employ 500-600 people and contribute about one million dollars to the local economy. Unfortunately, however, the plant would pollute the nearby river, and would contribute only $100,000 in tax revenues to help eliminate this pollution. Pupils are asked to vote on this issue. What evidence would you use in making the decision? What values are involved in your decision?

Among the special "excursions" at the back of the manual is one called "Depolluting Your Car" and one called "Anti-Litterbugging." In the former, the pupil investigates the use of afterburners to reduce emission pollutants. In the latter an organized campaign to reduce litter is discussed using scientific methodology and

SOURCE.   By permission of the author.

ideas like poster contests, unscheduled litter counts in classrooms, jingle and poetry contests, etc.

ERC—LIFE SCIENCE

The Educational Research Council of America (ERC) has developed a Life Science Course for seventh grade. It is a process program centered upon man and his relationship to the environment. The instructional materials were commercially distributed by Houghton-Mifflin Company in 1971. Here is an outline of the topics offered.

Topic I.   Variation
  Investigation
    1. Heartbeat
    2. Physical variations
    3. Variations in response to chemical stimuli
    4. Variations in behavior
    5. Variations in animals
    6. Variations in plants
Topic II.   Characteristics of Living Things
  Investigation
    7. Functions common to living things
    8. Experiments on life functions
    9. Cells—the units of life
    10. The heredity of the house fly
Topic III.   The Role of Living Things
  Investigation
    11. Producer-consumer relationships
    12. Abiotic-environmental factors
    13. The microscopic world
Topic IV.   Man's Effect on the Environment
  Investigation
    14. Man's effect on fresh water
    15. Man's effect on air

BIOLOGICAL SCIENCES CURRICULUM STUDIES

The Biological Sciences Curriculum Study (BSCS) at the University of Colorado is well known throughout the nation. They have produced three basic biology programs, the blue, yellow, and green versions. The Green Version—High School Biology, is produced by Rand McNally and Co. It is easily the most comprehensive ecology course available in America, despite the efforts of other text authors to elaborate on ecology. The Green Version, however, does not have a treatment of pollution problems to match its coverage of basic ecological facts, concepts, and processes.

ENGINEERING CONCEPTS CURRICULUM PROJECT

The Engineering Concepts Curriculum Project is located at Brooklyn Polytechnic Institute. The general purpose of the project is to improve the technological literacy of the average citizen. The approach is a problem-solving one, aimed at analysis of the technological and scientific roots of social, political, economic, health, and educational problems.

The crux of the ECCP program is a text called *The Man-Made World*, written by a group with diverse expertise. It emphasizes the importance of such concepts as (1) mathematical models, (2) sensing and measurement, (3) computers, (4) optimization with constraints, and (5) stability, instability, and control.

ECCP, with its stress on systems analysis and the use of analogies, offers an approach to pollution problems which is almost unknown to anyone but expert scientists and engineers. The need for rigorous problem-solving and decision-making approach should be obvious.

The project headquarters of ECCP is in Appendix D. By writing to this address, you can receive the ECCP Newsletter.

POPULATION CURRICULUM STUDY

The Population Curriculum Study of the University of Delaware has developed a conceptual scheme (K-12), expanded conceptual scheme, annotated lists for books, films, and periodicals, and other related materials.

This is a well-conceived, thoroughly executed study. The curricular outline is multidisciplinary. Anyone contemplating the multidisciplinary approach has much to learn from these materials.

EARTH SCIENCE
CURRICULUM PROJECT

Students in urban environments seldom study their own immediate surroundings. Usually in formal study of the environments of man, the examples are drawn from places beyond the experience of urban children, and thus beyond their care or concern.

The Environmental Studies program, a pilot effort from ESCP, focuses on activities and problems that involve students specifically with their own experiences and with information gathered by them from their immediate environment.

The materials will be designed for use in junior high school although they may be adapted to other levels.

Because the students create the goals, failure is impossible. The teacher's role is to encourage and assist students efforts in such a way that they will gain confidence in themselves and their future.

The Environmental Studies Program* is not a program about an environment. It is a program in an environment. That environment is the one in which the student finds himself. The student is the active force in observing it. He describes and defines problems as he observed them, and they may range from the motion of the clouds to the way the environment is being affected by man. Since these are his personal problems, the inquiries serve to

*This description is taken directly from the ESP brochure. Permission was granted by Robert Samples, Project Director.

enrich the student in the affective area as well as to strengthen his cognitive awareness.

The student feels and knows his own strengths, and he knows something about his environment. By becoming more knowledgeable about the situation closest to him, he not only understands it better but is better able to relate his surroundings to other parts of this country and the world.

Each set of materials will represent a starting point for investigation and inquiry. Once the materials are introduced, the student decides on his own course of action. He observes, analyzes, and eventually draws his own conclusions about the problem as he sees it. It is expected that these materials will open up many pathways, all leading into the student's environment. Divergence in the tasks should be expected and encouraged.

The Environmental Studies materials are designed in several packets, each independent of the other. Each packet contains a variety of beginnings for students studying their immediate environment.

The teacher's guide for the material, currently being tested, has a three-column format. One describes the materials used and student assignments; another contains a brief account of observations made during trial-teaching periods; and the third contains specific content qualities of the investigations carried out by students during the testing phase. Just as environments vary, so too do evaluative techniques in the various schools in our country. Teachers establish the evaluation criteria for themselves, but many suggestions for evaluation are included. Since the students set the course of action and establish the criteria for inquiry, it is necessary that they have a role in establishing evaluation techniques and criteria as well. The main evaluation relevant to the exercises is that which the teacher imposes upon himself as he looks at the students to see if, in fact, he has accomplished his prime objective . . . that his students have gained more confidence in themselves and in their abilities to interact with their own environment and will be better able to appreciate environments of others. Reactions to this program will be appreciated. Write to Environmental Studies c/o ESCP, P. O. Box 1559, Boulder, Colorado 80302.

Sample investigations from the ES project are included in Section 9, Part 3.

AMERICAN ASSOCIATION FOR THE ADVANCEMENT OF SCIENCE

The Commission on Science Education of the American Association for the Advancement of Science (AAAS) has established the Committee on Science and Society to strengthen environmental education at the secondary school level. The Committee's first major activity has been the production of *Science for Society: A Bibliography.** This bibliography consists of 2,000 recently published books and periodicals classified into the following topics:

1. General references
2. Population problems
    a. Cities
    b. Crowding and aggression
3. Agriculture, food, nutrition
4. Pollution of air, water, and food; pesticides
5. Medicine, health, drugs
6. Natural resources, conservation
7. Race
8. Biological engineering, eugenics
9. The nature of science and scientists
10. Science, technology, and society
11. War and peace

The Committee sees its future activities as threefold. First, it plans to issue

*Published through support of The National Science Foundation, The Battelle Memorial Institute, and The National Association of Secondary School Principals. Copies may be secured by sending your request to: Commission on Science Education, AAAS, 1515 Massachusetts Avenue, N.W., Washington, D.C. 20005.

environmental education Information Center Reports. These reports will consist of (1) information about projects for the production of instructional materials related to science-and-society topics, and (2) information about unique or innovative special projects for the study of science and society topics in local school systems and metropolitan areas. The Information Center staff will also attempt to find answers to specific problems posed by teachers and students, including references to sources of information, suggestions of names of lecturers, and so on.

Second, it plans to establish Environmental Education Councils. These councils would fulfill the growing need in high schools to use the diverse resources of the community in the study of environmental problems. They are planned to broaden the "school" beyond the classroom and the laboratory into the community. They would seek to coordinate the resources of community agencies (including industry) in the study of environmental problems. Councils would consist of autonomous organizations of school and community representatives. They would be associated with appropriate schools and develop coordinated study and action programs for students and teachers. They would serve as a clearinghouse for local problems that related to significant national and international activities.

Third, it plans to develop a series of study guides on science-and-society problems for high school science and social science teachers. Study guides will be produced by teams of prominent scientists, social scientists, science educators, and classroom teachers. Each study guide of the series will be produced at a place where significant research is going on, and heavy emphasis will be placed on scientific validity. Each guide will deal with both the scientific and social aspects of the problem and will include suggested projects for students and teachers as well as a bibliography including sources of films and other instructional materials. Work on the first study guide (atmospheric pollution) has started. Plans are now being made for the production of other guides on science-and-society topics.

The Information Center, Environmental Councils, and teachers' study guides projects would dovetail with each other. For example, Environmental Councils and study guides would use data from the Information Center. The Center would look to the Councils for identification of environmental problems on which data were needed. The study guides would contain ideas on the fullest possible use of community resources as suggested by Councils.

It can be readily seen that the concept for this triumvirate approach to environ- mental education is breathtaking in scope. If these plans properly materialize, a giant step will have been taken toward improved environmental education in our nation's high schools.

PATTERNS OF LIFE

Patterns of Life is a modern biology program, published by the American Book Company, which heavily emphasizes ecology, both in the text and in the laboratory and field investigations. The discussion of pollution problems is the most comprehensive yet available at the high school level. The teachers guide to this program contains ecotactics for biology classes. The ecology and pollution photography is excellent.

Cornelius J. Troost

CRITICAL THINKING IN ECOLOGY

If you are concerned about promoting critical thinking, environmental problems lend themselves well to such purposes. Issues such as leaded vs. unleaded gasoline, biodegradable vs. high phosphate detergents, internal combustion vs. steam or electricity, etc., are beautifully suited for critical analysis.

In Part 2 we have a fundamental issue under discussion. Paul R. Ehrlich, in "The Population Explosion: Facts and Fiction," takes a position contrary to that of Jean Mayer in "Toward a Non-Malthusian Population Policy." Basically, the two positions are as follows:

Ehrlich (E): No human effort will meet the demands upon our food and resources made by the vast population explosion underway. Ultimately, famines will result—almost inevitably, unless stringent population controls are enforced.

Mayer (M): Despite the tremendous rate of growth of the world's population, methods of food production can be developed which will result in feeding satisfactorily enough people to certainly avoid famines.

SOURCE. By permission of the author.

The two positions conflict in that E partly depends upon food shortage as a mechanism for ecological balance—the Malthusian position. M, however, contends that food shortage need not be a factor, and likely will not be a factor in limiting population growth. E is arguing that we must avoid famines by stringent population control measures now, while M is stating that use of starvation as a logical consequence of the fact of population expansion is by no means necessary. M means that premises other than starvation need to be used in the argument for population control.

Although E and M have a point of serious disagreement, careful reading will show that they do agree on population curtailment as a desirable end. Thus, it is only on the food shortage premise that they disagree. M is saying that since we can technologically conquer food shortages, food shortage is not a sound reason to use in defense of population control.

Further reading will show that E agrees with M about the matter of the rich being a much greater drain on food and resources than the poor. Thirdly, E and M agree that great increases in population will bring untold misery. Finally, the two authors do agree that immediate population curtailment policies need to be implemented.

Returning to their disagreement, it seems that Ehrlich is unaware of the current rate of per capita food production discussed by Mayer. Mayer's argument is enhanced considerably by the use of such relevant data, while Ehrlich seems not to substantially support his contention that land agriculture cannot do the job. M's expert nutritionists believe that up to 95 billion people could be supported if all available acreage was fully utilized. One may assume that these experts are in touch with technological developments which make them more optimistic than is E. A major factor M mentions is the role of fertilizers in food production, a point not mentioned by E.

M's argument, while impressive in a prima facie sense, is weakened by the many assumptions involved, such as (1) his assumption that the various nations will permit massive agricultural practices, (2) that even if they did, there would be enough farmers, equipment, etc., to do the job, (3) that extensive use of herbicides and pesticides would not have disastrous ecological side effects, and (4) that technological developments will continue to produce "miracles" (my quotes).

M sees space travel research as a mechanism for possibly producing new ways of producing food. While this is indeed possible, the current de-emphasis on space research, if continued indefinitely, would greatly reduce such a likelihood.

The preceding brief analysis demonstrates a comparison and contrasting of two vitally important positions. A few assumptions were identified, and a few limitations of each position were discussed. When you analyze such issues with your students, you may wish to separate out the value statements, concept statements, and facts.

If you examine the Ehrlich and Mayer articles again, you can identify at least the following as value statements:

1. It is not good to have a population growth rate which is above zero.

2. It is wrong to have a large family.

3. The famine "solution" is wrong but inevitable.

4. Those opposing birth control are morally wrong.

5. Birth control devices and techniques are good.

The above apply to E, while the following apply to M:

1. It is better to worry about food production than the population growth rate.

2. We ought to utilize far more land acreage for agriculture.

3. One ought to work for increased food production regardless of how fast population increases.

4. We ought to reduce the population of rich countries faster than poor ones.

5. It is better to decrease population as disposable income rises.

Value statements, as you can see, contain value terms like "good," "bad," "ought," "should," "wrong," or "right." These terms, however, may be used empirically. For instance, when we said birth control devices and techniques, including abortion, are good, we may have meant by "good" better at reducing population than no deliberate efforts. "Good," then, really did not have a moral meaning in this case. If "good" has an empirical meaning, then we can test the statement to determine its truth or falsity. Value statements probably cannot be determined to be true or false. As you can see, the writer had to infer the list of value statements, for often we do not state them explicitly and they may be called implicit assumptions, also.

Empirical statements in Ehrlich and Mayer are many. Some examples in E are:

1. The growth of the population is so rapid that the multitude of humans is doubling every 35 years.

2. For Columbia, with none of these things, with 30-40% of its population illiterate . . .

3. . . . the population of the Earth is growing, I repeat, by some 70 million people per year.

Some examples from M are:

1. The United States government rents 20 million acres from our farmers...

2. FAO's figures indicate that 3.4 billion acres are at present under cultivation.

3. Pilot plants are now in operation.

Empirical statements are testable and therefore can be judged true or false. However, some of the statements by E and M were not readily testable; for instance:

1. Today's technology could not maintain three and one-half billion people without "living on capital" as we are now doing. (E)

2. The problems entailed in passing from the theoretically possible to the economically feasible are formidable, but their solution is likely to be hastened from an unexpected reason. (M)

The above examples are not subject to solution by simple observation. These are general, theoretical statements whose truth could be determined, but at the time they are stated they are controversial (unproven).

Finally, you and your students ought to look for *conceptual statements*. Some examples are:

1. But even a miracle would be inadequate to meet the needs of the population growth. (E)

2. Excellent human beings will not be produced without abundance of cultural as well as material resources. (M)

Conceptual statements contain terms like love, democracy, man, God, etc. The rule is to analyze the statement by defining the concept first. Thus, in #1 above:

If by miracle you mean such and such, then it is indeed possible to . . .

Conceptual statements often have the truth-falsity element, but not always. Since conceptual statements are often difficult to fully justify or prove true, the use of authorities to support a position is a sound device. Professor Robert Ennis of the University of Illinois lists the following criteria for accepting a statement by an authority:

1. He has a good reputation.

2. The statement is in his field.

3. He was disinterested.

4. His reputation could be affected by his statement, and he was aware of this fact when he made his statement.

5. He studied the matter covered by the statement.

6. He followed accepted procedures in coming to decide that he was entitled to make his statement (although there are legitimate exceptions to this requirement).

7. He was in full possession of his faculties.

8. He is not in disagreement with those who meet the above criteria.

One readily can see that E and M meet nearly all of the above criteria. Both probably fail #3, and E is obviously less schooled in nutritional science (#5). Both E and M, consistent with innumerable authorities, agree on the absolute importance of population reduction.

The following are guidelines which may prove useful to you:

1. Compare the two basic positions.

2. Identify their underlying assumptions.

3. Judge which assumptions are most untenable.

4. Separate out factual claims, interpretations of facts, concepts, and value statements.

5. Determine whose position agrees most with the facts.

6. Look for statistical errors or errors in interpretation of statistical data.

7. Carefully weigh the reliability of the scientist who makes a prediction and evaluate the chances of the prediction coming true.

8. Look for logical fallacies like insufficient data, non-sequitors, false analogy, etc.

9. Look out for studies in ecology which are financially supported by those who are polluters.

A final comment on value discussions is important here. Your students may say things like:

1. Birth control is good.

2. It is better to reduce the rich to the level of everyone else.

3. We ought to fight against technology.

4. Litterbugs ought to stop littering.

These are value statements. The following are some of the critical criteria that are relevant:

1. Noncircularity
2. Level of sophistication
3. Proper function and type
4. Truth
5. Applicability

When you ask your students to justify the above value statements (and many others), you first ought to be sure they are not *circular arguments,* i.e., "Birth control is good because it controls birth." This helps us not one bit.

Second, the context in which the explanation is given is important. If the student says, "It is better to reduce the rich to the level of everyone else because egalitarianism is ultimately a superior form of politico-social system," and his listeners were fifth graders, the explanation would be at the wrong *level of sophistication.*

Thirdly, the criterion of *proper function* and *type* are applied. Proper function refers to when an explanation *justifies* or *accounts for* what is discussed. For example:

Teacher: Why ought we fight against technology?

Student: Because some of the young people in our technological society hate technology.

The term "technology" is a poor one, open to different interpretations unless defined. The explanation given, assuming nonambiguity, does not seem to meet the request for *justification.* The explanation simply *accounts for* the phenomenon. Justification explanations are those which prove a statement true, while accounting-for explanations are those which simply account for a statement which is already accepted as fact. For instance:

Why is Ralph Nader popular with consumers?

Because he is trusted by them.

Here you have an explanation which *accounts for* an obviously true statement.

What causes rain?

At a low enough temperature, water vapor condenses, forming droplets, which, when heavy enough, fall to the ground.

The above is a justification explanation.*

Let us look at the criterion of *applicability.* Here we might ask the student to think of examples of what is being called "bad," for instance:

Teacher: Why is it good that Southern California Edison did not build that power plant?

Student: Because it is a glowing example of an insatiable superorganism. (An insatiable superorganism is bad).

The term "superorganism" prevents us from thinking of concrete examples of this,

---

*Types of explanations are analytic, empirical, causal, reason-for-acting, and value. This is too large a topic for this paper. A detailed discussion can be found in *Logic in Teaching,* by R.H. Ennis, pages 300-337.

or nonexamples, instances where the situation was completely different. The explanation thus fails to meet the applicability criterion.

Here is a value statement: Litterbugs ought to stop littering. A teacher may ask: Why should litterbugs stop littering? A student reply could be: Because littering produces a disagreeable, ugly landscape. (Anything which produces a disagreeable, ugly landscape is bad.)

The explanation here is a value explanation, not a causal type. There are exceptions to it, like essential traffic signs. It may indeed meet the other criteria, but there are exceptions to its truth. As a teacher, you need not fear the incomplete truth of many value explanations. You may still have statements which are mostly true, and which meet the evaluative criteria. It is very important that in ecology disputes, you encourage the development of sound value explanations.

REFERENCES

1.   Ennis, Robert, *Logic in Teaching,* Englewood Cliffs, N.J.: Prentice-Hall, Inc., 1970.

2.   Salmon, Wesley, *Logic,* Englewood Cliffs, N.J.: Prentice-Hall, Inc., 1966.

SECTION 6

FIELD TRIPS

Field trips are essential to effective environmental education. There is no other way for students to systematically study actual pollution sites. In the first article field trip basic guidelines are listed. There is also a list of locations to visit on field trips.

In the second article, by Osborn and Spofford, specific field trip instructions are given for pond trips, along with suggestions for using the field trip as a vehicle for learning math, English, social studies, and reading.

Mr. Clifford Knapp, in the final article, provides three different field trip formats—teacher-oriented, modified, and student-oriented. Which of these a particular teacher uses will depend largely upon his purposes and his analysis of the needs of his students.

Cornelius J. Troost

FIELD TRIP GUIDELINES

Environmental education may be emasculated by lack of or absence of field work. It is one thing for students to make random observations of ecological disaster areas, but it is quite another thing to take them on field trips which are planned, systematic efforts to study specific ecological problems.

Since pollution problems exist nearly everywhere, few teachers in America will have difficulty locating interesting target sites for trips. Trips ought to include several teachers of specialized backgrounds, hopefully someone in either economics, history, social studies, art, etc., together with a natural science person (physics, chemistry, biology, or general science).

Before taking any field trip, the following basic rules need reviewing:

1. Plan the field trip carefully. Let the pupils help. For the more lengthy trips, parents should be invited to participate in the planning.

2. If the proposed route is a new one, go over it at least once prior to the field trip. Make preparations to take full advantage of the educational opportunities along the route. It saves time to know the route well. Plan the timing carefully. Make certain that the area to be visited will show everything you wish to teach. Make it a "doing" as well as a "seeing" trip.

3. Make certain of adequate and safe transportation whether you use school buses, parents' cars, or public carrier. If there are expenses not borne by the school, notify parents of the cost per pupil. Reliable older pupils can help materially in making collections. If water transportation is involved, make certain that sufficient life preservers are available for each occupant of the boat.

4. Insist on clothing and footwear suitable for the season and the type of trip. If a meal will be eaten, make certain that *everyone* has a lunch. Make provision for rest periods. Emphasize all safety rules and precautions. Pads and pencils are "must" items.

5. Before starting out, explain to the class the purpose of the field trip. Outline and discuss the important points. Test attitudes toward the resource to be studied.

6. Prepare a list of questions to distribute to the students. If the topic is off-shore oil, some questions might be:
    (1) What is the source of the oil?
    (2) Why does oil float?
    (3) What moves the oil along the coastline toward deposition on beaches?
    (4) How does oil kill waterfowl?
    (5) What do oil companies do to prevent leaks?
    (6) Why do leaks occur?

SOURCE.   By permission of the author.

(7) What can be done to prevent future oil-well spillage?

(8) How can high school students actively fight oil pollution in our oceans?

7. A few possible locations for field trips are:

(1) Polluted shorelines

(2) Large electric power plants

(3) Polluted lakes

(4) Rivers at the site of deposition of industrial effluents

(5) Water treatment plant

(6) Local air pollution control board office

(7) Nuclear reactor power station

(8) Any major industry which produces substantial pollutants.

8. During the trip, make full explanations of every point brought out. Make basic and important points stand out. If possible, have a conservation specialist—a forester, a soil conservationist, a county agent, a game warden, a ranger—accompany the class. Advise him fully of the objectives of the trip.

9. Utilize supplemental training aids. Maps of the area involved are most useful. If the class is studying erosion, a local soil map will be invaluable. Tree identification sheets will be of great help on a trip to the forest.

10. Before leaving the area, review the more important points. Ask questions and encourage the pupils to ask them.

11. After the trip, test the knowledge gained by the pupils. Let them discuss their experiences, write about them, and ask more questions. Specifically, compare their attitudes toward the resource with their attitudes prior to the field trip. Plan other ways and means for follow-through after the trip. Keep the pupils interested. Assign future work on the basis of the knowledge gained from the trip.

12. Invite constructive criticism from pupils. Study and improve your own performance.

13. For future reference and assistance to other teachers, keep a card record of each trip. List location of area, route, travel time, brief description of procedures on the ground, size of class, and any other information that will help in planning future trips.

Ron Osborn
Roger Spofford

INTERDISCIPLINARY INVOLVEMENT IN ENVIRONMENTAL FIELD TRIPS

Environmental studies increasingly have as their objective the creation of a concern for all environments. This leads to a commitment to preserve optimum environments and improve less desirable environments. Further, environmental studies develop situations and conditions where learning can flourish. By utilizing a nature center or other outdoor study area wherein an intense learning experience can be enjoyed by the students, opportunities for relationship to other parts of the curriculum can be developed. For this purpose we use the Fellows Hill Center.

Fellows Hill is a New York State reforestation area near Fabius. It has been set aside and managed by the New York State Conservation Department, in part, as a "wildlife refuge," for game birds, deer, and other animals. Seventh-grade classes of the Jamesville-DeWitt Middle School use the area as an outdoor laboratory to study the ecology of a pond environment, to observe animals in a natural setting, and, we hope, to awaken a sincere interest in the outdoor world. Though the full-day field trips are aimed primarily toward science, certain activities are arranged to include mathematics, reading, social studies, and English.

SCIENCE ACTIVITIES

The science activities include collection of some specimens that can be taken back to the classroom for study and on-site study of larger plants and animals that cannot be removed from the observation area. The students are divided into nine groups with the following assignments:

SOURCE. Reprinted, by permission, from *The Science Teacher,* April 1970, with slight abridgment.

EDUCATIONAL IMPLICATIONS

A—Study of microscopic organisms

B—Study of bottom-dwelling organisms

C—Study of larger plants

D—Study of larger animals

E—Collection of pond-water temperature data at various depths

F—Mapping the surface area and features of the pond

G—Measuring depth of pond along several different transects

H—Estimating heights of various plants and trees surrounding the pond

I— Estimating populations of various pond plants and animals

Below are field-trip instructions for several of the study activities undertaken by the youngsters in the Howland Island area of the Fellows Hill Center:

GROUP A: *Collection of microscopic organisms*

Materials:

Coffee cans and covers (labeled as follows:

"Surface-water Zone"

"Deep-water Zone"

Plankton net

Test tubes and plugs

Twine

At the pond, fill the cans about one-third full of pond water. Using the plankton net, collect samples of pond water, first at the surface, then in the deeper water. To use the plankton net, attach a test tube to the net by pushing it through the hole in the bottom (from the inside). Cast the net into the water and pull back and forth. If the net is pulled rapidly, it will stay near the top of the water. Then untie the test tube from the net and empty into the can labeled "Surface-water Zone." Collect three or four samples from near the surface. Then collect samples from the deep-water zone by allowing the net to sink to the bottom first, then pulling along slowly and evenly. Place three or four samples from the deep-water zone in the can labeled "Deep-water Zone." Leave

the cans in the shade until you are ready to leave.

GROUP B: *Collection of bottom-dwelling organisms*

Materials:

Three coffee cans (labeled as follows):

"Emergent-plant Zone"

"Submerged-plant Zone"

"Open-water Zone"

Three gallon jars (labeled as above)

Sieves (with wooden frame)

Unlabeled coffee can (for scooping up mud)

Twine

At the pond, fill each of the jars and cans about one-third full of clear pond water. With the cans, scoop up mud from the bottom from among the emergent plants (the ones coming up out of the pond above water level, near the shore). Dump this mud into the sieve; then shake the sieve in the water (at water level) until the mud is washed out. Remove dead sticks and leaves by hand. Pick out whatever organisms you find and put these into the larger jar labeled "Emergent-plant Zone." Repeat this procedure for the other two zones (progressively farther away from shore), placing the animals you find in the correctly labeled jar. Finally, scoop up a sample of mud from each zone and empty into the labeled coffee cans.

GROUP C: *Collection of plants*

Materials:

Three large plastic bags (labeled as follows with 3- x 5-inch cards dropped into each):

"Emergent Plants"

"Submerged Plants"

"Floating Plants"

"Twist-ems"—(wire ties for bags)

Hand trowels

Plant-grappling hooks

Twine

In each of the three plant zones, collect a sample of each kind of plant found. The "emergent plants" will be found closest to shore, the "submerged plants" out beyond the shore zone below water level, and the "floating plants" out in the open water. The plant-grapplers can be used to collect the plants in the last two zones. Whenever possible, try to get the whole plant. If the plant is too large, take the leaves and flowers only. Put the plants of each zone into the correctly labeled bag.

GROUP D: *Study of collection of certain animals*

Materials:

Four large pails (labeled as follows):
"Emergent-plant Zone"
"Submerged-plant Zone"

Ten small jars (labeled as follows):
"Emergent-and-floating-plant Zone"
"Submerged-plant Zone"

Dip nets

Two members of the group should record on paper the animals seen but not collected. This should include all animals that seem to be a part of the pond community, whether they live *in* the pond or not.

Use the dip net to collect some of the larger animals—for example, fish, crayfish, larger insect larvae, turtles, etc. First catch the animals in the shore zone near the edge of the pond. Insect larvae may be placed together in the same jar, with some sticks and leaves for shelter. Only a few fish should be placed in one jar. Be careful in handling animals; some may inflect painful bites. On return to the school, place the animals in a cool place, *not* in the open sun.

Choose one animal you find in or around the pond to observe and write a short essay describing, in detail, the behavior of the animal for the period of time you observed it. It would be easiest to choose some water insect you find. Draw or sketch one of the plants or animals you have seen on the Howland Island Game Preserve. If you do not have time, this can be done back in class. Make a map of one of the two ponds—show outline of

shoreline of pond, put in the location of the inlet and outlet streams, locate on the map shallow areas of pond and the probable location of deepest point. Mark your positions (locations), during both the morning and the afternoon session, on the map found in this field guide.

MATHEMATICS

The youngsters gather data for later use in class of the estimated numbers of certain plants and animals. They also measure the pond depths at various points as shown in the diagram and map the bottom of the pond.

ENGLISH

The English assignment includes making notes for use later in composing a short poem of the Japanese *haiku* type. These poems are usually about the world of nature and include the word for one of the seasons. Each haiku has three lines with five syllables in the first, seven in the second, and five in the third.

Another assignment for the English class is an imaginative composition, telling how one of the living things around the pond might perceive the world in which he lives.

SOCIAL STUDIES

In the social studies assignment, the students are asked to imagine themselves as a member of a pioneer family, as follows: The Blake family has just moved from Sturbridge, Massachusetts, to Fellows Hill, New York. The year is 1803.

The travel was mainly by horse and wagon, and the entire trip took three long weeks. Upon reaching their destination each member of the Blake family had a very different outlook or "umwelt" regarding their new home site.

Write a composition choosing *one* of the four possibilities:

EDUCATIONAL IMPLICATIONS

1. You are Sarah Blake, the mother of the family. How would you see Fellows Hill? What space patterns would you miss and what space patterns would you hope to create?

2. You are Noah Blake, the father. How would your "umwelt" affect your opinion of trees. What steps would you take to make this an acceptable homestead for your family?

3. You are Eliza Blake, an eleven-year-old daughter. You did not wish to leave Sturbridge, Massachusetts. You had many possessions you wished to bring with you and could not. Your mother told you that you could have one-eighth of the trunk. (Remember the trunk at Erie Canal Museum.) What did you bring with you and why?

4. You are Johnny Blake. You are the thirteen-year-old son. You were very anxious to leave Sturbridge, Massachusetts, since you felt it had been too crowded in the last few years. You were afraid that there would be no "open land" for you to start your own homestead. How would you see Fellows Hill and why? What area would you hope to make as your own homestead in the next few years? Do you think you would prefer to "stay on" with Pa? Why?

READING

One reading exercise is based on a magazine article on migrating birds, with questions covering both comprehension and vocabulary. Another includes a set of "Did You Know" queries about some of the unusual characteristics or name origins of plants and animals found near a pond in temperate zones. Following are a few of the queries. Students themselves might make up such a list for any environment to be studied.

—that the *liverwort,* a water plant, is simply a liver-shaped plant? "Wort" was the old English word for root or plant, and in ancient times people believed the liverwort would cure diseases of the liver.

—that the *plumatella* is also known as a "moss animal"? Can you guess why?

—that the life story of most water insects and the change which transforms them into winged creatures is called *metamorphosis,* an ancient Greek word that means "change of form"?

—that birds in open nests generally lay spotted eggs while dwellers in tree trunks, burrows, or buildings tend to produce white ones? Why?

Clifford E. Knapp

CONDUCTING A FIELD TRIP – ORGANIZATIONAL PATTERNS FOR INSTRUCTION

Teachers often express hesitancy about taking field trips. One reason may be that they tend to develop inflexible habits of thinking about the teaching process involved in these excursions. Mention of a field trip usually conjures up thoughts of 30 students clustered together being lectured to and going from place to place either in a bus or on foot. Teachers can picture the looks of boredom on the students' faces, the "horsing around" that inevitably occurs, and the difficulty encountered in managing and directing the group in a new and often unfamiliar setting.

The purpose of this article is to suggest some alternative patterns for organizing instruction during a field trip and to examine some of the advantages and disadvantages of each alternative. The term "field trip" is used broadly to include instruction conducted outside the school building under the auspices of the teacher. Field trips may be to indoor settings such as a factory, store, or fire station, and to outdoor settings such as a city street.

Three broad categories of instructional organization will be discussed. In each, the role of the teacher and student changes accordingly. The categories are designated as (1) teacher-oriented, (2) modified, and (3) student-oriented. The responsibility for direction is progressively released from the teacher to the student as the organization changes. Teachers may wish to experiment with variations of the three categories in order to achieve different objectives.

To illustrate the three organizational patterns, three approaches to handling a

SOURCE. Reprinted, by permission, from *Science and Children,* Vol. 8, No. 1, September 1970.

given problem can be examined. The problem may be stated: *Go outside and examine three different kinds of flowers carefully enough so that you can communicate some important characteristics of each to the rest of the class.*

TEACHER-ORIENTED

In the process of solving this problem, a variety of student objectives may be set up. One such objective may be: *To identify three different kinds of tree flowers, to record specific characteristics of each, and to tell three ways in which each plant relates to man.*

In this pattern, the teacher selects the three flowers to be observed and the specific characteristics of each and provides the information about the plants' relationships to man. The above objective appears to be best implemented by this organizational pattern for instruction and is typically identified with the traditional field trip.

MODIFIED

Another objective in the solution of the stated problem may be: *To observe and record specific characteristics of flowering plants (color, location, leaves, petals, sepals, size, and other characteristics) using a clue chart technique.*

In this pattern termed "modified" the teacher provides a data sheet (clue chart) upon which specific characteristics of flowering plants are recorded. The student is responsible for making the appropriate observations and recording the data through words or sketches. The teacher may organize small groups kept within established boundaries. He assists when students encounter particular learning barriers. The teacher's role becomes one of a facilitator. Classroom preparation is especially important in this pattern because the teacher should anticipate some of the learning problems and discuss them before they arise.

STUDENT-ORIENTED

A third objective, requiring a third organizational pattern, may be directed more toward the social ends involved in reaching decisions and carrying out a group task: *To make a group decision about how to select the flowers to be studied and to gather data to communicate to the class.* The data to be collected about the flowers become the vehicle for accomplishing the objective of cooperative human interaction in a group.

The responsibility for accomplishing the objective lies primarily with the student. The directive role of the teacher must necessarily be deemphasized in order for the student to progress toward the end of socialization skills.

SUMMARY

The three organizational patterns for instruction are evaluated in the accompanying chart. One important consideration in selecting the instructional pattern is the objective of the lesson. The assumption is that certain patterns of instruction can better accomplish certain objectives and that changes in organization should be made accordingly.

The students will respond to each instructional pattern in different ways. Certain students will be able to function more effectively in one particular pattern. It is to be expected that the student-oriented pattern will require more student responsibility and that the teacher should gradually work toward this goal. It is conceivable that all three patterns would be used with the class during one lesson if the teacher were to select the students best suited for each approach.

The field trip should be viewed as an opportunity to apply a variety of organi-

FIELD TRIPS

Comparison of Three Organizational Patterns of Instruction

	Teacher Role	Student Role	Possible Advantages	Possible Disadvantages
TEACHER-ORIENTED	(a) Selects the objectives, and concepts. (b) Directs student observation and data gathering personally. (c) Assigns responsibilities for completion of tasks according to knowledge of individual differences.	(a) Follows directions and records data suggested by teacher. (b) Analyzes data and draws conclusions.	(a) More detailed observations possible because teacher selects ideal specimens for study. (b) Much of trial and error of learning eliminated. More efficient from standpoint of time and amount of material covered. (c) More concepts revealed in sequential fashion.	(a) Range of observation limited largely to teacher's ability to select items. (b) Little opportunity for students to select relevant objects and information and reject irrelevancies. (c) Large pupil-teacher ratio. (d) Spontaneous and unplanned learning less likely to occur.
MODIFIED	(a) Selects important characteristics for observation by constructing a data sheet. (b) Divides the class into small groups and establishes physical boundaries for investigation. (c) Anticipates learning barriers and attempts to prepare the students in classroom for solving problem and meeting objective.	(a) Selects and observes appropriate specimens for observation. (b) Records data. (c) Demonstrates maturity and self-discipline in meeting designated task.	(a) Students may cooperatively solve problem and benefit from varied abilities of group members. (b) Students may work at their own pace. (c) The teacher can provide more individual attention in identifying and solving student problems.	(a) Students may not select the best specimen examples for examination. (b) Students may encounter problems which the teacher is unable to assist in solving. (c) Some students may not function well in self-directed learning situations.
STUDENT-ORIENTED	(a) Establishes boundaries of time, location, and student behavior. (b) Motivates students and presents preparation and follow-up activities.	(a) Clarifies task, establishes a plan for problem solution and meets human interaction situations that may hinder group effectiveness. (b) Plans to communicate findings to class.	(a) Provides for maximum application of creative thinking and group involvement situations. (b) Students can pursue aspects of the problem which interest them.	(a) Effectiveness is dependent upon the ability and motivation of the group participants. (b) Difficult to execute if all students are expected to adopt this pattern rapidly.

zational patterns for instruction selected on the basis of the desired student objectives and appropriate student and teacher readiness. The resourceful teacher will create ways of modifying these broad categories to better meet particular instructional objectives.

SECTION 7

URBAN ACTIVITIES

In the United States as in most other developed countries, the urban form of life has taken over from the rural. By 1975, 75% of this country's people will live in cities. It is expected that by the year 2000 (when most of us will still be alive), 85% of them will live in cities.

The activities and focus of the environmental movement have reflected this change in living style. Instead of the 4-H club farm boy emphasizing the dangers of the improperly plowed hillside, we now have the urban activist protesting the presence of polluted air.

Schneider's article explains how urban students can use the city as a laboratory for the investigation of environmental problems. The second article is an account of a project that provided inner city children with an opportunity to explore the wonders of nature in the country. The third article, from *Time,* tells about a group of architects who have developed manipulative materials for urban students to help them understand their man-made environment more fully. The fourth article provides samples material from *A Place to Live,* a work-text on the urban environment published by the National Audubon Society.

Gerald Schneider

CONSERVATION TEACHING IN THE CITY

GENERAL TEACHING PRINCIPLES

How do you teach the urban child? *You start where he is* and lead him forward step by step when he is ready for advancement. Forget "preaching" and accept him as he is. He may believe his way is right, too, until shown.

FOCUS ON PROBLEMS

A practical approach to teaching older youths, ages 12 and up, is to focus their attention on problems of city planning, waste disposal, water supply, pollution, ghettos and parks—things that affect their immediate, everyday lives. Save the forest management, soil erosion, hydrological cycle, and species identification business for later unless they ask about these things. Don't risk losing them before you begin; there are few chances available to reach them and no time should be wasted.

For younger children, ages 3 to 11, contact with live plants and animals can be most meaningful. Consider starting with the handling of bunnies and chicks since city children are often afraid of unfamiliar wild animals (and dogs). A simple introduction to the ecology of a vacant lot, patch of ground, sidewalk crack or a city tree is good. Stress the *fun, excitement,* and *adventure* of exploration outside the classroom. Leave the more structured science learnings and memorization for later years—especially with the very young.

And don't feel guilty when the kids are having fun outdoors and aren't being formally instructed. They are probably learning a great deal on their own and, best of all, discovering that the outdoors has *value.*

Contact with the out-of-doors outside the city is important for all age groups. Urban children need outdoor experiences in the country to contrast to their city lives and values. *Love* of out of doors (or

SOURCE. Reprinted, by permission, from *The Conservationist,* August/September 1969, published by the New York State Conservation Department, with slight abridgment.

Illustration repainted in black and white by Wayne Trimm from his original color illustration for *The Conservationist.*

any other thing) probably results from actual favorable experiences and can't be taught from a textbook or by osmosis.

City kids should have many opportunities to camp, hike, cycle, picnic, swim, and go boating in the out-of-doors. Teach safety, first aid and outdoor manners when necessary because it's necessary. But don't ruin the fun of "first experiences" by burdensome emphasis too soon on outdoor skill development. Learning to tie knots it not often important the first time out. Vigorous adherence to adult-made time schedules is also unwise. As little as possible should be done to restrict unbridled enjoyment of the out of doors.

Reinforcement of love of the out-of-doors and the development of conservation values comes from *involvement in conservation action projects*. Even as simple a beautification project as planting flower seeds and tending them in a flower box hung from a window may leave a child with a favorable lasting impression that no conservation lecture (such as is this article) can duplicate. While such projects may seem superficial and lack continuity, projects like these are the stuff on which children build their character.

Too many times, adults concerned with the problems of the world and the big issues of the day forget that little things mean a lot to a child.

THE KEY TO SUCCESS

Incidentally, the key to success in conservation projects involving youths is to let the youths do as much as possible of the planning, operation and follow-up for the projects. It is a common mistake to give young people unimaginative adult-planned work projects and use them as a cheap source of labor for dull manual work that adults won't do on their own or hire help to do. Adults working with children should *ask* pointed questions, answer questions asked of them, give technical assistance, "open doors" to resources and join

in like everyone else on work assignments. But the kids should be the bosses—they should make the major decisions and assume the major responsibilities on projects.

When working with children new to conservation, consideration should be given to avoiding use of the term "conservation" altogether. It is a confusing term that conjures up different images to different people, leads to arguments about its definition and can be omitted when teaching youths. Direct discussion of environmental problems such as pollution and poor planning without an overall label for the concerns included is possible. After some contact with study or action on environmental problems, youths can be exposed to the complexities of the term "conservation."

PLANTS AND ANIMALS

As H. Wayne Trimm's illustration on the next page shows, many kinds of plants and animals are found in cities—even in as big a place as New York City. These forms of life are valuable teaching resources that can be used to advantage.

What kinds of plants and animals are found around a school, a neighborhood or on a single street? How do plants and animals survive in the concrete jungles of cities? Can we learn anything of importance from these organisms that we can relate to our own survival? Do plants and animals contribute to the interest and charm of a community?

Discovering the answers to questions like these may generate greater awareness of the concept of *environment*. It may open up a whole new world for a child to explore between his school and the television set.

Going a step further, children can take local plant and animal censuses. A simple survey for the very young might be a count of the number of London plane trees near a school or the number of sparrows and pigeons in a five-block area.

Older youth can use fairly sophisticated sampling techniques to estimate the population of particular species in the total community. Such activities extend awareness of the environment and form the foundation on which many conservation *attitudes* can be developed.

Reinforcement of certain conservation values results from projects to improve the living conditions for plants and animals in the city. Shrubs can be planted near homes, around schools and in parks (with permission). Shrubs are not only attractive in themselves, but they provide cover for wildlife and, when properly selected, summer and winter animal food. Trees give shade, seclusion, beauty and wind protection and become nesting sites for birds and other animals—so, plant them. Flowers, such as sunflowers, produce seeds that children and birds enjoy—therefore, plant them. The affection of a young child for a shrub, tree, or flower *he* helped to plant is a wondrous sight.

The three basic needs of animals are food, water and shelter close enough for animals to get at. Food and shelter can be provided by the plantings mentioned above. Animal feeding stations can also be provided and kept stocked with suitable foods. Bluebird houses and other birdhouses can be built out of large tin cans, tar paper, nail kegs and wood scraps and put in place. Homemade bird baths become water sources in summer (keep them filled with warm water only in winter or let them stay dry; birds can obtain water from snow and ice). To a child especially, action speaks louder than words.

THE BOOKS ARE GLIB

While plantings and animal habitat improvement projects aren't difficult, books are often too glib in describing such projects. The author doesn't want to join them in their guilt. No two situations are exactly alike and, while you can use the above as a general guide for improve-ment projects, it's best to have professional advice on projects from experts on the scene—park department officials, landscape architects, conservation agency employees, science teachers, professional gardeners and others.

COMMUNITY PLANNING BY YOUTHS

Cities are rich sources of ideas for community planning. Environmental resources are stretched to the limit by the impact of thousands of people concentrated in urban living areas. Problems of noise, air pollution, water supply, slums, crowding, traffic, sanitation, space, and appearance plague cities. Solutions are difficult. However community planning on a youth-sized level can foster conservation values.

How about having kids make a conservation survey of their neighborhoods? Research should precede action to insure effectiveness. Are there garbage-strewn vacant lots that can be used and are needed as vest-pocket parks, tot-lots, and such? Is there a need for shade trees by schools, in parking lots and along streets? What can young people do, if anything, to make improvements?

Children can make a photographic survey that they can share with others and aid them in analyzing neighborhood needs. Using even the cheapest cameras, youths can go around their neighborhoods and take pictures of the things *they think* make the neighborhoods attractive and the things that they think are ugly. An exhibit of contrasts can be created from the collection of pictures taken. The exhibit can be discussed and followed up by environmental improvement projects when possible and appropriate. What a valuable conservation teaching resource the collection of pictures make!

Surveys and community planning analysis are "in" subjects that should appeal to urban youths.

Air pollution surveys need not be complicated. Children can study air pollution by use of their senses. Does the air have a funny odor in some parts of neighborhoods (a smell index of pollution might be developed)? Does dirt rub off bricks and stones of buildings at a touch (a touch index)? How often do windows at home need cleaning, or where can smoke be seen (visual indices)? Simple, but these measurements are fine for the young.

A DIRTY AIR INDEX

Children can smear sheets of acetate or bond paper with petroleum jelly and place the sheets in open areas such as on window sills. How dirty do the sheets get over a period of time (use magnifying glasses and microscopes to help look at them)? Compare the dirty sheets to clean sheets and a dirty air index may be created.

One-gallon, wide-mouthed jars filled with a pint of water and left open and exposed become traps for air pollutants. How dirty does the water get in a day, week or month? Boil off the water and the remaining solid materials can be examined. And another air pollution index can be made.

What can you find in the filter of an air conditioner? Do children or should children worry about breathing in the things they find trapped in filters? What are the local air pollution control regulations in the community, if any? Is enforcement of any laws good (make sure that this is researched before comment is made)? What can children do about air pollution? Discuss these questions with the youths of cities.

Where does the community's drinking water come from? Can the children take a hike to any of the water sources? Is there enough water for everyone and for every use? Has vegetation been affected by lack of water or too much water? Do local waterways smell, show visible amounts of garbage, seem choked with algae and debris, look muddy or unattractive to swim in?

Does the community treat its sewage? Is a visit to a sewage treatment plant possible? Is there primary, secondary, and tertiary treatment of sewage, if any? Can young people help improve things?

Noise! It may be killing us by degrees and affecting our hearing. How noisy is the neighborhood? Kids can find out for themselves. Their ears may not tell them because they've conditioned themselves to hearing only certain sounds important to them and screening out others. Are there reasons why selective hearing may be important to the psychological health of city dwellers?

Tape recorders won't discriminate among audible sounds. Noises heard in different parts of a neighborhood can be recorded on a tape recorder. Children can listen to the finished tapes. If they are surprised at the actual amount of noise there really is, why not discuss it? Can a noise index for the neighborhood be developed? (*Note:* Some noises on recording tapes are natural and allowance for static should be made.)

CURRENT EVENTS AND HISTORY

Today's newspapers are filled with articles having conservation implications. Examples include hunger at home and abroad in overpopulated countries, flood damage to homes built in flood plains, highways cutting across the last open spaces in a community, rising danger of respiratory diseases caused by air pollution, lack of recreation facilities in the inner-city and hot summers, houses sinking into filled swamplands, medical effects of crowding, the search for status and identity in a crowded world, controversies over the establishment of a redwoods park and more. All these current events should appeal to youths and are naturals for civics, social studies, sociology, geography, science and other courses.

Debates on the real issues behind conservation controversies—the kind that rarely get into conservation publications—can appeal to urban youths not otherwise sensitive to conservation concerns. With the frontier gone, rural land being swallowed up by urbanization, the value of rugged individualism undergoing scrutiny, an apparently rising welfare state, an increase in crime, violence and demonstrations in the streets and on college campuses, our entire socio-economic political life is being tested and questioned. We are forced to reevaluate basic issues affecting conservation:

With people so many and resources so endangered, should persons still have the right to be careless with property or do what they like with the land they own? Should people be allowed to build homes in flood plains and other unfavorable sites (ecologically unfavorable)? Should people be allowed to settle in places like Arizona where water problems are great and expect the rest of us to subsidize their water needs?

Should public money be given to private businesses to stimulate installation of air and water pollution control equipment in factories? Should restrictions be placed on visits to public parks and recreation areas? Should regional planning replace local autonomy on zoning regulations?

Also, consider the following: Does the concept of the greatest good for the greatest number, often associated with conservation, overlook minority interests? Does *The Conservation Pledge* so often used ("I give my pledge as an American to save and faithfully to defend from waste the natural resources of my country—its soil and minerals, its forests, waters and wildlife") need to be updated to take into account the *total* environment with such specifics as slum housing prevention, beautiful cities and others?

Questions, questions, questions! They all need to be asked and answered if we are to prepare for *tomorrow's* conservation problems. And, with freedom of discussion, urban youths can be turned on by these subjects.

History and resource use and conservation are closely linked. What role did beavers have in winning the West? Were resources the basis of the Industrial Revolution? How did the Homestead Act and land give-aways to railroads affect land-use policies in the United States? Why did such widespread poverty eventually come to Appalachia? These are but a few of the many conservation-linked history questions that can be explored.

Going further back in time, there may be interest in studying whether or not the downfall of the Roman and other empire was due to resource abuse. W. C. Lowdermilk's pamphlet, "Conquest of the Land Through 7,000 Years," available free from the U.S. Department of Agriculture, makes interesting reading on this matter.

CONCLUSION

This article only begins to investigate the opportunities for meaningful conservation teaching in the city. It is the result of successful conservation teaching in the city and much introspection and observation by the author who grew up in a slum area of Brooklyn. At least some of what the author has written is controversial and should cause some eyebrows to be raised. Certainly, the article should not be considered a final statement on the philosophy of teaching conservation to urban children.

Technique and approach to teaching in the city was emphasized for a Machiavellian reason: It works! The author did not want to suggest that traditional conservation teaching, study of the management of minerals, oils, forests, water and such, wasn't important to the urban child. But you don't communicate with anyone unless you *start where he is and build step by step* until he's ready for new ideas and concepts. Truth is what people want to believe, not necessarily fact.

Once a city child is aware of environment, has reflected on city environmental problems, has worked on interesting conservation projects, has had opportunities for fun and adventure in the out of doors, he may be ready for more traditional conservation teachings. Until such time, the city child must be met on his own ground.

Alice Dennis

CONSERVATIONISTS TURN ON FOR CHILDREN OF THE CONCRETE

The small black boy in the tree at the edge of the meadow looked around and called to a group of friends below, "Hey, man, it's beautiful up here!"

Two weeks previously this inner-city child was afraid to touch a tree and was even hostile toward one. Now he was graduating from a 2-week summer course in wading, climbing, stepping on stones, handling leaves, feeling grass, lying in the sun, and watching clouds drift across his vision. He had completed his degree in listening, smelling, touching, hearing, and noticing nature for the first time in his life. He rejoiced in harmony with his element, earth and her glory. And her reflection lighted his eyes.

The black lad was one of 105 youngsters who, in groups of 35 over a 2-week period, participated in the first ecology-oriented program of its kind for the ghetto child sponsored and administered by a conservation society. The small but enthusiastic Audubon Naturalist Society of the Central Atlantic States with headquarters in Washington, D.C., pioneered the program during the summer of 1969 as an offshoot of its already successful inner-city nature courses given by member volunteers to fourth and fifth graders in three D.C. public schools. Founded in 1897, the ANSociety is independent of the National Audubon Society.

The conservationists were able to offer a nearby wildlife sanctuary for the initial summer experiment. In 1968 the Society had received from the will of Mrs. Chester Wells her 40-acre estate, Woodend, in suburban Chevy Chase, Maryland, along with its 32-room Georgian mansion for use as headquarters. Built in 1928, the house was designed by John Russell Pope,

SOURCE.   Reprinted, by permission, from *National Parks and Conservation Magazine,* June 1970, which assumes no responsibility for its distribution other than through the magazine, with slight abridgment.

374

creator of the Jefferson Memorial and architect for the National Gallery of Art. Mrs. Wells, a nature lover, did not want her estate to be subdivided as a housing development; so she presented it to the Society, whose members she had admired during her lifetime. The property contains remnants of original farm planting, native woods, and grasses as well as decorative plantings, a pond, a small stream, and walking trails. Although surrounded by affluent suburbia, the estate is large enough that its wildlife remains abundant and varied.

The ANSociety's summertime program for the inner-city child has strengthened members' conviction that Americans are entering a new era in conservation education. Shortly after the assassination of Dr. Martin Luther King and the subsequent riots, the Society sought to create an experimental program in environmental education for children of the ghetto. Dennis W. Brezina and Mrs. Ann Morton, members of the Society's newly created Committee on Special Projects, began in 1968 to contact District of Columbia organizations to discuss such a plan. Contacted were the Urban Coalition, the Youth Program Unit of the D.C. Government, the United Planning Organization, the Washington Urban League, and the Public Welfare Foundation, as well as conservation education experts in the Departments of Interior and Agriculture and the Office of Education, and human resources experts in the Peace Corps, Teacher Corps, and area universities.

In August 1968 representatives of the Urban League, the Urban Coalition, and UPO met at Woodend with the ANSociety, where enthusiasm and a lively exchange of ideas predominated. By fall 13 conservation societies throughout the nation were contacted by letter to inquire what type program they offered deprived children. Few organizations had anything remotely comparable to the projected Society's program, but the replies strengthened the Society's

conviction that such a program was symptomatic of conservation's new role in bridging the gap between white and black citizens, between urban and nature-oriented environments. Mrs. Margaret Callihan, former teacher and school director, was asked to coordinate the program.

In May of 1969 with H Street still burned out and the hot Washington summer on the horizon, the Society announced completed plans for its Inner City Program in Environmental Education.

"This is a basic departure from traditional conservation education programs," wrote Mr. Brezina, volunteer chairman. "The approach and techniques are experimental; the classroom is the outdoors; nonverbal communications—feeling and sensing nature—will be emphasized; ecology, the relationship between man and nature, will be the backbone of the curriculum."

The Society received a $3,000 grant from the Hattie M. Strong Foundation to provide employment for six black group-leader college students from Federal City College and Howard University. These young men and women, who received training as well as a week's orientation at Woodend, had no natural science background but had worked with ghetto children in recreation programs. Gerry Schneider, the Society's first executive director, who arrived June 1, worked as coordinator with Mrs. Callihan. Part of the financial grant was also used to hire a bus to transport the children.

The first step in the spring was to locate a school that wanted to participate. Recent Congressional hearings as well as studies like the Riot Commission Report stressed that such a program was more likely to succeed if predicated on community participation. The Society opted to work directly with black community leaders. It was felt that a school in which the Society's classroom visitor program was already in action would open the door for enthusiasm for the summer session. Logan School near Union Station met all criteria.

Mrs. Callihan met with Mrs. Les Bowne, community coordinator at Logan, who stimulated community interest while Mrs. Callihan worked for ideas with the Neighborhood Planning Council and VISTA volunteers in the neighborhood. To learn more about the black community, ANSociety members attended Neighborhood Youth Corps seminars. Finally ideas from the school, community, and the Society were drafted into the Woodend Experiment.

Five objectives were listed: (1) to give a group of inner-city children of the fourth- and fifth-grade levels a 2-week-long summer learning experience at the wildlife sanctuary; (2) to develop a more effective conservation education source for Washington children; (3) to provide meaningful paid employment for six group-leader instructors; (4) to develop in the children a greater interest in and appreciation of the natural world; (5) to instill in them an enhanced sense of respect and responsibility toward their own environment.

Working with VISTA personnel in the inner city, Mrs. Callihan began her recruitment of the children. Sign-ups took place in alleyways, on doorsteps, on the radiators of cars, and in second-story tenements. The black community had approved the program, and the reception was good. For the three 2-week periods during July and August 1969, three groups of 25 to 35 children would spend 3 to 5 hours each day, 5 days a week, at Woodend. Individuals would bring their own lunches, but a beverage would be provided. The children would be divided into small groups of four to six for outdoor nature experiences, the heart of the study.

When the first bus filled with 33 children rolled up the long, winding approach to the parking lot behind the Wells mansion, the two were at last face-to-face: children of the concrete and Mother Nature. From the children's standpoint, they were unknowingly entering the ideal learning situation. The motto of the program was "Trust in the power of something other than the human voice."

"We wanted to teach them to trust and respond to nature," reported Mrs. Callihan. Many of the youngsters had never felt grass beneath their feet; most came from row houses whose back alleys were littered with trash; many had never had a carpet in their homes.

The pond terrified them. They were afraid to step on the grass. All their lives they had been shouted at not to do this or that. Suddenly here before them were rolling lawns of grass and wildflowers, meadows, a woodland where birds called, an intimate brook, and a smiling pond. In short, a miracle of invitation, and no one said, "Don't." No wonder they were wary.

Mrs. Callihan had great confidence that the introduction to nature would be felicitous. Since January, an experimental pilot group of fifth graders from Logan had spent one morning each week at Woodend under her direction as the Society and its volunteers moved toward a curriculum for the summer youngsters. The pilot students had also feared the pond at first but over the weeks had become acquainted with its wonders and finally reached the stage of hatching frog eggs in their palms as the gelatinous mass yielded squirming tadpoles. And best of all, they watched the seasons sweep over the countryside.

In the summer program the children of the concrete were to learn to frolic and rejoice in a natural setting. No plant or animal names were used in teaching sessions. Children were urged to use their senses to become acquainted with grass and bark, fur and feather exhibits. A raft was constructed. When bird nests were located, the youngsters were encouraged to try to build similar ones and to watch the progress of nestlings.

In addition to volunteering to help train the black group leaders, members also brought their own collections to share with the children, not as scientific exhibits but as examples of the wonders of the living environment—a rock collection to illustrate the beauty in stones, an extensive collection of bird nests, a pet raccoon, and pet skunks, who precipitated the only "serious" accident of the summer by biting Mrs. Callihan's finger.

One of the most important days of the 2-week "college" was the one spent back in the city in the child's home territory where with his group he remapped his own block; noting with a new perspective how his environment might be improved, even beautified.

At Woodend the learning procedure had been stimulated by games, scavenger hunts, mystery smell games, trail explorations. Dissecting microscopes were used to examine treasures from the wood. Mrs. Callihan reports that the children of the inner city also brought to nature their own form of definition, culled from the concrete childhood but nevertheless poetic. To a little girl, lying in a field of clover was like floating on popcorn, while a lad who had scooped up a handful of algae at the pond allowed that it smelled like collard greens.

After the summer was over, Logan School, as well as Gage and Kimball of the inner city, continued to participate in the classroom ecology project given by ANSociety volunteers for fourth- and fifth-graders. Here the child's own neighborhood is used as the laboratory with its own special ecosystem. The children are taken on one field trip to a nearby park or nature center.

The project consists of a 7- or 8-week course of 1-hour sessions in the autumn and spring with a different topic each week, including ecology, the green world, insects, pollination, birds, mammals. A slide show of common flora and fauna of the D.C. area is presented as a final summing-up of the course.

The hour begins with a 15-minute discussion of the day's subject, conducted as a question-and-answer period by a Society volunteer who has received a training course. Then the class breaks into five or six groups headed by a volunteer to take an outdoor walk. Each week the conservationists bring and leave three objects related to the topic, which the children may identify—two by sight and one, hidden in a mystery box which can be named only by touch. Books are also left to help identify the mystery.

Bridging the gap between a white middle-class conservation-oriented volunteer and a black inner-city child who often is hostile to nature requires a special adjustment by Society members, which comes partly from experience and partly from advice of earlier volunteers. For instance, sighting uncovered garbage cans in alleyways, new volunteers might be tempted to relate the prevalence of rats to the situation. But as Irene McManus, assistant editor of *American Forests* and a volunteer teacher, learned, it is "a good idea to stay off the subject of rats completely. It usually turns out that one child in the class has had a bad experience with rats—either they'd been bitten or some member of their family had, and it's just too traumatic for them."

In exploring a vacant lot, the teacher and her small group discovered tiny insects they could not identify until the team stumbled over a dead rat and realized they had viewed rat fleas leaving the corpse.

When a fire drill interrupted a class where flowers were being studied for pollination, the children were careful to carry the flowers outside to safety. The volunteers had thought that in identifying stamen and pistil the youngsters would tear the flowers apart, but to the conservationists' surprise, most of the flowers remained intact as some of the children announced their intention of taking them home.

In order to reach more inner-city children during the 1970 summer on its very limited budget, the ANSociety has shifted its emphasis to concentrate on leaders.

The summer budget will go exclusively into salaries to hire more black college students, who, after intensive training from the Society, will reach into the ghetto neighborhoods with a lively ecological program. Instead of transporting a mere 105 children to Woodend, the Society in the form of its black ambassadors hopes to reach hundreds of inner-city children in their home neighborhoods. Community nature centers will be headquarters of the movement.

"Our first summer's experience proved that Woodend is not the logical center for this type of program," Gerry Schneider reports. "The bus took $1,200 out of our budget; the drivers often became lost and didn't deliver the children until after noon; the chance of resentment building up in an inner-city child driving past the homes of affluent Chevy Chase is too great." The logistics of time and cost of transportation dictated that the Society shift its emphasis.

Bill Sessoms, a black sociology major at Federal City College, will be chief leader and Gerry's righthand man. Recruitment and training, as in 1969, was on a planned basis at the employment offices of Federal City and Howard University. Starting in March, the leaders received training at Morgan School Nature Center in Washington, a center underwritten by the Junior League. The Society also hopes to enlarge its volunteer courses in more city schools.

Working in the nation's capital directly with its black population, the ANSociety has great hopes for the children of the concrete. Moving quietly, scientifically, with careful preliminary planning and training, totally in harmony with the Negro leaders, with little or no fanfare, the ANSociety is sowing seeds of imagination, beauty, rapport, and responsibility for environment in the minds of ghetto youngsters. It is true that only 105 were reached last summer, but the successful small beginning was most provident.

What an opportunity for volunteer nature lovers across the country to share their lifetime of joyful observation with city children! What a bridge others might also build where the child of the ghetto may learn to walk in confidence toward a responsible acknowledgement of his environment and—more important—its resurrection. Thousands of bright lost children are waiting to be found and inspired. The conservationist is the extraordinary candidate who can, with no personal axe to grind and no affiliation but nature herself, offer to teach and to heal.

GEE: GROUP FOR ENVIRONMENTAL EDUCATION

Our Man-Made Environment: Book Seven is, quite simply, the best primer on architecture and urban planning yet published in the U.S. Designed to open the eyes of seventh graders to the world being built around them, the book has much to teach adults as well.

Aspiration. It was conceived in 1966 after some educators in the Philadelphia school system asked the local chapter of the American Institute of Architects to help explain architecture to kids. But the collaborators set even higher goals. "We wanted to make students aware of their environment," says Architect Alan Levy. "We wanted to give them confidence in their ability to make judgments about what they like and don't like. Finally, we hoped to give them a sense of aspiration beyond the limits of the environment they know."

The job took 3½ years and $60,000 in foundation grants. Last summer the educators and architects formed GEE! (the Group for Environmental Education) to work out, says GEE! Vice President William

 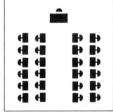

If a single room is used in a variety of ways, each use can cause a change in the environment. In a classroom, for example, different activities may require an entirely different arrangement of chairs and desks. At times the teacher may instruct the class from her desk or blackboard . . . other times she may lead a debate between one half of the class and the other, or she may want to oversee a number of smaller group discussions.

SOURCE. Reprinted, by permission, from *Time,* May 18, 1970, copyright Time, Inc., with slight abridgment.

Chapman, a complete teaching program and to distribute the book. All 20,000 copies have since been sold (at cost) to schools in Philadelphia—plus Houston, San Mateo, Columbus, Ohio, and six cities in New Jersey. Despite its grade school language, the book is used by sophomores studying architecture at the University of North Dakota.

See and Do. *Our Man-Made Environment* bristles with challenge. Many of its pages are lightweight cardboard punch-outs, which can be folded to make beams, roofs, and whole buildings. One of the first lessons asks students to punch out six geometric shapes and arrange them in a pleasing design within a rectangular frame. When the students turn over the shapes, they find that the pieces represent armchairs, a table, a TV set. The next step is to rearrange the shapes within a room, which entails thinking about how people best communicate.

The lessons soon get more complex. Students learn about weather topography and motion as determinants of design. They are required to see and draw the "rhythmic" elements of a streetscape like doors and windows. As if that were not demanding enough, the kids must also arrange identical punch-out "buildings" so that one—then two units stand out among the best. This done, they may never look blindly at a street again.

GEE! already has a series of similar workbooks in progress. "What we are trying to do is develop a program that gets students to recognize that the man-made environment is more than just dirty air and water pollution," explains Architect Richard Wurman. "In effect, we see the program as an invitation to a marvelous, continuous visual party." If GEE! succeeds, the day may come when kids will know why man-made America is ugly. Better still, they may know how to clean up the visual mess.

A PLACE TO LIVE

EDITOR'S NOTE: The following explanation is from a brochure issued by the National Audubon Society. It gives the overview, rationale, and organization of the study program on urban ecology.

A Place to Live is a 64 page work-text which covers basic ecological concepts, as found in any *urban* environment. While there are no discrete chapters, the book is primarily divided into the following sections: You, Where You Live, Other Living Things, Needs, Cities Change the Environment.

Over three-fourths of the nation's children live in cities. *A Place to Live* is a study program which provides material in ecology, relevant to these city and inner-city children. As future voters on solutions to problems in conservation, pollution and the quality of the environment, it is essential that they understand the interrelationships between living things, themselves included, and the total environment. *A Place to Live* stresses these interrelationships, as found in surroundings familiar and interesting to the city child.

In addition, the National Audubon Society, with the cooperation of naturalists and other educators, has produced this book in the belief that each child has a birthright to feel "at home" with nature, to marvel at the continuity of life, to delight in living things, and that an obligation exists to enable *every* child to enjoy, and preserve, that birthright through pertinent and satisfying study.

STUDY WORK-TEXT

A Place to Live is designed to be self-motivating and is written simply enough (third grade reading level) to be read independently by most fourth or fifth grade children. Woven into the text are "Try This!" activities which help to sustain the children's interest and to amplify the concepts introduced.

Generally, the "Try This!" suggestions fall into two categories; (1) those which involve children writing or drawing in their Work-texts; and (2) group activities or experiments around which class lessons can be built.

The book includes ten "Walks" related to the text (and not requiring transporta-

SOURCE.   Reprinted, by permission, from the Educational Services department of the National Audubon Society, with slight abridgment.

tion). This section is of prime importance, for it is from these first-hand discovery experiences that the greatest learnings will come. Ideally, the text of the book will provide the stimulation and the background for the children's own explorations of the living laboratories outside their school.

TEACHER'S MANUAL

In addition to the activities suggested in the children's book, many ideas for supplementary experiences are included in the Manual. Some of these projects aid in

reinforcing the ecological concepts presented in the children's text. Others indicate ways of correlating *A Place to Live*

with such curriculum areas as language arts, social studies, mathematics, and art.

The methods employed by teachers in using this work-text will vary according to each individual's preference, and to the level and needs of the class. One recommended procedure is to encourage the children to read the book individually, at their own pace, and to build group lessons around the "Try This!" activities, the supplementary ideas presented in the Teacher's Manual, and the Walks.

A sample chapter entitled, "Cities Change the Environment," with its accompanying environment walk, is presented from the student's work-text.

Cities Change the Environment

We said before that the city is your environment. All the buildings, cars, trucks and other people are part of it. The air, water, other animals, sunshine, and plants are also parts of it. These last parts were not made by people. They are part of the NATURAL ENVIRONMENT, because they come from nature. Cities change the natural environment. If lots of people walk on a street every day, there has to be a hard covering that won't wear out for a long time. That means there will be less soil for plants to grow in. And so there will not be as many plants. Our oxygen will have to blow over to us from other parts of the country, where there are more plants.

Cities change the natural environment in other ways too. Tall buildings cut down on sunlight. They change the climate. Where you see a twenty-story building now, perhaps there once was a pond. Instead of a woodchuck hole under the ground, there are telephone wires and water pipes. Other animals that need a large habitat have moved away because people took up more and more of the room they needed.

These are some of the changes man has made in the natural environment. The changes have made life easy for people in some ways. It is easier to buy food in a store than to hunt or grow your own. You keep warmer in a house with a furnace than in a house with only a fireplace. You can get water from the sink. Before the city was here, people had to get it from a well.

There are other changes that cities have made on the natural environment. These changes make life harder and not as pleasant. Because there are so many people in a city, there have to be a great many furnaces to keep them warm. One furnace pouring smoke into the air isn't too bad. But when there are hundreds, it makes the air dirty. The air is less healthy and makes clothes and paint dirty, too.

TRY THIS! Rub some vaseline on 4 pieces of paper (or 3 X 5 cards). Put the cards on a window sill, at home or at school. After one day take away 1 card and put it where it won't collect more dirt. The next day do the same thing with another card. Do this until you have taken away all the cards.

On the last day, look at all 4 cards. Compare the amount of dirt on each. Look at the dirt under a magnifying glass. Do you think the air in your city is clean or not?

This dirt makes water dirty too. Most of us have to pay to buy clean water from far away.

A river running through a city can be very pretty. Do you have a river in your city? What does it look like?

Getting rid of garbage is also a real problem in crowded cities. People have to get it out of their homes. Garbage men have to get it out of the cans in the street. and then it has to be put some place away from people.

Too often the waste from houses and factories is thrown into the river. This makes the water not fit to drink. The dirty water kills the fish and other animals which live in clean rivers and lakes. You cannot go fishing because there are no fish. Some rivers are so dirty that people cannot go swimming in them. They might get sick from the dirty water.

This kind of man-made dirt in air and water is called POLLUTION. Another kind of man-made dirt is called litter. One small candy paper on the sidewalk may not be so bad. When hundreds of people throw small pieces of paper on the ground it makes a big mess.

Noise can be another bother. Noise doesn't do anything to air, water, food and shelter but it does something to you. In the city you hear noise from trucks, cars, buses, trains, air hammers, horns, garbage cans, airplanes, and many other things. All this noise can make you feel mad or restless and uncomfortable. Too much noise is not good for anybody.

WALK #10 Some ways people are hurting the Environment

You have just looked at some of the parts of the environment that man has changed. Maybe man forgot to think ahead when he made some of these changes but man is PART of the environment. He is as important to it as the other living things found there. He is even more important in one way. Man has a mind which can think and plan ahead and choose what to do. Some of the man-made changes in the environment are not good. Something can be done but it will have to be done by man. You are a person. You can plan ahead. You can help change your environment. You can help make it a better place for all plants and animals.

WHAT ARE SOME WAYS PEOPLE ARE HURTING THE ENVIRONMENT?

I. Air Pollution:

1. Stand outside your school. Look all around. Check all of the places you can see that air pollution is coming from:

_____ factories   _____ buses
_____ apartment houses   _____ airplanes
_____ cars   _____ fires

2. Describe the sky. Is it clean?   _____ yes   _____ no
   Is it hazy?   _____ yes   _____ no
   Is it darker in some parts than others?   _____ yes   _____ no

3. Can you smell the air?   _____ yes   _____ no

EDUCATIONAL IMPLICATIONS

4. Do your eyes tear or smart? _____ yes _____ no

   If possible, watch a bus leave a bus stop.
   Can you see the exhaust? _____ yes _____ no
   Can you smell the exhaust? _____ yes _____ no

5. Try to collect some pollutants.
   a. Wipe a car with a tissue. Paste a piece of the tissue below.

   b. Wipe a window ledge with a tissue. Paste a piece of the tissue below.

   c. Go to a tree near a bus stop. Wipe a leaf with a tissue. Paste a piece of tissue below.

   d. Go to a tree as far away as possible from bus stops and heavy traffic. Wipe a leaf with a tissue. Paste a piece of tissue below.

6. Sandpaper a small section of the stones on the outside of the school building. Is there a difference in color? _____yes _____no

7. If there is snow on the ground, what color is it? _____white _____gray
How long ago did the snow fall?_____today _____yesterday _____a few days ago.

II. Litter:
Examine the litter under a tree, on the grassy strip between the sidewalk and the street, or in a vacant lot. Check the things you find. Some of these things will come apart soon. Some will last a long time and make the ground ugly.   Draw a line from each thing you found to the right group.

GROUP 1	GROUP 2
Things that will make soil soon:	Things that will not make soil soon.

newspapers
cans
glass
soda can tabs
foil
candy wrappers
cigarettes

The following informational material is from the teacher's manual. It provides additional background, suggested activities, and conceptual understandings for the chapter previously excerpted from the student's work-text.

Cities Change the Environment

INTRODUCTION

From the previous sections the child has learned not only about the other living things which share the environment with him, but also about the physical, life-supporting substances which comprise that environment. He has been introduced to the basic needs of all living things—including man—and knows about the interactions taking place in a natural environment.

In this final part of the book, the ideas of how and why the natural environment in cities has changed are suggested. One reason is the large numbers of people. As the population of a place grows, the need for housing, transportation, food and power grows, too. The more matter consumed, the more wastes must be disposed of. The more houses, factories and roads, the less space there is for oxygen-producing green plants, and for people to find the solitude necessary for enjoying emotionally healthy lives.

But, cities serve a purpose, and they are here to stay. Cities are not intrinsically undesirable. The problems encountered in cities stem from man's neglect to utilize constructively his most important attribute—his brain—which can permit him to coordinate his actions and plan ahead with vision, ecological understanding, and a sense of social responsibility.

As the book closes, children are reminded of the role they can play in combatting our environmental crisis, and are asked to "use your senses and your special brain so you can help make a better world for everyone."

UNDERSTANDINGS

1. Cities change the natural environment.
2. The wastes created by large numbers of people, consuming large quantities of matter in a small area, have resulted in the deterioration of the quality of our environment.
3. Our environmental problems include: air pollution; water pollution; noise pollution; solid wastes; littering; and over-population.
4. Our current environmental crisis is the result of man's neglect to plan ahead.
5. Man is the only animal that can make a conscious decision to save or to destroy his environment.
6. Improving the quality of the environment is the responsibility of every man, woman and child in the country.

SUGGESTED TOPICS

What does it mean when Lake Erie is called a "dead lake"? (All the high-quality fish have perished for lack of oxygen and the lake is left with coarse fish that can survive in degraded waters. This is a result of pollution of all sorts, including excessive organic matter, phosphates from detergents and fertilizers, all of which stimulate plant growth. The plants then decay, using up oxygen faster than it is replaced. All lakes and ponds tend to become silted in and "over-fertilized" by organic matter in time [a process called eutrophication] but this normally takes centuries or millenia. Man's pollution is shortening the process to a few years.)

How many ways do we use electricity every day? What effect does this have on environmental problems? (Air pollution; thermal pollution; lowered watersheds; depletion of oil and coal; radioactive wastes.)

What is the one, biggest environmental problem your city faces?

Discuss the advantages and disadvantages of living in a large city.

ADDITIONAL RELATED ACTIVITIES

1. Walk around the neighborhood of your school with a transistorized tape recorder. Record the sounds heard in five minutes. Play the tape back when you return to the classroom. How many sounds can the children recognize? How many sounds were unpleasant? Discuss how the noises made the children feel. If there are animals in the classroom, notice whether they showed any reaction to the noises. Encourage the children to discuss whether the unpleasant sounds were necessary or not. (There will be differences of opinion.) Elicit suggestions as to ways of trying to have unnecessary noises stopped.
2. Examine the filter of an air conditioner.
3. Wipe leaves of a classroom plant with a tissue. How long does the leaf stay clean? in the winter? in the summer?
4. Develop a map pinpointing the problem areas in the neighborhood. Use this map at a PTA meeting to encourage cooperation of the adults in trying to combat some of the problems.
5. Seek the help of the community in cleaning out and improving a vacant

lot. Keep a photographic record of progress.

6. Start a campaign in and around your neighborhood to cut down on solid waste. Recommend ways of utilizing materials more fully (e.g., writing on both sides of the paper; using scrap material for arts and crafts projects; using plastic food containers as refrigerator dishes).

Visit a supermarket to study different methods of packaging. Prepare a list for parents recommending those ways in which to create the least disposal problems (use deposit soda bottles instead of no return bottles; use waxpaper instead of plastic wrapping paper).

Set up a depot for collecting aluminum cans. Use the revenue from this project for a neighborhood beautification program.

Find out about legislation designed to discourage non-reusable or non-biodegradable packaging. Bring this information to the attention of parents and community.

7. Maintain a bulletin board on the *Quality of the Environment*. Divide the class into committees, each responsible for one environmental problem. Keep the bulletin board up-to-date. Include notices of radio and television programs.

8. Start an on-going study of the various environmental problems, their causes, consequences, and possible cures. Prepare a large chart like the one on the inside back cover.* Fill in the detailed information as the study unfolds.

9. On a large sheet of oaktag, draw a picture of the way your own area probably looked before it became a city. Include such physical features as ocean, rivers, lakes, mountains. Encourage the children to plan the kind of city they would like to live in. Have them prepare cutouts of apartment buildings, houses, factories, stores, schools, parks, playgrounds, theaters, railroads, museums, highways, bridges, etc. In developing their city they will encounter many situations which will highlight the need for long-range and joint planning.

When their city is completed, have them compare it with the real city in which they live. What are the differences? Why? Which city is preferable? Why?

WALK #10 What Are Some Ways People Are Hurting The Environment?

   I. General Hints (see Walk #2)

  II. Objectives:

     1. To develop an awareness of environmental problems.

 III. Materials Needed:

     For entire class: piece of white cloth; string

     For each group of 4-6 children:

       Ringelman Scale

 IV. Before The Walk

     1. Elicit from the class a list of the environmental problems they consider most severe in their city. (List might include: air pollution; water pollution; solid waste disposal; noise pollution; litter; congestion; unsightly vacant lots; etc.)

     2. Review some of the causes, sources, and effects of air pollution.

  V. Background:

     A. Air Pollution

       Air pollution is the result of incomplete combustion. The burning which causes air pollution takes place in one of several places, and results in the production of several different kinds of pollutants.

*Editor's note: See Appendix B of this book.

EDUCATIONAL IMPLICATIONS

SOURCES	POLLUTANTS
Automobiles & Buses	Carbon Monoxide
	Hydrocarbons
	Nitrogen Oxides
	Particulates (rubber dust, asbestos dust)
Space Heating	Sulfur Dioxide
	Nitrogen Oxides
Factories	Sulfur Dioxide
	Nitrogen Oxides
Incinerators	Particulates (soot ash)

The increased awareness of air pollution during the past few years is leading to two major types of controls:

Input—by limiting the sulfur (or, in the case of automobiles—lead) content of fuels.

Output—by installing devices in generating plants, automobiles, incinerators and space heaters which bring about more complete combustion of fuels.

In observing smoke rising from smokestacks, the characteristic to note is its color. The darker it is, the more harmful it is.

ON THE WALK
1. Use a Ringelman Scale to examine the smoke coming from smokestacks.
2. Tie a piece of white cloth on the tail pipe of an automobile. Run the motor for five minutes. Remove the cloth and have the children examine it.

B. Litter

Although all litter is unsightly, some has more lasting unpleasant effects than others. Articles of organic origin (food, paper) will eventually decompose to form soil. "Tin" cans (which are really tin-coated steel) will eventually rust and disintegrate. The most lasting scars on the landscape are items made from aluminum, plastic and glass, which remain intact for indefinite periods of time.

VI. After The Walk
1. Observe one factory or apartment house several times a day for a period of several weeks. Use the Ringelman scale to note the degree of pollution being spewed forth. Record this information and the day and hour of the observation. Discuss findings.
2. You may wish to add to this Walk, or to take a subsequent Walk, to investigate other aspects of environmental pollution raised by the class in the preliminary discussion of your city's problems. A checklist similar to the one below could be used.

CHECKLIST

LITTER AND DESTRUCTION
1. How many litter baskets do you see on the walk? _____
2. How many are_____empty_____partly filled_____full_____overflowing?
3. Is there litter_____along the curb_____on the sidewalks_____near the buildings?

URBAN ACTIVITIES

4. How many covered garbage cans do you see?_____
5. How many uncovered garbage cans do you see?_____
6. How many soda or beer cans do you see lying on the sidewalk?_____
7. How many soda or beer can flip-tops do you see?_____
8. How many of the soda or beer cans are made of iron? (use a magnet)_____
9. Is broken glass along the curb?_____yes_____no
   on the sidewalk?_____yes_____no
10. How many times do you see evidence that people do not "curb their dog"?
    _____
11. How many candy, gum or ice cream wrappers do you find on the sidewalk or along the curb?_____
12. Are there any pieces of furniture or other household articles lying on the side-walk or in the street?_____yes_____no
    If yes, how many?_____
13. Are there any abandoned cars in the street?_____yes_____no. If yes, how many?_____
14. Are newspapers lying on the sidewalk or flying around?_____yes_____no
15. How many vacant lots or strips of land do you see?_____
    How many are tidy and pretty?_____How many are ugly?_____
16. How many broken windows do you see?_____
17. In how many places do you see writing on walls, public signs or billboards?
    _____

NOISE POLLUTION

1. Stand still for two minutes and listen. Check all the sounds you hear. Add others not on the list.____fire engine____train____horn____ambulance____po-lice siren____airplane____bus engine____truck engine____screeching brakes ____fog horn____autos or trucks moving along the street____shouting____riveting____cement mixer
2. How do you rate the general noise level?
   ____very noisy____noisy____moderate____quiet

VII. Understandings
   1. The natural environment in cities is being severely affected by the necessity of providing for the needs of many people living in a limited area.

SECTION 8

ACADEMIC SIMULATION GAMES

Simulation games have recently become popular as a teaching tool. Before 1960 they were used primarily by the armed forces in war games, by business administrators in development of more efficient operations, and by behavioral scientists as a research technique. Today, there are a great variety of games available to elementary and secondary school personnel. Most of them are designed for the social science field and appeal to students from the upper elementary grades through to senior high school.

A simulation game is an operating model of a physical or social phenomenon, incorporating a game technique. Players assume roles, interact with other players, and make decisions based on those roles and interactions. As students become actively involved in problems similar to those encountered in real life, they gain insight into the attitudes, concepts, skills, and decision-making processes typical of that physical or social phenomenon.

Simulation games have disadvantages as well as advantages. They are time-consuming. Sometimes the concepts and skills are neglected as students concentrate more on the game element. Teachers accustomed to a formal classroom organization may feel "threatened" by the informality and classroom disorder that is likely to occur during a game situation.

For successful simulation activities, there must be a change in the teacher's role. He becomes a consultant rather than a judge. He does not rate participants since they can each evaluate their own performance in respect to the outcome of the game. Instead of the teacher being the supplier of all knowledge, the students and teachers begin to recognize that in some instances there are no "right" answers.

Simulation games can be used by all members of the class at the same time, or by a small group of players as part of a learning center. The way they are used depends on the type of game and the objectives of that activity.

ACADEMIC SIMULATION GAMES

The first article by Fred Rasmussen from the Educational Research Council of America (ERC) gives good background on the value of simulation games to the classroom. The second article is a synopsis of four environmental simulations devised by ERC. These simulations are part of their Life Science Program which is available in commercial edition from the Houghton Mifflin Company.

The third article is an action description of two environmental games, "Smog" and "Dirty Water." They are both produced by Urban Systems, Inc.

Fred A. Rasmussen

SCIENCE TEACHING AND ACADEMIC GAMING

EDITOR'S NOTE: This article is a slightly abbreviated version of the original.

How does the future adult learn to make appropriate judgments on social and political issues such as thermal pollution, supersonic transport, drug control, pesticides, or on the criminal who has a chromosomal imbalance? The hapless citizen is not likely to get much help from his present science courses. What he needs in order to make intelligent choices is not more bits and pieces of science knowledge but a better comprehension of the nature of science and its interaction with technology and society. To become a truly functional adult, he should have studied the provisional nature of scientific knowledge and its limitations. He should have engaged in activities that will help him realize that scientific expertise does not necessarily qualify one to be an unbiased judge on social and political issues. He should have had the kinds of encounters which allow him to understand scientific information within the context of the prevalent social forces.

How can these major deficiencies in our current science curriculum be corrected? Of course, a long range solution to the appropriate teaching of the interactions of science technology and society would entail not only a new revolution in science curricula, but a serious reorganization of the training required for science teachers. The narrowly trained science teacher is not well equipped to handle these cross-disciplinary topics with the conventional modes of instruction.

Short of teacher training and rebuilding the science curriculum, it may be possible to overcome this deficiency in science teaching to some extent by a significant shift in pedagogy. This will entail a reordering of priorities so that new, rather than additional, materials can be added to science curricula. The new materials would be appropriate simulation models from which students can learn the inter-relationships among science, technology, and society. The use of simulation situations

SOURCE.   Reprinted, by permission, from *The American Biology Teacher,* December 1969, with slight abridgment.

or simulation games in classrooms is a relatively new technique but one which is receiving a great deal of interest in the social sciences (Nesbit, 1968). The word "game" in no way implies play, but in current usage among behavioral scientists, the game is designated as a simulation situation where the winner is identified (Boocock and Schild, 1968).

This is not to suggest that educational games are a panacea that will solve our problems in science teaching. However they do offer an excellent method whereby students can be confronted with the many parameters of such complex problems such as pollution control, world population control, etc. This type of learning experience is very different from the traditional didactic method of instruction. The student involved in a simulation game has the opportunity to play roles in situations similar to ones he may encounter as an adult.

It is possible for a teacher, if he will do the necessary research, to provide a model for students so they can learn to make defensible and rational predictions on problems of world importance. Given the increased capacity for data storage and retrieval provided by access to computer terminals, students could be given the opportunity to manipulate real data and become familiar with the parameters of significant world problems.

Can the players involved in simulation games learn from their participation games?

Gordon (1967) indicates that educational games have a potential for motivating students in areas other than immediate concern because:

1. Games require active participation. Players themselves make things happen. They cause events and they know it immediately.

2. The player gets immediate feedback. When a player makes a decision, it has an immediate effect. Others respond to his decision.

3. Educational games are goal directed, i.e., (originally at least) the objective of winning seems to be a powerful motivating force.

4. Almost all educational games require interaction among players and physical movement. They provide an opportunity to expend physical energy as well as satisfy the need to communicate with peers.

5. Educational games provide new opportunity for other than the class leaders. The situation for class monopoly by the better students is less likely to happen.

6. Games provide new and interesting ways to convey information to children. Facts, when they can be used to support a position, take on a significantly different role than when they are to be memorized.

7. Games call for activity in the higher cognitive levels of synthesis, application, and analyses.

REFERENCES

Abt, Clark C. and V. H. Cogger. 1968. Educational games for the sciences. *The Science Teacher* 36 (1): 36-39.

Boocock, Sarane E. and E. D. Schild. 1968. Simulation games and learning. Sage, Beverly Hills, California.

Gatewood, Claude. 1968. The curriculum viewed nationally. *The Science Teacher* 35 (8):18-21.

Gordon, Alice K. 1968. Six booklets on Academic Games. Science Research Associates, Chicago, Illinois.

Nesbit, William A. 1968. Simulation games for the social studies classroom. The Foreign Policy Association, New York.

Peterson, Glen E. 1968. The challenges of our times. *The American Biology Teacher* 30 (9): 475.

Paul Holobinko

Frederick A. Rasmussen

Victor M. Showalter

SYNOPSIS OF GAMES AND SIMULATIONS IN THE COMMERCIAL EDITION OF ERC LIFE SCIENCE

THE POLLUTION GAME

The Pollution Game is a role-play game where students assume common roles from our own society, i.e., industrialist, property owner, citizen, etc. The game is played on a board so that relationships between participants can be visually represented. Just as in real life, resources are unequally allocated and financial success is due, in part, to chance.

In the Pollution Game students discover that there is positive correlation between significant financial success and being a pollutor. With each gain in affluence by an individual or team, there is an accompanying decrease in the quality of the environment. This record is kept on large dials as a Water Pollution Index and an Air Pollution Index. If, as a consequence of team action, either index exceeds a predetermined level of pollution, all players on the team lose.

The player that accumulates the most money is the class winner. The winning team is that team with the highest quality

SOURCE. Reprinted, by permission, from the paper, "Synopsis of Games and Simulations," Commercial Edition of *ERC Life Science,* by Paul Holobinko, Frederick A. Rasmussen, and Victor M. Showalter, with slight abridgment.

environment as reflected by the indices. Thus the goals of the group are in conflict with those of individuals with the greatest resources. To solve this dilemma, students must propose compromises that are based on mutual interest and mutual survival. If they do not, they lose.

THE REDWOOD CONTROVERSY

The problem of appropriate utilization of land becomes increasingly acute as populations increase in size and mobility. What kinds of factors should be considered when making decisions for a new park, a green belt, or local zoning ordinances? The Redwood Controversy is designed so students gain insights into political, geographical, and sociological issues which confuse and confound the solution of land utilization problems.

In the Redwood Controversy the class simulates the senate hearings and debates which preceded the establishment of a National Redwoods Park. The majority of the class members play the role of senators. Each senator is provided with a profile which describes his role and places constraints on his behavior. Other class members play the roles of witnesses representing lumber interests, conservationists, local politicians, federal bureaucrats, and the academic community..

Witnesses present their points of view and are questioned by senators. Eventually the senators must make a recommendation about the establishment of a National Redwoods Park using their profiles and the witness data as guidelines.

Input from the game materials and the interaction with other players along with individual concerns such as re-election, political debts, and partisan interests make a true consideration of the issue at hand difficult, but not impossible.

PLANT MANAGEMENT GAME

In this game, a team of three or four students manages the resources of a myth-

ical planet, Clarion. The management team is responsible for deciding how the planet's development budget will be spent for ten consecutive five-year cycles.

Feedback data from Clarion is provided at the end of each five-year cycle so that the management team may continue or change its development program. The management team may compete against another team (or teams) to determine who can direct Clarion to its highest level of development. Or, a team may play the game several times in an attempt to better previous performance.

Although the planet Clarion is mythical, the students get involved in many concerns that exist on Earth, such as: population expansion, food supply, standard of living, and environmental quality. The complexity and interrelationships of the problems become apparent to the student.

Playing Planet Management successfully depends on the management team's success in adopting certain scientific attitudes and procedures and applying them to a situation that has contemporary relevance.

THERMAL POLLUTION

Thermal Pollution is a simulation designed to help students understand the origin and perpetuation of thermal pollution in our water resources.

This simulation has two phases. In the first phase students play the roles of business owners, investors, and wage earners to learn how the actions of each group contributed to the origin and the growth of the thermal pollution problem from the turn of the century to the present.

In the second phase students play the roles of contemporary groups: a citizen's committee, an electrical power producer, an industrial association, a state health board, and city councilmen in deciding whether or not to continue practices which perpetuate the thermal pollution problem. The state board of health holds hearings to determine the conditions under which a permit may be granted to the power producer to discharge waste heat into a local lake. Testimony from witnesses who support and who oppose granting the permit serves as the basis for deciding the issue.

This simulation has no single winner. Winning players in Phase One are those who are able to accumulate the greatest wealth relative to the amount of assets with which they begin the simulation. Phase Two winners are those whose biases are adopted by the power producer and/or the state board of health

POLLUTION PLAY

The most recent—and most scientifically sophisticated—additions to the social-problem game field plunge players into the environmental morass of "Smog" and "Dirty Water." Both games come from a group that should know about such things—Urban Systems, Inc., a Boston think tank composed ot scientists and politicians, including former mayor John Collins and more than a dozen Harvard and MIT urbanologists. "Smog" requires each of two to four players to assume the role of a city's "Air Quality Manager," and the dice determine how many people and industries pollute the urban air and pay taxes for cleaning it up again.

"Smog's" rules oblige each player to move along a "Decision Tree," dealing with zoning, population, industrial growth and bids for Federal funds. To win the game, he must earn 2,000 "management credits"—and that is no easy task. On his way around the board, he gets frustrating Outrageous Fortune cards and must cope with car exhaust, incinerator smoke, sulphur-containing fuels, contamination from neighboring jurisdictions—and still please taxpayers enough to keep his job. It is neither wise nor possible to outlaw cars or arbitrarily restrict industry, the manager

inevitably discovers; instead, he must use abatement techniques and settle for realistic compromises.

Similar quandaries are posed by "Dirty Water," each of whose players is the Water Pollution Commissioner of a lake surrounded by industries and residential developments. A commissioner must choose between winking at polluting factories and wiping out a town's vital jobs. He does battle with effluent from paper, steel and power plants, thermal pollution, phosphates, herbicides, pesticides, detergents, overpopulation, and sewage. To add to his difficulties, all lakes on the board are connected by rivers, and noxious elements in each one travel downstream to plague adjoining waters. A player wins by staying economically solvent while maintaining the lake's plant-and-animal food chain, from bacteria through algae to fish.

Both games demonstrate that pollution inevitably attends technology and growth, and that there are no magical solutions to make it vanish. But they also suggest that persistence, ingenuity and purpose can remove pollution's lethal sting, if players at the table—or in real life—are willing to engage themselves fully in environmental complexities.

SOURCE. Reprinted, by permission, from *Newsweek,* June 22, 1970, copyright Newsweek Inc., with slight abridgment.

SECTION 9

EXPERIMENTS FOR ELEMENTARY SCHOOL STUDENTS

Most of the experiments presented in this section can be used with students from kindergarten through grade six. Modifications for differing maturity levels can easily be made.

Four of the experiments concern ecosystems of various sizes. Comparisons can be made between the ecosystems of a square meter of ground, an aquarium, a terrarium, and a city (man-dominated community). These diverse ecosystems can be used for purposes of observation to contrast normal and abnormal environmental conditions. They are helpful in a study of the water cycle and the oxygen-carbon dioxide cycle.

Certain experiments focus on pollution of air, water, and soil. One of them traces the movement of pollutants through air, water, and soil.

In two experiments fruit flies are used to demonstrate population growth and the relationship of population growth to food supply. These experiments provide one way in which children can study the controversial issue of population growth objectively. They follow through on the issues raised in "The Population Explosion," in Part 2, and "Critical Thinking in Ecology," Part 3.

The reader is reminded that in the article, "Environmental Education for the Elementary Classroom," the National Academy of Sciences recommended the Science Curriculum Improvement Study as "one of the most promising for environmental education." Accordingly, five representative lessons from this outstanding curriculum project are reprinted. It is emphasized that excerpts are from preliminary or trial editions. It is possible that there will be minor or major revisions in the final edition.

It is recommended that teachers use an inquiry approach in which students manipulate concrete materials to discover answers to pollution problems. As a result of experimentation, students gain insight into relevant concepts. These concepts may be applied to specific situations in order to evaluate cause and effect relationships, and to promote the solution of environmental problems.

398

CLASSROOM EXPERIENCE WITH AIR POLLUTION

The following activities related to air pollution are merely suggestive as to intent. It is hoped that they will stimulate ideas and lead to further activities. Some of them are demonstrations; some are capable of being made into experiments. In every case they are planned to illustrate, to clarify, and to dramatize the story of air pollution. They may be used with a variety of age levels of children.

It is hoped that elementary school teachers will seek the assistance of junior high or senior high school science teachers in planning certain of these activities. In this way, apparatus may be made available, variations on activities may be prepared, and in general another link in the program of science K-12 may be forged.

I. *The reality of air.* For children in the early primary grades it might be well to establish the reality of air with them before proceeding to more specific work with air pollution. There are many ways to show that air takes up space, has weight, and exerts pressure. In all probability such activities are part of the regular curriculum. Almost all elementary science books list such activities as well as "The Science for Children" series published by the New York State Education Department.

II. *Weather activities.* Students would do well to have a knowledge of the "hows and whys" of the weather, including something about how weather elements are measured. For the most part, such material is readily available. However, two demonstrations pertaining to the behavior of air masses and the nature of an inversion are not commonly included in most sources.

1. Fill a flat bottle half full of water; then fill the remainder of the bottle with heavy motor oil. Cork the

SOURCE. Reprinted, by permission, from *Air Pollution,* published by the Bureau of Elementary Curriculum Development, The University of the State of New York, New York State Education Department, Albany, 1966.

bottle tightly. When the bottle is tipped on edge, the water moves under the oil. The oil and water represent two air masses of different characteristics, and the junction between them represents a *front*.

2. Take a tall narrow container, such as a graduated cylinder or an olive jar, and fill it half full of motor oil. Now introduce water through a tube on the surface of the oil. If this is done carefully, it may be possible to fill the cylinder to the top. Normally, the water should be below the motor oil. In a like manner, cold air should be found nearer the ground than warm air. However, under certain conditions, there is an "inversion" of normal affairs and the cold air, like the water, is found on top.

III. *Photographic studies.* Take pictures of various situations in the community which show air being polluted. Remember the three major sources of air pollution involve trash-burning either at home or in community dumps, automobile exhausts, and industrially produced smokes and gases. Does the community have another source of air pollution not included in one of these groups? Perhaps it has ordinances pertaining to air pollution. It is interesting to note that a survey made in 1958 showed that many communities in New York State having severe air pollution problems had no antipollution ordinances.

IV. *Light intensity studies.* One of the unpleasant features of many situations involving air pollution is the reduction of light intensity. This not only interferes with visibility, but it also affects the photosynthetic process of green plants. Time can be profitably spent in class discussion dealing with matters of safety under conditions of poor visibility. How are airlines affected by excessive smoke over cities? Find out from the National Safety Council what hours of the day most auto accidents occur.

1. The school nurse-teacher may have a light meter which she uses to determine whether or not sufficient light is available for reading. Use this to show differences in light intensity on days when the air is clear and on days when there is fog or overcast. Be sure to make the tests at the same location in the room and at the same time of day. If the nurse-teacher does not have the light meter mentioned, a photographic light meter may be substituted. Some parent will have such a device.

2. In this age of plastics, radiometers have become relatively common as toys for children. How does a radiometer behave when set on a sunny windowsill? Compare this with the behavior of the instrument on a cloudy day.

3. Grow several approximately identical green plants under varying conditions of light. Place one in sunlight. This will be the control plant, and observations made on the other plants will be made with reference to the control. Place another plant in a rather dark corner of the room. This plant should not be in darkness but in subdued light. Place a third plant in a cupboard where it gets practically no light at all. Give them identical care except for the amount of light each receives. Carry out this experiment as long as is necessary to get information. Ask the pupils to make inferences about light intensity and green plant welfare.

V. *Photochemical studies.* It has been stated earlier that not only do the substances emanating from smoke-stacks, automobile exhausts, and incinerators supply materials to pollute the air, but that these materials react with one another in the presence of sunlight to make an even greater variety of pollutants. The reactions of chemicals caused by light are known collectively as photochemical effects. Such chemical activity is very common but not at all well understood by scientists.

1. Photographic prints can be made in a darkened classroom using "slow" print paper. These can be made from negatives or from placing opaque objects on the print paper and getting shadow pictures. Photography depends largely on the fact that certain compounds of silver react in the presence of light.

2. In a darkened room, add a solution of silver nitrate to a solution of sodium chloride. Have pupils observe the color of the precipitate which forms. Now expose the precipitate to strong light (sunlight) for about an hour. What happens?

3. If blueprint paper is available, it too may be used to demonstrate a chemical effect of light. Place a key or other opaque object on the blueprint paper and expose to the sun. The shadow picture may be preserved by washing the print in running water.

4. Many household products are sold in either brown glass bottles or in opaque plastic containers. Hydrogen peroxide and bleaches containing sodium hypochlorite are among these. Why?

5. Many curtains and drapes are guaranteed not to fade in the sunlight. What does this indicate about the nature of some chemical dyes?

VI. *Particulate studies.* Smoke, smog, soot, and dust are suspended particles of solids and/or liquids in the air. The largest of the particles eventually settle out of the air. Some particles, however, are small enough to be kept floating in the atmosphere by the bombardment of air molecules. These particles are apt to be of more serious consequence to living things than the larger ones. Since they do not settle out of the atmosphere, they can be carried great distances, inhaled by man and other animal life, taken into the leaves of green plants, or act as nuclei for other substances in the air to condense on.

1. Very small particles can often be seen by a very bright reflected light even though practically invisible in ordinary light. Have pupils observe the motes (small dust particles) in a beam of sunlight as it passes into a darkened corner of the room. Ordinarily, one would not be aware of the existence of these small particles.

2. Place a clean cloth over the intake of a vacuum pump or over the hose of a vacuum cleaner. Draw air through the cloth for several minutes. What is observed?

3. Use a perfume atomizer or an aerosol can of air freshener to spray a mist into a beam of sunlight coming in a window. Observe the tiny droplets of moisture. Caution! Do not use an insecticide bomb. Make sure that no open flames are in the room during the spraying or for several minutes thereafter.

4. Place a few drops of concentrated hydrochloric acid in a small dish. Close by, place a dish containing a few drops of concentrated ammonia. DO NOT MIX THESE CHEMICALS! The gaseous vapors

of these two substances will react to form a cloud of white solid ammonium chloride.

5. Smog can be produced by the condensation of water vapor (or other vapors) on solid particles like smoke. Insert a lighted match in a gallon jug to make a small amount of smoke. Blow, with your mouth pressing firmly on the mouth of the jug and release the compressed air quickly. A smog should form in the jug. Try this blowing activity without the smoke from the match. What happens?

6. If a microscope and a Brownian movement apparatus are available, have pupils observe cigarette smoke. This demonstrates that tobacco smoke is made up of solid particles. The smoke particles are small enough to be kept suspended in the air indefinitely and are in a constant state of vibration due to the bombardment of air molecules.

7. Remove the rubber bulb from a medicine dropper. Insert a small wad of cotton in the glass tube and replace the bulb. Insert the end of the dropper in a lighted cigarette. Squeeze the bulb a few times to draw the smoke through the cotton. What happens? What conclusions might be drawn as to the nature of tobacco smoke? While tobacco smoke is usually not produced in large enough quantities to constitute an air pollution problem *out-of-doors,* indoors it may be another matter to contend with. Compare the probable reactions of a heavy smoker with those of a nonsmoker living through an experience such as occurred in Donora, Pa.

8. Certain particulate pollutants may clog the stomata or openings on leaves of green plants and inter-fere with the passage of water vapor and other gases in and out of the leaf. Moderately heavy dusting of a few leaves of a geranium plant can be used to demonstrate this. Vasline, though not a particulate pollutant, may be used more effectively to demonstrate the clogging of leaf "pores." Select two or three leaves on a healthy green plant. Coat them with vasline making sure that all surfaces are covered. Observe the condition of these leaves as compared with the uncoated leaves on the same plant over a period of time. An interesting variation of this experiment would involve coating one leaf on the bottom surface only, one leaf on the top surface only, and one leaf on both sides. What conclusions can be drawn from the results of this experiment?

9. Place a clean, cold dish in a candle flame. Soot formed is a result of incomplete combustion of the candle fuel. Heating this soot in a hot Bunsen flame causes it to disappear. Why? What ideas for one kind of pollution control might be suggested by this demonstration?

The foregoing experiences and demonstrations are only a few that can be used in teaching about air pollution. Most of them can be done with equipment found in well-equipped schools. Many of the activities, particularly those for elementary schools, can be done with common household articles.

The best examples of air pollution, unfortunately, can be found in the great outdoors. Air pollutants can be found in practically all of New York State at one season or another. It is hoped that this will be a thing of the past in the not too distant future. Education for future leaders is a step in the right direction.

Robert B. Sund

Bill W. Tillery

Leslie W. Trowbridge

WHAT PRECAUTIONS SHOULD BE TAKEN IN THE USE OF INSECTICIDES?

MATERIALS

Pressurized can of insect spray

Fruit jar with a lid

DISCUSSION

What do insects do to plants?

What kinds of undesirable insects do you often find in your home?

How would you go about controlling them?

What does an insecticide do to insects?

What care should you take in using an insecticide?

How would you prove whether an insecticide were effective against an insect or not?

PUPIL INVESTIGATION

1. Obtain a fruit jar with a lid and collect several insects around home, such as flies, ants, and cockroaches, to bring to class.
2. Obtain an insect spray can.
3. Partially open the jar and spray a small amount of the insecticide into the jar. Recap your jar quickly.
    CAUTION: Do not spray the insecticide toward any pupils and only spray just a little insecticide into the jar. DO NOT BREATHE ANY OF THE INSECTICIDE. Wash your hands with soap and water immediately after spraying the insecticide. Why?

SOURCE. Reprinted, by permission, from *Elementary Science Discovery Lessons: The Biological Sciences,* by Robert B. Sund, Bill W. Tillery, and Leslie W. Trowbridge. Published by Allyn and Bacon, Inc., 1970.

4. Observe your jar for several minutes.
5. What does the insecticide do to the insects?
6. Which insects seem to be affected the most by the spray?
7. What purpose does an insecticide have around the home?
8. What precautions should be taken in using them?
9. Why wouldn't you want to use an insecticide near food or dinner plates?
10. Why should insecticides always be stored so that babies cannot get their hands on them?
11. Why shouldn't you play with insecticides?
12. What is a poison?

CONCEPTUAL SCHEME

There is a relationship between an organism and its environment.

PROCESS OBJECTIVES

Observing, hypothesizing, inferring, defining operationally.

CONCEPTS

1. An insecticide is a chemical that kills insects.
2. Insects vary in their resistance to insecticides.
3. Insecticides should be used with discretion.

COGNITIVE BEHAVIORAL OBJECTIVES

The student should be able to:

1. Use an insecticide, taking care to spray it only where needed.
2. Define operationally an insecticide.

3. State reasons why an insecticide should be used with care.
4. State why an insecticide should not be stored where a baby could easily obtain it.

TEACHER'S NOTE

It is very important that children become aware of the fact that there are dangerous chemicals present in the home. Insecticides, for example, may be toxic. They should never be sprayed indiscriminately on food nor on surfaces where food will be prepared, and they should not be breathed. Care should be used in their storage especially if there are small children around who might try to eat them.

The alteration of the environment by man must always be carefully considered. Insecticides may be used to kill undesirable insects but they also kill desirable insects such as bees and other animals such as birds. They should, therefore, be used with discretion. They may be used in the home to control disease-carrying insects such as the fly, mosquito, or cockroach. They also may be used in the yard to control harmful plant insects.

Insects vary in their resistance to insecticides. Some will die easily from an application while others may be completely resistant to a certain insecticide. In this case, other insecticides may have to be applied. By the careful use of insecticides, man helps to control insect infestations in his environment.

OPEN-ENDED POSSIBILITIES

How do farmers use insecticides? How do insecticides vary in the way they cause an insect to die? What is the best kind of insecticide to use to kill aphids, cockroaches, mosquitos, house flies, etc.?

Robert B. Sund

Bill W. Tillery

Leslie W. Trowbridge

HOW MANY ORGANISMS CAN BE FOUND IN A SQUARE METER OF GROUND?

MATERIALS

Magnifying glass
Paper cups
A metric or yard stick

DISCUSSION

If you went outside in the school yard or a nearby park and measured off a square meter of yard area, how many different kinds of living things would you expect to find?

How would you measure a square meter or yard area?

What should you do to determine how many organisms live in a square meter?

Would it make any difference where you counted the organisms?

PUPIL INVESTIGATION

1. Obtain a metric or yard stick, magnifying glass, and paper cups.
2. Go outside and measure one square meter or yard of ground as shown by your teacher.
3. Look very carefully at your square meter or yard of ground and collect one type of each kind of organism you find. Place what you find in the cup. For each type of plant, you need only take part of the plant.

SOURCE. Reprinted, by permission, from *Elementary Science Discovery Lessons: The Biological Sciences,* by Robert B. Sund, Bill W. Tillery, and Leslie W. Trowbridge. Published by Allyn and Bacon, Inc., 1970.

4. Take your material back into class. Count the total number of organisms, the number of plants and then the number of animals, and record these.
5. Compare your results with other members of the class.
6. How do your results compare?
7. What can you conclude about the area you studied?
8. In all probability you are missing a large number of organisms. What do you think they are?

CONCEPTUAL SCHEME

There is a relationship between an organism and its environment.

PROCESS OBJECTIVES

Measuring, classifying, reporting, interpreting data.

CONCEPTS

1. There is considerable variation of life in a small area of land.
2. Insects are one of the common animals found in a piece of land.
3. Microscopic life such as bacteria are also prevalent but cannot be seen.
4. Plant and animal life live together.

COGNITIVE BEHAVIORAL OBJECTIVES

The pupil should be able to:

1. Collect several forms of life from a small area of land.
2. Collect several insects from the same small area of land.
3. State that microscopic life such as bacteria are prevalent in soil.
4. Describe when given a list of plant and animals found on a field trip how these organisms live together.

TEACHER'S NOTE

In a plot of land there are several different living plant and animal organisms. The animals usually most visibly prevalent in a square area of a field are insects. There are many microorganisms such as bacteria found in the soil which may be more prevalent but can't be seen because they are so small. Many organisms may be found beneath the land. These may include bacteria, fungi, protozoa, worms, and insects. In the city if there is not planted land available on the school ground, a local park or large flower box may be studied as a substitute.

OPEN-ENDED POSSIBILITIES

How many organisms would you expect to find in a green lawn as compared to a dry field? Why? How would you find out?

Robert B. Sund

Bill W. Tillery

Leslie W. Trowbridge

HOW DO FRUIT FLIES REPRODUCE?

MATERIALS

A pint fruit jar
Cotton plug to stick in top of fruit jar
Filter paper or paper made like a funnel
Ripe fruit, such as a banana or a plum

DISCUSSION

Where would you expect to find a large number of flies?

What ways could the fly population be controlled?

Why should garbage be covered?

PUPIL INVESTIGATION

1. Obtain a pint fruit jar, a small circular paper, and a small piece of fruit.
2. Place the fruit in the bottom of the jar.
3. Make a small paper funnel out of your circular paper and place it on top of the jar. The opening at the bottom of this paper funnel should be about a half inch in diameter.
4. Place the jar near an open window or outside for 2-4 days.
5. What do you think will happen to the fruit?
6. What do you think will be attracted to the fruit?
7. How will they be stimulated to come to the fruit?
8. After you have several insects in your jar, cap it with the cotton plugs and observe the jar for several days. Record your observations.
9. What conclusions can you make about what flies eat?
10. How do fruit flies reproduce?
11. How do fruit flies develop?

SOURCE. Reprinted, by permission, from *Elementary Science Discovery Lessons: The Biological Sciences,* by Robert B. Sund, Bill W. Tillery, and Leslie W. Trowbridge. Published by Allyn and Bacon, Inc., 1970.

EDUCATIONAL IMPLICATIONS

CONCEPTUAL SCHEME

Life continues genetically.

PROCESS OBJECTIVES

Observing, hypothesizing, inferring.

CONCEPTS

1. Animals may be stimulated by odors.
2. The life cycle of the fly includes the egg, larva, pupa, and adult forms.
3. Flies eat decaying food, such as garbage.
4. Male flies vary in appearance from female flies.
5. Male flies fertilize female flies.

COGNITIVE BEHAVIORAL OBJECTIVES

The pupils should be able to:

1. State the life cycle of the fruit fly.

2. Describe the different stages of fly development.

3. State some ways the fly population may be controlled, such as covering garbage or using garbage disposals.

4. Describe how fruit flies reproduce.

TEACHER'S NOTE

If ample food is available, male and female fruit flies will be attracted to it where they will eventually mate. The females after mating produce eggs. In two or three days, the eggs will develop into crawling larvae. The larvae then develop into the relatively immobile pupa stage. If the pupae are kept warm, they in turn develop into adults. The larvae may be more easily seen if a piece of brown wrapping paper is placed near the food for them to crawl on.

Male fruit flies are identified by their black-tipped abdomen and are smaller in size than the females.

OPEN-ENDED POSSIBILITIES

What could be done to speed up the time it takes for the larvae to hatch from the eggs? What do other types of flies eat and how do they reproduce? What can be done in your community to better control the fly population?

Robert B. Sund
Bill W. Tillery
Leslie W. Trowbridge

WHAT CAN LIVE IN DIRTY WATER?

MATERIALS

A quart jar of pond water
Some hay
Medicine dropper
Glass slide
Cover slip
Microscope
(If possible, also collect a spoonful of
  soil from a dry pond)
Plastic wrap

Jar with
water and hay

DISCUSSION

Why shouldn't you drink dirty water?
What is in dirty water that might make
  you sick?
What are microorganisms?
Where do they live?

PUPIL INVESTIGATION

1. Obtain a quart jar and some hay.

2. Place about ten pieces of hay, four
    inches long, in the jar and a spoon-
    ful of soil from a dry pond bed.
3. Fill the jar with water.
4. Place the jar in a warm place for

SOURCE. Reprinted, by permission, from *Elementary Science Discovery Lessons: The Biological Sciences,* by Robert B. Sund, Bill W. Tillery, and Leslie W. Trowbridge. Published by Allyn and Bacon, Inc., 1970.

several days and cover it with plastic wrap.

5. How do you think the water will change?

6. After two weeks, look at your jars each day and note any difference in the appearance of the water and any other changes.

7. With a medicine dropper, place two drops of the water from your jars in the middle of a glass slide.

8. Cover the water with a cover slip.

9. Place the slide under a microscope.

10. Describe and diagram what you see on a piece of paper.

CONCEPTUAL SCHEME

There are biological roots to behavior.

PROCESS OBJECTIVES

Formulating hypotheses, observing.

CONCEPTS

1. Microorganisms are present everywhere.

2. Microorganisms are small organisms that usually can be seen only with the aid of a microscope.

3. There are great varieties of microorganisms.

COGNITIVE BEHAVIORAL OBJECTIVES

The pupil should be able to:

1. Hypothesize what will happen after a few days to a jar of water filled with several pieces of hay.

2. State that small living organisms (microorganisms) are present in dirty water.

TEACHER'S NOTE

Small inactive organisms may be deposited on hay or in the soil. When these organisms have a desirable environment they develop and reproduce. A hay infusion is made by placing some hay in a jar of water. The organisms on the hay then start to develop. After several days the hay infusion will have large collections of bacteria hardly visible under the microscope. These will appear as transparent dots. Small microscopic animals—unicellular and multicellular—will also be viewed. These can be differentiated from the smaller bacterial cells by their movement and size.

OPEN-ENDED POSSIBILITIES

What do you think will happen to the kinds of life you will find in the jar after a period of time? Have the class keep their culture for several months. What other cultures could be kept in class? Have the children collect some water escaping from a septic tank, or sewer, or stagnant water from a pool and put it in covered jars to watch the changes in its appearance. The children should try to determine why these changes occur.

FRUIT FLY POPULATIONS

SYNOPSIS

A population of fruit flies is started in the classroom. The children are led to consider increase or decrease of the population in relation to conditions in the container.

MATERIALS

For the class:
1 1-gallon plastic container with cover
1 vial of fruit flies with prepared food
1 label
banana*
cotton*
paper towels*
*(provided by teacher)

PREPARATION

Fruit flies should be introduced within two weeks after their arrival. Have some children help you prepare a 1-gallon plastic container for the fruit flies. With a nail or scissors make about ten holes (one-quarter inch in diameter) in the container lid. Fill the holes with cotton (this keeps the flies in while allowing for the passage of air). Peel a banana so that about half the pulp is exposed, and place it on a paper towel at the bottom of the container.

TEACHING SUGGESTIONS

The children will observe the increase and subsequent decrease in the number of fruit flies in the population container. Their observations serve to reinforce some of the ideas introduced in the daphnia, aphid, and cricket activities, such as (a) the size of a population depends on the number of young born in relation to the number of deaths over a given length of time; (b) the number of births and deaths varies depending on the conditions in the environment.

The observations may also lead to review discussions of certain concepts introduced in the *Organisms* and *Life Cycles* units; reproduction, generation, life cycle, biotic potential, metamorphosis.

Adding fruit flies to the container. Let the children watch as you put the fruit flies into the population container. First

SOURCE. Reprinted, by permission, from Chapter 10 of *SCIS Teacher's Guide* (preliminary edition) for "Populations" unit, 1969, published by Science Curriculum Improvement Study, University of California at Berkeley.

set the cover loosely on the container. Slide the cover back and place the vial on the bottom of the container. Snap the cap from the vial and securely close the container cover. When most of the adult flies have left the vial, have the children label the container with the number of fruit flies and the date. (You may remove the vial or leave it in the container.)

Observation of fruit flies. Allow the children time to observe the activities in the population container. Encourage them to report and describe their observations. You may also wish to have the children keep records of the approximate time it takes a fruit fly to go through its developmental stages.

Within a week after adult flies are put into the population container, some children should observe tiny, wormlike larvae crawling on the banana. A larva will grow for about five days and then attach itself to the banana peel or paper towel and form a yellowish case around itself. The children should notice these cases and perhaps recall from the *Life Cycles* unit that these enclose pupas. In four or five more days, a new generation of adults should begin to emerge from their pupal cases.

Population increase. When it appears that most of the new adults have emerged (i.e., most pupal cases are empty), have the children estimate and record the number of flies now in the container. Compare this estimate with the original number. Ask the children to predict what will happen in the container in one more week, two weeks, three weeks.

Population decrease. A third generation of adults may emerge in about two weeks, or a sharp decrease in population may occur soon after the second generation adults appear. A decrease is usually a result of the banana drying out, which creates a food shortage. (Adding more banana often increases the chances for the production of a third generation.) When the children notice the decrease in flies (in either the second or third generation), begin a discussion by asking the children what they think are the reasons for the decrease in number. Are the reasons for the decreased fly population similar to or different from the reasons for decreased daphnia or aphid populations? What could be done that might help the fruit fly population increase again? Where possible, help the children test their ideas, perhaps as described in the optional activity.

Clean-up. When the children finish the activities in this chapter, set the population container out of sight for about a week. When all the adults, pupas, and larvas have died, put them and any remaining food into a bag and dispose of it according to the supplier's instructions. (Setups used in an optional activity should be discarded by the same means.) Wash the gallon container and cover in warm water and store them for future use.

You may wish to let the children start small fruit fly populations to test the factors that they think affect population increase and decrease. For example, if children want to test the food and space factors, small populations can be set up in containers such as baby food or instant coffee jars. You may have to remind children about the need for a control setup in an experiment.

To allow air passage into a jar and to retain the fruit flies, punch two or three holes in the lid with a nail and plug the holes with cotton (the holes should be approximately one-quarter inch in diameter). In the bottom of the jar place a piece of banana for food and a small piece of paper towel to serve as a surface for egg-laying and pupating. Start a small population with four or five flies from the gallon container. Transferring the flies may be difficult, but either of the following methods should succeed:

A. Wrap the gallon container in a cloth to make it dark inside. Remove the cotton from one of the holes in the gallon container and place a jar over the hole. Fruit flies are attracted to light and should enter the jar. If the flies do not readily enter the jar, shake the gallon container to excite them.

B. If you do not mind flies flying around in the room for a day, there is another method of starting new populations that can be more fun. Place open jars (containing pieces of banana) near the windows of the classroom. Then release some of the flies from the gallon container. The released flies will disperse around the room, and most will enter the jars by the end of the day. Have the children look at the jars occasionally. When several flies have entered one, a child should quickly replace the lid—he now has a fruit fly population.

MAN-DOMINATED COMMUNITIES

SYNOPSIS

The community concept is developed further to show that man is *a part of* the biotic community, not *apart from it.* Attention is drawn to the plant and animal populations in the man-dominated community when children explore areas around their school and homes. They identify populations (including man) and their foods. The investigations and the questions which guide the children may be similar to those suggested in Chapter 16, but here man is the dominant animal in the community and the objective is to understand the effects of human activity on other populations.

BACKGROUND INFORMATION

Communities in which humans live—from the small rural village to the densely populated city—consist of many plant and animal populations in addition to man. Some populations are there because of

man; some are there despite man and his activities.

The most obvious man-altered, man-dominated community is the city. The sociologist views the city as a human community in which people perform specialized tasks—dispensing of goods and services, and governing. From the biologist's point of view, human activity is but one level of organization—the social organization of one kind of animal population which dominates other populations in the community. The city community also includes organisms deliberately introduced by man such as plants used in landscaping and pets. Roaches, rats, sparrows, and weeds too are part of the city community.

When we view an urban area as a man-dominated biotic community, we see many organisms in a new light. Most city plants are introduced into the area by man—sometimes accidentally. The most obvious plants in a city are trees which may have been selected because they offer the best combination of hardiness and shade. Often

SOURCE. Reprinted, by permission, from Chapter 17 of *SCIS Teacher's Guide* (preliminary edition) for "Populations" unit, 1970, published by the Science Curriculum Improvement Study, University of California at Berkeley, with slight abridgment.

these trees must be capable of surviving with little water because so much of the area around them is paved. Trees provide food and shelter for many kinds of animals. Insects eat the leaves or burrow into the bark. Birds feed on the insects, and both birds and squirrels eat the fruits. Parks, dwellings, and commercial buildings are landscaped with a wide variety of vegetation, which harbors many kinds of insects. The soil beneath shrubs, lawns, and along walls is often well populated with animals such as insects, worms, and sow bugs.

One interesting aspect of the man-dominated community is the large variety of uninvited populations which find an easier life near human activity. Some biologists refer to these populations as "camp followers." If organisms compete with man for food and shelter, or if they threaten man's health, they are considered harmful and are called pests. Rats, mice, roaches, and flies are among these unwelcome followers. They populate areas where food is stored, prepared, or served, and where garbage is dumped. Man's buildings and trash heaps provide many places where animals can dwell. Other "camp followers" are tolerated by man. House sparrows, pigeons, and squirrels thrive because, like the pests, they are able to eat the variety of foods and nest in the places that exist because of man's presence.

Weeds are the plant kingdom's representatives among the camp followers. A weed is defined as any plant which grows where a person does not want it to grow. The word *weed,* therefore, is a general term which describes man's attitude of rejection or indifference toward certain kinds of plants. But weeds are interesting organisms. Some kinds withstand mowing and thrive in lawns. Some have long tap roots and survive in the dry, hard soils of footpaths or in cracks in pavements. Although these hardy plants may be considered pests in some places, they provide the base of a food web in what otherwise might be a lifeless place.

The object of this chapter is to help children understand that man is an integral part of the biotic community and that towns and cities are man-dominated communities. Man influences the environment in areas where he is dominant, just as beech and maple trees influence the environment in forests where they are dominant. The ultimate goal is to help children recognize man's influence on the biotic community by finding out what other populations life there, what they eat, and the extent to which their food relationships affect and are affected by man.

TEACHING SUGGESTIONS

Ask the children to list the kinds of plants and animals they have seen outdoors around school and home. The children's list of animals may include:

people	butterflies
cats	rabbits
dogs	caterpillars
squirrels	roaches
rats	flies
mice	mosquitoes
horses	aphids
sparrows	crickets
pigeons	ants
moths	earthworms
spiders	

Listing plants may be difficult if the children try to identify each kind of plant. The task might be simpler if children list major forms (trees, shrubs, and flowers) and indicate how many kinds of each form they saw.

Introduce the term *man-dominated community* as an extension of the idea of community introduced in Chapter 16. Emphasize that a man-dominated community includes populations of many animals and plants, as shown in the children's own list.

The children's main tasks in the following activities are to find out through observation what each kind of animal eats, to construct food chains and webs, and to determine the extent of human influence on these chains and webs.

Gathering information. Trips outside the classroom may be taken and organized in ways similar to those suggested in Chapter 16. Much observation can be done by children on their way to and from school, around their homes, and in vacant lots and parks where they play. Some questions which can serve to guide their explorations are:

Where are the animals? (under rocks, in trees, etc.)

What do they eat?

Where do they find water to drink?

Which of the foods are deliberately supplied by people? (dog food, for example)

Which foods are accidentally supplied by man? (What happens to an ice cream cone dropped on the sidewalk?)

Which trees and shrubs bear fruit? What animals feed on the fruit?

Which of the plants are deliberately introduced by people? Which are not?

If a child does not know the name of a plant or animal, he may draw a picture or simply describe it.

Using the information. Help the children construct a food web on the chalkboard based on the data they have collected. Ask the children to name organisms they have seen and what these organisms eat. When you have listed all the children's suggestions, ask questions such as the following:

1. What food is in the web as a result of man's activity?

2. Which of these foods are plant products or are traceable to plants?

Draw lines through all food supplied by man.

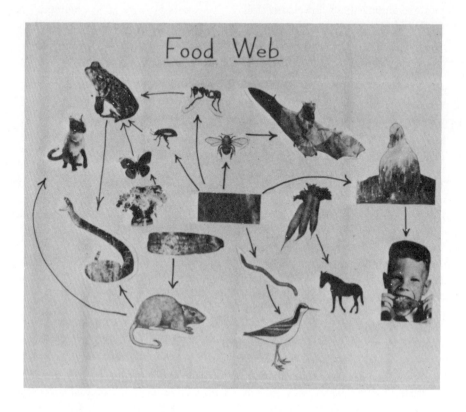

Food Web

1. Which animals are left without a food source?
2. If these animals disappear, which other animals (predators) will be without a food source?

The children might enjoy making a permanent record of this food web with drawings or pictures cut from magazines.

CONSTRUCTING TERRARIA

SYNOPSIS

Each team of three children builds a terrarium in which they plant wheat, radish, bean, clover, and grass seeds. The children speculate about what will happen to the plants when crickets, isopods, mealworms, and frogs are added. While most children have had some experience with animals eating plants, and animals eating other animals, they have little knowledge of the total dependence of animals upon plants for food. This chapter sets the stage for the study of the food transfer between plants and animals later in the unit.

TEACHING MATERIALS

For each child:
  2 bean seeds
  2 lima bean seeds
  2 sunflower seeds
For each team of three children:
  1 terrarium container
  6 bean seeds
  50 clover seeds
  50 grass seeds

  10 radish seeds
  20 wheat seeds
  1 medicine dropper
  1 water sprinkler
For the class:
  3 1-gallon plastic containers filled with soil
  3 paper trays
  3 scoops
  15 3-ounce plastic cups
  masking tape (provided by teacher)

PREPARATION

Provide at least three distribution centers for seeds, soil, and containers for terraria. Each distribution center should have a plastic cup containing each kind of seed. Using masking tape, label the seed containers. Fill three one-gallon plastic containers with soil and place a soil scoop at each soil distribution station. The paper trays may be used under the soil containers to catch spilled soil. On the chalkboard, list the number and kinds of seeds that each team should obtain: 6 bean, 50

SOURCE. Reprinted, by permission, from Chapter 1 of *SCIS Teacher's Guide* (trial edition) for "Communities" unit, 1970, published by the Science Curriculum Improvement Study, University of California at Berkeley, with slight abridgment.

clover, 50 grass, 10 radish, 20 wheat. Select a place near a light source for the children to store the terraria.

The other bean seeds, lima bean seeds, and sunflower seeds should be placed at a separate distribution station for use at the end of this chapter.

TEACHING SUGGESTIONS

Explain to the children that they will be growing plants from seed. Later they will add animals to the container of plants and investigate how the organisms live together. Tell them that this container is called a terrarium: an artificial place for land plants and animals to live.

Building terraria. Using one of the plastic containers, each team should add soil until the level is about 40 mm high. The seeds for each team can be planted in any order within the container. The children can use masking tape to label the terraria with their names, the number and kinds of seeds they planted, and the date. While one child is preparing the label, another should use the sprinkler to water the soil until it is quite moist. Have the children store their terraria in the location you have selected. Plan a schedule for watering and observing the plants three times a week.

On succeeding days the soil should be kept moist, but not so wet that the container is flooded. To test a terrarium for excess water, raise one corner of the container. If water forms a puddle in the opposite corner, show the children how to use a medicine dropper to draw up the water and discard it.

Discussion. Tell the children that crickets, isopods, mealworms, and frogs will be added to the terraria after the plants are growing. Ask them what they think will happen when the crickets are put into the containers. Follow this with the same questions about the isopods, the mealworms, and the frog. Questions such as these are designed to get the children thinking about the relationship between plants and animals.

Seed-soaking. After the children have planted their terraria and discussed the future addition of other organisms, make the bean, lima bean and sunflower seeds available to each child. Tell the children that because these seeds are larger than most of the ones they planted, they will be able to open and examine them. Give the children a moment to try opening the seeds. It will be very difficult, if not impossible, for them to open these dry seeds. Ask them what is making it difficult and how they could make the seeds easier to open. If the children suggest cooking the seeds, soaking in vinegar or salt water, or other methods of softening, let them try these techniques on a few seeds. Plan to dissect the remaining seeds after they have been soaked in water for about 24 hours.

OPTIONAL ACTIVITIES

Planting depth. Children in your class may disagree about how deep seeds should be planted. Some children will bury their seeds under several inches of soil, while others may barely cover them. Interested children can plant seeds at different depths in the soil near the inside edge of the plastic cups and observe any differences in germination.

Seed emergence. Children are curious about what kinds of seeds will emerge first. Some think large seeds are faster growing than small seeds. They can test different sizes of seeds, colors of seeds, or shapes of seeds to determine if there is any way to know which of several seed types will emerge first. They should keep a record of the date and approximate time of emergence of each seed.

Germination success. Children frequently believe that all seeds planted will germinate. This is usually not the case—seed growers are pleased if most of their seeds germinate. The children can test the percent germination of grass, clover or kidney beans from the grocery. At least 20 seeds should be

EDUCATIONAL IMPLICATIONS

planted (100 would be better and easier to calculate the percentage) to get enough data. Divide the number of plants emerging from the ground by the number of seeds planted and multiply by 100 to get the percent germinated.

THERMAL ENERGY AS A POLLUTANT

The children expose Daphnia in algae water to various temperatures and observe the effect of high temperature on organisms. On the basis of this experience, you introduce thermal energy as a pollutant and, thus, the idea that energy, as well as substances, can pollute the ecosystem.

TEACHING MATERIALS

For each child:
  Student manual pages 24 and 25 (Editor's Note: pages 24 and 25 are reproduced in the next article, pages 423 and 424.)
For each team of three children:
  2 14-dram vials
  1 medicine dropper
  4 Daphnia
  1 thermometer
For the class:
  algae culture
  5 light sources
  vial holders

TEACHING SUGGESTIONS

Review the effects of excess carbon dioxide on fish, the pollution of the snails' water by bacteria, and the effects of prolonged air pollution on organisms. Tell the students that in each instance the pollutant was a substance they could see, smell, or identify with bromothymol blue. Tell them that now they will be testing the effects of energy on the ecosystem.

The problem. Student manual page 24. Ask the children to read page 24, which presents the problem of thermal energy as a pollutant. After they have had time to read the page, encourage them to discuss how they could determine if warm water could be a pollutant for Daphnia.

The experiment. Tell the children that Daphnia, vials, thermometers, light sources, and medicine droppers are available. If the children do not suggest it, tell them they may use the medicine dropper to place two Daphnia in a vial half-full of algae

SOURCE. Reprinted, by permission, from Chapter 21 of *Teacher's Guide* (trial edition) for "Ecosystems" unit, 1970, published by Science Curriculum Improvement Study, University of California at Berkeley, with slight abridgment.

culture at room temperature. The children can slowly increase the temperature of the water in the vials by placing them close to the light sources. Each team should also prepare a control vial of Daphnia and algae culture which is kept at room temperature. Have the children record their experimental designs at the bottom of page 24.

After the children have completed their experiments, have a class discussion so teams can share their results.

Invention of thermal energy as a pollutant.

Student manual page 25. Tell the children that an increased temperature beyond that which is best for organisms may be considered a pollutant. The children may work on page 25 in their manual, where the effect of thermal energy on a food chain is considered. You might prefer to use page 25 for feedback, with the questions on that page serving as a basis for class discussion.

Cleanup. Return the Daphnia to the classroom aquarium and have the children clean the vials.

WARM WATER IN THE RIVER

An atomic power plant on a river uses water from the river to cool the atomic reactions. No chemicals or radiation are added to the water as it goes through the plant, but it is 20°F hotter when it comes out.

Many organisms live in the river near the plant. One of these is Daphnia, the main food supply for small fish. Is this water a pollutant for Daphnia and fish?

Draw or describe an experiment to find out if warm water is a pollutant for Daphnia.

SOURCE.   Reprinted, by permission, from Chapter 22, *SCIS Student Manual* (trial edition) for "Ecosystems" unit, published by Science Curriculum Improvement Study, University of California at Berkeley, with slight abridgment.

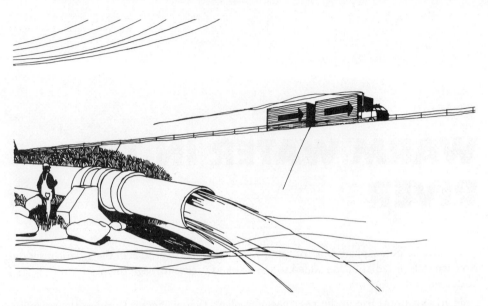

As a result of your experiment with Daphnia and algae in warm water, would you say that warm water from the atomic energy plant could be called a pollutant? What is your evidence?

_____

_____

_____

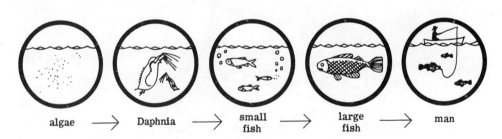

algae   →   Daphnia   →   small fish   →   large fish   →   man

If the Daphnia or the algae were killed by the warm water, how would this affect the other organisms in the food chain?

_____

_____

_____

MOVEMENT OF POLLUTANTS

The children investigate the movement of fertilizer through soil and water, and infer that substances or energy generated in one area can become pollutants in another.

BACKGROUND INFORMATION

The movement of pollutants through soil, water, and air affects the operation of the ecosystem. Pesticides that are sprayed on certain crops may get washed into waterways where they upset the food webs by killing organisms in a food chain. Smoke produced in one place is blown or moves elsewhere and is rained out of the air onto the soil.

TEACHING MATERIALS

For each child:
  Student manual pages 26 and 27 (Editor's Note: pages 26 and 27 are reproduced in the next article, pages 428 and 429.)
For each team of three children:

6 7-dram vials
1 vial holder
4 drinking straws
1 small cork stopper
1 rectangular plastic container (fluted)
1 rectangular label
1 sheet of white paper*
For the class:
  squeeze bottles of concentrated BTB
  1 pitcher
  1 plastic thimble
  soil
  fertilizer pellets
  1 baster
  cardboard trays
*provided by the teacher

ADVANCE PREPARATION

Prepare some BTB solution by filling the pitcher with tap water. Add one thimbleful of BTB to the water and stir. If the resulting color is green or yellow, use spring or distilled water. (The addition of baking soda to tap water will alter the results of the experiment.)

SOURCE. Reprinted, by permission, from Chapter 22 of *SCIS Teacher's Guide* (trial edition) for "Ecosystems" 1970, published by the Science Curriculum Improvement Study, University of California, Berkeley, with slight abridgement.

TEACHING SUGGESTIONS

The children will probably be familiar with fertilizers and how they improve the growth of plants. If all the children are not familiar with fertilizer, you might let some of them explain its function, or encourage them to fertilize some plants growing in the classroom and observe the results.

Ask the children what they think happens to fertilizer that is placed on the soil around plants or fertilizer which is washed into ponds. They may suggest that it sinks into the ground, sits on the top, dissolves, is used by plants, etc. After they have suggested several possibilities, show them a test for fertilizer presence. Using the baster fill two vials one-quarter full of BTB solution. Then drop a fertilizer pellet into one vial and stir each vial with a different straw. The water in the vial with the fertilizer will turn yellow. (This is a reaction of the BTB with the acid formed by the fertilizer and the water.)

Setting up the experiment. Tell the children they can experiment to find out if fertilizer spreads through soil by placing fertilizer pellets in the soil at one end of a container and later testing the soil at various intervals.

Each team should fill the plastic container with soil to a depth of one-half to three-quarters of an inch. The soil should be well-moistened, but there should not be water sitting on the surface. About fifty fertilizer pellets should be placed along one end and covered with a little soil. The children should label the systems with their names, placing the label at the end where they placed the fertilizer pellets.

After preparing the systems, have the children put the containers away for two days, and proceed to "Movement of fertilizer through water."

Movement of fertilizer through water. Ask the children if they think fertilizer would move through still water, such as that in a quiet pond. If they think it will

you may wish to skip this experiment. If they would like to find out, you will probably have to show them the following technique. Place the cork stopper in one end of a clean straw and secure it by giving it a slight twist. Then, using a medicine dropper, fill the straw with BTB solution. Place the straw on a sheet of white paper. Have the children obtain the materials they need. Tell them they can place a fertilizer pellet in the end of the straw so it just touches the BTB solution. By observing this system for a few minutes, they will see the BTB solution gradually change from blue to yellow along the length of the straw. They may wish to let the systems stand overnight.

Testing the soil. During the next science period, the children can examine the soil-fertilizer systems to see whether the fertilizer has moved through the soil. Each team will need a vial holder, six vials, two straws, and BTB solution. If they sample the soil at one-inch intervals in a line from one end of the soil container to the other, they will be able to compare any changes in color from soil which didn't get much fertilizer to soil that is saturated with fertilizer.

Each team should fill each vial one-quarter full with BTB solution. They should place the vials in a vial holder next to the soil-fertilizer system. Then as they test each soil plug, they can dip the straw into the vial opposite the location from which the soil sample was taken.

They should remove a small plug of soil from the classroom supply of soil (without fertilizer) for use as a control. A straw works well if it is pressed straight into the soil with a slight twist. Then the children should dip the end of the straw containing the plug into one of the vials, stirring it in the liquid so all the soil falls into the water. This sample should be labeled control and will show the color they can expect when no fertilizer is present.

426

The remaining five vials may be used to test soil samples taken from different places in the children's soil-fertilizer systems, so the children can find out how far the fertilizer has moved from where it was first placed. The characteristic yellow will appear in the vials if the fertilizer has reached the point from where the sample was taken.

Discussion. After the children have completed their observations, encourage a discussion of the movement of fertilizer in their experiments. Ask questions similar to the following:

Does fertilizer move through soil?

Does fertilizer move through still water?

If a field near a river were fertilized, what might happen to the fertilizer?

Remind the children that fertilizer is used to help plant crops grow. Tell them that if fertilizer gets into streams, it also helps the water plants grow, but kills some of the small animals. Thus, fertilizer is good for plants, but is a pollutant for many animals.

Now you might direct the children's attention to the movement of other pollutants in the ecosystem. Remember that these children have had a very limited exposure to pollution of the ecosystem in this unit, but encourage them to make educated guesses about the benefits and drawbacks of movement of pollutants. You might ask questions such as the following:

What happened to the smoke in the air a day after you smoked the terraria? Where do you suppose it went?

What might happen to the smog over cities if it is blown away?

A pesticide (chemical which kills pests) is sprayed on a crop of pea plants to kill the insects that eat peas so that there will be more peas left for humans, who also eat them. What effects might this have on the ecosystem?

The children may wish to discuss other examples of pollution that they are aware of such as sewage pumped into streams and oceans, and oil leakage from wells on land and in water.

Student manual pages 26 and 27. Pages 26 and 27 may be used as feedback about the children's understanding of pollution in an ecosystem. Use these pages for class discussion or independent work by the children.

Cleanup. The soil should be discarded. The equipment should be soaked and cleaned to remove all traces of fertilizer which may contaminate future experiments.

UTOPIA, U.S.A.

A group of people, who wanted to set up a perfect ecosystem, built a large, clear dome over their habitat. They wanted their system to be completely separate from the rest of the world. No organisms or other materials would be taken in or out of the ecosystem. They planned to grow their own food and live their lives as they had before.

What problems should they be aware of? Are there any problems that you don't think they can solve at all?

_____

_____

_____

_____

_____

_____

_____

_____

_____

_____

_____

_____

_____

SOURCE. Reprinted, by permission, from the *SCIS Student Manual* (trial edition) for "Ecosystems" unit, 1970, published by the Science Curriculum Improvement Study, University of California at Berkeley, with slight abridgment.

Elizabeth B. Hone
Alexander Joseph
Edward Victor

AN AQUARIUM COMMUNITY

It is usually not practical to build a home-made aquarium that will remain watertight. If the school cannot purchase an aquarium, set up several in wide-mouthed gallon pickle jars. One pair of fish needs at least a gallon of water. If possible, a 4-5 gallon tank is recommended. In the long run, good tanks usually cost less than cheap ones. The first step is to wash the tank with soap and warm water. Do not use hot water because it may loosen the aquarium cement. Rinse several times in cold water, fill two thirds full, and let stand for several days. Secure coarse sand (not beach sand) or gravel and wash in boiling water. You will also need some stones to hold down the sand and plants. Wash the stones in boiling water. As an additional precaution you may want to bake the sand and rocks to insure sterility. Get a half dozen pieces of water plants from the variety store or pet shop. The salesman or store owner usually is most helpful with regard to selecting appropriate plant and animal life and giving suggestions for planting and care.

While some children work on problems of securing and setting up an aquarium, others can participate in solving problems of aquarium housekeeping. The best way to fill or empty a tank without unduly disturbing the plants is to use a siphon. Let children *play* at siphoning long before they need to put it to use in the aquarium. Begin with drinking straws. Let children use some as dip tubes by closing the top end with a finger. The differential in air pressure, of course, allows the children to pick up a few drops of water just as a scientist uses a glass pipette in the laboratory. If possible, secure some 18" lengths of plastic or rubber tubing of ½-¾" diameter. These will be useful for daily removal of debris from the tank. Let the children

SOURCE. Reprinted, by permission, from *Teaching Elementary Science: A Sourcebook for Elementary Science,* by Hone, Joseph, and Victor, copyright 1962 by Harcourt Brace & Jovanovich, Inc., with slight abridgment.

practice using a tube to remove loose dirt from the bottom of a jar. Now let the children use rubber tubing to remove debris. Let them try different ways. Some may know the principle of siphoning liquids. They can fill the tube in the way already described or by immersion. Once a tube is filled, the ends are pinched while it is transferred into position to work as a siphon.

Adding water to replace that evaporated from the tank can be accomplished by pouring over a plate without scaring the fish or dislodging plants. Encourage the children to think of ways they can measure the amount of water which has evaporated. They will also think of ways to cut down the evaporation (i.e., by using glass or cellophane cover). How can fish have enough air even if tank is covered? The answer is that the plants produce oxygen.

A fish tank can illustrate one of the major conceptual schemes for the elementary school—namely, that under ordinary conditions matter may be changed but not destroyed. The carbon dioxide which all living creatures produce is put to use by the aquarium plants to make their food (sugar) in the presence of sunlight. We call this plant manufacturing process *photosynthesis.* Let the children discuss this word and its associations, *photography, synthetic,* etc., according to their level of understanding. Some may enjoy following the schematic symbols (chemical formula) for the process. (The power source is light energy.)

raw materials

$6CO_2$ (carbon dioxide *from* the fish)
$+6H_2O$ (water)

finished product

$C_6H_{12}O_6$ (glucose——sugar)
$+6O_2$ (oxygen to be used *by* the fish, snails, etc.)

Setting up an aquarium involves filling the tank 24-48 hours ahead of planting in order to bring it to room temperature. Let the children note and record water temperature as it comes from the tap. Compare with room temperature. Upper-grade children may record and graph the rate at which the tank water warms up.

Tank water is also drawn several days ahead of time in order to allow chlorine to escape from it. Store some in gallon jugs for future use. Using household bleach, the children may wish to experiment with the effect of varying amounts of chlorine on different organisms. They will find upon investigation that their municipal water department usually uses minute amounts of chlorine for water purification. Let the children experiment with a medicine dropper and several jars or tumblers of the same size to find the effect of different strength solutions on living things. Use similar sized samples of algae or other abundant small water plants.

Most children know that one should handle fish as little as possible, and when handling is necessary, one should moisten hands before touching. A small cloth dip net purchased at the dime store will facilitate any handling. Usually the fish can be "poured" into the tank from a container.

What can you learn from watching a goldfish? How a fish swims, of course, but more—how an organism adapts to its environment. Let the children tell you from observation about the way their goldfish moves, the number and location of fins. Which fin does what? Does your goldfish rest on the bottom or near the surface? Can it stay still without moving a fin? Does it tend to float? If so, why? Illustrate the action of a fish's air bladder with a small capped bottle or corked vial in which there is some trapped air. Vary the amount of trapped air to show how a fish can balance its buoyancy.

One of the observations your children should make is of gill movement. The fish appears to be continually opening and closing its mouth. If you can secure at the market a whole fish so children can examine the gills, they will see that the bright red color is due to the thin skin which permits the blood to come close to the surface. Oxygen in the water continually passing over the gills is taken up by the blood and carried to all parts of the fish's body. At the same time carbon dioxide is returned to the water. Here is an opportunity for discussion to help the children learn about their own respiratory system by contrast and counterpoint.

To be sure that children know there is air in water, draw some tap water and let stand in glass containers. In a relatively short time, depending on the difference between room and water temperature, they should begin to see air bubbles on the sides of the glasses.

Further, heat some water until most of the air is driven out. Then let it stand until cool. Draw a similar sized container of fresh water. All the containers and the aquarium should be within 2-3" of each other in temperature. Place a goldfish in each jar; watch carefully. Soon the fish in the water which was heated (and then cooled) will come to the top. Here at the top the water will have taken up more oxygen from the air and the fish will be better able to "breathe." (Watch that the fish in the airless water does not suffocate.) You may be able to help the children make the analogy to problems of air and space travel caused by the very narrow range of environments in which man can secure the oxygen he must have to live.

The next step may be to place some sprigs of a water plant such as elodea or anacharis in a container of water on a sunny window sill. Soon the children should see bubbles forming at the top of each leaf. Green plants give off oxygen when the sun's energy starts their food factories. An aquarium needs plants not only for their esthetic but also for their functional value. They supply oxygen to the animal life in the tank. This oxygen may be supplemented by that absorbed at the surface. This is why a widemouthed container or rectangular tank is desirable.

Using the aquarium as an example, you may wish to lead the children toward an understanding of the fact that plants and animals need each other—interdependence—and that there must be a proper amount of each in a successful community—balance.

Elizabeth B. Hone

Alexander Joseph

Edward Victor

A TERRARIUM COMMUNITY

A moist woodland terrarium provides a comfortable habitat for small snakes, frogs, toads, toy turtles, and salamanders or newts. Large specimens will disarrange and tramp down the miniature landscape in your terrarium. If your children ask, "What is a terrarium?," you can show them that it is a container for land-dwelling plant and animal life, just as an aquarium is for water life. A terrarium may be set up in a gallon pickle jar (widemouthed), a leaky aquarium, or a glass box especially constructed for the purpose. A glass globe tends to distort the interior view, and holds very little as well.

DESERT OR MARSH TERRARIUM

The children may also wish to construct a desert terrarium and a marsh terrarium. The techniques are much the same, except that for your desert you will select miniature cactuses and other thick-leaved plants which are planted in sand or sandy loam and seldom watered to prevent their growing too large for the container. In this case, do not cover the mouth of the jar except with screening to keep in desert visitors such as a horned toad or lizard. Botanical gardens sell miniature desert plants that can survive even on a radiator.

The marsh terrarium should contain such typical wet-foot plants as sphagnum, sedges, pitcher plants, and the like. You will need a watertight container if you build on an incline with a space for water at the end for your amphibian guests.

MAKING A PICKLE-JAR TERRARIUM

The pickle jar, though soon too small for many plants, makes a sturdy terrarium.

SOURCE. Reprinted, by permission, from *Teaching Elementary Science: A Sourcebook for Elementary Science,* by Hone, Joseph, and Victor, copyright 1962 by Harcourt Brace & Jovanovich, Inc., with slight abridgment.

It will need a simple wooden or cardboard box cradle or plaster of Paris base to keep it from rolling. If you have access to a woodland, look for small, compact, shade-loving plants such as moss, ferns, wintergreen, and liverworts. Dig them up with an old knife or trowel in order to get some soil with them. Take no more than one from each group of plants. Leave some to spread and eventually hide your "robbery." In your backyard there may be tiny ferns, baby tears, wandering Jew, or other shade lovers. Of course, the local florist or dime store will have an assortment of small plants in pots. Miniature ivy and the philodendrons are the safest investment. Buy only the smallest pots.

Having collected plants for your terrarium, you will need a small amount of woodland soil or leaf mold, some sand for drainage, and a few pieces of charcoal to go in the bottom. Beginners tend to use too much soil, making the terrarium too heavy and leaving too little room for plants. Use only enough to imbed your plants and cover their roots. The soil should be moistened before being spread in your container. In larger containers, contour the soil into a miniature hill. To save weight, use an aluminum foil pie plate to form a hollow core for the hill.

If you have bought potted plants, remove from pots by inverting with two fingers around stem of plant. Tap rim of pot to loosen soil and plant should slide out. If necessary push from bottom through drainage hole. Handle carefully to keep soil as intact as possible around roots. Set plants around on top of the soil to secure the best arrangement. If you use moss, plant some with the green side out. Meanwhile imbed a container for water, level with the soil base. A glass custard cup is about the right size lake for your miniature landscape. Now you are ready to set in the plants, covering roots completely and firming in place. Remove any bruised or broken leaves, trimming off with scissors to make a clean cut. Wipe the inside of the glass clean with paper toweling. Wet down with a sprinkler and close jar mouth with Saran Wrap or other transparent pliofilm. Discard the metal cover. It will rust and is not transparent.

After its initial "baptism" a terrarium should never have to be watered. Moisture evaporating from the plants and the water dish will condense on the glass inside and precipitate, a perfect example of the water cycle which takes place in nature. The first day or two, the terrarium will be so foggy or dewy one can scarcely see inside. Remove the cover and wipe the inside of the glass with paper toweling. Repeat when necessary, especially the "window washing." In proportion as you remove moisture, you may need to refill the water dish at long intervals. Be sure to remove moldy plants and to keep the glass clean. Succulents such as the sedums, ice plant, and the like will mold in a moist woodland terrarium. Use them in a desert terrarium for contrasting environments.

SECTION 10

EXPERIMENTS FOR SECONDARY SCHOOL STUDENTS

This section includes activities and experiments for secondary school students. The first activities provide an introduction to ecology. This introduction is by no means definitive, but should be helpful to most teachers.

Secondly, there is a series of experiments on air pollution. Specialized equipment can be obtained from local industries or via direct purchase from suggested commercial firms. You may have to "sell" your school administrator on the virtues of the items you wish to order.

Thirdly, water pollution experiments are less demanding, equipment-wise. You will enjoy doing these investigations with your students. One of the experiments, on bacterial pollution, requires a kit called The Environmental Microbiology Kit (Millipore), but it is well worth purchasing.

10A. Introduction to Ecology

C. A. Lawson
R. E. Paulson

FIELD ECOLOGY FOR THE TEACHER

INTRODUCTION

The purpose of this group of studies is to give the high school student a valuable field experience in ecology with a minimal use of apparatus. Seven field investigations are included in the unit. An attempt has been made to present them in such a manner as to allow flexibility in their use. A teacher may choose any one, any combination, or all of the parts, depending on local conditions. In addition, any part of any exercise can be modified by deletion or expansion.

In these studies, success will depend largely on the degree to which students learn to observe their natural surroundings. They should be stimulated to see the variations in different communities, search for examples of possible relationships between one species of animal and another, between plants and animals, between plant species, and between living things and their physical environment.

In addition to learning existing relationships, students should also be guided to observe seasonal changes. The teacher should further endeavor to stress any examples of succession found.

One of the most important concepts in ecology is that biotic communities are not stable, that there are continual changes in the kinds of plants and animals which occupy a given space. The series of communities which successively occupy an area is determined by the *total* habitat, which in turn is an integration of the physical factors such as light, water, and temperature, and of the biotic factors such as the superior competitive ability (called dominance) of some organism, the direct effects of one organism upon another through toxic secretions and disease, and many others. The series of replacements of one community by another at a given place is called a *succession*. There are two main types: *primary*, or succession develop-

SOURCE. Reprinted, by permission of the publisher, from Lawson, C.A. and Paulson, R.E., *Laboratory and Field Studies in Biology*, New York: Holt, Rinehart, and Winston, 1960.

ing in an area previously unoccupied by organisms; and *secondary,* or succession developing after an area has been denuded of existing organisms. Natural causes usually initiate primary succession; secondary types most often result from activities of man. Generally, the succession is determined by the sequence of *plant* communities, with animals playing a secondary role because of their dependence upon plants.

The succession is pictured as a series of recognizable steps, beginning with the *pioneer* stage and ending with the *climax* stage. In the climax stage, the biotic community tends to be stabilized with the rate of change at a minimum. The replacement of communities is relatively slow in the early stages and in those approaching the climax, and more rapid in the intermediate stages. But in the absence of a major change in climate, the entire succession is directionally and chronologically predetermined and the final climax community is predictable. In terms of time, the sequence of communities is toward those organisms which are best able to utilize all available necessary factors of the existing habitat. In terms of space, the community occupies or moves toward those areas whose physical factors exemplify or are being modified in the direction of the regional climate. Ideally, the organisms of the climax community will be essentially the same wherever the climate is essentially the same, but actually local factors such as soil and topography will modify the climax.

When an area is first exposed to colonization in primary succession, it generally is a very wet or a very dry habitat. Consequently, only a few organisms are able to invade. But as these pioneer organisms multiply, they modify the habitat in the direction of less wet or less dry conditions, for instance, by soil-building processes in water or on rock. In so doing, they make the area habitable by other organisms which previously were unable to survive the rigorous conditions. These organisms often are better competitors, i.e., are dom-

inant, under the improved conditions and replace the pioneers. As the new group of organisms in turn improves the habitat in the direction of more *mesic* (i.e., less wet or less dry) conditions, it creates a habitat which makes possible the entrance of new dominant species which in turn supplant the old. This process is repeated for the recognizable communities in each stage of the succession, and the final climax community will be essentially the same whether the succession started in a dry area (rock) or a wet area (pond). Secondary successions follow generally the same pattern as primary successions, but are usually shorter because typically the early (soil-building) stages are not necessary.

If you are fortunate enough to have a pond in your vicinity, look for the classical example of plant succession which might exist there. This might be something like the following: In the pond itself there would be such forms as algae and submerged plants, while along the banks would be found the partially submerged or intermediate plants, the sedges and rushes. The bank might contain low shrubs in contrast to the alders and willows farther back. The woods beyond would be typical of the area under observation, either hardwoods or evergreens.

At this point the teacher should make an effort to clarify to the student what he has seen in relationship to time. Walking through the sequence of communities from the pond back toward the woods should give the student an impression of what will happen to the area now containing the pond as it fills. Ponds are continually filling and becoming more shallow as materials growing in the water die and decay and as other materials wash or are blown in. As filling continues, the pond will eventually become an area describable as intermediate between aquatic and terrestrial, and the plants at this stage will include such species as cattail and bulrush. Later, as the pond dries completely, it may appear as an area of mixed grasses. Further succession will produce a shrub habitat, which, in its turn, will eventually give way to a woods, and finally the climax typical for the climate of the area will develop.

Thus, as students walk from the pond to the adjacent woodland, they should see the pond in terms of time, as though they were walking through time rather than through space and were watching each stage supplant the predecessor which produced it.

These field studies should be carried on in the late spring or early fall in areas where winter temperatures limit plant and animal populations and activities. Although it is instructive to study communities at all seasons, students will get a better general introduction to ecology if optimal periods are chosen.

Thorough and intensive field work requires concentration upon small, clearly limited samples of a habitat. Square plots called quadrats or strips called transects are commonly used for this purpose. If the area to be studied encompasses a variety of environments (e.g., aquatic site, marsh, field, and wood) a transect will be more instructive than a quadrat. If a single environment is being studied (e.g., forest or marsh or prairie), the quadrat is more useful. For an area of herbaceous plants or a prairie quadrats one meter square are appropriate. Quadrats five meters square are preferable for a shrub habitat, and for a woodland quadrats ten meters by ten meters.

Field work is greatly curtailed in many schools because of location, time, and other factors. In such cases teachers are urged to make use of the school grounds or to bring the out-of-doors into the laboratory. For example, many factors involved in the ecology of lakes find expression also in a large balanced aquarium. Indeed, the laboratory approach has certain advantages because it is easier to define conditions and establish experimental controls.

Before each field trip, appropriate time should be spent in the classroom acquainting students with the tools and equipment to be used in the field. Problems such as transportation, what to wear, the responsibilities of each student or group of students, instructions on field note-taking, and instructions on how to organize and write reports must all be discussed before leaving the classroom.

An analysis of the population of plants and animals in a given quadrat or transect gives students and teachers an excellent opportunity for developing original tools or techniques. Plants may be collected in the conventional manner, labeled and pressed. Much of the classification of specimens, if the teacher feels it is desirable, can be done in the field. Quantitative studies or counts of plants can be made in the field.

Counting animals is more difficult because of their ability to move about. The kinds and relative numbers of such small mammals as shrews and mice can be determined by trapping, using ordinary spring-type mouse traps or tall cans supplied with meat bait and left overnight buried to ground level. The number of hares or squirrels may be estimated from a counting drive through an area. Tracks, droppings, animals killed on highways, and other signs can be used as clues to kinds and relative numbers of larger mammals.

Given time, care, and some skill in field identification, birds, reptiles, and amphibians in an area can be counted or estimated fairly readily. Fish may be seen but cannot well be counted without seining, for which special legal authority is needed.

Populations of insects and other invertebrates can be sampled in several ways. A canvas or plastic tablecloth spread under a tree or shrub will catch specimens when the plant is shaken vigorously. A bait can left overnight is useful. Soil inhabitants may be captured by sifting the soil through a fine screen. Sweep nets, dip nets, or bottom samplers can also be used.

The Berlese funnel is another useful implement for collecting soil organisms. Berlese funnels can be purchased from supply houses but an adequate apparatus could be made by a student. It consists of a container, in which soil or leaf litter is placed; below it, a sieve; below the sieve a funnel with a wide neck; and below the funnel a collecting jar. After material is placed in the top container it is heated with a light bulb; the heat stimulates soil organisms to go down through the sieve into the collecting jar.

Collecting data on significant environmental factors is important. Here again teachers and students can develop tools and techniques. Temperature variations found by taking temperatures at varied sites and times may be revealing. Temperatures a few inches below the ground surface, on the surface, 1 foot above, and 6 feet above are suggested. Air moisture can be measured as relative humidity with a psychrometer. An imaginative student can devise an instrument to measure wind velocity. Chemical analysis of soil is complex and may be limited to reading pH with reagent papers. In aquatic environments, pH, free oxygen, and carbon dioxide are important and can be tested by good students with an interest in chemistry.

Since average classes have an hour or less in the field and students should collect a variety of data, students should work in teams, preferably in accord with their interests. A quadrat may thus be studied by insect, small mammal, herb, shrub, tree, and environment teams. On return to the classroom teams should pool information to provide a concise, meaningful ecological picture of the area studied. It is desirable to make several trips to each habitat, particularly to see seasonal variations.

USING THIS EXERCISE

Part A. The Lake or Pond Habitat

Students are divided into teams of four to six. Several teams will study the environmental factors of the area while the others, referred to as the *quadrat teams,* will gather living organisms from an assigned location.

Suggested materials include: dip net, plankton net, screen sieve, alcohol, a good supply of collecting jars and bottles, minnow pail, rubber boots, boat or collapsible life raft, thermometer, clip boards and note paper, chemicals and equipment for tests of pH, carbon dioxide, and free oxygen concentration. Be sure that some student in each team is responsible for the equipment taken into the field. Light is also an important factor but it is difficult to measure. Directions are given in Welch's *Limnological Methods* (see *Background Reading*). Light measurement is not suggested as general practice but may be done if you have the necessary equipment and interested students.

The teacher should make every effort to devise means for encouraging students to derive basic concepts from their field work. Students should come to realize that one living thing depends upon another for its existence and that there are environmental factors in play upon the organism which in part dictate the places in which the organism can live. The teacher should guide the discussion in such a manner as to allow the students to discover that some organisms collected in the field have habitats they fit into better than others. The class should also be led to attempt an analysis of the environmental factors which limit the distribution of specific organisms.

A discussion of the food habits of the organisms found will be necessary as background information for the construction of a food chain.

Further information on lake or pond habitats is given on pages 161-166 of *Workbook for Field Biology and Ecology* by Benton and Werner (see *Background Reading*).

EDUCATIONAL IMPLICATIONS

Part B. The Stream Habitat

Currents of streams vary. As the amount of material carried by the water in a stream is in part determined by its rate of flow, stream bottoms are varied. Bottoms of swift streams are characterized by rocks and pebbles; those of slower streams have smaller particles.

Rooted aquatic plants have difficulty surviving in swift streams. Animals in this environment are sometimes streamlined. Often they must be able to hide under or behind rocks to protect themselves from the current.

Large, slow streams are frequently shallow, and flood their banks after heavy rains or melting snow.

The field work can best be accomplished by dividing the class into teams as before. Refer to Part A for a suggested list of equipment and materials.

For further information, read pages 169-183 in *Workbook for Field Biology and Ecology* by Benton and Werner.

Part C. Bog Habitat

The bog environment presents a distinct contrast to a stream or pond, particularly in scarcity of calcium and a low pH, sometimes 4.0 or less. These conditions, plus a high water level during most of the year, act to limit the types and numbers of plants adapted to a bog existence. This is also true of plankton. Alder, red osier, and sphagnum are common. Good samples of plant succession are often to be seen at the edge of the bog.

See Part A for a suggested list of equipment and materials.

For further information, read pages 167-168 in *Workbook for Field Biology and Ecology* by Benton and Werner.

Part D. Prairie or Grass Habitat

Grasses are the dominant plants of the prairie. The dominant forms of animal life in this environment are insects and spiders. The soil is usually well populated with slugs, snails, and small nematodes. Some species of sparrows, larks, and other birds find this environment to their liking. Mice, shrews, gophers, and ground squirrels are the most common mammals, while some hares, woodchucks and an occasional deer may find the grass a good place to feed.

Have the students lay out several quadrats of one meter each. This study is best carried out by teams, as in the other parts of the exercise.

The Berlese funnel and mouse traps or bait cans are part of the field equipment, as they are for Parts E and F. Stakes and string should be on hand to mark the quadrats. A soil-testing kit is also a useful part of the laboratory equipment; such kits contain directions for use. The canvas or plastic tablecloth can be used here for catching insects.

Soil is a poor conductor of heat. As a result, temperature changes less rapidly in the soil than in the air above. With increasing depth, the temperature variation of the soil decreases until it becomes constant at two to three feet. This phenomenon can be partially tested by soil temperatures taken at six inches and one foot.

Information on the effects of light is given in Part F, *Forest Habitat.* For further information, read pages 117-119 in *Workbook for Field Biology and Ecology* by Benton and Werner.

Part E. Shrub Habitat

The plants which occupy this habitat are extremely varied, dogwood, blackberry, and hawthorn being widespread. Grasses begin to thin out, for they are sun-loving. This thinning allows occasional clear spaces which may create a favorable environment for tree-seed germination. The shrub stage, then, is usually a stage in succession, as students can see if tree seedlings are present in the area under observation. Where grass is less common, invertebrates are fewer in number. It follows that the animals which feed on the invertebrates are also fewer in number. Shrews and moles are common mammal types in this habitat. Thrashers, towhees, warblers, and some sparrows may frequent it. Amphibians are rare, toads being the most common. Some snakes may be present.

The quadrats for this part of the study could well be 5 meters square. Information on the effect of light is given in Part F. For further information read pages 120-122 in *Workbook for Field Biology and Ecology* by Benton and Werner.

Part F. Forest Habitat

As the trees mature, they begin to shade out many of the grasses and shrubs. Some few shrubs persist in this environment a long time, but eventually a stand of timber may be almost completely devoid of low-growing plants. The future of a wood may be in part predicted by the numbers and types of seedlings found under existing trees.

Again, a diversity of animal and plant life is evident. Fungi and woodboring insects are found in abundance on and in rotting logs. Spiders, sow bugs, millepedes, wasps, bees, and flies are usually abundant. Birds are less abundant than in certain other habitats, but many species inhabit the edge of a woody area. Deer mice and shrews are usually present, but in lesser numbers than in some other habitats.

The students should be advised to establish several quadrats, each 10 meters square. If the area under observation is on a hill, it is a good idea to make a transect of the slope.

A light meter can usually be provided by a student interested in photography. To see the significance of light in the ecology of an area, choose a situation which is relatively level, with soil of reasonably uniform color. This will to some degree eliminate variations in soil

fertility that might otherwise affect observed differences in the vegetation. The size of leaves, length of petioles, and length of internodes will be greater in the shady than in sunny areas. This is due to the fact that auxin (growth hormone) is destroyed by light. Also, plants wilt less in shady habitats, and this allows greater growth. Leaves, however, will be thicker in the sun; this may possibly be due to the increased photosynthetic activity.

For further information, read pages 123-125 in *Workbook for Field Biology and Ecology,* by Benton and Werner.

Part G. Succession

Many schools throughout the nation have set aside a tract of land for use by the biology classes as an outdoor laboratory. When such tracts of land are used to advantage, they become very useful adjuncts to a biology course, and their establishment should be encouraged. This study is suggested for teachers who have or will eventually have access to such an outdoor laboratory.

Early in the fall of the first year have a class clear a one-meter square in the area. It will probably be necessary to soak the soil with water in order to remove all roots. Take a census of all plant and animal life found there. Mark the area in a permanent manner as plot #1.

The following fall a class can move on to the next plot, completely denude the quadrat, mark it as plot #2, and take a census of both the freshly denuded quadrat and the quadrat cleared the year before. In succeeding years new plots can be started and data collected on those where succession has been going on for known periods.

There is no limit to the length of time for such study. A period of fifteen years will demonstrate a transect of natural succession of real ecological value. A walk taken along such a transect, starting with the area denuded that year, can in a few minutes allow the class to see natural, undisturbed succession as it takes place over a span of many years.

Yearly records of temperature and rainfall should be kept, so as to correlate the weather with the types of organisms and rate at which they invade the area.

The first class attempting this work may particularly enjoy being the pioneers in a project of lasting value and interest for future ecological observation and work.

Another possibility, where space permits, is to have each class denude two or more quadrats. Succession in several transects, perhaps in different types of situations (center of wood, edge of wood, near stream or pond, etc.), can then be compared.

Still another possibility is to develop two transects. One should be set up as described above. In the other, after the land has been cleared, turn over the entire area of top soil to a depth of six inches. Compare the invasion of organisms in this area with the first. Or, the six inches of top soil can be removed entirely. This may demonstrate effects of changes in the soil texture.

BACKGROUND READING

Benton, A. H., and Werner, W. E., Jr. *Workbook for Field Biology and Ecology,* Burgess Publishing Co., Minneapolis, Minn., 1957.

Buchsbaum, R., and Buchsbaum, M. *Basic Ecology.* Boxwood Press, Pittsburgh, Penn., 1957.

Clark, G. *Elements of Ecology.* John Wiley and Sons, Inc., New York, 1954.

Dice, L. R. *Natural Communities.* University of Michigan Press, Ann Arbor, Mich., 1952.

Odum, E. P. *Fundamentals of Ecology.* W. B. Saunders Co., Philadelphia, 1953.

Oosting, H. J. *The Study of Plant Communities.* W. H. Freeman and Co., San Francisco, Calif., 1956.

Storer, J. H. *The Web of Life.* Devin-Adair Co., New York, 1954.

Welch, P. S. *Limnological Methods.* McGraw-Hill Book Co., Inc., New York, 1948.

APPENDIX: SUGGESTIONS ON METHODS

Measuring relative humidity. If you have no hygrometer, you can use two thermometers. Wrap one in a damp cloth and keep the cloth damp during readings. The dry bulb of the other gives the true temperature of the air. The following directions will aid you in determining the percent of humidity by comparing the wet and dry thermometers.

Read the dry-bulb thermometer and the wet-bulb thermometer and find the difference between the two readings. On the relative humidity chart (Table 1), find the temperature indicated by the dry-bulb thermometer and read across to the difference in temperature between the two thermometers. The figure at this point is the relative humidity. For example, if the temperature of your school room is 22°C and the temperature difference between the two thermometers is 8°C, the relative humidity is 40 percent.

Determining concentration of oxygen in water (Rideal-Stewart modification of Winkler Method*). To collect water samples, 250-ml glass bottles with tight-fitting glass stoppers may be used. All glassware must be clean. Special water samplers can be purchased which enable one to secure water without introducing atmospheric oxygen. If a sampler is not available, the water should be obtained in such a manner as to avoid splashing or bubbling it. Siphons are useful in doing this. If the water is transferred from a sampler to a bottle, the water

*Adapted from Benton, H.B. and Werner, W.E., Jr., *Workbook for Field Biology and Ecology,* Burgess Publishing Co., Minneapolis, Minn., 1957.

TABLE 1.   Relative humidity chart for wet-dry hygrometer.

DIFFERENCE BETWEEN WET AND DRY BULB READINGS

°C	°F	C F 1/1.8	C F 2/3.6	C F 3/5.4	C F 4/7.2	C F 5/9.0	C F 6/10.8	C F 7/12.6	C F 8/14.4	C F 9/16.2	C F 10/18.0
10	50.0	88	77	66	55	44	34	24	15	6	
11	52.0	89	78	67	56	46	36	27	18	9	
12	53.5	89	78	68	58	48	39	29	21	12	
13	55.5	89	79	69	59	50	41	32	23	15	7
14	57.0	90	79	70	60	51	42	34	26	18	10
15	59.0	90	80	71	61	53	44	36	27	20	13
16	61.0	90	81	71	63	54	46	38	30	23	15
17	62.5	90	81	72	64	55	47	40	32	25	18
18	64.5	91	82	73	65	57	49	41	34	27	20
19	66.0	91	82	74	65	58	50	43	36	29	22
20	68.0	91	83	74	66	59	51	44	37	31	24
21	70.0	91	83	75	67	60	53	46	39	32	26
22	71.5	92	83	76	68	61	54	47	40	34	28
23	73.5	92	84	76	69	62	55	48	42	36	30
24	75.0	92	84	77	69	62	56	49	43	37	31
25	77.0	92	84	77	70	63	57	50	44	39	33
26	79.0	92	85	78	71	64	58	51	46	40	34
27	80.5	92	85	78	71	65	58	52	47	41	36
28	82.5	93	85	78	72	65	59	53	48	42	37
29	84.0	93	86	79	72	66	60	54	49	43	38
30	86.0	93	86	79	73	67	61	55	50	44	39
31	88.0	93	86	80	73	67	61	56	51	45	40
32	89.5	93	86	80	74	68	62	57	51	46	41
33	91.5	93	87	80	74	68	63	58	52	47	42
34	93.0	93	87	81	75	69	63	59	53	48	43
35	95.0	94	87	81	75	69	64	59	54	49	44

DRY BULB READING

should be allowed to overflow the 250-ml bottle two or three times, to flush out atmospheric oxygen. When the stopper is replaced, no air bubble should remain. Temperature of the water should also be recorded at the time and place the water is collected.

(a) Analysis. In steps 1 to 5 the reagents should be added quickly and the bottle restoppered immediately to prevent addition of atmospheric oxygen.

(1) To the water sample, add a glass bead (to aid mixing), 0.35 ml cone. H_2SO_4, and 0.5 ml $KMnO_4$ soln.

(2) Shake. A pale violet-pink color should appear and persist. If it does not, add a few ml more $KMnO_4$ solution. Allow to stand at least 40 minutes after the color is established.

(3) Add 0.5 ml potassium oxalate ($K_2C_2O_4 \cdot H_2O$). Let stand until color disappears.

(4) Add 0.5 ml manganous sulfate ($MNSO_4$) solution and 1.5 ml hydroxide potassium iodide solution. Shake. A yellow precipitate will form. Allow it to settle partially, then shake again.

(5) Add 0.5 ml conc. H_2SO_4. Shake. The precipitate should dissolve. If it does not, add 0.5 ml more H_2SO_4. A yellow color will remain, which represents iodine that replaced the oxygen dissolved in the water. At this point, the analysis may be suspended for several hours and completed in the laboratory.

(6) Measure out 100 ml of the sample, and titrate with N/100 sodium thiosulfate solution. *Make sure*

you read the level of the sodium thiosulfate before you start titrating. Write it down.

(7) Titrate until a very pale yellow color is reached, then add starch indicator (about 2 ml). The sample will turn blue.

(8) Continue titrating until the sample becomes clear. The clearness should persist for several seconds under agitation.

(9) Read the new level of the sodium thiosulfate, and calculate the amount used in titration.

(10) Multiply this amount by 2. This will give (roughly) the parts per million of dissolved oxygen in the water.

(b) *Reagents.* Use only distilled water in preparing solutions. Salts are usually first dissolved in small quantities of water, then diluted.

(1) Potassium permanganate solution: 6.32 gm $KMnO_4$ in 1 liter H_2O.

(2) Potassium oxalate solution: 20 gm $K_2C_2O_4 \cdot H_2O$; dissolved in H_2O; add 4 gm NaOH, then dilute to 1 liter with water.

(3) Manganous sulfate solution: 480 gm $MnSO_4$ in 1 liter H_2O.

(4) Hydroxide-potassium iodide solution: 500 gm NaOH and 135 gm NaI, diluted to 1 liter with water.

(5) Sodium thiosulfate (N/10): dissolve 25 gm sodium thiosulfate and 2-3 gm borax in H_2O and dilute to 1 liter with water that has been boiled and allowed to cool. This normality is fairly stable. For titrating, make N/100 solution by diluting 1 part N/10 with 9 parts H_2O.

(6) Starch indicator: 3 gm potato starch, ground with H_2O. Place in 500 ml freshly boiled H_2O. Allow to stand overnight, then use only the clear fluid.

Measuring pH of water and soil. Use litmus tests.

Measuring CO_2 in water. See next activity. [Editor's note: See also pp. 451-53 of this text]

10A. Introduction to Ecology

C. A. Lawson
R. E. Paulson

FIELD ECOLOGY FOR THE STUDENT

INTRODUCTION

There are many different ways of seeing the natural world. Most of us have sensed this world in a general way when we appreciate the out-of-doors. We may appreciate a beautiful lake, or a cool pine woods, or a flower-covered prairie. We may have a general feeling of pleasure, or we may note some particular shape of a tree, or observe interesting cloud formations or the graceful flight of a gull.

The landscape artist may approach the out-of-doors differently. He may paint or sketch the environment in a way which represents what was really there, or in a way which expresses his feelings or the moment, without regard to specific physical features.

The engineer may make a more systematic approach to the out-of-doors. He may plot the location of a new turnpike or a railroad. He may be only mildly interested in the beauty of the landscape, but will be concerned with measuring slopes and curves and streams so as to lay out his construction work intelligently.

The field biologist approaches the world of nature in still a different way. He uses a systematic appraoch, too, but a system designed to give him as much information as possible concerning the organisms which live in his chosen segment of the out-of-doors. He is interested in learning about the animals and plants in a given area, in describing how they interact with each other, finding which prey on which, where they live, how they reproduce, and what physical factors of the environment, such as temperature and moisture, affect the lives of these animals and plants. In these studies, the field biologist, attempting to obtain as accurate a picture as possible of the lives of all the organisms in an area, approaches nature with the systematic methods of science. For instance, the field

SOURCE. Reprinted, by permission of the publisher, from Lawson, C.A. and Paulson, R.E., *Laboratory and Field Studies in Biology,* New York: Holt, Rinehart, and Winston, 1960.

biologist may classify the different types of out-of-door environments, or habitats. He may speak of a lake or a pond, a stream, bog, prairie, or forest habitat. Each type of habitat has certain associations of animals and plants in which the biologist is interested.

In the next few weeks you are going to study some of the habitats mentioned above. You shall attempt to learn the kinds of animals and plants found in each habitat type. You will use some of the special analytical methods applied by the field biologist to the study of animal and plant associations.

In preparation for your excursions into the field, you should realize that the methods of study of a given habitat include both a study of the organisms themselves—that is, the animals and plants peculiar to that habitat—and of the physical environment of these organisms—the moisture conditions, the temperature, the nature of the soil, to name a few. In any given habitat we must, for complete understanding, study these factors. We must learn to know the organisms themselves and the environmental influences which guide and regulate their biological activities.

We can make such a study most conveniently by first picking one of the habitat types commonly studied by field biologists. Such habitats are the prairie habitat, in which the major vegetational type is grasses of various kinds, with occasional small herbs and perhaps a few shrubs, or the forest habitat, in which the main plants are trees and shrubs. The prairie seems a relatively lifeless place in terms of animal populations, but as you shall see, there are many types of animals living there. You can also study many of the physical factors in the forest or on the prairie: temperature, wind, soil type, and moisture conditions. It will be easiest for you to divide into teams of perhaps four or five persons, each of which will analyze one or a few of these factors in the habitat. Thus, there might be a group called the environment team, which would study the environmental factors. Others might include a plant team, a mammal, an insect, and a bird team. These latter teams are called quadrat teams in the foregoing instructions because the members will study specific areas called quadrats.

In a preliminary discussion with your teacher, you will be asked to state your preference as to which type of analysis you would like to make, that is, which team you would like to join. At this time, also, the teacher will settle on a particular habitat to which you will go, and may provide you with a map of the place.

After such a discussion, each team should meet together and write out a plan for its activities. For instance, the environmental team may want to list the various types of observations they wish to make. In deciding on these observations, they should select the few crucial observations of environmental factors which they think are of greatest importance in affecting the activity of the animals and plants in the forest or on the prairie. Then they should make up a list of the equipment they will need to measure these factors. The plant team will need to decide what kinds of plants it will collect, how to collect them, whether to bring back live or dried plants, the types of equipment needed. As it is difficult to record observations in the field, a table or form of some kind will facilitate recording. Prepare these forms before you leave for your field trip. Confer with your teacher concerning each team's plan.

Now try to imagine the situation you will find when you go into the field. When you arrive at the site, you will be expected to write out a description of the environment, some of the plants, or some special type of animal which you find there. Will you be able to describe all the animals, plants, and environmental factors on the whole area? Obviously not, and so you must devise some method of sampling.

For example, suppose you are to collect and describe the types of insects you find. Do you suppose that the prairie is fairly uniformly covered with these insects? If so, it is possible to devise a sampling method in which you study a small area of the prairie. Ecologists very often study small areas about a meter square. Then, by carefully collecting all the insects found on such a square plot of ground, they can describe what the probable content of the entire prairie is by doing a simple multiplication. So you will want to plan exactly which places and how many of them you will observe.

PART A. THE LAKE OR POND HABITAT

Environment team. Fill the sample bottles with water near the shore and at a depth of 1 foot, 10 feet out from the shore. These samples will be tested later in the laboratory for carbon dioxide, free oxygen concentration and pH. Take temperatures in the water near the shore, in the water 10 feet from the shore, in the air above the bank, and in the air above the water. Make notations describing the general weather conditions. Chart all your data on large cardboard sheets for the entire class to observe. Consult with your teacher during this process for clarity in expression.

Quadrat teams. Scatter the various quadrats in such a manner as to get samples from a variety of places in the pond. First, take a sample of water from the quadrat, using your quart jar. Take a tow net sample at various depths. Remove any plants floating in the water or rooted in the bottom in your one-foot quadrat. After this, carefully turn over any rocks on the pond bottom. Collect any organisms seen. Dig out the bottom and sieve the material for organisms. Continue this process until no more organisms are found, or until the water washes the hole full

again. Place half the organisms of each kind in jars containing alcohol. The others may be brought back to the laboratory alive, in jars containing pond water. Be sure to replace the rocks in their original positions.

In the laboratory the next day sort out all similar plants and animals found in a single quadrat. Chart kinds of organisms and their frequency in a clear manner on poster board. Consult your teacher on how to organize your chart.

Discussion and report. The class will now discuss the results of its findings under the guidance of the teacher. After the discussion you are to answer the following questions in writing.

(a) What plants and animals are common to all the quadrats?

(b) What organisms are found in the water near the shore but are not found any distance out?

(c) What kinds are found in the pond, but not near the shore?

(d) What different environmental conditions may be considered as possible causes for this variation in distribution?

From the discussion of food habits of the organisms found, construct a food chain of the pond. Do you think that most of the organisms found have a direct relationship to the welfare of some other organism in the environment?

PART B. THE STREAM HABITAT

Environment team. Collect samples of the water for analysis, as in Part A. Make collections in various locations in the stream. Take the temperature of the water near the bank and in the center of the stream, and in the air above both water and bank. Look for signs of the high-water mark made in times of flood. See if you can devise a means by which you can measure the swiftness of the stream. Consult your teacher as to the practicality of your proposals.

Can you devise a way to determine the grade or slope of the stream bed? Again check with your teacher.

Make your chemical tests when you return to the laboratory, and chart your results for the class.

Quadrat teams. Collect a sample of the water above your one-foot quadrat, using your quart jar. Collect any plants that may be growing in your quadrat. Holding a net downstream from the rocks, slowly turn over rocks or stones that make up the quadrat stream bed. Collect any organisms that are found there. Carefully dig down into the stream bottom and sift the contents for organisms. Place all the collected organisms in jars.

Back in the laboratory, sort your organisms into bottles. This should be done for each quadrat.

Make a list for each quadrat. Chart these for the class to see.

Discussion and report. Discuss the results of the trip with your teacher. After the discussion the following questions should be answered in writing.

(a) Is there a difference between the kinds of animals found in the stream and those found in the pond? What are these differences?

(b) What plants occur in the stream but not in the pond?

(c) Are there as many rooted plants in the stream as in the pond? Why or why not?

(d) What is the difference between the pond bottom and the stream bottom?

(e) What are the reasons for this difference?

(f) Are any living things found under the rocks?

(g) What adaptations of structure or behavior permit them to live in this environment?

PART C. BOG HABITAT

Environment team. Take temperatures below the bog level, on its surface, and in the air above the bog. If water is present, collect samples for laboratory tests of pH, free oxygen, and CO_2. Test the pH of the soil of the bog. Note its color. Make note of the plants growing back from the bog to find evidence of the plant succession which may have occurred. Make the chemical tests in the laboratory.

Quadrat teams. Each quadrat team should choose a position some distance away from the others. Stake out and string a one-meter square. Examine the kinds of plants in this quadrat. Take a census to determine the number of each kind. Bring one of each kind back to the laboratory. What animals or animal signs (tracks, runways, feces, nests) can be seen? Trap insects with a tin can buried level with the surface of the bog; bait the can with meat. You could also use a sweep net. Return to the laboratory and sort plants into separate jars. Do the same for the animals collected. Tabulate your results for the class to study.

Discussion and report. Discuss the discoveries of the field trip, and attempt to define significant ecological relationships. After this has been done, answer the following questions in writing.

(a) How did the pH and CO_2 readings differ from those of the pond and stream environments?

(b) In what way do pH and CO_2 content affect the types of plants and animals found in the bog?

(c) What is the dominant plant? Is this plant also found in the pond? In the stream?

(d) What is the dominant animal?

(e) Did you see any birds in the bog? Were they nesting there? What is there in the bog for them to eat? Do you often see these kinds of birds away from the bog?

(f) Are insects found in abundance? Are these the kinds you might usually find in a field or woods?

(g) Construct a chart showing a suggested food chain in the bog.

PART D. PRAIRIE OR GRASS HABITAT

Environment team. Take temperature in each of the quadrats six inches and one foot below the ground, on the surface, a foot above the ground, and six feet above the ground. Measure the humidity in the area with the wet and dry bulb thermometer. Make notes as to the weather conditions. Remove a sample of soil from each quadrat and test in the laboratory for pH and soil fertility. Gather information about the annual rainfall in the vicinity.

Quadrat teams. Take a plant census. Collect plants of the different kinds to take back to the laboratory. Set mouse traps and insect traps. Use the sweep net in the grass for insects. Observe birds in the vicinity. Look for signs of mammals, such as dusting places, trails or runs, nests, feces, etc. Take a sample of the soil for use in the Berlese funnel. Sift some of the soil through a piece of common window screen and gather the organisms present. Place all organisms in jars and return them to the laboratory.

Discussion and report. The environmental teams will make their soil tests upon return to the laboratory. The data that was collected in the field will then be charted by them for the other members of the class. The quadrat teams will separate the various kinds of plants and animals gathered, and chart their findings. The class is now ready for a discussion of the trip. After discussion of the data, write answers to the following questions.

(a) What is the variation in animals and plants found here as opposed to the bog?
(b) Are any woody plants present?
(c) Compare the soil samples in appearance and in pH with those taken in the bog.
(d) Is there any relation between pH readings and soil drainage?
(e) From your readings, class discussion, and your own observations, do you think that this is a climax grass stage, or an intermediate stage of plant succession? What are your reasons?
(f) In what way has man played a part in this succession?

PART E. SHRUB HABITAT

Environment team. Follow directions given in Part D.

Quadrat teams. Trap insects in the soil. Use the sweep net in the grass. Put a canvas or plastic tablecloth under the shrubs and shake the shrubs vigorously. Look for animal signs, such as dust beds, runways, or nests. Trap small mammals with mouse traps. (Be sure the mammals are not an endangered species!) Take samples of the plants back to the laboratory. Notice whether tree seedlings are growing under the shrubs. Is the grass here thinner or thicker than in other places studied?

Discussion and report. Quadrat teams and environment teams will chart their findings as before. After class discussion, the following questions may be answered in writing.

(a) Are signs of animals as frequent here as in the other areas studied? What might be the reasons for this?
(b) Compare the plants found in this habitat with those in the other areas?
(c) What is the ecological significance of tree seedlings growing under the shrubs?
(d) Construct a food chain for the area.

PART F. FOREST HABITAT

Quadrat teams. Establish your quadrat or transect in the location suggested by the teacher. Quadrats may be 10 meters square. If a transect is used, discuss its limitations with your teacher.

Trap the area for small mammals. Use a sweep net and bait-trap for insects. Gather samples of soil and leaf litter to be used in the Berlese funnel. Look for signs of animals, such as nests, runways, dusting spots, feces. Take a census of the plants found in the quadrat.

The various specimens will be placed in appropriate collecting jars or containers and taken back to the laboratory.

Environment team. Measure the depth of the top soil in each quadrat. Take samples of soil from each quadrat back to the laboratory for analyses of minerals and pH. Take temperatures, as in Part D. Take notes on general weather conditions. Measure humidity.

Soil samples will be returned to the laboratory for testing.

With a photographic light meter, measure the light intensity in a place which is in constant or almost constant shade. Measure the light intensity of an area of prominent sunlight.

Now follow one or more of these suggestions in both the shady and bright habitat:

Measure 50 violet petioles growing in the shade.

Measure 50 violet petioles growing in the sunlight.

Measure 100 leaves (from node to leaf tip or from leaf point to leaf point, as in maple) in the shady area. Do the same in a sunny area.

Measure the third internode from the end of a branch of 25 plants of a specific herb in the shade. Do the same for the same species in the sunny area. (An internode is the distance from the base of one leaf to the base of the next leaf.)

Calculate the average measurements taken in the sunlight and the average measurements taken in the shade.

Discussion and report. Both teams will organize their findings for presentation to the class as in Part A. After class discussion the following questions may be answered in writing.

(a) What animals and plants are found in this area that are not found in the other areas studied?

(b) What factors in this environment would you suggest as possible influencing factors for these organisms?

(c) What might the woods look like 30 years from now? What are the reasons for your opinion?

(d) What might the area have looked like 30 years ago? What are the reasons for your opinion?

(e) Construct a food chain for the area.

10A. Introduction to Ecology

C. A. Lawson

R. E. Paulson

A METHOD OF MEASURING CARBON DIOXIDE

USING THIS EXERCISE

This exercise lays a foundation for several quantitative studies of respiration and photosynthesis in aquatic organisms. It can well be handled as an exercise in simple chemistry to give the student experience in handling chemical symbols. The equations are no more complex than the equations for photosynthesis and respiration, and they deal with well-known chemicals that are a familiar part of daily living and are components of the human body. The fact that the exercise provides a useful method for study of metabolic rates makes it more valuable than some other exercises in elementary chemistry.

The stock solution of 0.4% NaOH and the phenolphthalein can be prepared by one or a few trustworthy students, who should report to the class on how they are prepared.

Instructions for preparation of 0.4% NaOH:

1. Place a clean 125-ml beaker on the pan of a balance and weigh it. Record the weight. Add 4.0 grams to the weight of the beaker and set the balance at the weight so computed. Using a clean forceps or spatula, place sodium hydroxide pellets in the beaker until the balance comes to equilibrium.

CAUTION: Sodium hydroxide is a strong alkali, so avoid contact with hands or clothing.

Since NaOH absorbs water from air, the weighing should not be prolonged unnecessarily.

2. Transfer the 4.0 grams of NaOH to a one-liter flask. Add distilled water

SOURCE. Reprinted, by permission of the publisher, from Lawson, C.A. and Paulson, R.E., *Laboratory and Field Studies in Biology,* New York: Holt, Rinehart, and Winston, 1960.

(or rain water if no distilled water is available) to make one liter of solution.

If graduated pipettes or burettes are not available, you can calibrate medicine droppers by counting the drops required to fill a graduated cylinder to the 5-ml mark. Then compute the volume of each drop and count the drops used when adding NaOH to the water sample. For example: If 82 drops = 5 ml, each drop = 0.061 ml.

The stock solution should be stored in a dispenser bottle (Fig. 1). This bottle makes it easy to draw a quantity of stock solution. The soda lime removes CO_2 from the air that enters the bottle, thus preventing the NaOH from being changed to $NaHCO_3$.

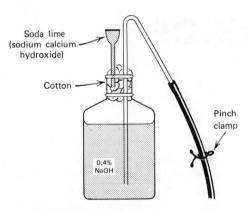

Soda lime (sodium calcium hydroxide)

Cotton

Pinch clamp

0.4% NaOH

FIGURE 1.   NaOH dispenser bottle.

The phenolphthalein solution is prepared as follows:

Weigh ¼ gram of phenolphthalein powder, put it in a screw-top dropper bottle of about 40-ml capacity, add 10 ml ethyl alcohol, and fill with distilled water.

CHECK-LIST OF EQUIPMENT AND SUPPLIES

For the class:
NaOH pellets
Phenolphthalein
Alcohol
Dispenser bottle

Soda lime (sodium calcium hydroxide)
Cotton
Absorption tube for air intake
Glass tube, rubber tubing, and pinch clamp
2-hole rubber stopper
Dropper bottle
100-ml graduated cylinder for filuting stock solution to 0.04%
125-ml beaker

For each student or group:
2 flasks or bottles, 150-250 ml capacity
1 graduated pipette (1 ml graduated in 0.1 ml; these cost about $1.15 each; since the medicine dropper substitute will seem inaccurate to good students, purchase of pipettes is recommended if at all possible)
Soda straws or glass tubes for aspirating water samples

INTRODUCTION

Carbon dioxide (CO_2) is a compound of great importance to life. Living organisms constantly produce it during respiration, and all green plants absorb large quantities of it when exposed to light. Thus, a method for measuring carbon dioxide quantities is a useful tool in biology. This exercise provides a method that requires only simple equipment.

A stock solution of 0.4% sodium hydroxide (NaOH) is provided for your use. An 0.04% solution can be made from the stock by adding 90 ml of distilled water to 10 ml of stock solution. Each ml of this 0.04% solution will combine with 10 micromoles of carbon dioxide. A micromole is a chemical quantity that contains 6×10^{17} molecules (600,000,000,000,000,000).

A solution of phenolphthalein is also provided. This is a dye which turns red after all the carbon dioxide has been removed from a sample of water.

PROCEDURE

To gain some experience in measuring carbon dioxide content of water, carry out the following experiment:

Measure 100 ml of tap water with a graduated cylinder and transfer it to a bottle or Erlenmeyer flask. Add 3 to 5 drops of phenolphthalein. Then bubble air from your lungs through the water, using a glass tube or soda straw, for about one minute. Now slowly add 0.04% NaOH, using a graduated pipette or burette, and mixing repeatedly by swirling the water around to insure complete reaction between NaOH and CO_2. When the solution turns pink, record the number of ml of 0.04% NaOH used. To compute the number of micromoles of CO_2 in the water sample, simply multiply the ml NaOH used by 10.

Repeat this exercise at least twice to give you experience in approaching the end point (color change) carefully, so that your determination of CO_2 content will be as accurate as possible.

CONCLUSIONS

Learn the chemical reactions that occur in this exercise:

1. While you are blowing air from your lungs through the water, carbon dioxide is combining with water to form carbonic acid:

$$CO_2 + H_2O - H_2CO_3$$

2. When you add sodium hydroxide, it combines with the carbonic acid, forming sodium bicarbonate:

$$NaOH + H_2CO_3 - NaHCO_3 + H_2O$$

These formulas all represent common substances:

H_2CO_3 (carbonic acid) is the acid in soft drinks, and is always present in your blood stream.

NaOH (sodium hydroxide), commonly called caustic soda or lye, is used in making soap.

$NaHCO_3$ (sodium bicarbonate) is commonly called baking soda. It also is always present in your blood stream, and prevents your blood from becoming too acidic.

H_2O is water.

10A. Introduction to Ecology

G. Peterson

S. Feldman

E. Green

J. Shouba

A. Nusbaumer

FOOD WEBS

Introduction

Even the simplest of communities have complex food relationships. Such relationships make up one type of "glue" that holds together the many organisms— plant, animal, and microbial—that form a community. Even if an organism consumes only one type of food, the picture may still be complicated by stages in the life cycle of the organism or by changes in the size of the population of secondary consumers or predators. For example, assume that we are considering one type of mammal that feeds on the leaves of only one type of tree. If the mammal happens to be quite young, its diet is milk. And the tree—is it a seedling, a sapling, or a mature tree with leaves beyond the reach of the animal?

Today you will set up a model terrestrial and a model aquatic community. You will examine it over a period of several weeks to determine the feeding relationships as the system develops. Bear in mind that the community or ecosystem, if you wish to consider the physical environment as well, is dynamic. If the community changes, so will the feeding relationships.

AQUATIC COMMUNITY

Materials
Aquarium
Sand
Unicellular algae culture
Daphnia
Hydras
Aquatic plants
Amphipods
Ostracods
Aquatic snails
Guppies

SOURCE. Reprinted, by permission of the publisher, from *Laboratory Guide for Biology*, by Peterson, G. et al, Morristown, New Jersey: Silver Burdett Co., 1969.

Procedures

A. Place a 2-inch layer of thoroughly washed sand in your aquarium, and then add water. Plant a few sprigs of the aquatic plants, but do not add other organisms until the water has aged 48 hours.

B. Add some algae to your aquarium. Give the algae ample light. Then add the snails.

C. As soon as the water has changed to a definite green color, add 10 *Daphnia*, 5 amphipods, and 10 ostracods.

D. Observe these organisms over a period of 1 week. Note their behavior when they are alone and when they come in contact with other species.

E. At the end of a week, count the survivors. Add 2 hydras. Examine to see whether any predator-prey relationships develop.

F. At the end of a second week, count the survivors. Add a pair of guppies to the aquarium and see how they affect the ecosystem. Do not feed any of the organiams; let the balance develop naturally.

G. At the end of a third week, count the survivors.

Discussion

1. Diagram the food webs that are apparent at Step C, Step E, and Step F.

2. How do the aquatic plants and algae affect your community, and how are they affected by it?

3. What food is consumed by each of the organisms in your community?

TERRESTRIAL COMMUNITY

Materials

Large container
Watering device
Soil
Seeds: grass, radish, pea,
    broad beans
1 small toad, or chameleon or
    other lizard
10 aphids
3 crickets (field or house)
1 spider
2 ladybird beetles
3 lacewings
Cheesecloth or nylon netting

Procedures

H. Add a 2-inch layer of soil to the bottom of your container. Scatter the grass seed but space out the other seeds according to the directions on the package. Cover the seeds with a thin layer of soil. Water them well and place the container in a lighted area.

I. As soon as the plants are about 3 inches tall, add 10 aphids. Cover your terrarium to prevent the aphids from escaping.

J. One week later, add the crickets, ladybird beetles, and lacewings. Observe the behavior of these organisms in relation to one another. Are there any feeding relationships among these organisms?

K. After the second week, add the spider. If it is a web-builder, note where it builds its web. Does the spider, or any organism, for that matter, show a preference for only one type of prey?

L. After the third week, add the vertebrate animal. Again, is there any food preference shown?

4. Diagram the food webs that exist at Steps I, J, K, and L. Include all organisms and all stages of these organisms.

10A. Introduction to Ecology

G. Peterson

S. Feldman

E. Green

J. Shouba

A. Nusbaumer

INTRODUCTION TO A QUADRAT

Introduction

In an effort to understand our natural environment, ecologists are devising and using means to make quantitative studies. Obviously, when attempting to study the complex relationships of even a relatively small area, some method of sampling must be used. One of the most common devices is to create study plots within the bounds of the area to be studied. These study plots are termed quadrats. The sizes of quadrats may vary depending upon the type of area to be studied. For example, forest quadrats are usually larger than those used on prairies.*

The shape of quadrats can also vary. Usually they are either circular or, as the name implies, square. The basic quadrat area is generally one square meter, and quadrats are usually distributed in some systematic fashion. A major question in any study area is how many quadrats to distribute. For this purpose a species: area curve is frequently used.

The number of species is plotted on the y-axis against the size or number of samples

*The class sets up quadrats in a variety of locations. Organisms studied may be taken back to the classroom for further study. Have a master data table set up in advance of this study.

SOURCE. Reprinted, by permission of the publisher, from *Laboratory Guide for Biology,* by Peterson, G. et al, Morristown, New Jersey: Silver Burdett Co., 1969.

EXPERIMENTS FOR SECONDARY STUDENTS

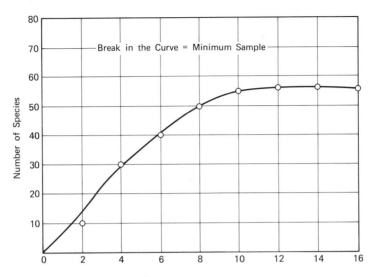

FIGURE 1. Number of one meter square quadrats.

on the x-axis. The break in the curve is the point of diminishing returns in relation to added information gained in the study. Usually an additional 10% is considered beyond this point. In your study you will use quadrats and make a species:area curve.

Materials
Meterstick
String
Trowel
Collecting bags and jars
Newspaper

Procedures

A. Once in the area selected by your instructor, make a class decision as to how to distribute the quadrats. When your location is established, measure off one square meter. Use small sticks to peg the corners of your square. Loop string around these corner pegs, outlining your quadrats.

B. Before you proceed further, make a data table for listing the kinds and numbers of all plants and animals in your study plot. Then carefully search the surface of your quadrat for all sur-

face animals. Also identify the plants present, and record all data as to number and kind. With a trowel dig carefully to a depth of about 5 cm and record in your data table all additional animals found. Use newspaper as a base for sifting through the soil. Collect samples of anything you cannot identify for further study in the laboratory.

C. Once back in the laboratory, at the completion of the study, each team will present its data to the class. From the class data of animal species, construct a species:area curve.

Discussion

1. How many quadrats were used by the class?

2. How many quadrats were needed to reach a minimum sample?

3. How many species were represented by the minimum sample?

4. How many quadrats were needed to go 10% beyond the minimum?

5. How many species were represented at 10% beyond the minimum?

6. How many square meters were represented by all quadrats?

EDUCATIONAL IMPLICATIONS

7. How many square meters were necessary to obtain the minimum sampling results?

8. How many square meters were necessary to obtain 10% beyond the minimum?

9. Give some objection to a strict reliance on the species:area curve as a determiner of sampling quantity.

10A. Introduction to Ecology

S. Weinberg

ECOLOGICAL SUCCESSION

PROBLEM

What changes take place in a laboratory aquatic community?

Introduction

In nature, many different kinds of organisms live together in any given environment. Under stable (or *climax*) ecological conditions, the various populations live in balance with each other and with the environment.

Under changing conditions, it may take a long time to reach this stable state of ecological balance. The community slowly changes, with various populations succeeding each other as the dominant and most abundant forms.

Working in groups, you will study an aquatic community set up in the laboratory. Succession in this artificial community will take place much more rapidly than it does in nature. The community may or may not reach stability by the time you terminate your study.

Materials

jar and cover
dried plant material from pond
sterile pond or spring water
microscope
pipettes
slides

Procedure

1. Clean a jar. Put into it a handful of dried grass, leaves, or other plant material, obtained preferably from the margin of a pond.

Fill with boiled pond water or spring water. (Why boiled?) Do not use distilled water or tap water. (Why not?) Cover the jar. (Why?)

2. Distribute the jars of the various groups in your class in a variety of places which differ in temperature and in light conditions.

3. Watch your jar. When the water begins to get cloudy—probably after

SOURCE. From Weinberg, S., *Laboratory Manual for Biology,* Boston: Allyn and Bacon, Inc., 1967, by permission of the publisher.

EDUCATIONAL IMPLICATIONS

several days—make a microscopic examination of water from various parts of the jar. Use a pipette to collect the samples.

The water samples will probably contain an abundance of bacteria. Describe them. What other organisms do you see? Which are most abundant?

Keep records of your observations— When you made them; where samples were drawn from (surface, bottom, sides, near plant matter, dark parts, etc.); what you observed.

4. Continue making observations every day or two.

Results

Keep a notebook of your observations, using headings like these.

Conclusions and Discussion

1. Where did the organisms which you observed come from?

2. How long did it take for the water to become cloudy? Why did it not become cloudy immediately?

3. What evidence did you see that succession was occurring?

4. What evidence did you see of population changes within the community?

5. Did a food chain or food web exist? Explain.

6. Did environmental factors affect your community? Did they cause differences among the various jars? Explain.

7. Did your community reach a stable or climax condition? Explain.

SAMPLE PAGE OF NOTEBOOK

Day and Time	Source of Sample	Organisms Observed and Their Abundance	Remarks

10A. Introduction to Ecology

ENVIRONMENTAL STUDIES INVESTIGATIONS

Editor's Note: The following collection of environmental activities is reproduced directly from the series of colorful cards which comprise the ES packets.

SOURCE. Reprinted, by permission of Robert Samples, Director of Environmental Studies, a special project of the Earth Science Curriculum Project, Boulder, Colorado.

THIS IS A DIRECT INVITATION TO ENGAGING VALUE SYSTEMS . . . DON'T VETO THEIRS WITH YOURS. . . .

the action:

Go outside and find objects in your environment that are representative of the following pairs of words:

hard/soft
ugly/beautiful
big/small
important/unimportant
high/low
on/off
threatening/calming
useful/wasteful
like/dislike
want/need
happy/unhappy
funny/sad
justice/injustice
wise land use/poor land use

more:

Have your students choose word pairs of their own and find objects to represent them.

notespace:

© American Geological Institute 1970

the action:

Get any ten photos taken at random—from the old picture box—and write or tell a story that includes all the pictures.

What they do:
— personal stories about kids in pictures
— stories about the neighborhood
— stories about a theme such as love, hate, trees
— conservation, pollution, etc.

This is great for a rainy day and when you are running out of film. Since these are the kids' pictures, they usually feel far more secure about writing or talking about them. With many kids the photography route has been a breakthrough in their going toward verbal communication.

This is a great assignment for you to collect personal data from the kids. Don't say anything; read their stories and learn. If you're really hung up in subject matter, you can make this into science, social studies, or even math.

more:

Use the same pictures and write a different story.
Entire class use the same set of pictures.

notespace:

YOU NEED A BATCH OF OLD PICTURES FOR THIS ONE.

the action:

Go outside with a tape recorder and
find and bring back sounds you like and dislike.
find and bring back morning, day, and night sounds.
What they do:
Record — traffic
— school announcements
— birds
— donut shop sounds
— police whistle

This is an invitation to explore the environment with essentially a single sense. This will be a new experience for students of all levels. It's a great way to break the monotony of a schedule. **LOW STUDENT THREAT**
. . . but be ready for them to record certain inane things around the school **HIGH TEACHER THREAT**

TAPE RECORDERS ARE TOOLS, NOT MUSEUM PIECES. LET THE KIDS USE THEM

more:

How does a sound make you feel?
Record sounds of work
Record sounds of play

notespace:

If the kids do the MORE on this one, keep the cassettes for SOUNDMAP and CITYSYMPHONY assignments.

YOU NEED A PORTABLE TAPE RECORDER

the action:

Go outside and prove that some living thing in your environment changes.

— trees
— ants
— pets
— people
— teacher

Some of the kids have dealt with living things in such abstract generalities that they never notice the available forms in their environment. The result is a life-apathy in terms of the environment. GET THEM INTO IT!

This is a low threat assignment that is perfect for an early venture into environmental studies.

more:

life what
life where
life when
life why
life wow!

notespace:

doityourself

the action:

Go outside and count something so you know more about it after you have
counted it than you did before you counted it.
  — bricks
  — broken windows
  — sand grains
  — how much garbage is produced by the school
  — how much gasoline is sold at a service station
  — cars in traffic periods
  — insects
  — leaves

(It is important that the kids choose the elements of their environment to count. The counting is a first step to some intriguing extensions. MORE is important in this activity.)

This assignment can be as fruitful as the kids make it. Your job is to be sensitive to the way the simple act of counting can heighten one's knowledge about something. If the kids seem puzzled, you can always try to count something yourself. Then don't let them count the same thing.

There may be some HIGH TEACHER THREAT or HIGH COMMUNITY THREAT, depending on what the kids decide to count.

more:

How can the various things that were counted be
related?
Should any of the things counted increase or decrease? How could they be made to increase or
decrease?

notespace:

the action:

Take some art materials of your choice outside and use them on some aspect of the environment so that you bring some of the environment back in. Really bring it back!

— paper
— fingerpaints
— charcoal
— clay

What they do:
— wall rubbings
— street rubbings
— textures in clay or fingerpaints

THIS GETS THE KIDS OUT TO CREATE ART. THE WIDE VARIETY OF MEDIA IS IMPORTANT. *(but messy)*

youdoit

notespace:

the action:

Go outside and collect as many seeds as you can find. Plant them and grow them. (The vacant lots and sidewalks are full of late summer plants from which you can get seeds.)

— dandelions and assorted flowers
— tree seeds (maple, Indian cigar, etc.)
— domestic flowers in yards

Let the kids determine what they will need, such as soil, containers, space near windows, etc.
DON'T HELP THEM TOO MUCH.

The weed garden might turn out to be HIGH THREAT to the people that run the school. Find out who they are!!!

more:

Which plants grow fastest?
What can you do to change how they grow?
Try to raise another plant from your own.
Which weeds are most beautiful?
Grow a weed garden of special and beautiful weeds along side the school.

notespace:

the action:

What is the youngest and oldest thing in the school?
(Photography optional)

The only hassle in this one is letting the kids run around the school. Thus it is probably better not to start the year with this one. *LET THE TRUST ENVIRON-MENT DEVELOP FOR A WHILE.* This is a good access route into historical developments and timeliness of all sorts.

Youngest
paint
repair work
kids
animals
plants
books
bulletin boards
--
--

Oldest
building stone
bricks
people
trees
sidewalks
chalk
chalkboard (slate)
--
--
--

Watch out for absolute vs. relative time relationships. We've found these brought up in fourth grade occasionally.

more:

Rank these things in order by age.
How is age determined?
Do you like newness or oldness best?

notespace:

Although the assignment is explicit, the tools are not. This results in a wide variety of techniques being used to examine the area. Each of the techniques intended by the students is correct. DON'T JUDGE THEM

the action:

Use some of the equipment provided and discover as much as you can about the area I'm sending you to. Select an area in the immediate school environment and provide students with a wide variety of tools such as the following:

string
sticks
paper
camera
film
pencils
pens
tape recorders
counter
etc.
etc.
etc.

If the kids seem bewildered, it is probably because you aren't doing the assignment too! Keeping off the kids' backs is a major expression of the art of teaching.

more:

Choose one of the things that you discovered and see if it changes throughout the year. Bring information about your home and neighborhood using each of your senses.

notespace:

the action:

Take a picture that is positive evidence that something natural happened.
What they come up with:
— roots cracking the sidewalk (caused by nature)
— paint peeling (caused by nature)
— litter on the school ground (natural condition)
— car fenders bent (natural condition)
— growth of self or other individual/or part of

CAUSED BY NATURE vs NATURAL CONDITION
The kids have a problem in determining what is natural. Part of the assignment is to let them clarify this point. What They see as natural may not agree with a natural scientist. After they finish the assignment work it out and repeat if you want to.
IF YOU ARE HUNG UP ON TERMINOLOGY YOU CAN BEAT THE KIDS TO DEATH WITH THIS ONE

WORDS DON'T MEAN. . . . PEOPLE DO! If you get hung up on semantics the kids will think that it is more important than it is . . . or than they are.

more:

Do it again within the context of the natural scientist. (if you can figure it out)

¹nat·u·ral \'nach-(ə-)rəl\ *adj* [ME, fr. MF, fr. L *naturalis* of nature, fr. *natura* nature] **1 :** based on an inherent sense of right and wrong (~ justice) **2 a :** being in accordance with or determined by nature **b :** having or constituting a classification based on features existing in nature **3 a** *chiefly dial* (1) **:** begotten as distinguished from adopted; *esp* **:** LEGITIMATE (2) **:** being a relation by actual consanguinity as distinguished from adoption (~ parents) **b :** IL-LEGITIMATE (~ child) **4 :** consonant with the nature or character of someone or something **5 :** INBORN, INNATE **6 :** of or relating to nature as an object of study and research **7 :** having a specified character by nature **8 a :** occurring in conformity with the ordinary course of nature (~ causes) **b :** inferred from nature rather than revelation (~ theology) **c :** having a normal or usual character **9 :** characterized by qualities held to be part of the nature of man **10 a :** growing as a native and without cultivation **b :** existing in or produced by nature **11 a :** being in a state of nature without spiritual enlightenment **:** UNREGENERATE **b :** living in or as if in a state of nature untouched by the influences of civilization and society **12 a :** having a physical or real existence as contrasted with one that is spiritual, intellectual, or mental **b :** of, relating to, or operating in the physical as opposed to the spiritual world **13 a :** closely resembling the object imitated **b :** free from artificiality, affectation, or constraint **c :** having a form or appearance found in nature **14 a :** having neither flats nor sharps (the ~ scale of C major) **b :** being neither sharp nor flat **c :** having the pitch modified by the natural sign — **nat·u·ral·ly** \'nach-(ə-)rə-le, 'nach-ər-lē\ *adv* — **nat·u·ral·ness** \-(ə-)rəl-nəs\ *n*
syn INGENUOUS, NAÏVE, UNSOPHISTICATED, ARTLESS: NATURAL implies lacking artificiality and self-consciousness and having a spontaneousness suggesting the natural rather than the man-made world; INGENUOUS implies inability to disguise or conceal one's feelings or intentions; NAÏVE suggests lack of worldly wisdom often connoting credulousness and unchecked innocence; UNSOPHISTICATED implies a lack of experience and training necessary for social ease and adroitness; ARTLESS suggests a natur ilness resulting from unawareness of the effect one is producing on others **syn** see in addition REGULAR

notespace:

Let the kids run free: they often have pessimistic views of the future and rich discussions come up.

the action:

Using photographs students have taken in earlier assignments, or pictures from magazines, study prints, etc. . . . ask the students to determine how the area in the picture will look a long time in the future . . . and how it looked a long time ago.

Materials for this would be:
— the pictures
— frosted acetate or tracing paper
— tape
— pencils (regular or colored), pens or grease pencils

Have the students fasten the acetate or tracing paper over the photograph and complete the assignment.

Kids sometimes want to prevent the inevitable . . . HELP THEM!! They don't want some of the unfortunate changes to take place!

more:

• Try using photographs of environments of varying degrees of abstraction such as:
— places far away
— ther countries
— photographs that show no evidence of man
— photos of the moon
— places near home
— inside your house
—
—

notespace:

Discovering patterns in the flow of people in the school is identical to the tasks of city planners, city managers and traffic managers of all sorts. Though this is sometimes a cumbersome activity because of schedules, etc., it's worth it.

the action:

Map the flow of people in the school.
- coming to school
- between classes
- lunchtime
- during classes
- going home

more:

Try these
- /teacherpatterns
- /pupilpatterns
- /boypatterns
- /girlpatterns
- /correct the flow problems
- Who does this for a living?
- How about field trips to where the professional traffic-watchers are?
  - AIRPORT
  - POLICE STATIONS
  - SUBWAY CONTROL OFFICE
  - etc.

notespace:

10B. Air Pollution

DETECTION OF ATMOSPHERIC CARBON MONOXIDE

BACKGROUND

Carbon monoxide, an odorless and colorless gas, has its origin in the incomplete combustion of carbonaceous materials; for example, auto exhaust. It has long been known as a noxious inhalant that has its effects because of a strong affinity for combining with the hemoglobin of the blood. When a sufficient amount of carbon monoxide attaches itself to the hemoglobin in the circulating red blood cells, it reduces the availability of the hemoglobin to combine with oxygen, and this results in the reduction of the amount of oxygen available to the tissues.

There are various methods for detection of carbon monoxide. One in particular is the use of N. B. S. Colorimetric Indicating Gel. (National Bureau of Standards manufactures this.) The air to be analyzed is passed through a tube containing a silica gel impregnated with ammonium molybdate, sulfuric acid, and palladium chloride. A yellow silicomolybdate complex is formed, and the palladium serves as a catalyst for the reduction with carbon monoxide. Upon reduction, the indicating gel turns from yellow to either a green or blue, depending on the concentration of the carbon monoxide present.

OBJECTIVE

To be able to detect carbon monoxide in the air.

STATEMENT OF THE PROBLEM

The purpose of this experiment is to familiarize the student with a simple method for detection of carbon monoxide in the air.

APPARATUS AND REAGENTS

1. Vacuum pump, hand bulb pump or vacuum line for drawing air sample through tube.
2. Absorbent cotton.

SOURCE. From *Air Pollution Experiments* (high school edition), by permission of the Cooperative Extension Service, College of Agriculture and Environmental Science, Rutgers-The State University, New Brunswick, N. J.

3. Guard gel*

4. Indicating gel*

5. Glass (filter) tube, about a 7 mm bore

6. Two 1-hone, No. 000 cork stoppers

7. Sufficient tubing to fit 7 mm bore tube

8. Two pieces of glass tube approximately 1 inch each.

Price list

Catalog #38530, Size 1P–Silica Gel Indicating (6-16 Mesh) . . . $2.70

Catalog #39532, Size 1P–Silica Gel Refrigeration (Grade 6-12 Mesh) . . . $2.10

PREPARATION OF FILTER TUBE

1. Clean 7 mm bore filter tube with sulfuric acid, rinse with distilled water. Make sure tube is dry before using.

2. Insert one glass tube into one hole No. 000 cork stopper.

3. Into filter tube, insert a small wad of absorbent cotton, so that it forms a loose pad against the cork.

4. Fill the tube with 5 cm length of guard gel.

5. Add 2 cm length of indicating gel.

6. Then add a second 5 cm length of guard gel.

7. Insert a cotton pad, tapping the side of the filter twice gently, making certain the filter is packed firmly.

8. Insert second one hole 000 cork stopper; then, insert the other glass tube.

*The guard gel and indicating gel may be purchased from:

Central Scientific Company
Division of Cenco Instruments Corp.
237 Sheffield St.
Mountainside, N.J. 07092

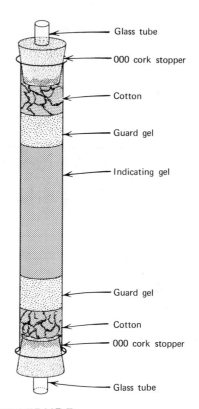

Glass tube

000 cork stopper

Cotton

Guard gel

Indicating gel

Guard gel

Cotton

000 cork stopper

Glass tube

PROCEDURE

Connect a hose leading to a vacuum pump or vacuum line to the end of the tube. Pull atmospheric air through the tube until the indicating gel turns to either green or blue. This is an indication of carbon monoxide.

Quantitative Test

In order to determine the amount of carbon monoxide in the atmosphere, known amounts of carbon monoxide are passed through indicating tubes, the resulting colors are used as standards to determine unknown concentrations by comparing the colors obtained from polluted air with standard colors.

REFERENCE

Bell, F. A., Jr., N. B. S. Detector Tube Method for Carbon Monoxide in Air, Technical Assistance Branch, Division of Air Pollution, R. A. Taft Sanitary Engineering Center, 1961.

10B. Air Pollution

CONSTRUCTION OF A FILTER AIR SAMPLER

BACKGROUND

Particulate matter will remain suspended for a certain length of time depending on the size of the particle, depending also on the desire of someone to filter the air. When air is passed through a filter, the particulate matter suspended in the air will be removed and collected on the filter paper. By constructing a filter holder, placing a piece of filter paper in this holder and connecting the holder to a source of vacuum, one can collect particulate matter from the atmosphere.

OBJECTIVE

To construct a filter air sampler that can be used with filter paper, such as Whatman No. 1, for obtaining samples of particulate matter from the air.

STATEMENT OF PROBLEM

A filter must be attached to a source of vacuum in such a way as to collect particulate matter from the air.

MATERIALS

1. One 5 in. diameter coffee can with lid which fits tightly.

2. One small piece of fine screening at least 4 in. square.

3. One rubber sealing ring for Mason jar (2½ in. inside diameter).

4. Four machine bolts, 1/8 in. diameter times 1/2 in. long, with wing nuts.

5. One metal ring 1/16 in. thick, with 2½ in. inside diameter and 4 in. outside diameter.

6. One short length of 1 in. diameter metal pipe.

PREPARATIONS

Construction of filter holder

1. In the center of the bottom of the coffee can, cut a 1 in. diameter hole and insert the short length of 1 in. diameter pipe securely to the can, forming an air-tight junction.

2. Cut a 2½ in. diameter hole in the center of the coffee can lid.

3. From the small piece of screening cut a circular piece 4 in. in diameter.

4. Drill four 5/32 in. diameter holes, spaced 90° apart, in the metal ring and four holes in the can lid, corresponding to those in the ring so that the two pieces can be fastened together with

SOURCE. From *Air Pollution Experiments* (high school edition), by permission of the Cooperative Extension Service, College of Agriculture and Environmental Science, Ruters-The State University, New Brunswick, N. J.

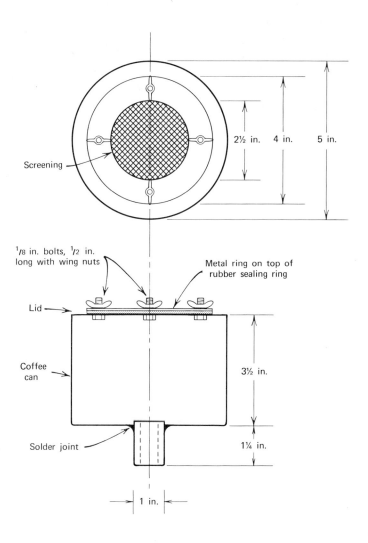

Screening

2½ in. 4 in. 5 in.

⅛ in. bolts, ½ in. long with wing nuts

Metal ring on top of rubber sealing ring

Lid

Coffee can

3½ in.

Solder joint

1¼ in.

1 in.

the bolts and wing nuts. (Since the screening will be placed between the ring and the lid, it will be necessary to punch four holes in it too.)

5. Assemble the filter holder as shown in the attached sketch.

PROCEDURE

Use of the filter air sampler

1. Place a piece of filter paper 3 in. in diameter between the screen and the rubber sealing ring. (The screen acts as a support for the filter paper.) Secure

these between the lid and the metal ring (screen against the lid) and fasten tightly with the four bolts and wing nuts.

2. Connect the 1 in. diameter pipe to a source of suction, such as the hose of a vacuum cleaner, and collect particles from the air on the filter.

3. If some type of flow measuring device can be obtained and incorporated into the system, it will be possible to obtain a quantitative determination of the amount of particulate matter in the air. To do this, the sampler should be run for a measured length of time (pre-

ferable at least 3 hours) and the volume of air sampled obtained by means of the flow measuring device. Then, by simply weighing the filter paper before and after sampling, the concentration, or weight of particulate matter per unit volume of air sampled, can be obtained. This con-

centration is commonly expressed in micrograms per cubic meter.

4. As a further use of the filter air sampler, concentrations can be compared from day to day, weekday vs. weekend, or by months or seasons of the year.

10B. Air Pollution

VENTURI SCRUBBER FOR PARTICULATE COLLECTION

BACKGROUND

Potential particulate air pollutants are often removed from effluent gas streams by means of Venturi Scrubbers. In this apparatus high collection efficiency is often obtained. A principal advantage of this type collector over other dust collectors is the relatively small size. In principle, the Venturi Scrubber accelerates the dust particles as they enter the Venturi throat, which is flooded with water or other absorbing liquid. Relative velocities between the dust and water allows the dust particles to collide with the water droplets. Upon collision the dust particles are, for all practical purposes, removed from the effluent gas stream. Upon leaving the collector the water droplets plus the dust particles contained within the water droplets are removed by some type of inertial separator.

OBJECTIVE

To demonstrate the above principles, using the Venturi Tube previously described as the Scrubber.

STATEMENT OF THE PROBLEM

You must pass polluted atmospheric air through a spray of water.

MATERIAL

1. Venturi Tube previously discussed
2. Coffee can, 2 lb.
3. 2 in. piece of 1¼ in. copper tubing
4. Vacuum cleaner

PREPARATION

1. Solder Venturi Tube at bottom of coffee can so as to produce tangential entry, as shown in the Figure.

SOURCE. From *Air Pollution Experiments* (high school edition), by permission of the Cooperative Extension Service, College of Agriculture and Environmental Science, Rutgers-The State University, New Brunswick, N. J.

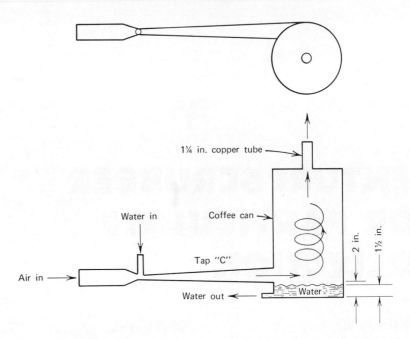

2. Solder short piece of 1/8 in. copper tubing in bottom of can, and connect to pressure tap "C" with rubber tubing.

3. Solder short section of 1¼ in. copper tubing in lid of coffee can.

4. Fill can with water to depth of 1½ in.

PROCEDURE

1. Connect the discharge air pressure side of the vacuum cleaner to Venturi Tube and pump air through the system. Increase air flow rate until water is sucked into venturi throat. Observe collection of water spray through top of can.

2. Seal top of can in place by means of solder or masking tape. Connect vacuum cleaner to coffee can and pull air through the system. Inject known quantities of dust into open end of Venturi Tube. Determine efficiency of collection by before and after weighings of vacuum cleaner bag or by visual inspection of bag.

SUPPLEMENTARY EXPERIMENTS

1. Determine efficiency of collection as a function of water injection rate. For this experiment a water reservoir of known volume is required. Water rate can be varied by means of pinch clamp on water inlet tube.

2. Determine efficiency of collection as a function of air flow rate. For this experiment a separate water supply is also required so that water injection rate can be maintained constant at a known value.

10B. Air Pollution

DETECTION OF ATMOSPHERIC ALDEHYDES

BACKGROUND

Aldehydes, principally formaldehyde, are produced by combustion sources such as incinerators, automobile exhaust, and photochemical reactions in the atmosphere. Formaldehyde has a characteristic pungent, suffocating odor and is intensely irritating to the eye, nose, and throat. Formaldehyde and other aliphatic aldehydes can be determined by reacting the aldehyde with reagent I (3-methyl—2-benzothiazolone hydrozone hydrochloride) and reagent II (1% aqueous ferric chloride) to form a blue dye.

OBJECTIVE

To determine whether aldehydes are present in the atmosphere.

STATEMENT OF THE PROBLEM

You are going to prepare a synthetic mixture of formaldehyde and air. You expose this controlled atmosphere to reagents I and II discussed below and observe the results. You now treat an air sample with reagents I and II and report whether or not aldehydes are present.

MATERIALS

1. Reagents:
   3-methyl - 2-benzothiazolone hydrochloride (Obtainable from Aldrich Chemical Co., Milwaukee 10, Wisconsin) (MBTH)
   1% aqueous solution of MBTH
   0.4% aqueous solution of MBTH
   37% aqueous formaldehyde solution
   Silica gel, dessicant grade, 100-200 mesh (can be obtained from Davison Chemical Co., Baltimore 3, Maryland)

2. Equipment:
   11 cm diameter filter paper
   glass tubing 5-6 mm inside diameter, 120-150 mm in length
   glass wool

SOURCE. From *Air Pollution Experiments* (high school edition), by permission of the Cooperative Extension Service, College of Agriculture and Environmental Science, Rutgers-The State University, New Brunswick, N. J.

suction pump
250 ml Erlenmeyer flask
2 hole rubber stopper

PREPARATION

Silica Gel Tube Procedure

The silica gel tube dimensions are shown in Figure 1. The silica gel contains 0.2 ml of 0.4% MBTH reagent solution mixed in each gram of silica gel.

1. Place glass wool in the constricted end of the tube.

2. Add the treated silica gel. (If kept in a sealed container, the packed tubes are good for about a month.)

3. Pull several liters of the polluted air through the tube.

4. Add enough 1% aqueous ferric chloride to wet the column of silica gel. (About 0.5 ml is usually sufficient.)

5. Read the color against a tube which has not been used. The blank will usually have a light green color throughout the tube. A blue color is evidence for the presence of aldehydes.

Preparation of a Synthetic Aldehyde Air Mixture

1. Place 100 ml of 37% formaldehyde solution into a 250 ml Erlenmeyer flask.

2. Fit a two hole rubber stopper with glass tubing as shown in Figure 2.

3. Attach amber rubber tubing to glass tubing.

4. Bubble air through the formaldehyde solution. The air emerging contains formaldehyde and can be used as a test gas for the filter paper and silica gel tube procedure for detecting aldehydes in polluted air.

PROCEDURE

1. Place one drop of the 1% MBTH reagent solution in the center of a sheet of filter paper.

2. Expose the spotted filter paper for a few seconds (if auto exhaust fumes) to a few minutes (for garages, bus terminals, or heavy traffic areas).

3. Do not allow filter paper to dry.

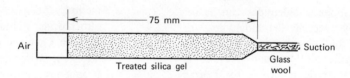

FIGURE 1.

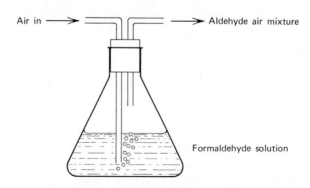

FIGURE 2.

4. Allow to stand one minute.

5. Add one drop of 1% ferric chloride solution.

6. Observe the color of the stain. If the color is blue the presence of aliphatic aldehydes is indicated. Identification limit is 0.1 mg for formaldehyde.

REFERENCE

Sawicki, E., et al., "Sensitive New Methods for the Detection, Rapid Estimation, and Determination of Aliphatic Aldehydes," *Anal. Chem.* Vol. 33, 93 (1961).

10B. Air Pollution

FABRIC FADING DUE TO OZONE AND OXIDES OF NITROGEN

INTRODUCTION

The stability of colors in dyed fabrics is extremely variable. Some of the causes of color fading are strong sunlight, washing, heat, and humidity. Recently attention has been given to air pollution as a cause of fabric fading. Oxides of nitrogen and ozone are suspected as being the air contaminants responsible. Included in the kit which you have received are two special dyed fabrics, one of which is sensitive to oxides of nitrogen and the other to ozone. Exposure of these two special fabrics will provide a rough measure or index of the concentration of all oxides of nitrogen and ozone in the atmosphere.

Simultaneous, similar exposure of samples of dyed fabrics from home, to contrast with the experimental fabrics, will provide a rough measure of the economic loss your family may be experiencing from the fading of dyes as a result of air pollution.

EQUIPMENT REQUIRED

1. Louvered Shelter 8" X 8" X 8"
2. Ozone sensitive fabric
3. Oxides of nitrogen sensitive fabric*
4. Plain fabrics (new)

EXPERIMENTAL PROCEDURE

Mount the fabric, to be investigated, on a piece of cardboard with a staple at each corner to hold it securely. A standard playing card makes a suitable holder. Suspend the card from the center post in the louvered shelter. The post has three hooks on it which makes it suitable for suspending three fabrics simultaneously. Use one piece of oxides of nitrogen sensitive fabric, one ozone, and one fabric from home.

*This Gas Fading Control Fabric is available in 2" rolls about 10 yards long from Test Fabrics Inc., 55 Vandam St., New York, N.Y. 10013. The price is 2 rolls for $5.00 and the price for 2 rolls of fabric for ozone is $7.50.

SOURCE. Reprinted, by permission, of Eduquip, Inc., from the *Eduquip Air Pollution Study Program Manual,* Boston: Eduquip, Inc., 1970.

Keep a similar piece of each fabric as a control in air tight containers, such as jars or stoppered test tubes, to enable comparison of your test samples with original samples. Place the louvered shelter outside. Nail it to a post or put a brick in the bottom to prevent the wind from blowing it over. Leave the fabrics out for a period of thirty days. Observation should be made of the fabrics each day and notes taken as to obvious fabric deterioration, such as strand snapping, color fading, etc.

10B. Air Pollution

THE EFFECT OF AIR POLLUTION ON NYLON

INTRODUCTION

The usable life of nylon goods, particularly women's hose, is often shortened by air pollution. Instances of severe nylon hose deterioration have been reported in the United States, Canada, England, and even aboard some ships. The pollutant causing this destruction is called "acidic soot." The known probable destructive agents of nylon are: (1) hot particles, contained in smoke, (2) soot laden with sulfuric acid, (3) acid aerosols, and (4) nitrogen oxides.

EQUIPMENT REQUIRED

1. Louvered Shelter 8" X 8" X 8"
2. 15 denier nylon hose
3. A 7X magnifier

EXPERIMENTAL PROCEDURE

Obtain some good quality (15 denier) nylon hose. Cut the nylon into a square and stretch it tightly over a standard playing card, or similar piece of cardboard. For this experiment the nylon must be taut before being stapled at each corner.

Place the nylon fabric into the louvered shelter, suspended from one of the hooks. Prepare a second sample in the same manner and store the sample in a closed container for the same period so that it may be used as a control for comparison purposes. Place the louvered shelter outside. Nail it to a post or put a brick in the bottom to prevent the wind from blowing it over. Examine the nylon daily for broken threads. A low power magnifying glass (7X) is suitable for this purpose. Record the number of strand breaks per day of exposure for each sample, including the control.

For comparative purposes, expose some samples of nylon to the outdoors without a shelter. Compare all three samples.

SOURCE.   Reprinted, by permission, of Eduquip, Inc., from the *Eduquip Air Pollution Study Program Manual,* Boston: Eduquip, Inc., 1970.

10B. Air Pollution

THE EFFECT OF AIR POLLUTION ON RUBBER

INTRODUCTION

Natural rubber is a colloidal suspension of tiny particles in a white milk-like fluid called latex. It is obtained from the bark of a tree, Herea brasiliensis, which grows in South America, by catching the liquid that oozes out. Each tree will produce about 6 pounds of rubber a year.

In 1826, Michael Faraday showed that rubber consists mainly of hydrocarbon molecules. Grenville Williams confirmed this in 1860 by distilling rubber and obtaining a liquid with the composition C_5H_8.

Natural rubber is highly affected by temperature changes; it melts when heated and becomes brittle when cooled. In 1839, Charles Goodyear discovered that if rubber is heated with a small quantity of sulfur, a chemical change takes place making the rubber much more resistant to temperature changes. This process is called vulcanization. With this discovery, rubber became a product which could be commonly used.

Ozone attacks natural rubber vigorously. The C_5H_8 radical contains a double bond which the ozone attacks. This double bond means that the molecule is unsaturated or that there is not a full complement of hydrogen atoms. The ozone attacks the carbon-carbon double bond, and eventually breaks the molecule. Ozone particularly attacks rubber at points of stress and cracking is readily observed at these points. Its ability to be stretched and return to original shape is greatly reduced after exposure to ozone.

The discovery of neoprene and other synthetic rubber substitutes partially overcome the ozone problem. They are more highly saturated and therefore less prone to attack but unfortunately they are more expensive than natural rubber. Other synthetic rubbers such as the silicones and butyls are also very resistant to ozone attack and are being used where deterioration of rubber must be avoided.

EQUIPMENT REQUIRED

1. Louvered Shelter
2. Test rubber plaques
3. A magnifier (7X)

SOURCE. Reprinted, by permission of Eduquip, Inc., from the *Eduquip Air Pollution Study Program Manual,* Boston: Eduquip, Inc., 1970.

EDUCATIONAL IMPLICATIONS

EXPERIMENTAL PROCEDURE

Place the louvered shelter in a convenient, safe, and unobstructed spot on the roof of your school or outside the window. Put a brick in the bottom to prevent the wind from blowing it over.

Cut a 2" long X 5/16" wide rubber strip from the sheet supplied with the shelter. Attach a book binder clip to each end. Hang one end from the hook in this shelter. Hang a lead weight of about 50 grams from a lower clip, putting the rubber between clips under tension.

After seven days of exposure to the atmosphere remove the rubber strip and examine it while under the same tension for degrees of cracking. Note any loss of elasticity in its ability to be stretched and then return to its original length from that of the unexposed strip. (Note that if exposure of seven days is not sufficient to cause noticeable cracking or other degradation, the period of exposure should be extended.)

Conduct several successive experiments over a period of weeks and apply an arbitrary numerical rating to the degree of degradation found in the rubber.

10B. Air Pollution

DUST AND PARTICULATE FALLOUT SAMPLING

INTRODUCTION

This experiment deals primarily with larger atmospheric particles. These are particles that settle and which can be readily seen with the naked eye after collection and range in size from approximately 2-100 microns. (A micron is one millionth of a meter or .00004 inches.) The data which is collected will be compiled to enable the class to determine which areas in his town are the worst. This data when sent back to Eduquip, Inc. will be compiled to form a master data sheet for the entire country. The results will be published and sent to each participating school so that statistical analyses may be made to allow you to compare the degree of pollution in your town with that in towns all over the country.

EQUIPMENT REQUIRED

1. The Eduquip Particle and Gas Sampler Kit

EXPERIMENTAL PROCEDURE

Take three frosted end glass slides and mark them #1, #2, and #3 on the frosted portion of the slide. On slide #1 place a piece of double sticky tape, approximately 2 inches long. On slide #2 place a drop or two of immersion oil and spread a thin even coat over approximately 2 inches of the slide. Leave slide #3 blank. Insert these in the particle holder and place the holder in some convenient location exposed to the environment which you are interested in. It may be placed on a window sill, outside in the school yard, on the roof of the school, or any one of hundreds of places. Simultaneously place three more slides, numbered 4, 5, and 6, indoors; in the classroom, the hallway, the cafeteria, etc. After twenty-four hours collect the slides, analyze, and record the results.

Take the magnifier which was supplied with the kit and observe the individual particles on the slides. What is their shape? Draw a square in the middle of the tape. Make the square 1 centimeter (or ½ inch) on each side. Count the total number of particles which you see in this area. If a microscope is available, try to determine the average particle size. Using this data try to extrapolate the amount of particulate matter which was deposited in one

SOURCE. Reprinted, by permission of Eduquip, Inc., from the *Eduquip Air Pollution Study Program Manual,* Boston: Eduquip, Inc., 1970.

square mile around the area of the sample for this 24 hour period. Express your results in number of particles per unit area.

Try to determine the count and size of all particles on 1 sq. cm. of the slides with oil and the plain slides. Compare the results of all slides.

PARTICLE COUNTING TECHNIQUE

1. When counting particles under a magnifier or microscope, count one row of particles from the upper left hand corner to the upper right of the square.

2. Index down and move back to the left hand side of the square.

3. Count another row of particles once again moving from left to right until you reach the right hand edge of the square.

4. Repeat steps 2 and 3 until you have reached the bottom line of the square. The technique is similar to the operation of a typewriter.

This method of counting particles minimizes counting a single particle more than once as well as minimizing the number of particles not counted at all.

PARTICLE SIZING TECHNIQUE

A microscope with a 100X magnifying capability and a calibrated reticle in the eyepiece is required for this analysis.

1. Focus the microscope on the slide in a random position near the left hand side of the slide.

2. Size the particles by traversing across the slide to the right.

3. Size at least 300 particles for a good statistical analysis.

4. A sample table of counted particles appears below:

SIZE RANGE	$<1\mu$	1μ-2μ	2μ-4μ	4μ-8μ	8μ-16μ	16μ-32μ	32μ-64μ	$>64\mu$
No. of particles in size range.	(tally marks)	(tally marks)	(tally marks)	(tally marks)	(tally marks)	(tally marks)	//	/
Total	16	80	100	75	40	10	2	1

10B. Air Pollution

LEAD COMPOUNDS FROM THE ROADSIDE (FOR THE TEACHER)

The thousands of tons of lead compounds emitted by the long lines of automobiles that crowd our highways must go somewhere. Lead-containing gasoline is used in many automobile engines. The lead does not accumulate in the engine. Rather it leaves the engine in the exhaust fumes. What becomes of the lead? We see no "white" colorless salt-like deposit of lead compounds along our highways.

The lead bromide or lead chloride leaves the tail pipe of the car as a gas and at a high temperature. The air cools the lead compounds and they soon become liquid and then solid. They are very tiny and very widely dispersed. A line of several hundred cars per hour, however, must put enough lead compounds into the environment to have a noticeable effect. Even if the condensed particles are tiny enough to be airborne for a while, eventually the action of wind and rain must cause some of them to settle out.

So we send the students out to gather samples. These may or may not contain a lead compound. Very likely most of them will not. We hunt for the lead in the samples by leaching them with warm water in which any lead compound dissolves.

At this point we are faced with a problem. Lead compounds react somewhat with water, a reaction called hydrolysis. In this case the reaction with water can be lessened if a few drops of an acid are added to the water. If an acid is added, we risk dissolving other metallic compounds or the elements themselves, especially iron, and introducing impurities. We could try acetic acid, a weak acid which reacts slowly with iron. If lead acetate forms, it is mildly soluble.

TEST REAGENT

If lead sulfide (PbS) is to be the compound of lead formed in the test, its solubility is small and its color is black. If lead chromate ($PbCrO_4$) is selected as the identifying compound, its solubility is smaller yet and its color is bright yellow.

SOURCE. Reprinted, by permission, from *Scientific Experiments in Environmental Pollution,* Elbert C. Weaver, Ed., published by Holt, Rinehart, and Winston, 1968.

EDUCATIONAL IMPLICATIONS

Tabulating:

Name	Formula	Color	Solubility (g/100 ml water)
Lead sulfide	PbS	black	0.00425
Lead chromate	$PbCrO_4$	yellow	0.000,005,8

Lead chromate is far less soluble by a factor of about 700 times (0.000,005,8 X 700 = 0.00406). Lead chromate is far more sensitive as a test agent.

RESULTS OF TRYOUT

As might be expected, some negative results were experienced. A visible bright yellow precipitate did form from one of the samples, giving hope that other samples will yield positive results.

$$PbCl_2 + K_2CrO_4 - PbCrO_4 + 2KCl$$

lead chloride	potassium chromate	lead chromate	potassium chloride
colorless, soluble	yellow, soluble	yellow, insoluble	colorless, soluble

FILTERING

Fold the paper circle in halves. Then fold the halves again to make quarters. Hold the flat side of the sector toward you. Make the filter cone-shaped by opening one fold half way around and leaving three folds on the other semicircumference.

Moisten the funnel. Put the paper in place with its cone within the cone of the glass funnel, points together. The filter paper should fit snugly. It may be moistened more to make it stay in place. The solid sample to be leached may reach to within ¼ inch of the top edge of the filter paper when the funnel is supported. See the diagram.* If a larger sample is to be used, use a larger funnel and larger paper or make several filtering arrangements using the same size funnel.

*Editor's note: Page 494 of this text.

THE PIPET

The simplest pipet is a medicine dropper. The ordinary dropper one-half inch full omitting the tip, contains about one milliliter (ml). Use one dropper for the sample and another for the potassium chromate test solution. Do not get the liquids mixed in any way until they come together in the test tube.

CONCENTRATION

If the lead chloride has 0.005 g in 200 ml, and the solution is evaporated so that only one tenth of the liquid remains, the 0.005 g is in 20 ml. The same operation repeated has the 0.005 g in 2 ml.

In this operation the concentration increases in steps tenfold and then 100-fold.

The test that might not make a precipitate form with 0.005 g in 200 ml might give a positive result with 0.05 g in 200 ml or 0.5 g in 200 ml. This is another way of expressing stepwise two tenfold increases in concentration.

This experiment is for a Sherlock Holmes of the highways. Take great care when you collect the samples.

PROJECTS

Does some lead bromide condense and stay near the end of the tailpipe of a car? Can you find out?

Lead may also be detected by spraying the places suspected of containing lead compounds with a solution of tetrahydroxyhydroquinone also called 1,2,3,4-tetrahydroquinoline. If lead is present, a red spot forms.

10B. Air Pollution

LEAD COMPOUNDS FROM THE ROADSIDE (FOR THE STUDENT)

Many brands of gasoline contain Ethyl fluid added to improve the performance of the gasoline in the high-compression engines used in modern cars. The fluid contains tetraethyl lead [Pb(C_2H_5)$_4$], and 1,2-dibromo ethane (or dichloro) ($C_2H_4Br_2$). Sometimes a dye is also added to identify the gasoline; other compounds are added for specific purposes. The lead compound acts as a catalyst which breaks the chain reactions in the combustion of gasoline and thus slows the rate of burning, diminishing engine knock.

In the burning, the carbon and hydrogen form carbon dioxide and steam respectively. The lead and the bromine (or chlorine) combine and form lead bromide or lead chloride. These used compounds form vapors at the temperature of burning gasoline, and these vapors pass out the tail pipe of the car.

When the vapors are cooled in the air, lead bromide or lead chloride are condensed to a solid. Lead bromide ($PbBr_2$) is 6.7 times as dense as water. It dissolves about one-half gram per 100 ml of water when cold and more readily in hot water. Lead chloride ($PbCl_2$) is 5.9 times as dense as water and has a similar low solubility in water.

When a car using leaded gasoline drives by your house, does it emit a little lead compound? This experiment seeks to find out.

MATERIALS AND APPARATUS

Funnel, filter paper, potassium chromate solution 0.25 M. (Dissolve 49 g of potassium chromate (K_2CrO_4) in enough water to make a liter. Use one ml of this solution from a pipet.) Breakers, acetic acid (H · $C_2H_3O_2$), medicine droppers, small test-tube (rack optional).

WHAT TO DO

Use a sample of roadside dust, especially from a low spot. Also take a sample of the sand or dirt left from the evaporation of a roadside puddle.

SOURCE. Reprinted, by permission, from *Scientific Experiments in Environmental Pollution,* Elbert C. Weaver, Ed., published by Holt, Rinehart and Winston, 1968.

Weigh out a 200 g sample of road dirt regardless of whether it is moist or dry. If this sample gives no test, larger samples should be used. Place the sample in a funnel which contains a filter paper. Arrange a tube with a small opening attached to a supply of warm water to which two drops of acetic acid have been added above the funnel and place a vessel beneath the funnel.

to be made because they are more soluble. Lead chromate ($PbCrO_4$) dissolves only 0.000,005,8 g in 100 ml of water at 25 C.

If no precipitate forms, evaporate (heat, or heat lamp) the solution to one-tenth its volume and try the test on a drop of this solution ten times more concentrated than originally with a drop of potassium chromate solution. If there still is no bright yellow precipitate, evaporate once more

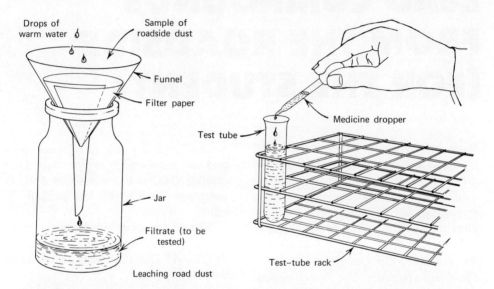

Leaching road dust

Let warm water trickle slowly through the dirt. Catch the filtrate.

Take 1 ml of the filtrate in a pipet. Put this into a test tube. Add a drop of potassium chromate solution to the filtrate. If a bright yellow precipitate forms, a lead compound is probably present. Some metal chromates other than lead chromate are yellow, but in this test chromates of zinc and strontium which are yellow are unlikely

to one-tenth the volume and repeat the test.

The intensity of the yellow color is a measure of the amount of lead chromate formed. A scale may be made and the relative amounts of lead chromate judged: 0 = none, 5 the most precipitate, 3 is between 1 and 5, 2 is between 1 and 3, and 4 is between 3 and 5 in intensity of yellow coloration.

10C. Water Pollution

Calvin R. Fremling

AN EXPERIMENT IN DIFFUSION, WATER POLLUTION, AND BIOASSAY USING POLYETHYLENE FILM AS A SEMIPERMEABLE MEMBRANE

INTRODUCTION

Water-filled polyethylene bags are permeable to oxygen. They thus provide excellent devices for measuring the oxygen concentration of waters which are so full of pollutants or particular matter that they are virtually impossible to test by conventional means. A water-filled bag is placed in the water to be tested and it is allowed to remain there for at least 24 hours. Oxygen diffuses through the polyethylene membrane until the concentration of dissolved oxygen in the water within the bag is equal to the concentration of oxygen in the water surrounding the bag. The water in the bag is then tested by standard methods for its dissolved oxygen concentration.

A small fish or other aquatic organism can be placed in another water-filled bag. By its living or dying in the test situation, the bioassay organism is also used as a

SOURCE. Reprinted, by permission of the editor, C.R. Fremling, "An Experiment in Diffusion, Water Pollution, and Bioassay," *The American Biology Teacher,* September 1968.

495

measure of the dissolved oxygen concentration of the surrounding medium.

I have found that modifications of these methods, which were developed for research work, provide a novel approach whereby students may learn, by experimentation, about water pollution, bioassay, and about the diffusion of a gas through a semipermeable membrane. The method is so flexible that its applications are limited only by the imagination of the instructor.

The experiment is easily adapted to large classes which have many sections. I use this experiment in a class of 120 students (5 lab sections), yet each student is an active participant—not merely an observer.

OBJECTIVES

The objectives of the experiment are; (1) to determine if oxygen will diffuse through a polyethylene membrane; (2) to determine how a high biochemical-oxygen demand pollutant such as milk will affect the dissolved-oxygen content of water; (3) to determine how apparently innocuous substances such as milk can kill aquatic organisms.

MATERIALS NEEDED

The following materials are needed to perform the experiment: polyethylene bags (8 in. x 15 in., 0.05 mm thick), aquarium aerator, dissolved-oxygen testing kit, hardy bait minnows such as fat heads or blunt-nose minnows, heavy string, 3 x 5 cards to make labels, a supply of tempered (dechlorinated) water, large containers such as tubs, garbage cans or aquaria and milk. The standard Winkler titration method of oxygen determination can be used, but I have found that a simple colorimetric modification of the test is best for this experiment (The Hach Chemical Company of Ames, Iowa, sells a very handy, inexpensive, colorimetric dissolved-oxygen testing kit). Tap water which has been allowed to stand for three days may be considered to be dechlorinated. If you are in a hurry, use hot tap water, let it cool over night, and aerate it prior to use.

PROCEDURE

The members of the class should work in pairs. Each pair will be a member of a group. There will be three groups. Determine, at this time, the dissolved-oxygen concentration of the water which is to be used to fill the bags. The simple directions for this procedure are provided with the kit.

Group I. One member of each pair in Group I should place a minnow in a bag which has been filled with two liters of dechlorinated water. Be sure that the water in the minnow bucket and the water in the bag are the same temperature, otherwise the sudden change of temperature may kill the minnow. The student's name and group number are written on a label in *pencil.* The label is placed *in* the bag so that it will not become lost later. Squeeze the air out of the neck of the bag and tie the neck of the bag securely with string. It will take two people to do this. Try not to have any air bubbles in the bag. Check the bag for leaks. If the bag leaks, discard it. The other member of the pair prepares a bag in exactly the same manner, but he leaves the minnow out. All members of Group I should leave their bags on a laboratory table where they will not be disturbed. Group I will thus determine if oxygen will diffuse from air through the polyethylene membrane into the water, thus enabling the fish to live. The bags should be left in place for at least 48 hours.

Group II. Use the same procedure as Group I except that all of the bags are placed in a large tank which contains tempered water. Group II serves as a control for experimental Group III. If over 20% of the volume of the tank is filled with water-filled bags, an aerator may be necessary. Allow five minnows to swim free in the tank.

Group III. Use the same procedure as Group II except that the bags will be placed in an identical container of water to which milk has been added (about one quart of milk per 20 gallons of water). The bacterial respiration concerned with the digestion of the milk will deplete the dissolved-oxygen supply of the water. If the room is very cool, however, or if the water still contains chlorine the process will proceed slowly. Best results are obtained if the milk is slightly soured at the outset. The bags should be completely immersed in the milky water lest oxygen diffuse in through an exposed portion of a bag. Five fish should be allowed to swim free in the milky water.

After 48 hours or more the bags from all three groups will be examined. The bags which contain fish will be examined to determine whether the fish lived or died. The minnows which swam free will also be checked. The water in all bags will then be tested for dissolved-oxygen concentration. All data will be recorded in tabular form on the blackboard. Each student will record the data from all laboratory sections into his notebook.

The oxygen determination is made in the following manner. Immediately after being removed from its test location, the bag is raised and held over a large funnel which rests in a standard dissolved-oxygen sample bottle. The stem of the funnel has previously been extended to the bottom of the bottle with rubber tubing. It is important at this point to not stand in line with bag in hand because oxygen diffuses very rapidly into the bag from the air. The bag is held over the funnel, the extreme tip of the lowest corner is cut off with scissors, and the bag is quickly lowered into the funnel. The weight of the water in the bag will make an airtight seal between the bag and the sides of the funnel. The first water to enter the bottle is undoubtedly oxygenated, but the quantity of water in the bag is sufficient to flush the bottle adequately. The sample is then treated for its dissolved-oxygen concentration according to the standard Winkler method. I prefer the simplified colorimetric version of this test for beginning students because they do not lose sight of the original objectives of the experiment as they do when they become involved in titration procedures. Even the slowest student quickly associates a white milky color with a low level of dissolved oxygen. It is equally easy for him to associate a bright orange color with a high dissolved-oxygen concentration. Advanced students may wish to titrate, however, to obtain more exact determinations (1, 3). Advanced students may also be referred to the theoretical considerations presented in an earlier paper (2).

DISCUSSION

The students will be quick to notice, as they observe all data recorded in tabular form on the blackboard, that milk is a pollutant. Somehow, it decreased the dissolved oxygen content of the water and killed fish. Each student should make a list of conclusions based on the experiment. The following are typical of some of the conclusions that students have drawn from this experiment; (1) polyethylene film is permeable to oxygen; (2) polyethylene film is not permeable to water; (3) polyethylene film is, therefore, a semipermeable membrane; (4) milk, which is nonpoisonous when taken internally, is a high biochemical oxygen demand (BOC) pollutant and as the milk undergoes bacterial decomposition it can kill sensitive aquatic species by depleting their oxygen supply; (5) conditions of oxygen depletion can be detected by using a fish as a bioassay organism; (6) oxygen diffuses faster from the air through a polyethylene membrane into water than it does from water through the membrane into water.

Equally important, the instructor should point out conclusions which *cannot* be drawn from the experiment. The following conclusions are typical of those which *cannot* be drawn from this experiment. Polyethylene film is permeable to carbon dioxide (although this is true, we did not test for it). All fish need at least 4 p.p.m. of oxygen to survive at room temperature (we can only be sure of the requirements of one species—the one which we used in the experiment).

SUGGESTIONS FOR OTHER EXPERIMENTS

The applications of this general method seem endless. The following are some modifications which I have used; (1) put different numbers of minnows in each bag to determine how many minnows it takes to exceed the diffusion rate of the membrane; (2) use 10 bags with a fish in each. Excite half of the fish so that they swim constantly. Allow the others to remain undisturbed. Check the dissolved oxygen content of the water in all bags to determine what effect increased respiration has had; (3) use small crayfish or other aquatic organisms as bioassay organisms; (5) use sugar or hamburger or too much goldfish food as a pollutant instead of milk (Don't we often kill aquarium fish by polluting the water with excess food?); (6) vary the temperature; (7) put 12 bags of water in soured milk and remove them all into the air after two days. The dissolved-oxygen concentration within the bags should now be very near zero. Check the dissolved-oxygen concentration of the water in one of the bags every two hours. Plot a diffusion-rate curve. The students should find that the rate of oxygen diffusion is a logarithmic function and that when equilibrium is approached the curve becomes asymptotic. Clever students will quickly devise a valid method by which no one has to stay up late at night to run the analyses.

LITERATURE CITED

1. American Public Health Association, *et al.* 1960. Standard methods for the examination of water and wastewater including bottom sediments and sludges. Amer. Pub. Health Assoc., New York.

2. Fremling, Calvin R., and John J. Evans, 1963. A method for determining the dissolved-oxygen concentration near the mud-water interface. Limnol. Oceanogr. 8(3): 363-364.

3. Welch, Paul S. 1948. Limnological methods, Blakiston, Philadelphia.

10C. Water Pollution

James O'Hara

A LABORATORY DEMONSTRATION OF OXYGEN DEPLETION IN POLLUTED WATERS

The continental death of aquatic organisms adds large amounts of organic material to the bottoms of lakes. This quantity of organic material reaches extremely high concentrations when domestic sewage and organic effluents from industries are discharged into the water. Since these organic materials are degraded by the aerobic activity of microorganisms, the consumption of the dissolved oxygen can be related directly to the amounts of organic matter present. The biological oxygen demand (BOD) of a water sample can be used to determine the amount of aerobic activity and therefore provide a technique which quantitatively describes the amount of organic matter present in the particular sample (1, 2).

Lakes with a naturally high production of plant and animal life generally have high rates of organic decay on or near the bottom of the lake. This decay can eliminate all oxygen from the deeper regions (hypolimnion) creating a condition that is unsuitable for most aquatic organisms. In heavily polluted lakes, such as Lake Erie, the bottom area made biologically useless by this anaerobic condition exceeds hundreds of square miles. In streams, the oxygen concentration can be reduced to drastically low concentrations within a few feet of the effluent discharge.

The concept of the biological oxygen demand in natural waters can be easily described in the classroom. However, demonstration of this phenomenon is difficult because it requires that dissolved oxygen determinations be made on the same water sample over a specified period of time in order to illustrate the rate of oxygen depletion. Unfortunately, the well-known Winkler method necessitates chemical fixation of the oxygen before titration can be done. To compensate for the individual sample

SOURCE. Reprinted, by permission of the editor, J. O'Hara, "A Laboratory Demonstration of Oxygen Depletion in Polluted Waters," *The American Biology Teacher,* September 1968.

EDUCATIONAL IMPLICATIONS

lost through chemical fixation, a large number of samples can be taken and determinations made periodically to establish the oxygen utilization rate. If more than one concentration of organic matter is examined or if more than one body of water is sampled, the number of determinations and the time involved become excessive.

The fairly recent development of the oxygen sensing probe allows a simple demonstration of BOD to be done in the laboratory or classroom. The accuracy of this method is extremely high and the extensive replication of samples is eliminated because the sensing probe does not alter the sample. One sample can then be used for a number of determinations.

In our laboratory, we assess the effect of different amounts of organic pollution on the oxygen concentration of water. To do this, a sample of water from a stream near a sewage effluent is brought into the laboratory and a dilution series is made with tap water. Each dilution of the original sample represents a different amount of organic pollution in the water.

A liter or two of water from a polluted stream is easily obtained and should be available at the beginning of the lab. If the stream is nearby, it is beneficial for the students to inspect the condition of the stream where the water is taken. A direct effluent from a sewage plant is extremely dramatic for this purpose.

The experiment is set up by adding a magnetic stirring bar and a measured quantity of effluent water to each bottle. The amount of effluent added can constitute a series of 1.0 to 100.0% of the bottle capacity. The rest of the volume of the bottle is filled with tap water. After filling, the oxygen probe is inserted in the neck of the bottle and the bottle is placed on the magnetic stirrer to create a slow current in the bottle. This insures proper gas exchange across the probe membrane and readings should be taken when the indicator needle on the oxygen meter is stable. Remove the oxygen probe and add a small amount of tap water to insure a water seal when the glass stopper is reinserted. This water addition and the stirring may affect a small

TABLE I. Oxygen Concentrations Obtained from a Sewage Effluent Dilution Series in Seven Days.

Bottle number	% effluent in test bottle	Oxygen concentration in mg/l							
		0 hr.	5 hr.	18 hr.	24 hr.	2 days	3 days	4 days	7 days
1	00.0	9.3	9.0	9.0	8.6	8.5	7.8	7.8	7.3
2	1.7	9.3	8.6	8.8	8.4	8.1	7.6	7.0	5.6
3	3.3	9.0	8.6	8.7	7.8	7.3	6.0	5.5	3.7
4	16.7	9.0	8.6	8.0	6.8	6.4	4.6	3.6	0.6
5	33.0	8.8	7.9	6.0	4.7	4.2	0.7	0.0	0.0
6	50.0	8.8	6.1	2.8	1.6	1.2	0.0	0.0	0.0
7	66.7	8.4	4.2	0.5	0.0	0.0	0.0	0.0	0.0

The materials needed to demonstrate BOD rates at different concentrations of organic pollution are:

    Oxygen Analyzer
    Magnetic stirrer with a stirring bar for each dilution
    Standard BOD bottles
    Graduate cylinders in 10 and 100 ml capacity
    Data sheets and graph paper

oxygen change but it will be nearly constant for all samples and the final values can be adjusted by running a control. The bottles should be kept in the dark to eliminate possible additions of oxygen from photosynthetic activity. Temperature fluctuations should be kept to a minimum.

The initial oxygen depletion in the heavily polluted samples will necessitate measurements every three or four hours for

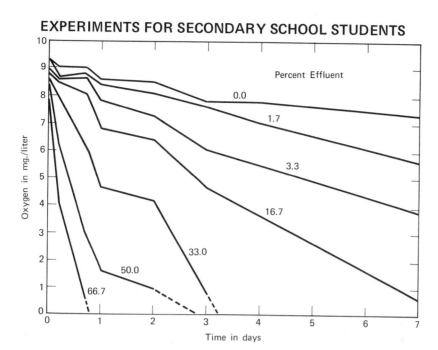

the first day. After that, daily determinations are sufficient and the total experiment should be run until clearly defined oxygen utilization curves are established.

The data presented in Table I indicate that the rate of oxygen utilization is nearly linear and the slight deviations from this may be due to variations in student technique in obtaining the data or to slight changes in the room temperature.

The BOD calculations (Table II) show that the microorganisms involved in the decay process have an average rate of oxygen utilization of approximately 0.03 mg/1 in each ml of the water sample. Thus, 30 rng of dissolved oxygen are required to completely oxidize the organic matter in a

liter of stream water. Extrapolation from these data indicates that in approximately seven hours, the total amount of oxygen in a saturated one liter sample (8.83 mg O_2 at 22 C) would be completely utilized in the breakdown of the organic matter contained in a liter of the stream water.

REFERENCES

1.   Ruttner, F. 1953. Fundamentals of limnology, Univ. Toronto Press, Toronto, Ontario, 295 p.

2.   Rainwater, F. H. and L. L. Thatcher. 1960. Methods for collection and analysis of water samples. U. S. Geological Survey Paper 1454. Washington, D.C. 301 p.

TABLE II.   Biological Oxygen Demand Determinations.

Bottle	Total Oxygen Depletion in mg/l.	Oxygen depletion corrected for control	Oxygen used per ml of effluent	Time in days	Oxygen used per ml per day (BOD)
1	2.0	0.0	0.00	7	0.000
2	3.7	1.7	0.30	7	0.043
3	5.3	3.3	0.33	7	0.047
4	8.4	6.4	0.13	7	0.019
5	8.8	6.8	0.07	4	0.017
6	8.8	6.8	0.05	3	0.017
7	8.4	6.4	0.03	1	0.030
				average	0.029

10C. Water Pollution

WATER ANALYSIS: pH (FOR THE TEACHER)

pH VALUE OF WATER

The members of the class do not need to understand the mathematical explanation of pH. Calculations based on pH may come later in their science work.

The class does need to know the fundamentals:

1. Pure water has pH value 7

2. Acids have pH value 7

3. Alkaline solutions (bases) have pH value 7.

4. A difference of one pH step, as from 7 to 6 is a difference of tenfold.

THE pH SCALE

Since the pH scale is a logarithmic scale, pH values when averaged give results that are inaccurate. For example, pH 6.0 and pH 7.0, averaged give 6.5. This is not the case. See a slide rule which has a logarithmic scale. Use the C or D scale, both of which go from 1 to 2. Is the 1.5 value midway between 1 and 2? Measure it and note that the midpoint is closer to 1.4.

MEASUREMENT OF pH

Liquids other than water can be measured for their pH value. In fact, here is an experiment that distinguishes acids from bases. Use solutions of alum, copper sulfate, zinc chloride, and ammonium chloride solutions, acetic acid, hydrochloric acid (omit sulfuric and nitric acids unless they are very dilute), and borax, sodium carbonate, sodium triphosphate, and sodium acetate solutions, ammonia water, and dilute sodium hydroxide solution. Milk, vinegar, soda water, and other liquids used as food may also be tested.

Students may wish to test body fluids such as saliva at several different times, tears, perspiration, urine (have a small anonymous sample ready in advance of class), and possibly blood. If blood is used, have a nurse take a sample.

PRACTICAL APPLICATION

The pH value of water is carefully controlled in paper-making, water purification, swimming pools, live fish tanks, and in

SOURCE. Reprinted, by permission, from the Teacher's version of *Environmental Pollution: Experiences, Experiments, and Activities,* Holt, Rinehart, and Winston, 1971.

large-scale agriculture. Blueberries thrive in an acid soil. Unless the pH value of the soil is low a good blueberry crop is impossible. Other plants have a pH range within which they grow well. Some grain crops grow in a slightly alkaline or neutral soil. Does liming the soil lower or raise the pH value? (raises)

The pH of drinking water should be close to 7.

Note: pH values of swimming pool water are checked. Many operators of swimming pools have pH testing equipment. Some students may be experienced in making such tests.

WATER INFORMATION KIT

A kit containing helpful information about water pollution problems is available free from Rex Resource Bureau, 300 E. 44th St., New York, N. Y. 10017.

10C. Water Pollution

WATER ANALYSIS: pH (FOR THE STUDENT)

Rain provides water, one of mankind's essential needs, to most areas of the globe. But it falls in Los Angeles and its vicinity, for example, only a few months of the year. The rest of the year the city is so dry that if you fall into the Los Angeles River, you get dusty and possibly bruised on the concrete apron. Los Angeles, therefore, brings water for its huge population from the Colorado river and from other remote places.

To help solve the water problem, careful investigations have been made into the process of desalting sea water. If the process eventually makes fresh water at a low enough cost, many water-needing places such as Los Angeles will use it extensively.

Water is so essential and drinking water so precious that some places have two water systems. One system supplies water for drinking, washing, and similar needs. The other system supplies water for flushing, cooling, and other needs which do not require water of the high quality required for drinking water. Let us find out how water quality is measured.

MEASUREMENT OF THE pH VALUE OF WATER

The pH scale is a measurement scale different from the sort found on a ruler. The pH scale goes from zero (0) to 14. The pH scale puts acids, water, and alkaline substances (bases) together on the same scale. Water occupies the position 7 on the scale, strong hydrochloric acid (HCl) is zero (pH 0), and strong sodium hydroxide (NaOH) solution has pH 14. Further, each whole number value on the scale shows a ten-fold change in strength compared to the next number. For example: pH 5 is ten times as strong an acid as one that has a value of pH 6, one tenth the acid strength of pH 4, and one one-hundredth the acid strength of pH 3. In acids, the smaller the pH value, the stronger the acid.

Pure water, neither acid nor base but occupying a position in between, has pH 7. Ordinary water, however, usually is not quite pH 7 because of substances naturally present. If the substances dissolved in water make it become alkaline, the pH value is more than 7. If the substances dissolved in

SOURCE. Reprinted, by permission, from the Student version of *Environmental Pollution: Experiences, Experiments, and Activities*, Holt, Rinehart, and Winston, 1971.

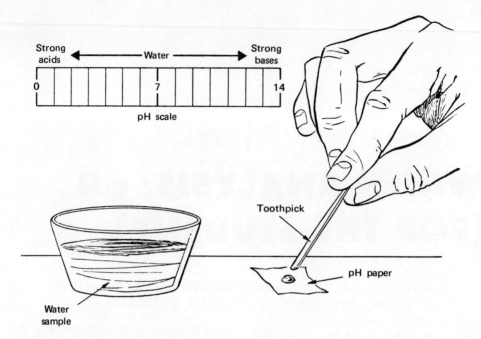

water are acid, the pH value is less than 7. Distilled water dissolves a little carbon dioxide from the air and thereby becomes slightly acid with a pH value between 6 and 7.

SUPPLIES

Toothpicks, pH paper and color comparison scale, several samples of water freshly collected in clean closed containers from several sources.

Note about pH: The kit used for measuring the pH of the water in a tropical-fish tank may be used. It contains an indicator dye, bromthymol blue, (pH 6.0 to 7.8) and a color-comparison chart, and it is available at Woolworth's, for example, for about 69 cents.

The equipment to measure pH in a swimming pool may also be available.

Test papers for pH are available. These include pHydrion paper available from many apparatus supply companies. Get the range that includes 6 through 8. Each student uses a small square of paper from the dispenser on which the color-comparison scale is printed. The same description applies to Alkacid paper from the Fisher Scientific Company.

WHAT TO DO

Each student has supplies of water from several sources available.

1. *Paper Test.* Use a square of paper on a clean surface. Dip a toothpick into a water sample and moisten the corner of the test paper. Compare the color produced and estimate the pH value of the samples. Give the name of the source of the water and its pH value in your report. Repeat the pH test for other samples.

2. *Comparison Test using Liquids.* Follow the directions that come with the kit. Report as above.

In case the run-off water from a mine is tested, low pH values are sometimes found if acids from sulfides are present. Extremely large departures from the expected pH value may indicate pollution.

REPORT

Prepare a paper, presenting the source of each water sample, how it was collected and stored, and the pH value you found.

Make a list of all the other pH values obtained by other members of the class.

10C. Water Pollution

BIODEGRADABILITY OF SOLIDS (FOR THE TEACHER)

APPROACH

Is sanitary land fill the whole answer to the problem of trash and garbage disposal? Is it merely a way to get the rubbish from modern living out of sight? Should some material never be put into a dump because it remains unchanged for 100 years or more?

The disposal of refuse is an amorphous problem, yet each town faces it, and each citizen should be informed of the limits and advantages of disposal of trash by burying it in a dump. How can such a problem be assessed? How can we find out what happens to the material in a dump? This experiment suggests one approach to the problem.

LIMITATIONS

It is difficult to simulate all the conditions in a dump within a classroom. The time factor also is too short and therefore unrealistic. Probably more instructive information could be gained if samples were lifted and measured at intervals greater than one week.

The daily watering is to keep the samples moist and to represent the soil moisture. Shallow samples of soil dry out quickly. Some students remarked that it does not rain every day at the dump. This is true, but refuse is buried deeper than one or two inches and is in soil that is continually moist.

It is not the object of the experiment to show mechanisms of bacterial attack—merely to show that some attack may take place and at different rates.

MATERIALS

One instructor obtained samples of the fill material used at the local dump for one group in the class. This "fill" was contrasted with the effect of rich garden soil. The sample of fill from the local dump used in a tryout made the conditions of the experiment close to those experienced in the town dump.

SOURCE. Reprinted, by permission from *Scientific Experiments in Environmental Pollution,* Elbert C. Weaver, Ed., published by Holt, Rinehart, and Winston, 1968.

Useful trays for the experiment can be made by cutting wax or plastic-coated milk containers lengthwise.

MEASUREMENT

Factors working against precise measurement are dirt sticking to sample, variable moisture content of sample, and growth of mold on a sample. If interference of this sort is an obstacle, dry each sample in a drying oven for one day before the measurement is taken.

RESULTS OF TRYOUTS

Irregular results are expected. The experiment shown below used garden soil which was not dried. The student criticized her own measurements, pointing out that the samples were dry at first and moist later.

The values within parentheses refer to the condition of the sample. These values are explained in the Student Book.

Notice the evidence that the steel can rust, and that the sheet aluminum is gradually changing to compounds.

One experimenter reported that he learned nothing new. "The experiment did not show anything, the conditions are not those of a dump, measurements are not accurate, materials absorb water, . . . measurements fluctuate."

Another experimenter said, "interesting, practice with micrometers, shows kind of work to find information on subjects we would normally find very unimportant, but are really quite important when you think about them."

OPEN ENDEDNESS

The amorphous nature of the experiment gives students a chance to review their work and to see whether or not the same techniques should be applied to all samples. What can be done to improve the accuracy of the measurements? What factors can be controlled to represent the conditions of the dump more closely?

Chemical corrosion may be a factor in the corrosion of aluminum and of iron, but bacterial corrosion is also known as a cause of the corrosion of iron.

Bacteria attack organic matter and remove two carbon atoms at a time in biodegrading. Straight chains of carbon atoms are in general more readily degraded than multi-branched chains.

A CONTROL

Use sterilized soil and sterilized samples, all enclosed so bacteria from the air cannot invade. Are bacteria responsible for the changes observed?

THE REPORT

Thickness of sample may be placed on a graph as a function of time of exposure to bacterial action.

	Initial	One Week	Two Weeks	Three Weeks	Four Weeks
Facial tissue	0.0055 mm	0.0054 (2)	0.0047 (4)	0.0056 (4-5)	0.0054 (5-6)
Paper towel	0.017	0.0122 (1)	0.0124 (1)	0.0134	0.133 (3)
Aluminum foil	0.0032	0.004 (1)	0.0032 (1)	0.0032 (1)	0.0025
Tin can	0.1332	0.1368 (2)	0.1340 (2)	0.1342 (2)	0.1041 (3)

10C. Water Pollution

BIODEGRADABILITY OF SOLIDS (FOR THE STUDENT)

THE PROBLEM

Sanitary land fill is sometimes used as a method of solid waste disposal. It has the advantage of causing relatively small amounts of air or water pollution. The method is simply to bury the trash and garbage (usually by the help of a bulldozer if municipal supplies are involved) and then to wait until bacteria in the soil disintegrate the rubbish. Sometimes this disintegration may produce unpleasant gases, but these gases are often in turn absorbed elsewhere in the soil. Water leaching through a fill may dissolve many undesirable materials, but subsequent seeping of the water through other layers of soil or rock tends to cleanse the water.

If the quantity of garbage and rubbish is not excessive, soil microorganisms dispose of many waste materials rather promptly. This experiment is designed to measure the relative rates of disintegration of various materials by soil microbes.

THE ATTACK

Tests are made on thin sheets of materials which are usually discarded after use. The rate of attack by soil microbes is measured by change in thickness and by visual estimation of the area remaining intact after attack. Thin samples of sheet material are used in this experiment because the attack by the microbes is slow. Hence, it is more quickly evident on thin sheets.

MATERIALS

Thin sheets of paper of various sorts, of aluminum, and of plastic wrapping materials.

Paper: toilet tissue, facial tissue, soft paper towels, wet-strength paper towels, typing paper, carbon paper, hectograph stencil paper (such as Ditto ® that has purple wax on it), notebook paper, magazine cover (glossy), rag-content writing paper, corrugated cardboard outside sheet,

SOURCE. Reprinted, by permission, from *Scientific Experiments in Environmental Pollution*, Elbert C. Weaver, Ed., published by Holt, Rinehart, and Winston, 1968.

kraft paper from a grocery store bag, label paper from a tin can, and other sorts. (The mark ® indicates a registered trade mark.)

Metal: Aluminum household foil, pieces cut from a tin can.

Plastic: Saran wrap ® , polyethylene (transparent), polyethylene (opaque), cellophane, coated cellophane, envelope "window," candy wrapping, cigarette package wrapping, and other sorts.

Garden soil or compost as a source of microorganisms, wick marker.

APPARATUS

Deep tray, bread pan, or milk carton cut lengthwise, machinist's micrometer, scissors.

PROCEDURE

This is an experiment that extends over a period of about one month. Observations are made at convenient intervals such as once per week.

The samples of wrapping materials are identified by numbers. A record of numbers alongside the names of the materials kept in a notebook.

Cut the sheets into strips of convenient size, about 1 by 3 inches. An assigned number is marked at one end of each piece.

Measure the thickness of each sheet. Use a machinist's micrometer that can measure one-thousandth of an inch or less. Place the sheet between the jaws of the instrument and bring the jaws together by means of the little knurled knob at the end of the shaft. This procedure provides equal tension for each measurement.

If a sheet such as toilet tissue is too thin to measure accurately, measure the thickness of ten sheets together and take one-tenth of the micrometer reading.

If the measurements on the same piece of material vary considerably, take ten measurements on different parts of the sheet and find the average of the readings.

Place the garden soil or compost in a deep pan, and mark off four equal areas. One sample of each numbered sort is to be placed erect buried about two inches deep with the numbered end projecting above the soil.

Each strip is separated from the next one by about 1/2 inch of soil. A pan ten inches long and 4 inches wide might have four rows of about 10 samples each projecting above the soil.

Keep the soil moist by watering it every day. Do not put so much water on the soil that the water accumulates. Simply keep the soil moist, not drowned. Also keep it as near 25°C as possible during the entire experiment. The classroom thermostat should be adequate for control of the temperature.

At the end of one week, one set of the samples is removed carefully without disturbing the others. The thickness of each sample is measured and recorded, also, record the extent of erosion of the surface, estimated as (1) no evident damage, (2) roughness, (3) noticeable irregularities, but no holes, (4) tiny holes, (5) Swiss cheese-like holes, (6) complete disintegration, or some similar scale.

At the end of the second, third, and fourth weeks the process is repeated.

RECORD

In your notebook make a tabulation as illustrated. Place scale number 1 through 6 in the table.

QUESTIONS

1.(a) Consider a sample which evidently became thinner. Which sample(s) did this? (b) What is the percent change in thickness each week?
2. Was any difference noticed in the rate of disintegration related to the sort of soil samples used?

EDUCATIONAL IMPLICATIONS

Sample No. Thickness	Date After 1 week		Date After 2 weeks		Date After 3 weeks		Date After 4 weeks	
	Thickness	Appearance	Thickness	Appearance	Thickness	Appearance	Thickness	Appearance
Facial tissue 1 0.001 in.								

3. Which samples (by names) disintegrated rapidly? Which show very slow disintegration?

4. Make a list of the samples by name going from the most actively disintegrated to the least easily disintegrated.

10C. Water Pollution

BIODEGRADABILITY OF DETERGENTS (FOR THE TEACHER)

BACTERIA

In this experiment the term bacteria is used broadly, referring to molds, yeasts, fungi, viruses, and any other microorganisms that can use carbon compounds as food.

If a strain of bacteria is needed, use the usual biology experiment to grow some. Prepare a sterile petri dish which contains agar, beef broth, and other nutrients as listed for the "basal medium." Expose the sterile medium to a source of bacteria (sneeze on it), and grow colonies of several kinds of bacteria by keeping the covered dish in a warm place until growth of colonies of bacteria is noticed. These bacteria may be used in place of purchased culture, No. 6880.

THE CULTURE MEDIUM

Notice that no carbon compound is included in the culture medium used in the student's experiment. This element is to be supplied by the detergent. Notice the caution that acetic acid, carbon containing, should not be used to adjust pH value.

RUN A BLANK (CONTROL)

In bacterial testing, it is good practice to include a closed dish which is put through the sterilizing steps and then is left in order to see whether or not the sterilizing was efficient. The effectiveness of each step may be tested similarly. Include one dish as a control and another really "loaded" with the material under study. By using these "blanks," each step of the process is tested as the experiment goes along.

THE EXPERIMENT

Weigh the amount of detergent added to each culture. Keep the detergent in a closed jar after the package is opened. This prevents excessive loss of moisture so that 1.0 gram of detergent contains approximately the same amount of water each time a sample is used.

SOURCE. Reprinted, by permission from *Scientific Experiments in Environmental Pollution,* Elbert C. Weaver, Ed., published by Holt, Rinehart, and Winston, 1968.

EDUCATIONAL IMPLICATIONS

MEASURING THE RESULTS

After an interval of 24 hours, the results may be evaluated. A scale can be devised in descriptive terms. For example: no effect, very slight effect, about one-fourth of maximum, one half, three quarters, the most. These six descriptive terms, or a better set devised locally and given numerical values, gives an estimate of the extent of bacterial action on the detergent. These terms could be assigned values 0 to 5 respectively.

A more quantitative measure may be devised. For example, a light beam from a constant source is focused so that parallel rays of light pass through the samples in which the bacterial action is going on. The light falls on a photoelectric cell which actuates a sensitive milliammeter. The reading of the meter is directly proportional to the transmission of light, which in turn depends on the degree of bacterial action. The zero point is established with a clean culture, so that readings that decrease progressively indicate the extent of bacterial action.

In a setup such as the one described it is important to keep the geometry of the arrangements identical during all the tests.

Fluorochemical surface-active agents may be tested for their extent of biodegradability. These compounds are used for detergents in environments which are hostile to soap and household-type synthetic detergents. If you want a sample for your class to test its biodegradability, write on school letter paper to M. R. R. Burford, Chemical Division, 3M Company, 367 Grove St., St. Paul, Minnesota 55101. Ask for small samples of FC-95 and FC-170.

10C. Water Pollution

BIODEGRADABILITY OF DETERGENTS (FOR THE STUDENT)

THE PROBLEM

Bacterial growth of aerobic organisms flourishes in locations which have proper conditions for that growth (warmth, moisture, food, oxygen). If any one of those conditions is lacking, the rate of growth of bacteria may become noticeably slower.

If a detergent is easily acted upon by bacterial enzymes, it biodegrades. That is, it furnishes food to bacteria readily. If a detergent biodegrades slowly, it is not readily consumed by bacteria.

THE APPROACH

Using these facts, a culture of bacteria is made with essentially no carbon-containing (organic) food for them. The samples of detergents to be tested are added, one sample to each culture. Those samples that are readily digested by bacteria are the biodegradables. The extent of biodegradability is related to the growth of bacteria. The greater their growth, the more turbid becomes the culture in which the experiment is performed.

MATERIALS

Culture medium as described later, 250 ml flask, sucrose ($C_{12}H_{22}O_{11}$), means of sterilizing, pH paper (range to include pH 7 to 9), source of light.

THE CULTURE MEDIUM

This bacterial culture, favored for growth, is the bacterial type called *Escherica coli*. It is one of the types of bacteria found in sewage, and is available as American type culture collection #6880 from suppliers.

The basal medium is made as follows:

A mixture is made of $NH_4H_2PO_4$ (1.0g), NaCl (5.0 g), $MgSO_4 \cdot 7H_2O$ (0.2 g) and K_2HPO_4 (1.0 g). This mixture is dissolved with stirring or shaking into 1000 ml of distilled or demineralized water.

SOURCE.   Reprinted, by permission from *Scientific Experiments in Environmental Pollution,* Elbert C. Weaver, Ed., published by Holt, Rinehart, and Winston, 1968.

TESTING THE CULTURE MEDIUM

Transfer 100 ml of the medium to a 250 ml erlenmeyer flask. Add 0.5 gram of common sugar (sucrose, $C_{12}H_{22}O_{11}$). Notice that this is the only carbon-containing ingredient.

The principles guiding this experiment are:

(1) bacteria + medium without carbon → limited growth

(2) bacteria + medium without carbon + carbon-containing material ⟶ abundant growth if the carbon compound is easily degraded by bacteria.

(3) bacterial + medium without carbon + carbon-containing material ⟶ limited growth if the carbon compound is not easily degraded by bacteria.

Close the mouth of the flask loosely by a wad of cotton, spun glass fibers (handle while wearing gloves), or by other means.

Sterilize the medium by heating it for 15 minutes in an autoclave or in a pressure cooker. After sterilizing, the medium is free from bacteria.

Sterilize a platinum wire in a glass holder by passing it through the flame of a bunsen burner: When it is cool, touch it to the culture of *Escherica coli.* Close the culture, and touch the wire to the surface of the medium in such a way that you transfer some of the bacteria from the culture to the medium. Rich garden loam may be used as a source of bacteria, but several sorts may be active in such an experiment.

Notice and record the effect on the sugar containing medium every day thereafter for as long as any change is seen. Keep this material in a location of steady temperature (about 30°C). Dispose of the material in the same way that any bacterial culture is treated. Avoid any personal contact with it. Wear glove and use a bactericidal rinse after washing both glassware and gloves.

TESTING DETERGENTS FOR BIODEGRADABILITY

Use the same culture medium as prepared previously. Instead of adding 0.5 g of sugar to it, omit the sugar but add 0.5 g of the detergent to be tested and stir it in. Adjustment of pH to 7.0 or 7.5 should be made by adding hydrochloric acid (HCl) or sulfuric acid (H_2SO_4) and mixing as needed, but do not add acetic acid. Use pH paper to test the pH value. If excessive suds arise, confer with your instructor.

Sterilize as before. Transfer the bacteria in order to inoculate the mixture. Close the mouth of the flask and let it stand at constant temperature. Repeat this process using other detergents, each in a labeled flask.

The extent of biodegradability is measured by how well the bacteria have lived on the food supply. If the bacteria are thriving, they degrade the detergent rapidly, growing, multiplying, and making a cloudy mixture in the flask. If on the other hand, the bacteria are only slowly degrading the detergent, the mixture in the flask is far less cloudy.

MEASURING THE RESULTS

While visual observation alone sometimes can rate the extent of bacterial attack on the detergent, more discriminating measures can be made.

One way to discriminate might be to pass a strong beam of light through the mixture and to observe the extent of transmission of light. It would, of course, be necessary in each test to use the same thickness of fluid through which the light passes. Pick up the transmitted light by a screen of some sort, perhaps a sheet of cardboard.

For further refinement, have the transmitted light fall on a photoelectric cell or photographer's light meter. The electric output of the cell, measured by the milliammeter (or the light meter reading), is proportional to the light energy that passes through the sample.

Since the extent of cloudiness is being measured, a turbidmeter such as the Part type might be used or a photo-nephelo-meter (a cloud measurer). The photo-ne-phelometer is much more sophisticated, costly, and complicated, but its results are precise within one percent or even a smaller value.

10C. Water Pollution

EFFECT OF GERMICIDES ON THE BIODEGRADABILITY OF SOAPS (FOR THE TEACHER)

THE PROBLEM

Soap is readily biodegradable. If soap is mixed with germicides, does this mixture biodegrade as readily as soap alone? Does the presence of the germicide hinder or stop the actions which cause biodegradation? Are germicidal soaps therefore a potential source of water pollution because of their slow biodegradation?

The use of germicidal soaps is being advocated by powerful advertising campaigns in several media of mass communication. It can be assumed that their use will increase. Does the use of such soaps also cause a nonbiodegradable or a slowly biodegradable material to enter sewage systems?

OPEN ENDEDNESS

Form no opinion on the matter in advance of the experiment. Approach the problem with an open mind. View the results suspiciously. Even if a conclusion is reached in one experiment, do not consider it to be positive proof. Check and double check each step of the experiment to be sure that it can be reproduced.

PERFORMING THE EXPERIMENT

Be sure that each culture medium is sterile. Run a "blank" with each sterilization into which 0.5 g of sugar was added. If this control shows no bacterial action, evidence is strong that complete sterilization was accomplished. Unless an experiment can be

SOURCE. Reprinted, by permission from *Scientific Experiments in Environmental Pollution,* Elbert C. Weaver, Ed., published by Holt, Rinehart, and Winston, 1968.

518

reproduced, its results are not firmly established.

If it is found that a soap contains phosphates as a "builder," then the K_2HPO_4 may be omitted from the culture medium.

If excess suds develop when soap is added, a drop of suds-breaker may be added. See for example Foam Breaker Kit, Chemical Products Division, Dow Corning Corporation, Midland, Michigan, 48641, and other anti-foaming agents.

The addition of soap to the culture makes it become cloudy, rendering measurement difficult. It is important, therefore, that an arbitrary scale of cloudiness be established.

INTERPRETING THE RESULTS

Somewhat irregular results may be anticipated from this experiment. Some soaps have germicides that destroy odor-producing bacteria. Such germicides need not be general germicides that destroy all bacteria. The results of the experiment may well show bacterial growth in cultures that contain a detergent and a germicide. Before drawing a conclusion (or being given the explanation above), students should question such a result and gather more evidence until they are convinced that their tests are reliable.

Class results make an interesting tabulation, especially if all soaps available locally are tested, and also if there is disagreement among students on the results of their tests.

CULTURES

The cultures are conveniently made in sterilized erlenmeyer flasks, stoppered with a loosely fitting wad of cotton or glass fibers. Each flask should be appropriately labeled as to contents.

The degree of cloudiness is a measure of bacterial action. Visual comparison is satisfactory if several samples are viewed at the same time. If viewing at different times is necessary, the use of instruments is almost essential if quantitative comparisons are to be made. One instrument for analysis is the Chemical Nephelometer, Catalog No. 4867, available from Welch Scientific Co., 7366 N. Linden Ave., Skokie, Ill. 60076.

10C. Water Pollution

EFFECT OF GERMICIDES ON THE BIODEGRADABILITY OF SOAPS (FOR THE STUDENT)

THE PROBLEM

Some soaps contain additives which are alleged to have bacteria-killing effects. Others have no such additives present. Does the presence of these germicides delay, deny, or have no effect on the rate at which soap biodegrades in sewage?

THE ATTACK

A culture medium is made which lacks carbon. The carbon is supplied by soap. The extent to which the bacteria attack the soap is measured by the extent of cloudiness in the culture medium. The method is like that used in Biodegradability of Detergents. In that experiment various detergents were tested for biodegradability.

It is assumed in this experiment that ordinary soap without germicides is readily biodegradable in sewage treatment. This assumption is essentially true, because soap in huge quantities has been discharged into sewage systems for more than a century with no evidence of accumulation.

THE APPROACH

A culture of bacteria is made with essentially no organic food for them. The samples of soaps to be tested are added, one sample to each culture. Those samples that provide food for bacteria are the biodegradables. The extent of biodegradability is related to the growth of bacteria; the greater the growth, the more turbid the culture.

SOURCE.   Reprinted, by permission from *Scientific Experiments in Environmental Pollution*, Elbert C. Weaver, Ed., published by Holt, Rinehart, and Winston, 1968.

THE CULTURE MEDIUM

See Biodegradability of Detergents for details on the culture medium and testing the culture medium.

TESTING SOAPS FOR BIODEGRADABILITY

Soaps such as Lux ®, Ivory ®, Camay ®, Sweetheart ®, and others do not mention a germicide on their wrappers or in their advertising. These soaps are to be compared with Zest ®, Dial ®, Safeguard ®, Praise ®, Cuticura ®, and others. (The symbol ® indicates a registered trade mark.)

Soaps emulsify dirt and the grease that holds dirt. By washing these foreign materials off the body along with dead cells, the surface of the body is left relatively free of bacteria after washing. On the other hand, complete sterilization of the skin by simple washing with soap is not accomplished. It is assumed that washing with a soap that contains a germicide will kill bacteria that remain on the skin even after washing. The question to be explored is whether or not the biodegradability of the soaps in the second group is affected by the presence of the germicide.

Use the same culture medium as prepared previously and tested with sugar. Instead of adding 0.5 g of sugar to it, omit the sugar but add 0.5 g of the soap to be tested and stir it in.

Sterilize as before. Transfer the bacteria in order to inoculate the mixture. Close the mouth of the flask with a wad of cotton or similar material and let it stand at a constant temperature, about 30°C. Repeat the process using other soaps, some with germicides and some without, each in a labeled flask.

As soon as a cake of soap is unwrapped and a sample taken from it, place it in a labeled widemouth jar and screw the cover on tightly. Soaps contain considerable moisture, and they will dry out unless they are kept in a closed container. By keeping the soap under cover, 0.5 g in one experiment is close to 0.5 g in another.

The extent of biodegradability is measured by how well the bacteria thrive on the food supply, the soap. If the bacteria flourish, they are feeding on soap, growing, multiplying, and making a cloudy mixture within the flask. If, contrasted to these conditions, the presence of a germicide kills the bacteria or makes the soap poisonous to the bacteria, they cannot thrive. Their food intake is limited and they cannot grow, and the mixture within the flask is far less cloudy.

MEASURING THE RESULTS

While visual observation alone sometimes can rate the extent of bacterial attack on the soap, more discriminating measures can be made.

One way to discriminate might be to pass a strong beam of light through the mixture and to observe the extent of transmission of light. It would of course be necessary to use the same thickness of fluid through which the light passes for each test. Pick up the transmitted light by a screen of some sort, perhaps a sheet of cardboard.

For further refinement, see the discussion in Biodegradability of Detergents.

10C. Water Pollution

DETECTING BACTERIAL POLLUTION IN WATER

In densely populated areas water pollution by sewage is an ever present hazard. Several serious diseases can be traced to polluted drinking water, among them typhoid fever and a group of intestinal disorders generally called "dysentery." The actual causative microorganisms, such as the typhoid producing *Salmonella typhosa,* may be extremely hard to detect. Consequently health authorities routinely check for the presence of certain bacteria that act as "indicators." These are known as "coliform" bacteria. Coliform are enteric organisms. This means that they are normally found in the intestines of man and animals. Even healthy people have an ample supply of coliform in their intestines. Furthermore, a number of these organisms are normally introduced into "raw" sewage water by excreted feces. Not only are coliform *always* present in sewage but they are always found in the presence of disease producing bacteria such as Salmonella.

Another reason that coliform are used as indicators of pollution is that they are very resistant organisms and are harder to kill off than the actual disease producers. So, if these organisms are not present in the test sample, health authorities can be reasonably sure that no other sewage pollution bacteria are present either.

Tap water, if properly treated, is of course free of coliform bacteria, while raw or untreated water contains an appreciable number. In this experiment, we will isolate and grow coliforms from a selected water source by trapping them on the surface of a membrane filter for culturing into identifiable colonies.

In addition to promoting growth of coliform organisms, the MF-Endo medium used for coliform culture is also selective in discouraging the growth of most other species of bacteria. This is a significant help in such tests because "raw" water sources contain hundreds of different species of microorganisms having nothing to do with pollution. These organisms would otherwise completely overgrow the test filter and mask the presence of any coliform colonies. How does MF-Endo medium work? Years ago, researchers learned that coliform bacteria have the particular ability to break down a complex "sugar" called *lactose,* forming a number of simpler substances, among which are a group of chemicals known as *aldehydes.* The MF-Endo medium contains lactose and other nutrients, and

SOURCE. Reprinted, by permission, from *Millipore Projects for Science Students,* February 1971, with slight abridgment.

also a stain—basic fuchsin—which reacts with the aldehyde molecules and forms a complex which appears as a shiny green coating. Because few microorganisms make aldehydes out of lactose, other than members of the coliform family, the "green sheen" colonies are quickly identified as coliform bacteria. The mere presence of coliform colonies, however, does not mean that the water is "polluted." Keep in mind that all open bodies of water are subject to animal excretion as well as seepage from soil. *What is important in assessing the possible pollution level of the water is the number of coliform found in the sample.* When health officials find that the number of coliform exceeds the standards set for particular areas and types of water, they assume that disease producing bacteria are also present. Additional tests are then performed to isolate and culture the pathogens.

PROCEDURE

The following procedure is very similar to the coliform test performed daily in pollution testing laboratories all over the world.

1. Sterilize a Sterifil filter holder in an autoclave or by immersing it in boiling water for 3 minutes. If this is not practical, such as in a field experiment, dip the Sterifil in 70% isopropyl alcohol (rubbing alcohol) for a few seconds, shake it off, and let it air dry. You can obtain rubbing alcohol at any drug store or supermarket.

2. Load the Sterifil holder with a Type HA (0.45 μm) membrane filter. When handling the filter, be sure to use flat-bladed (non-serrated) forceps that have been sterilized by dipping in alcohol.

3. Place a sterile absorbent pad in a 47 mm Petri dish. Absorbent pads are supplied in the same envelope with the membrane filters.

4. Break open an ampoule of MF-Endo medium* and pour the entire contents (2 ml) onto the absorbent pad. As an alternative, you can prepare a stock solution

from powdered MF-Endo medium and pipette 2 ml of this solution onto the absorbent pad. Close the Petri dish and set it aside until step 8.

5. To the Sterifil funnel, add about 20 ml of sterile water or tap water that has been boiled for several minutes. The exact volume added is not critical. Its purpose is only to evenly disperse the bacteria present in the measured sample.

6. Into the Sterifil funnel, pipette an aliquot of the sample water taken from a pond or stream. Swirl the funnel to mix the sample with the sterile dilution water. The size of the aliquot will vary with the contamination level of the water being sampled. To determine proper sample size, start with an aliquot of 1 ml. After your first cultures have grown, you can determine whether a larger or smaller sample size should be used. Adjust the sample size to get no more than 20 to 80 coliform colonies growing on the filter surface. The total of all colonies, including coliform, should not exceed 200. Alternately, your first experiment can be run with 0.1, 0.5, 1 and 2 ml to determine the optimum sample size.

Furthermore, you may want to determine the coliform level in water from different sources. As a general rule, the following sample sizes are recommended:

For untreated water (fresh or salt water), use 1 ml of sample added to the dispersion water prepared in step 5 above.

For well-water or natural spring water, use a sample size of 50 ml (omit step 5).

For chlorinated tap water, a much larger sample size is required, at least 500 ml (omit step 5). Here it is necessary to complete the filtration in several steps since the Sterifil receiver flask will only accommodate 250 ml. If your laboratory is equipped with an aspirator or vacuum pump, then the entire sample can be fil-

*Skin or clothing accidentally stained with MF-Endo medium can be cleaned with a dilute solution of sodium sulfite or household bleach followed by soap and water.

EDUCATIONAL IMPLICATIONS

tered at one time by attaching the top portion of the Sterifil unit to a standard 1 liter filtering flask. Ideally, you should find no coliform colonies in drinking water. If you do find coliform colonies in excess of 4 per 100 ml of original sample, you should suspect poor technique rather than polluted water.

7. Using a hand vacuum pump or some other suitable vacuum source (such as a water aspirator), apply vacuum to the Sterifil receiver flask. This will cause the water to flow through the filter leaving the bacteria trapped on the filter surface.

8. After filtration of the test sample, release the vacuum in the system by removing the vacuum pump tubing from the sidearm of the Sterifil receiver flask. Unscrew the funnel and, using alcohol-dipped forceps lift the filter from the Sterifil base and place it grid side up on the saturated absorbent pad in the Petri dish. Carefully line up the filter with one edge of the Petri dish and set it down with a slight rolling motion so that it is evenly centered. Replace the cover.

9. Invert the Petri dish and allow the culture to incubate for 48 hours at normal temperature, or 24 hours at 37°C in an incubator.

The medium will supply all areas of the test filter with needed nutrients, passing directly through the filter to the microorganisms on its surface. The Petri dish must be inverted because incubation often causes moisture condensation inside the closed dish. If the dish were right side up, droplets could form that might fall onto the filter surface, spoiling the appearance of the developing colonies. After the colonies have developed, remove the test filter and allow it to dry on a clean blotter or some other clean absorbent surface (paper towel) for ½ hour.

10. With a hand magnifier or low power microscope (10X), scan the surface of the filter for colonies having a shiny, greenish surface. Count the total number of these "green sheen" colonies on the filter.

Calculations. To figure the number of coliform bacteria present in the water tested, use the following formula.

$$\frac{\text{No. of Coliform Counted} \times 100}{\text{Mililiters of Sample}} = \text{No. of Coliform/100 ml}$$

Example: A two mililiter (2 ml) sample was added to the filter funnel containing approximately 20 ml of sterile water. After incubation, 48 sheen colonies were counted on the Millipore filter. Therefore, (48 x 100)/2 = 2400 coliform per 100 ml.*

NOTE: Standards vary from one municipality to the next. Check with your local officials to determine what the standards are for your area for different types of water (raw water, well water, drinking water and public swimming areas).

MAKING PERMANENT RECORDS

In some cases you may wish to preserve the results of your experiment for future reference or to attach to a report. The technique is as follows:

1. Saturate a piece of blotting paper or an absorbent pad with a solution of:
    20 parts glycerine
    40 parts formaldehyde
    40 parts water

2. Using forceps, remove the specimen filter from the Petri dish and set it down on the saturated blotter pad for at least 2 minutes.

3. Remove the filter and set it down to dry on a clean, dry blotter pad.

4. The dry filter can now be preserved between glass slides or carefully wrapped in an envelope made of plastic food wrap.

*The complete kit for this experiment is called Environmental Microbiology Kit ($48.00) available from Millipore Corporation, Bedford, Mass. 01730.

CLEANING UP

Cultures, whether on filters or in any other medium, should be considered potentially dangerous and handled with the utmost care. After completing the experiment and observing the results, you should destroy or deactivate the cultures that have not been preserved. The plastic Petri dishes should be resterilized using the following procedure:

1. Carefully remove the Petri dish covers using the back of the flat-bladed forceps as a prying tool. Put the covers and dishes (with cultures) into a large beaker or pan containing undiluted liquid household bleach for 10 minutes.

2. Then remove the Petri dishes and covers using tongs or a rubber glove. Rinse well under running water. Wet pads and filters should be put into a plastic bag and discarded.

3. Immerse the Petri dishes and covers in a solution of 70% alcohol for 10 minutes.

4. Remove the Petri dishes and covers and stack them on a clean surface. Once they are dry, assemble them and they are again ready for use.

SUGGESTIONS FOR FURTHER PROJECTS

You can study a variety of fresh water and marine microorganisms using the above procedure, but with different culture media that will allow other kinds of microorganisms to grow. A great deal of research has been carried out and published by professional microbiologists on the use of Millipore filters. The following bibliography will be helpful to you in planning additional projects in water microbiology.

1. Strong, C. L., "The Amateur Scientist." *Scientific American*, pp. 118-122, February '71.

2. Anderson, J. W. and Heffernan, W. P., "Isolation and Characterization of Filterable Marine Bacteria," *Journal of Bacteriology*, pg. 1713 December '65.

3. Sohn, B. I., "Membrane Microfiltration for the Science Lab." *The Science Teacher* 36:8, pp. 48-51, November '69.

4. Hershey, J. T., et al, *A Curriculum Activities Guide to Water Pollution and Environmental Studies.* Federal Water Quality Administ., U. S. Dept. of Interior,'70.

5. Rose, R. E., "Effective Use of Millipore Membrane Filters for Water Analysis," *Water & Sewage Works,* Reference Number 1966.

6. Clark, H. F., and Kabler, P. W. "Type Distribution of Coliform Bacteria in the Feces of Warm-Blooded Animals," *Journal of Water Pollution Cont. Fed.* 34: 295-301, '62.

7. Geldreich, E. E., and Clark, N. A. "A study of bacterial pollution indicators in the intestinal tract of fresh water fish." *Applied Microbiology,* 14: 429-437, '66.

8. American Public Health Association, Subcommittee on *Water Quality Control, Water Quality Standards of the United States, Territories, and the District of Columbia,* June '69.

bibliography

GENERAL REFERENCES AND ECOLOGY ACTION

Allee, W. C., and others. **Principals of Animal Ecology.** Philadelphia: Saunders, 1951.

Bates, Marston. **The Forest and the Sea: A Look at the Economy of Nature and the Ecology of Man.** New York: Random House, 1960.

Bock, Alan. **The Ecology Action Guide.** Los Angeles: Nash Pub. Co., 1971.

Carson, Rachael. **Silent Spring.** New York: Crest, 1969.

Commoner, Barry. **Science and Survival.** New York: Viking, 1967.

Darling and Milton, editors. **Future Environments of North America.** Garden City, New York: Natural History Press, 1966.

Dasmann, R. **Environmental Conservation.** New York: John Wiley, 1970.

Dasmann, R. **The Destruction of California.** New York: Macmillan, 1965.

DeBell, G., editor. **The Environmental Handbook.** New York: Ballantine, 1970.

DeBell, G., editor. **The Voter's Guide to Environmental Politics.** New York: Ballantine Books, 1971.

Dubos, René. **So Human an Animal.** New York: Scribner's, 1969.

Ehrlich, Paul. **The Population Bomb.** New York: Ballantine, 1968.

Ehrlich, Paul and Ehrlich, Anne H. **Population, Resources, Environment: Issues in Human Ecology.** San Francisco: W. H. Freeman & Company, 1970.

Ewald, William R. **Environment for Man: The Next Fifty Years.** Bloomington: Indiana University Press, 1968.

Farb, Peter. **Ecology.** New York: Time, Inc., 1963.

Farb, Peter. **Face of North America: The Natural History of a Continent.** New York: Harper & Row, Colophon Book, 1968.

Gates, Richard. **The True Book of Conservation.** Chicago: Children's Press, 1959.

Graham, Frank, Jr. **Since Silent Spring.** Houghton Mifflin, 1970.

BIBLIOGRAPHY

Hardin, Garrett. **Science, Conflict, and Society**. Readings from Scientific American with introductions by Garrett Hardin. San Francisco: W. H. Freeman, 1969.

Kormandy, B. **Concepts of Ecology**. New York: Prentice-Hall, 1969.

Leopold, A. **A Sand Country Almanac**. Oxford University Press, 1966.
Little, C. and Mitchell, J. **Space for Survival**. New York: Pocket Books, Inc., 1971.

Marine, G. **America the Raped**. New York: Simon and Schuster, 1969.
Marx, W. **The Frail Ocean**. New York: Ballantine, 1969.
Michelson, Max. **The Environmental Revolution**. McGraw-Hill, 1970.
Mitchell, W. **Ecotactics: The Sierra Club Handbook for Environmental Activists**. New York: Pocket Books, 1970.

Nickelsburg, Janet. **Ecology**. Philadelphia: J. B. Lippincott, 1969.

Odum, E. **Ecology**. New York: Holt, Rinehart, and Winston, 1969.
Osborn, Robert. **Mankind May Never Make It!** New York: New York Graphic Society, 1968.

Perry, John. **Our Polluted World. Can Man Survive?** New York: Watts, 1967.

Reveille, Roger and Landsberg, H. H., editors. **America's Changing Environment**. Houghton Mifflin, 1970.
Rienow, Robert and Train, Leona. **Moment in the Sun**. New York: Sierra Club and Ballantine Books, 1969.

Saltonstall, Richard. **Your Environment and What you Can Do About It**. New York: Walker and Co., 1970.
Sears, Paul B. **The Living Landscape**. New York: Basic Books, 1966.
Segerberg, Osborn. **Where Have All the Flowers Fishes Birds Trees Water and Air Gone?** New York: David McKay, 1971.
Shepard and McKinley, editors. **The Subversive Science**. New York: Houghton-Mifflin, 1968.

Udall, Stewart. **1976: Agenda for Tomorrow**. New York: Harcourt, Brace, and World, 1968.

Wood, Nancy. **Clearcut**. A Sierra Battlebook. New York: Charles Curtis, Inc., 1971.

POPULATION

Applebaum, Philip. **The Silent Explosion**. Boston: Beacon Press, 1966.

Bates, Marston. **The Prevalence of People**. New York, Scribner, 1955.
Borgstrom, Georg. **Too Many**. New York: Macmillan, 1969.

GENERAL REFERENCES AND ECOLOGY ACTION

Day, L.H. and Day, A.T. **Too Many Americans.** New York: Dell, 1965.

Ehrlich, P. **The Population Bomb.** New York: Ballantine, 1968.

Fraser, Dean. **The People Problem.** Bloomington: Indiana University Press, 1971.

Freedman, R., ed. **Population: The Vital Revolution.** New York: Doubleday, 1964.

Hardin, Garrett, ed. **Population, Evolution, and Birth Control: A College of Controversial Readings.** San Francisco, Freeman, 1964.

Hauser, P. M., ed. **The Population Dilemma.** Englewood Cliffs: Prentice-Hall, 1963.

Osborn, Fairfield, ed. **Our Crowded Planet.** New York: Doubleday, 1962.

Petersen, William. **Population.** New York: Macmillan, 1961.

Sax, Karl. **Standing Room Only: The World's Exploding Population.** Boston: Beacon Press, 1960.

PESTICIDES

Carson, Rachael. **Silent Spring.** New York: Crest, 1969.

DeBach, Paul, editor. **Biological Control of Insect Pests and Weeds.** New York: Reinhold, 1964.

Mellauby, Kenneth. **Pesticides and Pollution.** London: Collins, 1967.

McMillen, Wheller. **Bugs or People?** Des Moines: Meredith Press, 1965.

Rudd, Robert L. **Pesticides and the Living Landscape.** Madison, Wisconsin: University of Wisconsin Press, 1966.

WATER POLLUTION

Baur, Helen. **Water: Riches or Ruin.** Garden City, New York: Doubleday & Co., Inc., 1959.

Berrill, N. J. **The Life of the Ocean.** New York: McGraw-Hill, 1966.

Carr, Donald. **Death of Sweet Waters.** New York: Norton, 1966.

Carr, Donald E. **The Breath of Life.** New York, N. W. Norton & Co., Inc., 1965.

Carlson, Carl W. and Carlson, Bernice W. **Water Fit to Use.** New York: The John Day Co., 1966.

Carson, Rachel L. **The Sea Around Us.** rev. ed. New York: Oxford University Press, 1961.

Cowan, Edward, **Oil and Water: The Torrey Canyon Disaster.** Philadelphia: Lippincott, 1968.

Federal Water Pollution Control Administration. **Clean Air Publications.** 1967-1970.

Federal Water Control Administration. **A Primer on Waste Water Treatment.** (Free) Department of Interior, 1969.

BIBLIOGRAPHY

Grava, Sigurd. **Urban Planning Aspects of Water Pollution Control.** New York: Columbia University Press, 1969.

Halacy, D.S., Jr. **The Water Crisis.** New York: E.P. Dutton & Co., Inc., 1966.

Helfman, Elizabeth S. **Water for the World.** New York: McKay, 1960.

Hynes and Noel. **The Biology of Polluted Waters.** Liverpool, England: Liverpool Press, 1960.

Kneese, Allen V. **Water Pollution: Economic Aspects and Research Needs.** Baltimore: John Hopkins University Press, 1962.

Mannix, Daniel P. **Troubled Waters.** New York: Dutton Press, 1969.

Marx, Wesley. **The Frail Ocean.** New York: Ballantine Books, 1967.

National Wildlife Federation. **America's Shame—Water Pollution and** other pamphlets including **The Glory Trail, By Which We Live, The Three R's and Resources.**

Overman, Michael. **Water.** New York: (Doubleday Science Series) Doubleday and Co., 1969.

U. S. House of Representatives. Hearings before the Committee on Merchant Marine and Fisheries. **Oil Pollution.** Serial 91-4 Washington: U. S. Government Printing Office, 1966.

U. S. House of Representatives. Hearing before the Committee on Public Works. **Federal Water Pollution Control Act Amendments.** 91-1 Washington: U. S. Government Printing Office, 1969.

Wright, Jim. **The Coming Water Famine.** New York: Coward-McCann, 1966.

AIR POLLUTION

Battan, Lewis. S. **The Unclean Sky.** New York: Anchor Books, 1966.

Branley, Franklin. **Air Is All Around You.** New York: Crowell, 1962.

Carr, Donald E. **The Breath of Life.** New York: Norton, 1966.

Chandler, T. J. **The Air Around Us.** Garden City, New York: Nature and Science Library, Doubleday & Co., Inc., 1969.

Cheronis, Nicholas D., James B. Parsons and Conrad E. Ronneberg. **The Study of the Physical World.** 3rd ed. Boston: Houghton Mifflin, 1958.

Chester, Michael. **Let's Go to Stop Air Pollution.** New York: G. P. Putnam's Sons, 1968.

Edelson, Edward. **Poisons in the Air.** New York: Pocket Books, 1966.

Environmental Pollution Panel (PSAC). **Restoring the Quality of Our Environment.** Washington: U. S. Government Printing Office, 1965.

Forrester, Frank H. **Exploring the Air Ocean.** New York: Putnam, 1960.

Gamow, George. **Matter, Earth, and Sky.** 2nd ed. Englewood Cliffs: Prentice-Hall, 1965.

GENERAL REFERENCES AND ECOLOGY ACTION

Jacobs, Morris Boris. **The Chemical Analysis of Air Pollution.** New York: Interscience Publishers, 1960.

Kavaler, Lucy. **Dangerous Air.** New York: John Day, 1967.

Marshall, James. **The Air We Live In: Air Pollution, What We Must Do About It.** New York: Coward-McCann, 1969.

Preston, Edna. **Air.** Chicago: Follett, 1965.

Stern, A. C. **Air Pollution.** New York: Academic Press, 1968.

NOISE POLLUTION

Chedd, Graham. **The Power of Sound.** Garden City, New York: Doubleday & Co., Doubleday Science Series, 1970.

Committee on Environmental Quality of the Federal Council for Science and Technology. "Noise—Sound Without Value." Washington, D. C.: Government Printing Office, Sept., 1968.

Navarra, John G. **Our Noisy World: The Problem of Noise Pollution.** Garden City, New York: Doubleday & Co., Inc.

Redda, M. **Noise and Society.** New York: W. A. Benjamin, 1967.

Shurcliff, W. A. **SST and Sonic Boom Handbook.** New York: Ballantine—Friends of the Earth, 1970.

WASTE DISPOSAL

Hanks, Thrift G. **Solid Waste/Disease Relationships.** Public Health Service Publication No. 999-UH-6. Washington: U. S. Government Printing Office, 1967.

Laycock, George. **The Diligent Destroyers.** Garden City, New York: Doubleday and Co., Inc., 1970.

Packard, Vance. **The Waste Makers.** New York: David McKay Company, 1960.

Small, William E. **Third Pollution.** New York: Praeger Publishers, 1971.

URBAN ECOLOGY

Bellush, Jewel and Hausknect, Murray, eds. **Urban Renewal: People, Politics, and Planning.** Garden City, New York: Doubleday & Co., Inc., 1967.

Duhl, Leonard. **The Urban Condition.** New York: Basic Books, 1963.

Munzer, Martha. **Planning Our Town.** Alfred A. Knopf: The Conservation Foundation, 1964.

Munzer, Martha. **Pockets of Hope**. New York: Knopf, 1967.

McHarg, Ian. **Design With Nature**. New York: Natural History Press, 1969.

Rudofsky, Bernard. **Streets for People**. Garden City, New York: Doubleday & Co., Inc., 1969.

Weaver, Robert C. **The Urban Complex**. Garden City, New York: Doubleday & Co., Inc., 1964.

Whyte, William H. **The Last Landscape**. New York: Doubleday & Company (Anchor paperback), 1970.

BOOKS FOR CHILDREN

Branley, Franklyn M. **Air Is All Around You**. New York: Crowell, 1962.

Carlson, Carl W., and Carlson, Bernice W. **Water Fit to Use**. New York: Day, 1966.

Dudley, Ruth H. **Partners in Nature**. New York: Funk and Wagnalls, 1965.

Forrester, Frank H. **Exploring the Air Ocean**. New York: Putnam, 1960.

Gates, Richard. **The True Book of Conservation**. Chicago: Children's Press, 1959.

Hagaman, Adaline P. **What is Water?** Chicago: Benefic Press, 1960.

Harrison, William C. **Conservation: The Challenge of Reclaiming Our Plundered Land**. New York: Messner, 1963.

Helfman, Elizabeth S. **Land, People, and History**. New York: McKay, 1962.

Irving, Robert. **Energy and Power**. New York: Knopf, 1958.

Knight, David C. **The First Book of Air**. New York: Watts, 1961.

Laycock, George. **Wild Refuge**. New York: Doubleday & Co., 1969.

Lewis, Alfred. **Clean the Air! Fighting Smoke, Smog, and Smaze across the Country**. New York: McGraw-Hill, 1965.

Lewis, Alfred. **This Thirsty World; Water Supply and Problems Ahead**. New York: McGraw-Hill, 1964.

McCormick, Jack. **The Living Forest**. New York: Harper and Row, 1959.

Navarro, J. G. **Our Noisy World: The Problem of Noise Pollution**. New York: Doubleday & Co., 1969.

Preston, Edna M. **Air**. Chicago: Follett, 1965.

Spar, Jerome. **The Way of the Earth.** Mankato: Creative Educational Society, 1962.

Shuttlesworth, Dorothy. **Clean Air—Sparkling Water: The Fight Against Pollution.** New York: Doubleday & Co., 1968.

BOOKS FOR ADOLESCENTS

Aylesworth, T. G. **This Vital Air, This Vital Water.** Chicago: Rand McNally & Co., 1968.

Bates, Marston. **The Forest and the Sea: A Look at the Economy of Nature and the Ecology of Man.** New York: Random House, 1960.

Battan, Louis J. **The Unclean Sky; a Meteorologist Looks at Air Pollution.** Garden City: Anchor, 1966.

Bregman, J. I., and Lenormand, Sergei. **The Pollution Paradox.** Washington, D. C.: Spartan, 1966.

Bronson, William. **How to Kill a Golden State.** Garden City, New York: Doubleday and Co., 1968.

Buchsbaum, Ralph, and Buchsbaum, Mildred. **Basic Ecology.** Pittsburgh: Boxwood Press, 1957.

Blake, Peter. **God's Own Junkyard: The Planned Deterioration of America's Landscape.** New York: Holt, Rinehart & Winston, 1964.

Carr, Donald E. **Death of the Sweet Waters.** New York: Norton, 1966.

Carson, Rachel L. **Silent Spring.** Boston: Houghton-Mifflin, 1962.

Clawson, Marion. **Land for Americans: Trends, Prospects, and Problems.** Chicago: Rand McNally, 1963.

Clawson, Marion. **Man and Land in the United States.** Lincoln: University of Nebraska Press, 1964.

Douglas, William O. **A Wilderness Bill of Rights.** Boston: Little, Brown, 1965.

Farb, Peter, and the editors of Life. **Ecology.** New York: Time, 1963.

Friedman, R. **Population: The Vital Revolution.** New York: Doubleday & Co., 1964.

Helfman, Elizabeth S. **Water for the World.** New York: McKay, 1960.

Higbee, Edward. **The Squeeze: Cities Without Space.** New York: Morrow, 1960.

Hitch, Allen S., and Sorenson, Marian. **Conservation and You.** Princeton: Van Nostrand, 1964.

Landsberg, Hans H. **Natural Resources for U. S. Growth: A Look Ahead to the Year 2000.** Baltimore: Johns Hopkins Press, 1964.

Leopold, Luna B., Davis, Kenneth S. and the editors of Life. **Water.** New York: Time, 1966.

McMillen, Wheeler. **Bugs or People?** Des Moines: Meredith, 1965.

BIBLIOGRAPHY

McNall, P. E. **Our Natural Resources.** 2nd ed. Danville: Interstate, 1964.

Means, R. L. **The Ethical Imperative.** New York: Doubleday & Co., 1970.

Munzer, Martha E. **Planning Our Town.** New York: Knopf, 1964.

Munzer, Martha E. **Pockets of Hope.** New York: Knopf, 1967.

Udall, Stewart L. **The Quiet Crisis.** New York: Holt, Rinehart & Winston, 1963.

Wrong, Dennis H. **Population and Society.** 2nd rev. and enl. ed. New York: Random House, 1961.

ANNOTATED LIST OF BOOKS FOR CHILDREN AND ADOLESCENTS

GRADES K-3

An introduction to seasons and seed dispersal is offered in **The Tiny Seed** by Eric Carle. Readers will follow the life of a seed from autumn throughout the year. (Crowell, 1970, $4.50)

The small environment of a child's own garden is the subject of Ethel Collier's **Who Goes There In My Garden?** The ecological role of animals and insects is introduced in a simple text and illustrations by Honore Guilbeau. (Scott, 1963, $3.75)

In an allegory which presents man's irresponsibility toward nature, Bill Peet tells us of **The Wump World,** a verdant and peaceful planet which is invaded by Pollutians. Whimsical, Seuss-like illustrations help tell the tale. (Houghton-Mifflin, 1970, $3.95)

Millicent E. Selsam's **Birth of a Forest** describes the changes in the natural community as an area becomes a marsh and then a forest. Concepts of seed dispersal and animal migration are introduced. Excellent photographs by Barbara Wolff illustrate the text. (Harper, 1964, $2.95)

Similar in theme is Alvin Tresselt's **The Beaver Pond,** which gently explores the interdependency of animals, plants, and insects as it traces the life of a pond. Roger Duvoisin's full-page, full-color paintings illustrate the changes in the community as the pond forms from the work of beavers and then changes back when the beaver's dam is suddenly washed away.

The First Book of Swamps and Marshes by Frances C. Smith. Ecological interrelationships in the various kinds of wetlands—food web, distribution of wildlife, the need for conservation management. (Franklin Watts, Inc. 1969)

Marshes and Marsh Life by Arnold Dobrin. The ecology of a salt marsh. (Coward-McCann, 1969. $3.86)

In **Wilson's World** by Edith Thatcher Hurd and Clement Hurd, the earth is conceived by a boy-artist. He populates his world with beautiful people and landscapes, only to see the world become overpopulated and choking in wastes. Wilson rebegins his world more carefully, and shows that a cared-for environment is beautiful. (Harper, 1971. $4.50)

Earth and Sky by Mona Dayton focuses on natural processes in the air and on the earth. With a large variety of vivid, colorful illustrations, attention is drawn to the functional dialogue between earth and sky. The book would be especially useful for developing the receiving, responding, and valuing levels of the affective domain. (Harper, 1969, $3.79)

In a positive way, **Little Island** by Golden MacDonald describes and illustrates how an island functions in an environment. It tells how nature works without using an environmental crisis as part of the plot. Excellent for receiving and awareness levels of the affective domain.

Once There Was a Tree by Phyllis S. Busch. The tree and how it changed during its life cycle, as well as its effects on living things in the immediate surroundings. Highly motivating for young children. Encourages inquiry. (The World Publishing Co., 1968, $4.50)

GRADES 4-6

The world's vanishing wildlife is the theme of Robert Gray's **Children of the Ark** which describes each species in danger of extinction with a brief explanation of the causes. Illustrated by photographs. (Norton, 1968, $3.95)

A possible supplement to Gray's book is Ivah Green's **Wildlife in Danger,** which devotes its last chapter to the philosophy of the Audubon Society, "A Hopeful Outlook." Illustrated by photographs. (Coward-McCann, 1960, $3.50)

A fictional account of the problems of pollution is offered in **The Tree That Conquered the World.** Sybil Leek writes of a tree from outer space which comes to earth (Los Angeles in particular) to teach us how to fight air pollution. (Prentice-Hall, 1969, $3.95)

Air pollution is again the problem in James Marshall's **The Air We Live In, What We Must Do About It.** The text explains where pollutants come from, discusses what people can do to alleviate the problem, and describes some diseases caused by dirty air. There is a bibliography for interested youngsters. (Coward-McCann, 1970, $3.95)

Charlotte Pomerantz has combined ecological data and good artistry into her story-drama, **The Day They Parachuted Cats on Borneo** (A Drama of Ecology). Based on an article in the New York Times concerning the action of DDT in upsetting the ecological balance on Borneo, the book effectively shows that man needs to find ecologically sound methods of combating mosquitoes and other pests without ruining food chains. (Addison-Wesley, 1971)

Homes Beneath The Sea by Boris Arnov, Jr. An introduction to ocean ecology. Food chains, habitats, and population densities are discussed in the marine context. (Little, Brown and Company, 1969. $4.50)

Seeds by Wind and Water by Helene J. Jordan. How plants get into growth patterns as a group. Plant mobility as a function of animal, wind, and self-propulsion. (Thomas Y. Crowell Company, 1962)

The Only Earth We Have by Laurence Pringle. Effects of technology, definition of biosphere. The earth as a spaceship with limited supplies. Misuse of air and water. Container and poison accumulation. Perishing species of animals. Ecotactics for children. Index of conservation groups and glossary of important terms. (The Macmillan Company, 1967)

Alligator Hole by Julian May. The book is set in the Everglades region prior to 1968. Drainage projects dried the region, in combination with a drought. The book tells how the regional balance was upset and restored. The last page describes how the region has since been protected from human destruction. (Follett Publishing Company, 1969. $3.95)

Animals That Hide, Imitate, and Bluff by Lilo Hess. How animals adapt. (Charles Scribner's Sons, 1970. $3.95)

Unusual Partners by Alvin and Virginia B. Silverstein. Animals that live and work together in the environment—symbiosis. (McGraw-Hill Book Company, 1968. $4.95)

The Varmints by Michael Frome. Points out the value of wildlife forms, many of which are indiscriminately exterminated. Balancing in nature, services that animals perform. Plea for preservation. (Coward-McCann, 1969. $3.86)

Let's Go To The Woods by Harreit E. Huntington. General plant groupings and life cycles of specific ones. Description of animal life cycles. Interrelation of plants and insects. (Doubleday and Company, Inc., 1968. $3.50)

GRADES 7 AND UP

A lucid and interesting introduction to various eco-systems is presented in Natalie Friendly's **Miraculous Web; The Balance of Life**, illustrated by Bette Fast. Pollution and its consequences are also discussed. (Prentice-Hall, 1968, $3.95)

Natural History Press has published a series which offers a mature, scientific presentation of various aspects of ecology. Each book is well-written and contains superb color photographs. In New York, they are available at the American Museum of Natural History.

Joyce Hoffe, **Conservation** (1970, $6.95)
J. A. Lauwerys, **Man's Impact on Nature** (1970, $6.95)
George Laycock, **Wild Refuge** (an exception to the others, this book is illustrated by black and white photographs, 1969, $6.95)
Keith Reid, **Nature's Network** (1970, $6.95)

Dorothy Shuttlesworth clearly expalins mutualism, parasitism, commensalism in her book, **Natural Partnerships,** illustrated by Su Zan Noguchi Swain. (Doubleday, 1970, $3.95)

An excellent source for continuing study of the environment for all grades is **Ranger Rick's Nature Magazine** which is published by the National Wildlife Federation ($6.00 per year, monthly except June and September). Articles are well-written in exciting narrative and illustrated with color photographs of extremely high quality.

Elizabeth S. Austin points out that forty-nine kinds of birds cannot fly, even though they could in past ages. **Birds That Stopped Flying** tells the adaptational story of a fascinating group of birds that are managing to survive today without wings. The threat of civilization to some species survival is discussed, as well as the process of natural extinction. Photographs effectively supplement the solid content level of the book. (Random House, 1969, $2.95)

Spaceship Earth—A Space Look At Our Troubled Planet by Don Dwiggins. Describes the technological war against the destruction of the environment. Also emphasizes the directions and details of future space exploration in terms of watching earth's ecological events from outer space. (Golden Gate Junior Books, 1970)

The Living Community by S. Carl Hirsch. Traces basic ecological concepts back to Darwin, the book shows how biological needs and environmental conditions determine what species are successful in a particular region. Talks about man as dominant species, and ways in which technology threatens environmental communities. (The Viking Press, 1966, $3.56)

A Heritage Restored—America's Wildlife Refuges by Robert Murphy. Covers the past history of American wildlife and threats to its existence. Then the author discusses the fascinating varieties of live animals in America's refuges. (E. P. Dutton Co., Inc. 1969)

Shadows Over the Land by J. J. McCoy. Very high level. Current ecological problems. (Seabury Press, 1970. $4.95)

JOURNALS, MAGAZINES, AND NEWSLETTERS

The American Biology Teacher, National Association of Biology Teachers, 1420 N. Street, N. W., Washington, D. C. 10005. $10 per year.

Audubon Magazine, National Audubon Society, 1130 Fifth Ave., New York 28, N. Y. Free to members. $7.50 per year for schools.

Cornell Science Leaflets, Ithaca, N. Y., Cornell University Press. Many of these deal with conservation.

Elementary School Science Bulletin, National Science Teachers Association, 1201 Sixteenth St., N. W., Washington, 6, D. C. $1 per year.

Environment, Committee for Environmental Information, 438 N. Skinker Blvd., St. Louis, Mo. 63130, $8.50 per year. Excellent up-to-date discussions of environmental issues. A must for high school classes.

Environmental Education, Dembar Educational Research Services, Inc., Box 1605, Madison, Wis. 53701. $7.50 per year.

Environmental Quality, Environmental Awareness Associates, Inc., 6464 Canoga Ave., Woodland Hills, Calif. A fine effort by a group of young adults. Good analysis of eco-politics. $10/12issues.

Fauna, Fauna, 34th and Girard, Philadelphia, Pa.

Junior Natural History, American Museum of Natural History, Central Park West at 79th St., New York, N. Y. 10024. $1.50 per year.

Junior Scholastic, Junior Scholastic, 902 Sylvan Way, Englewood Cliffs, N. J. 07632. $1.25 per student per year.

BIBLIOGRAPHY

Natural History, American Museum of Natural History, Central Park West at 79th St., New York, N. Y. 10024. $7.00 per year.

National Geographic School Bulletin, National Geographic Society, 17th and M Sts. N. W., Washington, D. C. 20036. $2.25 for 30 issues.

National Parks, National Parks Association, 1701 18th St., N. W., Washington, D. C. 20009. $8.00 per year. Excellent magazine.

National Reporter, Zero Population Growth, 367 State St., Los Altos, Calif. $10 per year.

National Wildlife, National Wildlife Federation, 1412 16th St., N. W., Washington, D. C. (Publishes **Ranger Rick** for children.) $6.00 per year.

Nature Magazine, American Nature Association, 1214 Sixteenth St., N. W., Washington, D. C. 20006.

People, The Population Reference Bureau, Inc., 1755 Massachusetts Ave., N. W., Washington, D. C. 20036. A newsletter for teachers and researchers. Other publications are **Population Bulletins** and **This Crowded World.**

Public Information Workbooks, Scientists Institute for Public Information, 30 East 68th St., New York, N. Y. 10021. Excellent booklets on hunger, environmental education, air pollution, etc., for $1.00 each.

Ranger Rick's Nature Magazine, National Wildlife Federation, 381 West Center St., Marion, Ohio. 43302. $6 per year. Extremely valuable for elementary classrooms.

Science News Letter, Science Service, 1719 N. St., N. W., Washington, D. C. 20006. $5.50 per year.

Science and Children, National Science Teachers, Association, 1201 Sixteenth St., N. W., Washington, D. C. 20036. $5 per year, includes NSTA membership.

The Science Teacher, National Science Teachers Association, 1201 Sixteenth St., N. W., Washington, D. C. 20036. Membership is $10. Subscription is free to members.

Science, American Association for the Advancement of Science, 1515 Massachusetts Ave., N. W., Washington, D. C. 20005. $12.00 per year. Intelligent, often wise, discussions of the scientific, social, political, and moral aspects of pollution and population problems. Excellent way to keep well informed.

Sierra Club Bulletin, Sierra Club, 1050 Mills Tower, San Francisco, Calif. 94104. $5 per year. A very fine monthly bulletin useful to every teacher. Highly recommended. The best way to learn about urgent legislation and issues.

appendix A

GLOSSARY

Aerosol: particle of solid or liquid matter that can remain suspended in the air because of its small size. Particulates under 1 *micron* in diameter are generally called aerosols.

Algae: a large group of aquatic plants such as seaweeds or pond scums.

Air quality criteria: the varying amounts of pollution and lengths of exposure at which specific adverse effects to health and welfare take place.

Air quality standard: the prescribed level of a pollutant in the outside air that cannot legally be exceeded during a specified time in a specified geographical area.

Balance in nature: tendency of living things to maintain an equilibrium between themselves and their environment.

Biodegradability: the ability of anything that was ever part of a living organism to deteriorate.

Biocide: pesticide or herbicide.

Biome: climate, plants, and animals in a broad region such as a tundra or desert.

Biosphere: that part of the earth which supports life—the soil, oceans and fresh waters, and atmosphere.

Carbon monoxide: a colorless, odorless, very toxic gas produced by incomplete combustion of carbon-containing substances.

Carnivore: any animal that feeds on animal matter.

Community: an interrelated and interdependent group of plants and animals.

Condensation: a natural process in which water vapor becomes a liquid or solid such as rain or snow. Occurs when cooling takes place.

Consumer: in the food chain, all organisms other than green plants.

Daphnia: water fleas, a small fresh water crustacean.

Decay: reduction of the materials of plant or animal bodies to simple compounds through the action of bacteria or other decomposers.

Decomposers: organisms such as bacteria, yeast, or mold that break down other organisms into simpler forms.

Ecology: study of the relationship of living things to each other and to their environment.

APPENDIX A

Ecosystem: a community of living things that interact with each other and their special environment.

Effluent: liquid that comes out of a water treatment plant after completion of the treatment process.

Energy: the ability to do work.

Environment: all of the biological and physical components of a given place.

Evaporation: a natural process in which a liquid such as water becomes water vapor. Occurs when heating takes place.

Food chain: transfer of energy through an ecosystem through the action of food producers, food consumers, and decomposers.

Fossil fuels: coal, oil, and natural gas.

Habitat: the place where a plant or animal can find suitable food, shelter, water, temperature, and other things it needs to live.

Herbicide: a chemical used to destroy or inhibit plant growth.

Herbivore: a plant-eating animal.

Hydrocarbon: any of a vast family of compounds containing carbon and hydrogen in various combinations.

Hydrological cycle: the water cycle in which water condenses and evaporates within the biosphere.

Incineration: burning of household or industrial waste.

Inversion: the phenomenon of a layer of cool air trapped by a layer of warmer air above it so that the bottom layer cannot rise.

Landfill: a method of waste disposal in which refuse is covered with soil.

Marsh: a tract of soft, wet land, usually a place where salt and fresh water meet. Coastal wetlands.

Niche: the "job" a living thing does: its relation to its environment.

Nonbiodegradable: not capable of deteriorating through decomposition.

Ozone: a pungent, colorless, toxic gas. As a product of the *photochemical process,* it is a major air pollutant.

Particulate: a particle of solid or liquid matter.

Percolate: the action of water trickling through soil.

pH: a factor which denotes the acidity, neutrality, or alkalinity of liquids.

Photochemical process: the chemical changes brought about by the *radiant energy* of the sun acting upon various polluting substances.

Photosynthesis: process by which green plants, using light energy, combine carbon dioxide and water to produce basic food substance and oxygen.

Pollution: contamination of the environment by man.

GLOSSARY

Precipitation: condensed water vapor in the form of rain, hail, mist, sleet, or snow.

Predator: an animal that preys on other animals.

Primary treatment: Process of sewage treatment in which material that floats or settles is removed.

Producer: in the food chain, green plants, the only organisms capable of making food.

Ringelmann chart: actually a series of charts, numbered from 0 to 5, that simulate various smoke densities, by presenting different percentages of black. Ringelmann numbers are sometimes used in setting emission standards.

Secondary treatment: second step in the process of sewage treatment. Bacteria consume the organic parts of the wastes.

Smog: the irritating haze resulting from the sun's effect on certain pollutants in the air, notably those from automobile exhaust; see *photochemical process*. Also a mixture of *fog* and *smoke*.

Thermal pollution: pollution of water due to increase in temperature, usually caused by an industry which uses water for cooling and then returns it in a hotter condition.

Water cycle: continuous movement of water in its vapor, liquid, and solid forms between earth and air.

Watershed: a specific region within which water drains to a particular watercourse or body of water.

SOME EVIRONMENTAL PROBLEMS

Problem	Causes	Consequences
Water Pollution	Sewage and other wastes from cities, industries and boats; chemical nutrients and toxic chemicals; oil; acids; silt; heated water; radioactive wastes.	Deterioration of lakes, ponds and rivers; death of fish, birds and other wildlife; destruction of valuable estuarine regions, recreational facilities and source of food.
Air Pollution	Incomplete combustion: incinerators, spaceheaters, power plants, industrial plants, vehicles—autos, trucks, buses and airplanes. Some pollution caused also by grinding, drilling and spraying.	Increased illness and death rate; damage to crops and death to livestock; deterioration of building stones and metals; reduced visibility; increased cleaning costs; decreased amount and quality of sunlight; change in climate due to increased CO_2 in air.
Litter	Human carelessness and disinterest.	Streets and parks strewn with papers, soda and beer cans; roads cluttered with billboards; writing on buildings and sidewalks; dumping in vacant lots; "eye-pollution."
Population	Widespread control of infectious diseases has decreased the death rate, thereby increasing the population growth rate.	More strain on the already overtaxed environment; need for more housing, food, transportation, services and utilities all leading to more pollution and destruction of the environment.
Noise Pollution	Jets; air compressors; sirens; auto horns; loudspeakers; riveting; sanitation trucks; motorcycles; cars starting and stopping suddenly; cars with inadequate mufflers.	Health; hearing impediment, cardiovascular, glandular, respiratory, and neurological disorders; disruption of activities (schools, meetings, outdoor concerts).
Solid Wastes	Enlarging population; high consumption economy; wide usage of packaged and canned foods; consumer demand for convenience; planned early obsolescence of automobiles and household appliances; agricultural and industrial wastes; increased use of plastics and paper products containing impregnated chemicals.	Ugly dumping areas; no place to dispose of the undisposable; increased air pollution due to increased incineration; water pollution if rivers and oceans are used for dumping.

SOURCE. (Reprinted from *A Place to Live,* a publication of the National Audubon Society).

SOME ENVIRONMENTAL PROBLEMS

Possible Solutions	How You Can Help
More treatment works, new treatment methods; detergents without phosphates; rigorous controls to prevent oil spills; enforcement of existing anti-pollution laws.	Locate and publicize major areas of water pollution in your community; report sources of pollution to a conservation agent; boycott detergents containing phosphates; make posters illustrating water pollution and ask local merchants to display them.
Improving combustion to make it more complete; use of low sulphur and lead-free fuel; increasing mass transportation and decreasing use of private cars; emission-control devices in incinerators, power plants, factories and automobiles.	Use lead-free gasoline; don't race automobile motors or idle engines for more than three minutes. Keep car well tuned. Use good muffler and pollution-control device. Keep home heating systems in good repair. Cut down on electricity consumption where possible. Plant ground cover to eliminate erosion and dust blowing. Don't burn leaves or trash.
More trash receptacles; increased awareness of need for anti-litter campaigns; self-discipline concerning littering; enforced regulations about roadside advertisements and billboards.	Make a survey of trash receptacles in your neighborhood or local park, if insufficient, contact local authorities; clean up litter in local parks or in neighborhood; work with neighborhood group to clean up a vacant lot; plan a constructive use for this lot; plant trees and shrubs in your neighborhood. DON'T LITTER!
Changed attitudes concerning size of family; changes in welfare policy to benefit small families over large; tax rewards and incentives for small families.	Become informed about population problems.
Soundproofed air compressors; rubberized garbage trucks; improved automobile mufflers; rubber tires for subways; improved sirens; pressure to prevent further development of SST; committees against increased noise pollution.	Play radios and TV sets softly; avoid playing transistors on street; blow horn only for emergency; avoid sudden starts and stops in cars; form a Citizens for a Quieter City Committee; work for enforcement of anti-noise laws.
Change in consumer attitudes; use of waste as fuel for generating electricity or for space heating; reclamation and recycling as in paper products, aluminum cans and bottles.	Buy only returnable bottles; find out where aluminum cans, bottles and papers can be returned in your city; set up a service in your neighborhood to collect these items; work to eliminate an automobile graveyard; report abandoned cars to local authorities; use a shopping bag; don't accept unnecessary bags; buy economy sized packages; avoid using paper and plastic plates and cups.

appendix C

INSTRUCTIONAL MATERIALS

Instructional materials pertinent to environmental education are listed according to publisher. Each listing gives the address where orders may be placed, the type of materials offered, the subject matter titles, and the number of materials available on that title. The type of materials offered are the following:

Academic simulation games
Games
Filmstrips
Film loops (8 mm. cartridge)
Films (16 mm.)
Laboratory investigations
Multi-media packages
Overhead transparencies
Sound filmstrips
Sound recordings
Study prints
Wall charts

The number of materials available on a title appears within parentheses. Example: **Film loops:** Urban Ecology (10) means 10 film loops are available on the title, Urban Ecology.

Publishers are organized according to two major sources: commercial and noncommercial. The commercial publishers are profit-making firms that offer materials suitable for environmental education. The noncommercial publishers are generally governmental agencies or antipollution organizations. In most instances, their materials are free or inexpensive.

COMMERCIAL PUBLISHERS

ABT ASSOCIATES, INC., 55 Wheeler St., Cambridge, Massachusetts 02138.
Academic simulation games: Simpolis, high school or adult. ABT also designed Pollution (for elementary) which is available from Curriculum Development Center, Wellesley School System, Seawood Road, Wellesley Hills, Mass. 02181.

AIR POLLUTION CONTROL ASSOCIATION, 4400 Fifth Ave., Pittsburgh, Pennsylvania 15213.
Laboratory investigations: Air Pollution Experiments for Junior and Senior High School Science Classes.

544

INSTRUCTIONAL MATERIALS

AMERICAN EDUCATION PUBLICATIONS, Science Division, 55 High St., Middletown, Connecticut 06457.

> **Laboratory investigations:** Science in City and Suburbs (outdoor and urban education, activities and experiments), gr. 7-9.

AVID CORPORATION, 10 Tripps Lane, East Providence, R. I. 02914.

> **Filmstrips:** Ecology and Environmental Studies, primary grades (10). Ecology and Environmental Studies, middle grades (14), Ecology and Environmental Studies, high school (14).
>
> **Sound filmstrips:** Man and the Sea (2), Ecology for the Young Student (10) "Open Your Eyes" Environment and Ecology Studies (10).

EALING FILMS, 2225 Massachusetts Ave., Cambridge, Mass. 02140.

> **Film loops:** Urban Ecology (10), Backyard Ecology (6), Ecology of the United States (9), The Undersea World of Jacques Cousteau (13), Problems of Today's Cities (9), Elementary Science Study film loops include: Microgardening (7), Pond Water (2), Gases and Airs (4).
>
> **Sound filmstrips:** Pollution (6).

EDUCATIONAL COORDINATES, 432 S. Pastoria Ave., Sunnyvale, California 94086.

> **Sound filmstrips:** The Environment of Man—An Introduction to Ecology (4).

EDUCATIONAL PROGRESS CORPORATION, 8538 East 41st St., Tulsa, Oklahoma 74145.

> **Wall charts:** posters (12), teacher's guide, gr. 1-9.

EDUQUIP, INC., 1200 Adams St., Boston, Mass. 02124.

> **Laboratory investigations:** Air Pollution Study Program, high school. Excellent equipment for pollution experiments.

ENCYCLOPEDIA BRITANNICA EDUCATIONAL CORPORATION, 425 N. Michigan Ave., Chicago, Illinois 60611.

> **Film loops:** Aquatic Communities (21), Desert Community (4).
>
> **Filmstrips:** Conservation in the City (3), Discovering Life Around Us (5), Learning About Living Things (6), Living Things in the City (9), The African Lion—Disney (6), The Arctic Wilderness—Disney (6), Forests of Tropical America—Disney (6), The Living Desert—Disney (6), Living Things Through the Ages (4), Plant and Animal Relationships (6), True-Life Adventures—Disney (8), The Vanishing Prairie—Disney (6), Conserving Our Natural Resources (7), Soil Conservation (8), Using Natural Resources (3).
>
> **16 mm. films:** Environmental Science (10), Background for Basic Ecological Concepts (15).

EYE GATE HOUSE, INC., 146-01 Archer Avenue, Jamaica, N. Y. 11435.

> **Filmstrips:** The Interdependence of Nature (4).
>
> **Sound filmstrips:** Land Biomes of the World (8), Ecology: Land and Water (4), The Conservation of Our Resources (9).

EMC CORPORATION, 180 East 6th Street, St. Paul, Minn. 55101.

> **Multi-media packages:** Our Environment 1: Fresh Water Communities (4 filmstrips, record or tape cassette, 10 overhead transparencies, 1 teacher's guide, spirit masters for worksheet and follow-up assignments).

GRADE TEACHER REPRINTS, 23 Leroy Ave., Darien, Connecticut 06820.

> **Wall charts:** Pond Life (1), Oceanography (1), Seeds (1), Ecology (1).

APPENDIX C

H. WILSON CORPORATION, 555 W. Taft Dr., So. Holland, Illinois 60473.
Sound recordings: Issues in American Democracy (2 cassettes, 2 records, or 4 tapes), At Issue: The Quality of Life (4 cassettes, 8 records, or 8 tapes).

HAMMOND INCORPORATED, Education Division, 515 Valley St., Maplewood, N.J. 07040.
Overhead transparencies: Part of the "Hammond-Newsweek Visual Study Series." Sets deal with World Food Crisis, Urban Crisis, Urban Problems, Natural Resources, etc. (12 transparencies to a set).

HOLT, RINEHART, AND WINSTON, INC., 383 Madison Ave., New York, N.Y. 10017.
Laboratory investigations: Scientific Experiments in Environmental Pollution, Elbert C. Weaver, editor, gr. 7-12.

HOUGHTON MIFFLIN CO., Educational Division, 110 Tremont St., Boston, Mass. 02107
Academic simulation games: The Pollution Game (1), The Redwood Controversy (1), Planet Management Game (1), Thermal Pollution (1), (Part of the ERC Life Science Program for junior high school).
Project headquarters: Educational Research Council of America, Rockefeller Building, Cleveland, Ohio 44113.

IMPERIAL FILM COMPANY, 4404 South Florida Ave., Lakeland, Florida 33803.
Sound filmstrips: Ecological Systems (4), The Underwater Environment (4), Exploring the Seasons (4).

INSTRUCTOR PUBLICATIONS, INC., Dansville, N. Y. 14437.
Wall charts: Ecology (12).

JAM HANDY SCHOOL SERVICE, 2781 E. Grand Blvd., Detroit, Michigan 48211.
Filmstrips: Adventure in Nature (9).

JEWEL INDUSTRIES, INC., Jewel Aquarium Division, 5005 W. Armitage Avenue, Chicago, Illinois 60639.
Laboratory investigations: Experiences of the World in Plants.

KDI INSTRUCTIONAL SYSTEMS, INC., 1810 Mackenzie Dr., Columbus, Ohio 43220.
Multi-media packages: Water for Tomorrow, Land for Tomorrow, Air for Tomorrow (each of the 3 units contains a teacher's guide, sound filmstrips, transparencies, a student booklet, an activity guide, and a bibliography.

KING SCREEN PRODUCTIONS, 320 Aurora Ave. N., Seattle, Washington 98109.
16 mm. films: Search for Survival: Our Planet's Future (6 films).

LIFE (MAGAZINE) EDUCATION PROGRAM, Box 834, Radio City Post Office, New York, N. Y. 10019.
Filmstrips: Whales: Ecology (1), Insects: Ecology (1), Canopy of Air (1), Coral Reef (1), The Desert (1), The Arctic Tundra (1), Rain Forest (1), Woods of Home (1).

McGRAW-HILL FILMS/CONTEMPORARY FILMS, East: Princeton Road, Hightstown, N.J. 08520 Midwest: 828 Custer Ave., Evanston, Illinois 60202, West: 1714 Stockton Street, San Francisco, California 94133.
16 mm. films: Diverse topics such as natural resources, wildlife, agriculture, minerals, water and air pollution, chemical pollution, population, food problems, etc., (67).

INSTRUCTIONAL MATERIALS

MILLIKEN PUBLISHING CO., 611 Olive Street, St. Louis, Mo..63101.
   Multi-media packages: Ecology (12 overhead transparencies, 4 duplicating masters, teacher's guide).

MILLIPORE CORPORATION, Educational Division, Ashby Road, Bedford, Mass. 01730.
   Laboratory investigations: Detection and Analysis of Particulate Contamination, gr. 7-12, Experiments in Microbiology, gr. 7-12, Microbiological Analysis of Water, advanced manual. Kit *Experiments in Environmental Microbiology* is available.
   16 mm. films: Membrane Microfiltration—A New Tool for Classroom Science.

NASCO NATURE STUDY AIDS, Red Wing, Minnesota 55606.
   Laboratory investigations: Nature Study Aids: Conservation Education (exact replicas of leaves, plant structures, and feet of wildlife).

NASCO SCIENCE AND MATHEMATICS MATERIALS, Home Office: Fort Atkinson, Wisconsin 53538, Western Office, Modesto, California.
   Film loops: Introduction to the Coral Reef, Birds of Prey, and many others.
   Laboratory investigations: Materials such as living cultures, living materials, preserved materials, observation beehives, ant farms may be obtained for experimentation. Also kits for growing seeds, terrarium plants, aquarium plants, specimens of diseased plants, microscopic slides.

NATIONAL INSTRUCTIONAL TELEVISION CENTER, Box A, Bloomington, Ind. 47401.
   16 mm. films (also available on videotape):   If You Live in a City, Where Do You Live (5 films, 25 student activity cards, teacher's guide).

RAND McNALLY AND CO., Box 7600, Chicago, Illinois 60680.
   Film loops: Science Curriculum Improvement Study (1), Biological Sciences Curriculum Study Single-Topic Inquiry (40), high school.
   Study prints: Interaction of Man and His Environment (1 set of 20), Interaction of Man and His Resources (1 set of 20), gr. 1-4.

SCHOLASTIC BOOK SERVICES, 904 Sylvan Ave., Englewood Cliffs, N.J. 07632.
   Multi-media packages: Environmental Awareness Study Program Kits for gr. 1-3 and gr. 4-6; Ecology/Conservation Study Program Kits for gr. 1-2, gr. 3-4, and gr. 5-6.

SCOTT EDUCATION DIVISION, Holyoke, Mass. 01040.
   Multi-media package: Ecology: The Water Pollution Laboratory; includes investigation folders, apparatus, materials, filmstrips, cassettes, and teacher's guide, gr. 4-8.

SCOTT SCIENTIFIC INC., Box 2121, Fort Collins, Colorado 80521.
   Laboratory investigations: Water: Biological Pollution Test Kit (1), Water: Chemical Pollution Test Kit (1).

SOCIETY FOR VISUAL EDUCATION, INC., 1345 Diversey Parkway, Chicago, Ill. 60614.
   Filmstrips: An Ecological Approach to Nature Study (6).
   Sound filmstrips: Conservation for Today's America (7), Modern Biology: Environment and Survival, Group 1 (4), Modern Biology: Environment and Survival, Group 2 (4).

UNION CARBIDE CORP., P.O. Box 363, Tuxedo, N.Y. 10987.
   Laboratory investigations: Air Pollution Kit (1). Excellent study of Sulfur Dioxide, gr. 5-9.

URBAN SYSTEMS, INC., 1033 Mass. Avenue, Cambridge, Mass. 02138.
   Academic simulation games: Smog (1), Dirty Water (1), Clean-Up (1), Litterbug (1).
   Laboratory investigations: Why Are Leaves Green (1), Life in the Water (1),
   Predator-Prey (1), What Moves Life (1), Life From Death (1).

WARD'S NATURAL SCIENCE ESTABLISHMENT, INC., P.O. Box 1712, Dept. S, Rochester, N. Y. 14603.
   Filmstrips: Environmental Pollution: Our World In Crisis (6).

NONCOMMERCIAL PUBLISHERS (FREE OR INEXPENSIVE)

AMERICAN CANCER SOCIETY, obtain from local branch.
   Laboratory investigations: Biology Experiments for High School Students, Youth
   Looks at Cancer, gr. 10-12.
AMERICAN FOREST INSTITUTE, Education Division, 1835 K St., N. W., Washington
D. C. 20006.
   Wall charts: Forests and Trees of the U.S. (1 map).
AMERICAN PETROLEUM INSTITUTE, 1271 Avenue of the Americas, New York, N.Y.
10020.
   Multi-media packages: Conservation (picture and discussion kit of color plates
   with descriptive copy), Conserving Our Waters and Clearing the Air (booklets for
   students and teacher, poster, teacher's guide).
   16 mm. films: To Clear the Air (1).

THE CONSERVATION FOUNDATION, 1250 Connecticut Ave., N.W., Washington, D.C.
20036.
   16 mm. films: For All to Enjoy (1), A Matter of Time (1).

FLORIDA STATE DEPARTMENT OF EDUCATION, Tallahassee, Florida.
   Laboratory investigations: Sourcebook of Marine Science, high school.

THE GARDEN CLUB OF AMERICA, Conservation Committee, 598 Madison Avenue,
New York, N.Y. 10022.
   Multi-media packages: The World Around You (study guide, student leaflets,
   suggested lists of films, books, summer workshops).

KEEP AMERICA BEAUTIFUL FILMS, 99 Park Avenue, New York, N. Y.
   16 mm. film: Heritage of Splendor (1).

MARTIN COUNTY HIGH SCHOOL, Stuart, Florida 33494.
   Laboratory investigations: Laboratory Exercises in Marine Science; Also available
   from Val's Bookstore, Stuart, Florida are: *Let's Go Shelling*, and *Let's Go to the
   Beach*.

NATIONAL AUDUBON SOCIETY, Educational Services Department, 1130 Fifth
Avenue, New York, N.Y. 10028.
   Wall charts: Audubon Ecology Chart (principal biomes of North America).

INSTRUCTIONAL MATERIALS

NATIONAL WILDLIFE FEDERATION, 1412 Sixteenth St., N.W., Washington, D.C. 20036.
  Games: Ranger Rick's Forest Fire Game, Bird and Animal Jigsaw Puzzles, Wildlife Lotto, Wildlife Concentration, Songbird Dominoes, Wildlife Old Maid, Put a Bird Together.
  Multimedia packages: Wildlife Week Kit (poster and environment information), Teacher's and Leader's Kit (1 brochure), Adventures of Rick Racoon (book and record); Environmental Discovery Units (12), Gr. 1-9, Interdisciplinary.
NEW YORK STATE AIR POLLUTION CONTROL BOARD, 84 Holland Ave., Albany, N.Y. 12208.
  16 mm. films: With Each Breath (1).

RUTGERS UNIVERSITY, Cooperative Extension Service, College of Agriculture and Environmental Science, New Brunswick, N.J. 08903.
  Laboratory investigations: Air Pollution Experiments (High School Edition).

SIERRA CLUB FILMS, Available from Association Films, West: 25358 Cypress Avenue, Hayward, California 94544, East: 600 Grand Avenue, Ridgefield, N.J. 07657.
  16 mm. films: Various topics on land and forest conservation (10).
SOIL CONSERVATION SERVICE, MOTION PICTURE LIBRARY, U.S. DEPARTMENT OF AGRICULTURE, 701 Northwest Glisan Street, Portland, Oregon 97209.
  16 mm. films: Diverse topics such as Good Land Use, Natural Resources, Recreation, Soil, Water, General Environmental Education (64).

TUBERCULOSIS AND RESPIRATORY DISEASES ASSOCIATION OF LOS ANGELES COUNTY, 1670 Beverly Boulevard, Los Angeles, California 90026.
  16 mm. films: More Than Anger (1), Emphysema (1), Healthy Lungs (1), The Respiratory System (1).

U.S. GOVERNMENT PRINTING OFFICE, Superintendent of Documents, Washington, D.C. 20402.
  Wall charts: How a Tree Grows (1).

ENVIRONMENTAL FILMS—GENERAL

"For All to Enjoy"—20 min., color. $10.00 Conservation Foundation. 1250 Connecticut Ave., N.W., Washington, D.C. 20036. Satirical approach to uncontrolled development in National Parks.

"Man and his Resources"—28 min., B/W. $8.00. Contemporary, McGraw-Hill, Film Rental Office, 330 W. 42nd St., New York, N.Y. 10036.

"A Matter of Time"—27 min., color. $10.00 Conservation Foundation, 1250 Connecticut Ave., N.W., Washington, D.C. 20036. Historical approach to environmental deterioration.

"What Are We Doing to Our World?"—two parts, each 30 min. Each $11.00 Field Service, Indiana University, A-V Center, Bloomington, Indiana 47401.

"Tom Lehrer Sings 'Pollution'"—3 min., color. Free. Public Health Service. Audio Visual Facility, Atlanta, Georgia 30333. (PHS also has many other pollution films, all in heavy demand.)

APPENDIX C

"Environmental Pollution"—series of six excellent filmstrips covering air, water, and land pollution. Ward's Educational Filmstrips, Ward's Natural Science Establishment, Inc., P.O. Box 1712, Rochester, New York or P.O. 1749, Monterey, California.

"The Everglades: Conserving a Balanced Community"—11 min., color. $6.50. Encyclopedia Britannica, Educational Corporation, 425 N. Michigan Avenue, Chicago, Illinois 60611.

"The Crisis of the Environment"—series filmstrips. $97.50. New York Times Book and Educational Division. 229 West 43rd Street, New York, N.Y. 10036.
1. "Man—An Endangered Species"—How much can man tolerate.
2. "Breaking the Biological Strand"—Problems with technological advances.
3. "Vanishing Species."
4. "Preserve and Protect"—The last remnants of America's natural wilderness are disappearing. How much are we willing to pay to preserve them?
5. "The Population Explosion."

"The Biologist and the Boy"—15 min. State Fish and Game Comm., 270 Washington St., S.W., Atlanta, Ga. 30334. Narrated by Arthur Godfrey.

"House of Man"—15 min. Encyclopedia Britannica, 1150 Wilmette Ave., Wilmette, Ill. 60091. Man and how he has changed his environment since the Industrial Revolution; how man can positively rebuild the damage.

"Islands of Green"—24 min. U.S. Forestry Service, Suite 800, 1720 Peachtree Rd., N.W., Atlanta, Ga. 30309. Produced by the National Audubon Society.

"Problems of Conservation"—15 min. Rental fee unlisted. Encyclopedia Britannica, 1150 Wilmette Ave., Wilmette, Ill. 60091.

"The Redwoods"—20 min. Sierra Club, San Francisco, Calif. Awarded Oscar in 1968 as best documentary short.

"A Search for Ecological Balance"—28 min. $25.00 Radim Films, 220 W. 42nd St., New York, N.Y. 10036. (Also, $10.00. Kennesaw Mountain Historical Association, Box 1167, Marietta, Ga. 30334.)

"So Little Time"—28 min. Dept. of Interior, Conservation Education Department, Peachtree-7th Bldg., Atlanta, Ga. 30323. Disappearing wildlife.

AIR POLLUTION

"Air Pollution: Take a Deep Deadly Breath"—54 min., color. $35.00. McGraw-Hill, ABC Documentary, Film Rental Offices, 330 W. 42nd Street, New York, N.Y. 10036.

"First Mile Up"—28 min., B/W. $8.00. McGraw-Hill Contemporary. Film Rental Offices, 330 W. 42nd Street, N.Y., N.Y. 10036. Problems of air pollution and its effect on human health. Toronto and Los Angeles as examples.

"Air Pollution"—15 min., color. $8.00. Encyclopedia Britannica, Educational Corporation, 425 N. Michigan Avenue, Chicago, Illinois 60611.

WATER POLLUTION

"Beargrass Creek"—19 min., color. $15.00. Stuart Finley Productions. 3248 Mansfield Road, Falls Church, Va. 22041. The poignant tragedy of a small tributary stream, its promising start, and its sad end due to pollution.

INSTRUCTIONAL MATERIALS

"Clean Waters"—20 min., color. $9.00. Order #3972. Extension Media Center, University of California, Berkeley, California 94720. Illustrates dangers of water pollution and shows proper sewage treatment.

"Crisis on Kanawha"—20 min., color. $15.00. Stuart Finley Productions, 3428 Mansfield Road, Falls Church, Va. 22041. Shows sources of industrial water pollution and some methods of eliminating it.

"The Problem With Water is People"—30 min., B/W and color. $16.00. McGraw-Hill Contemporary, 330 W. 42nd St., New York, N.Y. 10036. Traces route of Colorado River from beginning to ocean and discusses its pollution and misuse.

"Water Pollution"—15 min., color. $8.00. Encyclopedia Britannica Educational Corporation, 425 N. Michigan Avenue, Chicago, Illinois 60611. Health problems posed by water pollution and steps being taken to correct them.

"The River Must Live"—21 min. Dept. of Interior, Conservation Education Department, Peachtree-7th Bldg., Atlanta, Ga. 30323.

POPULATION

"Multiply and Subdue the Earth"—60 min. B/W—$13.50. Color—$18. Field Service, Indiana University, A-V Center, Bloomington, Indiana 48401. World population crisis.

"Our Crowded Environment"—11 min., color. $6.50. Encyclopedia Britannica Educational Corporation, 425 N. Michigan Avenue, Chicago, Illinois 60611.

"People by the Billions"—28 min. B/W. $8.00. McGraw-Hill Contemporary Film Rental Office, 330 W. 42nd St., New York, N.Y. 10036.

"Population Ecology"—28 min. B/W. McGraw-Hill Contemporary Film Rental Office, 330 W. 42nd St., New York, N.Y. 10036, or Encyclopedia Britannica Educational Corporation, 425 N. Michigan Ave., Chicago, Illinois 60611. Ecological consequences if population not brought under control.

"Population Explosion"—15 min. B/W. $8.00. McGraw-Hill Contemporary Film Rental Office, 330 W. 42nd St., New York, N.Y. 10036, or Carousel Films, Inc., 1501 Broadway, New York, N.Y. 10036.

"The Squeeze"—10 min. B/W. $12.00. Hank Newenhouse, 1825 Willow Rd., Northfield, Illinois 60093. Throngs of people, jammed highways, rushing commuters, and starving children graphically portray population problem.

"Challenge to Mankind"—28 min., B/W. $8.00. McGraw-Hill Contemporary Film Rental Office, 330 W. 42nd St., New York, N.Y. 10036. Five world experts speak of threat of overpopulation.

LAND POLLUTION

"Bulldozed America"—25 min. B/W. Carousel Films, Inc., 1501 Broadway, New York, N.Y. 10036. Bulldozer and commercial interests tear apart countryside and turn it into supermarkets, highways, etc.

"By Land, Sea, and Air"—31 min., color. $5.00/day. Citizenship Legislative Dept., Oil, Chemical & Atomic Workers Int'l Union, 1126 16th St., N.W., Washington, D.C. 20036. Effects of pesticides on farm workers and environment of California.

"Poisons, Pests and People"—55 min., B/W. $16.00. McGraw-Hill Contemporary Film Rental Office, 330 W. 42nd St., New York, N.Y. 10036. Grim results of indiscriminate use of pesticides on wildlife and people. Plea for intelligent approach to the problem.

"A Day at the Dump"—15 min., color. Free. Environmental Control Administration, 12720 Twinbrook Parkway, Rockville, Maryland 20852. Story of Kenilworth Dump in Washington, D.C. and its planned conversion to a public park.

"The Third Pollution"—30 min., color. Free. Environmental Control Admin., 12720 Twinbrook Parkway, Rockville, Maryland 20852, attn: Tom Edgar. Excellent film which graphically describes America's $4 billion solid waste problem and demonstrates new techniques of solid waste management.

"Nation of Spoilers"—11 min. Encyclopedia Britannica, 1150 Wilmette Ave., Wilmette, Ill. 60091. Fee unlisted. Indicts littering.

"Silent Spring of Rachel Carson"—57 min. Rental fee unlisted. Contemporary Films, 267 W. 25th St., New York, N.Y. 10001. Produced by CBS.

CITY

"Green City"—23 min., color. $15.00. Stuart Finley Productions, 3428 Mansfield Road, Falls Church, Va. 22041. Civic action to preserve green space and open space as cities grow.

"Megapolis: Cradle of the Future"—22 min., B/W $9.00. Encyclopedia Britannica Educational Corporation, 425 N. Michigan Avenue, Chicago, Illinois 60611. Dynamics of urbanization and emphasis on need for careful planning.

"Our Changing Environment"—17 min. color. $8.00. Encyclopedia Britannica Educational Corporation, 425 N. Michigan Avenue, Chicago, Illinois 60611. Man's increasing power to control his environment has created new pressures and problems for the modern city.

"Pandora's Easy Open Pop-Top Box"—15 min. color. Free. Environmental Control Admin., 12720 Twinbrook Parkway, Rockville, Maryland 20852, attn: Tom Edgar. Dramatic presentation of effects of uncontrolled urbanization.

"Urban Sprawl"—21 min., color. $15.00. Stuart Finley Productions, 3428 Mansfield Rd., Falls Church, Va. 22041. Will we tolerate a continuing extension of urban sprawl? Or will we insist on something better?

"An African Essay"—narrated by Anne Morrow Lindbergh. 30 min. Guidance Associates, 1635 I St., N.W., Washington, D.C., contact Don Taylor.

"The Wisdom of Wildness"—narrated by Charles Lindbergh. 15 min. Guidance Associates, 1635 I St. N.W., Washington, D.C., contact Don Taylor.

"Man's Natural Environment, Crisis Through Abuse"—30 min. Guidance Associates, 1635 I St. N.W., Washington, D.C., contact Don Taylor.

"Cities in Crisis"—22 min., color. $13.00. Order #6812. Extension Media Center, University of California, Berkeley, California 94720. Impressionistic film of urban sprawl and unplanned growth.

appendix D

CURRICULUM PROGRAMS

Curriculum programs concerned with environmental education are listed according to publisher. This method is a convenience for the reader who desires to write directly to the publisher to get more information or to place an order.

Certain curriculum programs were developed by national projects supported by federal funds or foundation grants. In these instances, the project headquarters is also listed. Much valuable information can be obtained by contacting project headquarters.

THE AMERICAN GEOLOGICAL INSTITUTE, Box 1559, Boulder, Colorado 80302.

Earth Science Educational Program, includes the Environmental Studies Project, the Earth Science Teacher Preparation Project, and the Earth Science Curriculum Project. Projects are currently in process of development. Funded by the National Science Foundation: junior and senior high school.

Two packets of 25 cards each, produced by ESP, include such titles as: "Now You See It, Then You Don't," "Predator-Prey," "The Happening," "Power-picture," etc. Some of these cards are included in Part 3 of this text. The packets are available for $10.00 each from the address above.

CONSERVATION AND ENVIRONMENTAL STUDIES CENTER, Box 2230, R.D. 2, Browns Mills, New Jersey 08015.

Available are a K-12 curriculum outline, environmental education instruction plans, teacher's guides, and mini-curricula.

EDUCATIONAL CONSULTING SERVICE, 89 Orinda Way, No. 6, Orinda, California 94563.

The Environmental School. A guide which tells how to establish an environmental education program. Uses five conceptual environmental strands: Art, Communications, Math, Science, and Social Studies. Also available for purchase are 17 environmental lessons for upper elementary and junior high students.

GEE! GROUP FOR ENVIRONMENTAL EDUCATION, INC., 1133 Quarry Street, Philadelphia, Pa. 19107.

Our Man-Made Environment, Book Seven. Designed for grade 7 and deals with urban planning. Single copies from Joseph Fox Bookshop, 1724 Sansom Street, Philadelphia, Pa. 19103. Multiple copies from Gee! Group for Environmental Education, 1214 Arch St., Philadelphia, Pa. 19107.

APPENDIX D

HOUGHTON MIFFLIN CO., Educational Division, 110 Tremont Street, Boston, Massachusetts 02107.

Man and the Environment. Inquiry oriented life science course, grade 7. Includes teacher's annotated edition, student laboratory supplement book, checkpoints for evaluation, and form separately packaged academic simulation games. The games are: **Mouse in the Maze, Planet Management, The Redwood Controversy,** and **The Pollution Game.**

Project headquarters: Educational Research Council of America (ERC), Rockefeller Building, Cleveland, Ohio 44113.

J.G. FERGUSON PUBLISHING CO., 6 N. Michigan Avenue, Chicago, Illinois 60602.

People and Their Environment: Teachers' Curriculum Guides to Conservation Education. Eight volumes: Grades 1-3, interdisciplinary; Grades 4-6, interdisciplinary; Grades 7-9, science; Grades 7-9, social studies; Grades 10-12, social studies; Grades 9-12, home economics; Grades 9-12, biology; Grades 1-12, outdoor classroom and camping.

McGRAW-HILL BOOK COMPANY, Webster Division, Manchester Road, Manchester, Missouri 63011.

Elementary Science Study (ESS). Activities, experiments, and materials which include: Animal Activity, Behavior of Mealworms, Brine Shrimp, Changes, Crayfish, Eggs and Tadpoles, Gases and "Airs," Growing Seeds, Life of Beans and Peas, Microgardening, Pond Water, Small Things, and others, grades K-8.

Complete package includes teacher's guide, laboratory materials, teacher training activities, consultant service, films, film loops.

Project headquarters: ESS, Educational Development Center Inc., 55 Chapel Street, Newton, Massachusetts 02160.

Engineering Concepts Curriculum Project (ECCP). Examines impact of technology on today's world. Considers problems of air pollution, waste disposal, crowded environment, etc. High school level, laboratory-oriented, interdisciplinary. Text is titled, **The Man-Made World.**

Complete package includes text, laboratory manual, teacher's manual, teacher training activities, consultant service, laboratory equipment films.

Project headquarters: ECCP, Polytechnic Institute of Brooklyn, 333 Jay Street, Brooklyn N.Y. 11201.

NATIONAL AUDUBON SOCIETY, Educational Services Department, 1130 Fifth Ave., New York, N.Y. 10028.

A Place to Live. Study program in urban ecology, grades 4-5.

NATIONAL EDUCATION ASSOCIATION, Publications Division, 1201 Sixteenth Street, N.W., Washington, D.C. 20036.

Man and His Environment. An introduction to using Environmental Study Areas. Produced by Association of Classroom Teachers, NEA, in cooperation with Project Man's Environment, American Association for Health, Physical Education, and Recreation.

PENNSYLVANIA DEPARTMENT OF EDUCATION, Conservation Education Advisers, Box 911, Harrisburg, Pennsylvania 17126.

Guideline for Environmental Sensitivity. Grades K-6.

CURRICULUM PROGRAMS

School Site Development for Conservation and Outdoor Education. Interdisciplinary, grades K-12.

Science for Non-Science Majors (SNSM) and SNSM Scale. Pollution and population, grade 11.

RAND McNALLY & CO., Box 7600, Chicago, Illinois 60680.

Science Curriculum Improvement Study (SCIS). Materials-centered program in which scientific literacy in the life sciences is developed through an understanding of ecological concepts. The six year elementary level program for life sciences consists of six units: Organisms, Life Cycles, Populations, Environments, Communities, Ecosystems.

Complete package includes teacher's guides, laboratory materials, student workbooks, teacher training activities, consultant services, films, film loops.

Project headquarters: SCIS, Lawrence Hall of Science, University of California, Berkeley, California 94720.

Interaction of Man and the Biosphere. Life science program emphasizing environmental problems. Uses inquiry method. Includes teacher's edition, student text, lab materials, junior high level.

Biological Sciences Curriculum Study: BSCS Green Version. Emphasizes ecology. Uses methods of inquiry, observation, and experimentation, high school level. Related materials include BSCS single-topic inquiry film loops, and the BSCS pamphlet series.

Project headquarters: BSCS, University of Colorado, P.O. Box 930, Boulder, Colorado 80302.

RANDOM HOUSE/SINGER, 201 East 50th Street, New York, N.Y. 10022.

Science Through Discovery. Grades 1-6. Text series uses problem solving and discovery approach. Grades 5 and 6 emphasize environmental problems. Equipment and materials for lab activities are available for grades 4-6.

SAN DIEGO CITY SCHOOLS, Curriculum Productions, 4100 Normal St., San Diego, California 92103.

Man in His Environment. Grade 6.

SILVER BURDETT COMPANY, Morristown, New Jersey 07960.

National Environmental Education Development (NEED). A National Park Foundation Program created for the National Park Service and developed by the Educational Consulting Service. Grades 3-8.

Complete package includes teacher's guide and environmental school response book for grades 3-4, 5-6, 7-8. Six filmstrips and a picture packet supplement units.

Project headquarters: Educational Consulting Service, 89 Orinda Way, No. 6, Orinda, California 94563.

Intermediate Science Curriculum Study (ISCS). Developed units which are laboratory-centered, individualized, and sequential for junior high level. One of the units, The Environmental Crisis, deals specifically with pollution problems.

Complete package includes teacher's guides, student workbooks, laboratory materials, teacher training activities, consultant service.

Project headquarters: ISCS, Florida State University, Tallahassee, Florida 32306.

APPENDIX D

U.S. GOVERNMENT PRINTING OFFICE, Superintendent of Documents, Washington, D.C. 20402.

Education and Outdoor Recreation. Bureau of Outdoor Recreation, 75 cents, 1967.

ADDITIONAL SOURCES OF INFORMATION ARE THE FOLLOWING:

Environmental Education Communications, Science and Mathematics Education Information Analysis Center, 1460 West Lane Avenue, Columbus, Ohio 43221.

The Center serves as a clearinghouse for information on science education, mathematics education, and environmental education. Newsletters related to environmental education are released eight times a year on a monthly basis October through June. These newsletters contain information regarding instructional materials, educational programs, research grants, current events in environmental education, bibliographies of resource material, and information regarding federal programs. A limited number of back issues are available on request.

Apply to the ERIC Center to be placed on the mailing list for environmental education newsletters.

Henderson, Martha T. **Environmental Education: Social Studies Sources and Approaches.** A paper for the ERIC Clearinghouse for Social Science Education. Review Series No. 1. Boulder, Colorado: Clearinghouse for Education and Social Science, 1970, 39 pages.

This paper lists elementary and secondary social science programs in environmental education. Programs covering a wide range are grouped in four categories:
1. Projects especially suited to encouraging individual inquiry and exploration.
2. Projects to help the child understand the interaction between man and his environment.
3. Projects which feature a direct use of the local environment as an integral part of the study program.
4. Projects which concentrate on values and ethics and feature programs in law, politics, and economics.

Order from Clearinghouse for Education and Social Science, 970 Aurora, Boulder, Colorado 80302.

National School Public Relations Association. **Environment and the Schools: Pioneer Programs Set the Pace for States and Districts.** Washington, D.C.: The Association, a department of the National Education Association, 1971, 56 pages.

Tells what's happening in school districts, state legislatures, higher education, and nationwide programs concerning environmental education. Includes guidelines, sample programs, reading and film lists, and a summary of the Environmental Education Act of 1970. #411 - 12782. Cost is $4.00.

Purchase from the National School Public Relations Association, 1201 Sixteenth St., N.W., Washington, D.C. 20036. Orders must be accompanied by payment unless submitted on an authorized purchase order.

National Science Teachers Association. **Environmental Education for Everyone. Bibliography of Curriculum Materials for Environmental Studies, March 1970.** (Compiled by Ellie Snyder) Washington, D.C.: The Association, a department of the National Education Association, 1970, 38 pages.

CURRICULUM PROGRAMS

This bibliography was originally prepared for a two-day environmental work-shop preceding the 1970 meeting of NSTA. NSTA sent out over 800 inquiries to school districts, federal agencies, associations, companies, science curriculum projects, science teachers, and science supervisors. Over 200 replies were received and this information forms the basis for the report of environmental curriculum programs, courses of study, textbooks, single units, experimental activities, and suggested enrichment reading. #471 - 14600. Cost is 75 cents.

Purchase from the National Education Association, 1201 Sixteenth St., N.W., Washington, D.C. 20036. Orders must be accompanied by payment unless submitted on an authorized purchase order.

National Science Teachers Association. **Programs in Environmental Education.** Washington, D.C.: The Association, a department of the National Education Association, 1970, 51 pages.

This publication reports on a survey by NSTA of school systems having science programs related to the environment. Inquiry forms were sent to all state supervisors of science, all members of the National Science Supervisors Association, and all school systems represented in the NSTA Curriculum bibliographies. A variety of programs in all states of the Union are described, materials they have developed are listed, and mailing addresses are given. #471 - 14394. Cost is $1.50.

Purchase from the National Education Association, 1201 Sixteenth St., N.W., Washington, D.C. 20036. Orders must be accompanied by payment unless submitted on an authorized purchase order.

appendix E

ECOLOGY ACTION

Effective ecology action involves a concerted approach in which individuals and local groups coordinate their efforts with volunteer organizations and/or governmental agencies. These organizations and agencies offer technical ability in dealing with a particular environmental problem.

VOLUNTEER ORGANIZATIONS

The organizations listed are national in scope. In most cases they have local branches. These groups are highly motivated and can be counted upon for assistance in helping to solve local or national problems. They vary in membership from private organizations of lay people to professional organizations of specialists. Certain ones are designed specifically for young people while others are for adults. All of them provide some service or special resource to aid citizens everywhere in their attempts to enhance the quality of the environment.

AMERICAN FORESTRY ASSOCIATION, 919 17th St., N.W., Washington, D.C. 20006.
   Promotes conservation of forests and associated resources.
AMERICAN ASSOCIATION FOR HEALTH, PHYSICAL EDUCATION AND RECREATION, 1201 16th St., N.W., Washington, D.C. 20036.
   Professional group interested in improved environmental programs.
AMERICAN INSTITUTE OF ARCHITECTS, 1735 New York Avenue, N.W., Washington, D.C. 20006.
   Helps on problems of urban planning. Professional group.
AMERICAN SOCIOLOGICAL ASSOCIATION, 1001 Connecticut Ave., N.W., Washington, D.C. 20036.
   Produces units on population for teachers.

BOY SCOUTS OF AMERICA, National Council, New Brunswick, N.J. 08903.
   Interested in improved outdoor facilities. Open to boys 8 years of age and up.

CAMP FIRE GIRLS, INC., 65 Worth St., New York, N.Y. 10013.
   Encourages conservation and outdoor activities for girls 7-17 years of age.
CITIZENS FOR CLEAN AIR, 40 W. 57th Street, New York, N.Y. 10019.
   Action for cleaner air.

ECOLOGY ACTION

CONSERVATION FOUNDATION, 1250 Connecticut Avenue, N.W., Washington, D.C. 20036.
> Conducts research, information, and education programs. Publishes a monthly newsletter.

CONSERVATION LAW SOCIETY OF AMERICA, Mills Tower, 220 Bush Street, San Francisco, California 94104.
> Counsels litigants in cases of nationwide importance.

ECOLOGY CENTER, 2179 Allston Way, Berkeley, California 94704.
> Provides books, pamphlets, posters, reprints, and much other information on ecology action projects.

ENVIRONMENTAL DEFENSE FUND, INC., P.O. Box 740, Stony Brook, N.Y. 11790.
> Organization of scientists, attorneys, and others that takes legal action when necessary.

FOOD AND AGRICULTURE ORGANIZATION OF THE UNITED STATES, United Nations Headquarters, Suite 2258, 42nd St. and 1st Ave., New York, N.Y. 10017.
> Maintains 12 regional and liaison offices throughout the world. Part of the U. N. administrative organization.

FRIENDS OF THE EARTH, 451 Pacific Avenue, San Francisco, California 94133.
> International conservation organization. Maintains its independence for more aggressive action.

GARDEN CLUBS OF AMERICA, 590 Madison Avenue, New York, N.Y. 10022.
> Organization of local clubs promoting beautification, conservation, and open space planning.

GENERAL FEDERATION OF WOMEN'S CLUBS, 1734 N Street, N.W., Washington, D.C. 20036.
> Unites and serves affiliated local clubs. Its Conservation Department assists clubs with conservation and outdoor recreation projects.

GIRL SCOUTS OF THE UNITED STATES OF AMERICA, 830 3rd Ave., New York, N.Y. 10022.
> Informal education and recreation program for girls 7-17 years of age.

IZAAK WALTON LEAGUE OF AMERICA, 1326 Waukegan Road, Glenview, Illinois 60025.
> Membership organization with many chapters and state divisions. Provides speakers, literature, monthly newspaper, educational materials.

KEEP AMERICA BEAUTIFUL, INC., 99 Park Avenue, New York, N.Y. 10016.
> Public service organization for the prevention of litter and enhancement of urban and rural scenic beauty.

LEAGUE OF WOMEN VOTERS OF THE UNITED STATES, 1730 M Street, N.W., Washington, D.C. 20036
> National office can assist local Leagues in study and action programs to improve open space, parks, and recreation facilities.

APPENDIX E

NATIONAL ACADEMY OF SCIENCES–NATIONAL RESEARCH COUNCIL, 2101 Constitution Ave., N.W., Washington, D.C. 20418.
> Organization of scientists dedicated to furthering science and its uses for human welfare. Upon request, advises Federal Government. Professional group.

NATIONAL ASSOCIATION OF COUNTIES, Suite 522, 1001 Connecticut Avenue, N.W., Washington, D.C. 20036.
> Acts as a clearinghouse for information on county government administration. Publishes materials about parks, air pollution, water pollution, etc.

NATIONAL AUDUBON SOCIETY, 1130 Fifth Avenue, New York, N.Y. 10038.
> Membership organization with 150 local chapters. Operates 40 wildlife sanctuaries. Programs for schools. Field assistance. Provides teaching aids, bulletins, manuals, other publications. Furnishes films and speakers.

NATIONAL PARKS ASSOCIATION, 1701 18th Street N.W., Washington, D.C. 20009.
> Protects national park system and other natural environments. Leaflets for school use.

NATIONAL RECREATION AND PARK ASSOCIATION, 1700 Pennsylvania Avenue, N.W., Washington, D.C. 20006.
> Publishes monthly magazine, newsletters; public information programs and research services.

NATIONAL WILDLIFE FEDERATION, 1412 16th Street, N.W., Washington, D.C. 20036.
> Encourages wise use and management of natural resources. Graduate student grants. Informational material for media. Publishes newsletters, booklets, and magazines. Provides consultant services.

OPEN SPACE INSTITUTE, 145 E. 52nd St., New York, N.Y. 10022.
> Action group which stimulates open space conservation by working with land owners, municipal agencies, civic and regional groups.

PLANNED PARENTHOOD, 515 Madison Avenue, New York, N.Y. 10022.
> Programs to limit population growth.

SCIENTISTS' INSTITUTE FOR PUBLIC INFORMATION, 30 East 68th Street, New York, N.Y. 10021.
> Coordinates efforts of scientists to provide public with understandable scientific information. Particularly concerned with environmental problems. Professional group.

SIERRA CLUB, 1050 Mills Tower, San Francisco, California 94104.
> Devoted to study and protection of the nation's scenic resources. Very active and effective organization. Provides films, manuals, exhibits, speakers, conferences, and various publications suitable for schools.

SCIENCE AND MATHEMATICS EDUCATION INFORMATION AND ANALYSIS CENTER (SMAC) is one clearinghouse in the ERIC chain. Its address is 1460 West Lane Ave., Columbus, Ohio 43221.
> There is a newsletter on environmental education which is very informative.
> The coordinator for environmental education is Robert E. Roth.

SOCIETY FOR THE PRESERVATION OF BIRDS OF PREY, Box 293, Pacific Palisades, California 90272.
> Protects birds of prey, as the name implies.

ECOLOGY ACTION

THE NATURE CONSERVANCY, 1522 K Street, N.W., Washington, D.C. 20005.
Acquires and protects outstanding natural areas. Provides technical and financial assistance.

THE URBAN COALITION, 2100 M Street N.W., Washington, D.C. 20037.
Spurs people and groups to join together in action on the major problems of cities.

THE WILDERNESS SOCIETY, 729 15th Street, N.W., Washington, D.C. 20005.
Increases knowledge of wilderness.

WATER POLLUTION CONTROL FEDERATION, 3900 Wisconsin Avenue, N.W., Washington, D.C. 20016.
Devoted to advancement of knowledge on collection, treatment, and disposal of waste waters.

DEPARTMENT OF THE INTERIOR, Washington, D.C. 20240.
Bureau of Commercial Fisheries: Researches management and conservation of key marine and inland fishery resources.
Bureau of Land Management: Administers the public domain lands (500 million acres, mainly in the West). Conducts studies on use of public resources.
Bureau of Mines: Researches and develops action programs in conservation of mineral resources.
Bureau of Outdoor Recreation: Coordinates Federal plans and programs in out-door recreation areas.
Bureau of Reclamation: Develops water resource programs for the western states.
Bureau of Sport Fisheries and Wildlife: Works with state agencies to manage fish and wildlife resources. Responsible for migratory birds and rare and endangered species.
Federal Water Pollution Control Administration: Reviews state water quality standards. Interstate enforcement activities. Financial aid for municipal waste treatment projects.
Geological Survey: Conducts mapping and research on mineral resources and geologic structures.
National Park Service: Manages National Park System.

DEPARTMENT OF TRANSPORTATION, Washington, D.C. 20590
Develops and improves a coordinated national transportation system.

NATIONAL SCIENCE FOUNDATION, 1800 G Street, N.W., Washington, D.C.
Strengthens basic research and education in the sciences. Includes study of environmental programs.

ECOLOGY ACTION PUBLICATIONS

Individuals or groups interested in ecology action will find the following publications* worthwhile:

Clean Water—It's Up To You: A citizen guide to clean water action. 48 pages. Available free from the Izaak Walton League, 1326 Waukegan Road, Glenview, Illinois 60025.

---

*Lists of publications from **Community Action for Environmental Quality** Issued by The Citizens Advisory Committee on Environmental Quality (Washington: Government Printing Office, 1970), pp. 40-42.

The Big Water Fight: By the League of Women Voters' Education Fund. An informative discussion of citizen action on problems of water supply, pollution, floods and planning. 1966. 246 pages. $6.95 a copy. Available from the Stephen Greene Press, Brattleboro, Vermont.

Catalog of Federal Domestic Assistance: A definitive listing and explanation of all federal assistance programs. Available free from the Information Center, Office of Economic Opportunity, Executive Office of the President, Washington, D.C. 20506.

Challenge of the Land: Fine reference book for municipal officials and civic leaders on action to save open space. By Charles E. Little. 1968. 151 pages. $3.75. Available from the Open Space Institute, 145 E. 52 St., New York, N.Y. 10022.

Cluster Development: Comprehensive report on how better subdivision planning can provide more open space. 1964. 138 pages. Illustrated. By William H. Whyte. $4.50 hard cover, Published by American Conservation Association, 30 Rockefeller Plaza, New York, N.Y. 10020.

Community Action Program for Water Pollution Control: Community Action Program For Air Pollution Control: Two highly recommended books which discuss the problems of organization, enabling legislation, enforcement, staffing, financial and technical assistance, and how to drum up community support. $1.00 each. Available from the National Association of Counties, 1001 Connecticut Avenue, N.W., Washington, D.C. 20036.

Conservation Commissions in Massachusetts: Stimulating report on how commissions have prompted local action. By Andrew J.W. Scheffey. With supplementary report by William J. Duddleson on spread of conservation commission movement to other states. Published by The Conservation Foundation. 218 pages. $3.00. Available from New England Conservation Services Center, South Great Road, Lincoln, Mass. 01773.

Conservation Directory: Listing of principal national and state organizations, public and private. $1.50 a copy. Published by National Wildlife Federation, 1412 16th Street, N.W., Washington, D.C. 20036.

County Action for Outdoor Recreation: 48 page guide on practical steps for county park and recreational programs. Available for 25 cents a copy from the National Association of Counties, 1001 Connecticut Avenue, N.W., Washington, D.C. 20036.

The Electric Utility Industry and the Environment: A report to the Citizens Advisory Committee by a utility industry task force. Offers guidelines on better design of transmission lines, undergrounding of distribution lines, urban siting of nuclear plants, and other environmental challenges. 1968. 106 pages. $2.00. Available from Electric Utility Industry Task Force, Room 5600, 30 Rockefeller Plaza, New York, N.Y. 10020.

Federal Assistance in Outdoor Recreation: Summarizes programs of 30 federal agencies for cost-sharing, credit, technical aid, educational services, and research which are available to state, local governments, organizations, and individuals. Prepared by the Bureau of Outdoor Recreation. 1968. 99 pages. 35 cents a copy. Government Printing Office, Washington, D.C. 20402.

How to Preserve Your Area for Its Natural Value: Suggestions for landowners. 1962. 8 pages. Available free from The Nature Conservancy, 1522 K Street, N.W., Washington, D.C. 20005.

ECOLOGY ACTION

A Little About Lots: Excellent manual on how to make vest pocket parks of vacant lots, how to run them, how to organize tree planting and neighborhood clean-up programs. 1969. 62 pages. 50 cents. Available from the Parks Council, 80 Central Park West, New York, N.Y. 10023.

Manual for Municipal Conservation Commissions: Includes practical suggestions for specific projects. Available free from the Massachusetts Department of Natural Resources, 100 Cambridge Street, Boston, Mass.

More Attractive Communities for California: A practical handbook for community action for a better everyday environment. It is particularly helpful on landscaping techniques. $1.00 a copy. California Roadside Council, 2636 Ocean Ave., San Francisco, California 94132.

A Nature Center for Your Community: A basic handbook on the values, objectives, elements, and costs of a community nature center and how to go about establishing one. 1962. 40 pages. $1.00 a copy. National Audubon Society, 1130 Fifth Avenue, New York, N.Y. 10028.

Open Space for Urban America: By Ann Louise Strong. An excellent and very complete guide to all of the techniques available for conserving open space; extensive appendices include model statutes and legal forms. Free. Available from Office of Metropolitan Development, Department of Housing and Urban Development, Washington, D.C. 20410.

Planning in the Community: A useful check list of the basic elements of successful local planning efforts. 33 pages. 75 cents a copy. League of Women Voters of the U.S., 1730 M St. N.W., Washington, D.C. 20036.

Pollution by Pesticides: Some alternatives for better regulation. 50 cents. The Conservation Foundation, 1250 Connecticut Ave., N.W., Washington, D.C. 20036.

Power Lines and Scenic Values: How to pattern utility rights of way to the landscape. Free. Available from the Hudson River Valley Commission, 105 White Plains Road, Tarrytown, N.Y. 10591.

Recreation and Parks: Case Studies in Local Program: Down-to-earth reports on how 13 League of Women Voters groups appraised their areas' needs and worked with local officials, other citizens groups, and the voting public toward meeting them. 45 cents a copy. League of Women Voters of the U.S., 1730 M Street, N.W., Washington, D.C. 20036.

Signs Out of Control: Practical suggestions for solving billboard and other sign problems. 75 cents. California Roadside Council, 2636 Ocean Ave., San Francisco, California 94132.

So You'd Like to Do Something About Water Pollution: Concise guide for citizen action, with list of publications and films available. 20 cents. League of Women Voters of the United States. 1730 M St., N.W., Wash., D.C. 20036.

Solid Waste Management: Excellent series on new approaches to waste disposal, with strong emphasis on area-wide action possibilities. Free. National Association of Counties, 1001 Connecticut Ave., N.W., Wash., D.C. 20036.

Stewardship: Manual for showing landowners how they can conserve open space through gifts of land and of rights in land, and the legal and tax considerations involved. It has been very effective in the New York metropolitan region and should be helpful in any local open space program. $3.00 a copy. Available from The Open Space Institute. 145 East 52nd Street, New York, N.Y. 10022.

Successful Bond Election Campaigns: Outlines ways to promote support of municipal bond issues. Free. Available from Portland Cement Association, Old Orchard Road, Skokie, Ill. 60076.

Where Not to Build: How to provide open space in the face of urban growth. 1968. 160 pages. Technical Bulletin 1, Bureau of Land Management, Dept. of the Interior, $1.00. Available from U.S. Government Printing Office, Washington, D.C. 20402.

Wildlife Habitat Improvement: A clear, well-illustrated citizens guide to the management and increasing of wildlife in urban, suburan and rural areas. 1966. 97 pages. $2.50. Available from National Audubon Society, 1130 Fifth Avenue, New York, New York 10028.

Workbook for Clean Air: Instructive booklet on what citizens can do to spur action in their communities. Free. Available from The Conservation Foundation, 1250 Connecticut Ave., N.W., Wash., D.C. 20036.

Youth Takes the Lead: Lessons of the many community programs sparked by the National Youth Conference on Natural Beauty and Conservation. $1.95. Available from Urban Research Corporation, 5464 South Shore Drive, Chicago, Ill. 60615.

appendix F

FEDERAL AGENCIES AND RECENT LEGISLATION

The federal agencies often have local or regional offices. A quick survey of the phone book will enable you to determine if one of these agencies has a local office. You can obtain faster results by dealing with the local representative.

The phone book is also useful in locating the names of key state, county, or municipal agencies. Names of agencies concerned with the environment vary from state to state. A call to the office of your state legislator, county supervisor, or city alderman could quickly supply the desired information.

FEDERAL AGENCIES

Environmental Protection Agency (EPA).

EPA is to initiate and enforce pollution control standards so as to "protect the environment by abating pollution." EPA incorporates into one agency a variety of research, monitoring, standard-setting, and enforcement activities formerly dispersed among several federal departments and agencies. It is perhaps the most important of all the federal agencies.

According to the *Weekly Compilation of Presidential Documents,* Volume 6, Number 28, July 13, 1970, President Nixon states the following EPA guidelines to pollution control:

(1) Identify pollutants.
(2) Trace them through the entire ecological chain, observing and recording changes in form as they occur.
(3) Determine the total exposure of man and his environment.
(4) Examine interactions among forms of pollution.
(5) Identify where in the ecological chain interdiction would be most appropriate.

EPA roles and functions assigned are:

(1) The establishment and enforcement of environmental protection standards consistent with national environmental goals.
(2) The conduct of research on the adverse effects of pollution and on methods and equipment for controlling it, the gathering of information on pollution,

and the use of this information in strengthening environmental protection programs and recommending policy changes.

(3) Assisting others, through grants, technical assistance, and other means in arresting pollution of the environment.

(4) Assisting the Council on Environmental Quality in developing and recommending to the President new policies for the protection of the environment.

Council on Environmental Quality (CEQ).

CEQ is advisor to the President on environmental matters. It develops legislative proposals for the President to introduce to Congress. It reports to Congress annually on the condition of the environment. CEQ works closely with EPA.

Department of Agriculture, Washington, D.C. 20250.

Agricultural Research Service: Research in soil and water conservation, pest control.

Agricultural Stabilization and Conservation Service: Administers price stabilization and land conservation programs.

Federal Extension Service: Responsible for all general education programs. Field agents act as liaison between departmental research and action agencies.

Forest Service: Manages National Forests and grassland. Conducts research. Offers technical and financial aid.

Soil Conservation Service: Provides technical assistance in optimum land use.

Department of Commerce, Washington, D.C. 20230.

Business and Defense Services Administration: Consults with business on industrial problems including air, water, and waste pollution.

Department of Health, Education, and Welfare, Washington, D.C. 20201.

Office of Education: Curriculum development and grants to local school systems for innovative programs. Implements the Environmental Education Act of 1970.

Consumer Protection and Environmental Health Service: Coordinates research and action programs on the environment.

Environmental Control Administration: Conducts a national program to identify and control the problems relating to modern man's environment.

National Air Pollution Control Administration: Research, training, and dissemination of knowledge on the source and control of air pollution.

National Oceanic and Atmospheric Administration: Recognizing that the oceans of our planet cover three-fourths of the earth's surface, special research for environmental upgrading, oceanographic exploring, and marine resource developing this large portion of the earth is essential. Thus, the National Oceanic and Atmospheric Administration (NOAA) brings together in one administration federal programs dealing with the seas and atmosphere. Functions of NOAA include:

(1) Display leadership in developing a national oceanic and atmospheric program of research and development.

(2) Coordinate its own scientific and technical resources with the technical and operational capabilities of other government agencies and private institutions.

566

(3) Continue to provide those services to other agencies of government, industry, and private individuals which have become essential to the efficient operation of the transportation systems, agriculture, and national security.

(4) Maintain close liaison with the EPA and the Council on Environmental Quality as part of an effort to ensure that environmental questions are dealt with in their totality and that they benefit from the full range of the government's technical and human resources.

RECENT LEGISLATION

Population

Many environmentalists believe over population is at the core of earthly pollution problems. (More people means more car exhaust in the atmosphere, more detergent in the water, and more trash in the streets.) Keeping this in mind, the 91st Congress documented Title X–Population Research and Voluntary Family Planning Programs, an amendment to the Public Health Service Act, a new title which provides for a three-year birth control research and education program. Encompassed in the new Title X are provisions for family planning services, family planning research, and family planning information. Grants and contracts with public and nonprofit groups to establish and operate voluntary family planning projects and to train personnel to put into practice family planning service programs were approved. Also, funds will be allocated to public and nonprofit private and individuals for (1) research and research training projects in family planning and (2) to develop and make available family planning and population growth information (educational materials included). Topics qualifying for research grants include biomedical, contraceptive development, behavioral, and program implementation fields related to family planning and population.

Thus, the government has made an effort to control the population factor in the Population/Production/Pollution chain reaction.

Air

Automobile manufacturers must meet a 1975 deadline for 90% control of automobile exhaust emissions according to the National Air Quality Standards Act of 1970.

During the much debated deadline for automobile industries, Senator Edmund Muskie (D.-Me.) commented, "Detroit has told the nation that Americans cannot live without the automobile. This Legislation would tell Detroit that if that is the case, then they must make an automobile with which Americans can live." (Approximately 90 million vehicles are polluting the U. S. today.)

Included in Section 213 (awaiting signature) of the new air law is the provision for the procurement of special low-emissions vehicle standards for research and development purposes. The Section will enable researchers to determine whether technology is available for a low-emissions vehicle by 1975.

Another provision of the Act bolsters the public's role in fighting air pollution. Citizens can now instigate action against polluters under certain circumstances and participate in the development of implementation plans.

The bill also documents the establishment of national air quality standards for ten major contaminants. In addition, newly constructed sources of pollution, such as power plants and industrial mills, will be required to use the newest pollution control devices. Civil penalties will be charged for violations.

New concepts mentioned in the 1970 air amendment include national ambient air quality standards, standards of performance for industrial plants, and certification of performance. The new term "standards of performance," referring to the degree of emission control which can be achieved through process changes, operation changes, direct emission control, or other methods, enters federal legislation for the first time during the 1970's. This will apply to approximately 19 stationary emissions sources, including emission standards for 14 selected agents.

Appropriations monetarily amounting to more than last year's were granted to the Departments of Labor and Health, Education, and Welfare for the fiscal year of 1971 for air pollution.

Water

Control of water pollution by maintaining oil standards ranked high among the areas of water antipollution measures to be enforced through the Water Quality Improvement Act of 1970.

Section 11, added to the Federal Water Pollution Control Act, prohibits all oil discharges into or upon the navigable waters, adjoining shorelines, or the contiguous zone of the United States. On-shore and off-shore facilities plus vessels are included in this prohibition.

Whenever any discharge occurs, the person in charge of the vessel, on-shore or off-shore facility, must immediately notify the federal government. Failure to do so entails a fine of $10,000 or imprisonment for not more than one year, or both.

A revolving fund of $35 million is established to finance removal of oil and other hazardous materials.

The legal liabilities for the costs of cleaning up discharges are willful negligence or willful misconduct and all other situations ordinarily negligent. The Coast Guard may assess a civil penalty of not more than $10,000 for each offense.

Also stated in the provisions to control pollution by oil is a measure requiring a vessel over 300 gross tons to establish evidence of financial responsibility of $100 per gross ton or $14 million, whichever is less, before using U.S. ports or navigable waters.

Section 12 provides for the control of hazardous polluting substances.

Section 13 is concerned with controlling the discharge of sewage from vessels into the navigable waters of the U.S. Of major importance, new vessels are required to meet standards within two years after they are established and existing vessels have within five years.

Section 21 requires each federal agency having jurisdiction over any real property or facility or engaged in any federal public works activity to insure compliance with applicable water quality standards and the purposes of the Federal Pollution Control Act.

Other provisions of the Water Act include:

(1) Acid Mine Pollution
(2) Great Lakes Pollution Control
(3) Training Grants and Contracts
(4) Alaska Village Demonstration Projects
(5) Research, Development, and Demonstration
(6) Office of Environmental Quality

FEDERAL AGENCIES AND RECENT LEGISLATION

Public Works water pollution appropriations are to be used for construction of waste treatment facilities and research. Appropriations were also given to HEW for water hygiene. Housing and Urban Development (HUD) funds (awaiting signature) include money for water and sewage programs. Transportation's appropriations contain $35 million for oil spill cleanup, the amount authorized under the Water Quality Improvement Act.

Environmental Science & Technology, Volume 5, Number 1, January, 1971, cites the following major features of water control bills to be proposed in the next Congressional session:

(1) New environmental financing authority.
(2) Effluent charge considerations, earlier introduced by Senator William Proxmire (D.-Wis.).
(3) Speeding up the enforcement of conference procedures established by existing law, with elimination of hearing phase.
(4) Including of an effluent discharge requirement as an additional element in a state's implementation scheme to achieve its water quality standard.

(New statutory authority for water pollution control failed to pass since water legislation does not expire until June 30, 1971. Whereas, air and solid wastes expired June 30, 1970.)

Solid Wastes

The Resource Recovery Act of 1970 includes funds for: (1) construction of improved solid waste disposal facilities including innovative disposal facilities and (2) demonstration of area-wide resource recovery systems. Although funds for these purposes are deferred till fiscal 1972 and 1973, some grants to states as the demand compels are available for the fiscal 1971.

Also included in the Act are provisions for solid waste training grants to establish or expand training through support for personnel, student stipends and tuition, faculty expansion, facility improvement, necessary equipment and supplies, and other program expenses. Grants are allotted for work on advanced degrees in such fields as civil, chemical, sanitary, agricultural, and industrial engineering; the agronomic sciences; and urban planning.

The 1970 legislation provides for grants and contracts with eligible organizations offering training projects. Persons will be trained for the management, supervision, design, operation, or maintenance of solid waste disposal and resource recovery equipment and facilities. Training for instructors and supervisory personnel will also be provided.

Appropriations to HEW were granted for solid waste management.

Education

Educating man to live with his environment, is the goal of the Environmental Education Act.* Funds provide for the development of multi- and interdisciplinary curricula for levels ranging from preschool to graduate. Curricula for environmental studies will be pilot-tested before they are disseminated.

The Act stresses education dealing with the relationship of man to his environment—population, resource allocation and depletion, conservation, technology, and urban and rural planning.

*This Act (Public Law 91-516, along with related information, may be acquired by writing to the U.S. Office of Education, Dept. of HEW, Washington, D.C. 20202.

APPENDIX F

Grants will be available for:

(1) Preparation and dissemination of materials and development of programs.
(2) Preservice and inservice training programs on environmental quality and ecology.
(3) Community education programs designed especially for adults.
(4) Planning of outdoor ecological study centers.
(5) Initiation and maintenance of environmental education programs at the elementary and secondary school levels.

Relevant to this Act is the ERIC Information Analysis Center for Science and Mathematics Education (SMAC) environment program. ERIC Center personnel and selected consultants are developing a comprehensive information acquisition program for Environmental Education (EE) programs, instructional materials, and instructional resources. SMAC is one of the twenty clearinghouses in the ERIC (Educational Resources Information Center) network, a nation-wide information system established by the U.S. Office of Education. After acquiring environmental materials, SMAC staff analyzes and disseminates EE materials.

Index

INDEX

INDEX

INDEX

INDEX